KATIE WOOD is a n[...]
familiar with. Her do[...]
quality of her research h[...]
leading travel writers. Aut[...]g
the bestselling classics *Europ[...]p*, she
is also the Travel Correspon[...] Television
and for several newspapers, in[...] *Glasgow Herald*.

Educated in her native town [...]inburgh, she has now
clocked up over 87 countries and holds a fellowship of the
Royal Geographical Society. Married with two children,
she lives near Perth, Scotland.

THE 1996 GLOBETROTTER'S BIBLE

A Guide to Budget Travel Around the World

KATIE WOOD

Author of the bestselling *Europe by Train*

Researcher: Alexandria Katis

■ HarperCollins*Publishers*

HarperCollins*Publishers*
77–85 Fulham Palace Road,
Hammersmith, London W6 8JB

Published by HarperCollins*Publishers* 1996
10 9 8 7 6 5 4 3 2 1

A catalogue record for this book is
available from the British Library

ISBN 0 00 638688 1

Set in Linotron Meridien by
Rowland Phototypesetting Ltd
Bury St Edmunds, Suffolk

Printed in Great Britain by
HarperCollinsManufacturing Glasgow

CONTENTS

SECTION TWO: **Destinations**

SECTION THREE: **Round the World at a Glance**

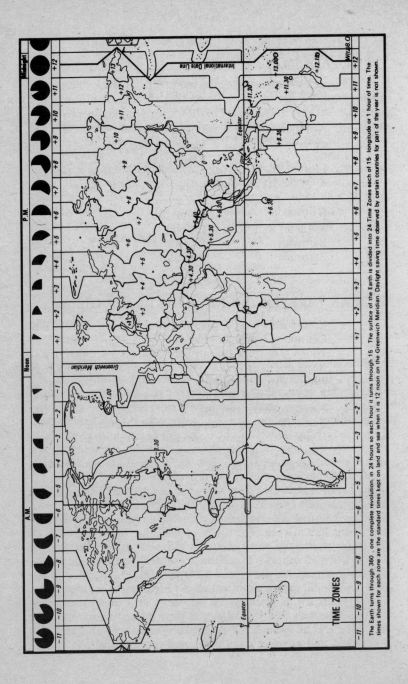

TIME ZONES

The Earth turns through 360°, one complete revolution, in 24 hours so each hour it turns through 15. The surface of the Earth is divided into 24 Time Zones each of 15 longitude or 1 hour of time. The times shown for each zone are the standard times kept on land and sea when it is 12 noon on the Greenwich Meridian. Daylight saving time observed by certain countries for part of the year is not shown.

INTRODUCTION

Isn't everyone's dream to travel the world? It was always mine and, judging from the figures, it's a dream that an increasing number of people are turning into a reality in the 1990s. Despite the recession, career worries and international crises, more and more people are taking time out to do the 'big trip' than ever have before. Good luck to them!

The great thing now is that modern communications have brought worldwide travel within most people's financial reach. Your dream can become a reality. Trekking in the Himalayas; shopping in Hong Kong; beach-bumming in Sydney; exploring in Peru; and paying homage to Mickey Mouse, all are there for the asking. And you *can* afford it. Yes, you. It *is* within your power – no matter how old you are, how broke you are, or what you did or didn't achieve at school – to pack a case, pop in the passport, raid the bank and head off, and this book will show you how.

Whether you need to work *en route* depends on how long you've got and how much you've saved. But the basic fact remains that what our parents' generation dreamed about is now here, waiting for you to grasp. So don't just dream, get out there and do it.

Why should you do it? If your feet are only moderately itchy as you read this, let me tempt you further: travelling the world, experiencing firsthand new and totally different cultures, hearing different languages, eating different food, meeting people you'd never otherwise encounter, will change you. Nobody comes back from a major trip quite the same. The good news is that 99.9% of people say that travelling has changed them for the better, given them a broader perspective on their life, made them reassess what they're doing, where they're going and why.

The old cliché that travel broadens the mind is true. But travelling is also great fun. There is nothing quite like setting your feet down in a new country. All five senses suddenly go into overdrive. Each day seems like a week. For many people, the 'high' gained from travelling (especially somewhere as different as the Far East or Africa) beats all others – it can make you feel you are really alive, not just existing. As you're out there inhaling the incense in the streets of Delhi, eating an all-American breakfast in a grotty diner in San Francisco, bargaining for souvenirs in a Mexican market, ask yourself: does this beat what you were doing back home? Isn't this what it is all about? Where would you rather be? And when you're old and grey (or even older and greyer), this trip will be what you think back to, the memories will stay with you for the rest of your life.

So, those are the highs of travel. But ask any experienced traveller and they will tell you that there are lows, too. One reason why I wrote this book was to make the lows less painful, less frequent, and to take away some of the hassles that every traveller encounters. I've stood at that last affordable hotel door as the Complet sign went up in my face; I've been mugged; walked round Osaka all night trying to decipher the map; missed the last train out of Jakarta; been bumped off the last plane out of an African hell-hole I never wanted to see again; had officious officials bugging me till I could scream; got ill; and all the rest. Because I've done all that, and learned the hard way, hopefully you won't have to.

This guide works through every aspect of serious travel, starting with the dreaming stage and taking you through the research, the travel itself, and on to the aftermath, the back-in-the-real-world stage (often quite a painful experience). Since coming down from the travelling high is no laughing matter, I've looked at that aspect too.

It is a hefty book, I know, but it does contain 15 years of solid travelling experience and I hope you'll be glad you took it along. Also, while prices and fares change, the theory doesn't — well, not a great deal — so you'll be able to refer back to the book before deciding on more trips in the future.

So, here's the definitive guide on how to travel through 28 countries and 45 cities — and keep smiling.

Happy travels!

Katie Wood
January 1996

SECTION ONE
ESSENTIAL PREPARATIONS

PLANNING YOUR TRIP

Independent travel means that it's up to you. You choose your mode of travel – be it plane, bus, bicycle, horse, foot or any other way to get around – where you go and how long you stay. However, the preparations that you make beforehand can make your travel experience much more enjoyable and worry-free. Take time to investigate what is available to you before setting off on your adventures.

Where to Go

What is your dream list of travel destinations? What do you prefer – large, cosmopolitan cities or the great outdoors? A little bit of each? Put a world map up on the wall. Where do your eyes immediately rush to? Don't let the glossy tourist brochures make your decisions for you, research the options carefully – your time and effort will be amply rewarded. What is the focus of your trip? The whole world is open to you, but don't forget what a big place it is. The selections below, taken from the countries covered in this guide, provide a starting point – a snap-shot rather than an exhaustive list of possibilities.

Wildlife and wilderness: Not surprisingly, these two invariably go together. East Africa's most popular destination for wildlife and big game is Kenya. This popularity has its disadvantages, but it's still possible to dodge the crowds, either on an organized safari or under your own steam. India offers unrivalled trekking: explore mountainous Ladakh (in the Himalayas, due west of Nepal) on foot; or take a camel safari from Rajasthan across the Thar Desert (and keep an eye out for the Bengal tiger *en route*). Outback Australia can be every bit as challenging as anything the developing world has to offer: its crowning glory, Ayers Rock, is a spectacle hard to match, as is the underwater world of the Great Barrier Reef.

Indigenous peoples and Old World civilizations: In some parts of the world it's possible to observe tribal societies still practising the old ways, in others only the relics of a bygone era remain. To encounter tribal villages, head to the northern hills of Thailand. Some 70,000 people do just this each year, but by searching out one of the less popular spots a world largely untainted by Western ways can still be seen. Alternatively, follow the nomadic Masai as they roam Kenya's Rift Valley. Extinct civilizations have left their mark on South America: the Peruvian lost city of Machu Picchu and the Mayan Pyramids of Mexico are but two examples. Elsewhere you can search out remains of the Roman Empire or Imperial China. You'll find as you travel that the past has a habit of making its presence felt amid the cacophony of the new world, whether in Athens or New Delhi.

Man-made beauty and chaos: Cities vary enormously in character and style. Sydney is laid-back, but the pace of New York will leave you inspired or exhausted – probably both. Berlin will provide a bite of contemporary history, while the sprawling metropolises of the developing world vibrate with a different kind of energy altogether. Yet amidst all the madness you will find proof of outstanding human achievement in the architecture and artistic treasures of the world's great cities, and in the thriving cultural life which gives each place a flavour of its own.

Island life: For pure escapism you can't beat tropical hideaways. Though few and far between, they can still be found: take a magnifying glass to the globe and search out hidden gems in Asia, Oceania and the dustier corners of the Caribbean. Or spend some time floating on water: rent a houseboat on Lake Dahl in Kashmir, or on the River Kwai in Thailand.

ECO-TOURISM

Justice cannot be done to this topic in a few lines. It covers everything from making as little negative impact as possible as you travel, to worthwhile working holidays involving everything from restoration to scientific studies. A wide variety of organizations has sprung up to promote the cause. The key campaigning group is Tourism Concern (tel. 0181 878 9053). See also *The Good Tourist* series by Katie Wood (Mandarin).

HOT-SPOTS

As with visa and inoculation requirements, no-go areas chop and change on a regular basis as trouble has a nasty habit of flaring up out of the blue. For up-to-date advice call the Foreign Office Help Line (0171 270 4129 Mon.–Fri. 9 a.m.–4 p.m.) before fixing your itinerary. Alternatively, for help on getting to particularly awkward places call the Bristol-based travel agent Regent Holidays (tel. 0117 921 1711); they won't fly you to a war zone but do pride themselves on giving the adventurous what they want.

How to Get About

The means of travel you choose is no insignificant matter. In addition to getting you from A to B, certain forms of transport can lend a new dimension to your experience of a foreign land. In some places it will be a camel safari that transports you back into the past, in others a felucca or dhow cruise. And who can resist a scenic train ride? A trip on India's rail network is as much a cultural experience as the Taj Mahal at sunset: arm yourself with a copy of the national timetable *Trains at a Glance*, or, to book seats and obtain Indrail passes, contact the London-based SD Enterprises (0181 903 3411 Mon.–Fri. 9 a.m.–5.30 p.m. and Sat. 9 a.m.–2 p.m.). The Trans-Siberian Railway will take you on an epic 9,000 km journey through Russia's darkest recesses from Moscow to Vladivostok, with connections onwards to Beijing on the Trans-Mongolian and Trans-Manchurian lines. Peru's El Tren de la Sierra through the Andes, South Africa's Blue Train, and the Bullet Train of Japan are some of the other memorable rides covered in Section Two.

Even road travel can possess a certain glamour: America's Highway of Hope, Route 66, snakes across the Union. Get on it and head due west until you reach Santa Monica. On the way read John Steinbeck's *The Grapes of Wrath*: among the road's first travellers were the desperate and hungry in search of work during the Great Depression. Western Australia's Eyre Highway stretches 2,575 km across the Nullarbor Plain between Perth and Adelaide. For this strictly been-there-done-that journey, take plenty of spare petrol and a copy of *Across Australia*, a driver's guide published by the Western Australia Tourist Board. While political instability to the west may prevent you from following the Grand Trunk Road from beginning to end as it traverses the Indian subcontinent from Kabul to Calcutta, join the road in India to trace the course of the River Ganges to the Bay of Bengal. The Kahkoram Highway and Silk Road are ancient caravan trading routes through Central Asia, a region yet to be exploited by popular tourism, though it has been known to intrepid travellers since time immemorial.

If you have more time, you might consider travelling at a slower pace on bicycle or on foot. These modes of travel bring you closer to the people and the land. Since you appear more vulnerable, you're more likely to be approached by local people. Josie Dew's *The Wind in my Wheel – Travel Tales from the Saddle* should be enough to inspire you. Bicycles can be taken on trains, planes and some buses all over the world. If half-way through you've decided that you've had enough, you can probably sell your bike for more than you paid for it in the UK (especially in New Zealand).

When to Go

CLIMATIC CONSIDERATIONS

If you intend to travel for several months, it's unlikely that you'll be able to visit everywhere at the optimum season. The trick is therefore to dodge the worst of the weather in as many places as possible. Beyond the temperate confines of Europe, seasonal changes can be very pronounced. Although few regions become total no-go areas, the climate inevitably determines what you can and cannot do; if you want to pursue activities such as hill-trekking, or to go on safari, you must time your arrival for the season in which these can be experienced at their best.

Putting up with daily downpours may be the price you pay for a bargain air fare (see **Cost considerations**, below); it can also make for an unforgettable experience in the best possible sense, as in southern India, where the monsoon season arrives each June bringing two months of death and disruption, yet is met with delight after weeks of arid heat. But think carefully before timing a trip at the height of the wet or hot season: the intense heat and humidity of tropical climates are not to everyone's taste. On an eastward round-the-world journey, it may be better to plan for a few cool, dry months in Asia followed by a wet Easter in autumnal Sydney, than to endure the orient at its most stifling in order to see Sydney in summer. Besides, in common with many tropical and subtropical countries, Australia hosts a variety of climates; sun worshippers need only head north into Queensland if they're suffering withdrawal symptoms. To experience that other sunshine state, California, at its best, head to America's West Coast in February or March. (Turn to the World Temperature Table in Section Three for a breakdown of other climates and seasons around the globe.)

Take into consideration, too, the timing of carnivals and religious festivals. Ramadan, the ninth month of the Muslim lunar calendar, is a time of daylight fasting and abstinence throughout the Islamic world. Many Christian countries, particularly those in South and Central America, have extravagant pre-Lent festivals when everything grinds to a halt amidst the celebrations. Such festivals don't make for easy travelling, but for the adventurous it's an opportunity to sample intense cultural and religious events firsthand.

COST CONSIDERATIONS

Air fares rise and fall with demand, so by avoiding traditional holiday periods – Easter, summer and Christmas – big savings can be made (both on flights and on costs once you land). Moreover, 'availability' (flexibility of flight dates) will be greater. However, travelling out of season isn't simply a case of dodging the school hols: off-the-beaten-track low-season bargains generally reflect the weather conditions that await you. The art is to pin-point precisely the right moment to make the most of the weather and bargain prices.

Rules of thumb: Air-fare seasons are well established and vary little between airlines. Demand for seats hots up as a more expensive season approaches, so book as far in advance as possible; fares go up overnight, even if the highest and lowest prices are separated by brief shoulder-seasons. Travel agents vary in their pricing policies on Round the World fares and other return tickets valid for up to twelve months: some set fares according to the initial date of outward departure, others split costs with anticipated onward/ return dates (even if these have yet to be booked); as a general rule, the best deals on RTW fares can be obtained in early spring, particularly from Campus Travel and STA. With this in mind, speak to several travel agents before parting with any cash, and keep an eye out for one-off bargains: long-haul fares have been known to drop by as much as 66%. Never forget, however, that price changes are invariably introduced in direct response to changes in demand. Bargains vary from sector to sector (i.e. different destinations), from carrier to carrier (i.e. different airlines) and at different times of the year. To take advantage of these special offers, you need to be as flexible as the air travel industry itself; it's a competitive business – be prepared to pounce when you spot a bargain. For advice on ticketing options, see p. 21, and **Buying a Ticket**, p. 36.

Timetabling Your Travels

If you're considering a lengthy overseas trip it's unwise to leave without making at least preliminary preparations for your return. In today's competitive job market absences from work or study cannot go unexplained. If the thought of planning ahead in this way kills the romance of wanderlust, think how much easier it'll be to relax – to really drop out for a few months – if everything back home is, as far as it can be, in good order.

Time off by no means spells the end of career success, but a lot can be done to prevent a year abroad from unnecessarily interrupting your long-term plans. A good starting point is considering what you'd like to do when you come home. Foreign travel has a reputation for altering aspirations, but it doesn't automatically clarify them, so it's worth taking stock of your options before going abroad. And though the timing of your departure will be predetermined by the seasonal conditions that await you in your chosen destination(s), try to combine these needs with ones that optimize your tax and benefits situation. If it looks likely that you're going to be unemployed for a while when you return home, make sure you can claim full unemployment benefit. The intricacies of the system are forever changing, so make sure you know what's what before setting off. Your entitlements will vary according to how long you've been working (i.e. how many national insurance contributions you've amassed) and whether you left your previous job voluntarily or not.

SIXTH-FORMERS

Sixth-formers considering a year out before going on to higher education will be glad to hear that most universities and colleges are enthusiastic about any experiences likely to enhance student independence and maturity. And although you'll have to sort out grant applications in advance, with something definite to come back to you won't have to worry unduly about the immediate future.

Technical and language faculties will expect students to brush up on the basics before returning to full-time education, but the only tutors likely to need serious cajoling into deferring your place for twelve months are those running lengthy vocational courses like dentistry, medicine or veterinary studies. Whatever your course, you must be back in time for the first term, and it goes without saying that you shouldn't leave the country before the exam results come out!

Backpacking isn't the only option. If you'd like a bit of variety, combine voluntary work overseas with independent travel. Adventure-project organizations, many of which specialize in trips for groups of school-leavers, combine overseas travel with work placements and aid projects: see **Arranging Work Abroad**, p. 64.

STUDENTS AND GRADUATES

It's worth setting aside some time to plan for the long-term future while you're still a student, even if the pressures of exams are bearing down on you. The first task is to identify the career area(s) most suited to your skills, interests and personality. No easy task, but help is at hand. Although college careers advisers can't make tough decisions for you, they can offer useful suggestions, and tapping into the knowledge of career-guidance professionals will never be so easy, or affordable, again.

Campus reference libraries are another invaluable source of information and will help focus your research. Newspapers and trade magazines are available, as are specific graduate publications like the excellent vacancy directories produced by Newpoint Publishing: *Graduate Opportunities* (*GO*) and, for postgraduates, the *Directory of Opportunities for Graduates* (*DOG*), available from all main libraries. A similar range of titles is available from Hobsons Publishing.

Having done the ground work and identified the careers that appeal to you, draw up a CV and application form tailored to those jobs. There's a definite art to this, so speak to a careers adviser before sending anything off. Also find out as much as possible about the sort of work you'd like to move into; keep an eye on current developments and read up on the companies most likely to have relevant vacancies. If you don't use all this information to find a job straight away, it'll be equally useful when you're back home from abroad. If you intend to work for a few months after graduation to raise some money before travelling, try to make useful contacts and acquire relevant skills: speak to people in the industry you're interested in and learn to type and use popular computer software packages. Someone, somewhere must have a computer you can use.

Deferred job offers before travelling: The ideal, if elusive, strategy for graduates hoping to move into mainstream employment – in the professions, management or engineering – is to secure a job offer deferred for twelve months. The Milk Round recruitment process, run by large blue-chip employers, screens final-year students and recent graduates between Christmas and Easter for jobs starting the following autumn. If, at the interview stage, you can present your time-out plans as worthwhile and useful, most organizations will be prepared to discuss a deferment. The majority of employers appreciate the character-building value of a year out, but the state of the economy and business optimism will influence how flexible they can be. Don't push hard for a year off until a definite job offer has been made, and avoid the subject altogether until your second interview.

Job hunting after your travels: If you want to give it a go when you get back from overseas, aim to be home by early December, but make sure you've done your preparation beforehand because you'll need to start filling in application forms immediately. For the bulk of law and accountancy vacancies, come back in the autumn.

Thanks to the Mutual Aid Scheme, recent graduates are entitled to use their nearest college careers service for several years after they graduate. It's a good way to get you out of the house, and you'll meet plenty of other job hunters. This will help to break the isolation of unemployment and, although current students have priority, brief interviews with careers advisers can also be arranged. Keep a look out for news about graduate recruitment fairs – few and far between as they may be – and any other useful careers seminars. Employers welcome Milk Round applications from graduates up to the age of 25, but won't be interested once you've passed that threshold. Most companies you apply to will want to see a reference. Will your college tutor remember you two years after graduation? A few strategic postcards sent from abroad might ensure that your name will ring a few bells. It's also a good idea to warn people that you've given out their name as a reference.

Of course, many careers openings aren't catered for by the Milk Round, not least because smaller companies recruit as and when staff are required. What's more, the only means of entry to many fields – the creative and media world, in particular – is through the back door. This is an upbeat way of saying you've often got to serve time in a less glamorous role before moving on to what you really want. You'll also have to spread your job search a lot wider.

Whatever your career plans, don't restrict yourself to official graduate vacancies. Most jobs have the potential to develop and it's always easier to find better work if you're already employed. Very little is certain any more in the search-for-work game, but late winter and spring have traditionally been the peak period for immediate-start vacancies. Late summer and autumn is a far less optimistic time. Vocational evening classes and unpaid work experience are a step in the right direction if you can't find any work in the areas – aim to have at least two – that interest you. Ask at the job centre about vocational courses organized by Training and Enterprise Councils (TECs) and local training agencies. If you're unemployed, sign up to join the nearest Job Club and look into government sponsored schemes like Employment Training (ET). For more ideas in the same vein, see **Returning Home**, p. 118.

Staying on in full-time education: Applications for popular postgraduate courses have to be submitted months before they begin. To avoid having to return unnecessarily early, leave instructions with a trustworthy friend who, nearer the time, can request application details on your behalf. Have the paperwork forwarded to you, and submit the forms from overseas – local post office facilities permitting. Remember also that requests for grants and bursaries generally have to be submitted by May of the year in which you plan to start your course.

CAREER-BREAK TRAVELLERS

The effects of taking a break from an established career vary with different occupations. A trip abroad will interrupt your immediate professional development and you won't be able to schedule your time off as easily as a student or graduate would, but with practical work experience you've potentially more to offer employers, and at the very least you'll be a seasoned job hunter. If you're working for an international company you may be able to avoid handing in your notice: some firms will be happy for you to combine travel with a stint in an overseas office.

Those looking forward to starting something new after their travels should take the same approach as a first-time job hunter. Do the groundwork before travelling and plan your return carefully. Likewise, if you want to pick up where you left off in the same career, is there any one particular time of year when vacancies are at a peak?

The thought of running the gauntlet of incredulous looks from colleagues when you announce your intention to depart may be more daunting than the prospect of looking for work when it's all over. And don't be surprised if you have to take a cut in salary when you first return home. On the flipside, however, companies looking to fill expatriate positions will value your international experience, and may pay a premium for it.

If you're concerned about your finances or would like to rent out your home while you're away, speak to the foreign department of your bank and contact a letting agency specializing in property management for overseas owners. If you live in a university town, you might consider renting out to academics or mature students. Staff at local hospitals are another good source of tenants. Funds permitting, bear in mind that a lick of paint and an electric shower do wonders for the rent potential. Ideally, keep the decor and furnishing fairly neutral, that way the place will appeal to the maximum number of people – landlords and property developers don't slap magnolia on walls just because it's cheap.

JOB HUNTING IN EUROPE

If you've been unemployed and claiming benefit for four weeks, you can go in search of work elsewhere in the European Community for up to three months and continue to receive dole money from the Department of Social Security in the UK. Before going, speak to your Job Centre, as they may have a list of continental vacancies. You'll also need to sort out tax and national insurance, so contact the DSS overseas office in Newcastle. Exactly what happens varies according to whether you find work, and if so, whether it's with a local company or a foreign branch of a UK firm. The job scene isn't any brighter on the continent, but at least it'll be a fresh start.

With the creation of the EC's single market, professional qualifications in different countries are now recognized across the region. That said, language problems remain. German is the most widely spoken first language, so unless you have a specific destination in mind, give it a go yourself. If you can't get enrolled in an evening class, see if the local library has some tapes you can borrow. Read some of the excellent books on this subject for further details, particularly those published by 'Vacation Work'.

Financing Your Trip

In a job market savaged by economic recession the task of saving for a trip abroad is not an easy one. You're probably prepared to try just about anything, perhaps working long hours with little to show for it; console yourself with the thought that any sort of work experience will be a bonus in the search for temporary employment overseas. Assurances along the lines of 'things on the job front can't be any worse when you get back' sound pretty hollow these days, but that's no reason to delay planning for life after travel – in fact it makes it all the more important. No matter how distant your homecoming, lay some foundations beforehand. See **Timetabling Your Travels**, p. 9.

Scrimping and saving for several months can be dispiriting, during which time your cost-conscious, anti-social behaviour will win you few friends. However, a sense of determination is no bad habit to acquire because you're going to need perseverance and imagination if you hope to find temporary work overseas. In the meantime, keep your morale high by opening a new savings account and watching your funds grow. The interest payments will help you on your way as well.

Set financial goals for yourself and stick to them.

CASUAL WORK
Keep your goals in mind as you pull that pint or stack those shelves having already slaved for a full working day. When you're working you're not spending, so no matter how poorly paid, an extra part-

time job is always worth taking. Not that all casual work pays pennies – silver-service waitering is a much sought-after skill. Teaching is another option. Do you have a talent which could be put to profitable use: sport, music, a foreign language, artistic skills?

DROPPING OUT

If you're giving up a permanent job to travel, raising the necessary cash won't be quite such a problem. Your career may be in mothballs, but isn't that half the appeal? What's more, you might be able to use your skills and experience overseas, see **Arranging Work Abroad**, p. 64.

WORKING YOUR WAY ROUND

There's a lot more than fruit-picking to be done, and earning a living overseas is as much a cultural experience as touring the wonders of the world. Finding a job won't be easy in the present depressed climate, but there's no motivation quite like being stone-broke and a long way from home. If jobs are in short supply, a little entrepreneurship will go a long way. If you haven't got a skill or service you can sell, try trading goods with fellow travellers: tents are ideal for Australia, next to useless in Asia. Sell what you no longer need and save money by buying necessities second-hand. Susan Griffith's *Work Your Way Round the World* (£9.95; Vacation Work), is essential reading. Also see **Arranging Work Abroad**, p. 64.

APPLYING FOR A BURSARY

A wide variety of organizations, companies and private benefactors contribute to and sponsor projects every year. But they don't reach for their chequebooks without asking a few searching questions beforehand, and as money has got tighter so the payees have become more discriminating – don't expect any miracles.

Companies like to be seen to be contributing to their communities – it's good PR. For this reason local firms are probably your best bet. Before approaching them, ask yourself what's in it for them? How will they benefit from being associated with your overseas jaunt? Backpacking isn't the stuff of front-page headlines, but are you doing anything particularly unique *en route*: socially, environmentally, culturally? Sponsorship by payment in kind is not to be sneered at. Does a company near you have a product you could use while overseas? If so, how can you generate local media interest? Needless to say, anything remotely political is not a popular business investment.

If nothing else, have a definite target in mind. Charitable

fundraising has grown into a highly professional business, and there have never been so many causes. What's eye-catching about yours? All of this planning is time-consuming, and with no assurance of financial success you may feel your efforts would be better spent earning a regular wage. That said, quizzing friends of friends who may be in the PR business costs nothing, and news-starved local papers should give you a fair hearing.

Grant-giving bodies, often set up at the bequest of a long dead philanthropist, distribute money annually to people and causes the trustees regard as worthy beneficiaries. Yes, they do receive thousands of requests every year – and not all of them will consider requests from private individuals – but *The Directory of Grant-Giving Bodies* (available at public libraries and careers centres) is a thick book, and you might just come across a lesser known organization prepared to consider your application. *A Year Between* (Central Bureau), offers advice on preparing your case for funding.

PLANNING YOUR BUDGET
Estimating the total cost of your trip, and deciding how much cash you initially need to bring away with you are two different things – not least because the former is virtually impossible to quantify. Costs will vary depending on how long you stay away, where and when you travel, and whether or not you work.

Your choice of destinations obviously has a direct bearing on expense. The poorer parts of the world are the cheapest to visit, but you won't have the option of looking for work, and they're often the most expensive when it comes to air fares and insurance cover. North America and Europe aren't cheap, but are relatively inexpensive to reach from the UK. Air fares to popular long-haul destinations are good value relative to the distance flown, especially those on the main RTW highway through Asia and Australasia – and if work can be found, the Aussie minimum wage makes virtually any temporary job well worth the effort. South America has traditionally been an expensive place to reach, but fares are dropping fast, and like Africa it's cheap once you've landed. The following notoriously expensive destinations should be given a wide berth unless you have a particular yearning to visit: Nordic Europe, Ireland, Middle Eastern oil countries, Japan, and the likes of Brunei.

Expenses also vary over time. The first few days in a new country will be pricey: cost-cutting of any kind is difficult until you've had a chance to gauge average prices for essentials like food, accommodation or transport – especially when it involves a new, confusing currency. If you arrive by air, you'll almost certainly touch down in a city. Capitals are particularly expensive places, and there are plenty of dodgy characters determined to bump up your costs. Assuming you aren't going to be counting every penny – or cent, baht, rupee or yen – from day one, you needn't worry about this. A fortnight relaxing on the beach or in the countryside often costs little more than an overnight stop in a town or city. Over the months your expenses will even themselves out, and you'll get used to economizing. There'll also be times when you pay out a lot of money, but recoup on the investment later: if you buy a secondhand car to save on transport and accommodation costs; or put up the deposit on rented accommodation; or buy some new clothes for a temporary job; or if you pay in advance for an all-inclusive overland tour.

Wherever you go and however you do it, don't let hidden costs like entry visas and departure taxes slip your mind – on a round-the-world trip they soon mount up. For more on cost-cutting travel, *The Budget Travel Handbook*, Pat Yale (Horizon), is full of useful tips.

Who to Go With

TRAVEL COMPANIONS

Travelling with someone else can be a dream or a nightmare – or both. It isn't necessary that you travel with your best friend, but you should know your companion well if you'll be travelling together for a long period of time. More importantly, however, is that you understand each other's expectations of the trip and of each other. Though it may sound silly, you really need to ask each other questions such as: What do you hope to get out of this trip? Why are you travelling? How much time do you imagine spending together while on the road? Are you open to sudden changes in plans – how structured are you? What accommodations do you feel comfortable staying in? Are you a morning person or a night owl? Would you consider splitting up for a period of time? It's better to find out these answers before you leave rather than in the middle of Zambia. Constantly finding places to stay, figuring out public transportation systems, listening to broken English, and general travel-stress can ruin a friendship if you let it.

There are a number of ways of tracking down potential travelling companions if you don't already have a particular person in mind. Students and recent graduates can advertise through their colleges. Members of the YHA and Globetrotters Club can advertise in the organizations' publications. (For membership details, contact: YHA

National Office, Trevelyan House, 8 St Stephen's Hill, St Albans, Herts AL1 2DY (tel. 01727 855215).

Alternatively, there are companion-matching agencies who, for a fee, will fix you up with someone whose details and travel plans tally with your own. No matter how carefully selected their list of prospective partners may be, there's no rush to come to a decision. Take your time finding the right person – anyone worth knowing will be equally selective. For more information, contact one of the following:

> Odyssey International (tel. 01223 861079). A £25 membership fee (£20 for the unwaged) gives you access to a 2,000-name database. Partners are usually of the same sex. Deals primarily with long-haul trips for people in their twenties.

> Travel Companions (tel. 0181 202 8478). Short-haul trips, 30-plus age group. Membership: £40.

If you're in London, *TNT* magazine has a new Travel Match service. Travel companions are sought and found weekly. Contact TNT Traveller's Noticeboard, 14–15 Child's Place, London SW5 9RX (tel. 1717 373 3377). This service costs £5.

Another option is to sign up for an organized tour with an overland adventure tour group. Most of these firms attract 20- to 35-year-olds, and tour for anything up to six months in groups of about a dozen. Though free and easy, they're not (officially, at least) a dating agency. One option is to book a short tour at the beginning of your trip, before heading off on your own – it is possible to split from a group midway through a tour. Are you any more likely to get on with a group of people than you are with just one other person? Well, you know whether or not you're a muck-in-and-meet-them type, and you'll have a chance to mix with everyone beforehand. For additional information see **Adventure Tour Specialists**, p. 40.

SOLO TRAVEL

Some people travel alone by choice – and revel in it. Of course, until you've given it a go, you won't know if it's for you. One thing's for sure, you don't need to be a hardened loner to travel solo. Anything but. In fact, you'll almost certainly meet more people than you would travelling with a companion. Think about it: it'll be you asking for directions, or enquiring if the spare chair at the table is free. As a single person, you'll also seem more approachable to others – locals and travellers alike. So although facing the world single-handed may be daunting at first, it has distinct advantages: your plans can be more spontaneous, and changes of heart won't be drowned out by sideswipes of 'I told you so . . .' Not that you'll ever be alone for long. Unless you decide to head way off the beaten track you'll be bumping into fellow travellers all the time.

If this freewheeling sounds enticing, remember that you'll have to shoulder the lows as well as the highs. Solo travellers certainly need to be more vigilant. Belongings have to be kept close at hand at all times, which isn't easy inside a cramped toilet on a jolting train. Inevitably, lone travellers provide an easier target for professional tricksters and muggers. It can be costlier too: unless you sleep in dormitories, or find a hotel with single rooms, you'll have to pay the dreaded single room supplement. Sharing rooms with fellow travellers is a simple enough way to cut costs on expensive double rooms, but not if you're robbed in the night – sadly, such thefts do happen. Falling ill is one thing, suffering alone quite another. It's both demoralizing and inconvenient – life's never so bad when there's someone to nurse you, and keep up supplies of toilet paper. That said, because you're setting your own pace, you'll be in no rush to get back on the road. Just don't forget to pack your sense of humour for the occasional lonely moments.

Women Travellers

Women are at risk from the more base instincts of males the world over. The lone woman traveller will often be flouting convention simply by her presence. In some Muslim countries, such as Egypt, women are at greater risk since they are seen as stereotypical Western women – free and easy. Thanks to pornography and trashy soap operas, verbal harassment sometimes spills over into physical harassment. However, in countries like Japan, The United Arab Emirates and Bahrain, women may feel quite safe.

All in all, it may sound none too inviting, yet plenty of women recommend travelling alone or without a male partner – even if they have had to ward off unwanted attention. For tactical advice, turn to **Staying Safe Overseas**, p. 100. For reassurance, remember that plenty of decent, honest people do still exist. Natania Jansz and Ludmilla Tueting have written a number of articles and books on the subject, including: *Women Travel*, ed. Natania Jansz (Rough Guides/HarperCollins), a wonderful collection of stories from women travellers, with an introduction packed with practical advice – at the time of writing, an updated version of this guide is

due to be published; and *The Traveller's Handbook*, ed. Sarah Gor-
man (Wexas), which has a chapter contributed by Ludmilla Tuet-
ing. A great sourcebook for women travellers is Thalia Zepatos, *A
Journey of One's Own: Uncommon Advice for the Independent Woman
Traveller*. This is available from the Eighth Mountain Press, 624
Southeast 29th Ave., Portland, Oregon 97214, USA.

Travellers with Disabilities

Disabled access in public places is on the increase, though at an
infuriatingly slow pace. Take a trip off the beaten track, however,
and what few facilities there are will disappear very rapidly. Nevertheless, an adventurous holiday is still a possibility. Holiday carers
can be 'hired' to accompany you and, given advance warning, airport authorities and airlines are generally very accommodating —
though how this enthusiasm translates into practical assistance may
vary. You'll doubtless be only too aware of the challenges posed
by cramped and crowded conditions, but all special-needs passengers are entitled to the following: an escort at airports; additional
information concerning departure and arrival times; plus, with
luck, the use of loading equipment to help them on and off planes.
If you're blind or partially sighted, check which airlines carry
guidedogs free, and if you'll be allowed to take yours with you into
the cabin rather than have it stowed in the hold.

Those with special needs of any kind will know the relevant
associations to contact for general information, but listed below
are organizations which specialize in meeting the recreational and
travel needs of people with disabilities:

> Royal Association for Disability and Rehabilitation (RADAR),
> 12 City Forum, 250 City Road, London EC1V 8AF (tel. 0171
> 250 3222). Provides help and information on special-needs
> holidays, and disabled access at airports.

> Holiday Care Service, 2 Old Bank Chambers, Station Road,
> Horley, Sussex RB6 9HW (tel. 01293 774 535). A national
> charity that offers free advice and support regarding special-
> needs holidays and travel, including insurance cover (SAE with
> all enquiries).

> Scottish Information Service for the Disabled (tel. 0131 229
> 8632) Mon.–Fri. 10 a.m.–4 p.m.

> Heathrow Airport Travel Care (tel. 0181 745 7495).

Mobility Car Rental (tel. 01992 87462). Specialists in self-drive car hire for the disabled.

Can Be Done Limited, 7–11 Kensington High Street, London W8 5NP (tel. 0181 907 2400). Arranges UK holidays for groups/individuals.

Guidebooks and information:

Nothing Ventured: Disabled People Travel the World, ed. Alison Walsh (Rough Guide/Harrap Columbus). A collection of stories by disabled travellers.

The Access Holiday Guide, Ian MacKnight. Lists accessible UK holiday centres. Contact him at: 7 Roundberry Drive, Salcombe, South Devon TQ8 9LY.

Radar Guides, ed. John Stanford. Published by the Royal Association for Disability and Rehabilitation (see p. 19 for address). Guides to travel in Britain and abroad.

Airports Guide International (Thomas Cook). Lists facilities in airports worldwide, including those for disabled travellers.

A List of Guidebooks for Handicapped Travellers (The American President's Committee on Employment for the Handicapped, Washington DC 20210). A directory of almost a hundred cities in North America and Europe.

In Touch Care Guide (BBC Radio 4). Available in standard or large print/braille/cassette formats. Contact: In Touch, PO Box 7, London W3 6XJ.

Plane Easy. This free tape, produced by the Royal National Institute for the Blind (RNIB) in association with British Airways, helps prepare blind/partially sighted travellers for air travel. Contact: RNIB Customer Services, PO Box 173, Peterborough, PE2 6WS (tel. 01345 023 153).

The Ticket to Suit Your Needs

ROUND THE WORLD TICKETS

RTW tickets are convenient to use and competitively priced. Valid for up to twelve months, they're an easy way to string together visits to destinations a long way apart. No single airline circles the globe, but forty companies have combined forces to offer more than 200 off-the-peg RTW fares. It's also possible, though it may be more expensive, to piece together your own itinerary of connecting flights. You can trawl through airline schedule directories such as *The Airline Passenger Guide* and *ABC Air Travel Guide* – available in most libraries – or enlist the services of a specialist long-haul travel agent, see **Buying a Ticket**, p. 36. These agencies are well versed in tailoring RTW trips; simply explain your needs and pick the best package. Some enthusiastic travel consultants will assure you that any routing is possible – and it's true that many restrictions on RTW tickets have indeed been relaxed – but they may play down the fact that if you want to zigzag around the globe, you'll have to pay for the privilege. Convoluted routes may also prove time-consuming in terms of the hours spent up in the air between destinations, so don't be surprised if your travel agent suggests a more manageable alternative.

Check the quality press for special offers on set RTW itineraries: they'll either be advertised, or mentioned in the news columns of the travel pages. These are often short-term promotions aimed at people able to travel at a moment's notice; they may carry additional restrictions, such as set dates for onward travel between destinations, but if money is your main concern it's worth putting up with the limitations.

If you want to keep costs down, avoid backtracking. Travel in a straight(ish) line – in an easterly or westward direction, as opposed to north or south – and limit the framework of your journey to gateway destinations on international flight paths. Most advertised itineraries follow these rules and still offer plenty of scope for adventurous travel; treat each stopover city as a starting point from which to explore. It's possible to split your journey and travel overland between onward flights – Bangkok to Singapore, for example – and extras like regional air passes and occasional spur-leg flights off your main route will help you make the most of large countries like America and Australia. Generally, the more stops, the more expensive the ticket will be. See **Additional Options**, p. 27.

Fares increase with the number of continents visited, the total distance travelled, and how far afield you go. Economy-class fares start at £700 and rarely exceed £2,000; most cost about £1,000. The most established and affordable RTW routing is Asia–Australasia/the Pacific–North America. It's possible to include Africa, South America and the Caribbean on an RTW trip, but because they're not on the main 'circuit' you won't be able to get rock-bottom prices. Direct flights between South America and Africa are particularly limited, and are usually routed via the US. The Australasia long-haul routing is a very lucrative one for the airlines, which explains their enthusiasm for discounting tickets to this region. Spring 1993 prices were, in real terms, 35% lower than those in 1987, and many of the best deals were with the top carriers.

Most travel agents require RTW fares to be paid for in full a fortnight to a month in advance. The standard proviso requires at least three stopovers and, although minimum-stay requirements at each destination have by and large been abandoned, the complete trip must last at least two weeks. The dates of onward flights may have to be provisionally booked, but can be changed, subject to availability (though a charge may be levied by the local handling agent). On busy sectors and at peak times, beware of leaving final decisions too late; after several weeks away from it all, it's easy to forget that Christmas or Easter is fast approaching and that long-haul routes passing through your present destination will be clogged up by festive travellers coming and going. Avoid the bottle-necks by flying at other times, or by booking well ahead.

Unlike agent-originated RTW fares which rise and fall depending on the season of initial departure, off-the-peg RTW trips offered by officially co-operating airlines rarely fluctuate in price. These itineraries are often more expensive than ones pieced together ad hoc with a travel agent, but some airlines throw in a few nights of free accommodation or a complimentary domestic flight *en route*, so it's worth keeping an eye out for perks and special offers. Whatever your plans, for suggestions on getting the best deal see **Buying a Ticket**, p. 36.

Sample itineraries:

Northern hemisphere orientated:

London−San Francisco−Honolulu−Tokyo−Bangkok (£740)

London−Toronto−Honolulu−Fiji−Sydney−Hong Kong (£925)

Southern hemisphere orientated:

London−Johannesburg−Perth−Sydney−San Francisco−London (£839)

London−Bangkok−Brisbane (*overland* to) Melbourne/Auckland−Vancouver−Toronto−London (£840)

London−Nairobi (*overland* to) Harare−Johannesburg−Perth−Sydney (*overland* to) Brisbane−Cairns−Hong Kong−London (£1,030)

ALTERNATIVE LONG-HAUL OPTIONS

Circling the globe certainly has an air of romance, but it's not obligatory to circumnavigate. There are plenty of other ticketing options.

LONG-HAUL RETURN FARES

Valid for up to twelve months, these tickets allow stopovers *en route* to and from the furthest destination you wish to visit (Australasia is about as far as you can get from Europe). Standard long-haul return fares include one stopover each way, but more elaborate trips taking in several continents are also available (see **Multi-Stopover Tickets**, below). Fares vary according to the itinerary. The most elaborate discounted economy-class trips are roughly on a par with the cheapest RTW tickets. As with RTW fares, be prepared to pay in full anything up to a month prior to departure. Dates for onward flights can be provisionally booked in advance.

Depending on your route and airline, if you're using a standard return ticket you may not be able to fly non-stop between destinations – but what's a few hours in a transit lounge if you're going to be abroad for up to a year? Do bear in mind, however, that you may not be able to fly into one destination and out of another, so your overland travel may involve a certain amount of backtracking to and from the gateway airport. That said, use your imagination and you won't have to retrace your steps exactly. Long-haul return tickets are especially useful if you want to spend a lot of time in one particular country. You have the freedom to travel for up to a year, plus the bonus of stopovers *en route*.

Sample itinerary:

London–Los Angeles–Papeete–Sydney–Auckland–Fiji–London (£820)

OPEN-JAW TICKETS

With an open-jaw return you fly in to one destination and home from another, allowing you to travel overland between the two. The price is set at either the fare for the more expensive of the two places, or at half the combined cost of both tickets. Open-jaw journeys can be arranged to just about anywhere and the two destinations needn't be close together, or even in the same country. Open-jaws are ideal if you want to travel overland extensively in one particular region. They save backtracking to and from a single arrival/departure destination, and let you see several neighbouring countries. Tickets are valid for up to a year, though travel for this length of time will usually involve two one-way tickets.

Sample itinerary:

London–Cairo–Nairobi–London (£460)

MULTI-STOPOVER TICKETS

These string together several destinations and can be either long-haul return or one-way tickets, or tours that circle a specific region.

Fares vary according to the itinerary, but for less than the price of the cheapest RTW ticket you can see much of the Far East. More elaborate still are return trips to Australia which combine several Asia stopovers with domestic flights in Oz. Overland sections between destinations can be incorporated too. Tickets are valid for 3, 6 or 12 months.

Sample itinerary:

Return fares

London–Boston–Los Angeles–Sydney–Honolulu–San Francisco–London (£710)

Regional circuits

London–Hong Kong o'land Beijing–Bangkok–Helsinki–London (£710)

OTHER RETURN TICKET OPTIONS

CHARTER FLIGHTS

Traditionally confined to European and transatlantic flights, charter services now operate on many long-haul routes, most notably the Far East, Australasia and tourist destinations such as Goa and the Gambia. Less flexible than scheduled airline tickets but often considerably cheaper, charter flights are ideal if you're looking for a shorter trip and can live with limited flexibility and hefty cancellation fees. Flights often operate weekly – predominantly Mar.–Oct. – and they don't have stopovers *en route*. Some travel agents can piece together trips flying out on a charter and onward/home via scheduled services. Even with the collapse of Dan Air, over-capacity in the charters market is likely to be around for some time, especially in the wake of the liberalization of European Community law (which is likely to lead to an increase in continental European charters operating out of the UK). Keep an eye out, too, for currency fluctuations. A weak pound against the dollar, for example, will make the United States less popular with visitors, so charter flights will be moved over to European destinations, thus reducing the price of continental tickets. Austravel (0171 734 7755/0117 927 7425 Mon.–Fri. 9 a.m.–7 p.m.; Sat. 9 a.m.–5 p.m.) is the sole operator for Britannia Airways' winter charter flights. As their name implies, Austravel specialize in Antipodean destinations, but in conjunction with Britannia they cover most parts of the world.

COURIER FLIGHTS

Savings of between 10 and 45% can be made on air fares by offering your services to international courier companies responsible for the swift delivery of documents and packages worldwide. It is all perfectly legal (don't think there are any bundles of white powder stashed about your person!). Usually, you just carry documents or computer software and simply escort the baggage in-flight and carry the paperwork to your destination, in order to circumvent the air cargo clearance procedure, which can take days.

You must travel alone (courier offers are always for single seats), and on many routes you'll have to travel with just hand luggage. You will be expected to dress smartly and act sensibly, and must fly from London as companies only operate from there. Most companies require you to be ready to leave at fairly short notice and, if you want to change dates, a cancellation fee will be charged and no other flights offered. The main drawback is the limited amount of time you'll be able to spend abroad: round trips are usually less than 28 days and you should book well in advance for specific dates and locations. However, it is sometimes possible to string several one-way courier journeys together. Most of the destinations on offer are business cities, but they are located right around the world. To get to Paris from London could cost £60, New York around £150 return, Hong Kong £350 return, and all large US cities, major European capitals, Far East and Australian cities are possible. If you want to take this further, try Courier Travel Services (tel. 0171 351 0300 Mon.–Fri. 9 a.m.–5 p.m.).

FREEWHEELING
Buying tickets as you travel opens up endless possibilities and there are several ways it can be done. DIY-ing doesn't necessarily work out cheaper than following a prepaid, prebooked itinerary – and it'll certainly involve more work – but it's an obvious option if you don't like the idea of keeping to a set route. Likewise, if you intend to work your way round the world, it makes sense to keep restrictions on your plans to a minimum.

ONE-WAY TICKETS
Fares vary considerably in price, so it pays to hunt around before booking as some cost nearly as much as a return, see **Buying a Ticket**, p. 36. Tickets bought in the developing world are often very good value, especially for routes between Third World countries. Be cautious about buying tickets from dodgy foreign bucket shops, but don't reject the idea out of hand as bargains can be had. Do, however, resist the temptation to buy a secondhand ticket from another traveller (the second leg of their return ticket, for example): airport security is much tighter than it once was, and passengers' names

are closely checked on tickets and passports – they'll have to match up if you're to be allowed to fly.

MULTI-STOPOVER ONE WAY FARES
These can get you half-way round the world, usually to Australasia. Again prices vary, but cheap ones cost roughly half the price of comparable RTW fares and allow stopovers in two or three countries *en route*. For good deals on one-way long-haul flights, contact Quest Worldwide (tel. 0181 547 3322 Mon.–Sat. 9 a.m.–6 p.m.; Sun. 10 a.m.–4 p.m.).

Sample itinerary:

London–Bangkok–Hong Kong–Perth–Sydney (£590 (£170 in high season))

Unfortunately, many countries require proof of onward travel plans before granting tourist visas, so there are limits to where you can go on a one-way ticket, especially if you enter a country by air. However, depending on the vigour with which these regulations are enforced, there are ways to get round the problem. Often a clean-cut appearance and sufficient money to finance your stay and onward travel will do the trick. See **Formalities**, p. 52, for information on specific countries. If you want to maximize your chances of unhindered travel, a Miscellaneous Charges Order (MCO) is a worthwhile, and refundable, investment. Similar to an air ticket, MCOs are vouchers that can be exchanged for flights. Ask travel agents for information.

ADDITIONAL OPTIONS

AIR PASSES
Offering generous concessions for extensive travel with domestic airlines in foreign countries, air passes are valid for anything between 7 and 60 days. Often sold in conjunction with international return flights, they're only available to visiting non-nationals and you may be required to buy them in advance from outside the country you want to visit. Some offer unlimited travel, though most put restrictions on the number of flights that can be taken. A number of coupons are issued, which are then exchanged for tickets as you need them.

Air passes can be used in America, Africa, Australia, India, the Far East, the Caribbean, South America and the Pacific. With discounts of up to 50% off normal fares, they're a very economical way to jet around large countries. Trips to neighbouring nations are often permissible; some United States passes are good for travel to destinations in Canada, Mexico, Hawaii and the Caribbean. Prices vary with different host countries, but start from around £150. For specific details, turn to the destination chapters in Section Two (or ask your travel agent).

SPUR-LEGS
These detours to destinations off your main route (and away from international flight paths) can be incorporated into pretty much any itinerary. On your way to Australia via Asia, for example, you could visit Hong Kong or China. Spur-legs can be booked in advance, or as and when you decide to take them. If you know you definitely want to add one to your itinerary, it's often easier (and sometimes cheaper) to buy them with your main ticket.

SURCHARGES AND CANCELLATION FEES
Discounted tickets come at the expense of flexibility. Pay the full fare on a scheduled flight and you have the right to cancel your trip without incurring any penalty charges, or to change to another flight. Buy the same seat at any other price and amendments are subject to cancellation fees and surcharges as soon as a deposit is put down. Charges start from 25% if you cancel within a month prior to flying, increasing to 50% or more should you change your plans once you're abroad.

Regulations vary from airline to airline, but substantial adjustments to journey plans – different destinations and routings – always incur charges. On a discounted scheduled flight, depending on seat availability and the conditions of your ticket, a small handling fee is all that's charged if you change the day of your journey, provided your new flight date doesn't fall in a more expensive season. It's when the ticket has to be reissued that costs start mounting up. This has to be done if you change your route, especially should you require additional stopovers; if your ticket is lost or damaged; or if your new departure date falls during a more expensive season.

Some cheap RTW tickets are non-reroutable, which means you won't be refunded for unused portions of your ticket if you change your itinerary midway through the trip. Unless you're 100% sure about your itinerary, these tickets should obviously be avoided; but even with refundable fares, don't expect more than 50% back. To make sure you get what you're entitled to, cancel any onward flights with the airline(s) and return the ticket to your travel agent as quickly as possible, preferably by registered post. If you need the money urgently, have the cheque made out to someone back home who can then forward it to you. Even so, it could take three months to come through. Refunds offered after the validity of the ticket has expired are rarely more than 10%, if that. Airlines have discretionary powers to waive these charges – if you have been forced to change your plans for reasons beyond your control, illness for example, they may take pity on you – but this is strictly a courtesy provision. Needless to say, it pays to give a lot of thought to how and where you want to travel, see **Deciding on an Itinerary**, p. 33.

TRAVEL BY SEA
Air travel may be swift and efficient, but planes can't offer sunbathing and cocktail hours. If you want to travel for the sake of travelling, consider taking a cruise. Black-tie for dinner and your best foot forward in the ballroom probably isn't your idea of adventure, but the Cruise Advisory Service maintain there are trips to suit all ages, tastes and budgets. Not all passenger-carrying ships are exorbitant luxury liners; many are affordably priced cargo vessels. Most cargo ships carry eight to twelve passengers with destinations almost anywhere in the world. Excursions to the Mediterranean, Europe, Bermuda and the Far East are fairly formal affairs, while the Caribbean and Mexican Riviera are classified as casual/semi-formal trips – though you can bet that standards are above and beyond backpacker scruffiness.

Your cruise needn't be a round trip; one-way excursions can be arranged, or you can hop aboard at one of the ports of call. Unlike most cruise liners, cargo ships sail regularly, year round. For information covering all the major shipping companies, contact the Cruise Advisory Service (tel. 01722 335 505), for cargo-ship voyages speak to The Strand Cruise Centre (tel. 0171 836 6363). Seven-night, one-way cargo-ship cruises to or from the West Indies start from £700 (full board). They also offer 3-month, around-the-world trips for £5,300. Other sources are The Geest Line (tel. 01703 334 415); Batary Cruise Club (tel. 0171 251 3389); Cruise World (tel. 01907 45162) and Gray Dawes Travel (tel. 01206 563 895).

PRACTICALITIES

Choosing Your Airline

NORTH AMERICA

Canada's airlines, which are all involved in RTW partnerships, tend to have fairly modern fleets and, by and large, enjoy a sound reputation for service and fair pricing. This is particularly true of Wardair, which retains its own identity despite having been taken over (along with Canadian Pacific) by Canadian Airlines; its RTW partners are Philippine Airlines and Cathay Pacific. Canadian Airlines' fares seem very susceptible to change, but they do have a wide variety of routes. Air Canada is still an independent carrier and an excellent one at that; for one thing, it's the world's first completely non-smoking airline. Air Canada's RTW partners are: JAL, Air New Zealand, Singapore Airlines, Cathay Pacific and Qantas.

Most American airlines operate to good standards, but in general they have fallen short of the first-rate reputation their Canadian counterparts enjoy. They do offer, however, a wonderful selection of routes. With the demise of Pan Am and TWA, the main US carriers are: American Airlines, North-west Airlines (which have a very good reputation and are teamed with numerous RTW partners, and offer some of the cheapest deals), and Continental Airlines. United serve useful Pacific routes and offer a wide range of excursions. North-west have recently opened up routes for the use of RTW tickets, and because of their extensive domestic schedules they're a good option for anyone planning several stops in the States.

Agreements between Continental, Thai International, All Nippon Airways and SAS mean that passengers can now fly either non-stop or with just one transfer almost anywhere in the US, South America and much of the Pacific Basin, including Australia and New Zealand.

CENTRAL AND SOUTH AMERICA

Caribbean carriers have small fleets and most of their business is conducted inter-island or between the USA and neighbouring South American countries. Air Jamaica, Bahamasair and BWIA, affectionately known as Bee Wee, are the best known of these. The South American lines have a poor reputation for service, reliability and comfort. The main carriers are Aerolineas Argentinas and the Brazilian carrier, Varig. Both have come in from the cold of late and though they do not as yet have offices in the UK, cheap tickets can be obtained through British consolidators (bucket shops) and some of the adventure travel agents. Aerolineas Argentinas has an RTW partnership with KLM and, more recently, with BA and Qantas. Avianca, the Colombian airline, also offers very cheap rates on South American routes.

AFRICA
Few African airlines are blessed with a good reputation. Ethiopian Airlines and Air Tanzania are the worst culprits, mainly because they don't always book their planes in advance and therefore can't say what type of aircraft they'll be using. Other national carriers in the region have a better image, especially South African Airways (SAA), which competes with the best in terms of comfort and service, and as the largest African airline it also serves the most destinations.

THE MIDDLE EAST
Outstanding among a generally poor assortment in the Middle East are Emirates, Gulf Air and Saudi Arabian Airlines. All three offer a truly luxurious service which caters for even economy passengers at an exceptional level. However, with continued troubles and upheaval in the region, these high standards are not always enough to entice Western passengers.

ASIA
Asia has some of the best airlines in the world – and some of the worst. As a rule, the Far Eastern airways are superb in virtually every respect. They have refined customer care to an art form which the Western world is hard put to imitate. Worthy of the highest recommendation are: Cathay Pacific, Singapore Airlines, Thai Airways, Malaysian Airline System (which has a cancellation fee of only 10%), plus JAL and ANA – Japan's two largest airways. That said, some of these airlines do tend to have a lot of stops, which may or may not operate to the benefit of the RTW traveller. Furthermore, owing to their popularity, there are seldom vacant seats at short notice. Cathay Pacific's RTW partners are American Airlines, Continental, Qantas, Pacific Airlines and United Airlines.

The Republic of China's national airline is as basic as can be, but it's the only domestic carrier for mainland China. China Airlines has RTW partners in American Airlines and Sabena.

Garuda Indonesian Airlines has a very small, modern fleet. It is fairly cheap and has a very high number of stopovers on some of their routes. It tends also to be quite heavily booked and, because the fleet is so small, flights are often subject to delays.

Air India is generally a sounder prospect than its immediate neighbours. It doesn't promise luxury to economy-class passengers, but what is offered is more than adequate. Air India has RTW links but does not seem at pains to advertise them.

AUSTRALASIA
Qantas of Australia is highly respected. It has an extensive network, very good RTW connections and, in addition to being highly rated in terms of comfort and service, it has never been involved in a crash. Qantas' RTW partners are: BA, United Airlines, North-west, Air Pacific, Delta, Air Canada, American Airlines and Aerolineas Argentinas. New Zealand's airlines also merit their good reputation. Other Australasian carriers tend to be very small, and only Air Pacific has significant RTW links.

EUROPE
Aeroflot enjoys the distinction of being the world's largest airline. Very little is ever publicized about it. Its flights are very cheap, but involve a large number of stops (invariably through Moscow) and the service is notoriously basic. Although Aeroflot (and other Eastern European airlines) may come to play a far more significant role in RTW travel once glasnost takes effect, in the short term they have taken something of a step back in recent years. The exception to this is Aeroflot's London to Tokyo route: not only is it the cheapest connection between the UK and Japan, it's also the most direct. Moreover, although it stops in Moscow, this is only to collect other passengers, so the famed 48-hour delays between connecting flights are avoided. Aeroflot's general handling agent in the UK is British Airways (tel. 0181 897 4000, or visit them at 156 Regent Street, London, W1R 5TA).

The Western European airlines enjoy varying reputations. Of the main carriers, BA is by far the largest and covers a huge number of destinations. It has recently introduced two new economy classes: Euro Traveller and World Traveller. BA tend to be amongst the most expensive, but occasionally they have amazing offers: at the time of writing, their non-stop flight to Mexico is one of the cheapest around. In early 1993, after being accused of orchestrating a smear campaign against close rival Virgin Atlantic, BA had a hefty fine slapped on it, and amid a shroud of mystery and allegations BA's Lord King retired early from his post as chairman. Virgin is Britain's youngest international airline, and is fast developing a reputation for good service, value for money and comfort, as has been proved by the awards it has won as the leading Business Class carrier. Virgin offer many exceptionally good deals on low-season transatlantic crossings.

France now has only one large airline, Air France, which bought out UTA in 1990. UTA had the best connections of any airline within Africa and these routes have not been affected by the takeover – they are now maintained by Air France. The Italian, Belgian and Greek airlines are Alitalia, Sabena and Olympic. SAS of Scandinavia is one of the biggest handlers of RTW flights and offers a large number of connections. Swissair, which has 32 RTW connections, and Lufthansa of Germany both enjoy a good reputation for service and punctuality, and are the only two airlines to offer first class within Europe. Lufthansa, in spite of being such a large carrier, does not have RTW partners. Spain's airlines tend to come and go, with the exception of Iberia, its national airline, which is well established. TAP of Portugal is a friendly carrier which has recently updated its fleet; it has very good connections with Brazil and parts of Africa. KLM Dutch airlines shares the honours with Lufthansa for having Europe's most modern fleet. It is a very big, highly regarded airline, with worldwide connections from its Schipol base. KLM's RTW partners are: North-west, United Airlines, Continental Airlines, Air New Zealand, Canadian Airlines and Aerolineas Argentinas.

Deciding on an Itinerary

Before planning your itinerary, be clear about the sort of trip you want to take. Are you going to focus on one particular region or string together several contrasting cultures? Do you want to travel continuously or are you planning to work for some of the time? Your budget will influence your decision to some extent, but whatever your plans, it's possible – indeed, vital – to tailor your itinerary to meet your needs and interests.

Freedom of choice is the great advantage of independent travel, and the longer you're abroad the more relaxed your itinerary can afford to be. Although variety is important, a whirlwind tour of as many countries as possible isn't the best way to see the world. The busier your timetable the less you'll actually see, and it's easy to fall behind schedule; what use are three remaining stopovers if you've only a week to go?

By visiting fewer places and spending more time in each of them your trip can be spontaneous – fellow travellers are an invaluable source of information on worthwhile detours – and with more time on your hands you'll be able to dig beneath the tourist gloss. A year-long journey focusing on two or three contrasting continents – half a dozen countries at most – offers plenty of scope and sufficient variety to add spice to your trip and help sustain your enthusiasm for travel. The obvious mix is a combination of Western nations and developing countries, which are found (predominantly) in the southern hemisphere.

The developing world – basically Asia, Africa, South America and the Caribbean – is intriguing, exotic and often challenging; the perfect cocktail for the adventurous traveller. Each of them has a distinct identity, but it's true to say that Africa is characterized by tribal allegiance, Asia by its sheer diversity of cultural and religious influences, South America by its Spanish and Portuguese inheritance, and the Caribbean by the legacy of the colonial slave-trade. It pays to do a bit of research in order to find out which parts of the world will best suit your tastes and interests (see **Where to Go**, p. 5). More detailed information on individual destinations is listed throughout Section Two, and travel agents – do consult more than one – will be able to offer you additional advice.

ROUTE PLANNING
Throwing yourself into alien cultures unlike anything you've experienced before can be a disconcerting experience, so an itinerary that initially dodges the more demanding parts of the world is a good idea. Avoid making India, one of the most notoriously difficult destinations, your first stopover; if you're on an RTW journey heading east, ease yourself into it with a stopover in Egypt or Kenya before tackling India. Though, in the light of current political differences, these places cannot be guaranteed safe destinations. An alternative could be found in some of the Middle East states, but these do not lend themselves easily to backpackers. Not all of Asia is hard going: Singapore represents the other end of scale, Indonesia lies somewhere in between, and visits to any of the popular Southeast Asian destinations will be fairly relaxed. Because they've not been included in traditional east–west RTW routes, many travellers overlook Africa and South America or place them way down on the list of places to be visited. Although authoritarian rule and civil strife have been common to both regions – not to mention grinding poverty – don't let sweeping generalizations put you off now that they're becoming more accessible.

It may seem hard to believe, but complacency of the oh-no-not-another-day-in-paradise variety can set in surprisingly quickly once the initial buzz of being away has fizzled out. Soon after this you may become bored and frustrated and experience an overwhelming desire to move on to somewhere new. These feelings hit different travellers at different times: on average, two to three months of non-stop travel in one country or continent is enough for most people. Not everyone is afflicted, but if when planning your route you build in some flexibility, you'll be able to combat this fatigue should it arise. Or you can plan a route that takes you from chaotic Bombay to the tranquillity of the Kerala backwaters; from the emptiness of the Australian Outback to the tidy suburbia of Adelaide. Build contrasts into your schedule by planning some time on the beach after an arduous spell of city-sightseeing, or a scenic train ride as an antidote to all those obligatory visits to not-to-be-missed national sights. Don't stick to one mode of transport for too long: hitch-hiking and camping will make a change after endless buses and backpacker hostels. And there's no rule that says you have to stick to the main tourist route, ask around once you're out there for alternative places worth a visit. If you end up anywhere interesting, write and tell us.

BUDGETING

Long-haul and RTW tickets on the popular Asia—Australia—North America 'highway' are always good value; it's a competitive routing and there are plenty of flights. Side-stepping jaunts to Africa, South America and the Caribbean can be incorporated into an RTW itinerary, but only at considerable additional expense. If you're particularly interested in one of these regions, and your funds or time are limited, you'd be better off taking a more direct route. Air fares to South America have dropped in price recently. Keep an eye out for one-off bargains on all routes in the national press. In general, RTW fares across the northern hemisphere are cheaper than RTW tickets for journeys south of the equator, but countries in the southern hemisphere tend to be less expensive to travel through.

The affordability of the developing world has long attracted budget-conscious travellers. Although prices vary from country to country, accommodation, food and transport are always remarkably good value. There are plenty of ways to stretch your budget, see **Working Your Way Round**, p. 15. When the constant upheaval of travel starts getting to you, it can work wonders to settle down for a while. Temporary work will boost your funds, and after a few weeks back at the nine-to-five you'll be craving the open road again. But bear in mind that opportunities for casual employment are severely limited in the developing world and even lands of opportunity like Australia have been hit by the economic recession. Legal restrictions on aliens seeking employment are strictly enforced the world over these days. Europeans are free to roam fellow EC member states for up to three months in search of work and, thanks to Working Holiday visas – if you're aged between 18 and 25 – you can legally hunt for temporary employment in Australia and New Zealand. Elsewhere it's a different story – unless you're on an official student vacation scheme, or indentured (sponsored) by a local company, above-board casual work will be virtually impossible to find in the United States and Canada.

Nevertheless, the constraints imposed by travelling on a tight budget are one of the major causes of travel fatigue, so try to allow some flexibility in your purse strings: a slap-up meal or a soft bed every now and again will do wonders for your morale. Put it on credit card if you can't afford the cash.

Buying a Ticket

Wherever you travel, the framework of your itinerary will be tied to the international flight paths that link the major countries and cities of the world. Airlines operate on different routes, but all of the big names fly via regional gateway destinations which serve local and international air traffic. It's these routes that are most likely to be discounted, and these are the airports with the greatest variety of onward flights. Whether you opt for a set itinerary arranged by a travel agent or decide to piece together your own route will depend on what sort of trip you have in mind.

RTW itineraries, though a popular choice, are by no means the only option. If you do use one, consider stitching together your own itinerary rather than picking up an off-the-peg route put together by a travel agent. But don't commit yourself to anything until you have looked into all the other possibilities. See **The Ticket to Suit Your Needs**, p. 21 for details of tickets that take a circular route round individual continents; open-jaw tickets that allow you to arrive at one destination and fly home from another, even if it's in another country; open-return tickets with stopovers *en route* each way; and the pros and cons of setting off with a one-way ticket and the intention of buying additional tickets as and when you need them.

WHERE TO BUY YOUR TICKET
The good news is that value-for-money air fares are widely available. Unfortunately, it's up to the bargain hunter to track them

down. The travel trade is fiercely competitive; special offers and new deals spring up all the time. If you can be flexible about dates and routings, you can take advantage of discounts and deals as and when they arise. Put another way, if you can't be flexible, you may miss out. RTW deals are available all year, but many bargain flights on competitive transatlantic and long-haul routes are short-term initiatives that come and go. Keep an eye out, too, for charter deals – they're a lot more widespread on long-haul sectors than they used to be. Equally, by planning ahead you can deliberately pick a cheap season to fly. As a rule, the best deals go to those who either book very early or very late. See **When to Go**, p. 8.

Most bargain flights out of the UK are from Heathrow and Gatwick, but if you're prepared to change planes *en route* in Europe, it's possible to fly from local provincial airports without travelling via London, and the transfer between planes will probably be a lot smoother. Whatever your plans, keep an ear to the ground for news on current trends in the months leading up to your travels, especially if you're planning a long trip. It's worth keeping an eye on the London offices of the major airlines for any special promotions (addresses in section 3).

Word-of-mouth recommendations are a useful short cut, but don't forget to look elsewhere, too. Even the most attentive and friendly of travel agents will be pushing a particular brand or product, so don't expect the whole story from a single company – although a good one will have access to literally hundreds of deals. There's no need to brace yourself for the hard sell, just check the alternatives before parting with any cash. Once abroad, check the notice boards of local youth hostels; many of them, particularly in the USA, advertise schemes enabling you to travel one-way across the Atlantic very cheaply, getting you home for next to nothing.

Bucket shops: Once the obvious option for budget travellers, these are now just one of several possibilities. Bucket shops started up in the 1970s as unlicensed outlets for heavily discounted air fares; they operate through a loophole in the law which allows them to buy cheap tickets in bulk from airlines and to make a profit by selling these tickets separately at a discounted yet marginally lucrative price to individual customers. It's also a convenient way for airlines to dump unwanted seats, though they invariably deny any link with bucket shops because the arrangement breaks established ticketing agreements. A very small percentage of flights are sold illegally, but the majority of bucket shop tickets are safe to use and completely above board, despite their anonymous offices (which are as much an attempt to avoid expensive high-street rents as they are a deliberate ploy to keep a low profile). Many operate on a tele-sales only basis, so you won't always be able to visit in person. For the same reason, advertising is often limited to word of mouth and small classified ads in the press (see **Sources**, p.60). Alternatively, ring round the airlines and ask for details of their consolidators – it's the title they prefer to use when talking about bucket shops.

Initially bucket shops were shunned by IATA (International Air Travel Association) and ABTA (Association of British Travel Agents), two of the travel industry's governing bodies, not least because of their disreputable image – some outlets offered tickets that were dirt-cheap because the flight simply didn't exist. Now, however, many reputable bucket shops are licensed IATA/ABTA members, and these are the ones you should deal with (it's a good idea to check that the membership is legitimate: simply phone IATA/ABTA and quote the agent's IATA/ABTA number). See also **Security**, p. 44.

Because they're out to sell as many fares as possible, bucket shops are not a source of detailed information on places to go or advice concerning inoculations and visas. And don't assume they're automatically the cheapest travel agents, or that the scruffiest-looking outfit is keeping its costs to a minimum. 'Discounted' can mean a variety of things as well as low cost – officially discounted tickets usually come with restrictions; a bucket shop may simply be selling these without advertising the added rules concerning when the ticket can be used. The other myth which has no foundation in truth is the one about bucket shops only selling flights on dodgy Eastern European and developing world airlines. Yes they do but, depending on which consolidators they work with, they also deal with mainstream carriers, and sell business and first-class seats.

The major airlines, in a bid to halt mid-season price wars, have recently cut fares: 1995 prices were generally at or below the levels of the previous year. This may seem like good news for the traveller, but if the trend continues, airline promotions and other discounts are likely to be less impressive than hitherto. How far this affects the bucket-shop market depends on passenger demand and the number of flights being operated. Bucket-shop flights on European routes are already limited because of tighter controls and excellent official deals and discounts. Details of flights offered by bucket shops (and other last-minute bargains) can be found on teletext's travel pages.

Adventure travel agents: These agents combine low, though not always rock-bottom, air fares with a variety of other services. The three main companies – Campus Travel, STA and Trailfinders – arrange flights worldwide, and they specialize in RTW routings to off-the-beaten-track destinations. Each operates slightly differently, but between them they offer a variety of supplementary facilities including inoculation centres, visa agencies, emergency help-lines and travel shops.

You can expect well-travelled consultants to talk you patiently through all the options, especially when it comes to intricate RTW routings and multi-stopover itineraries. Visit in person, or make arrangements by phone. They're bonded by IATA/ABTA and generally use mainstream airlines on direct routes. Each company caters for budget-minded travellers of all ages, but Campus Travel in particular is closely linked with universities. It has offices on campuses around the country, and offers many good student and under-26s discounts – and they're often tied in with university holidays.

As part of an upbeat marketing strategy, each company produces a detailed brochure. They're available free from display bins outside tube stations in central London, or you can join the mailing list and have them posted to your home. Call the following numbers for details:

Campus Travel: These specialists in student and youth travel are definitely worth checking out for your round-the-world trip. Not only are they well versed in selling long-haul travel but they can offer you advice on how to plan your route, what to see, and the best time to travel. Being one of the largest chains of specialists in Britain means they have access to a wide range of competitive fares. They can also book you on a myriad of adventure tours or trekking holidays, provide internal travel passes (by air, train and coach), design a tailor-made itinerary to suit your needs and offer travel insurance geared for young independent travellers. Campus Travel has an extensive network of UK branches, on many college and university campuses, in university towns and in YHA adventure shops. For more details, contact their head office at: Campus Travel, 52 Grosvenor Gardens, London, SW1. European destinations (tel. 0171 730 3402), North America (tel. 0171 730 2101), worldwide (tel. 0171 730 8111). Manchester office (tel. 0161 273 1721); Edinburgh office (tel. 0131 668 3303). See **Getting the Best Deal**, p. 42.

STA: Offices overseas and in Bristol (tel. 0117 929 4399); Manchester (tel. 0161 834 0668); and London–North American destinations (tel. 0171 937 9971), European destinations (tel. 0171 937 9921), rest of world (tel. 0171 937 9962).

Trailfinders: Offices in London and Manchester. London office contact details: Long-haul destinations (tel. 0171 938 3366/3939); Transatlantic and European destinations (tel. 0171 937 5400/938

3232). Manchester office contact details: Long-haul destinations (tel. 0161 839 6969); transatlantic and European destinations (tel. 0161 839 3636).

Travelbag (tel. 0171 497 0515/0420 88724). Open Mon.–Fri. 9 a.m.–7 p.m.; Sat. 9 a.m.–5 p.m.

Bridge the World (tel. 0171 911 0900). These travel consultants can help with RTW tickets and adventure travel worldwide.

Adventure tour specialists: These cater for people who want to travel overland as part of an escorted group, though some also tailor individual tours and offer flight-only departments. They either cover worldwide destinations, or focus on a couple of continents. If you're thinking of travelling alone you could incorporate into your itinerary a stint with one of these tour groups. They'll take you well off the beaten track and their all-inclusive rates can work out cheaper than going solo. If you're headed for Australia, look out for trips organized by Contiki and Top Deck once you're out there. Also see **Who to Go With**, p. 17.

Explore Worldwide (tel. 01252 319 448 – 24 hrs)

Exodus (tel. 0181 637 0859 – 24 hrs)

Dragoman (tel. 0171 370 1930 – 24 hrs)

Guerba (tel. 01373 827 046 – 24 hrs)

Steamond International (tel. 0171 978 5500)

Journey Latin America (tel. 0181 747 8315)

Passage to South America (tel. 0171 602 9889 – 24 hrs)

Travel clubs: WEXAS International is a London-based travel club with over 35,000 members. In exchange for an annual subscription of £39.58, a variety of services, value-for-money flights and tours worldwide are on offer, as are discounts on certain hotels and car rental firms. WEXAS travel insurance premiums are particularly competitive. Several publications are mailed to members, including a quarterly newsletter and *Traveller* magazine. Well-travelled staff are on hand to offer advice and, with a lowest-price policy, their pledge that you can save your subscription many times over is no idle boast. (For details, tel. 0171 589 3315.)

High street travel agents: With so many budget and specialist outlets to choose from, visiting your local travel agent may seem unnecessary. In fact, they're a useful starting point, if only to gauge average prices. Of the big four – Thomas Cook, Lunn Poly, Pickfords and Hogg Robinson – Thomas Cook is probably your best bet for general information and advice. Their larger branches have extensive libraries of books, directories and leaflets. Whichever travel

·agent you choose, remember to ask for discounted air fares because the first price to appear on the consultant's computer screen is unlikely to be the cheapest they have. All four sell RTW tours officially provided by co-operating airlines. They also sell packaged round-the-world holidays, for those lucky enough to be able to afford a couple of thousand pounds on what's essentially just a holiday. These two to three week adventures take in all the major stop-off points and cost around £2,000. Trailfinders and Thistle Air's offerings are worth a look, but the position changes from month to month, so the best advice is to get a good travel agent to give you up-to-the-minute information.

Alternatively try one of the small, independent travel agents that are scattered all over the country. As ever, personal recommendation is a good way to track them down. Often reliant on a high turnover to make a profit from slim margins, some provide a tele-sales only services, so check your local press and business directories. Try several – some operate like their big-name counterparts, others more like bucket shops. The Travel Group is an independent London-based tele-sales/flights only operator offering worldwide destinations/RTW itineraries (tel. 0181 313 0333).

Flight Bureaux: If you'd like a quick overview of who's offering what in terms of cheap deals, contact an air-fare information bureau. Different outfits operate in different ways, but the principle is the same: you can either telephone and request lists of travel agents offering cheap flights to specific destinations, or pay an annual subscription and receive a monthly directory of worldwide flights. Either way, the information covers fares available at that moment, so it'll go out of date fairly quickly, though the directory will be a useful source for tracking down independent travel agents and bucket shops. Most bureaux work on the system that only travel agents who pay to advertise with them get a directory entry – firms often sign up for a short period, while their special offer is available – so don't expect an exhaustive list.

The two main outfit is:

The Air Travel Advisory Bureau (ATAB). London-based, offers free telephone service on 0171 636 5000, Mon.–Fri. 9 a.m.–6 p.m.

Press Advertisements: National and local publications are a good source of budget travel advertisements (the broadsheet weekend press have particularly useful travel sections which often include full pages of budget airfare offers). Listings magazines like *Time Out*, *City Limits* and their regional counterparts are another option. In London, a traditional haven for Australasians, several free weekly publications for Antipodeans have sprung up. Packed with travel offers and information, they're available from display bins outside tube stations, or for about £10 you can subscribe for three months. Contact: *Southern Cross* (tel. 0171 244 6529) or *TNT* (tel. 0171 373 3377). Another possibility is the *Insider's Guide to Discount Air Fares*. This quarterly publication costs £49.50 annually and claims to contain information on the lowest airfares anywhere. For more details contact: Insider's Guides Ltd, PO Box 290, Southampton SO9 7XS.

Courier Work: If you can get involved with this, the perks are amazing – as long as you're not too bothered about the destination you travel to and the length of time spent there. Check your local telephone directory, just in case, but the London directory will have a wider selection of such companies.

GETTING THE BEST DEAL

Often, the biggest cost to the budget traveller is the initial outlay spent on flights. With a little planning and some prior knowledge, however, you can avoid burning a hole in your pocket. Increased competition amongst flight operators means that good deals abound for the holidaymaker. One way of keeping abreast of all the latest news in the flight industry is through 'Air talk', a regular column in the newly revamped Lonely Planet travel newsletter. To obtain a free one-year subscription to this quarterly newsletter, contact Lonely Planet on 0181 742 3181.

The following are details of various budget flight operators and some samples of the bargains being offered at the time of going to press. Please bear in mind that prices in the travel industry are subject to fluctuation, and this is particularly true of airfares; treat the fares quoted below as a rough guide only.

Connections (tel. 0171 495 5545) do a great variety of cheap deals on RTW and multi-stop tickets. For example:

London–Istanbul–Cairo *overland* to Tel Aviv–London (£310)

London–Bangkok–Manila–Hong Kong–London (£540)

London–Delhi *overland* to Khatmandu–Bangkok–London (£540)

London–Johannesburg–Harare–London (£555)

London–Bali–Australia–Singapore–London (£610)

Airline Ticket Network (tel. 01772 727272): the national sales centre for over 100 leading airlines. They offer scheduled flights to Australia with stopovers in Bangkok, Singapore, or Hong Kong from £600, and RTW tickets from £765.

Other great prices include:

London–San Francisco (£420 – high season)

London–New York (£350 – high season)

London–Johannesburg (£560)

Farebusters (Jupiter Travel): (tel. 0171 436 2711). Offers RTWs from £689 and multi-stopovers from £375.

Flightbookers (tel. 01500 212200) offer a number of excellent last-minute deals at scheduled prices. Specially priced itineraries include:

London–Boston–San Francisco–Toronto–London (£350)

If you're not too fussy about exactly when you go or are flexible about destinations, then last-minute deals can be positive eye-openers:

Direct Line Flights (tel. 0121 626 0013; open seven days a week, 9 a.m.–9 p.m.) claim to offer savings of up to 65% on scheduled airline standard prices. They offer direct flights to many US airports:

London–Dallas (from £275)

London–Minneapolis (from £275)

London–Seattle (from £280)

London–Denver (from £285)

Dial a Flight (tel. 0161 962 9799): flights to Orlando start at £175.

Super Travel (tel. 0121 606 1979). Flights to the Caribbean from £239.

Flightline (tel. 0171 323 4203). Flights to the Americas from £200, and to Asia from £350.

Australia Warehouse (tel. 01117 947 7700). London to Sydney from £539.

Worldwide Travel (tel. 01493 440239). Will try to undercut prices quoted by other operators on Virgin flights.

Skytrackers (tel. 0171 931 7000). Very cheap deals on returns and singles.

The high street chains also periodically offer good deals on round the world tickets:

Campus Travel (tel. 0171 730 8832). An example of one such high season offer is the very tempting:

London–Abu Dhabi–Jakarta–Bali–Cairns (*overland* to) Sydney–Auckland–Buenos Aires–London (£958)

Trailfinders (tel. 0171 938 3366) quote similar prices for the high season, when seat availability is limited, and have sporadic low-priced deals throughout the rest of the year, e.g:

London—Hong Kong—Tokyo—San Francisco—New York—London (£878).

RESERVATIONS PROCEDURES

If you book a flight several weeks in advance – the maximum is usually four months – try to pay promptly so that the ticket can be issued without delay. Fares go up roughly three times a year – aside from seasonal air-fare variations – and unless you 'kill that fare' to use the jargon, you may have to pay more than the price originally quoted. If you're using a bucket shop, other considerations have to be taken into account when paying in full, see **Security**, below.

Reservations and bookings can be made in person or by telephone. If you're arranging a particularly complex routing it might be best to pay a visit. Once a provisional booking has been made, a reservation slip will be issued. Quote these details when paying in full or reconfirming.

For advance bookings of eight weeks or more a personal cheque is acceptable, though it will have to arrive within three days, and clear, before the agent will issue your ticket. This process can take up to two weeks, so last-minute arrangements – less than a fortnight prior to departure – often cannot be paid by personal cheque unless accompanied by a Special Payment Provision (which costs £10). Payment by cash, credit card, traveller's cheques, banker's or building society draft, is always acceptable. If it's a very late booking, you may have to collect the ticket yourself, or pay for a courier.

Whenever you break your journey – 'stop off', in other words – you must reconfirm your next flight at least 72 hours before departure. Failure to do this will automatically cancel your reservation. Make sure, too, that you request any special in-flight dietary needs well in advance, and double-check the arrangements at least 24 hours before departure. Trips within the same country (domestic flights) have less stringent reconfirmation requirements, but it always pays to be well organized. Nowadays, many airlines will let you preselect your seat, so get a good window/aisle booking while you can.

SECURITY

Despite the existence of several trade associations and regulatory bodies, there is very little financial protection for passengers travelling on flight-only scheduled airline services. If you book through a travel agent bonded to ABTA (Association of British Travel Agents) or a member of IATA (International Air Travel Association), your money will be safe should the agent stop trading, provided a confirmed reservation has been made. But if an airline goes bust – which will be your main concern if you're travelling independently – you can expect little recompense. Credit-card bookings over £100 offer some security under the Consumer Protection Act 1974, but only for passengers who have booked direct with the airline; so unless you've been able to book months in advance and got a good discount on an Apex/Super Apex ticket (see **Travel Jargon**, p. 46) this will be an expensive precaution to take.

If you stick with mainstream airlines and reputable, bonded travel agents, there's little cause for concern. But when using a bucket shop, take additional precautions:

- If possible, visit the shop in person. Does it look like a reputable outfit?
- Check which airlines will be used, the routes they offer, and whether there are any minimum-stay restrictions governing stopovers etc. Will you have to change flights *en route* to your chosen destination? Remember, the cheapest airlines often fly the most convoluted routes – is this compatible with your plans?
- Compare the fare quoted against other travel agents.
- Check for any surcharges and cancellation fees that may not have been mentioned.
- Avoid paying anything more than a deposit before the ticket is issued. And keep the deposit down to 10%, paying by cheque or credit card if possible. With their slim profit margins, bucket shops sometimes charge an additional fee for credit cards.
- Once a reservation has been made, get written details of the airline(s)/airport(s) involved, the flight numbers, dates and times. Think twice before proceeding if you're refused any of these.
- Having got all this information, make a quick call to the airline(s) involved to check that your name appears on their central computer records.
- If your details are not known to the airline, query it with the bucket shop and, if necessary, cancel your deposit.
- Make sure that your ticket has 'OK', 'NK' or 'KK' written in the status box – it means your reservation has been confirmed. 'RQ' stands for reservation requested. See **How To Read Your Ticket**, p. 47.

TRAVEL JARGON

Fares

Apex/Super Apex: Advance Purchase Excursion fares are cheap flights issued by airlines. Restrictions include advance booking up to two months prior to departure and 100% cancellation fees. No longer so popular with shoestringers as a variety of alternative student/youth fares offer greater flexibility.

Pex/Super Pex: the instant purchase, short-haul equivalent of Apex fares. Serving mainly European destinations, they tend to involve a Saturday night stay (to discourage business travellers from using them).

Standby fares: most common on busy transatlantic routes, these cheap tickets can be bought at any time as singles or returns, but offer no guarantee of travel on specific flights/days because they're only valid if there are spare seats.

See **The Ticket to Suit Your Needs**, p. 21, for details of other fare categories.

Terminology

Bucket shop: An unlicensed travel agent dealing in unofficially discounted tickets.

Bumped: Because many passengers cancel flights or fail to turn up (no-shows), airlines double-book a certain percentage of seats on each flight. Seats are allocated on a first-come-first-show basis, if you're late and all the seats have gone you've been 'bumped'. This happens only very occasionally on popular routes, and you'll be offered the next available flight and/or compensated depending on the delay. See also **Know Your Rights**, p. 83.

Business class: On a plane, this class comes between Economy and First. For the extra money, you get extra frills. This is a 'C' or 'J' ticket code.

Carrier: An airline.

Departure tax: Imposed by some countries when you leave, prevalent across the developing world. Flight-only air fares rarely include this additional cost.

Fifth Freedom: When the airline that you are travelling on has no relation to the country you departed from, nor to the country you will arrive in (e.g. if you fly Qantas between London and New York).

Gateways: Major airport centres for regional and international traffic. London and Paris are gateways for Europe, Singapore and Hong Kong service Asia.

MPM: Maximum Permitted Mileage. This is used when you pay full fare. It allows stopovers at no extra charge.

Option: A provisional booking held open by an airline, awaiting confirmation and payment.

Sixth Freedom: When you fly between two countries on the airline of another country but go through that country en route (e.g. if you fly Qantas from Bangkok to London via Sydney).

Stopover: A break in your journey from which you can stay over, as opposed to 'via' which is the route taken by an airline, usually a refuelling stop.

HOW TO READ YOUR TICKET

Airline tickets are all printed and made out to a standard format – usually in English. Even so, they can look incredibly complicated so the following guide should help you translate your Round the World ticket.

1. **Endorsements/Restrictions** – Indicates whether you have an off-peak ticket which disqualifies you from certain peak-time flights. Shouldn't affect Round the World travellers.
2. **Name of Passenger** – Your surname, initial and title. Should coincide with that on your passport.
3. **Coupon Not Valid After** – As it says, though this will normally be 180 days or a year.
4. **Date of Issue**
5. **Fare Calculation** – Will show the price for each additional sector but may not itemize costs for each scheduled Round the World sector. Will also detail the carrier for each sector abbreviated to two letters (e.g. BA would indicate British Airways, CX for Cathay Pacific and so on. They are not always obvious.)
6. **Date and Place of Issue** – Agency or airline stamp which is essential to validate a ticket. Keep a note of this information in case you lose your ticket.
7. **Routing** – Departure and destination airports. You will probably need two or three actual tickets so keep them all safe and in order.

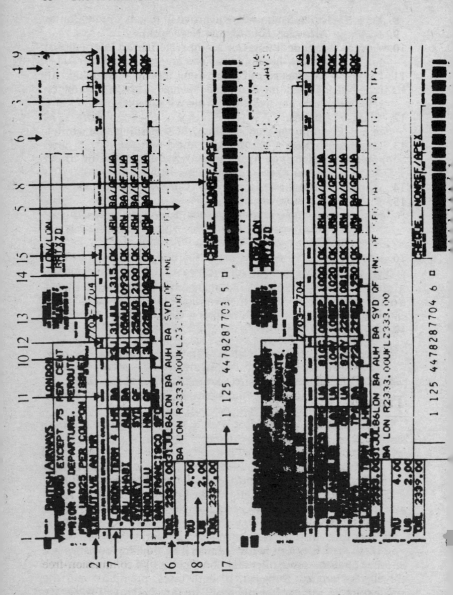

8. **Fare Basis** – Will show fare being used.
9. **Baggage Allowance** – Usually 23 kilograms.
10. **Actual Baggage Weight** – Number of pieces (and weight) filled in by check-in desk.
11. **Carrier** – Airline identification code and flight number. All scheduled flights have unique numbers which should be remembered at departure airports until called.
12. **Class** – Ticket class: F – First Class; J or C – Club Class; Y, M or B – Economy or Tourist Class; R – Supersonic (Concorde).
13. **Departure Date** – The first date must be filled in, but obviously successive ones may be left to your own discretion. Don't forget to reserve onward flights when you land!
14. **Departure Flight Time**
15. **Status** – OK – confirmed seat reservation; RQ – space requested but not confirmed; NS – infant not occupying a seat; SA – subject to space being available; OPEN – reservation not requested.
16. **Total Fare** – May be broken down already (at 5) into local currencies. This box will show total fare paid in whatever currency you paid in.
17. **Ticket Number** – Keep a note of this unique number safely. It shows the airline code number and ticket serial number.
18. **Tax** – Will show any taxes which must be collected before ticket issue, e.g. US Departure and Security Tax.

Travel Insurance

Don't risk an arm and a leg – financially as well as physically – by scrimping on travel insurance. It may not come cheap, but should the unexpected occur, your insurance will more than likely pay for itself, and peace of mind is priceless whatever happens. That said, ensuring that you're adequately covered for what you want to do, and understanding what's expected of you as the policy-holder, is a little less cut and dried.

Mainstream insurance companies are worth approaching if you're already a policy-holder. Banks and building societies are another option – some offer additional perks like commission-free traveller's cheques. However, in both cases, premiums and the small print of the exclusion clauses frequently prove prohibitive when compared to the policies offered by the insurance departments of adventure travel agents such as WEXAS, STA, Trailfinders and Campus Travel (see pp. 38–9). These agents have policies tailored to meet the particular needs of independent, off-the-beaten-track travellers:

WEXAS offers a few schemes: their £99.50 offer is valid for a year, including all trips up to 10 weeks in duration.

Travel World (tel. 0171 739 3444) has policy costing £95, no membership necessary (no trip may exceed 120 days).

Campus Travel (tel. 0800 262 299) offers rates from 3 days in Europe (£9.50) to 24 months worldwide (£54).

Club Direct (tel. 01730 817533) offers several schemes. 'Club Classic' and 'Club Choice' offer policies for an unlimited number of trips during a 12-month period. Backpackers can get a policy for £35 for travel within Europe and £45 worldwide. They offer the option of 17 or 31 days maximum per trip.

Cover varies according to the individual policy, but look out for hazardous-hobbies insurance if you're planning on anything more adventurous than straightforward sightseeing. Hill-trekking (which is sometimes classified as an alpine sport, regardless of altitude or location) is one example, skiing is another. Twenty-four-hour medical help-lines offer advice if you fall ill, and the duty staff can confirm your insurance details with foreign doctors (American medical care is totally reliant on private health cover). Likewise, the services of a chartered air-ambulance could be vital if you were to become seriously ill in a part of the world without adequate medical services. Consider specialist US automobile cover if you're going to be hiring a car in America. And wherever you're going, check that the claims limit for individual items is sufficient, especially if you've got an expensive camera.

Typical premiums: Depending on the type of insurance cover offered, expect to pay around £25 for a month in Europe; £80–£220 for six months, and in excess of £170 for a year. Premiums for worldwide cover start at about £45 for a month; £150-plus for six months or more. Apart from the WEXAS members' premium of £99.50 for twelve months, most 12-month policies will cost between £300 and £600, depending on the cover.

Making a claim

- Carry with you a couple of photocopies of all important documents – passport, traveller's cheque proof-of-purchase papers, insurance documentation, receipts for valuables – leaving the originals at home. If you have to cancel a flight or need to return home earlier than planned, you'll also need ticket/deposit receipts.

- A clean bill of health from your doctor or dentist will smooth the way should you need to claim for unexpected treatment abroad. Check what cover there is for any existing ailments before taking out a policy. Often the cost of urgent treatment, if not routine work, is refundable.
- Get as much paperwork as possible to substantiate your claim: a police report for lost or stolen property (within 24 hours of noticing anything missing); an explanatory note from the carrier (airline, bus/train/shipping company) if anything happens while you're on the move); a medical report if you're examined by a doctor or dentist.
- Claims usually have to be made asap, and certainly within a month of the policy expiring. Not all holiday insurance companies will let you renew your policy indefinitely, but if you need to extend your cover while you're away (most are valid for a year) phone through and pay by credit card, or rely on someone back home to sort it out and send you the documentation. Without proof of current cover you may not get medical treatment as swiftly as you need it.
- Opt-out clauses: the big grey area with all insurance claims is the matter of 'due care and attention' on behalf of the policyholder. The simple solution is not to do anything foolish, which is easier said than done once you've relaxed into your travels. Ultimately, as soon as you've allowed something out of your sight it becomes subject to this clause, but there are ways to minimize the risks, see **Keeping Healthy** and **Staying Safe**, pp. 91, 100.

Ludicrous requests for unsubstantiated amounts of cash that have mysteriously gone missing aren't going to get very far, neither will claims for financial losses incurred at the hands of a skilled poker player, but if you do feel you've a legitimate case and the insurance company aren't co-operating, contact the Insurance Ombudsman Bureau, 31 Southampton Row, London WC1B 5HJ.

For general information, request a copy of the guide *Holiday Insurance* from the Association of British Insurers, Aldermary House, 10–15 Queen Street, London EC4N 1TT.

Formalities

PASSPORTS

Correct, you will need one of these! Post offices stock the necessary application forms, the instructions are self-explanatory. Allow at least a month for the paperwork to be processed, longer between February and September, and over the Christmas period. UK passports cost £15 for the 32-page version, £22.50 for the 48-page. Both are valid for ten years, which one you choose is up to you: 32 pages should be sufficient unless you're planning a lengthy journey through lots of countries – overland across Africa, for example. A smaller passport won't take up so much space in your money belt, and will look a little less conspicuous.

If you already have a valid passport, make sure its life-span exceeds your planned return date by at least six months. This is a prerequisite for entry into many countries, and gives you the freedom to prolong your travels should you wish. If you lose your passport while you're away, replacements can be obtained from overseas British consulates and embassies, though don't let this lull you into a false sense of security. See **What to Do if You . . .**, p. 116.

Israeli or South African visa stamps in a passport will prevent you from entering certain countries (most notably the Arab world and Black Africa). One way round this is to apply for a replacement or duplicate passport. If you're planning to visit either of these regions *en route* to other parts of the world, ask to have visa stamps recorded on detachable sheets that can be slipped temporarily into your passport. These days, immigration officers will usually oblige.

VISAS

Entry visas are a legal requirement in many parts of the world. Some countries issue them to visitors at border-points, others expect the necessary paperwork to be sorted out in advance. Most visas cost between £5 and £20 and will be valid for single, double or multiple visits during a set period. They usually have a limited life-span: for example, you may have to enter the country within three months of your passport being stamped. Because of this, if you're planning to travel for several months, you'll probably have to sort out some of your visas *en route*, or where permissible at border-points when you arrive.

Rules and regulations change, so contact all the relevant embassies for up-to-date advice before you leave home. Find out exactly what's required, and the cost. If the visa must be applied for before you set out on your travels, check the embassy's office hours; whether there are any imminent national holidays when they will be closed; what the preferred method of payment is; and how many passport photos are required. Whatever the procedure, be prepared to queue. Most visas take at least 24 hours to be processed, so you'll probably have to come back in a day or two. If you haven't got the time to do this, ask about postal services (always send your passport by recorded delivery), or enlist the services of a visa bureau. For a handling fee, usually about £11 per visa, these agencies do all the leg work for you. Contact the Rapid Visa Service (tel. 0171 373 3026) or Visa Shop Ltd (tel. 0171 379 0419/0376). Adventure travel agents invariably have their own service, see p. 37.

Where visas are to be applied for *en route*, make sure you have plenty of passport photos to hand, and expect to encounter the usual administrative wrangles. Don't be surprised if you need to produce a so-called letter of introduction from the nearest British consulate confirming your identity. It's nothing more than a formality, but will cost you an additional £5 or so.

Border-point visas are issued by some countries automatically at airports or border crossings. Be prepared to answer a few questions about where you've been and what you intend to do during your stay. Looking reasonably presentable will smooth your way, as will a co-operative attitude. Hippy attire isn't always appreciated; indeed, Thai immigration law explicitly states that visitors who develop any such tendencies during their stay will be expelled! Long hair (tied back) is generally okay, but a little decorum when it comes to clothes goes a long way. Immigration officers at the borders of developing countries may expect a financial incentive to nudge them along, but *never* volunteer a bribe unless it's made clear that a gift would be appreciated (other travellers can often advise on what's required). Brief visits of a week or two may not incur a charge, otherwise expect to pay a visa fee.

For details of visa formalities around the world, turn to Section Three.

INOCULATIONS
Seek advice about inoculations at least 2 months before your travels, and be prepared for a course of injections. GPs won't necessarily know what's currently required for different parts of the world so, for up-to-date information, contact one of the following:

MASTA (Medical Advisory Services for Travellers Abroad) West

Yorkshire (tel. 01274 531 723). Open Mon.–Fri. 9 a.m.–5 p.m.
Hospital for Tropical Diseases, London (tel. 0171 636 6099).

Common travel illnesses and preventative inoculations

Typhoid	new oral vaccine is available.
Cholera	vaccination optional as present serum doesn't provide much, if any, protection. If you decide not to have it, at least request an official exemption form or get hold of a certificate claiming that you have been injected.
Hepatitis A	painful gammaglobulin jab required. If you opt for the short-term cover, have it just before you travel. New 10-year cover is now available.
Hepatitis B	disease spread by blood and blood products. See **Keeping Healthy**, p. 95.
Yellow fever	vaccination lasts 10 years, but doesn't take effect until 10 days after inoculation.
Rabies	a pre-emptive vaccination is now available, though not needed unless you're going to be working directly with animals
Polio and tetanus:	yes, you did have a jab and a sugar cube at school, but boosters are required.
Anti-malarial tablets:	these offer some protection against a disease which has claimed several tourists' lives in recent years. Contact the Malaria Reference Laboratory, London (tel. 0171 636 7921) for malaria conditions in the areas you'll visit: some strains are resistant to normal tablets. Tablets should be taken immediately before and after your trip as well while you're away. See **Sickness**, p. 94.

International certificates of vaccination are officially no longer required, except for proof of inoculation against yellow fever, but the paper work is still worth having. GPs may charge for completing them.

Not all inoculations are free under the NHS these days, so if you go to a GP or health clinic for your jabs expect to have to pay for your pain. What's more, doctors are not licensed to administer yellow fever jabs. Because of this, a trip to one of the specialist immunization clinics scattered around the country may make more sense. Ask about local clinics in your area, or call the following numbers for information and an appointment:

British Airways Travel Clinics (tel. 0171 831 5333 for details of your nearest clinic).

Trailfinders Immunization Centre, London (tel. 0171 938 3999).

The Department of Health (toll-free tel. 0800 555 777) can provide additional information, including a free leaflet *The Traveller's Guide to Health* (ask for leaflet T1). It's also available from post offices and travel agents. Those planning an off-the-beaten-track jaunt for any length of time should consider investing in Dr Richard Dawood's excellent guide, *Traveller's Health: How to Stay Healthy Abroad* (Oxford University Press, £7.99).

How to Take Your Money

The more adventurous and lengthy your trip, the more money you're likely to need, and the more advisable it becomes to spread your funds. There are a variety of options, and such is the competitive nature of the financial services industry that new ones are springing up all the time. *Holiday Which* magazine (published quarterly and available in libraries), and the personal-finance pages of the national press (especially over the spring and summer) are good sources of objective travel-money advice.

TRAVELLER'S CHEQUES
Traveller's cheques are easy to purchase, widely accepted and easily replaceable if lost or stolen. They also have an indefinite life-span, and in many places foreign-currency traveller's cheques can be used like cash. That said, you'll have to pay for this convenience. Shop around, but expect to pay commission and/or handling fees when buying and selling (cashing in) cheques.
Buying: The commission rate when buying sterling traveller's cheques is around 1%; foreign-currency cheques are charged at 1.75%. Banks invariably charge a minimum fee of about £3 (more if you don't hold an account with them). Building societies tend to forgo minimum charges and their commission rate is often lower. Bureaux de change are another option: their rates vary enormously, but some will buy back − commission free and at the

same exchange rate – one-third of unused foreign currency cheques purchased from them.

Local banks usually stock traveller's cheques in a dozen or so popular currencies; you may have to order more obscure ones three days in advance. Main branches, bureaux de change, and exchange centres run by Thomas Cook and the like generally stock a wider range of currencies (in cash and traveller's cheques).

Selling: Avoid places where moneychangers are likely to charge high rates of commission for their convenient location – airports, border crossings, railway stations, popular tourist spots, etc. And don't be surprised if rates deteriorate when the banks are closed. For all these reasons, it pays to buy some local currency in advance, to tide you over when you first arrive.

What to take: US dollars are accepted worldwide; sterling can be less welcome. Where appropriate, local-currency cheques are a good idea, especially for trips to America and Western Europe. But only sterling ones can be paid straight back into a British bank account without incurring additional costs. £20 and £50 cheques (or the equivalent) are ideal for everyday use. A few £10 ones will save you from changing too much towards the end of a stay, while one or two £100 ones will cover hefty expenses.

Using cheques issued by two different companies can be useful. That way, if you're robbed or lose your traveller's cheques, you won't be reliant on one company for reimbursement. But do stick to big-name issuers like Thomas Cook, Visa and American Express. In the more remote parts of the world, obscure building society cheques will be carefully scrutinized, and often refused. Holders of American Express cheques can have their post sent to Amex offices, which in some parts of the world will be more reliable than the local poste restante.

If you're travelling with a friend, always take your own traveller's cheques in case something happens to the other person. And when selling, always count the money in front of the changer.

CASH

For convenience, cash can't be beaten, but it's the least secure way to carry your travel funds. Check how much your holiday insurance covers you for, but remember that if your money does go missing you won't be reimbursed until you're able to put in a claim with the insurers at home. Sterling is widely accepted but, as with traveller's cheques, US dollars are welcome worldwide. It's also worth having a small amount of local currency for when you first arrive. Buy it before you leave or *en route* in other countries. Oddly enough, exchange rates abroad usually favour traveller's cheques over cash.

As with traveller's cheques, a mix of denominations is advisable; single dollar bills will oil bureaucratic cogs and open doors, crisp one hundreds get the best black-market rates. See **Streetlife**, p. 106. Small emergency cash reserves stashed away in your camera case and rucksack are worth the risk in case you lose your money-belt; that way you'll have enough money to get you to the nearest phone or British consulate.

CREDIT CARDS

As useful for what they signify as what they can actually do, credit cards are a useful addition to traveller's cheques and cash. You can put a deposit down on a hire-car without actually parting with any money, and in the developing world a credit card will help smooth your journey whether you're trying to nip into a posh hotel for an air-conditioned high-tea or enter a country without sufficient hard currency or the regulatory onward ticket.

If you don't own a credit card, acquire one well in advance of your trip because the life-span of your first card is likely to be quite short. Most banks charge an annual fee for issuing Visa and/or Mastercard (Access) cards. Your own bank is an obvious choice, but check out the competition, especially Barclaycard (issued free to students) – ask how many days of interest-free credit the card offers. Visa is the most widely accepted credit card, but as with traveller's cheques, it can be useful to have more than one.

Existing card-holders should make sure the expiry date on their card(s) doesn't fall while they're away. If you're going abroad for several months contact the credit-card company and explain the situation. Either leave your account in credit, or arrange a standing order with the bank to cover minimum monthly payments and the annual fee. Alternatively, have someone pay off monthly bills on your behalf. And memorize your PIN number because you can often use credit cards in foreign cashpoint machines.

The interest rates charged for credit-card purchases and cash withdrawals (from cashpoints or over the counter) abroad are identical. Each credit-card company sets a recommended rate, but banks – the middlemen – invariably add their own commission on top. The amounts aren't outrageous but they can add up, especially with cash withdrawals because interest on these is charged from the moment the transaction is made, not after a set period of time once your monthly statement has been issued. A typical transaction charge is 1.5%.

Travel in Europe and America, in particular, can be paid for almost exclusively by credit card. Elsewhere, plastic is a good standby for both emergencies and the occasional luxury. A £1,000 credit limit will be enough to get you on a one-way flight home from just about anywhere.

BEWARE: credit-card fraud is a major problem. To make matters worse, the onus is on the card-holder to prove that a transaction was fraudulent. If your card goes missing contact the issuing company as quickly as possible. Once that's done, your liability is limited to £25, though you may have to pay up if the card has been used in the meantime.

A tougher fraud to trace is phantom bills that start appearing on monthly statements even if your card hasn't gone missing. To minimize this risk, don't allow credit cards out of your sight. It doesn't take two seconds for someone to run off a few extra bills, and once you're long gone it's easy for them to duplicate your signature. More serious than the opportunist thief are the syndicates that make up duplicate cards, though as yet this isn't widespread.

Feeling paranoid? Don't be, the potential risks may be higher than at home, but there are ways to limit the pitfalls. Keep a record of your card number and the credit company's international helpline separately from your credit card. For an annual fee of £7, Card Protection Plan (tel. 0171 351 4400) will cancel all your cards and request replacements in the event of theft. See also **What to Do if You . . .**, p. 116.

LINK CARDS

Link cards are cashpoint cards that can be used overseas in machines on the Plus-network. Issued by building societies, Girobank, and the smaller high-street banks, they allow you to borrow up to £250 a day from your account back home. They aren't credit cards, so the potential risks of fraud are lower, but do keep your PIN number secret.

Other British cashpoint cards can sometimes be used overseas; ask your bank for details. Obviously the developing world does not have many 'hole-in-the-wall' machines.

EUROCHEQUES

Eurocheque-books containing ten cheques, plus a eurocheque guarantee card (good for amounts up to £100), can be purchased from British banks. They are valid throughout Europe, including some Eastern bloc countries. With a PIN number, the card can also be used in cashpoints on the continent.

The big advantage of eurocheques is that you can write cheques in local currency. This service is free at the point of use, but your bank will charge you commission on each transaction, usually 1–2%, though additional handling charges may also be levied. Furthermore, you'll pay an annual fee of £4–10 for the guarantee card. Rates may be cheaper if you apply outside the holiday season, between November and April.

SENDING MONEY ABROAD

If you're going to be away for several months and don't want to carry all your money, there are various ways to spread your funds. Likewise, if you run short, money can be sent out to you.

Money transfers: Speak to the international department of your bank. They will have a list of representative agents abroad who will accept and hold your money. Expect to pay about £15 for the service, regardless of how much you're sending. It's also a good idea to check that the agent is still at the same address and that they are prepared to hold the money until you arrive, which may be several months after your initial departure. Ideally, get all this in writing from your bank. Depending on the efficiency of the foreign agent, you'll be able to pick up your money quite easily, but expect to pay a small administrative fee (regardless of what your own bank may tell you). And if you want to turn your cash into traveller's cheques, you'll pay the usual commission.

Foreign bank accounts: These are useful if you intend working overseas, say in Australia. Speak to your own bank about it, or contact the British head office of the relevant national bank, which will usually be based in central London. Expect to pay about £15 to telex the money (send it all in one go because you'll be charged each time, even when your account is set up). You'll be given some paperwork to pass on to the foreign branch when you arrive, but apart from that it's no more difficult than setting up a money transfer.

Obviously, it's best to pick a central branch in a city you intend to stay in for some time, though you can also travel around the country using local branches just as you would at home. The Commonwealth Bank of Australia pays interest on many of its accounts, so if you're heading slowly to Oz you may recoup the cost of the initial transfer of funds.

The big bonus of money transfers and foreign bank accounts is the security it offers. It's also an easy way to budget. But it's not cheap and can be inconvenient if you set up too many – one per continent is more than sufficient. And easy as it all sounds, the more remote your destination, the less straightforward it could prove to be.

HAVING MONEY SENT OUT TO YOU

Wiring money: Banks call this a telegraphic transfer. As with transferring money abroad before you leave, once a designated bank to receive the money has been agreed, the process is quick and easy. The sender pays for the telex; as the recipient, you may have to pay a handling fee. These fees vary. Banks charge senders a flat £15. Western Union charges £14 or under for amounts up £100, more for larger sums. Thomas Cook offers a similar service. Banks have a wide network of foreign agents, but check all the options for the best deal, including: Western Union (toll free 0800 833 833), Thomas Cook (tel. 01733 63200 and ask for the Telegraphic Transfer Service).

Banker's draft: A postal service that offers a cheaper (and slower) alternative to wiring money. A designated bank has to be agreed and forewarned, or a foreign bank account opened. The sender will pay about £10 for the cheque to be issued, £12 if the bank posts it. As the receiver, you should expect to pay a fee as well.

Girobank (based in post offices) provides a similar service. Prices vary according to what's required. Call 0151 933 3330 for details.

Researching Your Trip

SOURCES OF INFORMATION

Speaking to someone who's recently visited the place you're thinking of going to is a useful source of information and advice. If you draw a blank with friends and relatives, ask around at college or work. Tracking down useful people is not as difficult as you might think, and few travellers need much prompting when it comes to recounting their foreign jaunts.

Tourist boards are another source of useful information, though they inevitably play down any bad points. For politically sensitive areas, it might be wiser to phone the Foreign Office (tel. 0171 270 3000). That said, tourist offices are remarkably knowledgeable. Make your queries as specific as possible, and don't be surprised if you have to call several times before finally getting through.

When it comes to objective information and honest advice, you can't do better than a central library or a good bookshop. Both will have extensive travel sections. At the library, begin your browsing at the 910-shelves for general travel and tourism; the 610s for medicine and health; the 330s for working overseas. London, like many major cities, has several specialist travel bookshops:

The Travellers Bookshop, 25 Cecil Court, London WC2N 4EZ (tel. 0171 836 9132).

Edward Stanford Ltd, 12–14 Long Acre, London WC2E 9LP (tel. 0171 836 1321). Map centre in basement.

Waterstone's Mail Order Division, 4 Milsom Street, Bath BA1 1DA (tel. 01225 448 595).

A wide range of publications is available dealing with every conceivable aspect of travel. Background reading material is dealt with on a country-by-country basis in Section Two, but here is a brief overview:

Guides to countries and regions

Lonely Planet Publications: These guides are written from a resolutely see-and-survive perspective. The Shoestring Guides cover whole regions (South-east Asia, Africa or Eastern Europe, for example), while the Travel Survival Kits provide information on specific countries. A quarterly newsletter is also available. Australian head office: Lonely Planet Publications, PO Box 617, Hawthorn, Victoria 3122, Australia. London office: Lonely Planet Publications, Devonshire House, 12 Barley Mow Passage, Chiswick, London W4 4PH. (tel. 0181 742 3161 – mail-order enquiries only).

Rough Guides: Aimed (though not exclusively) at youthful independent travellers, Rough Guides cover cities, countries and regions. Having worked their way through Europe, Africa and America, Rough Guides are branching out into Asia and elsewhere. The nightlife sections are particularly well researched! Contact Rough Guides Ltd on 0171 379 3329.

Vacation Work: In addition to a range of Travel Survival Kits covering a number of countries and continents, Vacation Work also publishes several invaluable guides to working overseas, for further details, see **Arranging Work Abroad**, p. 64. Simon Calder, one of Vacation Work's most prominent writers, contributes regularly to the travel section in Saturday's *Independent*.

Travel and Trade Publications: The Handbook series provides information of interest to travellers of all ages and budgets in hardcover format. *The South America Handbook* is much praised. Head office: 6 Riverside Court, Riverside Road, Lower Bristol Road, Bath BA2 3DZ (tel. 01225 469 141).

Handbooks offering general advice

The Traveller's Handbook, ed. Sarah Gorman (WEXAS Ltd). A comprehensive planning-to-travel book. WEXAS also publish *Trouble-Free Travel*, Richard Harrington. Both are available at a reduced price to Wexas members, see p. 40 for details.

Culture Shock!: A series of guides to peoples and customs of countries overseas, published by Kuperard (London) Ltd.

The Budget Travel Handbook, Pat Yale (Horizon). Focuses on how to cut travel costs.

Additional reading

Cadogan Guides: informative, but not specifically geared at budget-minded travellers.

Fodor's Guides: the upmarket presentation reflects the intended readership.

Insight Guides: From APA Publications, these guides have useful information and good photographs.

Prolific contemporary travel writers to look out for include, in no particular order: Paul Theroux, Jonathan Raban, V. S. Naipaul, Redmond O'Hanlon, Bill Bryson, Colin Thubron, James Fenton, Eric Newby, Alexander Frater, Bruce Chatwin. A classic travel writer worth delving into is Wilfred Thesiger. After a healthy resurgence over the past decade, travel writing has again fallen prey to the critics' sneering challenge: 'Is it real writing?' True, travelogues are often a lot more enjoyable if you've visited the place yourself, but the best of them are observant, knowledgeable and often very witty.

There's no need to confine yourself to professional travel writers; reading novels by foreign-born authors is an excellent way to get a feel for a country, as are history books.

Magazines

Granta: A quarterly book-cum-magazine of contemporary creative writing and photography. Most editions include at least one travel-related piece. *The Best of Granta Travel* is a collection of travel reportage, essays and short stories. Both are available from bookshops, but regular readers will find it cheaper to subscribe. Back copies are available, and there's a no-obligation book club. Head office: Granta, 2/3 Hanover Yard, Noel Road, Islington, London N1 8BE (tel. 0171 704 0470).

World Magazine: A monthly publication combining travel with cultural, anthropological and environmental issues. It also follows up BBC programmes. Available from newsagents, or by subscription.

National Geographic: An enduring international monthly magazine from America, and arguably *the* overseas-interest publication. Famous for its photographs, some of the articles can be heavy going. Available from larger newsagents and by subscription.

The Traveller: Published quarterly by WEXAS International. Available to members only. For further information, see p. 40.

Marie Claire: A monthly women's magazine with an acclaimed (and adventurous) travel section. Regular holiday-related features over summer months. Available from all newsagents and by subscription.

A number of free weekly travel magazines and newspapers, such as *TNT* and *Southern Cross* are available from display bins outside tube stations throughout Central London, or by mail order (see p. 42).

The broadsheet weekend papers have travel sections mixing descriptive features with up-to-the-minute information on cheap flights. On Saturdays, check the *Independent, Guardian* and (surprisingly enough) the *Financial Times*. For detailed European news and features, turn to Friday's *Guardian* and the weekly *European* newspaper.

Television series dedicated to travel

Rough Guide: BBC2 midweek

Travelog: Channel 4 midweek

Lonely Planet: Channel 4 midweek

The Travel Show: BBC2 midweek in summer

Wish You Were Here: Carlton/ITV Monday (winter)

Traveller's Tales: Channel 4 midweek

Scottish Passport: STV Monday

Holiday: BBC1 Tuesday (winter)

Around the World in 80 days : BBC, one-off series starring Michael Palin, now available on video and in paperback from bookshops and video stores.

Pole to Pole: BBC sequel to Around the World, also starring Michael Palin; video and book available.

Look out, too, for mid-week documentaries (BBC2's Under the Sun, for instance) and foreign-film festivals.

Radio

Breakaway: Radio 4 Saturday 9.30 a.m.

The Art of Travel: Radio 4 midweek

A Case for Packing: Radio Scotland (tel. 0131 255 3131)

Other radio programmes with a foreign focus include:

Europhile: Radio 4 Saturday

Letter from America: Radio 4 Friday p.m./Sunday a.m.

From Our Own Correspondent: Radio 4 Saturday/midweek

In addition, check out programmes by investigative journalists like Michael Buerk, and adventurous presenters such as Andy Kershaw. Radio 5 often has offbeat programmes on the world at large.

Arranging Work Abroad

TEACHING ENGLISH

TEFL: Teaching English as a Foreign Language is big business. Native English speakers are in demand wherever people want to learn the language. To meet this need, a large number of TEFL training colleges have sprung up in the UK to equip would-be teachers with the necessary skills. A TEFL certificate isn't essential, but language schools abroad are getting fussier, and the best pay and conditions inevitably go to most eligible employees. Training courses and qualifications on offer include:

The Royal Society of Arts (RSA) certificate is universally recognized and highly regarded. Courses are intensive and costly: about £700 for a month of rigorous training. For details of RSA affiliated colleges, contact:

The Royal Society of Arts, 8 John Adam Street, London WC2N 8EY.

The British Council, English Language Information Unit, 10 Spring Gardens, London SW1A 2BN.

Introductory TEFL courses are offered by a growing number of organizations. They don't have the kudos of an RSA qualification, but many of the colleges have direct links with overseas language schools. Introductory courses last a week, cost £150 on average and are offered all over the country. Courses by correspondence are cheaper. Contact the following prominent companies for details of their regional courses, or look for small ads in the national press.

Lingurama, New Oxford House, 16 Waterloo Street, Birmingham B2 5UG (tel. 0121 632 5925).

Inlingua Method Courses, Rodney Lodge, Rodney Road, Cheltenham, GL50 1JF.

TESL: Teaching English as a Second Language to ethnic minorities in Britain (on a voluntary basis) is a rewarding way to acquire relevant experience. You won't end up with a formal qualification, but all it costs is time and effort. Contact the voluntary-services unit of your local authority or other local community groups that may be co-ordinating TESL programmes. After several evening classes, you'll be placed with a student whom you'll visit and teach. Arrangements are flexible, but there is a degree of commitment, so sign up as far in advance of your foreign trip as possible.

Direct recruitment: JET (Japan Exchange and Teaching) is an organization which selects and sends people under the age of 35 to teach in Japan. No experience necessary. Contact the JET Programme Desk, Council of International Exchange, 33 Seymour Place, London W1H 6AT (tel. 0171 224 8896).

Finding a job: If your training college can't find you a vacancy, check the national press. Alternatively, look for work once you're abroad. Local English-language papers often advertise vacancies, as do noticeboards in backpacker hostels. Ask around: many people land jobs on the strength of little more than a presentable appearance, enthusiasm, and the inability to speak the local language – it's a guarantee that you'll talk nothing but English in the classroom. A degree or similar qualification goes down well, so take copies of any relevant certificates.

Finding out more: Courses and worldwide foreign vacancies are advertised in the national press, especially the *Guardian* (Tuesdays and Saturdays), and the *Times Educational Supplement*. Books worth reading include:

Teaching English Abroad, Susan Griffith (Vacation Work).

How to Teach Abroad, Roger Jones (How to Books).

Coming Up Roses, Michael Carson (Black Swan Books). An offbeat novel about a TEFL teacher in the Middle East.

SUMMER CAMP WORK

In spite of being notoriously hard work, camp courier jobs have boomed in popularity over recent years. Summer vacancies for placements in Europe and North America, working either with the general public or schoolkids, begin appearing in the press the preceding autumn, so keep an eye out and plan well ahead.

At Summer Camps in the USA, two types of counsellor are required. General ones serve as basic supervisors for the campers, and specialist counsellors are able to teach one of a vast array of sporting and non-sporting activities. A basic knowledge and ability to do your chosen activity, along with great enthusiasm for working with children, will get you just as far as a whole load of coaching certificates would. If you really can't think of anything you could teach the campers, try working on the kitchen or maintenance program or in the camp office as a general clerk or secretary. There are various types of camp, most of which are privately owned. Some are specifically for handicapped children, others for under-privileged inner-city kids or those with other special needs and are usually either run by charities or funded by the state. Though probably harder work, these could well be very rewarding.

North America and environs:

BUNAC, 16 Bowling Green Lane, London EC1R 0DB (tel. 0171 251 3472). For positions in America, Canada and Jamaica.

Camp America, 37A Queen's Gate, London SW7 5HR (tel. 0171 581 7373, or brochure line: 0171 581 7333).

Europe

Canvas Holidays, 12 Abbey Park Road, Dunfermline, Fife KY12 7PD.

KeyCamp Holidays, 92–6 Lind Road, Sutton, Surrey SM1 4PL.

EuroSites Overseas Recruitment, Wavell House, Holcombe Road, Helmshore, Lancs BB4 4NB.

Freedom of France, Alton Court, Penyard Lane, Ross-on-Wye, Herefordshire HR9 5NR.

Eurocamp (uses a PO Box number for recruitment, check press adverts for latest contact details).

Publications

Directory of Summer Jobs (Vacation Work).

Cruiseship Job Guide. Send an SAE to Cruiseships, Suite 401, 29 Margaret Street, London W1N 7LB.

WORKING AT SKI RESORTS
There are many jobs available in this area, both connected with the skiing itself and with the hospitality industry. It is possible to get a job as a ski instructor, a courier, a rep for a tour company or a ski-lift operator. If you do not manage to lay your hands on one of these more glamorous positions then you could try for hotel or restaurant work, work as a chalet girl/boy where you cook and clean for groups of skiers, or even as a nanny or au pair with a family or with one of the larger hotels. The following agency will help you to find a job with a reasonable employer: Jobs in the Alps, PO Box 388, London, SW1X 8LX (tel. 0171 235 8205), open Mon.–Fri. 9 a.m.–12 p.m.

If you want to hit the slopes in other parts of the world, then Australia, New Zealand and the United States would be your best bet. For Australia, all you need is a working holiday visa. If you are British and under 26 you will have no problem getting one for Australia, but it may be a little more difficult for New Zealand. To go to the States, you need a J-1 Exchange Visitors' Visa or a normal tourist visa and work casually (which is illegal, but not difficult).

WORK AMERICA PROGRAM
This scheme is run by BUNAC and is only available to British students. It gives them the chance to work legally for up to five months in the United States from June to October. Most opportunities are available within the hotel and catering industry, but other popular alternatives are to work with travelling carnivals, in shops or on farms.

KIBBUTZ WORK
Kibbutzim are small communities in Israel that accept volunteers every year to supplement the permanent workforce. Volunteers must be between 18 and 32, physically fit and prepared to work hard for their full board and pocket money. Average wages are low, so people tend to go for the atmosphere rather than the money. Be prepared to share the experience: although kibbutzim vary in size and style, they're always very communal places. Depending on where you go, expect to pick fruit, help out in the kitchen/canteen,

or work in a factory. Moshavim are like kibbutzim, but less communal; moreover they pay wages in exchange for your labour.

In order to join one, you will need the following documents: a valid passport with several spare photographs; medical insurance cover; a medical certificate from your doctor attesting good health; two letters of reference; your return ticket — but don't worry too much if you don't have one as this is not vital.

For kibbutz placements contact: Kibbutz Representatives, 1A Accommodation Road, London NW11 8EP (tel. 0181 458 9235) or Project 67, 10 Hatton Gardens, London EC1N 8AH (tel. 0171 831 7626).

For moshavim placements contact: Gil Travel, 65 Gloucester Place, London W1H 3PE (tel. 0171 935 1701).

VOLUNTARY WORK AND ADVENTURE PROJECTS

Volunteers on overseas placements can work on projects with a variety of themes: leadership and self-discovery, conservation, teaching, community service, youth work, and Christian service. Not all projects are self-financing, so you'll have to raise the cash before going on some of them. Generally they're involved with overseas-aid projects. Some are specific year-out options for sixth-formers or recent graduates, others are longer placements for qualified/skilled people.

Project organizations include:

Operation Raleigh, Venturer Division, The PowerHouse, Alpha Place, Flood Street, London SW3 5SZ (tel. 0171 351 7541).

GAP Activity Projects Ltd, 7 Queen's Road, Reading, Berkshire RG1 4BB (tel. 01734 594 914). Open Mon.–Fri. 9.30 a.m.–4.30 p.m. Projects for sixth-formers.

Christians Abroad, 1 Stockwell Green, London SW9 9HP (tel. 0171 737 7811).

VSO (Voluntary Service Overseas), 9 Belgrave Square, London SW1 (tel. 0181 780 2266). The VSO are increasingly focusing on placements abroad (usually for two years) that require volunteers with practical skills and experience: teachers, doctors and nurses, etc.

The United Nations Association, Temple of Peace, Cathays Park, Cardiff CF1 3AP (tel. 01222 223088). Operates work camps and voluntary placements abroad for suitably qualified and skilled young people.

World Challenge (tel. 0181 964 1331). Open Mon.–Fri.

9 a.m.–5.30 p.m. A tour operator who offers leadership training and planning for 16- to 20-year-olds who want to join summer expeditions to the developing world.

OTHER INTERESTING OPTIONS

Hot-air ballooning: Societie Bombard, Chateau de Laborde, Meursanges 21200, France (tel. 00 33 80 26 6380).

Crewing on ocean-going yachts: Travelmate Crewfinder Service, (tel. 01202 431520); The Cruising Association, Cruising Association House, 1 Northy Street, Lime House Basin, London; Crewit, PO Box 91, Poole, Dorset BH12 3PR (tel. 01202 721 188).

Overland Expeditions: places available for expedition leaders, drivers, mechanics and cooks. Possible contacts are Dragoman, Camp Green, Debenham, Suffolk IP14 6LA (tel. 01728 861 133); Encounter Overland, 267 Old Brompton Road, London SW5 9JA (tel. 0171 370 6845); Trek America, The Bullring, Deddington, Oxford OX15 0TT.

Sources of information: The Central Bureau is a UK agency which provides information and advice on all forms of educational visits and exchanges. For further details contact:

The Central Bureau, Seymour Mews House, Seymour Mews, London W1H 9PE (tel. 0171 486 5101).

The Central Bureau, 3 Brunsfield Crescent, Edinburgh EH10 4HD (tel. 0131 447 8024).

Books and directories:

A Year Between (Central Bureau).

The International Directory of Voluntary Work (Vacation Work).

PERMANENT OVERSEAS EMPLOYMENT

Career-break travellers have the option of tasting life as an expatriate. Foreign employers looking to fill permanent positions generally want skilled and/or experienced staff, so this is not really an option for recent graduates – though suitable vacancies do arise, most notably for technically qualified staff. Aside from the EC countries, Hong Kong welcomes job-hunting British passport holders. It's also one of the few places that still has career opportunities up for grabs, as does the Far East as a whole. Sought-after skills include: engineers and oil industry personnel, accountants, management accountants, financial services personnel, medical staff, teachers.

Useful organizations

Overseas Placing Unit, Department of Employment. Can provide worldwide job market information.

Job Centres have EC vacancy lists.

Business Libraries (for example, City Business Library, 1 Brewer's Hall Gardens, London EC2).

Travellers' Contact Point Australia provide complete lists of available work at 8th Floor, 428 George St., Sydney (tel. 221 8744) Mon.–Fri. 9 a.m.–6 p.m., Sat. 10 a.m.–2 p.m.

Books

How to Get a Job Abroad, Roger Jones (How to Books).

The Daily Telegraph Guide to Working Abroad, Godfrey Golzen (Kogan Page).

Other useful sources of information include careers offices, the broadsheet press, international publications (*The Economist* etc.), trade press. A number of placement publications and recruitment agencies have been advertising their services recently; do send off for information, but an agency brought to your attention by personal recommendation is a safer bet.

Finding work once abroad: The economic climate being what it is, you are unlikely to stumble across paid employment, but there are jobs – and ways of raising money – for those who persevere. Initiative and entrepreneurial flair will be required, and may impress prospective employers when you eventually return home. For imaginative ideas for earning a crust or stretching your budget, read *Work Your Way Round the World*, Susan Griffith (Vacation Work), and any title from the *Working Overseas* series published by How to Books.

Vacation Work, 9 Park End Street, Oxford, OX1 1HJ (tel. 01865 241 978).

How to Books Ltd, Plymbridge House, Estover Road, Plymouth PL6 7PZ (tel. 01752 695 745).

What to Take

HOW TO CARRY IT

Backpack: Durable, strong and almost 100% waterproof, a back-pack is the most efficient way to carry your kit. For added comfort, modern designs feature internal frames and adjustable straps. Some new models even convert into suitcases: a flap zips over the outside, improving appearances should the need arise, and protecting vulnerable straps and waistbands against the rough treatment they usually receive from airline baggage-handlers. Ingenious as they are, the design of these backpacks is less geared to the human anatomy than the traditional shape: they don't taper inwards to keep the bulk of the contents at the top, which, with the waistband adjusted to hip-height, is the most comfortable way to carry heavy loads. Backpacks specifically for women are also available.

When it comes to practical sizes, a 45-litre pack is about as small as you dare go. A 65-litre one will leave plenty of space for souvenirs, but resist the temptation to over-fill it before you leave. Economy class passengers are restricted to a 20 kg weight allowance, and you'll be charged for anything over this. Officially, there's also a size restriction of 53 x 21.5 x 35.5 cm for hand luggage, though if you're discreet you can get away with more.

Stuff-bags: By keeping your possessions in several plastic bags they're more likely to stay dry, and unpacking will be easier.

Daypack: A lightweight draw-string shoulder bag is ideal for carrying your camera and other essentials. The stronger and more inconspicuous the better. Determined thieves will know precisely what it's likely to contain, but if the actual bag doesn't look especially expensive you may be okay. Avoid black, it holds the heat.

Money-belt: Anything kept next to the skin day after day is going to get pretty hot and smelly, but a poly-cotton mix is the most comfortable combination. A strong waistband and clasp are also important. Bigger, though more conspicuous, are the money-pouches that can be strapped over clothing.

WHAT TO WEAR

This obviously varies according to your destination and what you intend doing. Use the climate chart on p. 595 as a general guide to likely weather conditions, and remember that culturally acceptable clothing is as important as style and comfort. See **Culture Shock**, on local customs p. 104.

HOT TROPICAL CLIMATES

Two pairs cotton trousers/skirts

Two pairs shorts

Two pairs socks

Five pairs underwear

Two cotton T-shirts

One cotton shirt/blouse

One sweat-shirt/jumper for cool evenings

Light-weight waterproof jacket

Sandals and flip-flops (useful at shower-time)

shoes/trainers

Water bottle

Sun glasses: UV protection essential and needn't be expensive

Plain, durable watch: a Swatch is ideal

Option: one smart/work set of clothes (Black skirts/trousers and white blouses/shirts are interchangeable for office and bar jobs.)

Sheet-sleeping bag (as required by Youth Hostel Association), useful on overnight trains and when hotel bedding looks unsavoury.

COOL TEMPERATE CLIMATES

Use the above as a guide, but replace most of the lightweight items with warmer clothing. Jeans or heavy cotton trousers and additional pairs of socks will be essential. Jogging bottoms are good for cold nights. Sleeping bags can prove handy, if bulky. Should you decide to take one, it's worth investing in a feather-down filling: it packs smaller and is warmer than cheaper man-made alternatives. If you're going to be trekking, take broken-in boots. Synthetic uppers are lighter than the heftier leather ones.

THINGS TO BUY EN ROUTE

Sun-hats and umbrellas (both invaluable)

Sarongs/lungis: these lengths of fabric used as body-wraps – especially in Asia – are very handy when modesty should prevail: at the beach, *en route* to the shower, or in temples.

Mosquito nets: not readily available at home or abroad, but a lot cheaper overseas if you can track one down. Vital for occasions when hotel rooms in affected areas don't have them.

Electronic goods: very cheap at 'shopover' destinations like Hong Kong, Bangkok, and Singapore.

Tent/sleeping bag: if not needed immediately, wait and buy from fellow travellers.

Work-clothes: Asia is a good place for well-made, affordable clothing, particularly in large cities like Bangkok where a lot of fake designer wear is available. Elsewhere, secondhand shops are an option.

SECURITY

Padlocks: for hotel rooms and backpacks.

Chain: useful for securing backpacks to bus roof-racks and when travelling on night trains.

Door wedge: for hotel doors when you can't use your own padlock on the inside.

Luggage tags: keep address details hidden from casual passers-by. Always have a second set of details inside backpack.

Women would do well to carry a wedding ring and 'husband and wife' photograph. (For more information aimed at women travellers, see p. 19 and p. 102.)

FIRST AID

Trip-kits: basic first-aid kits (including sterilized needles), available from chemists (or see p. 99 for what to include in a home-made kit).

First-aid booklets: useful to have, make sure you read instructions thoroughly *in advance* of an emergency.

Medicine: depending on your destination(s), a variety of antibiotics are essential.

USEFUL EXTRAS

Mini torch (plus spare bulb/batteries) Maglites are ideal

A candle

Matches (keep them, and the strike-strip, in an empty film canister)

Swiss Army knife: worthy addition, if a bit of a cliché

Small sewing kit

Universal sink plug

Travel detergent for washing clothes

Elastic clothes line (you don't need clothes pegs with these)

Nylon garden twine: good for hanging mosquito nets

PVC tape: good for covering holes in old mosquito nets

Travel alarm clock
Cutlery/chop sticks

LUXURIES

Walkman: one with a record function is useful for capturing local 'atmosphere'. Radio-alarm versions are available.

Worldwide radio for picking up the BBC World Service

Travel games/pack of cards

GIFTS/ENTERTAINMENT ITEMS

Old yet useable make-up and lipstick is often appreciated in the developing world and Eastern Europe. Family photographs and postcards from home are often of interest to foreigners, especially if there's a language problem. Within reason, avoid pictures displaying obvious signs of wealth.

Skills like juggling are face-savers if you get embroiled in a talent half-hour as a guest in someone's house.

BARTER AND TRADING

Duty-free money-spinners are many and fabled. Johnny Walker Red Label whisky and 555 cigarettes are perennial favourites in Asia. Brightly coloured clothes with prominent labels and logos are popular across the developing world. Wealthier residents may even ask to buy your camera, and in shops you can sometimes barter rather than pay for expensive goods, but be sure of the value of what you're buying.

Despite this thriving demand for all things Western, or perhaps because of it, many countries stipulate that imported goods have to be for personal use only. Still, if the landlord at your hotel doesn't have a taste for whisky, he'll know a man who does. See **Financing Your Trip**, p. 14.

PAPERWORK

It's a good idea to carry a diary containing the following personal information:

Passport details: number, place and date of issue, expiry date. Carry a photocopy of your passport.

Airline ticket details: number, place and date of issue, current reservation number for reconfirmation.

Travel agent: name and address, contact name and telephone number.

Airline: home head office and relevant local agent addresses.

Traveller's cheques: international cancellation hot-line number and relevant foreign country address; proof of purchase details; serial numbers – crossed through as used.

Credit cards: international cancellation hot-line telephone number – and dates when used.

Insurance: address and telephone number details, policy number and dates of cover.

Identification numbers: of camera, Walkman, etc.

Medical information: generic names, formulas of any prescription drugs taken on regular basis, details of allergies and blood group, etc., record of 'medicine days' for anti-malarial tablets etc. which need to be taken on a regular basis.

Personal emergency numbers: home addresses and telephone numbers of friends and relatives.

Correspondence: names and addresses for letters/postcards. Plus dates of when sent.

Mug-shots: half-a-dozen passport photos for visas etc.

Employment: photocopies of academic qualifications (degrees especially), any vocational qualifications, CV, references (optional).

Carry all paperwork safe and dry in a document bag: a zip-up A4-size wallet is ideal.

DISCOUNT CARDS

International Student Identity Card (ISIC): Available to students currently in full-time education. Holders qualify for a wide variety of discounts from shopping and entrance fees to bus fares. Cost: £6

The Under-26 card: Supported by the British Council, offers similar discounts to the ISIC card – not least because in the more remote parts of the world it's often mistaken for one. Also available to members is a free 24-hour international legal advice line. Cost: £6

Youth Hostel Association Card: Entitles you to the YHA's worldwide budget accommodation network. Cost: £9 (for over 18s)

Student Coach Card: Available to full-time students, offering a third off bus fares on trips with National Express, Scottish Citylink, Supabus, Continental and Irish services. Cost: £6

Young Persons Railcard: Young people between the ages of 17 and

23 get a third off most rail journeys with this card. Cost: £16

WHAT TO LEAVE BEHIND
Anything valuable or conspicuous, like expensive jewellery and watches. Take a hard look at your backpack before you go. Do you really need all that stuff? Also, think of space-saving ideas – like taking the cardboard tubes out of the middle of toilet rolls.

CAMERA EQUIPMENT
What you take will be dictated by the sort of results you're after and what you can afford. Great photographs can indeed be taken with virtually any camera, but unless you're after little more than holiday snaps, you'll do best to take a 35mm Single Lens Reflex (SLR) camera – ideally with at least two zoom lenses and a flash. Modern 35mm compact cameras are also very good, and less expensive. They're lightweight, often have a built-in zoom and flash unit, and are just about pocket-sized. The big advantage of an SLR, however, is that it can be used with interchangeable lenses, powerful flash units, and the viewfinder 'looks' straight through the lens – so what you see is what you get.

Most modern SLRs are semi or fully automatic and feature auto-focusing plus a variety of functions for different shots and conditions (bright or dull, action or portrait, etc.). Made from (durable) plastic, they're also much lighter than traditional metal cameras – though sticklers maintain that these predecessors are real cameras as opposed to hand-held do-it-all-for-you computers. The new generation of automatic cameras have bridged the gap between compacts and SLRs, though their lenses are not detachable. Ideally, take an SLR (of any description) and a point-and-shoot compact – that way you're covered for occasions when you've got time to think and when speed is paramount.

Lenses: A zoom of any description is useful as it allows you to home in on your subject (although purists prefer fixed-length telephoto lenses). Superzooms straddle focal lengths of 28mm to 210mm. Standard (fixed-focal length) lenses are 50mm, so a versatile zoom can handle wide-angle shots and close-up telephoto work. A superzoom basically combines two less powerful ones, so you'll have less to carry; but these benefits come at the expense of design compromises – especially in terms of focusing ease and accuracy – so if you can afford it, you'll do better to buy two separate lenses: a 28–70 and a 70–210. On a safari, if you want to get decent close-up shots of animals, you'll need a 300mm lens (or a 'times two' adapter for your existing lens). Automatic/autofocus SLRs often have a motorized zoom which shifts in and out from wide angle to telephoto at the flick of switch – great fun, but like auto film-winders they're a big drain on battery power, so buy one with a manual override.

Film: The other advantage of having more than one camera is that you can have more than one type of film at your disposal. There are different formats (colour transparency, colour or black-and-white print film) and also different 'speeds' of film.

Colour transparencies (slides) look great when they're projected onto a screen, but they're not as easy to flip through as prints – which when you come back home raises the spectre of slide-show dinners with friends and family! Black-and-white prints can look very atmospheric. But most people opt for colour, and carry at least two speeds: 64 and 200 for transparencies, and 200 and 400 (or more) for prints. The slower the film (and the lower the number) the more light you need – daylight in the above cases. Faster film is useful when the light is poor, and for flash photography.

The make of film is considered important by many enthusiasts. Kodachrome is popular for transparencies; Fuji and Kodak Gold for colour prints; Ilford for black-and-white shots. A popularly held belief is that Fuji (green box) is best for jungle/grassy shots, and Kodak Gold (Yellow box) is better for beachy/sandy pictures. Ask any camera shop assistant and they'll probably have their own preference, so don't worry unduly about such intricacies. Do, however, make a concerted effort to practise taking pictures before your trip; there's nothing more disappointing than unsatisfactory results.

The other important rule is to take as much film as you can carry. Buying it abroad is rarely cheaper than striking up a deal for a bulk purchase from a shop back home, and you won't have to worry about the quality (which can be a problem in the developing world). For further tips, see **Sightseeing and Photography**, p. 109.

Last-minute Reminders

Make sure you've got:

A current passport with a life-span of at least six months longer than your proposed home-by date.

All necessary visas – plus plans for getting any others you need *en route*.

Your plane ticket(s) and airline confirmation of all bookings.

A selection of traveller's cheques and hard and soft currencies, as required.

A stash of reserve cash.

Sufficient insurance cover.

Details of the above, carried in a diary or notebook (along with other useful telephone numbers/addresses in case of emergencies).

Life at home sorted out – your possessions in safe hands etc.

Your future plans sketched out for when you return – career/jobwise etc.

TRAVEL SURVIVAL

Negotiating Airports

DEPARTURES

Checking-in: Visit your airline's check-in desk in the departures terminal as soon as you've arrived at the airport. The earlier you check-in the better, you'll stand less chance of being 'bumped' (see **Know Your Rights**, p. 83) and there'll be a bigger choice of seats: aisle or window, smoking or non-smoking. Get confirmation that any special dietary needs you may have are being catered for. This should have been requested when you booked your flight, but badger the airline with a few phone calls to make sure. The check-in staff will detach the first page of your ticket, and give you a boarding pass. Keep this paperwork and your passport to hand until you're on the plane, it'll be examined several times before you board.

Luggage: Economy-class passengers are permitted 5 kg. of hand luggage, and up to 20 kg. stowed in the hold. Make sure that your backpack is identifiable. Your name and address, and (that day's) flight and destination details should be clearly visible. Buy a durable luggage tag beforehand (only the flimsy card variety are available at check-in desks). As an additional safeguard, tuck a piece of paper under the flap of your backpack with the same details. To protect vulnerable straps and buckles, wrap your pack in a clear plastic bag. Once you've landed, conceal all luggage tags.

Baggage-check: Unless they're expressly labelled as camera-safe, assume security X-ray machines will damage photographic film. Even if they're said to be okay, avoid putting fast film through. Exposed and unexposed film of all speeds will be affected if scanned enough times, so if you're going to be in the air a lot, ask to have your film checked by hand. This won't be appreciated by harassed security staff, but persevere.

Airport geography: The air- and landward sides of a terminal are separated by Passport Control in the departures area, and by Immigration and Customs Control in the arrivals hall. In large airports, you'll have walked a fair distance by the time you finally make it on to the plane. Apart from duty-free shops, there are generally far fewer distractions to help pass the time on the air-ward side of a terminal, and it's often a point of no return. Be that as it may, don't loiter on the landward side too long – in smaller airports

Passport Control may close once it's assumed all passengers have gone through. From the departure lounge, you'll be called when it's time to take your seat on the plane.

Airport amenities: These vary considerably. Sadly, some airports do little to promote favourable first impressions of a country. Modern terminals are starting to incorporate shopping precincts, but airports in poorer countries are fairly spartan. Catering facilities also vary. Snack bars are universal; restaurants common. But prices are as unpredictable as the quality of the food being served. Overnight accommodation is sometimes on offer, as are shower facilities, mothers' rooms and creches. Modern airports have access for people with disabilities, and staff who are well versed in assisting disabled travellers, though how efficiently this operates in practice is less predictable. Medical centres and interdenominational chaplaincies may also be on site.

Duty-free: Airport shops selling duty-free merchandise are found on the air-ward side, and are generally for departing passengers, though outside Western Europe and America they may also be open to arriving travellers. If you're leaving home on the outward leg of your trip, check on any restrictions imposed by your host nation. With the exception of Bahrain, which permits visitors two bottles of spirits for personal consumption, most Muslim countries in the Middle East forbid the importing of alcohol. Duty-free in developing countries will probably have to be paid for in hard currency. Wherever you are, don't automatically assume that duty-free prices undercut local dealers.

ARRIVALS

Luggage claim: Once you've landed, head for the luggage claim carousel. Expect to wait at least 15 minutes before anything comes trundling through; longer at peak season. If your gear doesn't turn up, keep calm – irritating as it is – and go in search of the Lost Luggage Desk, ideally having first spoken to a representative from your airline (see **Know Your Rights**, p. 83).

Transit lounges: If you're changing planes *en route* to your destination, you'll sit out the wait in an airport transit lounge. With luck there'll be a few shops and a café or restaurant. If the airport is in a country with a reputation for poor hygiene and sanitation, be cautious about what you eat and drink. If you have to wait several hours for a connecting flight, the airline might provide a complimentary meal (this food should be safe enough, but see **Keeping Healthy**, p. 91). Before buying an especially cheap air ticket, ask if the journey involves swapping planes, and if so, how long the delay incurred is likely to be. Always carry a few American one-dollar bills. In some countries US dollars are the only currency accepted in transit lounges, and everything will cost at least a buck. **Immigration:** A mere formality, most of the time. Have at the ready your passport (with visa stamps, as required) and a landing pass stipulating your identity and the proposed nature of your visit (this will have been handed to you on the plane). It's not much fun if you're interrogated by immigration officers, but if this happens keep cool and be co-operative. Although a tidy appearance always helps, unwittingly flouting local laws won't do you any favours. Before taking anything out of the ordinary away with you, always check that you're entitled to bring it into the country you're visiting.

Customs control: Customs officials are on the look out for smugglers – professional or otherwise. Permitted duty-free goods needn't be declared, but anything above and beyond this limit should be. In the developing world – where there is often a thriving black market for Western goods – personal items such as watches and camera equipment may also have to be presented, and may be listed in your passport. This is to ensure that they're re-exported, rather than sold locally. When you're homeward bound, duty-paid goods bought in another country will have to be declared – and VAT paid on them – if they exceed the nominal permitted value of £32 per person.

Choose the green channel if you don't have anything to declare, the red one if you do. If you're at all uncertain, play safe and take the red channel. With the exception of very expensive items, honesty is often rewarded with only a minor charge, while fines for evading payment are punitive. Indeed, legal proceedings may follow, and you could find yourself having to buy back the confiscated items. If you send home unaccompanied goods by sea or air, you'll have to pay both VAT and import duty, adding about 30% to the cost.

Customs officials monitoring the green channel pick out the occasional passenger for random inspection. If you're the unlucky one, accept it and allow your bags to be searched. Customs officers will be watching your reactions as much as examining the contents of your luggage, so don't prolong the ordeal by acting aggressively and raising suspicions.

EC update: EC citizens should opt for the blue channel when travelling directly between Community countries. Since the creation of the EC free market in 1993, limits on tax and duty-paid goods carried between member countries have effectively been abolished, although indicative levels for alcohol and tobacco have been introduced. These distinguish between amounts that can reasonably be expected to be for personal use (which can lawfully be bought abroad and imported) and larger quantities which it is assumed are for resale (and should therefore have UK duty paid on them). Duty-free limits remain unchanged, but are to be phased out entirely in 1999, except for travellers heading to other countries.

For further information on travellers' imports within the EC, contact: The Single Market Unit, HM Customs and Excise, 11th Floor East, New Kingsbeam House, 22 Upper Ground, London SE1 9PJ (tel. 0171 865 4796 – call well in advance, they like to leave the answerphone on).

AIRPORT FACILITIES

Flight information: Check the overhead destination board for up-to-date flight information. Look for your flight number (as listed on your ticket) and the departure time and gate number. Video screens dotted around airports display the same details. Flight Enquiry Desks are another source of advice, and the major airlines operate passenger help-desks. Smaller carriers may be represented by another, larger airline, or the airport authority. If you're lost, ask for help – groundstaff of any description can usually point you in the right direction.

Tourist and accommodation information: Visitor information desks of one sort or another are operated by all airports. Some will have stacks of tourist literature, helpful staff, and an accommodation bureau which will book you into a hotel – ideal for a bit of first-night extravagance. Others will be smaller and less well-equipped. As a rule, don't expect too much when visiting poorer countries.

Banks and bureaux de change: Most airports offer 24-hour banking and exchange services. But beware: bureau de change rates may be poor – arriving visitors are a captive market – and they worsen outside banking hours. This is most likely to be the case in developing world destinations but, wherever you land, always check your money before leaving the sales counter. Weary passengers, unfamiliar with the local currency, are an easy target for unscrupulous clerks. To avoid the problem altogether, bring a small amount of local currency with you, just enough to tide you over for the first few days.

Meeting points: Most airports have prominent meeting points and, in cases of emergency, there's generally a public address system which can make contact with incoming passengers. To have a message relayed, contact the passenger's airline and leave details of their flight and expected date and time of arrival; they'll be paged when they land.

Post and telephones: Communication facilities vary. Airports in remote locations will provide little more than a letter box and an international telephone link. If there's a post office, it should be possible to send an international telegram, telex or fax. Outside North America, expect far fewer public telephones on the air-ward side of an airport.

Onward transport: In some parts of the world – Bombay, for example – arriving visitors can book a city-bound taxi through an official airport agent. The traveller pays a set fare and is allocated a driver. This ensures good value and personal safety. Elsewhere it's a question of queuing at a taxi rank or opting for public transport, which can be extremely efficient. For specific information on airports worldwide, consult Thomas Cook's *Airports Guide International*.

Know Your Rights

Delays: No airline guarantees to operate punctually and, in the event of a delay, none are obliged to offer compensation. Thankfully, however, most companies issue snack vouchers to travellers kept waiting for up to two hours, and a hot meal if the delay drags on. Overnight accommodation should be provided if the problem arises between 10 p.m. and 6 a.m. It pays to be wise to all this because you may have to ask before it's offered.

Generally, the more reputable the airline, the better you'll be treated. Cheap tickets are often fix-dated – the initial date of departure on an RTW ticket, for example, is set and cannot be changed – this means that you cannot announce you're dissatisfied and demand a refund, or that you want to come back another day. If it looks like being a long delay, the airline may arrange to have you flown by another carrier – if a comparable one with availability can be found. However much you paid, the airline has an obligation to get you to your destination, but don't expect a full refund if you didn't pay the full listed fare.

Bumping: Safe in the knowledge that a fair proportion of customers alter reservation dates, airlines overbook many scheduled flights. This arrangement usually runs without a hitch, but when it doesn't, the carriers are faced with a problem and passengers with time on their hands could find themselves with an opportunity: if you're the one bumped, you may be upgraded to a higher class or flown by another airline (they generally help each other out). Every carrier operates differently, but after a hold up of more than four hours Denied Boarding Compensation is generally granted – either in cash or travel vouchers. If you're in possession of a confirmed reservation and you get delayed at an airport within the EC, provided you checked in at the right time, you're entitled to refreshments, compensation and, if necessary, accommodation. If it isn't offered, mention your rights under EC Council Regulation no. 295/91. Compensation for short-haul flights should be in the region of £200 (double for long-haul trips of 3,500 km or more). This applies to all airlines operating out of European Community airports. Even if you're not the one who's bumped, there are possibilities: when someone who's been left behind kicks up a fuss, an appeal will be made to seated passengers for someone to give up their place in exchange for compensation and overnight accommodation (as necessary). If you're not in hurry, this is a chance to live it up at the airline's expense.

Lost luggage: If your luggage fails to arrive at your destination, it could be just about anywhere: temporarily mislaid onsite, loaded onto the wrong plane or, if your flight was continuing after you got off, it may have been mistakenly left on board. All you can do is fill out a Property Irregularity Report (PIR) Form and hope it'll turn up soon. Airport staff will contact you once they've traced it; give them 48 hours to sort everything out. In the meantime, most holiday insurance covers policy-holders for the replacement of essential items (usually for amounts up to £50). Better still, keep a spare set of the bare essentials with you as part of your hand baggage.

If your luggage doesn't turn up after a couple of days, you'll have to fill out a claim form against the airline. You must complete this within 21 days of your flight, even if you're still on holiday. Under international law, you're entitled to compensation to the tune of £15 per kilogram of baggage weight. This adds up to a surprisingly disappointing sum, so always carry expensive items separately. To speed up the process, provide proof of ownership of the pricier items, including receipts confirming their value. Not everything goes missing by mistake: adept baggage-handlers can rifle through personal belongings in seconds – another good reason for keeping hold of prized possessions. If you have any complaints when you land, speak to a representative of the airline there and then, and follow this up with a letter to the Customer Relations Office. If that draws a blank, contact the Air Transport Users Council (AUC), 5th floor, Kingsway House, 103 Kingsway, London WC2B 6QX (tel. 0171 242 3882).

Although loss or damage to property incurred while in transit is generally the responsibility of the carrier, check whether you're covered under your holiday insurance.

Customs: If you're searched by customs officers and feel you have grounds for complaint, speak on the spot to the senior customs official. If you're still unhappy, write a formal letter as soon as possible. The vast majority of innocent passengers look just that, so you'll probably never be pulled over. If you are, remember that it's part of a concerted effort to stem organized, international crime. Firearms and explosives, drugs and pornography, endangered plant life or anything likely to be a health hazard cannot be carried lawfully.

Buying secondhand air tickets: Don't be tempted to buy a cheap ticket from another traveller. Airport security is much tighter than it once was and it's no longer possible for the original ticket holder to check in your luggage (showing their passport) before handing you the boarding pass. The name on the boarding pass will checked against the one in your passport at least once before you get on the plane. If the two don't match up, you won't fly.

On Board the Plane

Hand luggage: Cabin baggage must be small enough to tuck under a seat or be stowed in an overhead storage bin. Apart from obvious things like drugs, contraband and firearms, a variety of apparently innocuous items are not allowed on planes: anything remotely likely to explode or catch fire, for example. A leaflet, *The Air Travellers' Code*, available free from travel agents, lists lots of do's and don'ts. For specific advice, speak to your airline, or contact the Cabin Safety Co-ordinator, Flight Operations Department, Civil Aviation Authority, Aviation House, Gatwick Airport South, West Sussex RH6 0YR.

Cabin geography: Economy-class seating is located in the rear two-thirds of a plane. Noise levels vary little throughout the cabin, but the seats at the tail end, behind the engines, are slightly noisier. If you're sitting over the wing, your window view will be obstructed; if you're close to the toilets (at the front and rear of the fuselage) or the galley, expect to be disturbed more often than you would elsewhere. Window seats provide the best view, but can be cramped. If space is your priority, take an aisle seat or one next to an emergency exit. Another good spot is right at the front of economy class, behind business class, though you may have to move for a better view of the in-flight movie screen. If the plane has empty seats, look around for a quiet spot where you can stretch out and sleep – taking your valuables with you, of course.

Creature Comforts: Reclining seats, and blankets and pillows (on request) are standard on long-haul scheduled flights. For added comfort you might like to bring a small horseshoe-shaped inflatable travel-pillow. Feet tend to swell on long flights, so kick off your shoes and wear an extra pair of socks instead. To cut out the light, an eye mask is a good idea. Before buying any of these items, however, check if they're offered by the airline as complimentary in-flight gifts. Loose-fitting clothes are the most comfortable and will still look presentable at the end of a long journey. It's a good idea to do a little exercise once you're airborne: walk around occasionally, and flex your joints every now and again while seated.

Air sickness: Motion sickness is a common ailment. If you suffer from car sickness you may be prone to similar symptoms in a plane. Avoid cigarette smoke and alcohol in the hours leading up to your flight. Eat a starchy, low-fat meal beforehand and, once airborne, nibble on a dry biscuit every half-hour or so – it gives the stomach something to do instead of producing the hormones which induce nausea. The problem is that your eyes and ears won't be picking up the same signals. The inner ear – which controls balance – will be detecting shifts and movements caused by the plane's motion, but your eyes won't. The confusion that results starts the stomach churning. The worst conditions are usually encountered at take-off and landing. Choose a window seat, because by keeping an eye on the ground your eyes will start to believe what your ears are telling them. Distractions are useful, too. Anything that will (discreetly and lawfully) take your mind off the situation should help. Travel sickness drugs are widely available, but they're by no means perfect and can have side-effects akin to the symptoms you're trying to avoid. Luckily, motion sickness lasts only as long as the journey. For additional advice, speak to your doctor and, once on board, the cabin crew.

Jet lag: This occurs as a result of crossing time zones, and is not directly related to the distance of your journey. For every zone passed, it's thought 24 hours is needed to adjust fully. Fatigue and disorientation set in because the body's natural bio-clock is confused: the regular routine of sleeping, waking and eating is in a state of chaos. Jet lag is worse on eastward journeys, when travellers are 'losing' time and find themselves ahead of their biological schedule – at breakfast when they should be fast asleep, for example.

Deliberate preventive action is required to limit the ill effects. Theories and aids (tablets, aromatherapy potions and pocket gadgets) abound. There aren't any miracle cures, however, not least because everyone is affected differently. It may help if you exercise before the flight, because this will help the body relax during the hours of confinement on board the plane, and should promote sleep. Once you've landed, adjust to local time as quickly as possible, and try to go to bed at the correct hour on the first couple of nights.

Boring as it may sound, one of the main ways to decrease jet lag and discomfort of all sorts is to cut out in-flight alcohol, coffee and carbonated drinks. Each of these either dehydrates the body – especially alcohol – or accentuates problems such as ear-popping. With airlines bending over backwards to offer complimentary fizzy drinks and alcohol, it'll take great determination to opt for still water or orange juice – especially if you're celebrating the start of an RTW trip – but your moderation will pay dividends. Ideally, drink a glass of orange juice once an hour while awake on the plane.

Abstinence from alcohol has other benefits, too. You may not consider yourself a heavy drinker, but booze at altitude is thought to have approximately three times the kick it has on land. Inebriated and disruptive passengers can be forced to leave at the earliest stopover, and penalties as high as a £2,000-fine and/or two years in prison can be levied: a sobering thought to take your mind off the motion sickness.

For more tips on health in the air, read *Why Flying Endangers Your Health*, Farrol Khan (Aurora Press).

In-flight food: Despite its poor reputation, the standard of airline grub has greatly improved over recent years. Most airlines offer a choice of meals on scheduled services (usually one dish verging on the exotic and another which is quite bland) and the larger airlines – given advance warning and plenty of reminders – can cater for a variety of dietary preferences: Kosher/Kedassia, Muslim, vegetarian, vegan, infant, diabetic, fat-free, salt-free, gluten-free, low calorie, low sodium. But no matter what you chose, don't raise your hopes when it comes to flavour. The food will have been cooked up to 24 hours beforehand, and your tastebuds will desensitize by 50% in the pressurized cabin of the plane. *Bon appetit.*

Fear of flying: This phobia is thought to affect 20% of British adults. The affliction takes two forms: fear of an air disaster, and fear of the anxiety that air travel may induce. If you can relate to these feelings of dread, you'll be glad to hear that there are several courses available to help sufferers come to terms with the problem. In the meantime, remember that the chances of a plane crashing are statistically about one in a million. The sensation of rising and descending at speed can be disconcerting, as can the occasional bump because of turbulence. But, like ear-popping, this is nothing to worry about. Three deep breaths, each held for five seconds, is a simple way to calm fractious nerves and it will help you take control of the situation. Cabin crews are well trained in these matters and will be only too willing to help. And, yes, flying really is safer than crossing the road. In the meantime, look out for a repeat of Channel Four's *Plane Scared* programme, or contact British Airways or Guy's Hospital: both run courses to help people cope with the stresses of air travel.

Transport

Taxis: As well as the four-wheeled variety, you can expect to ride in three-wheeler rickshaws (motor- or pedal-powered), and two-wheeled horse- or bullock-drawn traps. Anything motor-powered will be speedy, if hair raising. No matter how it's driven, fix a price with the driver before getting in.

Public transport: This can be a delight, or a nightmare. Railways are by far the most romantic and usually the most comfortable option. Buses are more cramped, though not if you're sitting on the roof. Indian video-nightbuses are a unique experience you won't want to relive too soon – whatever the title of the film, the boy gets the girl but not before several hours of angst.

Car hire: Ask around for local car-hire operators based away from airports and prime city centre sites, they'll be considerably cheaper. Also check for flexible terms like one-way rental. International hire companies allow customers to drive one way across national boundaries, and may offer foreign customers preferential 'leisure rates'. An international driving licence won't necessarily be needed, but check beforehand. In any case, take your ordinary licence: it's a valid source of identification and, if you have to surrender it (when hiring a car, for example) less valuable to you than your passport.

Buying a car: This offers plenty of freedom, but can be a headache if you buy too cheaply. For places like Australia it's one of the best ways to see the country, though in spite of hours of driving it will seem as though you've barely moved across the map. For added authenticity buy a Holden station wagon – the Aussie equivalent of a Ford Cortina. Sleep in the back and carry plenty of spare petrol. AA members will be able to extend their cover with Australia's national recovery company. The only other dilemma is whether or not to pick up hitch-hikers. If you don't want to buy your own car, look out for notices at hostels placed by vehicle owners looking for people to share expenses and shifts behind the wheel.

Hitch-hiking: This is travel turned into an art form. For some connoisseurs it's the only way to see a country. After six fruitless hours on the edge of the highway in Outback Australia you may not be quite so enthralled, but do give it a go. The characters you meet along the way will often stick in your mind long after other memories have faded. Of course there are plenty of people you'd prefer never to have come across in the first place, let alone have to forget, so take care. Women especially shouldn't hitch alone, and don't feel embarrassed about turning down an offer of a lift. For inspiration and practical advice read Ken Welsh's and Katie Wood's *Hitch-hiker's Guide to Europe* (HarperCollins), it's a useful starting point no matter where in the world you may be heading.

City–airport connections: Always establish a price with taxis; rip-offs on these sort of journeys can be particularly horrific. Courtesy buses provided by airlines and larger hotels are another option, but be prepared for the circuitous route they may weave between pick-up and drop-off points. Public transport is clearly one of the cheapest options. Direct rail and bus links between city centres and out-of-town airports are widespread. They run regularly, and generally on time. If you're relying on a standard service, add the usual margins in anticipation of delays or cancellations. Always arrive in plenty of time for your flight – two hours before an international trip, no less than forty minutes prior to a domestic journey.

Accommodation

YHA hostels: Youth Hostel Association dormitory accommodation is scattered across the world. Open to all members of the YHA, it varies in style from large, purpose-built places to small buildings with only a handful of bunks. Generally less regimented than they once were, YHAs are still clean, safe places to stay. Self-catering communal kitchens are usually available, or a cooked meal can be bought. You will meet fellow travellers from all over the world, but apart from the staff you're unlikely to come across any locals. In Europe, it is possible to fax requests for reservations between many hostels.

Backpacker hostels: These dormitories are run along similar lines to YHA hostels, and are widespread in Australia. While the quality is generally good, standards are less predictable than at YHA establishments – though the nightlife is often better. Cooked food is usually available, but self-catering facilities may not be. In some places – Sydney's King's Cross district, for example – you may be sharing an individual bedsit with a handful of people. On the downside, hostels of all sorts can become claustrophobic places night after night. Beware of the school holidays (especially in Europe), when they'll be full of youngsters. Even if you're not a guest, always check hostel noticeboards for useful information and advice – especially if you're looking to sell or buy anything.

Budget hotels and guest houses: Across the developing world, this cheap accommodation will take the form of anything from ramshackle but grandiose hotels to dreary, anonymous dumps. Many have a great deal of atmosphere and are a delight to stay in, so much that you hardly notice the cockroaches. In hot climates, expect to share your room with a couple of lizards and a solitary, though large and hairy, spider. This is no bad thing because, after dark, both will be on the look out for other undesirable visitors. Some 'as recommended in the guidebook' hotels have been taken over by Western travellers. In others, you may be the first foreign guest in weeks.

Private accommodation: Families with a spare room or house often rent it out to travellers. Apart from cost, the advantage of such places is that you're going to be experiencing the country first-hand, but check how far from town your hosts live. Few families who are obliged to let rooms are wealthy enough to live close to city centres. On occasions, you may be offered free accommodation out of hospitality. This can be a great experience, and the generosity of many people is overwhelming. Don't take advantage of people, though. Friendly hosts will appreciate a gift, if not always money. Should the situation look at all risky, however, don't feel obliged to accept an offer of accommodation.

Bamboo beach huts: Bamboo bungalows are found in places like Goa in India, and on the few remaining quiet islands dotted across South-east Asia. You'll have to share the experience with the local creepy crawlies and do without most of the comforts of modern living but, on quiet islands, it's as close to Desert Island Discs as you'll ever come.

Long-term accommodation: If you decide to settle down for a while midway through your trip, perhaps to try and find work, it makes sense to move into a flat or shared house. Hostel noticeboards may advertise vacancies, but you're more likely to find somewhere by looking in the small ads of the local press, the *Sydney Morning Herald*, for example. University noticeboards are another good source. Hostels offer special rates for long-term residents, but can never provide the same amount of freedom as having your own place. Be prepared to pay a deposit and a month's rent up front before moving in. In Australia, a deposit is called a bond.

Keeping Healthy

DIET

Eating and drinking abroad is one of the great pleasures of travel. Unfortunately, it can also be a risky business. The main problem is contaminated water and food prepared in unhygienic conditions. It's an unsavoury thought, but because human excrement is used as a fertilizer in much of the developing world, and because effective sewerage systems are few and far between, most food will have come into contact with faeces (often diseased). For the same reasons, the water supply will be affected. Food that has escaped the water supply will have been handled by people with germs on their hands.

Don't let your guard slip because a restaurant looks clean or has up-market prices – germs don't have to dress for dinner. To minimize the threat of serious illness, certain foods are best avoided altogether. Going vegetarian isn't a bad idea. Cold, lightly cooked or reheated meals of any description – including vegetables – should be studiously avoided. Away from coastal regions, fish isn't a good idea, either. And wherever you are, if the sanitary conditions are primitive, skip the following: untreated water, ice and ice cream, fruit juice, salads, raw vegetables, and fruit (unless you can peel it). Eggs, butter and hard cheeses are normally safe, but soft cheese and milk can cause problems. Avoid them if they're unpasteurized.

Being realistic, dodging these 'don'ts' altogether is going to be all but impossible. If your will breaks, or you're forced to compromise, always put safety first – even if this means severely limiting your choice. If you can get a good look at the food's preparation, so much the better. Fried snacks made to order by street venders are generally okay, if only because they have been cooked at an extremely high temperature. Your egg intake will probably skyrocket, so leave the low-cholesterol diet at home. Basic accompaniments like rice, noodles or beans will be consumed in large quantities. When it can be found, fresh cake and bread straight from a bakery is generally okay.

At some stage you'll be offered food or drink as a gift, or invited to try something. Chances are, it'll be one of the must-avoids, or be served on a grubby plate or in a dirty cup. Refusing hospitality will almost certainly sour the moment, but the next few days won't be too sweet if you accept contaminated food or water. Never consume anything offered to you by a stranger in the street or on a train – it may be drugged.

It's not all doom and gloom, though. Far from it in fact. In even the most obscure places you'll stumble across safe-to-try treats that will delight. Any fresh, well-cooked vegetable meal with hot tea, fizzy pop or treated water will be fine. Food throughout the developed world is less of a threat, but can be as risky as anything back home – shellfish are best given a wide berth wherever you are.

Keeping your strength up is also important. Supplement a lack of protein with nuts you've shelled yourself and vitamin tablets. A bout or two of diarrhoea may be par for the course on an adventurous budget trip, but if you take the necessary precautions, few stomach bugs need develop into serious tropical diseases. If available, comfort food like chocolate will help boost your morale on days when there seems no hope of finding anything tasty.

EATING CHECK-LIST

AVOID:

Untreated water, including ice and ice cream

Shellfish

Uncooked or peeled produce: meat, vegetables, salads

Food that's been left out, including buffet snacks etc.

Reheated food – if it looks it, leave alone

Gungy sauce bottles

SAFER BETS:

Piping hot tea

Hot, fresh vegetable meals

Coconut water

Fruit with an unbroken peel bought from market vendors

Fresh bread

Fried food made to order

Cooked eggs

Packaged products untampered with and within their sell by date: ice cream, fizzy drinks etc.

BEWARE:

Dirty hands (yours and theirs)
Swarms of flies near food
Anywhere particularly dirty for that part of the world
Anywhere particularly clean, it's no guarantee of hygiene
Fresh fruit juices (unless made to order from peeled fruit – never from street vendors, never from sugar cane)

ETIQUETTE

Don't be afraid to turn something down, even though refusing hospitality can be embarrassing for host and guest.

Don't be afraid to walk out of a restaurant (if you haven't ordered) or leave food uneaten.

Don't be fobbed off with dodgy-looking fruit from market vendors.

Don't be surprised if restaurateurs in far-flung places are honoured, if slightly bemused, to serve you.

HYGIENE

Personal cleanliness: This will greatly reduce the risk of illness, wherever you travel. Wash your hands before meals, and always keep dirty fingers away from your mouth and face (if you floss your teeth, scrub your hands first). Only clean your teeth in safe water. When taking a shower, keep the water out of your eyes and try not to swallow any. Wear flip-flops (thongs) in washrooms and toilets, they'll help guard against verrucas and warts. Don't leave toothbrushes or razors lying around in hotel rooms: they may attract creepy crawlies, or be used by hotel staff. A fork and spoon will be a godsend if cutlery is unavailable or looks too dodgy to use. Handi-wipes are useful for a quick clean up. When buying bottled water check the seal hasn't been tampered with.

Cuts and grazes, no matter how minor, should be cleaned with antiseptic, and kept clean till they heal. Use gauze, not cotton wool, to clean and dress deeper wounds. Seek medical advice for serious cuts, but make sure all needles etc. are sterilized (ideally you should carry your own).

Feminine hygiene: Tampons and sanitary towels are best brought with you. They're hard to find in the poorer parts of the world, and those that are available may not be very effective or safe (inducing toxic shock etc.). It can be difficult and embarrassing to ask for them if there's a language barrier. A plastic lunch box will keep them dry and safe from damage.

Sickness

Diarrhoea: Don't reach for the antibiotics at the first sign of tummy trouble — more than likely it'll be nothing more serious than a reaction to a change in diet, in which case, it'll pass naturally in a day or two. If you have caught a mild stomach upset, by letting nature take its course you'll acquire a degree of immunity which will ward off problems in the future. If you aren't feeling better in two to three days, seek advice from doctors or use medicine from your medical kit (see below for symptoms). Drink safe water and take electrolyte rehydration powders. If you can hold it down, try some plain toast and black tea. Rice is also helpful. Avoid dairy products and eggs. Until fully recovered, stick to plain foods. Fruit like bananas and papaya often helps to settle stomachs, as does curd (yoghurt).

Cholera: The 1990s has seen a resurgence in the developing world of this severe water-borne disease, the main symptom of which is acute diarrhoea. Fostered by poor sanitation and overcrowded conditions, cholera spreads via contaminated water and food. Inoculation serums are woefully inadequate and, for travellers, no longer mandatory — though there's no harm in having it. A course of two jabs offers some sort of protection for about six months. Highly contagious, cholera can also be caught from carriers who aren't actually suffering themselves. The latest strain of cholera, El Tor, is so called because it originated in an Egyptian aid camp by that name. That it has spread to parts of Latin America, Africa and Asia is testament to cholera's ferocity and durability. Seek medical advice immediately if symptoms don't abate.

Typhoid: Common in areas with poor sanitation and low levels of hygiene, typhoid is transmitted by contaminated food and water. It induces fever, which can be fatal. Preemptive vaccination is very effective, though flu symptoms may knock you out for a day or so after the jab.

Dysentery: This stomach bug comes in two forms — bacillic and amoebic. Both induce severe diarrhoea, stomach cramps and fever. If treated, the symptoms will clear up in a few days, but amoebic dysentery is more worrisome and harder to get rid of. The tell-tale signs are blood and/or mucus in faeces. Seek medical advice; failing that take the strongest antibiotic in your medical bag (Flagyl is commonly prescribed for this purpose). Track down a doctor as soon as possible.

Giardia: In gut-wrenching terms, this stomach upset lies somewhere between diarrhoea and dysentery. It generates a bloated feeling akin to heavy indigestion. Extremely pungent flatulence is common, too – so you'll soon know if you've caught it. Look out for yellowish, frothy diarrhoea. Take Flagyl (or something slightly milder if you have it) and seek medical advice.

Bilharzia: Caught (easily) from infected fresh-water snails. Debilitating though rarely fatal, it enters the bloodstream through the skin. To avoid it, don't paddle, wash or bathe in fresh water in high-risk areas. Swim in chlorinated pools or salt water only. The disease does not immediately take hold, so have a routine check up as soon as possible after leaving a contaminated area.

Hepatitis: Hepatitis A is a disease of the liver, spread by water infected with faeces. Hepatitis B is spread by dirty syringes and casual sex. Gammaglobulin guards against Hep. A, though its protection is short-lived, so have the jab as close to departure as possible. There is a drug for Hep. B, but for general preventive measures, see **AIDS** below.

Constipation: This may not immediately spring to mind when contemplating the health risks associated with travel to far-flung places, but don't be surprised if it's a problem every once in a while – and not only because of an unbalanced diet. The sight of a particularly unsavoury toilet can be enough to inspire days of lavatorial abstinence. Sufferers should stay clear of eggs and eat lots of fruit and vegetables. Drink more, too. Failing that, take a mild laxative.

Some final don'ts:

Don't get too worried at the prospect of illness, stress is also bad for your health.

Don't let your appetite drop because the food looks less than enticing, always try to eat something.

Don't travel without consulting a doctor first – the information here is for general guidance only.

BITES
Malaria: This well-known and widespread tropical disease is spread by mosquitoes. Western visitors are particularly susceptible as they haven't any acquired immunity. To make matters worse, the Anopheles mosquito has been busy developing its own resistance to traditional anti-malarial drugs, so it's vital that your fight against contracting the illness takes two forms: a course of tablets (to reduce the potency of an attack) and preventive precautions. Different doctors prescribe different medicines, but usually two types of anti-malarial drugs (in tablet form) are combined and taken frequently – on a daily or weekly basis depending on your

destination; the course starts before you travel and finishes after your return. For full protection, do complete the programme. A potent repellent (look out for ones which include Deet) should be applied to exposed parts of the body in the evening: wrists and ankles are particularly susceptible (special bracelets and anklets are also available). At night, sleep under a mosquito net (the latest designs are steeped in repellent), and burn a mosquito coil (some hotel rooms will have electric vaporizers). Self-adhesive DIY tape is an easy way to cover tears in mosquito nets. Additionally you may wish to spray the room with repellent, but avoid breathing in heavy fumes night after night. Mosquitoes are particularly attracted to water, so after dark avoid lakes, rivers and the beach.

The first signs of malaria are typical flu symptoms. If you're in any doubt contact the nearest doctor. You're bound to get bitten – and you'll know it, the bites are extremely itchy – but not all mozzies carry malaria. With vigilance the disease can be avoided.

Though Africa is a malaria hot-spot at the moment, all tropical developing countries should be treated with care. Speak to a tropical disease specialist before travelling.

Yellow fever: Another virus spread by mosquitoes. Widespread in Central Africa and Central America. Inoculation is mandatory for visits to these regions. The cover lasts ten years. Proof of vaccination is required worldwide for travellers who have visited an infected region up to six days prior to their arrival elsewhere.

Rabies: A potentially fatal disease. Pre-emptive inoculation is only necessary, however, for travellers who are certain to come into close contact with animals. Any animal bite or scratch – from a domestic or wild creature – must be taken seriously. The wound should be cleaned immediately. If possible, apply antiseptic or alcohol. Then head to the nearest doctor or hospital. Take down details of when and where the incident occurred. If the animal has an owner, do your utmost to have the person contact you should the animal get sick or die in the next fortnight. Contact your own doctor on your return.

Other bites: Although snake bites can be fatal, if you're travelling on a budget, you're far more likely to suffer at the jaws of bedbugs and other microscopic mites. There's little that can be done about this. See a doctor if any bites and rashes persist or swell. Africa, in particular, is notorious for bugs whose bites have serious repercussions.

SUNBURN AND SUNSTROKE

The effects of these can be serious, and so they should be avoided. Sustained, unprotected exposure to intense sunlight can lead to skin cancer, and the relatively minor short-term effects are none too pleasant, either. The basic precautions are well known: build up your exposure to the sun a little at a time, protect all exposed parts of the body with sun-screen, and start off with a strong UV factor screen. However, independent travel is considerably more arduous than trotting off to the beach on holiday, and if you're on the move you may not be able to dodge the midday sun, so wear a hat and, ideally, a T-shirt with a collar, as this protects the nape of the neck. If you wear shorts, keep bare legs well doused in sun-screen because they probably won't have seen the light of day, let alone the piercing sunshine, for quite some time. Lip-bloc is essential too. The effectiveness of some sun-tan lotions has been questioned lately. *Which!* magazine is a good source of information (if there hasn't been a recent survey, trawl through some back issues). Over the summer months, the better women's glossies are worth looking at. Most popular magazines can be found in the reference section of larger libraries. Clinique cosmetics don't come cheap, but are effective and long-lasting. After-sun lotion will soothe any painful bits.

If you're going to be beaching it in the developing world, take ample supplies of sun-screen. Locally available products will be of dubious quality, if they're available at all. Traditional home-spun remedies may be a better bet. If you over-do the sun, apply plain yoghurt to burns and allow it to dry before washing off with a cool shower. Serious sunburn/heatstroke requires medical attention. Beware of dehydration. Wherever you're going, invest in a pair of quality sunglasses. They don't have to be expensive to be good.

HIGH ALTITUDES AND COLD CLIMATES
Altitude sickness is very unpleasant. Usually associated with skiing and mountain trekking, it can take its toll in any high places. As far as the destinations in this guide are concerned, this includes parts of Mexico and India, and excursions to places like Machu Picchu in Peru. As with all acclimatization, take it in gentle stages and you'll come to no harm. If you begin to feel queasy or giddy, backtrack to a lower altitude immediately. The thinner air holds less warmth and the wind factor will give it an added chill, so have plenty of warm clothing: thin layers that can breathe; a wind-resistant, waterproof jacket, and stout footwear. If you become very chilled avoid alcohol, as this directs heat away from vital organs. Don't smoke, either.

AIDS

HIV, the virus that can lead to AIDS, is not contracted via everyday contact with people and the world. It is spread by having sex with an HIV positive person, by intravenous drug use, and by contaminated blood products. Swimming pools, toilet seats and insect bites (including mozzies) are okay. So, unless you're injecting drugs, or are given a transfusion of infected blood, you have nothing to worry about – provided you practise safe sex. To be completely safe, stay clear of casual sex altogether. Prostitutes of both genders should definitely be avoided. Also forgo anything that will break the skin and possibly bring you into contact with the HIV virus: ear-piercing and tattooing, etc.

Don't be fooled by the identification of high-risk groups, everyone is in danger: ignorance and promiscuity are the real threat. AIDS is a global disease affecting some 7 million men and 5 million women. A Harvard University report in 1993 revealed that it is still spreading in Europe and North America; that Asia will have overtaken Africa as the worst-hit region by the turn of the century, and that the Caribbean and South America are also infected.

It's not a bad idea to carry an AIDS pack with you while travelling (especially in Africa, the CIS and Asia). This can be put together with the help of a health clinic or bought ready-made. It should contain: hypodermic needles, suture material (for stitches), intravenous drip needles and alcohol swabs. It should also contain a label with your blood type and a typed, offical-looking letter stating that it is only for medical use.

For up-to-date, confidential advice on safe sex and other AIDS-related issues, call an official help-line before travelling:

Terrence Higgins Trust (tel. 0171 242 1010: 12–10 p.m. daily)

Body Positive (tel. 0171 373 9124)

National Aids Helpline (tel. 0800 567 123)

CONTRACEPTION

Condoms are not only vital for safe(r) sex, they're one of the few contraceptives worth taking abroad. The disorientation caused by flying between time zones can render the pill ineffective. If you're going to be taking several flights in quick succession, not only will it be difficult to keep track of the days but jetlag can cause problems, too. And if you become ill while you're away, your body will be flushing away the pill along with everything else. As an additional safeguard to condoms, the coil is one option, but have it fitted several months before your trip to avoid possible complications once abroad. Needless to say, a woman traveller's partner(s) should also take responsibility for methods of contraception − at the very least by carrying some condoms.

For details of what inoculations and malarial tablets are required around the world, see the country-by-country medical table in Section Three.

Medicine

A variety of electrolytes (rehydration powders of salt, sugar and glucose) and antibiotics are available, and will be issued to you when you have your inoculations. With care, few travellers catch serious diseases, but the occasional stomach upsets are pretty much unavoidable. Seek medical advice if the symptoms persist longer than two or three days, or appear to be full-blown. Any over-crowded, poorly sanitized area should be treated with caution. Grubby hands and cooking/eating utensils carry as much bacteria as the food itself.

FIRST AID
Speak to a doctor about specific medicines and inoculations (see also **Formalities**, p. 52. The following will be needed for most parts of the developing world:

Medicine Kit

Diarrhoea tablets (various strengths from mild preparations to strong antibiotics)
Electrolyte sachets (rehydration powders)
Anti-malarial tablets (usually two types)
Sterile needles and syringes
AIDS kit (see p. 98)

First Aid Kit

Assorted sticking plasters
Gauze bandages (use these, not cotton wool, to clean/dress deep wounds)
Small pack of cotton wool
Crepe (elasticated) bandage for a sprained wrist/ankle

Small plastic bottle of antiseptic
Small tube of antiseptic cream
A pair of blunt-ended scissors
Small roll of elastoplast and safety pins
Small bar of medicated soap
100 soluble aspirin (not codeine, as it is banned in some countries, and some people are allergic to it)
Antihistimine tablets (a decongestant)

Other Items

Sun-screen of sufficient amounts and strength
After sun or calamine lotion
Bite and sting treatment
Insect repellent (Deet is best for mosquitoes)
Water purification tablets
First aid manual: read it before an emergency happens

Optional Extras

Portable water filter
Thermometer (not a mercury one as they are banned on aircraft)

Staying Safe Overseas

A minority of professional tricksters and con-artists do eke out a living by ripping off travellers. The good news is that it's done mainly by stealth rather than force. Unfortunately, this also means those involved are both adept and highly organized. You'll almost certainly never find out until it's too late. That said, a few simple precautions will limit the dangers.

THEFT
Don't take many valuables with you in the first place. Keep those you do bring close at hand, and don't flash them about. Ostentatious displays of money will either irritate or inspire: avoid both. Don't leave bags hanging on the backs of chairs in restaurants, but at the same time don't cling to your property for dear life, creating the impression that you're hoarding gold bullion. Instead, slip a

strap from your bag under a chair leg as this will inconspicuously ensure it doesn't walk off. Likewise, in hotel rooms and on night trains, a padlock and chain will make life difficult for opportunist thieves. Hotel rooms are never very safe, whether you're in them or not. If possible always put your own padlock on the door – most budget hotels have a latch that can be bolted. It's also a good idea to chain your backpack to the bed. Is the window safe? If not, ask to see another room (always view a place before agreeing to stay). Even if all looks well, keep money and valuables close by at night. If someone can't creep in they may find other ways: poles with hooks on passed through windows are not unheard of.

Street crime: South America is notorious for this. Pickpockets work alone or in teams. While someone creates a diversion to distract your attention, an accomplice will relieve you of your wallet, or snatch your bag as they pass on a scooter. There's not a lot you can do about this. It happens in the best and the worst of places – whether you're relaxing after a hard day's travelling, or preoccupied by the sights. Think twice before accepting food or drink from affable strangers in the street or on trains. If it's been drugged you'll wake up with little left but a headache.

DECEPTION

Rip-offs don't only take the form of robbery. Unscrupulous taxi drivers are notorious the world over, but in poorer countries the scams are a lot more sophisticated than a convoluted route to boost the fare. Upon arrival in a new country or city, you're going to need transport to get you to a hotel. This is where the fun could start. Having agreed a price (always do this; if you have no idea what the fare should be aim for at least a third off), you may be told that the hotel you want is full, closed or even flooded – anything to get you to agree to go to the place that offers the driver commission for bringing guests. Alternatively, if there is one particular hotel that is very popular, don't be surprised if there are lots of places with similar names.

Even if your driver is very co-operative, he may well escort you to the hotel lobby and expect commission from the manager, an additional expense that will more than likely be added to your bill. To some extent this is acceptable; after all, you've arrived safe and sound at the right hotel, but some touts will latch onto you in the street. Others may even have a friend masquerading as the manager. He'll meet you and apologize profusely about the lack of rooms – then suggest you try his cousin's place down the road. If you haven't got a specific hotel in mind, don't tell the driver how much you can afford. He can strike a deal with a hotelier (in their own language) and put you in a cheaper room.

More irritating still are the taxi drivers at some national monuments. Agra, in India, site of the Taj Mahal, is a classic example. Having driven you to your hotel, taxi drivers offer a personal day-long tour of the sights. This can be a great way to see the place, but can also involve being shepherded from carpet shop to silversmith to 'very cheap place'. Your escort picks up commission on the way whether you buy anything or not, so you needn't make purchases – but will you arrive at the Taj in time to see the sunset? If this sort of treatment seems likely – listen out for horror stories from other travellers – hire a bicycle for the day instead.

Women Travellers

Women are often well versed in coping with unwanted male attention before they ever set foot abroad. That said, while few places are totally safe, some parts of the world are a lot tougher going than others. Many local people, men and women, will be extremely courteous and kind, but outside Western societies women will have to take into account more than just the libidos of predatory males. Women in the developing world don't have the independence that their Western counterparts take for granted. For this reason, your presence (especially if unaccompanied) will generate interest within local people of both genders. The often-asked question regarding your marital status is one of genuine interest – and bemusement if you reply that you're single. It will also make you a target in the eyes of some men, so a white lie and a fake wedding ring are a useful pretence.

Male-dominated Muslim countries are frequently cited as the most difficult places for a woman to visit: the Middle East, North Africa, Pakistan and parts of India. South America is another place to be wary of. However, macho societies the world over – from Italy to the Australian Outback – can present problems, if not always danger. Although many women travel alone and greatly enjoy the experience, listed below are some action-points to help smooth your way in the developing world. If it feels like you're 'playing it their way' by adopting this strategy, remember that as a guest in another country it always pays to follow local convention – if only for purposes of self-preservation.

● Clothing should be conservative and presentable: shapeless but not too scruffy. Arms and legs should be covered, especially when visiting temples and national monuments. Across the Arab world, and in other Muslim countries, hair should be covered by a head scarf.

- Avoid eye contact, it will be read as a come-on by many men. Dark sunglasses will limit this problem.
- Try to be inconspicuous yet confident. If challenged, adopt an assertive, dismissive manner.
- Give straightforward reasons why you're alone/without your 'husband'. Are you working or studying abroad? Are you on your way to meet him, or other relatives? Be prepared to back this up with a wedding ring or family photograph. Is your husband a very important man, a guest of the government? That should frighten most men away.
- If confronted about your lifestyle as a lone woman, stand your ground but resist controversial statements attacking centuries of culture and ideology. It won't change anything.
- Be prepared for lingering stares and 'helping hands' in crowded places. One response to this is to publicly denounce the offender. Often (hypocritically) other men present will be equally annoyed by the intrusion.
- Don't become paranoid, but always size up situations.
- Before travelling, consider signing up on a women's self-defence course run by your local adult education college. Check lists of local evening classes (available in libraries).

The above ideas are suggestions only. Speak to other women travellers for additional ideas. See also **Who to Go With**, p. 17.

Cultural Indigestion

Don't be surprised if it takes time to adapt to life on the move. The sense of freedom is exhilarating, but there's also a distinct lack of certainty, and you won't have your familiar circle of friends and family to fall back on. Some days will prove more memorable than others, not least because a lot of time will be spent grappling with officialdom of one sort or another: arranging transport, getting visas, confirming onward flights. Also, no matter how overcrowded a country may be, sometimes you'll feel extremely lonely. But not for long: that's the beauty of independent travel. It's the highs and lows that make it such an adventure. In some countries, you'll have to keep a close eye on your health. If your budget's tight, money worries will never be far away, either. Yet life is rarely dull for long, neither is uncertainty all bad: that dodgy-looking restaurant could serve the best food you've tasted in weeks. Will your trip also be a journey of self-discovery, the unearthing of the real you? Who can say, but you'll certainly enjoy finding out.

A BACKPACKER, FOR BETTER OR WORSE

A shoestring budget will keep you on the look out for cost-cutting opportunities, but where does economizing end and miserliness begin, and what are the repercussions of travelling in this way? It's easy to slip into a routine: spend as little as possible and assume the worst of everyone. This makes life very easy – whether you're beating down the price of a bag of oranges, or kicking up a fuss over a restaurant bill. Bartering is a way of life in many developing countries, as is corruption (and there's certainly no need to kow-tow to petty criminals squeezing as much as they can from foreign visitors), but don't remonstrate any more mockingly and dismissively than you would at home with someone of your own strength and size.

Travellers have an impact on the places they visit, however they behave. You could avoid imposing yourself on vulnerable societies by staying at home, but that won't actually solve the problem. Learning to respect distant cultures by experiencing them first-hand, and being prepared to give and take a little – even if it is occasionally at your own expense – is a far more constructive approach. For information on the wider debate concerning the problems associated with travel – ecological and social – read Katie Wood's *Good Tourist* series (Mandarin paperbacks). There's a popular, if somewhat trite saying that goes 'take only photographs, leave only footprints'; wishful thinking it may be – but well worth aiming for.

CULTURE SHOCK

This 'illness' takes many forms. There aren't any antibiotics to ease the discomfort, but the worst symptoms usually wear off quite quickly. At first you may feel vulnerable in your new surroundings, even a little jittery. Don't worry, this is a perfectly natural reaction. The butterflies will pass as your confidence grows. Life won't always run smoothly, but don't let frustration turn into anger or indignation. That said, an all-forgiving saintliness is as inadvisable as cynicism – at times you'll be well advised to be assertive (if not aggressive). But if misfortune – illness or theft, for example – does tarnish part of your trip, elsewhere the selfless generosity and friendliness of local people will be equally unforgettable.

After several weeks of roughing it and doing your utmost to soak up local culture, there's no shame in spending a night in a decent hotel, or scoffing chips in front of a TV in a backpacker hostel. At other moments, these easy-going times will seem a lifetime away: head off the beaten track and you'll soon know what it feels like to be the centre of attention. Some questions will become tedious in the extreme: Where are you from? What is your name? Are you married? Others will be a lot harder to answer with any honesty, especially in the poorer parts of the world: How much did it cost to get here? What's your camera worth? Do you practise family planning? If the bluntness of such questions takes you aback, remember that when two cultures meet the wrong impression is easily made by both sides – often unwittingly. Cultural do's and don'ts are outlined on a country-by-country basis in Section Two. Abiding by them will smooth the wrinkles from your travels.

Respecting local customs is not only a painless way to show appreciation, it also makes a foreign visit easier and more pleasurable. Body language and subtle social nuances characterize all cultures, and outside the Western world – particularly in rural regions – local conventions should always be followed. As a rule, public displays of affection should be avoided. Skimpy clothing (on both sexes) isn't welcome, especially in temples and at national monuments. If you're travelling as a couple, pretending to be married will save upsetting people who know nothing of the more relaxed ways of the Western world. Indeed, as a young couple people may even feel more kindly towards you. Assertive eye-to-eye contact with strangers may be misconstrued as aggressive behaviour. Likewise, no matter how severe the language barrier, it won't be difficult for local people to pick up on damning comments regarding their foolhardy ways and inefficiency. Poor countries inevitably run at a slower pace than we're used to. There's nothing that can be done about this, so just accept it – even if the bureaucracy is infuriating. The same places are often very cheap to visit. Fixed exchange rates keep the traveller's purse bulging, even if local people are suffering rocketing inflation. With this in mind, don't discuss at length over dinner the amazing value of your visit, especially if you then squabble with the waiter over the bill – perhaps he assumed you could afford a little extra.

Useful additional reading: Culture Shock (Kuperard). A series of guides to countries and their social conventions.

Streetlife

BEGGARS

You'll encounter poverty and squalor, to varying degrees, all over the world. Part and parcel of this is begging. In poor countries, desperate-looking mothers will ask for money; lepers and disabled people will shuffle up to tug your sleeve, and occasionally you'll stumble across cripples lying passively alongside begging bowls. What to do? It's shocking and impossible to avoid, especially in large cities in countries like India. Stories abound that beggars are making a small fortune, that street barons take a large cut from the money the beggars earn, and that people deliberately mutilate themselves to generate pity. Regardless of this, the choice to give money or not is yours. Some travellers decide to send cash – enough to make a real difference – to an Aid agency when they return home. In the meantime, you'll often find yourself touched by someone's plight, or cornered – in railway carriages or in queues – at which point it might be a good idea to have a small amount of money to hand. Take care though, you could be swamped if others spot your philanthropy. Some begging is directed especially at travellers. Schoolchildren often ask for pens. At first this might strike you as worthwhile, but you'll soon realize that it's a popular demand – and how many pens are you likely to have? You may prefer to ignore it, giving to beggars can never be a long-term solution to social and economic problems.

BRIBES AND TIPS

In many parts of the world, there's a thin line between bribery and tipping. Bribery is a crime but tipping isn't, and for better or worse it often oils administrative cogs in the developing world. You won't always realize when it's needed, but once you do, railway tickets and the like will miraculously become available. Another way to smooth your journey is to pay people to run errands or carry your luggage. In some respects it's patronizing, in other ways it provides employment that otherwise wouldn't exist. Because of this you may find yourself swamped by helpers. Ignore them if you wish, but always pay up if you do use them. At border posts, however, beware. Here a bribe becomes a serious crime as well as a moral dilemma. Some overland immigration controls are notoriously corrupt, in which case by the time you reach them you'll know what to expect, having heard stories from other travellers. Make no attempt to offer money unless it is expressly suggested. Even then, don't give in to ridiculous demands for money from people who make a tidy profit preying on foreign visitors.

THE BLACK MARKET
Changing money on the black market is not only illegal, it's also a lot less lucrative than it used to be. However 'the black' is still an easy way to stretch a shoestring budget. The soft currencies of poorer countries are so called because they aren't recognized internationally and cannot be converted into hard currency. Unlike sterling and the American dollar, soft currencies are also prone to hefty inflation, making them worthless as a way of saving money. As a result, a lot of people are more than happy to pay over the odds to turn their local earnings into (your) hard currency. Although many governments and police authorities turn a blind eye to small-time dealing, discretion is still absolutely essential.

You'll soon find out what the going rates are from other travellers. If you can get more than this so much the better, but don't take any unnecessary risks. If possible, change money with your hotelier – he'll offer if he's interested, usually as you're booking in! If not, ask other travellers if they know of any reliable changers. Shopkeepers are a safe bet because they can't disappear too easily if they try to rip you off. Jewellers, and the like, are especially good because you'll have good reason for having so much money in your hand if anyone walks in. Above all, avoid going down dark alleys with strangers off the street, and always count the money before handing over your note(s). Large denominations – particularly US $100 bills – fetch the most, especially if they're crisp and clean. No black marketeer is out to do you any favours. Some magicians can swap notes for less valuable ones without a twitchy traveller even noticing, until it's too late. So don't let anyone offer to add to your money once you've exchanged currencies.

There's one other hitch to be aware of. Many poor countries now require visitors to account for their holiday expenditure by retaining the exchange forms given by banks when money is changed officially. In practice, when you're at a border and about to leave, few immigration officers are too concerned with this, but be prepared to show at least a few pieces of paper. Perhaps you lost the rest.

DRUGS
WARNING: The consequences of being caught in possession of drugs overseas are considerable. Stiff prison sentences and death penalties are imposed for possession of even the mildest drugs. As the war

against narcotics and trafficking focuses on harder substances, some Western governments are tacitly relaxing laws on softer drugs, and letting offenders off with official warnings. Elsewhere, there is no such distinction – most notably in regions that were once very liberal. Traditionally, India was relaxed about drugs; Sadu holy men have long smoked hashish as part of their religion. But beware – although drugs are still freely available, don't be lulled into a false sense of security. It's easy to get caught out, and bribes, if any use at all, will have to be substantial. Police raids on popular backpacker hotels are not uncommon. Dealers may be in collusion with the authorities, who, it is often alleged, are prone to planting drugs and demanding extortionate pay-offs. Failing that, the penalty for possession of upwards of just five grammes of cannabis or marijuana is 10–20 years – and that's provided you can prove it was for personal use only. Not surprisingly, foreign prisoners – guilty and innocent – welcome visits from passing travellers. Notices are often put up in hostels by friends of detainees.

For more information contact:

Prisoners Abroad, 82 Rosebery Avenue, London EC1R 4RR (tel. 0171 833 3567). This is charity which campaigns on behalf of British prisoners overseas.

Travel Advice Unit, Room CL 635, Consular Department, Clive House, Petty France, London SW1H 9HD (tel. 0171 270 4129; 0171 261 8712 for leaflets). Open Mon.–Fri. 9.30 a.m.–4 p.m. Emergency phone line open after 6 p.m. every day: 0171 270 3000.

Journals

Keeping a journal while you travel ensures that the memories will be kept alive long after the trip has finished. However, keeping a journal doesn't have to be the usual, everyday, written rundown of what you've seen. There are many other creative ways to keep track of what you want to remember. Taking along a mini tape-recorder will allow you to capture the sounds of your trip and the voices of people you met along the way. Sending postcards home to a friend (or even to yourself) with instructions to keep them safe for you means that you won't have to carry around your journal – you can put it together when you get home. Embroidering words and pictures on jeans or a T-shirt doesn't require a quilter's licence and is a great way to flaunt your travels.

Sightseeing and Photography

Indulging in either of these will, for the most part, be pleasurable and straightforward. But beware of sticking your nose or lens anywhere it's not welcome. Sensitivities vary, but military bases are obviously something to stay clear of. At border posts, the photographing of bridges and buildings may irritate immigration officials. In some countries, the same is true for trains, planes and ships. If in doubt, avoid the wrath of the local police or army by not loitering or taking pictures of anything that might be considered strategically important, especially in politically sensitive countries. Religious sites, antiquities and works of art may be out of bounds. Great care should also be taken when the subject of your interest is human. Most of us feel self-conscious when we're photographed, for many people in the developing world a sense of confusion is added to this bashfulness. They may believe part of their soul is being taken away; they may disapprove of their image being preserved for others to look at; they may just be sick of foreigners intruding into their everyday lives. Judge each situation for yourself. If you can't get a decent shot from an inconspicuous position some distance away, always ask/gesture for permission before sticking your camera in someone's face – and respect their wishes if they want to be left alone, no matter how good a picture it might be. If you're asked for money, the decision to give is yours, but never fool someone into posing and then walk off without paying. If you're asked for money after taking the photograph, it's up to you. Begging shouldn't be encouraged but, if the person is obviously poor and malnourished, it may be difficult to refuse – especially if they're persistent.

PHOTOGRAPHIC HINTS

Keen photographers will know how to make the most of the pictures they take. If you're a novice, it's worth getting a good photography book from the library. Back issues of *Amateur Photographer* magazine are usually available on the reference shelves, and have useful handy-hints columns. Local camera clubs are another source of sound advice; if they're holding a competition, pop along to the judging to hear some constructive criticism. Your scope for creativity will be limited by the quality of your camera, but it still pays to come to grips with the basics, both technical and artistic. Areas worth understanding include: depth of field (the portion of the picture that will appear in focus), light metering (how to avoid under- or over-exposure and heavy shadows), film speeds (what to use and when), use of filters (especially UV and polarizers), composition and style (capturing atmosphere).

General points to remember

Unless it's a spur of the moment snap, compose your shots carefully. A portrait should fill the frame, while wide-angle shots of buildings etc. may need something in the foreground to add perspective – the branch of a tree, for example.

Keep horizons horizontal, and verticals (doorways and lamp posts, etc.) vertical (though without a special lens this won't always be possible with wide-angle shots of buildings). Look at photos in the quality national press and in coffee-table picture books for plenty of examples of this.

Busy pictures capture hussle and bussle, but simple shots made up of a few bold shapes and colours can say a lot as well.

Avoid taking too many posed shots of people.

Natural light can be very intense in the tropics. Avoid taking pictures around midday; early morning and late afternoon is preferable.

Taking interesting photographs isn't difficult, with practice you'll soon learn the basics. If you'd rather just snap away, however, fine. You'll have more time on your hands to soak up all those precious moments you'd otherwise be trying to capture for posterity.

CAMERA CARE
Your camera will take more than a few knocks. Dust will find its way into grooves and notches, and screws may loosen. There's not much that can be done about this but, by keeping your camera clean, serious damage can be avoided. At all costs make sure the lens(es) aren't scratched. A UV (skylight) filter screwed onto the lens will protect the glass. For the same reason, a lens hood is a good idea – it also cuts out glare from the sun. Camera cleaning kits are small yet invaluable.

Humidity and extremes of temperature are the other main threats to guard against. Sachets of silica gel tucked into camera bags will soak up moisture that might otherwise collect. The worst effects of temperature can be avoided by keeping the camera out of direct sunlight in hot climates, and packed away when not in use if the temperature drops below freezing. To avoid theft, keep your camera discreetly hidden – but with you – at all times.

PROTECTING FILM
Film can be damaged by airport baggage-security X-ray machines
(see **Negotiating Airports**, p. 79). Date every roll of film as it's
finished; this will help keep track of how many shots you've taken
at different stages of your travels, and will separate exposed film
and those rolls yet to be used. Quality processing and developing
is essential for top results, and will be hard to come by off the beaten
track and in the poorer parts of the world. Have the occasional roll
processed and developed to check that the camera is functioning
correctly, but save the bulk of the developing until you're home
again (if that's going to be within six months) or until you've
reached a country likely to have good photographic facilities. Avoid
the fast one-hour developers, and don't put all your film in at the
same time. Otherwise, if the machine breaks down, you've lost the
lot. For further information and advice, check back issues of *Which!*
magazine.

Buying and Bargaining

Buying to wear or keep: As well as souvenirs and memorabilia,
there are lots of opportunities to pick up fabrics that can be shipped
home as presents, or made into clothes. Asian tailors can run up
suits, shirts and shorts in a matter of hours, but keep a close eye
on the styling. With off-the-peg clothes remember that oriental
people are commonly petite, so sizes can be problem. And dyes
may not be colour-fast.
Buying because of the discount: Hong Kong, Bangkok and
Singapore are the main 'shop-over' destinations for cheap(er) electronic goods, watches and designer wear (fakes and authentic factory pieces). Don't expect a lot of help and assistance. When looking
for cameras and the like, know what you want and buy it. Customer
care is not a high priority with shop owners determined to shift
stock at low prices. Whatever you're after, gauge the average prices
before parting with any cash, and make sure you're paying a lower
price than at home or from duty-free shops. Never buy expensive
electronic goods unless they come with a full international guarantee. And get a receipt – you'll need it for insurance purposes.
Buying to resell: Strictly speaking, you should declare at customs
any goods you intend to resell when you return home, but if you're
going to bend the rules make sure that whatever you're bringing
back will be in demand – if you've been away for several months
fashions will have changed. For up-to-date ideas, speak to travellers

who have only recently left home. Bags, belts, hats and other accessories are an obvious choice because they're small, light and cheap. Buy as many different items and styles as possible because colours that don't appeal to you may do something for someone else. Also grab any Westernized items. These will appeal to the more conservative of your customers. See also **Profiting from Travel**, p. 120.

WHERE FOR WHAT

Europe: French lingerie, cotton separates, Italian quality off-the-peg clothes (budget permitting), Spanish bridal lace, Greek jewellery and rugs, Portuguese ceramics.

The Americas and Australasia: Australian and North American beach and casual wear, Australian gems, Central and South American ethnic clothes and accessories, Caribbean batik prints.

Africa: Soapstone ornaments, glass and silver. Also tribal fabrics and Westernized accessories. Board games.

Asia: Affordable designer and tailored clothes, silks and cottons and electronic goods in the Far East. Also tribal fabrics, embroideries and artefacts. Indian marble, carvings and carpets. Board games.

BARGAINING TACTICS

Bartering doesn't come naturally to Westerners used to paying a set price for virtually everything. However, haggling over goods is basic economics elsewhere in the world, and not to do it would be unthinkable. It's a cross between a game and a battle, and there are certain rules that should be obeyed:

Bargaining is not an excuse for getting something for nothing, a mutually acceptable price has to be reached.

Don't bargain at length unless you are genuinely interested.

Keep your cool, try to avoid pouncing on something with great delight. Unless you're after a specific camera or similar item, having spotted something you like, look at a few other bits and pieces before casually picking it up.

Ask how much it is. Look discerningly at it again. Ask if that's the best price.

If asked how much you're willing to pay, your answer must be serious but, depending on how expensive it is, offer between a third and a half of the original price – and take it from there.

If you're interested in several items, ask for a special deal for the whole lot. Alternatively, suggest paying in hard currency as this should be worth a further reduction, or offer something of your own in part exchange.

Keep the bargaining good humoured but, as a last resort, try walking away and see who cracks first.

The ferocity of the duel will vary depending on whom you're dealing with – but don't be either bombastic or intimidated.

Barter for clothes, goods and souvenirs, also taxis and rooms in cheap hotels. But accept set prices for meals, medicines or public transport (however, do question any prices that seem excessive, or ones that have been deliberately bumped up).

Think twice before accepting offers by shops to ship home expensive purchases like carpets. If it doesn't arrive there's little you can do once you're a couple of thousand miles away.

If something you want heralds from a particular region of a country, buy it when you're passing through. It'll be cheaper than in other towns and cities elsewhere.

Taxi drivers will take you for a ride unless a price is set in advance. In places like Bangkok, aim to knock at least a third off the asking price.

Keeping in Touch

Sending mail: How you send post back home will depend on where you are. In the developed world it'll be straightforward enough, but elsewhere expect things to be a little trickier. As a rule, letters arrive quicker than postcards, but both should be sent by air mail. Ask to see the stamps franked before leaving them in the hands of the post office – otherwise they may be peeled off and resold.

Sending parcels: Unless there's a big rush, send heavy packages by surface mail. It'll take a long time to arrive – count on at least two months – but will cost a lot less. Local and international conventions will also have to be abided by. In India, for example, the package will have to be wrapped in cloth, with the seams stitched and sealed with beeswax. The cost of sending the parcel will probably be set according to multiple units of several kilograms. To avoid paying unnecessarily because your package just falls into a higher price category, try to have it weighed before it's finally wrapped and sealed. In accordance with customs regulations, you'll also need to fill out and attach a declaration form stating the contents and confirming that none of it is for resale. Animals, foodstuffs, plantlife and protected products like ivory cannot – and should not – be sent.

Receiving post: For travellers on the move the easiest way to receive mail is via a post office holding facility. Poste restante services are offered by the main post offices in all capitals, large cities and towns. Letters should be addressed clearly, thus: first initial followed by surname (which should be in CAPITALS and underlined), Poste Restante, main post office name/address, name of city/town/country. Local post offices in popular tourist spots – beach resorts, etc. – may also offer this service. There shouldn't be a handling fee, but how you collect your mail will vary from place to place. In Bangkok you'll be given a shoe box full of letters, in Sydney before anything's handed over you'll need to show your passport.

A similar service is offered by American Express for its card and traveller's cheque holders (a good reason for buying their traveller's cheques). Other organizations which may hold post are Consulates and Embassies. Check first, though, because they are not obliged to. Post offices in Britain stock useful booklets on posting and insuring packages for international delivery. Whatever method you chose, poste restante is not a safe way to send money. For advice on money transfers see **How To Take Your Money**, p. 55.

Telecommunications: In developed countries, dialling direct internationally from a phone box should present few problems; ideally use a phonecard. Elsewhere, you may have to use specific international telephone booths, or phone from a large hotel. International direct dialling (IDD) may not be possible. If you have to call via the operator, expect a surcharge. You may have to book your call, and wait to be connected. Check if you will be charged in bands of several minutes, and time your call appropriately – otherwise, for example, you'll pay for six minutes even if you only speak for four. If your message is urgent, telegrams, telexes and faxes are another option. The Australian postal service has an agreement with its counterparts in the UK, and faxed 'greetings' can be transmitted and delivered like post.

Radio: The BBC World Service, Voice of America and Australia Today are the three main international broadcasting stations. They can be picked up on shortwave radios. Information and programming schedules for the World Service are available in *Worldwide*, a BBC monthly magazine available in W. H. Smith. For additional information contact the BBC World Service, Bush House, Strand, London WC2 (tel. 0171 240 3466).

Newspapers and Publications: English-language papers are available in the major cities of most countries. They may be local publications (*The Bangkok Post* or *Times of India*); they may be international magazines/papers (*Newsweek* or the *International Herald Tribune*); or foreign papers imported from abroad (*The Times*, etc.). For a real wallow in what's happening back home pop into reference libraries in major foreign cities, which usually hold British papers. Or see what's on offer at your nearest Embassy or Consulate. British Council offices abroad generally stock a lot of the UK press, and have extensive libraries.

Helpful Organizations

CONSULATES
In the words of the Foreign and Commonwealth Office, Consulates exist to 'help British citizens abroad to help themselves . . .' Which is a diplomatic way of saying, don't expect very much. That said, although consulates don't dish out a lot of sympathy to travellers who have run out of cash through over-spending or under-budgeting, they will assist in the following ways:

Issue emergency replacement passports.

Contact friends and relatives – if you need help with money or air tickets, or if there has been an accident or death.

Advise on international money transfers.

Advance money against a sterling cheque for £50 supported by a bank card.

Offer repayable loans for repatriation to UK, but only in exceptional circumstances, and only as a last resort.

Provide local assistance: lawyers, interpreters, doctors.

Contact British nationals held in prison. Offer some guidance for tracing missing persons.

They cannot, however:

Get preferential treatment for British nationals in prison or hospital (though they can insist that you are treated as well as the locals are).

Interfere with the local judicial procedure, give legal representation or investigate crime.

Formally assist dual nationals in the country of their second nationality.

Help obtain work or work permits.

If you're arrested, insist on the British Consulate being informed. If you're seriously assaulted, robbed or lose your valuables (money, passport, etc.), report the incident to the local police first, then contact the Consulate if you need further help. Not all consular services are free. When arranging entry visas for a future destination from another foreign country, you may be required to produce a letter of introduction confirming your identity. Consulates can do this while you wait, but will charge a fee. A leaflet *Consular Assistance Abroad* is available from travel agents and post offices throughout the UK.

STUDENT ORGANIZATIONS
Student unions overseas are likely to be a good source of useful information and local nightlife. Check the accommodation board if you're looking for somewhere to live. Check college careers offices for part-time and temporary work.

TOURIST BOARDS
Most countries have a tourist office in their capital city. Some club together and also provide a regional service – The Latin American Tourist Association, or East Caribbean Tourist Board, for example. The quality of service will vary but, at the very least, they'll have a bundle of brochures worth reading. Use them for basic information before and during your trip.

What to Do if You ...

Miss your flight: The outcome of this will depend on your ticket type, the airport from which you're trying to fly, and the season in which you're travelling. Few budget travellers, if any, pay the full fare. This limits your options and you won't be entitled to a full refund – very cheap tickets are often specifically non-refundable because they are fix-dated, which, with an RTW ticket, means you might lose that sector of your journey. Hub airports like Heathrow are especially busy, and availability on future flights may be limited, particularly at peak season when planes are often fully booked several weeks ahead. Ask your travel agent before booking about restrictions on refunds. If you miss a plane because of an unforeseen disaster, the airline may bend the rules on compassionate grounds, but the only fail-safe solution is to arrive at the airport in plenty of time.
Lose your ticket: The repercussions of this vary with different

airlines. As with any loss or theft, report the incident to the local police, then get in touch with the nearest branch of the airline. They will contact the issuing agent (the travel agent you bought the ticket from), and may or may not charge for reissuing a duplicate ticket. Apart from being expensive and extremely inconvenient, if you have to buy this new ticket you will not get a refund until the validity of the old one has expired and it can be proved that it wasn't used. This treatment of passengers is endorsed by the best and the worst in the airline industry, so you might like to check on the situation before booking with a particular carrier. In case you do lose your ticket, keep a record of the following details: when you bought it; from where and when; the telephone number of the travel agent; all the ticket details, including the period of validity; its serial number; the itinerary you were following.

Lose your passport: Consulates issue emergency replacement passports, but don't let this lull you into a false sense of security. Guard passports as closely as cash and traveller's cheques. Never be tempted to sell your passport to local crooks.

Lose your money: Report the incident to the local police as soon as possible. For insurance purposes, ask for a copy of their official report. If anything is lost or stolen in a hotel or aboard a plane or ship, notify the management as soon as the problem is discovered. If you lose everything, ask for assistance from the nearest British Consulate.

Fall ill: If the symptoms are serious (see **Keeping Healthy**, p. 91) or are lingering after a couple of days, seek medical advice. Don't worry about wasting people's time – most doctors are sympathetic to the plight of foreign visitors. If you can walk, go in search of the nearest hospital or doctor's surgery. Failing that, try a chemist. If you're admitted to hospital anywhere in the developing world, supply your own needles and syringes. Also notify the nearest local Consulate.

To ease the problems caused by any of these mishaps, it's worth keeping a record of important personal details and information. If you're travelling with someone else, swap lists with your partner. See p. 74 for a list of what to include. A secret stash of cash will be equally useful. That way even if you lose everything else you'll have enough to get you to a Consulate. Never rely on reciprocal health agreements between countries – always take out full medical insurance before travelling anywhere. Form E111 covers EC citizens travelling within the European Community – and is available from DSS offices and post offices – but treatment won't always be free at the time of need, neither is a full refund guaranteed.

RETURNING HOME

Back to the Future

If you've been away for several months, don't under-estimate the shock you'll feel at being back home again. Even if you were glad to be leaving behind the rigours of life on the road as you boarded your final plane, those feelings may sink with a thud – either as soon as you touch down, or several weeks later. A lot depends on what you get up to once you've settled in again. This is why planning for your life after the homecoming is so important. Dropping back into the world of work may not sound very exciting, but getting stuck into anything beats sitting around waiting for your life to kick-start itself.

How will others react to you? Sadly, the novelty of your travel-talk will wear thin all too soon. This can cause problems because you'll have little else to talk about at first, especially if you're unemployed for a while. Your photographs and memorabilia will acquire a new status: a fix of African music; the whiff of Indian sandalwood, and a peak at those ethnic trousers that already look too ridiculous to ever try on, can all too easily become essential daily rituals. Like any addiction, this isn't very healthy behaviour. If there doesn't seem much to look forward to, treat the problem as a bonus: it's a fresh start, and that's the next challenge (no matter how uninspiring it may initially appear). Never forget either, that everyone around you may be equally fazed out, particularly if you're living back home with mum and dad for the first time in years – especially if you still owe them half the air-fare money.

Jobhunting

EMPLOYERS' ATTITUDES

Few companies have the time or inclination to adopt specific policies towards job applicants who have had time off from the nine-to-five – and the whole issue is laid to rest remarkably quickly once work is found. However, do be prepared to 'justify' your decision – on application forms and in the interview room – when you first return home. Employers will need reassuring that you're here to stay, they may also want to know why you went overseas, and how it might be of benefit to them. For better or worse, much rests with the likes and dislikes of individual companies – even the interviewers – but some general points can be made. If you're interested in specialist or technical jobs, some employers may fear you lack up-to-date knowledge, in which case, a brief refresher course will bolster your appeal and reconfirm your interest and commitment. For jobs reliant on broader life-skills, such as general management, catering/hospitality and (not least) the travel trade, a character-building few months abroad can be a positive plus in your favour.

MARKETING YOURSELF

Itchy feet were probably your main reason for wanting to travel. Few employers will be disgruntled to hear this – few worth working for, that is – but they will want to know how you have developed as a result of this self-indulgence. Be clear about your motives. Why was it worth doing? How can it be put to good use? Try to focus on specific new skills you've acquired. You'll have had an eventful time; if relevant experiences don't immediately spring to mind think how you coped when things didn't go according to plan. Remember, resilience and maturity are twin qualities much sought after by employers.

By justifying your decision to travel – professionalizing your time off, if only to create the right impression – you can also explain how it 'officially' fits into the scheme of things: recent graduates are getting wanderlust out of their system; career-break travellers are taking a break at an opportune moment. As well as specific job-related interview questions, open-ended discussions are a popular way to assess personality and motivation. Having been abroad you might be asked any of the following: How did you chose the itinerary for your 'journey of a lifetime'? How did you budget your money? Did you travel alone or with friends? Did you ever wish you were back home? Although there's no need for too earnest an explanation, independent travel is a real achievement and can be promoted as such. Did you finance it yourself? Did you do anything worthy of note: voluntary work or something particularly adventurous?

Always list your time abroad on CVs and application forms – otherwise you'll be leaving suspicious gaps – but highlight qualifications and relevant skills more prominently. A brief summary of your travels under a heading like 'International Experience', or listed with previous employers as part of a 'Career Chronology', if you've acquired a lot of work experience, is sufficient.

WHAT'S A CAREER ANYWAY?

Careers develop over time and rarely in a predictable manner, especially during economic recession. If a minority of employers dismiss you as work-shy, it's worth remembering that the whole nature of employment and the jobs market is changing. Careers are more flexible than ever before and opportunities often arise unexpectedly. It all comes down to the gloriously hit-and-miss business of job hunting. Basically, anything that helps boost the number of applications you have on the go is worth a try. One thing's for sure: well-targeted, speculative applications are at least as likely to land you an interview as the appointment pages of the national press. Personal contacts are also well worth quizzing.

If friends have moved up in the world in your absence – and are driving a 'you know the sporty-version' car – remember that travel is inspiring and you'll more than likely return with a fresh lease of life, and possibly new aspirations. Your interests will have widened and you may come back with specific jobs in mind that you hadn't previously even considered. Whatever happens, you won't regret taking time off; leaving others to ponder, later in life, what might have been if they'd followed in your footsteps.

Having recently returned from a career break, you might feel in need of some re-orientation before easing back into the corporate world of backbiting and oneupmanship. If this is the case, read *Neanderthals at Work*, Dr Albert Bernstein (John Wiley). A serious yet irreverent look at office careers, it explains at length the best procedures for climbing the corporate ladder in today's large organizations.

Profiting from Travel

SELLING GOODS YOU'VE BROUGHT BACK

If you've got the right stuff and can set up a stall at a local market, this can be quite profitable. And skills like hair-braiding can be as lucrative as selling. What's more, a bit of entrepreneurship will perpetuate the feeling of freedom generated by independent travel – it can also be a complete (if not expensive) disaster, but you won't know until you try. Major markets in London, like those at Camden and Greenwich, are worth getting in on. Although both are well booked up, it should be possible to get a stall at Camden on a Friday: the stalls are cheaper to rent than at weekends, and over the summer and school holidays there'll still be plenty of passing custom.

If self-employment appeals – and you'll certainly have learnt a thing or two about bargaining – enquire about the Enterprise Allowance Scheme at your local Job Centre. There are also a variety of affordable small business courses worth attending – speak to your nearest TEC.

TRAVEL WRITING

Successful freelance journalism of any description requires business acumen as much as creative flair, and this certainly holds true for travel writing. There can be few people who after several months abroad and many lengthy airmail letters home haven't felt inspired to pursue the two pastimes more seriously. This makes it all the harder to succeed. The statistics speak for themselves: travel editors on national publications receive a dozen or more unsolicited manuscripts a week; vacancies for roving researchers on top-notch budget travel guides inspire a thousand or more applications – and past the first paragraph very little of anything submitted gets read, let alone published. Feeling demoralized already? Don't be, but do be realistic about your chances. The first step forward is to find out about the market for your product. It's no good sending a piece on steak tartare to a vegan magazine. Scale down initial aspirations – your objective should be to get something published: anything; anywhere. Check the local free press in your area, the stuff that's shoved through the letter box without being asked for. If you think you've got a good story, but no one will offer you a commission to write it, see if you can sell the idea instead. It gets you known, and that's a vital first step.

Improve your skills with the written word. There are mountains of books on the subject, and evening classes are particularly useful. Ask local colleges and universities for details of any courses they run. Ideally speak to a journalist or someone in publishing. Feedback and first-hand knowledge are essential. Often a lot of the must-do's listed in books (especially in terms of presentation) are completely ignored in reality – don't look the novice because you are being too 'professional'. Books worth using as a starting point, include:

The Writers' and Artists' Year Book (Black).
The Way to Write . . . series.
Fowler's *Modern English Usage*.

Read a decent newspaper and listen to a quality radio station; keeping up with current affairs is essential, and will add topicality to anything you write. Always be on the look out for a news peg on which to hang a story, even if it's only a local event. With this in mind, several radio and television programmes are worth tuning into:

What the Papers Say: Channel 4 Friday/Saturday p.m.

Hard News: Channel Four Sunday p.m.

Right to Reply: Channel Four Saturday p.m.

A Week in Politics: Channel Four Saturday p.m.

Newsnight: nightly midweek BBC 2

Stop Press: Radio 4 Friday p.m.

The News Quiz: Radio 4 Saturday lunchtime/Monday p.m.

PHOTOGRAPHY

Photography is as tough an industry to break into as travel writing and journalism, but equally rewarding. Again, appearing professional is all important, as is flexibility. Don't confine yourself to one market. If possible, make a habit of taking your camera around with you. Quirky, interesting shots are welcome in many publications. When it comes to travel photography, if you're going to approach a photo library you first need a bank of at least 200 pictures, usually transparencies, and ideally some should have been taken with a larger format camera than 35mm. Well composed, unusual pictures are the ones likely to appeal. So while abroad, do snap the Eiffel Tower and the Taj Mahal, but also be prepared to go looking for pictures, and grab opportunities as they arise. This may mean getting wet and going hungry on occasion from waiting for the right moment, but that's part and parcel of the job. As with freelance journalism, careful targeting of your efforts is crucial. It can be dispiriting, but just plug away at getting your first published pic – with luck, success will breed success. You've also got to harness creative skills with technical knowhow. Speak to local colleges about evening classes and short summer schools. Camera clubs are well worth joining, particularly for the competitions. Further reading:

The Writers' and Artists' Year Book.
The Freelance Photographers' Market Handbook.

PUBLIC SPEAKING

Rarely a profitable pastime, but useful experience and quite good fun, if more than a little nerve-racking the first time. If you've taken a year out after school or university, you might suggest to the careers office that you give a benefit-of-hindsight talk to others thinking of doing the same.

SECTION TWO
DESTINATIONS

EUROPE

Europe's appeal lies in its diversity. Nowhere else in the world can you find such a diverse mix of races, cultures, languages, history and peoples packed into such a small area. It's a traveller's dream: easy, efficient and fascinating. Everything, from landscape to weather, from culture to cuisine, seems to change every 81 km in Europe. You could spend a year touring this beautiful continent alone, so don't be put off just because it's on your own doorstep. Why do you think all the Aussies and Americans come over to savour its delights? Once you've travelled the world, and toured continents as homogeneous as the USA, you'll begin to appreciate all the more the delights of your own continent.

WHERE TO GO FOR WHAT

For history and heritage, the UNITED KINGDOM takes some beating. Some of the world's greatest museums and art collections are to be found in its major cities, and almost every small town has something to offer in the way of ancient churches, or stately and historic homes. London is particularly rich in fascinating relics of bygone days – the Tower of London, Westminster Abbey, Buckingham Palace, etc. – but don't neglect the rest of the British Isles. Scotland, Wales and Northern Ireland are as culturally diverse as you could wish for and the lush green countryside is enchanting (though sun-worshippers may curse the wet summers that keep the land so green). In spite of the miserable weather, the UK is popular with hikers and is also small enough to enable the keen cyclist to pursue his or her travels by bike.

The UK's closest neighbour, FRANCE, also has a large slice of history on offer. Not just in Paris but in the wealth of beautiful monuments and architectural delights of Gothic, medieval or Roman origin which are dotted round the country – the Roman remains in Provence are amongst the best known. The French retain strong regional identities and each part of the country provides a different atmosphere and culture – from the cosmopolitan city of Paris, to the beautiful scenery and chateaux of the Loire Valley, to the small villages dotted throughout the unchanging rural countryside. The French riviera is justifiably famous for its beaches, where you can lap up the sun alongside the rich and famous, while France's ski resorts are among the best in the world.

GERMANY is a nation of enthusiastic hikers, and no wonder with such beautiful landscapes as the Black Forest, the Bavarian Alps and the Rhine valley to entice them. The major cities are modern

— many were rebuilt after the war — and it tends to be the smaller cities such as Heidelberg and Regensburg and those on the Romantic Road which have retained their quintessential German charm. Re-unified Berlin, which continues to exert its own peculiar fascination, is the exception to the rule.

THE NETHERLANDS is a cyclist's paradise as the entire country is geared towards two-wheel tourists. If you have the time, a bicycle is *the* way to travel. Amsterdam is crammed with art treasures and is a delight to explore on foot. Outside of the cities, while it lacks the spectacular scenery of some other European countries, the Netherlands has a beauty all of its own, with golden beaches, miles of canals and fields of gorgeous flowers providing blankets of colour.

For those who want to experience something a little different and are not too bothered about creature comforts and gourmet food, much of the fascination of a visit to RUSSIA lies simply in being in a country that has spent forty years as the idealistic and militaristic enemy of the West and is currently undergoing fascinating changes. In addition to the fascinating architecture of Moscow and St Petersburg, which is unlike anything to be seen in the West, reminders of Russia's past can be seen in the Golden Ring of ancient villages encircling Moscow, where time has virtually stood still.

TAKE HEED

There are a few things which must be kept in mind when travelling through Europe as much as in the rest of the world. Firstly, keep a close eye on your luggage at all times. This is particularly important around such places as airports and stations, where potential thieves can spot their potential victims a mile off, and soon get lost in the crowd. Beware of being fooled into looking in the opposite direction by one person while another steals your luggage from behind your back. Try not to keep all important documents such as passport, travellers' cheques and travel tickets all together as you may well lose everything to one thief.

A warning should go out to women who are travelling alone. In the developed Western society in which we live, it may well be quite safe for women to travel alone, but as you get to the further reaches of the world, it can become more dangerous. Even within Europe, it may be worthwhile to carry a fake wedding ring and photo of your 'husband', and not to flaunt the fact that you are travelling alone, in order to avoid harassment.

Those of you who think that it is easy to smuggle the odd drug across European borders now that customs inspections have disappeared should also be warned. Police are still looking out for anyone who might be tempted to break the rules (this is especially true on Dutch borders).

EMPLOYMENT OPPORTUNITIES

There are many options available to those wanting to take time off from work or study and live abroad. Central Bureau publications aimed at paid and voluntary jobs abroad include: *Working Holidays*, a guide to legal requirements for employees, travel and accommodation in 70 countries; *Study Holidays*, a guide to language courses in Europe; and *Volunteer Work*, which offers information on voluntary organizations in over 120 countries.

The Directory of Summer Jobs Abroad and *Work Your Way Around the World* (both from Vacation Work) offer information on job opportunities, along with details of legal requirements and likely wages. The *How to* series (How to Books) includes among its titles: *How to Spend a Year Abroad*, *How to Live & Work in France*, *How to Live & Work in Germany* and *How to Teach Abroad*.

INTRA-CONTINENTAL TRAVEL

If you are planning a prolonged spot of travelling across Europe, the continent is well catered for in terms of travel passes and cheap coach and rail deals, though there are at present no European air passes. (For details of travel passes covering individual countries, see the **Internal Travel** section for the relevant country.)

TRAIN

There are a number of rail passes on offer, primarily aimed at those under the age of 26. Deals available to Europeans over the age of 26 include the Euro Domino (non-European wrinklies can take advantage of certain Eurail deals – see below for details).

If you decide to do most of your travelling by rail, *Europe by Train* (Fontana) is essential reading (see **Further Information**, p. 129). Another useful book to have by you is Thomas Cook's *European Timetable*, which contains details of train and ferry services throughout Europe. You can purchase a copy at any Thomas Cook travel agency or by post from Thomas Cook Ltd, PO Box 36, Peterborough PE3 6SB (they publish summer and winter schedules, so make sure you buy the right one).

InterRail: Anyone under 26 and living in Europe is eligible for an InterRail pass giving a month's unlimited second-class travel in various combinations of European countries (Britain and the former Soviet states are not covered, though the pass does give you a 34% discount on rail travel in the UK, as well as concessions on some European ferry routes, including those operated by Sealink, P&O and B&I ships). In the UK, InterRail passes can be bought from appointed British Rail stations or through authorized BR agents. Prices range from £179 for 15 days in any one zone, £209 for two zones in one month, £229 for three zones in one month, and £249 for all zones in one month. Take your passport when you book. For further details and up-to-date information contact the International Rail Centre.

Eurotrain: This UK operator offers generous discounts on normal rail fares to 200 destinations in Europe for those under 26. Tickets (which also cover ferry crossings) are valid for up to two months. You must specify your outward and return routes, but you can start your journey from any UK station and stop off when and where you wish. It is therefore important to pick the route which takes in the places you most want to see. The popular Eurotrain 'Explorer' tickets offer a number of set combinations of European cities: the Capital Explorer, for example, links London, Paris, Brussels and Amsterdam for £120. For full details contact Eurotrain, Victoria Station, Platform 2, London (tel. 0171 630 8132).

Route-26: A UK subsidiary of Wasteels, Route-26 offer a similar deal to Eurotrain. They are based at 121 Wilton Road, London SW1 (tel. 0171 834 7066).

Euro-Youth: A British Rail International venture catering for the under-26s. For details contact British Rail International, Victoria Station, London SW1V 1JY (tel. 0171 834 2345).

Euro Domino: The Freedom Pass gives unlimited rail travel in a single country for 3, 5 or 10 days in any one month. There are 19 countries to choose from including France, the Netherlands and Germany. A 10-day French pass, for example, costs £221 (or £200 for under-26s). For more details call or write to British Rail International, Victoria Station, London SW1V 1JY (tel. 0171 834 2345).

Eurail: Only those living outside Europe and North Africa are eligible, and you should purchase your Eurail pass from a travel agent at home, as it is not usually permitted for agents within Europe or North Africa to sell them. Passes on offer include the Eurail Youthpass, which gives under-26s unlimited second-class rail travel in 17 European countries (not including the former Soviet Union or the UK – the latter is covered by a separate Britrail pass) for 15 days (£329), 1 month (£479) or 2 months (£665). Alternatively, the Eurail Youth Flexipass permits second-class travel for any 5, 10 or 15 days within a two-month period. Prices are £215, £330 and £446 respectively. Eurail passes for the over-26s are available, but for first-class travel only, so prices are correspondingly dearer. Groups of two or more travelling together can purchase Eurail

Saver tickets. For further details of these and other Eurail tickets, enquire at your travel agent.

COACH
Eurolines operate a coach service to more than 15 European countries, including France, Germany and the Netherlands. Fares are inclusive of cross-Channel travel and on many services there are special discounts for the under-26s. In addition to tickets for individual destinations, a range of 'Euro Explorers' are available whereby you can visit a set combination of cities for a fixed price, e.g. London–Amsterdam–Brussels–Paris–London for £70. Eurolines' UK agent is National Express. Bookings can be made either at your local National Express agent, or at one of Eurolines London offices:

Eurolines, 52 Grosvenor Gardens, Victoria, London SW1W 0AU.

Eurolines, Victoria Coach Station, Buckingham Palace Road, London SW1.

The Coach Travel Centre, 13 Regent Street, London W1.

FURTHER INFORMATION
In addition to their range of individual country and city guides, the publishers of *Let's Go* (Pan Books) and *The Rough Guide* (Harrap Columbus) both offer budget overviews of Europe. Other invaluable guides to those travelling on a shoestring budget include:

The Hitch-Hiker's Guide to Europe, Ken Welsh (Fontana), which gives tips on successful hitching in Europe as well as information on sights, eating out, accommodation and internal travel.

Europe by Train, Katie Wood and George McDonald (Fontana), the Inter-Railers' bible to travelling by train around 27 European countries, with advice on preparing for your trip, what to see and where to sleep.

The Cheap Sleep Guide to Europe, Katie Wood (Fontana), a detailed guide to budget accommodation in 27 countries, including Eastern European destinations.

Kuperard's *Culture Shock!* series will provide an insight into the customs, characteristics and lifestyles of the countries you plan to visit. *Time Out* and *Rough Guide* also cover more than just the sights in their in-depth guides to individual cities such as Paris and Amsterdam, but in terms of books to carry with you on your travels, the handy little pocket guides published by *Berlitz* are ideal.

The Central Bureau publishes *Working Holidays*, a guide to employers for both paid and voluntary work in 70 countries, which includes information about legal requirements, travel and accommodation; *Study Holidays*, a guide to language courses in Europe; and *Volunteer Work*, which offers information on voluntary organizations in over 120 countries.

FRANCE

VITAL STATISTICS

Red tape: British and other EC nationals require only a valid passport. If, however, you plan to stay for more than three months, a *carte de séjour* will be needed. US and Canadian nationals may also enter the country without a visa provided they do not intend to stay for more than three months. Other nationalities should check with their nearest French embassy or consulate.

Customs: With the implementation of the Single Market, EC nationals are now permitted an unlimited amount of excise goods as long as they are for personal use. Some EC countries have introduced guidelines, i.e. if you exceed certain limits you could be stopped and asked to provide evidence that your goods are for personal use only.

Visitors from other countries are permitted 200 cigarettes or 50 cigars or 250 g tobacco; 2 l still wine and either 1 l drinks over 22% or 2 l up to 22%; 50 g perfume and 25 ml toilet water; plus other goods not in excess of 300F per person.

Health: EC nationals are entitled to medical and hospital treatment within the French social security system. British citizens should obtain and take with them form E111, available from any DSS. Check the booklet that comes with it to ensure you know the rules for getting your money back; you must pay for treatment and then claim it back while still in France – and you won't be able to recover the full amount. E111 only covers you for accident or unexpected illness, so it's advisable to take out adequate medical insurance to cover other costs that may arise. All other nationals should ensure they take out insurance beforehand.

Language: French.

Population: 55 million.

Capital: Paris, population 11 million.

Political system: Democratic republic.

Religion: Predominantly Roman Catholic.

Time: An hour ahead of GMT in winter and two hours ahead in summer. Time is based on the 24-hour clock.

Money: The currency is the French Franc (F), divided into 100 centimes (c). Coins: 5c, 10c, 20c, 50c and 1F, 2F, 5F, 10F. Notes: 20F, 50F, 100F, 200F, 500F. £1 = 7.7F.

It is easiest and safest to carry the bulk of your money around in traveller's cheques (preferably in francs or US dollars). You can find bureaux de change in most banks, as well as in airports and railway stations. Visa and Mastercard are widely accepted, as are Eurocheques.

Communications: Some public telephones are still coin-operated, but the majority now take phonecards which can be purchased at tobacconists, métro stations or post offices. You can make long-distance or international calls from any phone box. Cheap rates to the UK operate Mon.–Fri. 10.30 p.m.–8 a.m.; Sat. from 6 p.m.; and all day Sunday and public holidays.

You can buy stamps at any post office or tabac. Main post offices in towns and cities have poste restante counters.

Electricity: 220v AC. Occasionally 110 in older hotels. Plugs are the round two-pin variety, so you will need an adapter.

Business hours: BANKS: Mon.–Fri. 9 a.m.–4.30 p.m. Closed at noon the day before public holidays.

POST OFFICES: Mon.–Fri. 8 a.m.–12 p.m. and 2.30–7 p.m.; Sat. 9 a.m.–12 p.m.

SHOPS: Large stores generally open Mon.–Sat. from 9 or 10 a.m.–6 or 7 p.m. Small food shops are open Mon.–Sat. 9 or 10 a.m.–8 p.m. and on Sunday mornings. Some small shops close for lunch from 12–2 p.m. and all day on Mondays.

OFFICES: Mon.–Fri. 9 a.m.–6 p.m., with a one or two hour lunch break.MD1

Holidays: 1 January; Easter Monday; 1 and 8 May; Ascension Day; Whit Monday; 14 July (Bastille Day); 15 August; 1 and 11 November; 25 December.

Climate: Temperate in the north and Mediterranean in the south. Cooler in the mountains with heavy snowfall in winter.

DO'S AND DON'TS

Despite the efforts of Jacques Delors to convince us that European unity is at hand, many people still approach the French with trepidation: their reputation for rudeness goes before them and a long history of niggles between the English and the French casts perennial doubts on the *entente cordiale*. A little effort towards avoiding cultural *faux pas* will help smooth your path.

The French consider it rude to arrive in a shop or restaurant without a liberal sprinkling of *bonjours* and *mercis* and *madames* and *monsieurs*, so don't forget your phrasebook! A little French, however poor, will elicit a warmer welcome than if you take the attitude that it's down to them to speak English. 'Tu' or 'toi' is reserved strictly for family and friends; the correct form of address is the more formal 'vous'. Shaking hands is *de rigueur*; the 'double kiss' – a peck on each cheek – is usually reserved for close family or friends. Politics is an eternally popular topic of debate, and don't be alarmed if heated arguments flare: it's all considered part of good conversation.

Something else the French are passionate about is food. Shops close for an hour or two at lunchtime and meals are eaten at a leisurely pace, so don't expect to be in and out in an hour. Service (at 15%) is usually included, but a little extra on the table shows appreciation. And, despite what you learnt in school, don't call the waiter 'garçon': 'Monsieur' is the polite expression.

WHERE TO GO FOR WHAT

France's appeal lies partly in its diversity. The capital, PARIS, is a must, both for its cultural and historical richness and for the unique flavour of the metropolis. Outside the capital there are numerous points of interest each meriting a day's visit at least.

NORMANDY has the Bayeux tapestry and the D-Day beaches, and the provincial capital, ROUEN, boasts many fine churches and other 12th-century buildings, as well as the market place where Joan of Arc was burnt at the stake in 1431. The breath-taking MONT ST MICHEL is difficult to get to, but this ancient abbey and 12th-century village perched precariously on a small island which gets periodically swamped at high tide is well worth the trouble.

The neighbouring province of BRITTANY has clung to its Celtic identity and hosts a number of festivals celebrating its cultural heritage. Don't miss the impressive walled port of ST MALO, formerly a pirates' stronghold, and DINAN, a beautifully preserved medieval town. Brittany's outstandingly beautiful coastline combines fine beaches with rugged windswept cliffs; particular beauty spots are CAP FRÉHEL on the northern Côte d'Emeraude and COTE SAUVAGE on the southern coast. Here you can also see the 300 standing stones which make up the French equivalent to Stonehenge.

The pastoral countryside, beautiful châteaux and palaces of the LOIRE VALLEY attract thousands of visitors. If you want to see all the major châteaux allow at least five days – most lie between Angers and Blois (a distance of about 129 km) in an area which is well served by train.

CARCASSONNE in the Languedoc region is a gem of a walled fortress city which is perhaps the best preserved relic of the Middle

Ages in Europe. Stroll round the town to get an impression of what life was like in medieval Europe.

Roman remains are scattered throughout PROVENCE, a region whose tranquil blue skies and fertile countryside have inspired countless artists and travellers. There are fine amphitheatres and other impressive Roman buildings in ARLES and NÎMES. Time your visit carefully – AIX-EN-PROVENCE and AVIGNON hold arts festivals in July and August which make pre-booking essential.

For relaxation of another kind, the FRENCH RIVIERA is unsurpassed. Despite overcommercialization, the coast still manages to retain its own alluring beauty. Your best bet is probably to base yourself in the cosmopolitan and comparatively cheap town of NICE. In July (Jazz Parade time in Nice) and August you may have trouble finding a spare bit of sand on which to lay your towel, but you can always take excursions to MONTE CARLO, CANNES, ANTIBES and ST TROPEZ and mingle with the rich and famous.

Your renewed energy can be put to good use in the ALPS, where there are excellent hiking and skiing to be had, winter or summer. CHAMONIX offers spectacular scenery all year round – lakes, waterfalls, snow-capped peaks – as well as excellent regional food and wines. Take the mountain railway for dramatic views and picturesque mountain villages.

BORDEAUX is a quintessentially French town, renowned for its wines, culture and gourmet restaurants. It's also a good base from which to make excursions into the Lot and Dordogne regions, where you can enjoy sleepy villages, remote castles and prehistoric remains. BURGUNDY is a wine lover's paradise, as well as possessing some of the finest abbeys in France.

INTERNAL TRAVEL
Air: Flying is comparatively expensive and there are no passes available. If you must travel by air there is a comprehensive internal network. Air Inter, the main domestic carrier, links all the major cities of France, and there are several smaller domestic airlines. There are discount passes for under-25s – 'Ait-Jeune' – which offer a 10–20% reduction.

Rail: The French railway system (SNCF) is one of the world's leading railways both for comfort and speed, and is justifiably the most popular means of travel in France. There are four different types of train: high-speed TGV, Eurocity, Corail and Turbo-train. There is a supplementary charge for travel on all TGVs (approximately 20F) and Eurocities, and reservations are compulsory. If you are using a ticket bought in France, make sure you date-stamp it at the orange machine – otherwise you may be fined.

If you haven't bought one of the international rail passes (see Intra-Continental Travel), there are several useful domestic passes you can buy:

The Carrissimo offers under-25s a 50% discount on all off-peak trains and a 20% reduction on most other services. It's valid for one year from the date of your first journey and costs £24.50 for four journeys or £38 for eight, but you can buy as many as you like. In Britain it's available from French Railways Ltd, 179 Piccadilly, London W1V 0AL — take your passport and a passport photo — or call 0891 515 477. In France you can buy it at any railway station.

The Euro Domino pass is relatively new. It offers 3, 5 or 10 days unlimited rail travel within a given month. Prices are £96, £125 and £200 respectively for under-26s.

BritFrance Railpass is for those who live outside Britain and France. It gives you 5 days unlimited travel within a 15-day period or 10 days in any month on both the British and French rail networks. This pass can only be purchased in the USA or Canada.

Bus: Buses are slow and cheap but of limited usefulness since there is no national network (though the cities have their own networks). Bus terminals are usually located adjacent to railway stations.

Bicycle: One of the best ways to enjoy the French countryside is to cycle through it. The SNCF 'Train et Vélo' scheme enables you to hire a bicycle from over 250 stations in France (and in most cases you can hand it in at a different station). Rates start from 50F per day plus 500F deposit. For more details get the SNCF pamphlet 'Guide du train et du vélo', available from most stations. If you want to take your own bicycle with you, it may be carried free on shorter routes, but on long-distance trains you'll have to pay a fee — and it may be carried separately and arrive some days after you.

Car hire: Car hire is widely available and a number of major international chains have offices in France. Overseas driving licences are valid in France but you will also need your vehicle registration document, and it is essential that you take out insurance. Make sure you know the rules of the road before venturing out — in particular, give way to traffic from the right. Roads in France are at their busiest in the summer months when vast numbers set off on their holidays.

Taxis: Taxis charge supplements on journeys from stations and airports as well as for luggage. All charges should be displayed inside the taxi.

Hitching: Legal except on motorways, though it is permitted on sliproads. The French are not especially 'hitcher-friendly', particularly in the big cities – you'll probably have more luck on the secondary roads.

ACCOMMODATION

For details of different types and lists of accommodation, contact your national French tourist office or regional tourist offices in France, or one of the organizations listed below. If you're planning to visit in the summer, book well ahead.

Youth hostels: Standards vary, but most hostels are open all year round, there are no age restrictions, and prices are usually around 55–75F per person, according to the type of room. IYHF cards are required, but if you don't have one you'll usually be able to pay a small supplement instead. Relations between the major hostel organizations are a little sticky – the IYHF handbook lists the FUAJ hostels but few of the LFAJs.

FUAJ (Fédération Unie des Auberges de la Jeunesse), 27 rue Pajol, 79018 Paris (tel. 1 46 07 00 01).

LFAJ (Ligue Française pour les Auberges de Jeunesse), 38 boulevard Raspail, 75007 Paris (tel. 1 45 48 69 84).

UCRIF (Union des Centres de Rencontres Internationales de France), 4 rue Jean-Jacques Rousseau 75001 Paris (tel. 1 42 60 42 40).

Foyers: Aimed at providing residential accommodation for young workers and students, Foyers des Jeunes Travailleurs are generally found in the larger towns and are often of higher quality and less strictly run than youth hostels. Your best chance of getting a place is during the student vacations. Rooms go for around 70F.

Hotels: Hotels are rated from 1–4 stars or are unclassified. The cheapest will charge around 120–160F for doubles (probably with communal washing and toilet facilities) and can thus work out cheaper than two dorm beds in a hostel. Always take a look at the room first, and check whether breakfast is included. A useful scheme is *Accueil de France* which is operated by around 50 French tourist offices. This allows you to book hotel accommodation in any other town which is also part of the system up to eight days in advance.

Rural accommodation: Gîtes de France are low budget self-catering accommodations let by an association of French families, always in the countryside. A four-bed accommodation would cost around 900–1,500F per week. Gîtes d'étapes offer basic cheap accommodation, usually in the form of bunk-bedded dorms with simple cooking and washing facilities for about 25–45F. They're ideal for cyclists and hikers. Another option is chambres d'hôtes: B&B in rural homes. For lists of these and other rural options, see the leaflet 'Accueil à la Campagne', available from your national French tourist office.

Private accommodation: Renting a flat can work out cheaply for a group who plan to stay a while. Go through an agency (ask at the tourist office) or look at university or public noticeboards.

B&B: Bed and breakfast is available, but expensive. Café Couette provides a list of B&Bs (8 rue d'Isly, 75008 Paris tel. 1 42 94 92 00); Accueil France Famille offers a minimum of one week's stay to foreigners only (5 rue F-Coppée, 75015 Paris tel. 1 45 54 22 39).

Campsites: Campers are well catered for in France. There is a campsite in virtually every town and they are usually clean and well maintained. Campsites are rated from 1–4 stars and range from around 15–30F per person per night.

FOOD

You should have no trouble finding out what's on the menu in France: restaurants must by law display their prices outside. Typically, as well as the *à la carte* menu there will be a fixed-price menu of two or three courses (usually a good bet for around 65–120F). Most restaurants also offer a *plat du jour* (dish of the day) for around 50F, which may be more interesting as it is often a regional speciality. Table wine is usually cheap and good value.

Brasseries are similar to restaurants but tend to serve quicker meals at all hours of the day, but for a real flavour of France, you can't beat cafés. Menus are fairly limited – outside lunchtime don't expect much more than a *croque monsieur* and a couple of desserts – and you can pay just as much for a snack as for a three-course meal in a small bistro. However, cafés are not just for eating: you're paying to sit and watch the world go by. Buy one cup of coffee and you can sit for hours undisturbed. Remember that prices will vary according to where you sit: at the counter is cheapest, outside on the terrace the most expensive. If in doubt, check the price before you order.

France has been slow in catering for the needs of vegetarians – usually you'll have to trust to luck that there will be something suitable on the menu. Self-service restaurants which allow you to make up your own menu according to taste and budget may offer more scope for vegetarians. Expect to pay around 45–85F.

For lunch it's as much fun (and far cheaper) to head for the nearest boulangerie and pick up a baguette. Cremeries offer a huge selection of cheeses, while charcuteries specialize in ready-made food such as cooked meats and salads. Supermarket chains to look out for are Prisunic, Monoprix, Uniprix or Codec. Alternatively, try the local markets – usually low-priced, colourful affairs. For bargain deals, go near closing time when traders are trying to offload their perishable products.

As in most European countries, fast-food chains abound for around 35–50F a head – if you must.

BUDGETING

France is not an outrageously expensive place to visit – at least no more so than most Western European countries! Put a little effort towards choosing the right places to eat, sleep and drink and you can probably get by on around 350F per day.

If you make hostel dorms your primary source of accommodation, you can reckon on around 65–90F per night. Your biggest problem may be with food – all those tempting French cafés! A few reckless decisions and costs can start to add up alarmingly. But if you stick to the set menus, avoid terrace snacks, and grab a baguette for lunch, you should be able to get by on around 100F per day. Choose your evening entertainment equally carefully: clubs and discos can set you back between 65–160F for the entrance fee alone, with expensive drinks to match. A beer can cost anything from 15–40F.

Travel is relatively cheap if you buy and make good use of a travel pass. Monuments and museums are pricey (20–30F per visit), but if you can brave the queues many are half-price on Sundays, and some tourist attractions offer a 50% discount to under-25s.

If you want to earn some extra cash, there are a number of possibilities, particularly for EC nationals who are now legally entitled to work anywhere in the Community. (Remember that EC nationals staying more than three months will need a *carte de séjour*.) Teaching English is probably the most common source of casual work, though you will generally need a degree, and preferably (though it's not compulsory) an English-teaching qualification such as TEFL. It's probably easiest to find a job from Britain: look for ads in the *Times Educational Supplement*. The French Embassy in London also publishes a leaflet: 'Teaching Posts in France'. If you aim to set up as a freelance, it's worth putting up notices at colleges. The British Council office in Paris also holds a list of language schools (tel. 1 49 55 73 12).

Au pairing is always an option, but landing a 'good' family is very much down to luck. If you think this is for you, there are several agencies both in France and the UK that will try and match potential families and au pairs. Most UK agencies don't charge a fee, but the French ones will. Buy a copy of *The Lady* for names of

agencies in this country, or ask at the main tourist office in Paris
for French agencies.

Finally there are the usual array of casual jobs that may scrape
you a living – grapepicking, waitering/waitressing, washing up,
typing and so on, though some of these may depend on your command of French. In Paris there are a couple of useful agencies you
could try: the CIDJ (Centre d'Information et de Documentation de
la Jeunesse) at 101 quai Branly (métro: Bir Hakeim) and CROUS,
39 avenue Georges Bernanos (métro: Port-Royal). Both are youth
agencies which have addresses and lists of jobs.

FURTHER INFORMATION

The French Government Tourist Office, 178 Piccadilly, London
W1V 0AL (tel. 0891 244 123) will provide useful information on
where to stay, eat, sightseeing etc. Getting through by phone is
difficult – you would be better off writing or dropping by in
person.

French Embassy, 58 Knightsbridge, London SW1X 7JT (tel. 0171
201 1000).

French Consulate, 21 Cromwell Road, London SW7 (tel. 0171 838
2000).

For visas, contact 6 Cromwell Place, London SW7 2EW (tel. 0171
838 2050).

Background reading: Useful guides for the budget traveller
include: *France: The Rough Guide* (Harrap Columbus) and *Emplois
d'Eté en France* (Vacation Work), a guide to summer jobs in France.

Paris

AIRPORT FACILITIES

The main international airport is Roissy–Charles de Gaulle, 26 km
north of Paris. There are two terminals: most international airlines
operate out of Terminal 1; the second terminal is split into 2A, 2B
and 2D. Tourist information is available from 7 a.m.–11 p.m. in
terminals 1, 2A and 2B. All terminals have the usual shops and
duty-free outlets, as well as currency exchanges (open from
6.30 a.m.–11.30 p.m.), cafeterias, restaurants, car rental and left-
luggage facilities; terminals 1 and 2D also have post offices.

Check-in time is usually 90 minutes before international flights,
30 before domestic. There is no airport tax. For departure information call 1 48 62 22 80.

The secondary international airport is Orly, which handles mainly charter flights. An Air France coach service links the two airports, running every 20 minutes. Journey time is 50 minutes at a cost of 64F. Alternatively you can go by rail (RER line B).

CITY LINKS
You should have little trouble getting from either airport to the city centre.

ROISSY–CHARLES DE GAULLE
Rail: This is the quickest and cheapest way to get to the city. RER trains (line B) run daily every 15–20 minutes to Gare du Nord where you can change for the métro. Tickets cost around 30F and the journey time is 30 minutes. You can get a courtesy bus to the train station from any terminal.
Bus: Air France buses leave from both terminals and stop at Etoile (Arc de Triomphe) and Porte Maillot. Tickets are 50F and may be bought on the bus. Average journey time is 40 minutes with buses running every 15 minutes. Alternatively, the number 350 RAPT bus will take you to Gare du Nord and Gare de L'Est, while the number 351 bus goes to Nation.
Taxi: It costs between 180–240F to travel into the centre by taxi, and the journey can take anything from 40 minutes to over an hour, depending on the traffic.

ORLY
Rail: Take the courtesy bus to RER station Pont de Rungis, then take line C to Paris, where you can switch to the underground. Tickets cost about 25F and trains run every 15–20 minutes daily.
Bus: Air France buses depart daily from both terminals every 10–15 minutes, stopping at Les Invalides and Montparnasse. Tickets cost around 35F – buy them from the Air France Terminus. Alternatively, the number 214 RATP bus will take you to Denfert Rochereau, as will the Orlybus, which costs around 20F; both run every 15 minutes and tickets are available from machines in the airport hall. Journeys last 30 minutes.
Taxi: A taxi costs around 170F and will take 30–40 minutes (allow longer in the rush hour).

USEFUL ADDRESSES
Tourist office: 127 avenue des Champs Élysées (tel. 1 47 23 61 72). Open 9 a.m.–8 p.m. daily. Métro: Etoile-Charles-de-Gaulle.
CROUS: 39 avenue Georges-Bernanos (tel. 1 40 51 37 10). Métro: Port Royal. Organization offering cheap accommodation and eating options for students.

Main post office: 52 rue du Louvre. Open 24 hours for services including poste restante. Métro: Louvre or Les Halles.

British Embassy: 35 rue du Faubourg Saint Honoré (tel. 1 42 66 91 42). Métro: Concorde.

US Embassy: 2 avenue Gabriel (tel. 1 42 96 12 02). Métro: Champs Élysées or Clémenceau.

Emergency Services: Dial 17 for police, 15 for ambulance, 18 for fire.

Medical/Dental emergencies: 24-hour doctor tel. 1 47 07 77 77; 24-hour dentist tel. 1 43 37 51 00.

Pharmacy: Pharmacie Dhéry, 84 avenue des Champs Elysées (tel. 1 45 62 02 41). Open daily 24 hours. Métro: George V.

GETTING ABOUT

Public transport within Paris is comprehensive, efficient and easy to understand. For individual journeys on the métro or RER, a single ticket costs around 5.50F and will allow you unlimited changes to get to your final destination. A cheaper option is to purchase a book (carnet) of 10 tickets for around 35F from any métro station or tobacconists.

There is a tourist pass, the Paris Visite, which gives unlimited travel on zones 1–3 (if you travel within the city limits you will only be using zones 1 and 2) of the métro, buses and central Paris RER trains. A 3-day pass costs 85F, a 5-day pass costs 135F; both are available from main métro and RER stations. The Paris Visite also entitles you to discounts at certain tourist attractions.

The 7-day Coupon Jaune pass costs 60F for two zones, valid Mon.–Sun. regardless of when you buy it. There is also a monthly pass, the Carte Orange, which costs 201F for two zones (or 460F for all zones) and is valid from the first day of the month. Both of these require passport photos.

Carry your passes with you: as in England, there are spot checks.

Rail: RER, the mainline railway, operates daily. Trains run every 15 minutes from 5.30–12 a.m. You need separate tickets for journeys outside Paris.

Métro: Your best bet for quick and easy travel, the métro runs daily from 5.30–12.30 a.m. Lines are identified both by their numbers and their final destinations. A connecting station is termed a correspondence. You'll find a map of the underground system in each métro.

Bus: Buses run Mon.–Sat. between 6 a.m. and 8.30 p.m., with a limited amount of night services. Single bus rides require one ticket per two sections, more for longer journeys.

Bicycle: Despite the frightening spectre of Paris traffic, French law protects cyclists and a bike can offer you a wonderful bird's-eye view of the city. There are several hire shops in the city: try Paris Vélo at 2–4 rue de Fer-à-Moulin (métro: Censier-Daubenton) (tel. 1 43 37 52 22). You can take your bicycle on the train for free on short routes.

Taxis: When travelling late at night or when you feel like treating yourself, why not take a taxi? Their rates are very reasonable and three small lights on top of the taxi will tell you which fare rate the meter is switched to: A (passenger side) is daytime, B (centre) is night time, and C (driver's side) is out of town.

SIGHTS

Begin your tour on the Right Bank at PLACE DE L'ÉTOILE – so named for its 12 avenues shooting out to form a dramatic 12-pointed star – located at the western end of the Champs Élysées (métro: Etoile). For a view of both the star and the resulting traffic chaos, climb the 277 steps of the ARC DE TRIOMPHE, Napoleon's 50-metre triumphal arch built as a tribute to his armies and himself. At the foot of the Arc, the TOMB OF THE UNKNOWN SOLDIER and an eternal flame commemorate those killed in the two World Wars.

The tree-lined CHAMPS ÉLYSÉES is still one of Europe's most elegant avenues and one in which you can enjoy window shopping in boutiques displaying some of the most expensive fashions in Paris. It's a pleasant stroll up the avenue to the PLACE DE LE CONCORDE, the vast square in which many prominent figures of the revolution met their death under the guillotine, among them Louis XVI, Marie Antoinette and Robespierre (métro: Concorde).

No trip to Paris is complete without a visit to the LOUVRE, even if you just head straight for the *Mona Lisa* and out again. The controversial 212-metre glass pyramid in the central courtyard now serves as the main entrance. The Louvre is free on Sundays, but be prepared for long queues (métro: Palais Royal or Louvre). Remember, most museums are closed on Mondays.

It's a short walk from the Louvre to the PONT NEUF, Paris's oldest bridge and one of five bridges you can cross to get to the ÎLE DE LA CITÉ (métro: Cité), the tiny island where Paris started life in pre-Roman times. The Pont Neuf leads you to the PALAIS DE JUSTICE (law courts), former home of France's medieval kings. Within the Palais gates is the SAINTE-CHAPELLE, built almost entirely of stained glass. The CONCIERGERIE, on the other hand, still strikes a chilly note; this gloomy prison is where Marie Antoinette, Robespierre and over 2,000 other revolutionary figures sweated it out before their execution. At the far end of the island lies

NOTRE-DAME, the 13th-century cathedral where Napoleon was crowned and where all national celebrations are still staged.

The Left Bank is traditionally home to the more Bohemian side of Paris. It was the focal point of the student demonstrations of the 1960s, and the long line of notable ex-residents include Hemingway, Picasso, Sartre and Henry Miller. Today the area is still busy with students and young people, and the LATIN QUARTER (round the boulevards St Michel and St Germain) in particular is packed with cafés, bookshops, restaurants, galleries, antique shops and more up-market boutiques. Just off the boulevard St Michel is the SORBONNE university, whose ex-students include Molière and Victor Hugo. The PANTHÉON is a secular mausoleum and the final resting place of French heroes such as Hugo and Voltaire (métro: Cardinal-Lemoine).

MONTPARNASSE is another well-trodden area, still trading off the fame of those who used to hang out there, including such literary and political figures as Hemingway, Fitzgerald, Lenin and Trotsky. You won't see many visible reminders of them, but if you have a sense of history you'll be interested to see their former café haunts. Many of these former residents ended up in MONTPARNASSE CEMETERY, one of two cemeteries of note in Paris (the other is PÈRE LACHAISE, where you can visit the graves of celebrities such as Sarah Bernhardt, Oscar Wilde and Jim Morrison (métro: Père Lachaise).

Also on the Left Bank is the HÔTEL DES INVALIDES, built by Louis XIV to care for wounded soldiers, now housing the tomb of Napoleon himself (métro: Invalides). The other main attraction is the EIFFEL TOWER. The tower opens till late but gets millions of visitors every year so be prepared to queue (métro: Bir Hakeim).

A short ride out of the city centre is MONTMARTRE, the artists' quarter which flourished in the late 19th century when many of the Impressionist painters lived and worked (métro: Anvers or Abbesses). Despite being overrun by tourists, the area still manages to retain its own sleepy atmosphere. On the hill stands SACRÉ-COEUR, whose large and bulbous white dome dominates the Parisian skyline. Climb to the top for a panoramic view of the city. For a contrasting atmosphere nip down the hill to PIGALLE, Paris's equivalent of Soho, where you'll find street vendors, respectability and sleaze intermingled.

East of Montmartre lies one of the most interesting and cosmopolitan districts in Paris. BELLEVILLE has a lively mix of peoples from all cultures: Arabs, Algerians, Tunisians, Moroccans, Chinese and more. It's a vibrant, colourful part of Paris, filled with the sounds of foreign tongues and foreign food. A day's walkabout will be rewarded with a decent lunch.

If you're interested in something a little more offbeat, the CATACOMBS at place Denfert-Rochereau were used as resistance headquarters during the war and are now a popular attraction. Or you could try the SEWERS (entrance at the corner of Pont d'Alma and Quai d'Orsay) if you can put up with the smell.

There are over 100 museums in Paris – pick up a leaflet from tourist information. Aside from the Louvre, the best of the bunch are probably the MUSÉE D'ORSAY (métro: Solferino), with its excellent collection of Impressionist paintings; the RODIN MUSEUM, a tribute to the sculptor's life and work; and the MUSÉE DE CLUNY, where medieval art is housed in a beautiful 15th-century mansion next to Paris's Roman baths. The distinctive POMPIDOU CENTRE on the Rue Beauborg contains a cultural mish-mash of just about everything – paintings, books, films, videos and records – and there is usually some form of free entertainment going on. All state museums in Paris are shut on Tuesdays, and those owned by the city close on Mondays. Entrance fees are around 20–30F. Many are half-price or free on Sundays, but consequently packed out. An ISIC card should get you a 50% discount, or you can buy a museum pass, valid for 1, 3 or 5 days, which gives direct access to most museums without the need to queue. Prices are 55F, 110F and 160F and you can get them from museums, tourist offices or métro stations.

Paris is a shopper's paradise, and if you fancy restocking your backpack but can't afford the *haute couture* of the Champs-Élysées don't despair! Check out Paris's flea markets: there's a market on Place d'Aligre (métro: Ledru-Rollin), and another on Carreau du Temple (métro: Temple). Even if you don't find anything worth buying, they're good fun in themselves. For books, the place to go is Shakespeare & Co., 37 rue de la Bucherie (métro: St Michel); this bookshop is so well known that it's become a bit of a traveller's haunt. In addition to having the widest selection of second-hand English books in Paris, it holds regular poetry readings and such like.

For gastronomical bargains don't miss the many open-air food markets, which are usually at their liveliest on Saturday mornings. You'll find entertainment not only in the colourful display of every conceivable type of produce but also in the raucous hard sell and equally hard bargaining that goes into every transaction. Try the market at rue de Buci (métro: St Germain des Prés), or the one at place Monge near the métro of the same name.

For a good picnic venue where you can devour your bargains,

there are plenty of attractive parks and gardens. The BOIS DE BOUL-
OGNE is a former royal park at the western end of the city with
seven lakes, a waterfall, restaurants and cafés. At the south-eastern
end is the BOIS DE VINCENNES where you can also go boating or
cycling. The two most central picnic parks are the JARDIN DES
TUILERIES and the JARDIN DES CHAMPS ÉLYSÉES.

The best means of transport for this tour is a combination of the
métro and your own feet. You can, however, take bus tours or one
of the famous bateaux-mouches which sail down the Seine and
give a different view of many of the sights.

ACCOMMODATION
Your best option is to try a room-finding service which can save
you both time and money.

The Accueil des Jeunes en France (AJF), provides a free booking
service for budget accommodation in hostels or foyers and has
8,000 beds in Paris, rising to 11,000 during the summer – prices
are around 110F including breakfast. It has four offices located
at:
Gare du Nord, (tel. 1 42 85 86 19). Open daily June–Oct.,
8 a.m.–10 p.m.
Beaubourg, 119 rue St Martin (tel. 1 42 77 87 80). Open all
year, Mon.–Sat. 9.30 a.m.–7 p.m. (métro: Les Halles or Ram-
buteau).
Hotel de Ville, 16 rue du Pont Louis-Philippe (tel. 1 42 78 04
82). Open all year, Mon.–Fri. 9.30 a.m.–6.30 p.m. (métro:
Hôtel de Ville or Pont Marie).
Latin Quarter, 139 Boulevard St Michel (tel. 1 43 54 95 86).
Open Mar.–Oct., Mon.–Fri. 9.30 a.m.–6.30 p.m. (métro: Port
Royal).
Bureaux d'Accueil, 127 avenue des Champs-Élysées (tel. 1 47 23
61 72) will also make reservations. There are several other offices
at various train stations: Gare du Nord; Gare de l'Est; Gare d'Auster-
litz; Gare de Lyon; Gare Montparnasse, as well as the Eiffel Tower.
The Bureaux charge a small commission and are not quite so geared
to the budget-conscious as the AJF.
Youth hostels: There are only two IYHF youth hostels: the Jules
Ferry at 8 Boulevard Jules-Ferry, Paris 11 (tel. 1 43 57 55 60), and
the D'Artagnan at 80 rue Vitruve (tel. 1 43 61 08 75). In summer
both need to be booked well in advance and there is a maximum
stay of 3 or 4 nights. One very useful aspect of the IYHF hostels:
you can fax reservations between them and a number of other

European hostels, which is quicker and easier than writing.

UCRIF (Union des Centres de Rencontres Internationales de France) has 18 hostels in or near Paris. Prices range from 60–200F. Go to their main office at 4 rue Jean-Jacques Rousseau (tel. 1 42 60 42 40) métro: Palais Royal or Louvre.

Student residences: The Cité University, 19 boulevard Jouran (tel. 1 45 89 35 79) offers cheap accommodation when term is out (métro: Cité Universitaire). For other student accommodation ask at CROUS (see Useful Addresses).

Hotels: For cheap hotels look around the Place de la Bastille, Nation, St Paul, Gare de Lyon, Place de Clichy and Pigalle.

Private accommodation: If you are considering renting a room or flat for a longer stay, check out the Cité University noticeboard. You might also find it useful to make your way to Shakespeare & Co. at 37 rue de la Bûcherie (métro: St Michel), a bookshop favoured by travellers, which often has notices of flats to let.

Campsites: Camping is not recommended since the sites are not central and involve convoluted commuting. If you are determined to use your tent, however, you could try the Bois de Boulogne, alleé du Bord de l'Eau (tel. 1 45 24 30 00), though this is certainly not the safest of places to stay. To get there, take the métro to Port Maillot, then bus 244 followed by a short walk.

For all types of accommodation, make sure you get there early in the day for the best chance of success.

FOOD

Paris restaurants are varied and many. (See **France: Food**, p. 136 for a rough guide to the types of eating places available.) One of the best areas to nose around for cheap meals in Paris is the Latin Quarter, particularly the areas near rue de la Huchette and rue Mouffetard. The Latin Quarter reflects the huge gastronomic influence of France's many immigrants: here you can eat Greek, Vietnamese, Italian or Japanese style. For North African cuisine (Algerian, Tunisian, Moroccan, etc.), the central point is the area between the rue St Jacques and boulevard St Michel. Cheap eateries may also be found in Marais and Bastille. (If you have an ISIC card, you are entitled to tickets for student restaurants where you can pick up a meal for around 25F. CROUS (see Useful Addresses) will supply you with both tickets and lists of venues.)

If you're looking for a quick snack, keep an eye out for the many street stands – crêpes are particularly plentiful in the Montparnasse area, while in Marais you can buy pitta bread jammed with falafel for only 15F. Those who want to cook for themselves will find plenty of the usual supermarkets, boulangeries, épiceries, charcuteries and cremeries around, and the smaller shops seldom close before 7 p.m. There are also markets selling cheese, sausage, bread, etc. – popular choices include the market on rue Mouffetard in the Latin Quarter and the huge covered market on rue Mabillon in Saint Germain. Most markets open from 8 a.m.–1 p.m. and are at their best on Saturdays.

In keeping with the rest of France, Paris is weak on veggie options, though it does have some vegetarian restaurants (the Piccolo Teatro at 6 rue des Ecouffes is one of the best).

ENTERTAINMENT

For full entertainment listings, check out the weeklies, *Pariscope*, *7 à Paris* or *l'Officiel des Spectacles*. You can book tickets for all types of entertainment at the Alpha-FNAC – ask the tourist office for your nearest branch. Amongst other things, the listings magazines will carry details of the 250-plus films showing in Paris each week: VO means the film is being shown in its original language. Tickets are around 40F, cheaper on Mondays.

There is also a thriving live music scene. Jazz afficionados will fare best in the rue St Benoît, home of such clubs as the Bilboquet and Montana, and rue des Lombards, whose clubs include the Sunset and Duc des Lombards. As in any major city, there is a wide range of nightclubs and discos. Popular venues include the Locomotive (90 boulevard de Clichy) and the Rex Club (5 boulevard Poissonnière). Nightclubs are usually closed Mondays and/or Sundays; entrance fees are around 80–100F. Try the Pigalle area for clubs with cheap or free entrance. As for the internationally famous Moulin Rouge, Folies Bergeres and Lido: these have retained their fame but not their character – don't bother unless you have around 500F to spare.

Notable opera and theatre venues include the recently opened Opéra Bastille, built to house opera 'for the people' and the Paris Opéra, home to the French national ballet. You can buy half-price theatre tickets for same-day performances at the Kiosque Theatre at 15 Place de la Madeleine, open daily from 12.30 p.m.

If you don't feel like splashing out on any particular event, wandering through the Latin Quarter will probably afford you as good an evening's entertainment as any.

EXCURSIONS

Most visitors to Paris include a trip to VERSAILLES PALACE, 20 km outside the capital, in their itinerary. The palace was once the official royal residence of Louis XIV, and subsequently Louis XVI and Marie Antoinette. Its main attractions are the Hall of Mirrors, where the Treaty of Versailles which ended World War I was signed in 1919, the Queen's bedroom and the King's apartments. Outside you can stroll through the palace gardens and visit the royals' individual hideaways. The palace is open Tues.–Sun. from 9 a.m.–5.30 p.m. (until 6.30 p.m. May–Sept.) Entrance is 31F and there's a 50% discount for under-25s and students – but everyone gets in half-price on Sundays. It's usually overrun with tourists so arrive early if you want to avoid the worst of the queues. To get there take the RER line C5 to Versailles-Rive Gauche, a journey of around half an hour.

Still crowded but older and more beautiful is the palace of FONTAINEBLEAU, dating from the 12th century and famous for its gardens and surrounding forest. The forest has excellent walking and cycling trails and you can hire both bikes and horses. Fontainebleau is 65 km outside Paris and opens daily except Tuesdays. Entrance is 25F, half-price on Sundays and for under-25s (to see the whole site, however, extra tickets must be purchased). Take the RER from Gare de Lyon and change at Fontainebleau-Avon for bus A or B.

Just an hour away from Gare Montparnasse is the world-famous Gothic cathedral of CHARTRES with 137 of the finest stained-glass windows in France. The smaller but equally attractive château of CHANTILLY can be reached by train from Gare du Nord (closed Tuesdays).

Other places of interest within easy distance of the capital include the early Gothic basilica at SAINT DENIS, which contains many royal tombs from the Middle Ages; and the FORÊT DE COMPIÈGNE, 81 km from Paris, where you can relax and enjoy a picnic amidst beautiful natural surroundings.

France's newest and much discussed attraction, EURODISNEY is 32 km east of Paris. If you're tempted by the charms of Mickey Mouse and company, be prepared to pay for the pleasure. A one-day pass will set you back 250F; a two-day pass 475F; and a three-day pass 630F. The numerous fast-food places and restaurants inside are equally dear, and if you plan on bringing your own sandwiches, be warned: there's a ban on picnics inside the park! There is, however, a picnic area outside. To reach Eurodisney from Paris, take RER line A; the journey takes around 40 minutes. The park opens daily at 9 a.m. but get there much earlier to beat the queues. Avoid weekends and French holidays.

GERMANY

VITAL STATISTICS

Red tape: A valid passport is all that is required of EC nationals and citizens of the USA, Canada, Australia and New Zealand. If you plan to stay for more than three months you will have to apply for a residence permit. Other nationalities should enquire at a German embassy or consulate for information on visa requirements.

Customs: With the implementation of the Single Market, EC nationals are now permitted an unlimited amount of excise goods as long as they are for personal use. Some EC countries have introduced guidelines, i.e. if you exceed certain limits you could be stopped and asked to provide evidence that your goods are for personal use only.

Non-EC nationals are permitted 200 cigarettes or 50 cigars or 250 g tobacco; 1 l spirits and 2 l wine.

Health: EC nationals are entitled to free medical care (though a charge may be made for prescription drugs) provided they have with them form E111, available from DSS offices. However, the system is not user-friendly – see the accompanying booklet with E111 for full details – and you are only covered for accidents or emergencies. It is strongly advisable to take out full medical insurance before you go. The same applies to non-EC nationals, who have no such rights to free health care.

Language: German. English is widely spoken.

Population: 79 million.

Capital: Berlin, population 3.5 million.

Political system: Parliamentary democracy. Germany has a coalition government led by Chancellor Helmut Kohl. The ongoing integration of East and West remains the outstanding problem.

Religion: About 45% Protestant and 45% Roman Catholic.

Time: An hour ahead of GMT in winter, two hours ahead in summer.

Money: The currency is the Deutsch mark (DM), divided into 100 pfennigs. Coins: 1, 2, 5, 10 and 50 pfennig; DM1, 2 and 5. Notes: DM10, 20, 50, 100, 200, 500, 1,000. £1 = DM2.20.

Eurocheques and DM traveller's cheques are the preferred methods of payment. Credit cards are not widely accepted except in the major hotels, shops or restaurants. You can change money at banks and currency exchanges (*Wechselstuben*), as well as hotels and travel agencies, though rates here tend to be lower.

Communications: In the West you can make international

telephone calls either from phone boxes with a green square or from main post offices. Most pay phones are now card-operated. Phonecards (*Telfonkarte*) can be bought at any post office. Cheap rates to the UK operate 6 p.m.–8 a.m. weekdays and all day Saturday and Sunday; to Canada and the USA midnight to noon. For the domestic operator dial 010; international operator 0010. You cannot make transfer charge calls.

In former East Germany, the phone system is still pretty limited and confusing. Overseas calls are best made from a post office via the operator. It's also possible to make transfer charge calls.

Poste restante mail can be sent to main post offices in any town, East or West. Take your passport or ID when you go to collect it. Expect East German mail to take a little longer.
Electricity: 220v AC.

Business hours: BANKS: Mon.–Fri. 9 a.m.–12.30 p.m. and 2.30 p.m.–4 p.m.; Thurs till 5.30 p.m.

POST OFFICES: Mon.–Sat. 8 a.m.–6 p.m.

SHOPS: Mon.–Fri. 8 a.m.–6.30 p.m.; Thurs. till 8.30 p.m.; Sat. till 2 p.m. (6 p.m. on the first Saturday of each month). Some smaller shops also close from noon till 3 p.m. Those near train stations generally stay open later.

OFFICES: Mon.–Fri. 8.30 a.m.–5 p.m.
Holidays: 1 and 6 January; Good Friday; Easter Monday; Labour Day; Ascension Day; 1 May; Whit Monday; 3 October; 1 November; third Wednesday in November (Day of Prayer and Repentance); 25 and 26 December.
Climate: Temperate throughout the country with warm pleasant summers and cold winters, especially in the south and east. Rain falls throughout the year but is at its heaviest in the winter. Conditions in the mountains can be severe.

DO'S AND DON'TS

The Germans have a reputation for formality and reserve. While this is gradually being eroded by the more easy-going younger generation, your safest bet is to take the lead from your hosts rather than risk offence by barging your way around mindless of all social graces.

Don't call anyone by their first name unless invited to do so – using the correct form of address is considered very important: 'Herr' for a man and 'Frau' or 'meine Dame' for an adult woman, regardless of whether she's married or not. If you're talking to someone with a title, it's 'Herr Professor', for example, with or without the family name. In conversation, use the more formal 'Sie' rather than 'du' to address all but your closest friends. German greetings are nothing if not thorough – the appropriate 'Guten Morgen', 'Guten Tag' or 'Guten Abend' together with a firm handshake, followed by an 'Auf Wiedersehen' and another handshake when saying goodbye. You'll soon discover that shaking hands is an important social ritual both in formal and informal situations. Use 'Bitte' (please/you're welcome) and 'Danke' (thank you) often.

If you're invited to someone's house, don't think you have the traditional British half-hour leeway; in Germany, eight o'clock for dinner means exactly that. Make sure you bring a small gift – flowers or chocolates will do – and remember to write a thank you note afterwards.

In German eyes, laws are there to be obeyed; if the sign says don't sit on the grass, don't! If the road is clear for miles but the pedestrian lights are red, stay put! Jaywalking can actually land you with a fine.

WHERE TO GO FOR WHAT

BERLIN, the newly appointed capital, is a must on anyone's touring list, but what are some of the other highlights of unified Germany?

Focal point of the north and the second largest city in Germany, HAMBURG took a terrible battering in World War II but has since been completely rebuilt and boasts many fine buildings, notably the Renaissance Rathaus. Its principle attraction, however, is the infamous nightlife of the St Pauli Reeperbahn – the red light district where the Beatles slogged it out before they found fame and fortune. The Reeperbahn contains a phenomenal concentration of bars and clubs offering just about every kind of service you care to think of.

Fill your lungs with purer air in the legendary RHINE VALLEY, an area of great natural beauty endowed with legends from yesteryear. River trips through the Rhine Gorge take you past a fascinating landscape of hillside vineyards, mythological rocks and ruined castles. At the head of the Mosel Valley in Koblenz is Ehrenbreitstein Fortress, one of the world's largest, which houses a youth hostel. If you have time, catch a river barge along the Mosel to TRIER, the oldest town in Germany and one of the oldest in Europe.

West of Koblenz is COLOGNE. Decimated by the Allies during the war, Cologne has survived to become one of Germany's largest cities and plays host annually to the popular pre-Lent carnival; this is the best time to visit. There are some excellent Roman remains as well as the visually stunning Gothic Dom – one of the world's most visited cathedrals.

HEIDELBERG is a beautiful riverside town, renowned for its university and for the drinking habits of. its students. The town is dominated by the 13th-century castle housing the Heidelberg Tun, a giant wine barrel with a capacity of around 50,000 gallons – enough to satisfy the greatest thirst – and the student inns are popular with students and visitors alike. The annual drama festival takes place in July and there are plenty of open-air concerts.

Tucked into the south-western corner of Germany is the BLACK FOREST. Wonderful scenery, a host of charming villages and the best climate in Germany combine to make this one a most popular resort area. Encircled by the forest is FREIBURG, offering yet another spectacular cathedral and a number of lovely market squares. Take the cable car up Schauinsland mountain for some stunning views. Further north you can visit the elegant spa resort of BADEN BADEN, once the therapeutic playground of the rich, where you can soak away your aches and pains in one of the remaining baths.

MUNICH is the swinging capital of Bavaria and a great centre of art and culture as well as the German national pastime – beer drinking. The city is well supplied with beer gardens where you can wallow happily. Munich enjoys perpetual celebrations, from the winter carnival to the summer seasons of the State Opera and Theatre to the famous Oktoberfest, when beer drinkers and brewers from all over the world descend on Munich for a happy fortnight. The Mariahilfsplatz is always at the heart of things and three times a year hosts a fantastic flea market of junk and antiques.

Bavaria also has its share of excellent scenery as well as some fairly bizarre castles. If you fancy a sporting weekend, head for the Bavarian Alps or the Bavarian Forest for some good skiing and alpine walking. The ancient cities of PASSAU and REGENSBURG make fine bases from which to explore the area. For picture-postcard beauty, take one of the special buses along the so-called ROMANTIC ROAD between Fussen and Wurzburg, a 325-km trail featuring some of the most stunning medieval towns in Europe.

In general, the smaller cities are more picturesque than the larger ones. Since they weren't bombed in World War II, they've maintained their medieval flavour.

INTERNAL TRAVEL
Air: The national carrier is Lufthansa, but air travel is expensive. Contact their UK office (tel. 01345 737747) for information on air passes.
Rail: German railways, once divided into separate Western and Eastern networks, have now united to form German Rail. If you

don't already have an international rail pass, there are several options available:

The Euro Domino pass allows 3, 5 or 10 days unlimited rail travel in any one month. Prices are £131, £144 and £198 respectively, or £98, £107 and £148 for under-26s.

Regional Passes are available only to residents of Britain and Ireland. There are 15 such passes covering different areas within Germany. Each pass is valid for 21 days and allows you unlimited rail travel (including S-Bahn trains) for any 5 or 10 days within that period. Supplements for ICE trains are not included. A second-class Regional Pass costs £54 for 5 days and £85 for 10. There is no Youth Pass equivalent.

If you plan on buying single tickets rather than a pass, there are a number of different options. Ask at your nearest travel agent for details or contact German Rail, Passenger Services, Suite 4, The Sanctuary, 23 Oakhill Grove, Surbiton, Surrey.

Bus: German buses are efficient and prices are comparable to those of the railways, but there is no national network. You can use German Rail Passes on the DB-run Bahnbusse.

Taxi: Widely available, with compulsory meters.

Bicycle: Cycling is popular in Germany and therefore well catered for. There are cycle paths in most cities and you can rent bikes cheaply from most country stations and return them to a different station later on.

Car: The German autobahn (motorway) network is extensive – and the fastest in Europe, as speed limits do not apply. Car hire is widely available and you can use your national or international driving licence for up to a year. Like most Europeans, Germans drive on the right. Seatbelts are compulsory.

Hitching: Although common in Germany, it is prohibited on autobahns except on entry and exit roads. On entry roads you are not supposed to stand beyond the blue sign showing the white auto. If you're trying to get out of a big town, check the student Mensa (university cafeteria) noticeboards – most carry offers of rides. Special bureaux known as 'mit fahrgelegenheiten' hook drivers up with passengers who need rides. It's like 'hitching' through an agency.

ACCOMMODATION

For all types of accommodation, you'll maximize your chances by getting there early. Bear in mind that you're likely to face problems in eastern Germany, where budget accommodation is in short supply. Tourist offices are very helpful, both the ones overseas – most national tourist offices hold lists of hotels, pensions and campsites – and those within Germany, some of which provide a booking service.

Youth hostels: Youth hostels (Jugendherberge) originated in Germany. You'll find an IYHF hostel in virtually every town you wish to visit, particularly now that the East and West's associations have merged. Hostels are open to all ages (except in Bavaria, which has an age limit of 27). Curfews (usually 10 p.m.) are rigorously enforced, except in the larger cities where doors may stay open till midnight or 1 a.m. Always try to book in advance, especially during the summer. German hostels are comparatively group-orientated – particularly the Jugendgasthäuser – and if you turn up unexpectedly you may find them overrun with hordes of school trippers. If the hostel is busy, you'll usually be limited to a three-night stay.

There are six different types of youth hostel with prices varying according to the hostel's standard, facilities and location. Most either provide cooking facilities or offer meals. The most basic Jugendherberge (grade I) charge between DM14–18, while the top of the range Jugendgastehäuser (youth guest houses) usually charge DM26–32. If you're a non-member or over 25 expect to pay around DM5 extra. For further information, contact YHA, 14 Southampton Street, London WC2.

Hotels, pensions and gasthäuser: Widely available in the West, expect to pay around DM27–35 per person (more in Berlin) for a room (breakfast included, in many case). In the East such rooms are comparatively rare.

Private accommodation: In the East, private rooms are easier to come by than pensions and they cost less, at around DM25–35 per person for singles or doubles. Ask at the tourist office or look for a 'Gasthof' or 'Zimmer frei' sign. If you're looking for a longer-term stay, the Mitwohnzentrale agency will find you rooms or apartments that are available to rent for anything from a few days to a few months. German tourist offices should be able to provide you with agency addresses.

Campsites: Recommended as an excellent alternative to hostel life when the noise of screaming schoolkids starts to wear you down. West Germany has around 2,000 campsites covering all the main places of interest and most towns and villages. Standards are high and prices low: around DM7–12 per tent and DM6–9 per person. East Germany has fewer sites but new ones are opening up rapidly. Prices are similar to those in the West, though standards are lower and sites are likely to be crowded due to the general shortage of accommodation in the East. It is illegal in both West and East to camp outside an official site. An official list of campsites can be obtained from D.C.C., Mandlestraße 28, Munich 40, D 80802.

FOOD

Traditionally Germans enjoy simple but tasty cooking. Strictly speaking there is no such thing as a national cuisine; each region has evolved its own specialities. However, all tend to be rich and meaty, featuring pork (*Schweine fleisch*), beef (*Rindfleisch*) or veal (*Kalbfleisch*). And of course you can't forget the ubiquitous sausage: avid sausage-eaters need look no further than the word *wurst* on any menu – *Bockwurst* (boiled), *Bratwurst* (grilled) and *Currywurst* (grilled with curry sauce), are just three of the many varieties you're likely to come across. Other specialities include *Schweinebraten* (roast knuckle of port), *Schnitzel* (fried escalopes of pork, veal or beef) and *Sauerkraut* (pickled cabbage). Soups are always a popular choice: *Gulaschsuppe*, *Zwiebelsuppe* (a version of French onion) and *Bohnensuppe* (spicy bean) are common.

In a nation of established carnivores, vegetarians may have a tough time, particularly in the East and outside the major cities in the West. You can, however, enjoy the desserts: look for Konditoreis serving rich cakes with mounds of whipped cream. *Käsekuchen* (cheesecake) and *Apfelkuchen* (spicy apple pie) are real treats.

German beer also enjoys a deserved reputation. Both German wines and beers are excellent, with different regions offering their own speciality brews (*helles* is light lager while *dunkeles* is dark). If you're trying to dry out, go for *Saft* – fruit juice – instead.

German restaurants tend to offer generous portions at reasonable rates, though you can expect lower standards in the East. Menus and prices are displayed outside and will often include a set menu (Tagesmenu) for around DM15–25, typically comprising soup, a side dish and a main course. Good places to eat are simple traditional establishments – Gasthaus, Gaststätte and Kneipe – which serve as both pubs and restaurants. In the cities you'll also find a variety of ethnic restaurants – Turkish, Italian and so on – which offer decent food at reasonable prices. Alternative watering holes are Bierkellers (inside) and Biergartens (outside). If you drink at one of the beer gardens, don't be surprised to be charged a deposit for your glass – just remember to claim it back.

Germany has the usual fast-food chains, as well as its own Schnell Imbiss stalls and shops. If you plan to save deutschmarks by making your own snacks, the endless variety of breads should provide sufficient stimulation. Visit your nearest bakery (Bäckerei) and pick up some cold cuts from the butcher (Fleischerei or Metzgerei).

The food halls of the large department stores – notably Hertie and Kaufhof – also offer an excellent choice of produce.

BUDGETING

Prices in Germany are much the same as those in the UK – the higher costs of Berlin and London cancel each other out. If you stay in hostels, accommodation should cost in the region of DM15–30 per night (you're more likely to pay top prices in the big cities). You should be able to eat for around DM25–30 per day, less if you eat nothing but Imbiss food. Drinks can add up: expect to pay DM3–7 for a bottle of beer. Public transport in cities is expensive (around DM7–9 for an all-day ticket, DM2.50 for a single). Admission to places of interest costs from DM2–5, though some museums are free. The cost of enjoying German nightlife depends entirely on what you want and how much you are willing to pay.

Only EC nationals are entitled to work legally in Germany without a special visa, and even they should get a residence permit if planning to stay more than three months. Good sources of temporary work are hotels, pubs and restaurants, which often take on extra hands – for fairly menial jobs – during the tourist season. If you're looking for farm work, it's generally a question of being in the right place at harvest time. Teaching English is always a popular option but it's best to fix up a job before you go. Check out the ads in the *Times Education Supplement*. You will need a TEFL qualification and preferably a degree. For au pair jobs, a useful organization is Verein für Internationale Jugendarbeit, 39 Craven Road, London W2 3BX.

To find any kind of job once in Germany, your first port of call should be the nearest state-run Arbeitsamter (employment office). If you want to set something up before you arrive, write to the Zentralstelle für Arbeitsvermittlung (Central Placement Office), the arm of the German Employment Service which deals with overseas applications, at Feuerbachstraße 42–6, W-60325 Frankfurt am Main. If you're still out of luck, try door-knocking.

FURTHER INFORMATION

German National Tourist Office, Nightingale House, 65 Curzon Street, London W1Y 8NE (tel. 0891 600 100).

Germany Embassy, 23 Belgrave Square, London SW1X 8PZ (tel. 0171 235 5033).

German Consulates General, Westminster House, 11 Portland Street, Manchester and 16 Eglington Crescent, Edinburgh EH12 5DG.

Background reading: Useful guides for budget travellers include *Germany: The Rough Guide* (Harrap Columbus) and *Let's Go: The Budget Guide to Germany, Austria and Switzerland*. For information on work opportunities, try *Work Your Way Around the World* by Susan Griffiths (Vacation Work).

Berlin

AIRPORT FACILITIES

Berlin has three airports: Tegel and Tempelhof in the West and Schönefeld in the East. Most international flights, however, land at Tegel airport, 8 km from the city centre. Tegel has an airline information and a tourist information desk (both are open daily 5.30 a.m.–11.30 p.m.). If you need to change money there is a currency exchange and a branch of the Berliner Bank. All the other usual facilities are also there: post office, restaurant, duty-free outlets, car hire and left-luggage facilities. For flight information, tel. 41 01 23 06.

CITY LINKS

Bus: The number 109 bus runs from Tegel airport right into the city centre, calling at Kurfürstendamm, U- and S-Bahn Zoologischer Garten and Budapester Straße along the way. Buses run every 10 minutes, journey time is 40 minutes and it costs DM3.70.
Taxi: Takes much the same time as the bus, but costs about DM40.
There are direct bus and U-Bahn connections between Tempelhof Airport and the city.

USEFUL ADDRESSES

Tourist offices: There are branches of Verkehrsamt Berlin in the Europa Center, Budapester Straße 45 (tel. 262 60 31), open daily 8 a.m.–10.30 p.m.; at Bahnhof Zoo (tel. 313 90 63), open 8 a.m.–10.30 p.m.; and at Tegel Airport. It's worth making a detour to the Informationszentrum to pick up their excellent free booklet *Berlin for Young People*, which contains a wealth of useful information for the young traveller, from city walks to entertainment venues to accommodation options.
Main post offices: Bahnhof Zoo, West Berlin. Open Mon.–Sat. 6 a.m.–midnight, Sun. 8 a.m.–midnight. Poste restante mail should be addressed to Poste Restante/postlagernd, Postamt Bahnhof Zoo, D-10623 Berlin 12. East Berlin also has a 24-hour post office at

Postamt Berlin 17, Straße der Pariser Kommune 8–10, 10243 Berlin (at the main train station).
UK Consulate: Uhlandstraße 7/8 (tel. 309 52 92).
US Consulate: Clayallee 170 (tel. 832 40 87).
Emergency services: Police 110 (West and East); Fire 112 (West and East); Ambulance 112 (West) or 115 (East).
Medical emergencies: 31 00 31 (West); 280 91 28 (East)
Pharmacy help line: 11 41 (West); 160 (East)

GETTING ABOUT
Berlin has an exceptionally efficient transport system, comprising the U-Bahn (underground), S-Bahn (overground train) and city buses. If you are ever really stuck, go to Bahnhof Zoologischer Garten (Bahnhof Zoo), the main train station in West Berlin, from where you can get U or S-Bahn services, buses and taxis to just about any other Berlin district. Contact BVG at Potsdamer Straße 188, D-01773, Berlin.

Tickets generally cover the whole network: a short distance single ticket (Kurzstreckentarif) costing DM2.50 is valid for six bus stops or three U-Bahn stations and allows a single bus transfer or two transfers on the U-Bahn. A regular single ticket (Normaltarif) allows you two hours unlimited travel on the buses and the U and S-Bahn, and costs DM2.70. Alternatively you can buy a short-distance multiple ticket (Sammelkarte) with four fares for DM8.50, or a normal Sammelkarte with four fares for DM12.50. The same criteria apply to Sammelkartes as to the equivalent single fares. Both single and multiple tickets must be stamped in the red invalidator on the bus or by the ticket officer at station entrances before each use.

Another option is the Berlin Ticket, which gives you a day's unlimited travel on the BVG network within Berlin. If you plan to stay longer, you can buy the Umweltkarte. The Berlin 'Welcome Card' costs DM29 and is valid for three days on all transport.

Bus drivers sell only single tickets; all others can be bought from station ticket counters and from vending machines in stations or at bus stops.
U- and S-Bahn: U- and S-Bahn lines are identified by both their numbers and their final destinations. Maps are readily available and fairly simple to understand. Both systems run from 4–1 a.m., with the exception of lines U1 and U9, which run all night.
Bus: Enter from the front and exit from the middle. Look for bus stops with the yellow route number on a green background. All night buses start at Bahnhof Zoo.

Taxi: Taxis carry up to four people and there's a flat rate of DM3.40 before the journey starts, with a supplement for luggage.
Bicycle: There are several bike rental shops. Try Fahrradbüro (bicycle office) at Haupstraße 146 (U-Bahn Kleistpark) or Räderwerk (Wheel Works) at Körtestraße 14 (U-Bahn Südstern). A day's rent will cost about DM12, and you'll usually have to pay a deposit too. On weekends and public holidays you can take your bike on the U-Bahn at any time; on weekdays you're limited to 9 a.m.–2 p.m. and after 5.30 p.m. There are no restrictions on S-Bahns.

SIGHTS

There are few cities whose very name strikes such an evocative chord as Berlin. From the radicalism of its roaring 1920s to Hitler's Third Reich and the dramatic felling of the Berlin Wall – it's not so much the sights that are worth coming for as the atmosphere.

The most famous street in post-war West Berlin is the KURFÜR-STENDAMM or Ku'damm. Crammed with shops, cafés, cinemas and theatres, this is a street where you can sit and watch the world go by – if you can afford the price of a coffee. The Ku'damm is worth a visit even though it will give you only a superficial impression of Berlin. A popular meeting place is the GEDÄCHTNISKIRCHE, where the new church stands beside the bombed ruins of the old, reflecting Berlin's mix of old and new.

Just off the Ku'damm are some of West Berlin's most enjoyable sidestreets, full of interesting little shops, restaurants and cafés and beautifully restored aristocratic apartments – in particular the area round Ludwigkirchstraße and Bleibtreustraße. On Fasanenstraße is the JÜDISCHES GEMEINDEHAUS (Jewish Community Centre), which stands on the site of the synagogue which the Nazis destroyed on the infamous Kristallnacht of 1938.

Keen marketeers should consider taking the U-Bahn to NOLLEN-DORFPLATZ, where the main attraction is the flea market in the station. It's become rather touristy, but is nevertheless worth a visit to rummage through the old U-Bahn carriages in which the goods are sold. The writer Christopher Isherwood (the film *Cabaret* was loosely based on some of his characters) lived here in the 1920s and you can visit his house at 17 Nollendorfstraße. For some real bargain hunting keep going until you get to the street market on WINTERFELDPLATZ, where everything from fruit and veg to clothing is sold (Wed. and Sat. 8 a.m.–1 p.m.).

The ZOOLOGISCHER GARTEN leads into the Tiergarten, the beautiful park right in the heart of the city. Inside is the SIEGES-SÄULE (Victory Column), which was built in the 17th century by Emperor William I to commemorate Prussian war victories and topped with an 2.4 m statue of Victoria. If you can manage the 300 steps to the column's summit, you'll be rewarded with an impressive view of the city.

Follow the Straße des 17 Juli to the end for one of Berlin's great landmarks, the BRANDENBURGER GATE, formerly a symbolic divide between West and East Berlin. The nearby REICHSTAG is home to Germany's Parliament and its burning in 1933 sparked a wave of Nazi persecutions. Just behind it you can still see the line of DIE MAUER (the wall) which divided Berlin from 1961 to 1989 and cost many lives in attempted escapes.

Further south, POTSDAMER PLATZ is the once thriving square which was transformed into an empty wasteland during the Cold War years. A small grassy mound marks the site of the bunker where Hitler committed suicide in 1945. The remains of the head-quarters of the SS and Gestapo are on Stresemannstraße behind the MARTIN GROPIUS BAU MUSEUM. An exhibition documenting their history has been built on top of the former Gestapo cellars which you can still walk through (Tues.–Sun. 10 a.m.–6 p.m.). On Friedrichstraße is the site of Checkpoint Charlie, the former crossing-point between East and West. The nearby HAUS AM CHECKPOINT CHARLIE has a fascinating exhibition on the history of the wall and the sometimes extraordinary attempts to cross it (daily, 9 a.m.–10 p.m.).

If you want to get away from wars and walls, take a trip to EAST KREUZBERG, West Berlin's 'alternative' district with its mix of Turkish immigrants, drop-outs, artists, left-wing activists and other 'counter-culturalists', who were originally attracted by the area's low rents. From Kottbusser Tor walk towards Oranienstraße to get the feel of the place and the ever-present social tensions. MARIANNENPLATZ is a popular meeting place in summer. Even better, postpone your walk until late evening when the district really comes alive.

A popular attraction in the north-west of the city is SCHLOß CHARLOTTENBURG. Originally built in 1695 for Queen Sophie Charlotte, wife of Emperor Friedrich I, it's a beautiful palace with spacious grounds. The living quarters are worth the tour and you can also visit the palace's museums, of which the ÄGYPTISCHES MUSEUM (Egyptian Museum) is highly recommended. Ardent museum fans shouldn't miss the DAHLEM MUSEUM complex in the south-west of the city, with its large collection of Rembrandts.

North of Charlottenburg, the PLÖTZENSEE MEMORIAL on Hüttingpfad is another grim reminder of Germany's past. It's located in the former execution compound of Plötzensee prison, where more than 2,500 people were executed during the Hitler regime.

The execution chamber itself has been restored, complete with execution chamber (open daily, 8.30 a.m.–6 p.m.). If you can stomach more, there's a MEMORIAL AND EDUCATION CENTRE in Stauffenbergstraße outlining the resistance movement in Germany.

When you've had your fill of the city, there are plenty of open spaces within easy reach. The GRUNEWALD FOREST is popular with Berliners, and STRANDBAD WANNSEE, Berlin's largest beach, is a great place for a swim, drawing thousands of visitors in summer (S-Bahn 1 or 3 to Nikolasee station followed by a 10-minute walk).

UNTER DEN LINDEN is the obvious place to start your tour of East Berlin and an enjoyable way to spend a couple of hours walking. Running east from Brandenburg Gate, this tree-lined boulevard was once Berlin's most prestigious avenue. Many of its neo-classical buildings have since been beautifully restored. After the cluster of embassies comes the STAATSBIBLIOTHEK (library), followed by the HUMBOLDT UNIVERSITY and the GERMAN STATE OPERA. The infamous book burnings of 1933 were carried out opposite the university. The 19th-century NEUE WACHE (New Guard) building stands as a memorial to the victims of fascism and militarism, while next door the former Prussian arsenal has become the DEUTSCHES HISTORISCHES MUSEUM (German history museum). Just off the Unter den Linden is the GENDARMEN MARKT, currently undergoing restoration. Its main attractions are the SCHINKEL PLAYHOUSE, the French and German cathedrals and the SCHILLER MONUMENT.

MARX-ENGELS PLATZ was once the site of the Kaiser's palace. Behind the 19th-century BERLINER DOM (cathedral) is the area known as MUSEUMINSEL (Museum Island). The PERGAMON MUSEUM is home to numerous ancient masterpieces of Islamic, Asian and Near Eastern origin; the magnificent 160 BC Pergamon Altar fills one entire hall of the museum and the 6th-century BC Ishtar gate is also a must-see (daily 9 a.m.–5 p.m.).

Many of East Berlin's districts retain a strong flavour of old Berlin. The NIKOLAI QUARTER includes the 13th-century Nikolaikirche, which has recently undergone attempts to restore it to its former historical detail. The narrow streets and tenement buildings of the SCHEUNEN QUARTER were home to Berlin's Jewish immigrants from the 17th century onwards. Next to the site of the destroyed Jewish cemetery on Grosse Hamburger Straße stand sculptures of concentration camp victims.

PRENZLAUER BERG is East Berlin's equivalent to Kreuzberg. A 19th-century working class area, its cobbled streets and tenement rows now play host to all those 'alternatives' who haven't yet moved to the West. It is still vibrant with streetlife and a profusion of bars, shops and cafés. Finally, don't miss ALEXANDERPLATZ, East

Berlin's answer to the Ku'damm. Its international clock is a popular meeting place.

ACCOMMODATION

Although Berlin has a wealth of accommodation options, it can still be tricky finding what you want, particularly in the East. Since the demolition of the Wall, the city has grown enormously in popularity and it's advisable to book in advance if you can. The main tourist office holds maps and lists of what's available.

Youth hostels: For reservations write (preferably a month in advance) to DJH Landesverband Berlin, Berlin 61, Tempelhofer Ufer 32 (tel. 262 30 24), making clear how much you are prepared to spend. The Informationszentrum Berlin (Information Centre) at Hardenbergstraße 20 (tel. 31 00 40) will make group bookings at no charge. Berlin hostels are expensive – around DM30 for juniors and DM35 for seniors – and you'll need an IYHF card.

Jugendgästhaus, Kluckstraße 3 (tel. 261 10 97). Bus 29 from Ku'damm to Oranienplatz or Hermannplatz. Centrally located. Juniors DM28.

Jugendgästhaus Wannsee, Badeweg 1, Kronprinzessinnenweg 27 (tel. 803 20 34). S3 to Nikolassee, then a 10 minute walk to the beach. A clean modern hostel, out of town but close to Strandbad Wannsee beach. Juniors DM27.

Ernst Reuter, Hermsdorfer Damm 48–50 (tel. 404 16 10). U6 to Tegel, then number 15 bus (direction: Frohnau) to the fourth stop. Quite far out from the centre. Juniors DM25.

Privately run hostels include:

Jugendhotel am Tierpark, Franz-Mett-Straße 7 (tel. 510 01 14). U-Bahn Tiergarten. A vast 700-bed hostel in East Berlin, situated near the Tiergarten. DM29–32.

Jugengästhaus am Zoo, Hardenbergerstraße 9a (tel. 312 94 10). U-Bahn Ernst-Reuter-Platz or a short walk from the zoo. A very popular hostel whose higher prices are offset by its central location. Dorms DM29; singles DM44; doubles DM38 per person.

Studenthotel, Meiningerstraße 10 (tel. 784 67 20). U-Bahn Rathaus Schoneberg. Prices from DM38 per person.

Internationales Jugendcamp, Waidmannsluster Damm, Ziekowstraße 161 (tel. 433 86 40). This is in fact a huge tent with mattresses and sheets provided. U6 to Tegel, then number 20 bus. DM10 and three day maximum stay. Open from June until the end of August. Age limit 26.

Bahnhofsmission in Zoo station. One night only for DM15.

Hotels and pensions: The easiest way to find a room is to pay DM3 to the Verkehrsamt Berlin tourist office (see **Useful Addresses**, p. 156) in the Europa Centre, and let them do the hunting for you. If you want to reserve, write a month ahead and say how much you're willing to spend. Prices are steep. The cheapest single goes for around DM40 and doubles start from DM56.

Private accommodation: The Verkehrsamt Berlin can book these for you in West Berlin for around DM35 pp. In East Berlin private accommodation is a growing market and prices are cheaper at around DM18–30 per person; you can book rooms through the Reisebüro on Alexanderplatz (see **Useful Addresses**, above).

For long-term private accommodation, the Mitwohnzentralen agencies provide vacant rooms or arrange flat-shares. Prices start at around DM35 pp for an apartment. Their main office is at Ku'damm-Eck, Kurfürstendamm 227–8, 2nd floor (tel. 882 66 94) near Bahnhof Zoo.

Campsites: Campers will pay around DM10 per person. All campsites have good facilities. The following sites are open all year round:

Haselhorst, Pulvermühlenweg (tel. 334 59 55). U-Bahn to Haselhorst, then walk along Daumster to Pulvermühlenweg.

Kladow 22, Krampnitzer Weg 111–17 (tel. 365 27 97). Bus 35, then bus 35E.

Dreilinden, Albrechts-Teerofen (tel. 805 12 01). Number 18 bus, then a 20 minute walk along Kremnitzufer to Albrechts-Teerofen.

FOOD

Berlin's culinary offerings reflect the cosmopolitan nature of the city. If you've developed a particular 'foreign' taste during your travels, you should be able to satisfy it in Berlin. The city's cafés are something of an institution and can be particularly useful for late-nighters – not only can you sit and idle your time away in them, many now serve breakfast day and night.

West Berlin's cheap eateries, where you should be able to get a sit-down meal for around DM15, are located in areas like Kreuzberg, away from the city centre. The streets around Savignyplatz are popular for affordable restaurants, fast-food joints, pizzerias, Kneipen and cafés. East Kreuzberg is the place for Turkish food. The cheapest option, however, are the numerous Imbiss stands dotted around the city where you can buy kebabs, *Currywurst* (curried sausages) and other snacks for around DM5. Some even sell salads. If you have an ISIC card you could have lunch at one of the Mensas (student cafeterias) for around the same price: there's one at Ernst Reuter Platz and another at Hardenbergstraße 34.

Vegetarians shouldn't have too much trouble as veggie restaurants are increasingly popular. If you're having difficulty finding one, try Einhorn at 5 Wittenbergplatz or Baharat Falafel on Winterfeldstraße. Those who want to devise their own picnics could do worse than KaDeWe on Wittenbergplatz, which has Europe's largest grocery department and is surprisingly good value. Pennymarkt is one of the cheapest supermarket chains in town. Or you can combine sightseeing with shopping and take in one of Berlin's many market halls: Eisenbahn-Markthalle on Eisenbahnstraße is one of the best. Almost every district has a health food shop (Bioladen) which should sell veggie options.

East Berlin doesn't enjoy the same profusion of budget restaurants but you can still get by cheaply. Alexanderplatz is packed with street sellers offering all types of cheap eats. For cafés and restaurants your best option is Prenzlauer Berg, which offers both good food and lively company.

ENTERTAINMENT
Berlin is the place for action day and night. There's no particular 'in' area, but thriving hot-spots include the area round Winterfeldplatz and Nollendorfplatz. One of the best known of the many bars and clubs is Metropol at Nollendorfplatz 5, which has live music until the early hours – definitely not for MORs. The area round Schlütterstraße and Savignyplatz (near the Technical University) is strong on Kneipe and cafés.

For a more 'alternative' scene, head for Kreuzberg. Round Yorckstraße, Mehringdamm and Gneisenausgrasse is a good place to start, but do be careful and try not to go alone. Kreuzberg's Eastern equivalent, Prenzlauer Berg, is also making a name for itself. Take a walk down Schönhauser Allee and look for the Lotus Bar at no 46 or the Wiener café at no 86.

There are a wide selection of cinemas showing both mainstream and less commercial films. To see all the big name films, look no further than the Ku'damm. Tickets cost DM10–15, often half price on Wednesdays. For theatre tickets, the main ticket office is Theaterkasse Centrum at Meinekestraße 25. Some tickets are cheaper for students and you can often get discounted tickets direct from the theatre half an hour before the performance starts. The same goes for some of the big concert houses such as the German Opera. The Reisebüro on Alexanderplatz also sells tickets for classical music and drama.

To find out exactly what is going on and where, buy either of the bi-weekly listings magazines, *Tip* or *Zitty*. An excellent publication is the tourist office's *Berlin for Young People*, which gives detailed lists of cafés, bars, cinemas and theatres, music venues and more. You can pick it up from the Informationszentrum (see **Useful Addresses**, p. 156). You should also be able to buy *Checkpoint Berlin*, an English-language listings magazine.

EXCURSIONS
German reunification has opened up several fascinating excursion opportunities from Berlin, but if you only have time for one outing, POTSDAM is the perfect choice for an enjoyable day-trip. Less than an hour away from the city centre, Potsdam was a favoured residence with Prussian royalty and has been the centre of many historical events since. Its beautiful SANSSOUCI PARK contains four palaces, of which the most outstanding is SCHLOß SANSSOUCI, built in 1745 by Frederick the Great as his summer residence and considered a classic of German Rococo. Next door, the BILDERGALERIE displays paintings by Rubens, Van Dyck and Caravaggio, while further afield lies the ORANGERIE-SCHLOß with its 67 fake Raphaels and the extraordinary gold-plated CHINESICHES TEEHAUS (Chinese teahouse).

Potsdam also has a second park, the lakeside NEUER GARTEN, whose main attraction is the SCHLOß CECILIENHOF. It was here that Churchill, Stalin and Truman signed the Potsdam Treaty dividing Germany. A further historical curiosity is GLIENICKER BRÜCKE, the bridge that separates Potsdam and West Berlin, and a favoured Cold War trading place for spies between East and West. The most famous exchange involved the downed American U2 pilot Gary Powers in 1962.

Potsdam is a short ride on the number 53 or 57 S-Bahn to either Potsdam-Stadt, the closest station to the town centre and tourist office, or Potsdam West, nearest to Sanssouci. If you plan to travel on a Monday, check with the tourist office first — many of the sites close on certain Mondays in each month.

A little further out (two hours from Berlin) is DRESDEN, one of the world's most beautiful cities until its controversial destruction by over 1,500 allied planes in February 1945 at a cost of an estimated 100,000 civilian lives. Though the city remains scarred, many of its most important buildings have been carefully reconstructed. Once the cultural capital of the DDR, it has a wealth of museums, galleries, palaces and churches. Its centrepiece is the ZWINGER PALACE, which contains half the city's museums. Pride of place goes to the portrait gallery housing Raphael's *Sistine*

Madonna. The ALBERTINUM is Dresden's other museum complex and includes the popular GRÜNES GEWÖLBE (Green Vault) containing a fabulous collection of the treasures of Saxon dukes. Dresden is easily accessible by train to either the Hauptbahnhof or Neustadt. The main tourist office is near the former on Prager Straße. If you want to stay a few days, try to arrive early as cheap accommodation is scarce.

The SPREEWALD FOREST (100 km outside Berlin) is ideal for for a relaxing day in the country. This vast woodland is criss-crossed by numerous canals while the local Sorbs have retained their own language and traditions. A grimmer reminder of Germany's past can be found 20 km away in Oranienberg, where SACHSCH-HAMSEN concentration camp was opened as a memorial in 1961 to commemorate the camp's victims. (S-Bahnhof Oranienberg). Closed Mondays.

NETHERLANDS

VITAL STATISTICS
Red tape: Citizens of the EC, Australia, Canada and the USA need only produce a valid passport and proof that they have sufficient funds to cover the cost of their stay. EC nationals planning to stay more than three months or to seek employment in the Netherlands should apply for a residence or work permit from the Aliens' Police in Amsterdam (see **Amsterdam: Useful Addresses**, p. 173). It is essential to get your passport date-stamped on entering the country if you plan to work. Non-EC citizens must obtain residence or work permits from their nearest Dutch Embassy before travelling.
Customs: With the implementation of the Single Market, EC nationals are now permitted an unlimited amount of excise goods as long as they are for personal use. Some EC countries have introduced guidelines, i.e. if you exceed certain limits you could be stopped and asked to provide evidence that your goods are for personal use only.
Health: No immunizations required. EC citizens are entitled to emergency medical treatment provided they can produce form E111 – UK nationals can pick one up from a DSS office. Check the booklet that comes with it to ensure you know the rules for getting your money back; you must pay for treatment and then claim it back. Since only emergency care is covered, it is a good idea to to take out private medical insurance.
Language: Dutch, English and German are widely spoken.

Population: 15 million.
Capital: Amsterdam, population 1 million.
Political system: Democracy. There has been coalition rule since the end of World War II. The current government is a Labour and Christian Democrat coalition.
Religion: A fairly even divide between Catholic and Protestants.
Time: An hour ahead of GMT (two hours in summer).
Money: Dutch guilder (f) divided into 100 cents. Coins: 5, 10 and 25 cents; f1, f2.50 and f5. Notes: f9, f10, f25, f50, f100, f250 and f1,000. £1 = f2.47.

The best way to carry your money is in traveller's cheques. Eurocheques are also widely used and are more popular than credit cards in the Netherlands. Currency exchange facilities are available at banks, bureaux de change, VVV (tourist information) offices and at railway exchange offices (*Grenswisselkantoren*) which often open late, even 24 hours in some cases (tel. 060566).

Communications: International calls can be made from many phone boxes, but the easiest and cheapest way is to call from a post office. Most pay phones still take coins: 25 cents, f1 and f2.50, though phonecards are increasingly common. Buy them from post offices or VVV (tourist information) offices in units of 20 (f5), 40 (f10) or 100 (f25). Cost f1 per minute in Europe; f4 outside Europe.

Poste restante mail can be sent to any main post office.
Electricity: 220v AC.

Business hours: BANKS: Mon.–Fri. 9 a.m.–4 p.m.; late opening on Thurs. 7p.m.–9 p.m.

POST OFFICES: Mon.–Fri. 9 a.m.–5 p.m.; Sat. 9 a.m.–12 p.m. in the main cities.

SHOPS: Mon.–Fri. 9a.m.–6p.m.; Sat. 9 a.m.–5 p.m.

OFFICES: Mon.–Fri. 8 or 9 a.m.–5 p.m.
Holidays: 1 January; Good Friday and Easter Monday; 30 April (Queen's birthday); Ascension Day; Whit Monday; 25 and 26 December.
Climate: The Netherlands has a pleasant, if unpredictable, maritime climate. Average temperatures range from 16–26°C in the spring and summer; and from 4–16°C in the autumn and winter. The late spring, when the days are sunny and the tulips in full bloom, is a good time to visit.

DO'S AND DON'TS
The Dutch are keen Europeans and have a gift for mastering languages, particularly English. Don't be surprised to be greeted in

your mother tongue at every turn and for people you meet to be well versed in your culture and traditions.

Despite its liberal reputation, the Netherlands is not a free for all where drugs are concerned. While police may go easy where soft drugs are concerned, it is only in Amsterdam that attitudes are very liberal – elsewhere you may find police taking a harsher line. If you are caught carrying or supplying hard drugs, you will almost certainly be arrested.

WHERE TO GO FOR WHAT

The Netherlands may lack the rugged scenery to be found in other European countries but its golden North Sea beaches, fields of flowers ablaze with colour, its many lakes and 8,000-km network of canals have a beauty of their own. The landscape is dotted with picturesque villages and windmills, ancient churches and castles, and all bear testament to the country's rich and varied past. The Dutch are obviously proud of their cultural heritage and there are more museums in the Netherlands per square kilometre than in any other country.

The joy of such a compact country is that once you've had your fill of colourful and cosmopolitan AMSTERDAM, none of the country's other attractions should be beyond your reach – whether by bike or public transport. A stone's throw from the capital are the historic villages of MONNICKENDAM and MARKEN, where the inhabitants still wear traditional costume, and just 24 km to the west is the lively town of HAARLEM with its preserved gothic buildings.

South of Amsterdam is the university town of LEIDEN, where Descartes first published his *Discourse on Method*. The university is still considered one of Holland's finest. Leiden is a good base from which to visit LISSE, home to the largest flower gardens in the world. Between the end of March and the end of May, some 7 million flowers in full bloom are on display.

THE HAGUE's attractions include the model city of Madurodam, which has been visited by over 30 million people since it was first opened in 1952; the Binnenhof – Holland's Westminster – which is open to the public; and the International Court of Justice, housed in the Peace Palace. The Hague is not one of the liveliest places at night, but its close neighbour ROTTERDAM has about 600 cafés which are open well into the small hours, after which you can dance till dawn at one of the city's nightclubs. By day, you can visit the zoo or scale the 607ft Euromast Spacetower, or spend your cash at SCHEVENINGEN, an island entertainment complex offering all the usual facilities including a beautifully restored casino.

Between The Hague and Rotterdam the small historic town of
DELFT is famous for the blue-and-white china produced there since
the 17th century. KINDERDIJK is one of the Netherlands' most
noted landmarks with its 19 windmills, and GOUDA, 20 km north-
east of Rotterdam, is best known for its delicious cheese but also
boasts many fine houses built in early Dutch styles.

Near the Belgian border is MAASTRICHT, the town whose name
has become synonymous with one of the most debated issues of
recent times. Aside from the treaty, Maastricht is famous for its
nine castles and 193-km network of man-made tunnels.

ARNHEM suffered great damage and was the site of thousands of
Allied deaths in the Allied operation of 1944, immortalized in the
film *A Bridge Too Far*. North of Arnhem lies the Nederlands Open-
luchtmuseum – an open-air museum where working farms, mills
and houses provide a glimpse of traditional Dutch rural life – and
the HOGE VELUWE NATIONAAL PARK, the largest uninterrupted
nature reserve in Holland. Deer, wild boar, badgers and foxes all
live within the reserve, which has some 40 km of cycling paths.

Nature lovers should go north to FRIESLAND – Groningen is a
good base from which to explore – a land of lakes and forests
teeming with wildlife. Friesland has its own language and history,
and is almost like a separate country. The Wadden Islands – VLIE-
LAND, TERSCHELLING, AMELAND and SCHIERMONNIKOOG – are
nature reserves of outstanding natural beauty off the north-west
coast. Visitors are not permitted to drive on Vlieland and Schiermonnikoog, so you can cycle or walk undisturbed exploring the
woods, dunes and beaches as well as several bird-breeding areas
that can be visited between mid-May and mid-June.

INTERNAL TRAVEL

Air: Distances in the Netherlands are too small to warrant air travel.
Domestic air services are operated by KLM Cityhopper.

Rail: Holland is so small, and its rail service so frequent, fast and
reliable, that you could travel the entire country in a single day. If
you want a long-term pass and don't have an InterRail, there are
a number of useful ones you can buy, either in your own country or
from the 'National' (*Binnenland*) ticket counters at Dutch stations,
where English-speakers should be able to advise you. Note that in
Holland you cannot pay for train tickets by credit card. Phone Holland Rail's UK office on 0196 277 3646 for further details.

The new Euro Domino pass allows you 3, 5 or 10 days unlimited
rail travel within any one month and costs £34, £52 and £93
respectively or £25, £37 and £65 for under 26s. The one-day Rail
Rover gives you unlimited travel and costs £25 (second class). You

can combine this with a Public Transport Link Rover which entitles you to travel on all public buses and trams, as well as Amsterdam and Rotterdam metros for £2.50. When buying a Rail Rover or Euro Domino Pass in the Netherlands, you will need to provide a passport photo and show your passport. Disabled travellers requiring special attention should call 30 355 555 about 24 hours ahead.

Groups of between two and six travelling together should consider the Multi Rover, which gives a day's unlimited off-peak travel. Prices range from £37 for two people to £63 for six. The Summer Tour Rover allows two people 3 days' unlimited travel within 10 days in June, July or August and costs £43. This can be extended to include buses, trams, metros (£52 for two).

If you plan to travel throughout the Benelux countries, the Benelux Tourrail gives you 5 days' unlimited travel within a period of 17 days throughout Holland, Belgium and Luxembourg. A second-class pass costs £84 or £63 for under-26s.

To save money on train, boat and bus travel when visiting the islands off the north coast, ask about a 'Wadden Ticket'.

For more information, pick up the free leaflet 'Touring Holland by Rail' from any train station in Holland.

Bus: Bus and rail timetables are integrated and bus terminals are usually located adjacent to railway stations. Ticketing runs on the same 'strippenkaart' system as local transport (see **Local Transport**, p. 170).

Bicycle: There are 15 million bikes in Holland. No surprise that it's an ideal country to tour by bike. Distances are relatively short and the land is flat. Cyclists are extremely well catered for: there are many special lanes and paths for bicycles, even in the big cities. The VVV will give you maps and cycling routes, and Netherlands Railways can supply details of routes for nature enthusiasts, but maps aren't necessary. Distances and destinations are clearly marked on red-and-white signs throughout the network of bike paths. Look out for the round blue sign with a white bicycle in the middle or a board saying 'fietspad'. You are not allowed to use the main road if a separate cycle lane is available.

You can hire bicycles almost anywhere in Holland; ask at VVV offices for lists of hire companies within the local area. A hired bike costs around f5 per day, plus a refundable deposit of between f50–f200; you will need to provide proof of identity. Bicycles can also be hired at railway stations for around f7.50 per day or f30 per week, less if you have a valid rail ticket. Again a deposit will be required together with some form of ID. If you want to transport your bicycle by train at any time, you must buy a separate ticket for it and use off-peak trains only. Hired bicycles must be returned to their original point of hire. A station will reserve your bike until 11 a.m. unless otherwise arranged.

Car hire: Car hire is widely available as long as you have your driving licence. Drive on the right and give way to cyclists coming from the right. Seatbelts are compulsory.

Local transport: Towns have bus and sometime tram networks. Amsterdam and Rotterdam also have metros. Tickets are in the form of strip cards (*strippenkaart*) and will take you on all three methods of transport in any part of the country. The country is divided into zones and the driver will cancel strips on the card according to how many zones you are travelling through. If you do not intend to use public transport very much, small strip cards can be bought direct from the driver. You can buy them at bus or railway stations, post offices, or tobacconists where they're available in strips of 15 (f11) or 45 (f32.25).

Taxis: You will have to find a taxi rank or local taxi centre, as cabs cannot be hailed on the street. Costs are high but tips are included in the price.

Hitching: Generally good, though you may find getting out of Amsterdam tricky. Hitching is illegal on motorways but permitted on the slip roads.

ACCOMMODATION

There is a well-organized network of budget accommodation in the Netherlands but it tends to get very crowded in summer. It is advisable to book ahead wherever possible. The price for most hostels and hotels includes breakfast. The National Reservations Centre will book hotels, B&Bs and even campsites all over the country for a £7 booking fee (per reservation). Contact the NRC in London: PO Box 523, London SW1E 6NT (tel. 0171 931 0801). The Netherlands Board of Tourism in London and other major cities issues brochures on accommodation options.

Youth hostels: Holland's IYHF hostels are run by the NJHC (Dutch Youth Hostel Federation) and offer good value all round. They're usually spotlessly clean, equipped with a bar and games room, and they tend to stay open later than is the norm for official hostels. Some provide cooking facilities, and many offer good meals at reasonable prices. Those in the major towns stay open all year round, the remainder tend to open from Easter to late September (though a few open in summer only). Prices range from f20–23 including breakfast, depending on the location and time of year. Non-members pay about f5 more. The VVV can supply you with a full hostel list, or write to: NJHC, Professor Tulpstraat 2, 1018 HA, Amsterdam (tel. 20 551 3155).

In addition to the 'official' hostels there are many private hostels, though beds tend to be more expensive.

Sleep-Ins: Amsterdam led the way in establishing these vast dorm hostels which offer basic dormitory accommodation for about f22. Some Sleep-Ins are open in summer only. Enquire at the local VVV.

Hotels and pensions: Hotel rooms can be found from around £20. For a small fee, most VVVs will make same day or advance hotel reservations for you anywhere in the country.

B&B: Bed and breakfast in a private home costs around f35 per night. The VVV will advise you on availability.

Campsites: Wherever you stay in Holland, you should be able to find a campsite nearby. There are about a thousand campsites around the country, ranging from the most basic to luxury sites with extensive washing, recreational and eating facilities. Campsites are classified according to their facilities. Prices start from around f5 per person plus f5–10 per tent. The VVV holds lists of sites. It is illegal to camp outside an official site.

Hiker's cabins: Some campsites also have basic wooden cabins (*Trekkershutten*) which sleep four and are equipped with cooking facilities, though you must bring your own sleeping bags and utensils. Cabins are available from Apr.–Oct. The maximum stay is three nights at around f48 per night for four people.

FOOD

Dutch food is plain and filling: meat and potatoes, vegetables, hotpots and soups. The dairy produce is justly famous – try the butter and delicious cheeses at breakfast (a hearty meal), or at lunch, when the Dutch go for a *koffietafel* (sandwich and coffee). There are plenty of coffee shops and cafés, as well as bars known as eetcafés which serve at least sandwiches and soup. With over 26 types of cheese, there's no excuse for sticking to just Edam and Gouda.

Another option in university towns is the student 'mensa' cafeterias which sell generous portions of cheap food. Alternatively, try one of the many types of fast food. These include chips (*frites* or *patates*) served with salt, mayonnaise and numerous other dressings; pancakes, sweet or savoury; and fish specialities sold at street stalls. One of the best is *nieuwe haring* (new herring) – salted herring roe – which is surprisingly tender and savoury and at its best during the first weeks in May. Also sold at street cafés are *broodjeswinkels* – soft bread rolls with various tasty fillings.

In the evenings, the Dutch tend to eat early – many restaurants are closed by 10.30 p.m., though you can get a snack in the big cities throughout the night. Popular specialities include *erwtensoep* (pea soup) and *hutspot* (winter stew). A good choice is the dish of the day (*dagschotels*), which is usually a huge helping of meat and vegetables for around f17.5. Vegetarians should have few problems: most restaurants have at least one veggie option and there are many vegetarian restaurants.

Though Dutch cuisine is not exotic, the Netherlands is noted for its outstanding selection of Indonesian restaurants, a legacy of its imperial past. A favourite speciality is *Grote Rijsttafel* (rice-table) which consists of rice served with a selection of up to 30 spicy dishes. Chinese and Italian restaurants are also good value.

To wash down your meal, Dutch beer is excellent – Heineken is probably the best-known brand – as are the many Dutch liqueurs. *Jenever* (the Dutch version of gin) is the indigenous spirit. For cheap booze, the supermarkets are unbeatable.

BUDGETING

If you plan to stay in hostels, accommodation will set you back around f20–23 per day. You can spend as much or little on food as you like, but allow a minimum of f35 per day (and take full advantage of the 'dish of the day' offered by most restaurants). Beer costs around f2.50 a glass. Nightlife can be cheap if you choose carefully: some clubs are free, others charge around f8 for admission. Likewise, many sights are free, but expect to pay around f5 for those that charge. Transport is reasonable if you choose the right ticket for your needs.

Work opportunities in Holland are hard to find, though EC nationals holding a residence permit are entitled to seek employment, and wage rates are generally respectable. Non-EC citizens need a work permit, which must be applied for by a Dutch employer (see **Vital Statistics**, p. 165).

Most temporary jobs are in agriculture (particularly during the bulb season between mid-June and October) and there is hotel work in the tourist season. Teaching English is a possibility, but budding teachers are plentiful and competition fierce. Au pairing is becoming increasingly popular. The youth agency Exis sets up au pair placements for foreigners (Postbus 15344MH Amsterdam tel. 020 262 664). Private recruitment agencies (*Uitzendbureau*) such as Manpower and Randstad can be a good source for a variety of short-term work. The agency ASA Studenten Uitzendbureau specializes in placing students.

There are in addition several work camp organizations that organize projects for young people from all over the world. These include IVN (Institute for Nature Protection Education), Postbus

20123, 1000 HC Amsterdam; and SIW (International Volunteer Projects), Willemstraat 7, 3511 RJ Utrecht.

FURTHER INFORMATION

The Netherlands Board of Tourism, PO Box 523, London SW1E 6NT (tel. 0891 200 277 – calls charged at premium rate). A wealth of useful brochures on accommodation, transport etc. in the Netherlands.

Holland Rail, Gilbert Street, Ropley, Hampshire SO24 0BY (tel. 0196 277 3646). Provides information on various Dutch rail passes, which can also be purchased via this office.

Dutch Embassy, 38 Hyde Park Gate, London SW7 (tel. 0171 585 5040).

Background reading: *Holland, Belgium and Luxembourg: The Rough Guide* (Harrap Columbus) and *Amsterdam: The Rough Guide* (Rough Guides Ltd) are both useful guidebooks for the budget-conscious traveller.

Amsterdam

AIRPORT FACILITIES

Amsterdam's international airport is Schipol. In the arrivals hall there are an information desk (open 24 hours) and money-changing facilities. The airport also has a post office in the waiting lounge (open 7 a.m.–10 p.m.) and a huge tax-free shopping centre with over 40 shops, plus the usual bars, cafés and restaurants. For flight information dial 20 511 0432.

CITY LINKS

Amsterdam-Schipol is 15 km outside the city centre. There are frequent trains to Amsterdam's Centraal Station (every 10 minutes for f5.50) and other city destinations from the railway station opposite the terminal. A taxi ride to the city costs around f75.

USEFUL ADDRESSES

Tourist office: VVV Amsterdam Tourist Information, Stationsplein 10, outside Centraal Station (tel. (06) 340 34066). Open daily; May–Sept. 9 a.m.–11 p.m.; Oct.–Apr. 9 a.m.–5 p.m. There's another branch at Leidsestraat 106, open May–Sept. 9 a.m.–5 p.m. daily; Oct.–Apr. Mon.–Sat. 9 a.m.–5 p.m. The VVV can tell or sell you just about everything you need to know, including information on accommodation and maps.

For listings information and tickets for cultural events, visit Uitburo in the Stadsschouwburg on the corner of Marnixstraat and Leidseplein (tel. 621 12 11). Mon.–Sat. 10 a.m.–6 p.m.; Thurs. 10 a.m.–9 p.m.

Main post office: Singel 250–56 (tel. 556 33 11). Mon.–Fri. 8.30 a.m.–6 p.m.; Thurs. 8.30 a.m.–8 p.m.; Sat 9 a.m.–3 p.m.

UK Consulate: General Koningslaan 44 (tel. 676 43 43).

US Consulate: Museumplein 19 (tel. 664 56 61).

American Express: Amsteldijk 166 (tel. 540 1999). Mon.–Fri. 9 a.m.–5 p.m., Sat. 9 a.m.–12 p.m.

Emergency services: Dial 0611 for police, ambulance or fire.

Medical/Dental emergencies: Dial 664 21 11 for doctors, dentists or chemists on duty 24 hours.

Bookstores: The English Language Bookshop is at Lauriergracht 71; and W. H. Smith have a branch at Kalverstraat 152.

GETTING ABOUT

Amsterdam is a compact city and ideal for exploring by foot. When need arises, however, there are ample transport facilities.

Bus, tram and metro: As in the rest of the country, *strippenkaarte* (strip cards) are used in a zonal system. Strips are cancelled on your ticket according to the number of zones you pass through. Fare dodging is *not* recommended since Amsterdam's bus inspectors are zealous and fines are heavy. Tickets can be bought direct from the driver but this works out expensively. It's cheaper to buy a multi-ride strip of tickets, valid on all services and usable throughout the Netherlands. (See **Netherlands: Internal Travel**, p. 168.) Alternatively, invest in a pass which allows you unlimited travel on bus, tram and metro for up to 9 days. Prices start at f9.50 for a 1-day pass, rising to f18.50 for a 4-day pass, and f3.10 for each further day.

Services run until midnight, when hourly night buses take over until 4 a.m. Route maps and an English guide to the ticketing system are available from the GVB public transport office in front of Centraal Station.

Bicycle: Cyclists in Amsterdam enjoy a well-established route of cycle paths (*fietspaden*), so cycling is not the hazardous occupation it is in most major cities. There are plenty of hire shops; try Damstraat Rent-a-Bike at Pieter Jacobsdwarsstraat 11 off Damstraat, or Koenders Take-a-Bike at Stationsplein 33. Make sure you keep your bike locked up – bicycle theft is rife. For guided bike trips, contact 'Yellow Bike' (tel. 620 6940).

Water Bicycles: If you prefer to be on the water rather than dry land, you can rent 'canal bikes' (pedal boats) from four moorings in the city centre: at the Leidseplein between the Marriot and American Hotels; on the Singelgracht between the Rijksmuseum and the Heineken Brewery; on Prinsengracht at the Westerkerk; and on the Keizersgracht, near Leidsestraat. Boats must be picked up and dropped off at one of these points. Prices start at f20 per hour for a two-seater.

Canal Boats: A canal trip in one of the many glass-topped boats is a gentle and pleasant introduction to the city. You have a choice of four embarkation points, all fairly central: Damrak, Rokin, Amstel and Nassaukade. Rides start from around f10 per person.

There is also a Canalbus route between Centraal Station and Rijksmuseum, which makes three stops, with departures every 20 minutes. A day ticket costs f12.50. The Museum Boat combines a canal trip with a museum visit: a boat leaves every 30 minutes, making seven stops in the area where 20 of the city's major museums are located. A day ticket costs f15; a combination ticket including entrance to three museums of your choice is f25.

Taxi: Taxis are expensive. You can't hail them; ranks are located on the main city squares including Dam Square.

Cars: Hiring a car is easy; your biggest problem is likely to be parking: fines are steep and the Dutch traffic police are keen clampers.

(For more information, see **Netherlands: Internal Travel**, p. 168.)

SIGHTS

Amsterdam is a compact and tolerant city where the old 17th-century canals, winding streets and tall houses co-exist comfortably if incongruously with today's red-light areas, an open market for sex and drugs. It's a friendly city with a terrific streetlife, and a bicycle or a pair of feet are all you need to get you round. The four main canals – the Singel, Herengracht, Keizergracht and Prinsengracht – wind their way past the main sights, so in many ways the canal boats give you the best introduction to the city (See **Getting About**, p. 174).

The heart of Amsterdam is DAM SQUARE, lying at the end of the main shopping thoroughfare, the Damrak. Dam Square is always lively, a popular theatre for street artists and buskers and a common meeting place for tourists. Across the square, the KONINKLIJK PALEIS (Royal Palace) is a former town hall built in 1640 to demonstrate the city's commercial success. Most impressive is the sumptuous interior. (Open daily July–Aug. 12.30–4 p.m.; Sept.–June Wednesdays from 2–6 p.m.)

Leading off the Dam, Nieuwe Zijds Voorburgwal and its surrounding area retains much of the old Amsterdam charm. One delightful attraction is the BEGIJNHOF. Set in Spui, this is one of Amsterdam's many *hofjes* – 17th-century almshouses with picturesque courtyards built for the poor and elderly. The tranquil Begijnhof also includes two churches, one of which dates back to the 14th century. By contrast, Spui itself is a lively part of town packed with bars, cafés and bookshops.

Further south on Singel is the famous BLOEMENMARKT, the floating flower market where traders sell their wares from floating barges (Mon.–Sat. 9 a.m.–5 p.m.).

West of the Dam on Prinsengracht is the 17th-century WESTERKERK (Western Church) whose tower dominates the surrounding square. Outside the church stands a small statue of Anne Frank, and a few yards away at Prinsengracht 263 is the ANNE FRANK HUIS. Inside the house is the annexe in which the young Jewish girl wrote her diary of life in hiding with her family, until their betrayal to the Gestapo and subsequent incarceration. Anne died of typhus in Belsen concentration camp just a week before the German surrender. Adults f8. (Open June–Aug., Mon.–Sat. 9 a.m.–7 p.m. and Sun. 10 a.m.–7 p.m.; Sept.–May open Mon.–Sat. 9 a.m.–5 p.m. and Sun. 10 a.m.–5 p.m.)

Prinsengracht is one of the roads bordering the old immigrant and working-class quarter of JORDAAN, along with Brouwersgracht, Marnixstraat and Elandsgracht. Jordaan has recently taken on a more Bohemian character, and it makes for an easy and enjoyable stroll along narrow canals and streets dotted with interesting shops and a growing profusion of bars and cafés. Watch out for the *hofjes*, in particular, the Van Bienen Hofje at Prinsengracht 89–133. There's also a good Saturday market on Lindengracht.

East of the Dam lies the old city centre, stretching over two canals: Oude Zijdse Voorburgwal and Oude Zijdse Achterburgwal. With buildings dating from the 14th century, there remains much to be admired if you can find it. Unfortunately, the area – known as WALLETJES – has achieved notoriety as the city's red-light district and people come to look not at the history but at the prostitutes and peepshows that line the streets.

A few streets over and you come into the start of what was historically the city's Jewish quarter, the JODENHOEK. The principal centre of activity was the Jodenbreestraat, though today it holds a few signs of the past. At Jodenbreestraat 4–6, however, you can still find the house where Rembrandt lived from 1639–60. A collection of 250 of his etchings are on display here, including some of his most famous Biblical illustrations. (Open Mon.–Sat. 10 a.m.–5 p.m.; Sun. 1–5 p.m.)

Running parallel to Jodenbreestraat is WATERLOOPLEIN, site of the first Jewish settlement and once the biggest and busiest market in Amsterdam. The flea market which has now re-established itself on the site is an enjoyable place to browse and it's particularly good for secondhand clothes. (Open Mon.–Fri. 9 a.m.–5 p.m.; Sat. 8.30 a.m.–5.30 p.m.) Waterlooplein leads into Mr Visser Plein, where the 17th-century PORTUGUESE SYNAGOGUE still stands, having survived the war (Sun.–Fri. 10 a.m.–4 p.m.). Nearby is the JEWISH HISTORICAL MUSEUM, which recounts the history of Holland's Jews from 1752 (Sun.–Mon. 11 a.m.–5 p.m.). Between the two buildings, on JD Meijerplein, is a statue commemorating the rounding up and transportation to Mauthausen of 400 Jewish men in reprisal for the killing of a Nazi sympathizer. The arrests triggered a countrywide general strike known as the February Strike.

No visit to Amsterdam would be complete without a visit to the RIJKSMUSEUM at Stadhouderskade 42. This is one of the world's greatest museums with the largest public collections of Rembrandts anywhere in the world, including the famous *Nightwatch* (Tues.–Sat. 10 a.m.–5 p.m.; Sun. 1–5 p.m.). The RIJKSMUSEUM VINCENT VAN GOGH at Paulus Potterstraat 7 is probably Amsterdam's most popular museum and houses a magnificent collection of Van Gogh's works, including *Still Life with Sun Flowers* and *Self-Portrait as a Painter* (daily 10 a.m.–5 p.m.). Adults f10.

Another much-visited museum is the VERZETSMUSEUM AMSTERDAM at Lekstraat 63. Housed in a former synagogue, it's dedicated to the Dutch Resistance movement against the Nazis during World War II (daily 10 a.m.–5 p.m.). Adults f10.

If you plan to visit a lot of museums, it may be worth investing in a museum card which gives you free entry to most museums in Amsterdam and in the rest of the country. The card costs f40 and is available from VVV offices. Or consider the 'Amsterdam Culture and Leisure Pass' for f29.90. This gives free entry to five museums plus other discounts.

ACCOMMODATION

Since Amsterdam is such a compact city, you are unlikely to find yourself very far out from the centre of things, no matter where you stay. Summer crowds mean early booking is advisable, or else try and turn up early on the day.

Youth hostels: There are two official IYHF hostels:

3 Vondelpark, Zandpad 5 (tel. 683 17 44). The better of the official hostels with bar, restaurant, TV rooms and kitchen. Best arrive early. Tram 1, 2 or 5 from the station to Leidseplein. f22 for dorms; f27 for doubles. 2 a.m. curfew.

Stadsdoelen, Kloveniersburgwal 97 (tel. 624 68 32). Good facilities. Take tram 4, 9, 16, 24 or 25 from the station to Muntplein. f22–27.

Private hostels include:

Bob's Youth Hostel, NZ Voorburgwal 92 (tel. 623 00 63). Popular hostel near Dam Square with cheap dorms. A short walk from the station or tram 1, 2, 5, 13 or 17. B&B from f21. This is *the* place to stay.

Christian Youth Hostel Eben Haezer, Bloemstraat 79 (tel. 624 47 17). Cheap and cheerful. Tram 13 or 17 to Marnixstraat. B&B f15.

Kabul Young Budget Hotel, Warmoesstraat 38–42 (tel. 623 71 58). Noisy hostel in the red-light area, 5 minutes' walk from Centraal Station. Dorms f24, doubles from f70–90.

Sleep-In: 's-Gravesandestraat 51 (tel. 694 74 44). A little way out but very cheap. Tram 3, 6, 9, 10 or 14 to Mauritskade, then back along Sarphatisstraat. Large dorms with mattresses on the floor for f14 per person. No curfew.

The VVV holds a more complete list of hostels.

Hotels and pensions: Lists are available at the VVV, together with a reservation service. Cheapest doubles start at around f55.

Pax, Radhuisstraat 37 (tel. 624 97 35). A 10–15 minute walk from Amsterdam Centraal, or take tram 13 or 17. Doubles from f70.

Weber, Marxinstraat 397 (tel. 627 05 74). Tram 1 or 2 from Amsterdam Central to Leidse Plein, then a short walk along Marnixstraat. Doubles from f75.

Amstel Boat Hotel, de Ruijterkade pier 5 (tel. 626 42 47). Moored a short walk from the rear exit of Amsterdam Centraal. Doubles from f119. With TV and private bath.

Schröder, Haarlemerdijk 48b (tel. 626 62 72). A 5–10 minute walk from Amsterdam Centraal. Doubles from f60.

Old Nickel, Nieuwe Brgsteeg 11 (tel. 624 1912). Singles from £45, doubles from f70.

Canal Boat B.B., DA Costakade t/o 1 (tel. 689 0426). Singles from f55, doubles from f120.

Private accommodation: Enquire about the availability of private rooms at the VVV. Expect to pay around f45 p.p. per night. Long-term accommodation is horrendously difficult to find in Amsterdam, where there is a severe shortage of property to rent. Your best bet is in the run-down area of Amsterdam Zuid-Oost, since few people want to live there. Expect rents of f400–600 per month. It's also worth keeping an eye on the noticeboards and scouring the 'To Let' (*Te Huur*) sections of the newspapers.

Campsites: Open April to September:

Zeeburg, Zuider-Ijdijk 44 (tel. 694 44 30). Aimed at young travellers, with regular live music. Direct ferry from Centraal Station or Tram 3 or 10 to Muiderpoort, then bus 22 or 37 followed by a 10 minute walk. Night bus 71 or 76. Cost: f6 per person with tent.

Vligenbos, Meeuwenlaan 138 (tel. 636 88 55). Another youth site. Bus 32 from Centraal Station. f5.50 per person with tent.

Gaasper, Loosdrechtdreef 7 (tel. 696 73 26). Metro to Gaasperplas or night bus 75. f8.35 per person with tent.

FOOD

Amsterdam has traditionally been a haven for refugees from all over the world and they have left their culinary mark on the city, particularly in the Leidseplein/Jordaan area, where good cheap restaurants abound – Dutch, Chinese, Italian and Indonesian – in lively surroundings. There's also a glut of cafés and restaurants near Dam Square and in the red-light district. Avoid restaurants advertising 'tourist menus' as these are generally uninspiring. Go for the *dag's menu* (dish of the day) at f18–20, and fill the gap with deep-fried *poffertjes* (mini-doughnuts) from street stalls.

For Indonesian *rijsttafel*, avoid the more expensive restaurants around Damrak and head for Binnen Bantammerstraat to the south-east of Centraal Station. This street is excellent for good value authentic Indonesian and Chinese food. The Azie and the Ling Nam are just two of many good restaurants there.

Dutch cuisine can be found at the Blauwe Hollander, Leidsekruisstraat 28; Haesje Claes at Spuistraat 275; Leto at Haarlemmerdijk 114; and Moeders Pot at Vinkenstraat 119. For cheap beer, head away from the town centre to the Leidseplein, Rembrandtsplein or Thorbeckeplein. If it's atmosphere you want, try one of the city's famous brown cafés (*bruine kroegen*). These sparsely decorated pub-like affairs are full of character.

Vegetarian restaurants are plentiful. Bolhoed in Prinsengracht 60–62 (near Anne Frank's House) and Harvest in Govert Flinkstraat 251 are two possibilities. Amsterdam also has two mensas (student cafeterias) where you can get a full meal for around f10: Atrium at Oude Zijdse Achterburgwal 237 and Agora at Roeterstraat 11. Fast-food outlets and street kiosks are scattered liberally throughout the city.

The Mignon supermarket chain has a number of central branches ideal for picnic supplies. Several street markets also sell food, including the Albert Cuypstraat and the Lindengracht in Jordaan.

ENTERTAINMENT
Amsterdam's red-light area is a tourist attraction in its own right these days, and a major source of free entertainment – free, that is, if you go just to look. In a more traditional vein, Amsterdam's clubs, bars and discos play host to a wide range of live jazz, rock and pop performers, the vast majority being located around the Leidseplein and Rembrandtsplein squares. The Melkweg on Lijnbaansgracht 2341 and Paradiso on Weteringschans 6–8 are two good live music venues. The Bimhuis on Oude Schans 73–7 is excellent for jazz. If you're missing the pub, try one of the famous 'Brown cafés', where you can sit and have a drink and watch the world go by. Hoppe at Spui 18–20 is one of the most popular and is always crowded.

Cinemas are well represented in the city and English-language films are nearly always subtitled rather than dubbed. Classical music lovers will be drawn to the Royal Concertgebouw Orchestra at the Concertgebouw; while ballet and opera buffs should make for the Musiektheater, home to both the Dutch Opera and the National Ballet. Theatre addicts will enjoy Amsterdam's 60 theatres, the best known of which are the Stadsshcouwburg and the Koninklijk Theater Carré. There are also two companies that put on plays in English at venues around the city: the English Speaking Theatre of Amsterdam (Leidsestraat 106, tel. 622 97 42) and the American Repertory Theatre (Kerkstraat 4, tel. 625 94 95)

Tickets for all venues can be booked at the VVV Amsterdam Tourist Office and the UitBuro (see **Useful Addresses**, p. 173). You can also buy your listings magazines there; the best are *City Life* and *What's On*, and the *Time Out* guide to Amsterdam, available from the better London newsagents.

FESTIVALS AND EVENTS
You may want to time your visit to coincide with one of Amsterdam's many festivals:

1–30 June	Annual Holland Festival of music, drama and dance
12–15 Feb	Great Carnival Festival

| mid March | Blues Festival |
| 29/30 April | Queen's Birthday. Huge open-air markets, Europe's largest street party. Busiest weekend of the year. |

During the summer months there are also music, cabaret and theatre performances in the Vondelpark Open-Air Theatre.

EXCURSIONS

Distances are so small in the Netherlands that you can easily travel the whole country. But you don't have to go far from Amsterdam to discover the charming town of MONNICKENDAM, where little has changed over the last 200 years and you can still visit the 15th-century Gothic-style church, the 17th- and 18th-century gabled houses and the town hall, built as a private house in the middle of the 18th century.

MARKEN and VOLENDAM are two small picturesque towns where the inhabitants still wear traditional costumes. A short drive from Volendam or a bus ride from Amsterdam's Centraal Station is the town of EDAM. Only a handful of working cheese warehouses are left, many dating back to the 18th century, but you can still see the age-old process of cheese-making. The town's main attraction is the 15th-century GROTE KERK, a vast church with 30 remarkable stained-glass windows.

Other excursion possibilities include the Wesfriesian former ports of ENKHUIZEN and HOORN, which retain much of their charm with their pretty 16th- and 17th-century harbours and canals. Enkhuizen contains the Pepperhouse, the only remaining warehouse of the Dutch East India Company which played such a crucial role in the Netherlands' colonial development. Nearby, or an hour from Amsterdam by train, the small town of ALKMAAR is popular for its fine old buildings and, in summer, for its Friday cheese market where the participants wear costume.

West of the capital lies HAARLEM, with its historical inner city and dozens of courtyards and antique shops. Haarlem also has the oldest museum in the Netherlands, the TEYLER MUSEUM. Lisse, 17 km south of Haarlem, is home to the KEUKENHOF GARDENS, the largest flower gardens in the world. From the end of March till the end of May, Holland's most magnificent open-air flower show displays around seven million flowers in full bloom.

Finally, along there are a number of fine beach resorts along the North Sea coast, all with excellent water-sport facilities. ZAND-VOORT is a modern seaside resort with a wide beach, surfing, cafés and new casino.

(See **Netherlands: Where to Go for What**, p. 167, for additional options to those covered here.)

RUSSIA

VITAL STATISTICS

Red tape: Despite the general relaxation of official bureaucracy in Russia since the downfall of the Communist regime, there is still an abundance of red tape to circumvent. Visas are required of all foreign nationals, and in order to obtain one you must specify all destinations you intend to visit and produce proof that your travel and accommodation has been booked in advance (see **Accommodation**, p. 189). Dealing with the Russian Embassy can be a frustrating experience — it's much easier to get a travel agent to handle the visa application for you. Unless you are willing to pay an 'express fee' (which can be as much as £80) in addition to any other visa fees, the Embassy takes six weeks on average to issue a visa. There is nothing spontaneous about a trip to Russia! The completed application, together with three passport photos and your passport (which must be valid for at least three months after your proposed return date), will therefore need to be submitted five weeks before departure. (In some cases a photocopy of your passport will be OK.) Watch out! Depending on where the visa is issued, its validity may start on the day of issue rather than the day you actually enter the country. Be sure to ask about this.

One post-Glasnost improvement is that you now have the option of travelling independently, organizing your own itinerary, accommodation, meals and entertainment — it is even possible to arrange a home-stay whereby you lodge with a Russian family as a paying guest. On the other hand, signing up for a group package tour has the advantage of being cheaper, simpler and far less time-consuming than going it alone. See **Further Information**, p. 191 for details of specialist travel agencies.

Customs: Visitors can take into Russia: 1 l spirits; 2 l wine; 250 cigarettes or 250 g of other tobacco goods. If cash in excess of US$500 is being imported it must be declared on a currency form on arrival. You cannot bring in Russian currency. When leaving the country it is illegal to export computer hardware, currency, more than 1.5 litres of vodka, 2 litres of wine and 100 cigarettes. Don't ever be tempted to smuggle anything that looks like an icon.

Health: No immunizations are required, though if you are coming from an infected area you may be asked for proof of vaccination.

A diptheria vaccination is recommended and an HIV certificate is required if you're spending more than 3 months in Russia. It may not be safe to drink tap water; stick to the bottled variety (St Petersburg's water is particularly hazardous: don't even use it for cleaning your teeth!) Make sure you take out private medical insurance before you go. On the whole, few problems exist, but to be on the safe side, carry your own AIDS pack (see **Medicine**, p. 98).

Language: Mainly Russian with some local dialects and languages. Try to learn a little before you go, especially if you plan to travel alone, and take a decent phrase book. This is particularly useful since the Russians use the Cyrillic rather than the Roman alphabet.

Population: 155 million.

Capital: Moscow, population 9 million.

Political system: Following the unsuccessful coup attempt in 1991, Boris Yeltsin has taken over the helm and is trying to steer towards a market economy. However, Russia, like the rest of the CIS, is at present embroiled in confusion and economic hardship, and still faces an uncertain future both in terms of its own well-being and its links with other former Soviet republics.

Religion: Mainly Russian Orthodox, with a number of minority religions. Since Glasnost, the Russian Orthodox Church has grown tremendously.

Time: Three hours ahead of GMT (four hours Apr.–Oct.).

Money: The currency is the rouble (R), divided into 100 kopecks. Because of Russia's rampant inflation, it is impossible to give a likely exchange rate. Coins have become almost worthless and there are now few in circulation. Notes: R1, R3, R5, R10, R25, R50, R100, R500 and R1,000. Foreign currency can only be exchanged at state banks and official bureaux. The US dollar is the preferred currency to take, though the tourist exchange rate fluctuates wildly. You'll probably be approached by black marketeers wanting to change money, though strictly speaking this is illegal. Be careful not to get too many roubles as you may find it difficult to use them all, especially as tourists are often asked to pay in hard currency. Moscow in particular has many hard currency shops, restaurants and bars (which will usually accept credit cards, but at a less advantageous exchange rate than you would get for cash). Traveller's cheques are not widely accepted. However, if you do bring them, make sure that they are in US dollars. On the whole, the most convenient (though not the safest) way is to take a few traveller's cheques for emergencies and carry the rest in US$20, 10, 5 and 1 bills

Communications: The telephone system is hopeless. Phones now take jetons since coins are no longer available. Local calls can be made free of charge in hotels. Apart from Moscow, where limited direct-dialling facilities exist, international calls must be made through your hotel or at post and telegraph offices, where you will need to book well in advance.

International telegrams can be sent from most hotels and post offices and usually arrive within a day or two at most. Look for the blank forms and print your message clearly. Fax connections to Moscow are good, providing a quicker way of making contact with the outside world.

You can buy postcards and stamps from post offices and large hotels. Letters take two or three weeks, less from Moscow. International parcels may be sent only from international post offices.

Electricity: Mostly 220v AC. Plugs are the European type with two round pins.

Business hours: BANKS: Mon.–Fri. 9 a.m.–12 p.m. and 1–5 p.m., longer in the big cities.

POST OFFICES: Mon.–Fri. 9 a.m.–8 p.m.; shorter hours Sat. and Sun.

SHOPS: Usually Mon.–Sat. 11 a.m.–8 p.m.; major department stores open 9 a.m.–8 p.m.; food stores Mon.–Sat. 8 a.m.–9 p.m. and Sun. 8 a.m.–7 p.m. Smaller shops may close for lunch.

OFFICES: Mon.–Fri. 9 a.m.–6 p.m.

Holidays: 1 and 2 January; 8 March (International Women's Day); 23 April (Orthodox Easter Day); 9 May (Victory Day); 12 June (National Independence Day); 31 December.

Climate: Summers (May to September) are warm, but expect long cold winters with snowfalls from December to early April. Moscow and St Petersburg range from 18–24°C in summer, while temperatures in the Black Sea coastal resorts reach 20–27°C. Winter temperatures average -5°C in Moscow (St Petersburg is usually a few degrees warmer).

DO'S AND DON'TS

The Russian are a very hospitable people, though in these days of perpetual shortages it is hard not to feel guilty at the enormous spread which will invariably be laid before you if you are lucky enough to be invited to a Russian's home for dinner (the trick is to eat enthusiastically and appreciatively but not to deplete too many of the optional extras). Great importance is placed on gift-giving. Wherever you go, expect to give presents and receive them. If you are invited to dinner, for example, you should take gifts not only for the host but for each member of the family – so before you leave home stock up with luxury (but not ostentatious) consumer goods such as decent soaps, good quality writing materials, chocolates, and tinned goodies from Fortnum & Mason. Recent books on Britain or English as a foreign language are another good idea, as are introductory books on business studies (in this fledgling free-market economy, many people are immensely keen on starting their own business).

Drinking is one of the cornerstones of Russian life — Russian vodka is famous the world over. If you get taken in hand by a group of happy Russians in a restaurant or at someone's house, they are quite likely to embark on a long round of vodka toasts. Unless you are a very hardened drinker, either go slow or expect severe after-effects. And don't be taken aback if you find yourself locked into a Russian bear-hug — it's okay (though not obligatory) for men to embrace one another. Just follow your host's lead; in most cases a handshake will be sufficient greeting.

The most important thing to remember when travelling in Russia is that it is a time of enormous transition. This is the most exciting and the most frustrating part of travelling there. Prices are continuously going up and down, businesses are opening and closing. Unofficially, the Russian mafias run the country and bribery is rampant. Sadly, using a US$5 or $10 bill is often the only way to speed up the bureaucracy. Remember, though Russia is no longer Soviet rule, some habits are hard to break. Don't be surprised if not everyone is happy to meet someone from the West.

WHERE TO GO FOR WHAT

Even without the fifteen former Soviet republics, Russia is still the world's largest country. Aside from the obvious attractions of the great cities of Moscow and St Petersburg there exists a wealth of 'real' travel experiences for the intrepid tourist — but this is not easy travelling; conditions are at best basic, and occasionally perilous.

The GOLDEN RING refers to the ancient Russian cities which form a loose circle around Moscow. Famed for their architectural riches, towns such as SERGEYEV POSAD, YAROSLAVL and KOSTROMA with their 11th-century churches, SUZDAL, with its complete set of wooden 'dachas', and BURYATIA, the centre of Russian Buddhism and site of the splendid Ivolginsk Monastery, each present a beautiful visual display of Russia's past and seem oblivious to the 20th century as they continue to enjoy life at a snail's pace.

One of the best ways to explore the Golden Ring is to take a boat trip along the VOLGA, Europe's longest river and certainly one of its most beautiful, bordered by forests, mountains and lush countryside. You can book a cruise of your choice, though it will have to be part of a group package.

NOVGOROD, some 966 km north of Moscow, dates from the 10th century and was once Russia's largest and most powerful city. Despite suffering terrible devastation at the hands of some of the Tsars, notably Ivan the Terrible, it still possesses a range of fine architecture. North of Novgorod is the charming and elegant city of ST PETERSBURG (now reverted to its original name after a post-Revolutionary spell as Leningrad). See p. 192 for details of its many attractions.

The vast CAUCASUS mountain range straddles the republics of Russia, Georgia, Armenia and Azerbaijan. Some of the most commonly visited towns, such as Dombay and the villages of the Baksan Valley, are within Russian territory. Chair lifts ensure that even the unfit don't miss out on the spectacular mountain views. A number of mineral water spas are located in the central Caucasus. Their alleged recuperative powers have been drawing visitors since the 18th century. Even if you're in perfect health, it's still a lovely area in which to enjoy the waters, the peaceful atmosphere and the scenic walks. However, to get into many of the baths you will need to book through Intourist.

When Russians, including many of the top brass, want to get away from it all they make for the Black Sea resorts; SOCHI and DAGOMYS are two of the most popular. With their attractive summer climate, pebble beaches, warm sea and numerous bars, restaurants and cafés, both are good places to recuperate after some hard walking up in the mountains. Dagomys is the more modern of the two.

SIBERIA, once the frozen dumping ground for those who had fallen out of favour with the State, is a land of endless rivers and forests. IRKUTSK, as well as being fascinating in its own right, is a good city from which to make excursions. The prime attraction is LAKE BAYKAL – the world's deepest lake and one of its oldest, at around 25 million years. Crystal clear and so pure that you can drink the water, it's one of the most beautiful sights in Russia, arguably in Europe.

INTERNAL TRAVEL

If you're with a group, your internal travel arrangements will be taken care of. If you're planning an independent trip, you must specify on your itinerary how you wish to get from A to B, and you should pre-book to save time and trouble (not to mention visa hassle) and to ensure you get the ticket you want. As travelling restrictions for both nationals and foreigners have reduced, public transport has become very crowded and it may be difficult to get seats. Once inside Russia, foreigners are sometimes allowed to purchase tickets in hard currency for prices way above those paid by the Russians.

Technically it's illegal to deviate from your itinerary, and by law you should be required to show your visa when purchasing a ticket. However official watchfulness has declined markedly, particularly at train stations, and it's become much easier to take an unscheduled trip without having your documents checked.

Air: Aeroflot, the state airline, covers the country with a network of regional and local flights. If buying a ticket in Russia, either from an Aeroflot office or Intourist, you may be able to pay in hard currency. For speed, air is a good way to travel between cities and tickets are rarely more expensive than their rail counterparts. You must, however, book well in advance. The service is surprisingly good.

Rail: Russia has an extensive rail system and trains are generally reliable. There are four classes: two- or four-bed 'luxury' sleeping compartments; four-bed open or closed couchettes; and bog standard bench seating. If you have a reservation you will normally be given some kind of sleeper. In Russia you can book tickets through Intourist or direct from the station.

The famous TRANS-SIBERIAN RAILWAY will take you from Moscow right across Russia to the port of Vladivostok (from whence many travellers catch the ferry to Japan), or to Beijing. It's the world's longest continuous rail journey and is regarded as an experience in itself. As such it's well used by travellers, but for all that it involves being stuck in a carriage with a bunch of strangers for a week, enduring limited eating and washing facilities, and with very little to do except stare at the sometimes less than spectacular scenery as it passes by (though for a higher price there are a few stopovers you can make if you wish to break the journey). Intrepid travellers can book a first- or second-class sleeper but must make reservations as far in advance as possible (two to three months at least). Intourist and Regent Holidays are two firms that handle the bookings. There are three routes to choose from: the TRANS-SIBERIAN ROUTE leaves every two days from Moscow at around 2 p.m. and finishes in Vladivostok. The trip covers 9,000 miles and takes eight days. A one-way ticket starts from around £215 second class/£382 first class. The TRANS-MONGOLIAN ROUTE leaves every Tuesday from Moscow at around 7.50 p.m. and finshes in Beijing. You must obtain a transit visa for Mongolia in advance as this cannot be purchased at the border. You will also need a Chinese visa. The route passes by the Great Wall of China and lasts about seven days. Prices start at £275 second class/£435 first class. The TRANS-MANCHURIAN ROUTE leaves every Friday from Moscow at around 8.25 p.m. and finishes in Beijing without passing through Mongolia. You will need to obtain a Chinese visa in advance. The route takes eight days and also passes the Great Wall. Prices start at around £260 second class/£405 first class. The *Trans Siberian Handbook* by Bryn Thomas should tell you all you need to know.

Bus: Buses are mostly used for short distances within cities, not for long-distance travel.

Car: Road travel in Russia can be very rewarding. Strictly speaking, you are supposed to stick to the route you've pre-arranged with Intourist. In practice, however, a car provides the means to enjoy some short excursions of your own. Tourists can take their own vehicle or rent one there, but if travelling in your own car, you must have an international driving licence, registration certificate and insurance papers. These may enable you to jump the queues at some petrol stations. Read up on traffic rules extremely carefully before you set off. Seatbelts are compulsory and you're not supposed to carry extra passengers.

Hitching: Not permitted.

Local transport: Once you've arrived in a city you're allowed to make your own trips within the city limits. With the slackening of official watchfulness, however, it's fairly easy to take a day-trip beyond the city limits without having your papers checked.

Local buses, trams and metros offer you good cheap service in getting round within cities. Bus stops are shown by a roadside 'A'. Tickets can be bought at newsstands, outside metro stations, or from the bus driver. They must usually be validated on the bus using the hole-puncher. Buses are overcrowded and can be tricky for a visitor who doesn't know exactly where to get off – metros are much easier. Stations are indicated by a large 'M', tickets cost 400R, but are increasing regularly and, as with phones, payment is now by jeton since coins have gone out of circulation. Put the jeton into the machine to get to the trains and look for the name of your destination to find the right platform. If in doubt, ask. Make sure any map you buy is up to date – there have been so many name changes that if it is printed before 1992 it will be of little use.

Local trains are useful for day-trips further afield. You can buy a ticket in roubles at the station – often there will be a ticket machine on the platform. Also, one station may have two names, depending which line you are travelling on.

Taxis: State taxis are those with a 'T'. Make sure you establish the price before you set off. If you want to flag down a cab on the street, stick out your hand and wait to see what stops. Many Russians moonlight as taxi drivers to earn a bit of extra cash. Most will try for dollars rather than roubles.

ACCOMMODATION

All accommodation must be booked in advance, whether you are on a tour or travelling independently. The hostel in St Petersburg is very helpful. If you write or fax the dates that you would like to stay, they'll send you a confirmation letter to use when applying for your visa. In most cases, this is all that is necessary.

Group travellers will be allocated hotels, depending on who they have booked their tour with. Individual travellers should have some choice in the matter.

Hotels: Standards are not up to those of the West, but most hotels offer comfortable rooms with private washing and bathing facilities, one or more restaurants and a bar, depending on the category. Independent travellers get a choice of hotels within a chosen price bracket. Accommodation in Russia can be expensive, which is one reason why packages often work out cheaper. Now that the Intourist monopoly on booking accommodation has been broken, however, rooms in 2–3 star hotels can be pre-booked for £30–£40 (whereas a double room booked through Intourist can range from £50–£100 in a 2–3 star hotel, usually including breakfast).

On arrival you hand in your passport and accommodation voucher in return for a pass with your room number on it. This is then given to the lady responsible for your stretch of corridor, who will give you your room key. Every time you go out you must exchange the room key for the pass, which will have to be shown to the doorman when you return. For further information, contact Russian Youth Hostels and Tourism, 409 N. Pacific Coast Highway 100, Suite 390, Recondo Beach, CA 90277, USA.

B&B: You can stay in a private Russian home at a very reasonable cost if you book a homestay holiday. See **Further Information**, p. 191 for organizations offering this option.

Campsites: If you are travelling by car in summer, you have the additional option of staying at an Intourist campsite. There are only nine open to tourists at present, however, and current concerns about crime and shortages of supplies on campsites make this a tough option that cannot be recommended.

FOOD

Russian food is notorious for its blandness – no one goes there for the cuisine! Meals generally consist of various types of salad, potatoes, poor quality meat and cabbage, with tea or coffee to drink. Soups are usually a good bet. Vegetarians will find the going particularly tough. Surprisingly, in view of the climate, the one reliable food is ice cream, for which the Russians have developed a year-round passion.

If you're on a package tour, your meals will be arranged for you, often in the hotel restaurant with some form of floor show thrown in. If you're travelling independently or just want to find a meal on your own, you can expect dismal service wherever you go. Your options are a hotel or state-run restaurant (both of which usually offer a cabaret in the evenings), or privately owned co-operative restaurants (which tend to offer slightly better food). You may have to queue to get in for lunch, and for dinner you must book well in advance (before midday, at least). Intourist will book co-operatives free of charge, but they charge a hefty booking fee for state restaurants so you'd do better to phone or call in yourself. Try and establish how you are going to pay for the meal beforehand, preferably when you book. Expect to pay the equivalent of a meal in any standard restaurant in the UK.

On the cheaper side are cafés (*Kafe*) which have limited menus, no entertainment and which should accept roubles. If you don't mind eating on the move, there are some excellent snacks available outside metro stations. Try *piroshki* (meat pies) and *blini* (savoury pancakes). You can also buy delicious breads and sweet rolls at the bakery for a few kopeks, or fruit and veg at the markets, though be sure to wash it in bottled water before you eat. Buying food at the markets, as the Russians themselves do, is the cheapest way to eat. Everything is usually weighed. Write your desired quantity on a piece of paper and point at it. Be just as assertive as the locals — after years of waiting in breadlines they are quick to push and shove.

If you are lucky enough to be invited to a Russian's house for dinner, you'll probably enjoy the best meal of your trip.

On the other hand, should you want to forget what you've just eaten in a hurry, one of the many brands of famous Russian vodka should do the trick. State and hotel restaurants serve vodka, and most Intourist hotels have hard currency bars. Co-operatives aren't allowed to sell liquor but you can normally bring your own.

BUDGETING

Russia is one of the few places where it is probably cheaper to take a package tour than to travel independently. If you take a package, nearly everything — accommodation, transport, dinner — will be taken care of. A three-night break costs from around £300–350. For independent travellers, the flight alone will cost around £250, depending on who you fly with and your destination. The lack of budget accommodation also means that hotels are expensive: the cheaper hotels in Moscow or St Petersburg still cost from £30 a night for a twin room.

Accommodation aside, living costs in Russia can be incredibly cheap for foreigners – if you can get by spending roubles. Food, local and national travel costs are minimal when paid in roubles. Shopping with the Russians you'll be able to purchase a lot for, by Western standards, very little. (It's pointless to list current prices here, since Russia's rampant inflation means that they will almost certainly be out of date by the time you read this.) Prices rise, however, if you have to spend hard currency – as you probably will in the big cities, particularly Moscow. Train fares are not so cheap when paid for in hard currency; air travel is a comparatively better bet. Taxis can be expensive: up to US$10 in Moscow. In the same city, a full meal in a local restaurant demanding dollars will cost around US$22, including wine. Other areas are likely to be much cheaper. Hard currency shops set up for foreigners are expensive but better stocked than their Russian counterparts.

The opportunities for picking up work in Russia to earn extra money are extremely limited and the pay is likely to be appalling by Western standards. Probably the only possibility is teaching English: VSO is a good starting point for further enquiries.

FURTHER INFORMATION

The Russian Embassy, 5 Kensington Palace Gardens, London W8 4QX (tel. 0171 229 8027)

Russian Tourist Information Service, 219 Marsh Wall, London E14 9PD (tel. 0891 516 951)

Background reading: The 1991 edition of Lonely Planet's *USSR*–Travel Survival Kit is out of touch with recent changes but still excellent on background and sights. *Alternative Moscow* (available from The Institute for Social Inventions, 20 Heber Road, London NW2 6AA tel. 0181 208 2853). At £4.95 this annually updated guide to Moscow is a bargain. Aiming to bring you into closer contact with Russians, it includes information on how to stay with a Russian family, recommends restaurants that still accept roubles and suggests interesting ways to spend your time beyond the more obvious tourist attractions.

SPECIALIST TRAVEL AGENCIES
Both group and independent visits can be booked through Intourist, the former state-owned travel agency which has long been the dominant name in Russian travel and is now an independent

company (tel. 0171 538 8600). Intourist offers a wide choice but tends to be expensive. Other agencies with large programmes offering group travel include:

Thomson Holidays (0171 433 3444).

Page and Moy, 136–140 London Road, Leicester (tel. 0116 252 4463).

STA Travel (tel. 0171 938 4711).

Travel Cuts (tel. 0171 255 1944).

Goodwill Travel (tel. 01438 716 421), tours on offer include one called 'Meet the Russians'.

Regent Holidays (tel. 0117 921 1711) specialize in arranging trips for individuals.

Progressive Tours (tel. 0171 262 1676) also cater for individual travel.

Adventure travel specialists, offering walking and explorer holidays in Russia, Soviet Central Asia and Siberia:

Explore Worldwide (tel. 01252 319 448).

Exodus (tel. 0181 673 0859).

Out There Trekking (tel. 0114 258 8508).

Homestays can be arranged through:

Room with the Russians (tel. 0181 472 2694).

Russkies (tel. 0114 258 3591).

Moscow

AIRPORT FACILITIES
Moscow's international airport is Moscow-Sheremetyevo (tel. 578 9101), about 29 km from the city centre. Terminal 1 handles domestic flights and Terminal 2 international flights. Money-changing facilities are available at two banks and there is an Intourist information desk, plus the usual airport shops, duty-free outlets, eating facilities and a post office. There is no airport tax.

CITY LINKS
It is advisable to book transfers before departure (package tours are usually inclusive of coach transfers). If you are making your own way, bus 551 for metro Rechnoi Vokzal departs every 15 minutes

from just outside the arrivals ramp. The journey takes about 50 minutes. Alternatively you can take a taxi, which is quicker but more expensive. Taxi drivers will charge US$20 minimum, but expect to pay US$30–40 on average.

There is a shuttle bus service between Sheremetyevo's two terminals, as well as between Sheremetyevo and Moscow's other main airports – Domodedovo and Vnukovo.

USEFUL ADDRESSES
Tourist office: Central Excursion Bureau, ul. Tver'skaya 3/5 (tel. 203 6962).
Main post office: ul. Tver'skaya 7 (formerly Gorky Street), next to the Intourist Hotel).
British Embassy: Naberezhnaya Morisa Toreza 14 (tel. 231 8511).
US Embassy: Ulitsa Chaikovskovo 19/23 (tel. 252 2451).
Emergency services: Dial 02 for police, 03 for ambulance, 01 for fire.
Medical assistance: Walk-in medical care available at US Embassy. There is also an American Medical Centre (tel. 095 256 2212), and the British Embassy has a doctor (tel. 095 230 6333).

GETTING ABOUT
Metro: This is the quickest and most efficient method of getting round the city. Trains are frequent and very cheap. Buy a jeton – current price 400R – and drop it in the barrier at the entrance. One potential difficulty is that so many stations have been renamed that maps are often out of date; check with Intourist or your hotel for the most recent information. To find a metro, look for the large 'M' on the street. Many stations are so ornate they're tourist attractions in themselves. The Metro runs from 6 a.m.–1 a.m.
Tram and bus: Tram stops are marked by a 'T'; bus stops an 'A'. As with the metro, jetons are now used instead of tickets; buy them from news kiosks or from the driver. If you plan to spend any length of time in Moscow, you can buy a monthly pass which allows you to use the metro, trams and buses. Buses are very crowded in Moscow, so be prepared to push your way on and off.
Taxi: There are plenty of taxis on Moscow's streets since most Muscovites are happy to moonlight as taxi drivers. A state taxi will be marked with a 'T'. Make sure you agree a price before the journey starts. Most unofficial taxi drivers will want to be paid in hard currency rather than roubles. Two recommended taxi firms can be contacted on 227 000 and 227 0040.
Car hire: You can hire a car in Moscow but it is advisable to make

arrangements in advance – ideally at the same time as you book your holiday.

For more information, see **Russia: Internal Travel**, p. 186.

SIGHTS

Moscow is a huge and overwhelming city, and vastly different from what it was a few years ago when the Communist Party still ruled the roost. Today it epitomizes the changes and tensions that have characterized Russia and the former Soviet Union over recent years. Muscovites have broken free of their past and tried to come to terms with democracy and free enterprise and the clash between the two systems – the relics of Communism and the new capitalism (neither of which are working properly) – produces a curious atmosphere. Out have gone the old revolutionary place names and statues of past leaders, and in have come the new bars, advertising hoardings, Western goods and pavement entrepreneurs. Unfortunately there's still a long way to go. Freedom has not improved the average Muscovite's lot and the city is still gripped by severe economic hardship.

Despite its problems, Moscow remains a great city. Most of its palaces and mansions lie within an inner ring, which is easily negotiated on foot. Its streets are impossibly wide – in the thirties some buildings were pulled down and re-erected further back so that Stalin could have wider streets and thereby bigger parades.

To most people, Moscow signifies RED SQUARE (Krasnaya Ploschad), site of the vast Communist parades and, further back in time, of some very public executions, particularly during the era of Tsar Ivan the Terrible. Red Square lies in the heart of the city and contains three important monuments, of which the most distinctive is perhaps ST BASIL'S CATHEDRAL, with its multi-coloured domes. This splendid 16th-century church was built for the notorious Ivan the Terrible and is now Russia's most famous landmark (closed Tuesdays).

In the days of Communist rule, Soviet citizens used to queue for hours outside the LENIN MAUSOLEUM to glimpse the body of the great man. Today it's relatively easy to get in (except on Mondays and Fridays, when it's closed to the public), though it is rumoured that plans are afoot to remove Lenin and give him a proper burial in the near future. The nearby KREMLIN WALL holds the tombs of other Heroes of the Soviet Union, including Stalin, Maxim Gorky and American Communist John Reed, on whose life story Warren Beatty based the film *Reds*.

The KREMLIN is a huge fortress of ancient cathedrals, palaces and museums, surrounded by a thick brick wall. Inside, the ARMOURY

CHAMBER's priceless Tsarist collection includes jewels, gowns and silver. Also on your itinerary should be CATHEDRAL SQUARE (Sabornaya Ploschad) and its six cathedrals. Make sure you buy a ticket for the cathedrals before you enter – there's a kiosk in the Alexander Gardens. Archangel Michael Cathedral contains the tombs of the Tsars from the 13th to the 18th centuries while the Assumption Cathedral is where they were crowned. The 15th-century Annunciation Cathedral is the most visually outstanding and contains two famous icons.

One of the best ways to acclimatize to the new Moscow is to walk along TVERSKAYA (formerly Gorky Street), Moscow's main thoroughfare. The street has become a open-air marketplace, with pavement entrepreneurs offering everything from flowers to underwear in the relentless struggle to earn money. PUSHKIN SQUARE, at the southern end of Tverskaya, is a popular arena for soap-box lecturers. It's also the site of Moscow's first McDonald's and a favourite Muscovite meeting place.

Another popular street is ARBAT, one of Moscow's oldest areas and now a pedestrianized zone with a thriving scene of its own: you'll find buskers and street theatre, food stalls, and souvenir sellers offering a selection of very Russian wares, such as furs and Lenin memorabilia. The best arts and crafts market in town, however, is the ISMAILOV, which takes place on Sundays in the park of the same name.

Okhotny Ryad is lined with former Party offices and leads into Teatralnaya Ploshchad (Theatre Square), dominated by the BOLSHOI THEATRE. To the right of the Bolshoi is PETROVSKY PASSAGE, a new Western-style shopping mall which has been a big hit with the Muscovites. The biggest department store in Moscow is known by the acronym GUM and stands directly opposite the Kremlin on Red Square. For more up-market goods, Moscow's smartest shopping street is PROSPEKT KALININA.

Back on Teatralnaya Ploshchad, follow Teatrainy Proezd and you'll arrive at LUBYANKA, headquarters of the KGB. One of Moscow's most chilling façades, the building is not signposted but is opposite the Dyetskii Mir (Children's World) department store.

Moscow's museums seem to be going through rather an erratic period, so don't be surprised if you find several closed or only partially open. The PUSHKIN GALLERY houses an exceptional collection of Impressionist paintings, the TRETYAKOV GALLERY is known for its icons. Some of Russia's greatest writers are commemorated by their former houses or flats which have been converted into museums bearing their name – among them Leo Tolstoy, Chekhov, Gorky and Dostoevsky.

NOVODEVICHY CONVENT, an outstanding monument to Russian architecture of the 16th and 17th centuries, is where tsarinas were sent when their husbands died, and where Khrushchev, Gromyko and Chekhov are buried. There are some outstanding frescoes inside.

Finally, GORKY PARK, immortalized in the novel of the same name, is a popular place to unwind – come winter the lake freezes over and Muscovites get their skates out. Opposite the park lie the statues of the fallen heroes Stalin, Lenin and Dzerzhinsky – torn down in the aftermath of the failed coup against Mikhail Gorbachev in August 1991.

If you are making your own way round Moscow, the best way to see the city is on foot, taking the metro where necessary. Try to obtain an up-to-date map since street and metro names are changing all the time. A tourist boat on the MOSKVA RIVER will give you an excellent view of the Kremlin, while the LENIN HILLS across the river provide a fine panoramic view of both old and new Moscow.

However you choose to get around, the metro is worth a visit because many of the stations are sights in themselves. The most ornate are the earliest, built in the 1930s under Stalin. Some feature immense candelabra, stained glass, sculptures and mosaics. KOMSOMOLSKAYA and NOVOSLOBODSKAYA are among the best.

ACCOMMODATION

Officially, all accommodation must be pre-booked, whether you are on a package tour or travelling independently. If planning your own tour, you do at least have a choice of hotels within your chosen price bracket, though in summer you should book well in advance if you don't want to end up with the dregs. Note that the cheaper hotels tend to be further out from the city centre. Alternatively you can stay with a Russian family. For more information on all these options, see **Russia: Accommodation**, p. 170. There are no campsites in Moscow.

Hotels: The following examples provide a rough guide as to what you can expect to pay for hotel accommodation in Moscow. There are few single rooms proper (the single price given here normally indicates what an individual will be charged for a twin room). All include breakfast, except the Belgrade. Ratings are Russian, not Western standard.

Cosmos (4 star): A modern, impersonal hotel 30 minutes from the centre. Good recreational facilities, including a pool, sauna and bowling alley. From £68 for a single or twin.

Intourist (4 star): Good central location and lively nightlife with a bar that's open until 4 a.m. £68 for a single or twin.

Belgrade Hotel (3 star): Centrally located with a reasonable restaurant. Prices start at £48 per night for a double (decreasing if you stay longer). Tel. 248 1643.

Izmailovo Hotel (3 star): Large hotel with several restaurants and bars. £24 for a single; £28 for a twin.

Sevastopol Hotel (2 star): £89 for a single; £98 for a twin. Tel. 119 6450.

Solnechnaya Hotel (2 star): a long way out, but has several restaurants. £55 for a single; £70 for a twin.

Salyut Hotel (2 star): also far out but with several restaurants. £55 for a single; £70 for a twin.

FOOD

The food in most hotels is generally bland and uninspired. There are some good restaurants, though many of the best are hard currency only. It's always advisable to book in advance and to establish whether you'll be paying in roubles (which works out far cheaper) or dollars. (See **Russia: Food**, p. 171, for some general advice on restaurants.) A full meal in a local hard-currency restaurant will cost around US$30–40.

New restaurants are opening all the time in Moscow. Your hotel may be able to offer some recommendations in addition to those outlined below, all of which should be reserved.

Aragvi, ul. Tverskaya 6 (tel. 229 3762). State restaurant serving good Georgian cuisine in a hospitable atmosphere.

Delhi, Krasnaya Presnya 23b (tel. 252 1766). Co-operative offering high quality Indian menu with excellent service.

Praga, ul. Arbat 2 (tel. 290 6171). Expensive state restaurant with luxurious open-air roof terrace and good food. Reservations essential.

Uzbekistan, ul. Neglinnaya 29 (tel. 924 6053). Popular state restaurant with reasonable food and swift service.

Slavyanskiy Bazar, ul. Dvadtsat' Piatovo Oktyabrya 17, behind GUM (tel. 921 1872). State restaurant serving substantial Russian meals.

Cheaper options, which you should be able to get into without booking and where you may pay in roubles, include:

Kafe Sinaya, Ptitsa, ul. Chekhova 23. A stand-up café serving excellent Russian food, especially *pokjlebka* (sausage soup with breaded puffy crust).

Kafe Russkiye Pelmeni, ul. Arbat 52. Low-priced classic Russian food.

Kafe Sever, ul. Tverskaya 17. The best ice-cream sundaes in Moscow.

Moscow has not been immune to the American fast-food wave. McDonald's in Pushkin Square and Pizza Hut on ul. Tverskaya are both well established. But if you prefer to eat with the Soviets there is plenty of street food, always cheap and usually of reasonable quality. Snacks on sale outside metro stations can be delicious. Watch out for *blini* (savoury pancakes filled with spicy cabbage and onion).

To make your own lunch, visit the local markets and super-markets. Ask Intourist for directions. You can also shop at the hard-currency supermarkets.

ENTERTAINMENT

It has to be said that Moscow is not exactly throbbing with nightlife. There is nothing resembling a pub or bar scene, though there are a few jazz clubs around the city – try the *Sinyaya Ptitsa* at ul. Chekhova 23. An average night's entertainment, however, will consist of the cabaret that comes with your evening meal – good or bad. Alternatively you can wallow in one of the hard-currency hotel bars.

On the other hand, it is rich in cultural pursuits. Moscow offers some of the finest classical music, opera and ballet. The world-famous Bolshoi Ballet performs to full houses in the sumptuous Bolshoi Theatre, though in summer the company is usually away on tour. Tickets are cheap: even on the black market the maximum price is US$30. Another popular attraction is the Moscow State Circus – if you can stomach the hair-raising stunts of the performers (many of them animals). The best concert venues are the Tchaikovsky Conservatory and the Tchaikovsky Concert Hall.

Sports fans are also well catered for. Moscow has three well-known football teams which often figure in European competition – Torpedo, Dinamo and Spartek – as well as several ice hockey teams. Both sports are usually played at the Lenin Stadium complex.

Tickets are available either at the venues themselves or from kiosks (*Kassa*) around the city. Keep your eye out for posters adver-tising where tickets for a certain event are on sale. Intourist sells tickets for most events and is definitely the easiest route, but prices will be much higher and you will have to pay hard currency. How-ever, for popular performers such as the Bolshoi, Intourist may offer the only realistic opportunity of getting seats.

EXCURSIONS

Intourist arrange trips to a number of places of interest. Your visa must state each destination you intend to stay overnight. For day trips you can leave the city limits without a visa. In practice, however, such rules are seldom enforced these days and so you may want to go it alone and join the Muscovites riding the suburban trains out of the city.

Top of the excursion list should be the TROITSE AND SERGIEV MONASTERY at Sergeyev Posad. A remarkable monument of Russian history and religion, it comprises several beautiful cathedrals as well as a functioning seminary which plays a key role in Russian Orthodoxy today. Sergiyev is about 70 km outside Moscow – take an Intourist excursion or catch a train from Moscow's Yaroslavl station, journey time around 90 minutes.

Slightly nearer, just 25 km from Moscow, ARCHANGELSKOYE is a reminder of the bygone days of imperial Russia. One of the grandest estates in the region, it boasts a palace (which may or may not be open) and beautiful grounds, including a church and a theatre, which alone make the trip worthwhile. To get there by yourself, take the metro to Tushinskaya and then ask which bus to take.

YASNAYA POLYANA, 200 km from Moscow, is the birth and burial place of Leo Tolstoy. The house where he lived and wrote *War and Peace* and *Anna Karenina* is now a museum. An Intourist trip is expensive but the only viable way to get there.

ST PETERSBURG, an hour and a half's flight from Moscow, merits a trip in its own right rather than an excursion. Built by Peter the Great as a great Russian showpiece and known as 'The Venice of the North', it's a city of extraordinary beauty with its parks and palaces, cathedrals and canals. The PETER AND PAUL FORTRESS houses the marble tombs of 16 tsars, while the stunning WINTER PALACE on Dvortsovaya Polschad (Palace Square) was home to the tsars from 1762 right up until the Revolution in 1917. This palace forms just one part of the magnificent HERMITAGE MUSEUM, which houses a vast art collection which includes Rembrandts, Rubens and Gauguins among its endless treasures. If you don't want to fly to St Petersburg, you can take the train from Moscow – journey time around 8 hours.

UNITED KINGDOM

VITAL STATISTICS

Red tape: EC nationals and citizens of the USA, Japan and most Commonwealth countries require a valid passport but no visa. Nationals of all other countries should check visa requirements with their nearest British Embassy or Consulate.

Customs: With the implementation of the Single Market, EC nationals are now permitted an unlimited amount of excise goods as long as they are for personal use. Some EC countries have introduced guidelines, i.e. if you exceed certain limits you could be stopped and asked to provide evidence that your goods are for personal use only.

Health: No immunizations required. If travelling from an area where yellow fever is prevalent, an international certificate of vaccination is required. EC citizens are entitled to free emergency medical care but it is recommended that they also take out private medical insurance.

Language: English; some Gaelic in far-flung parts of Scotland and Northern Ireland; some Welsh in north and mid-Wales. The British are notoriously inept at mastering other languages.

Population: 68 million.

Capital: London, population 7 million.

Political system: Democracy. The Conservative party has been in power now since 1983. The current Prime Minister is John Major.

Religion: Predominantly Protestant.

Time: GMT (plus one hour Mar.–Oct.).

Money: The currency is the pound (£), divided into 100 pence (p). Coins: 1p, 2p, 5p, 10p, 20p, 50p and £1. Notes: £5, £10, £20, £50. All the major credit cards are widely accepted, as are traveller's cheques. Currency exchange facilities are available at banks and bureaux de change.

Communications: International calls can be made from any public phone box. Public phones take either coins (from 10p upwards) or phonecards, which can be bought for £1–£20 from post offices and newsagents. In general, international calls are charged at a cheaper rate from Mon.–Fri. 8 p.m.–8 a.m. and at weekends.

The postal service is efficient. EC letters are automatically sent airmail but you should specify if you want other overseas mail to go by air, as it will otherwise go surface. Stamps can be bought at post offices, from vending machines and at some newsagents.

Electricity: 230/240v AC.

Business hours: BANKS: Mon.–Fri. 9.30 a.m.–4.30 p.m.; Sat. 9 a.m.–12 p.m.

POST OFFICES: Mon.–Fri. 9 a.m.–5.30 p.m.; Sat. 9 a.m.–12.30 p.m.

SHOPS: Mon.–Fri. 9 a.m.–5 or 5.30 p.m.; many shops stay open later on Thursdays and Saturdays, some also open on Sundays. On Wednesday some shops in small towns close at 1 p.m.

OFFICES: Mon.–Fri. 9 a.m.–5 p.m.

Holidays: 1 January (and 2 January in Scotland); 18 March (in Northern Ireland); Good Friday; Easter Monday (except in Scotland); the first and last Mondays in May; 12 July (in Northern Ireland); first Monday in August (in Scotland); last Monday in August (not Scotland); 25 and 26 December.

Climate: Unpredictable. The south usually has the best of the weather; in the north and in Scotland temperatures tend to be lower. Rain is common and temperatures seldom exceed 21°C.

DO'S AND DON'TS

The British were once renowned for their manners, but standards have slipped somewhat in recent years. Nonetheless, good manners continue to be appreciated and expected. Do say please and thank you, don't queue jump – barging to the front of the queue when a bus arrives will earn you distinct mutterings of disapproval if not a loud verbal accusation.

Notoriously reserved, the Brits consider a handshake to be sufficient greeting; women may kiss each other if they are good friends, men never. Don't take it as an insult if your friendly 'hello' elicits little response – the British are unaccustomed to striking up conversations with strangers. The weather is always a safe starting point if you do feel like persevering in talking to the natives. And once you get chatting, there are few subjects which are taboo (bragging about how much you earn is one). Popular talking points, depending on whom you're talking to, include politics, the Royal Family and football.

Great British traditions include afternoon tea at 4 o'clock; roast Sunday lunch; talking about the weather; always carrying an umbrella; 10% tip to taxis, hairdressers and waiters.

WHERE TO GO FOR WHAT

The capital, LONDON, as the former heart of one of the world's greatest empires, is a city worth getting to know. Moreover it provides a good (if expensive) base from which to see some of England's most attractive towns. Follow the Thames south-west to

WINDSOR, site of a huge castle still used by the Royal Family, despite being badly damaged by fire at the end of 1992. Nearby ETON is a famous public school which can be seen as one of England's finest institutions or not, depending on your political point of view.

An hour's journey from London will take you to OXFORD, home of Britain's (some say the world's) most prestigious university. The university colleges buildings are some 700 years old and the sort of sights overseas visitors have in mind when dreaming of 'Olde England'. Oxford's great rival, CAMBRIDGE, has a university that dates back to the 13th century. Darwin, Byron and Newton are among its more illustrious former students.

The COTSWOLDS show England's green and pleasant land at its best. Here quaint villages with outlandish names such as Stow-on-the-Wold, Chipping Norton and Shipton-under-Wychwood are dotted amongst the rolling green hills – ideal rambling country. STRATFORD-UPON-AVON is the birthplace of England's greatest playwright, William Shakespeare. You can still visit the house in which he was born and that of his wife, Anne Hathaway. The Elizabethan town is also home to the Royal Shakespeare Company.

The elegant Georgian spa town of BATH was, in its heyday, one of the most fashionable places in the land. Successive generations of the aristocracy came to 'take the waters' and left behind them a rich architectural legacy. SALISBURY is dominated by its outstanding 13th-century cathedral, and on the outskirts of town (16 km north) is the ancient religious site of STONEHENGE, which remains a source of mystery and speculation. The stone circle dates back to at least 1500 BC, and one theory has it that the 5-metre stones were an astronomical calendar which was subsequently taken over by the Druids for their sun-worshipping festivals. Because of vandalism, the monument is cordoned off and can only be seen at a distance.

In the western-most corner of England is the wild and rugged countryside of DEVON, and the rocky coastline and sandy beaches of CORNWALL – Britain's answer to the French Riviera. This part of England enjoys an unusually mild climate. Good bases from which to explore it are Exeter, Plymouth or Penzance.

There's spectacular scenery in the north-west of England, too. The LAKE DISTRICT has attracted a long line of admirers: William Wordsworth lived in the tiny village of Grasmere; a few kilometres further on is Keswick, where Lamb, Keats, Shelley, Tennyson and Ruskin all stayed at one time. Hikers and climbers will readily understand the attraction.

Although many of their inhabitants would prefer that it were otherwise, Wales and Scotland come under British rule. Referring to the whole of the UK as 'England' will not go down well; these are, after all, historically distinct nations with their own culture and language. About a fifth of WALES' 3 million inhabitants speak Welsh, and you will see many signs in the native tongue. For a small country it provides some outstanding opportunities for getting away from it all, such as the SNOWDONIA NATIONAL PARK. The terrain is ideal for climbing, hiking, camping or hostelling. The 13th-century town of CAERNARFON has a well-preserved medieval castle where the investiture of Prince Charles (Prince of Wales) took place.

SCOTLAND, too, has some outstanding scenery. The glens and mountains, lochs and islands of the SCOTTISH HIGHLANDS are unique in their unspoilt beauty. EDINBURGH, the capital, has a most dramatic setting: its fairytale castle sits on an extinct volcano, dominating the city, with hills and sea all around. The New Town dates from the Georgian era; the Old Town to the days when Scotland was an independent nation and bloody battles with the English were fought on the cobbled streets.

INTERNAL TRAVEL
Air: Expensive and unnecessary. Unless you're in a hurry, Great Britain is not big enough to warrant extensive air travel.
Rail: British Rail has an extensive network and its InterCity trains connect all major cities. The catch is that it's expensive — British Rail is not covered by Eurail or Inter-rail — and there are a baffling variety of tickets and passes to choose from, depending on when you travel (Fridays and weekends tend to be more expensive than other days). For individual journeys, a cheap day-return (valid only on the day of purchase, after 9.30 a.m. on weekdays and any time weekends) is often the best buy. If you are under 24 or a full-time student in Britain, the Young Person's Railcard is good value. It costs £16 from any station and offers 30% off all rail tickets for a year.

There are several rover tickets you can buy:

The British Rail All-Line Rail Rover offers unlimited travel throughout the UK for 7 days (£230) or 14 days (£375).

The BritRail Pass can be purchased only in North America and is available from travel agents or by writing direct to BritRail Travel International, 10th Floor, 1500 Broadway, New York, NY 10036. It entitles you to unlimited rail travel in England, Scotland and Wales, excluding the London Underground, and is valid for 8, 15, 22 days or one month (days must run consecutively). Prices are $219, $339, $425 or $495 respectively. If you are 25 or under, prices drop by 30%.

The BritRail Flexipass is subject to similar restrictions to the BritRail Pass and available from the same agents. It permits second-class travel on 4 days from 8; 8 from 15; or 15 days in one month. Prices are $189, $269 or $395. Youth passes are 30% cheaper. Under-25s are elibible for a pass giving 15 days over two months, which costs $309.

If you plan to spend a lot of time in a certain part of England, Wales or Scotland, regional rover tickets are available for 7 or more days between Easter and October. For example, the Freedom of Scotland Pass offers unlimited travel in Scotland for 8 consecutive days (£99), 8 days of travel over a 15-day period (£115) or 15 consecutive days (£139).

Bus: Coach travel is far cheaper than rail travel. The main operator is National Express, which links all major cities and most tourist areas. The centre of the network is Victoria Coach Station, Buckingham Palace Road, London SW1 (tel. 0171 730 0202). Services are frequent and coaches reasonably comfortable. Again, the ticket price often depends on your time of travel (Fridays and weekends are more expensive). It's advisable to reserve your tickets in advance as coaches are often crowded. Cheaper standby tickets can be bought on the day of travel but you will not be guaranteed your preferred departure time.

If you are a full-time student in Britain or under 23, you can buy a Young Person's Coach Card which qualifies you for 30% off standard fares. The card costs £7 and is valid for a year. Overseas visitors can purchase a Britexpress Card which give 30% off standard fares over 30 consecutive days. The card costs £12 and can be bought in Britain or overseas. The Tourist Trail Pass provides unlimited travel for periods from 3–15 days at prices ranging from £39–145 for under-26s.

The Slow Coach links youth hostels throughout England, Scotland and Wales on a 1600 km trip. The ticket is £88 and is valid for two months. This is a 'jump-on, jump-off service'. You get off at any stop and stay as long as you want, then jump on the next Slow Coach coming through. For further details, contact the Slow Coach, 71 Brandenstoke, Wiltshire SN15 4EL (tel. 01249 891 859)

Bicycle: There are no facilities for hiring bikes at British Rail stations, so ask at a tourist office for local suggestions. If you want to transport your bike by train, check with the station first. Cycles may not be carried at all on some routes and on others reservations are compulsory, sometimes for a fee.

Taxi: Some form of taxi service operates in all towns. Both taxis and minicabs have fitted meters. Taxis may be hailed in the street or found at taxi-ranks, minicabs must be booked by telephone.

Car-hire: Rental facilities are available in all towns. Remember that Britons drive on the left.

Hitching: Hitching in Britain is generally good except on Sundays when lack of traffic can mean long waits. Hitching is not permitted on motorways but is allowed on exit and entrance roads and at service stations.

ACCOMMODATION

Budget accommodation in the UK is widespread but relatively expensive. Tourist Information Centres will book a room for you, though booking fees vary from office to office: £2 is the norm but you can pay £5 or more in London. Tourist Information Centres also operate a useful book-a-bed-ahead service for around £2.50, which enables you to make a reservation at your next destination. In places popular with tourists, booking ahead is essential.

Youth hostels: Britain has an extensive network of IYHF hostels, run by separate English, Welsh, Scottish and Irish associations. Prices vary according to the standard of facilities available, the time of year and the age of the user, but tend to range from £7–12 (more in London). Non-members pay a supplement. Most hostels operate a curfew – usually around 11 p.m.

There are also a number of independent hostels in the main places of interest – their prices and facilities are generally on a par with IYHF hostels, except in London where standards can be poor. YMCA/YWCA hostels are generally of a high quality but expensive.

Student residences: Rooms in student residences are often available during the Easter (mid-March to mid-April) and summer (mid-June to early September) vacations. Students with ID will pay around £12. Universities may also rent out student flats during the vacations – which can work out economically for groups, though you may be expected to stay at least a week.

Hotels and pensions: Hotels in the United Kingdom are amongst the best and, therefore, the most expensive in the world. There is a vast array of different types of hotel in Britain, ranging from huge five-star establishments in the centre of the cities, to small family-run hotels with only three or four bedrooms. These are more likely to be called guesthouses and it is possible to get hold of a very nice room with en-suite facilities for less than £20.

B&B: Bed and breakfast is a traditional British institution: you get a room in a family home and a hearty English breakfast of sausage, eggs, bacon and tomatoes, etc. Prices usually start from £15 but range from £20 in London.

Campsites: Camping is the best option if you want to keep costs really low. Most main points of interest will have a campsite, though standards and prices vary dramatically. On average expect to pay around £5–8. In small towns and villages, local farmers will usually let you pitch your tent on their land if you ask permission first. The main drawback to camping is the wet climate – make sure your tent is waterproof and your sleeping bag warm!

The tourist offices publish lists of approved B&Bs and campsites.

FOOD

British cuisine has improved dramatically over the last decade and eating out need no longer be an expensive and tasteless affair. The best examples of traditional British fare are the roasts (lamb and beef) often served in hotels as set-lunch menus or buffets at reasonable cost – around £7 per person including dessert. Deliciously stodgy British puddings are not to be scoffed at – 'spotted dick' (raisin sponge) and custard is a perennial favourite. Treat yourself at least once to a traditional afternoon tea consisting of scones served with jam and clotted cream, and a pot of tea. Afternoon tea is served in many hotels or, more cheaply, in some of the big department stores.

'Pub grub' is another favourite with the Brits. Served at lunchtime – only a few pubs offer evening menus – it's usually a range of home-cooked quiches, pies, baked potatoes, or sausage and chip combinations.

For evening meals, the best value meals can be found in the enormous range of ethnic restaurants, a welcome legacy of Britain's immigrant communities. In particular, Chinese and Indian restaurants usually offer excellent menus at around £3–£5 per dish. Or there are the usual pizza and fast-food chains, together with the traditional takeaway fish'n'chips shops.

For picnic lunches, all the major supermarket chains (Sainsbury's, Tesco's, Asda, Safeway's) sell an impressive variety of British cheeses – Cheddar, Stilton, Cheshire, etc. – together with fresh bread, as do bakeries and delis.

The classic complaint about British beer is that it is warm. Nevertheless the British are proud of their beers and a wide variety will be sold in any pub. Bitter is a dark rich beer, sold on tap; stout is sweet and rich; light ale is lighter and more akin to lager; lager is lager; and real ale is the naturally fermented brew that enthusiasts will walk miles to get a pint of. Beers, spirits and wines can also be bought at 'off-licences' or supermarkets.

BUDGETING

Britain can eat away at your budget – especially if your trip includes a visit to London. Even if you stay exclusively in hostels, a bed for the night will cost you around £9 (£15–18 in London). Food is less of a problem: if you choose carefully, you can buy a decent meal in a restaurant, particularly an ethnic one, for around £5. Fast-food outlets are even cheaper, and fish'n'chips should only cost you a couple of pounds. Booze is expensive: beer costs around £1.60 a pint. Wine is better value (you can get a drinkable bottle for around £2.50). Prices rise sharply in clubs and discos, where you should also watch out for cover charges of about £4 (more in London).

Transport is not cheap, though costs can vary considerably according to which method you use and which of the bewildering variety of tickets you buy. Coach travel is generally the cheapest and the best deals tend to be those available to students. Admission to the sights can cost £1–2 outside the capital and up to £4 in London, though many are free.

Work opportunities in Britain are good in the major tourist areas. EC nationals are legally entitled to work here; there are also working holiday schemes for young people from America, Canada, Australia and New Zealand. Good possibilities for casual work exist in pubs, fast-food outlets, restaurants and hotels. If you know where to go and when, you may also be able to catch up with the harvests. For those with office skills, particularly typing and word processing, there are numerous temporary agencies such as Manpower and Brook Street Bureau. These agencies can be very successful in setting you up with a temporary office job for good wages. Word processing operators get around £7–8 per hour, more in London. Some temporary agencies also sign up people for warehouse and labouring jobs. Newspapers are also a good source of job vacancies. Failing that, try your luck at the nearest Jobcentre, which holds information on local vacancies.

Au pairing is an option for girls. *The Lady* and the free magazine *TNT* (free at various places around London: check outside Campus Travel, Grosvenor Gardens) list job vacancies including au pair work. Teaching English is a popular choice since there are hundreds of English language summer schools in Britain, but budding teachers will need a formal EFL qualification or, at the very least, a university degree, and you must apply to your chosen school well in advance of the summer rush. A list of schools approved by the British Council is available from ARELS-FELCO, 2 Pontypool Place, Valentine Place, London SE1 8QF.

FURTHER INFORMATION

United States Embassy, 24 Grosvenor Square, London W1A 1AE (tel. 0171 499 9000).

Canadian High Commission, McDonald House, 38 Grosvenor Street, London W1X 0AB (tel. 0171 258 6600).

High Commission of the Commonwealth of Australia, Australia House, The Strand, London WC2B 4LU (tel. 0171 379 4334).

Embassy of the Republic of South Africa, South Africa House, Trafalgar Square, London WC2N 5DP (tel. 0171 930 4488).

New Zealand High Commission, New Zealand House, 80 Haymarket, London SW1Y 4TQ (tel. 0171 930 8422).

British Tourist Authority, Thames Tower, Black's Road, Hammersmith, London W6 9EL (tel. 0181 846 9000).

The Northern Ireland Tourist Board, 11 Berkeley Street, London W1X 6LN (tel. 0171 493 0601). Mon.–Fri. 9 a.m.–5.15 p.m.

The Scottish Tourist Board, 19 Cockspur Street, London SW1Y 5BL (tel. 0171 930 8661). Mon.–Fri. 9 a.m.–5 p.m.

The Wales Desk, British Travel Centre, 12 Regent Street, London W1 (tel. 0171 409 0969).

Background reading: *Let's Go: Britain & Ireland* (Pan Books Ltd) is a good budget guide to the UK, while the *Directory of Summer Jobs in Britain* (Vacation Work), lists employment opportunities.

London

AIRPORT FACILITIES

London has five airports: Heathrow, Gatwick, Luton, Stansted and City Airport. Bus and coach services link Heathrow with Gatwick, Stansted and Luton Airports.

LONDON HEATHROW

Heathrow, 24 km west of London, is one of the world's busiest airports. It has four terminals, all of which have currency exchange facilities, information desks offering tourist information, eating facilities and duty-free outlets. Terminals 2 and 4 also have post offices.

Rail: The Piccadilly line on the Underground (tube) runs from all terminals into London and vice versa from around 5 a.m.–11.30 p.m. The journey from Heathrow to Piccadilly (the heart of London) takes around 50 minutes and costs £3.80. It's quick and cheap but not recommended for people with a lot of luggage.

Airbus: There are two routes operating from all terminals: the A1 to Victoria railway station and the A2 to Euston railway station. Journey time to either destination is 60–80 minutes, depending on the traffic and which terminal you leave from, and costs around £5.

Bus: Green Line bus 701 runs to London Victoria via Hyde Park Corner and Kensington High Street. If you arrive by night, the N97 nightbus runs to Trafalgar Square.

Taxi: Expensive. You'll pay around £30 for a 40-minute ride to the city centre.

LONDON GATWICK

Gatwick Airport lies 44 km south of London. There are two terminals: North and South. Both have information desks in the International Arrivals Concourse, as well as eating facilities, shops and duty-free outlets. Banks located in the Arrival and Departure Halls of both terminals stay open 24 hours on alternate nights. South Terminal also has a post office. For flight enquiries, call 01293 535 353.

Rail: British Rail's Gatwick Express is the easiest way to get to London, with departures every 15 minutes for Victoria, where you can then change on to the tube. Services run from approximately 6.20 a.m.–11 p.m. and the journey lasts 30 minutes. A single ticket costs £8.60. There is also a service to London Bridge.

Bus: There is a direct express coach, the number 777, which runs between Gatwick and London Victoria coach station. This service runs every hour and the journey takes about 60 minutes. A single ticket costs around £7.50.

Taxi: Expensive; it costs about £50 to the city centre.

LUTON

Luton lies 52 km north-west of London and deals mostly with charter flights. It has the usual facilities, including currency exchange, eating facilities and duty-free. Take the British Rail's Luton Flyer to King's Cross station or bus 757 to Victoria.

LONDON STANSTED

London's newest airport lies 50 km north-east of the city centre and is aimed primarily at the short-haul business traveller from Europe. It has far more limited facilities than its older and larger counterparts, but there is a direct rail link operating every 30 minutes to Liverpool Street station. Journey time is 40 minutes. There is also an infrequent coach service to Victoria coach station.

CITY AIRPORT
City Airport has relatively limited facilities compared to the major airports, but does offers duty-free, currency exchange and eating facilities. To get there, take the tube to London Bridge followed by the D11 bus. Alternatively take the River Boat to Canary Wharf, from where you can get a shuttle bus. A taxi costs around £15–20.

USEFUL ADDRESSES

Main tourist office: The British Travel Centre has branches at Victoria railway station forecourt and 12 Regent Street, London W1. Open Mon.–Fri. 9.30 a.m.–6 p.m.; Sat.–Sun. 10 a.m.–4 p.m.

Accommodation agencies: There are a few accommodation agencies in London which will provide you with a private room, usually for a minimum stay of two or three nights. Alma Tourist Services, 21 Griffiths Rd, Wimbledon (tel. 0181 542 3771); Best London Homes, 126 Lower Richmond Road (tel. 0181 780 9045).

Main post office: 24–8 William IV Street (near Trafalgar Square) has extended opening hours (8 a.m.–8 p.m.)

US Embassy: 24 Grosvenor Square, London W1A 1AE.

Emergency Services: Police, fire and ambulance: 999

There are two late-opening chemists in London: Bliss at 5 Marble Arch W1H 7AP, which is open Monday–Friday, 9 a.m.–midnight, while their branch at 50–56 Willesden Lane NW6 7SX is open daily between 9 a.m. and 2 a.m. In the event of medical/dental emergencies, immediate first-aid treatment is available for all visitors, after which charges are made unless the visitor's country has a reciprocal health agreement with the UK. If urgent treatment is required, go to the nearest hospital casualty department, where you will be seen as soon as possible.

GETTING ABOUT

Transportation in London is fast and efficient. Unfortunately it is also expensive, and tends to be overcrowded. Don't despair: if you invest in a decent map, you may be surprised at how much you can see on foot.

London underground (the tube): The tube runs from 5.30–12 a.m. and is the quickest way to travel round London. It operates on a zonal system: tickets are priced according to the number of zones you pass through and can be bought at tube stations, either over the counter or from ticket machines. Most stations have automatic barriers in which you must insert your ticket – make sure you retrieve it from the slot on top of the machine, though, as you'll need to pass through a barrier at the end of your journey.

Large maps are located within the stations showing the extensive network which covers the whole capital and its environs. The twelve tube lines have different names and are colour coded. As long as you have a map – available free at any station – it is quite easy to find your way around the network. If you need to change trains, simply follow the signs for the line you want.

Bus: London buses tend to get snarled up in heavy traffic, so allow plenty of time for your journey. Tickets operate on the same zonal system and must be bought on board, either from the driver or, if there is one, from the conductor, who will come round to your seat. Most useful are the night buses operating on certain routes, which depart hourly from Trafalgar Square between midnight and 5 a.m.

If you intend travelling around London by public transport, it is a good idea to invest in a Travelcard (one-day, weekly and monthly cards are available), which gives you unlimited travel on all London Transport buses and the tube; you can purchase them from underground stations and from certain newsagents (a London transport logo will be displayed in the window of newsagents selling Travelcards). British Rail stations sell a Travelcard which will cover you for suburban rail services as well tubes and buses (useful if you're planning an excursion to Greenwich or Hampton Court, for example). One-day Travelcards have certain restrictions: they are not valid on night buses, and on weekdays they can only be purchased after 9.30 a.m. (they are available all day at weekends). A one-day Travelcard costs from £2.80 (for zones one and two only) to £3.80 (all zones). An all-zones weekly Travelcard costs from £31.20; you will need to take along a passport photo when applying.

Information leaflets are available from London Underground stations and travel centres such as those in Piccadilly and Oxford Circus stations. The 24-hour London travel information line is on 0171 222 1234.

Taxi: London's black cabs can be hailed on the street, provided the yellow FOR HIRE sign on the front of the cab is illuminated. Fares are metered and expensive, and if your destination is more than six miles from the city centre they are not obliged to take you (if your accommodation is on the outskirts, you may have problems getting home by taxi late at night: expect to be refused by several cabbies before you find one who'll take the fare). Cabbies usually know London's streets backwards and can be an excellent source of information.

Bicycle: Cycling in London is a precarious activity. There are few cycle paths and you will have to contend with heavy traffic and fumes. However, the London Cycling Campaign is lobbying to make the city safer and more accessible to cyclists. They publish *The London Cyclists Map* for £3.95, available from Waterstones bookshops (branches throughout the city) or from the LCC (tel. 0171 928 7220). Bicycle theft is rampant in London; anything, including wheels, seats and pedals, will be stolen if not bolted on or locked up. Look in the Yellow Pages phone directory for hire shops. Expect to pay around £12 a day.

Car-hire: All the international car-hire companies have offices in London. Look in the phone directory or ask at the tourist board.

SIGHTS

A combination of a thousand years of history and tradition, plenty of open green spaces and the buzz of being Europe's biggest city make London an experience not to be missed. In fact, there are three Londons to take into account, each with a different feel: the CITY OF LONDON (the financial and administrative centre of Great Britain); WESTMINSTER (the political, royal and religious centre); and the WEST END (home of the British theatre and cinema, smart shops and clubs).

Despite its size, London is a walking city. To make the most of it, try to use your feet rather than public transport.

THE CITY OF LONDON

The London of the 11th century is that area known as the City. In this 'square mile', the wheelings and dealings of the Stock Exchange and big business take place, and it is here that the Bank of England and Royal Exchange have their headquarters. At its heart is the Renaissance cathedral of ST PAUL'S. Built by Sir Christopher Wren in the aftermath of the Great Fire of London of 1666, St Paul's impressive dome dominated the city skyline until the intrusion of modern office developments. Wren, Wellington and Nelson are buried in the crypt. (Mon.–Sat. 8.30 a.m.–4 p.m. Admission £2.50; U: St Paul's). Nearby is the OLD BAILEY, Britain's foremost criminal court. You can watch 'mi learned gentlemen' in their wigs and gowns from the court gallery when court is in session (Sept.–July).

TOWER BRIDGE is one of London's most famous landmarks, and when they're not busy repairing it you can go inside. Virtually next door stands the TOWER OF LONDON. Dating back to William the Conqueror, the Tower has served as prison, palace and mint. Two of Henry VIII's eight wives, Anne Boleyn and Katherine Howard, were executed in the courtyard on his command. Inside the maze-like rooms you can see the Crown Jewels, as well as a magnificent collection of armoury and relics from many of the monarchs and noblemen who lived and died in the Tower. (Mar.–Oct. Mon.–Sat. 9 a.m.–6.30 p.m.; Sun 2–6 p.m.; Nov.–Feb. 10 a.m.–5 p.m. U: Tower Hill.)

WESTMINSTER AND THE WEST END
This area stretches roughly from HYDE PARK – whose Speakers' Corner is a national venue for impromptu free speech on Sundays – to WESTMINSTER ABBEY, a stately edifice built and rebuilt between the 11th and 13th centuries. Since William the Conqueror, almost every British monarch has been crowned here, and it has been the site of all royal burials since Henry III. Many of Britain's most famous citizens are also buried here, including Chaucer, Tennyson and Charles Dickens (Mon.–Fri. 9 a.m.–4 p.m., Sat. 9 a.m.–2 p.m. and 4–5 p.m. U: Westminster).

Directly opposite the Abbey is the Palace of Westminster, more popularly known as the HOUSES OF PARLIAMENT. The famous chime of BIG BEN, the bell housed in the huge clock tower, is known the world over. The Palace itself was almost totally destroyed by fire in 1834, and the Chamber of the House of Commons was wrecked by German bombing in World War II. Ironically it is Westminster Hall, the oldest part of the Palace which has survived the longest; this enormous hall, dominated by huge oak beams, was built originally by William the Conqueror in the 11th century. The abdication of Edward II was declared in the hall and both Charles I and Guy Fawkes were found guilty of treason here. The interior is steeped in history and the architecture and the fittings are suitably dramatic. Tickets to watch debates from the public galleries are issued on a first-come-first-served basis; alternatively you may be able to obtain tickets from your Embassy in London (visiting Brits can apply to their MP).

WHITEHALL – the location of British government offices – occupies the area adjoining the Palace of Westminster. The Cenotaph war memorial and 10 DOWNING STREET, official residence of the Prime Minister, are only a short stroll from the Houses of Parliament, but security precautions may prevent you from getting more than a glimpse of No. 10's famous black door. You can, however, visit the CABINET WAR ROOMS in Whitehall, where Churchill's War Cabinet met at the height of World War II. (Daily 10 a.m.–5.15 p.m. U: Westminster.)

THE MALL is the tree-lined boulevard which leads from TRAFALGAR SQUARE, site of NELSON'S COLUMN, to BUCKINGHAM PALACE, home of the monarchy. The Palace itself is open to the public (at a price) during August and September (daily 8.30 a.m.–5.30 p.m.), but you can view the Changing of the Guard for free (daily

Apr.–Aug. 11–11.30 a.m.; alternate days Sept.–Mar. U: St James Park).

LEICESTER SQUARE is the hub of London's nightlife. The area just north of it is SOHO, the old red-light district, which is crammed with restaurants and small clubs. Nearby lies the centre of London's CHINATOWN (U: Leicester Square), and the CHARING CROSS ROAD, which is packed with bookshops. Also within easy walking distance is COVENT GARDEN, a former vegetable market which has been transformed into a touristy shopping arcade. There's still a buzz in the air, though, and a constant stream of excellent street performers who put on shows for the punters in the piazza before passing round the hat (U: Covent Garden).

London has so many museums and galleries that it would be impossible to list them all here. Choose carefully rather than trying to fit them all in. Among the best is the BRITISH MUSEUM in Great Russell Street. Huge as it is, only a fraction of its vast collection of predominantly medieval antiquities can be shown at any one time. (Mon.–Sat. 10 a.m.–5 p.m.; Sun. 2.30–6 p.m. U: Russell Square.) In Exhibition Road are the NATURAL HISTORY MUSEUM and the SCIENCE MUSEUM (Mon.–Sat. 10 a.m.–6 p.m.; Sun. 11 a.m.–6 p.m. U: South Kensington). The IMPERIAL WAR MUSEUM has a huge collection of documents and artefacts from the two World Wars (daily 10 a.m.–6 p.m. U: Lambeth North.) And even museum-haters will enjoy the MUSEUM OF THE MOVING IMAGE MOMI, a lively and very 'hands-on' exhibition covering the history of cinema and TV.

As far as galleries are concerned, the NATIONAL GALLERY has one of the world's finest collections of Western European art, including greats such as Rembrandt and Raphael. (Mon.–Sat. 10 a.m.–6 p.m.; Sun. 2 p.m.–6 p.m. U: Charing Cross.) The NATIONAL PORTRAIT GALLERY holds several thousand portraits of distinguished British men and women spanning several centuries. (Mon.–Fri. 10 a.m.–6 p.m.; Sat. 10 a.m.–6 p.m.; Sun. 12–6 p.m.)

If you are in the mood to shop, the most famous department store is HARRODS in Knightsbridge. For a good day out as well as a shopping expedition, try one of London's many markets: the PORTOBELLO (in the road of the same name) sells fruit and veg, general goods or antiques, depending which day you visit (U: Notting Hill Gate); CAMDEN, by the Regent's Canal, is a weekend favourite with both Londoners and tourists alike. The market is spread out over several locations and sells clothes, accessories, antiques, jewellery and general bric-à-brac, and there are some pleasant canalside eateries (U: Camden Town).

ACCOMMODATION

There is a serious shortage of cheap places to stay, especially in the summer, so it is essential to book ahead as you will struggle to find a place in a hostel, hall of residence or one of the cheaper B&Bs if you leave it until your arrival. A useful source of information is the *Cheap Sleep Guide to Europe* (HarperCollins). Outside the IYHF and a few independent hostels, it's near impossible to find accommodation under £18 per night. Student and youth hostels average £12–15, halls of residence £20 for a single (and not much less per person for a double). B&Bs average £18 for a single and £30 for a double.

All the tourist offices operate a booking service but charge £5 for the privilege (see **Useful Addresses**, p. 210). If you are telephoning for a reservation, the main number is 0171 730 8101. The London Tourist Board also runs an advance booking service from 26 Grosvenor Gardens which takes credit-card bookings on 0171 824 8844.

Youth hostels: London IYHF hostels will only admit members and therefore require to see membership cards.

Oxford Street, 14–18 Noel Street (tel. 0171 734 1618). Juniors £16; seniors £18. (U: Oxford Circus)

Carter Lane, 36 Carter Lane (tel. 0171 236 4965). Juniors £16; seniors £19. (U: St Paul's)

King George VI Memorial Hostel, Holland House, Holland Walk (tel. 0171 937 0748). Juniors £15; seniors £17. (U: Holland Park or High Street Kensington)

Earls Court, 38 Bolton Gardens (tel. 0171 373 7083). Juniors £14.50; seniors £16. (U: Earls Court)

Hampstead Heath, 4 Wellgarth Road (tel. 0181 458 9054). Juniors £13.50; seniors £14.50. (U: Golders Green)

Highgate Village, 84 Highgate West Hill (tel. 0181 340 1831). Juniors £9.60; seniors £11.30. (U: Archway)

Other hostels/student residences:

International Students House, 229 Great Portland Street (tel. 0171 631 8300). Hundreds of beds in a huge complex. Singles and doubles £19.75–23.40 with breakfast. (U: Great Portland Street)

C/E/I International Youth Hostel, 61 Chepstow Place, Notting Hill Gate (tel. 0171 221 8134). £11.50–50.00. (U: Bayswater)

Allen Hall Summer Hostel, Allen Hall, 28 Beaufort Street (tel. 0171 351 1296). Open July–Aug. From £20.

B&B: There are vast numbers of B&Bs in London. Some of the cheaper ones are soul-destroying places which will make you wish you'd booked a hostel. There are cheap B&Bs in the following areas: Victoria, Earls Court, Notting Hill Gate, Paddington and Bayswater. Some of the better ones (which may need to be booked ahead) include:

Beaver Hotel, 57–9 Philbeach Gardens (tel. 0171 373 4553). Doubles from £40. (U: Earls Court)

Cheviot Hotel, 8 St George's Drive (tel. 0171 834 6018/5993). Great budget B&B in heart of city, 2 mins from Victoria station. All rooms en-suite, colour TV, tea/coffee-making facilities. Prices from £12 per person per night in a triple, £15 in a twin. Book ahead if possible. (U: Victoria)

York House, 28 Philbeach Gardens (tel. 0171 373 7519). Doubles from £40. (U: Earls Court)

Luna-Simone Hotel, 47 Belgrave Road (tel. 0171 834 5897). Doubles from £35. (U: Victoria)

Gower House Hotel, 57 Gower Street (tel. 0171 636 4685). Doubles from £42. (U: Goodge Street)

Private accommodation: Staying with a local family is an increasingly popular option, and there are agencies which will arrange this type of accommodation. Ask for leaflets at the London Tourist Board offices at Victoria station.

For longer-term accommodation, check out the 'Rooms to Let' or 'Flatshare' pages of the *Evening Standard* newspaper or *Loot*, a daily paper available from newsagents. Newsagents' windows are also good sources of accommodation ads.

Campsites: All the sites listed below are outside the city centre, so remember to budget for Travelcards or daily fares back and forth into London:

Hackney Camping, Millfields Road, Hackney Marshes (tel. 0181 985 7656). June–Aug. £4.50 per person. Bus 22 from Piccadilly.

Crystal Palace Camp Site, Crystal Palace Parade (tel. 0181 778 7155). £3.50 per person. BR from London Bridge or Victoria to Crystal Palace.

Tent City, Old Oak Common Lane, East Acton (tel. 0181 749 9074). June–Sept. £5.50 per person. Dormitory accommodation also available. (U: East Acton).

FOOD

There is no food that cannot be had in London. The capital has a staggering choice of restaurants representing just about every cuisine and nationality – Chinese, Indian, Thai, Italian, Japanese, Turkish, Greek . . . the list goes on. And nearly all can be sampled for less than a tenner. Chinese and Indian restaurants are particularly good value.

The West End has always been packed with eateries but now every London high street has its share of good restaurants. Food tends to be cheaper outside the tourist areas like Covent Garden and Piccadilly. For the biggest choice of Chinese restaurants, head towards Soho. Some suggestions:

Stockpot, 40 Panton Street, SW1Y 4CA (tel. 0171 839 5142). Cheap food such as spaghetti and sausage, egg and bacon fry ups. Also traditional English puddings like apple crumble and custard.

Chelsea Kitchen, 98 King's Road, SW3 4TZ (tel. 0171 589 1330. Run by the same people as above.

Pollo, 20 Old Compton Street, W1V 5PE (tel. 0171 734 5917). Cheap pasta restaurant always packed out.

Jimmy's Restaurant, 23 Frith Street, W1V 5TS. Cheapest Greek restaurant in Soho.

Wong Kei, 41–3 Wardour Street, W1V 3HA (tel. 0171 437 6833). Good value Chinese restaurant notorious for its rude waiters. You can fill up for £3.

Khans, 13–15 Westbourne Grove, W2 4UA (tel. 0171 727 5420). Good curries at reasonable prices.

The usual chain restaurants abound all over London – Pizza Hut, Pizzaland, Garfunkel's – together with fast-food chains such as Wimpy, McDonald's and Kentucky Fried Chicken where you can get a meal for a couple of quid. Greek and Chinese takeaways are also popular for their good value. However, workers' cafés and pubs (provided you avoid the tourist pubs) are without doubt the best places to eat cheap filling meals for between £3–5. At lunch time, cafés, pubs and sandwich bars also offer a wide range of sandwiches for £1–2.

Sainsbury's, Tesco and Safeway are the cheapest supermarkets, and if it's a good day you can't do better than to get a picnic together and head for one of the parks. The small corner shops offer a more personal service, but are more expensive.

ENTERTAINMENT

The best way to work your way round the myriad of entertainments London has to offer is to buy one of the weekly listings magazines, *Time Out* or *City Limits*. Both offer comprehensive coverage of what's going on around town.

First port of call for many Londoners on a Friday night is the pub. There are countless pubs in the capital, many of which are packed out on Friday and Saturday nights as Londoners welcome in the weekend. Most open from around 11 a.m.–11.30 p.m.

Avid club-goers will find plenty of choice in the capital. Popular rock and pop venues include the Marquee at 105 Charing Cross Road (U: Tottenham Court Road), and the Wag Club at 35 Wardour Street (U: Piccadilly Circus). Ronnie Scott's at 47 Frith Street is internationally known for jazz (but it's expensive); cheaper is the Bass Clef at 35 Coronet Street (U: Old Street). Avoid flashy places like the Hippodrome, where the prices are high. Check your listings magazine to find out which clubs play which kind of music and on what days. To see the major international bands, check out the bigger venues, like Wembley or the Apollo Hammersmith (formerly the Hammersmith Odeon). Expect to pay for the privilege.

London has a thriving film culture and a wide range of current and past releases can be seen around town. Expect to pay around £7 for a ticket – less for the first (matinée) performance on weekdays and all day Monday. The most expensive cinemas are those centred around Leicester Square (with the exception of the Prince Charles, just off Leicester Square, which has seats for £1.50–3.00; tel. 0171 437 8181). Independent cinemas tend to be located just outside the West End: the Screen on the Green (U: Angel), the Screen on the Hill (U: Belsize Park), the Everyman (U: Hampstead), the Ritzy (U: Brixton) and the Scala (U: King's Cross). These independents are not only much cheaper than mainstream cinemas, they offer terrific double bills and special all-night programmes where the audience is as entertaining as the movies – especially at the Scala!

London is famous for its theatre. Pick up the fortnightly *London Theatre Guide* from any theatre or information office to see what's on. The National, the Aldwych, the Royal Shakespeare Company at the Barbican, and the Royal Court usually put on the classics. In summer there's open-air theatre in Regent's Park. Prices range from around £15 to as much as £45 for top seats. Take along your ISIC to any theatre displaying an (S) in its write-up and you can buy cheap standby tickets shortly before the curtain rises. There's also a half-price ticket booth in Leicester Square where you can queue for shows listed on the board from 2.30–6.30 p.m. on the day of the performance. If you can't get discounted tickets, sitting in the 'gods' (high up in the gallery), is the cheapest way to view a show.

Classical music has several London homes including the Royal Festival Hall on the South Bank (U: Waterloo, Embankment or

Charing Cross) which often stages free concerts in the foyer; the Royal Albert Hall in Kensington Gore (U: Kensington High Street); and the relatively new Barbican Centre. The two major ballet venues are the Royal Opera House in Covent Garden (home to the Royal Ballet), and Sadlers' Wells Theatre in Rosebery Avenue, Islington (U: Angel) (for more contemporary dance). The Royal Opera House also stages opera, as does the nearby Coliseum (English-language productions only). Tickets are available from the box office and there is sometimes standing room available on the day.

For sports lovers, London has plenty of action but the overriding sports passion of the capital is football. The forthcoming battles of London's football teams are recorded in *Time Out* – call the stadium or, provided the match isn't sold out, turn up on the day to get a ticket.

EXCURSIONS

You can reach just about any part of mainland UK from London and get back again within a day. But unless you're really pushed for time, it's advisable to save the far-flung places like Edinburgh for a separate trip. The following sights are all within a 30-kilometre radius:

HAMPTON COURT PALACE was the riverside Tudor residence of Henry VIII. Built in 1525, the palace is surrounded by beautiful gardens and has an authentic Tudor maze. You can travel the 20 km from London by rail, Green Line coach, or boat. Be warned that it's expensive: there's a £7.50 entrance fee for adults. Also near the Thames, RICHMOND PARK, west of London, is the perfect place to enjoy a summer picnic or a relaxing day's walking in the countryside overlooking the capital. A royal hunting ground since 1637, it has been open to the public since 1758. The park is so huge – over 2,000 acres – that you can drive round it. It's famous for its deer and for its interesting flora and fauna. Nearby are the peaceful KEW GARDENS, where you can stroll amongst over 45,000 different plant species.

GREENWICH, home of the Maritime Museum and the *Cutty Sark*, is best reached by boat. In summer, river buses leave from Westminster Pier or Tower Hill for the 50-minute trip down the Thames to the village of Greenwich (or you can, if you must, take the train from Charing Cross). Along with a vast collection of astronomical and navigational equipment, the works of such outstanding architects as Inigo Jones and Christopher Wren can be seen here. Combined tickets are available allowing entry to several places of interest.

BRIGHTON is only 50 minutes from London and makes an

enjoyable day trip. A popular 18th-century seaside resort, it retains the easy-going atmosphere of a pleasure-seeking town. Sights include the opulent ROYAL PAVILION which was built in 1783 when the Prince Regent came to settle here and the winding shopping area of the 'Lanes'.

AFRICA AND
THE MIDDLE EAST

Africa, the 'dark continent', holds a fascination for most people. Many visit to see animals they would usually encounter only in zoos roaming freely through the game parks. Others take up voluntary work, hoping to relieve the extreme poverty experienced by so many natives. Some travel to sample the 'simple native life' for themselves. It's a continent where breathtaking beauty and outrageous injustice go hand in hand.

Egypt is something of a crossover point between Africa and the Middle East. This region, home to three of the world's major religions, has great historical and religious interest, but Israel/Palestine — considered sacred by Jews, Christians and Muslims — is characterized by political unrest. Anyone visiting Israel will not be permitted to enter any of the Arab states, with the exception of Egypt.

WHERE TO GO FOR WHAT
The dismantling of apartheid means that travellers can now visit SOUTH AFRICA without the fear of being barred entry to other African nations. The main draw is undoubtedly the fantastic Kruger National Park, with its superb opportunities for viewing game. The beaches and landscapes of Cape Town and Durban are also outstanding attractions, as are Johannesburg and the nearby, infamous township of Soweto. Everybody has their own opinion about the South African situation; but to have a realistic one, you need to see the country for yourself. Though expensive in African terms, South Africa is cheaper than most Western countries. It's not yet geared towards the budget traveller, but it's possible to find reasonably cheap accommodation.

KENYA is the most popular safari destination in Africa, though attacks on tourists in recent years have driven many tourists away to Tanzania, Zambia, Botswana and Zimbabwe. If you intend to visit Africa solely for a safari, look around to see which country offers the best current deals. Kenya's Masai Mara and Samburu game parks continue to attract the largest number of tourists, but as a result, they can get extremely crowded; other countries may have less sophisticated and therefore more 'wild' game parks. Seeing a lion or leopard is bound to be thrilling, but many tourists complain that the commercialized game parks have become something like zoos. Salt licks are left outside lodges to tempt the animals, the jeeps go right up to the wildlife, and the animals have become used to the gawping tourists.

Kenya's other main attraction is its beaches: the coastal resorts of Mombasa and Malindi are beautiful, but are heavily commercialized as a result and prices are inflated. That said, there is no shortage of budget accommodation in Kenya, though standards do vary considerably.

EGYPT presents a completely different side of Africa; historians and religious pilgrims will be enthralled by the land of the Pharaohs. Attractions include the Pyramids and the Sphinx, the tomb of Tutankhamun, the Sinai peninsula and the Nile valley. If you've money to spare you can treat yourself to an unforgettable experience such as a Nile cruise or a balloon ride over the Valley of the Kings. And for all that the capital city of Cairo is chaotic and crowded, it's definitely worth a visit. There's plenty of budget accommodation in Egypt, but you really need to see the room before agreeing to take it: cleanliness and amenities vary considerably!

If you want to try a desert safari, head for the UNITED ARAB EMIRATES or BAHRAIN. These countries are safe to visit and attitudes towards Westerners, including women, are more positive than in Gulf states like Iran and Iraq; moreover the laws on alcohol are not so strict. In addition to desert safaris, the UAE and Bahrain offer camel racing and fascinating old *souks*. The major drawback with both countries is that they're prohibitively expensive to visit so far as the majority of budget travellers are concerned. There are YHA hostels, though, which will help to save money.

TAKE HEED
When travelling in Africa and the Middle East, please respect the people, traditions, history, wildlife and culture of the country that you are in. Learn as much as you can beforehand about the country, and take care that you don't do anything that would offend the locals. Be very careful about getting into religious or political arguments, especially in the more sensitive parts of the Middle East and North Africa. It's probably wise not to mention either the Gulf War or your personal solution to the Israel/Palestine situation.

If you're in a Middle Eastern country where alcohol is banned, then don't drink. Penalties are harsh. And remember to respect religious festivals like Ramadan – if you're the type who enjoys eating out regularly as part of your travels, then it's best to avoid Muslim countries at this time. Many restaurants are closed.

Unfortunately, tourists and sites visited by tourists in Egypt have recently become the target of Islamic fundamentalist terrorists.

Recent well-publicized bomb attacks may deter many travellers from visiting Egypt.

The rules about keeping your wits about you and an eye on your valuables apply the world over, but in places like Nairobi, where the crime rate is high, you should be especially vigilant. Many travellers lose their valuables before they've even made it from the airport into Nairobi's city centre!

Female travellers should take particular care in these parts of the world. Lone women are perhaps at risk wherever they are, but in certain parts of Africa and the Middle East they can be regarded as 'fair game'. Don't walk about in shorts or a short skirt. When visiting religious sites in the Middle East or Egypt, make sure that your legs and shoulders are covered. If you're on your own in a hotel room, make sure your door can't be unlocked from the outside. And a lone female should never hitch-hike.

Healthwise, a number of inoculations may be required beforehand. Make sure you check out well in advance of your travels what medical precautions you should take. And when you're there, remember to safeguard against infections from water, fruit and vegetables.

EMPLOYMENT OPPORTUNITIES
Both Africa and the Middle East offer good working opportunities, though these tend to be long-term rather than of a few weeks or months' duration. English teachers are in demand in both Africa and the Middle East, though fully qualified applicants are preferred. Various charities send workers to the poorer African nations. Nurses should have no trouble finding appointments in most Middle Eastern countries. Remember, though, that the culture in both Africa and the Middle East couldn't be more different to the West, and two to three years can be a very long time if you're unhappy in a country.

INTRA-CONTINENTAL TRAVEL
There are no passes covering Africa or the Middle East – and intra-continental travel can, in any case, often be difficult because of political tensions and unrest between and within the various countries. (For details of travel passes covering individual countries, see the **Internal Travel** section for the relevant country.)

FURTHER INFORMATION
Lonely Planet publish some excellent books on Africa such as *Africa on a Shoestring; East Africa; West Africa;* and *Central Africa.* As always, you can't go far wrong with your Lonely Planet guide for company!

In addition, Lonely Planet, Fodors, etc. produce a range of guides to individual African countries (see the following sections for details).

Lonely Planet also publishes one of the few guides for budget travellers to the Middle East. Their *Arab Gulf States – A Travel Survival Kit* is a must if you are going to this region.

KENYA

VITAL STATISTICS

Red tape: A full passport is required by all visitors. A visa is required by all apart from nationals of Commonwealth countries (except Australia, New Zealand, Nigeria and Sri Lanka, and British passport holders of Pakistani and Bangladeshi origin), Ethiopia, Germany, Ireland, Italy, Spain, Norway, Sweden, Finland, Denmark, Turkey, San Marino and Uruguay. Those who don't need a visa are issued on entry with a Visitor's Pass, usually valid for three months.

If you enter Kenya via a land border it's unlikely that you'll be asked to produce an onward ticket or proof of 'sufficient funds' to cover your stay. If you arrive by air, however, you will be. Jobs are hard to find in Kenya, so working permits are difficult to obtain.

Customs: 200 cigarettes or 50 cigars or 225 g tobacco; 1 l spirits or wine; 76 ml perfume. Special restrictions apply to gold, diamonds and skin or game trophies unless they have been authorized by the Kenyan government department. Personal effects are free, but there's a duty tariff on gifts. There are no restrictions on the amount of foreign cash or travellers' cheques brought into the country, which is noted on a currency declaration form issued on arrival.

Health: Immunization against cholera, typhoid and polio is recommended but not mandatory. Visitors from smallpox-infested areas should be vaccinated and certified. Those intending to travel to the Kenyan coast or bush should take precautions against malaria. Tap water is generally safe to drink, and the sea and swimming pools are safe for bathing. Take care about swimming in lakes, rivers and reservoirs, as they may be infected by bilharzia parasites. Health insurance is essential, and it's best to ensure that it covers entitlement to free air transport and Flying Doctor services. It's a good idea to take an AIDS pack with you (see **Medicine**, p. 99).

Language: Kiswahili and English are the official languages, but a number of major and minor tribal languages are also spoken. It's useful to acquire some knowledge of Kiswahili if you're planning to travel in the more remote parts of Kenya.

Population: About 25 million.
Capital: Nairobi, population 1.5 million.
Political system: Independent republic within the British Commonwealth. Democratic system, but in effect a one-party state; there are moves to rectify this, but as the other parties are predominantly tribal, this has led to some rioting within the country. The President is Daniel ArapMoi.
Religion: Most Kenyans living on the coast and in the eastern part of the country are Muslim, while other areas have a Christian majority.
Time: Three hours ahead of GMT.
Money: The Kenyan shilling (Ks) is divided into 100 cents. Coins: 5, 10 and 50 cents, 1Ks and 5Ks. Notes: 10Ks, 20Ks, 50Ks, 100Ks, 200Ks and 500Ks. £1 = 76.30Ks.
Communications: Kenya's telephone system is pretty good, and international calls are easy to make from Nairobi, Mombasa and Kisumu: either go through the operator, or dial direct by using a phonecard. These can be bought from post offices, and come in denominations of Ks200, Ks400 and Ks1,000.
Post: Mail can be sent c/o poste restante in any town. Incoming letters take about a week to reach Nairobi, and usually make their way to the right person: tell your friends to write legibly, and to write your name in block capitals and underline it. When letters go astray at the huge poste restante in Nairobi, it's almost always the fault of the letter writer.

Letters sent from Kenya rarely go astray, but can take up to two weeks to arrive at their destination. Similarly, parcels sent by surface mail can take almost five months to arrive, but arrive they do! If you want to send a parcel home, it has to be presented unwrapped to the customs people at the post office. Take along your own cardboard, paper, tape or string to wrap it up afterwards. There's usually someone selling things like that outside the post office in Nairobi.
Electricity: 110v AC/60 Hz, 210–240 v.

Business hours: BANKS: Mon.–Fri. 8.30 a.m.–1 p.m. On the first and last Saturday of each month, they open from 9–11 a.m. (Branches of Barclays Bank stay open until 4.30–5 p.m. in Nairobi and Mombasa, and the Barclays at Nairobi airport is open 24 hours a day.)

POST OFFICES: Post offices are open 8 a.m.–7 p.m. Mon.–Fri., and 8 a.m.–1 p.m. on Saturdays.

SHOPS: Mon.–Sat. 8.30 a.m.–12.30 p.m. and 2p.m.–4.30 p.m.

OFFICES: Mon.–Fri. 8 or 8.30 a.m.–5 p.m., with a break between 1 and 2 p.m. Some businesses open on Sat. 8.30 a.m.–12.30 p.m.
Holidays: 1 January; Good Friday; Easter Monday; 21 February (Eid-el-Fitr); 29 April (Eid-el-Adha); 1 May; 1 June; 10 and 20 October; 12, 25 and 26 December.
Climate: The coastal belt is hot and humid all year round, with temperatures ranging from about 22–30°C. The humidity is tempered by the breeze from the Indian Ocean. Western Kenya also tends to be hot and humid, with high rainfall (up to 200 mm) usually occurring in April. Northern and eastern Kenya suffer extreme temperature variations; it can reach 40°C during the day and fall to 20°C or less at night, with occasional violent rainfalls. November is usually the wettest month and July the driest. The central highlands and Rift Valley areas enjoy a fairly agreeable climate with average temperatures ranging between a maximum of 22–26°C and a 10–14°C minimum. Here there are two rainy seasons: the 'long rains' fall between March and May, and the 'short rains' between October and December.

DO'S AND DON'TS
Theft from tourists has become increasingly common in Kenya, so you need to keep your wits about you. You are particularly vulnerable when you first arrive, when your lack of familiarity with the place is very easy for would-be thieves to spot. The trick is to form a crowd round the victim, jostle them and slash their bag or money-belt strap. So it's advisable not to carry any valuables or large amounts of cash around.

There have been some unpleasant clashes between locals and tourists on Lamu, and also some incidents of rape on the beach. Women travellers should try to sunbathe near other people, and should definitely avoid topless bathing in a Muslim culture where local women are clad in black from top to toe.

Don't be tempted to sample *changa:* these illicitly distilled liquors can leave you blind – or dead.

Whether you like it or not, you'll have to get into the habit of bargaining. Look around and get a grasp of the price ranges before you start.

WHERE TO GO FOR WHAT
Safaris are Kenya's major tourist attraction and if it's safaris you want, there are plenty of options to choose from, lasting from two days right up to twenty-five! Ideally you should join a safari which lasts at least five days, as you're guaranteed to see a lot more

animals and all your time won't be taken up with driving to and from the national parks.

A three-day safari starting from Nairobi will most likely be restricted to either AMBOSELI or MASAI MARA. A five-day trip would allow you to visit two parks, such as Amboseli and TSAVO or Masai Mara and LAKE NAKARU. A seven-day safari might take in a couple of Rift Valley lakes, plus Masai Mara and Amboseli. An eleven-day itinerary might head south from Nairobi to take in a Rift Valley lake or two, Masai Mara, Amboseli and Tsavo, or head north to MOUNT KENYA, SAMBURU and BUFFALO SPRINGS, MERU and LAKE NAKARU. The general rule is that the longer you spend on safari, the less it costs per day.

Just as there are plenty of options for the length of your safari, there are numerous tourist companies competing for your money. Basically, there are two types of safari available: those which involve camping beneath the stars with only canvas between yourself and the wandering wildlife; and the kind where you stay in game lodges or luxury tented camps. For budget travellers (and for those who want an authentic experience of the African bush) camping safaris are the only real option. You might be rewarded for putting up with such hardships as no flush toilets or showers by seeing a lion or elephant wander through the camp at night. However, for those with much more money to spend, the lodges are beautiful and you can watch the nocturnal wildlife from the verandah, with a drink in your hand. The luxury tented camps are in the same price range as the lodges.

A word of warning: some of the safari companies touting for business are not safari companies at all, but agents – and if anything goes wrong, you won't see a penny of your money back. Reputable safari companies, highly recommended by travellers, include Safari-Camp Services, PO Box 44801, Nairobi (tel 330130, 328936); Yare Safaris Ltd, 1st Floor, Union Towers, Mama Ngina St, PO Box 63006, Nairobi (tel. 214099); and Special Camping Safaris Ltd, Gilfillan House, Kenyatta Ave, PO Box 51512, Nairobi (tel. 338325, 220072). Advance booking is essential, especially with the really good companies. Two Nairobi-based firms to avoid are Kiwa Safaris and Parrot Tours – both are frequently in trouble with the authorities.

Apart from safaris, Kenya's main attraction is its coastline. After leaving NAIROBI, most tourists head for the ancient trading port of MOMBASA, which is very much the capital of the coast. Its Old Town and Fort Jesus are well worth exploring. South of Mombasa there are unspoilt beaches right the way down to the Tanzanian border. North of Mombasa lies MALINDI, a major coastal resort centre which dates back to the 12th century. South of the town is the MALINDI MARINE NATIONAL PARK, where you can rent a glass-bottomed boat and snorkelling gear to enjoy the coral reef. The GEDI ruins are also a short bus ride south of Malindi, and are a must for anybody even slightly interested in archaeology. Only discovered in the 1920s, the site features a number of magnificent buildings such as the palace and the Great Mosque, and is believed to date from the 13th century. A small museum houses items uncovered during the excavations, including Ming Chinese porcelain, and glass and glazed earthenware from Persia. The largely Muslim-populated island of LAMU, with its narrow streets and traditionally robed locals, started to become popular – some would say over-run – with tourists in the 1970s and 80s, and this has lead in recent years to friction with the local population who fear that the culture which gives the island its charm is under threat from tourism.

Climbers should head for the CENTRAL HIGHLANDS to scale MOUNT KENYA (5,199 m) the highest mountain in Kenya, and the second highest in Africa, behind MOUNT KILIMANJARO, which looms just over the Tanzanian border. Kenya's second highest mountain, MOUNT ELGON (4,321 m) is near the border with Uganda.

And if you're touring the world's major cities, then the capital NAIROBI has plenty to offer, including colourful parks and gardens, bustling shopping and market areas, a superb National Museum and a Snake Park, featuring most of the species of snake to be found in East Africa.

INTERNAL TRAVEL

Air: Kenya Airways provides internal air services between Nairobi, Mombasa, Kisumu and Malindi. In addition there are several private airlines which connect the main cities with smaller towns and the national parks. Fares are expensive, so budget travellers will probably find themselves using the train or bus instead.

Rail: Kenya's railways are pretty efficient, and much safer than the buses. The main passenger line runs from Mombasa to Malaba on the Ugandan border, via Voi, Nairobi, Nakuru and Eldoret. There is also a line between Nakuru and Kisumu.

The Nairobi–Mombasa route is not to be missed. Two trains run daily, passing through Tsavo National Park. Tickets cost about US$45 (first class), US$30 (second class), and US$12 (third class).

Most journeys are made by night and there are three classes of travel: first class consists of two-berth compartments with a washbasin, wardrobe, a supply of drinking water and a drinks service.

Second class offers four-berth compartments with a washbasin and drinking water. In both first and second class the sexes are segregated unless you book the whole compartment. Third class is seats only – not the best way to spend an overnight journey.

Bus: All the bus companies are privately owned, so some buses are more expensive and better maintained than others. Bus fares cost somewhere between what you would pay for second and third class rail travel, but journey times are quicker and because buses run during the day you get an opportunity to see the countryside. On the minus side, they are often overcrowded. Goldline, Malindi Bus and Garissa Express are among the better options if you decide you want to travel by bus.

It's best to avoid travelling by *Matatu* (minibus) if you can avoid it. Reckless driving and overcrowding mean that horrific smashes are not uncommon (especially along the Nairobi–Mombasa route).

Car hire: Unless there are three or four of you to share the costs, this is an expensive way of touring Kenya, for all that it does give you the freedom to explore the country thoroughly and in your own time. Before hiring a vehicle, check out the hire and distance charges of as many companies as possible and decide which type of vehicle will be most suitable for your plans – for example, a 2WD won't be much good if you're going upcountry to some of the big reserves. Also, make sure you're properly insured. Obviously, an international – or your own national – driving licence is required, and some companies won't hire vehicles to people under 23 or, occasionally, 25.

Hitching: It's fairly easy to find a lift on the main roads, though the driver will expect a contribution unless you make it clear at the outset that you want a free lift. Hitching is not advisable for women and it is not a good idea to try to hitch to one of the national parks – most people either join a tour or hire their own vehicle, so rides are hard to come by (and walking is forbidden inside the parks).

ACCOMMODATION
Kenya has a wide range of accommodation, from £3-per-night budget lodgings to wonderfully luxurious but very expensive hotels in the national parks.

Youth hostels: Hostelling is very much in its infancy here – there are only eight IYHA-affiliated hostels in Kenya. Dorm beds cost from US$4, per night depending on the hostel. They are closed between 8 p.m. and 6.30 a.m. and open in the day at the discretion of the warden. You cook your own food, and it's best to carry your own plate, cup and cutlery. Cooking is mainly on charcoal stoves, although the larger hostels do have gas cookers. The hostels are good places for meeting other travellers, but cheaper accommodation can be found.

'Board and lodgings': At the bottom of Kenya's accommodation league, these tend to be brothels first and hotels second – they're often dirty and noisy, and definitely not the type of place your mother would like you to stay! But they are also cheap, from as little as US$6.

If you can afford to pay a little more, there are some better board and lodging establishments where US$10 will get you a clean single room with private bath, and soap and towel supplied. But the establishment will probably have a noisy bar. Women travelling alone should make sure their bedroom door can be locked from the inside. Some women travellers have reported problems with men knocking on their bedroom door at night – in the top hotels as well as in the cheaper accommodation.

Hotels: All the usual international chains can be found in Kenya, with prices starting at about US$25 for a single room. Some of the hotels are in old colonial buildings, which makes for a wonderfully atmospheric stay. If you want to watch the animal nightlife from the comfort of a verandah, the lodges in the game parks cost from US$50.

Campsites: The campsites in the national parks and game reserves are very basic – no flush toilets, no showers. Camping out in the bush is sometimes possible, though before pitching your tent it's best to check whether you need permission. It's not advisable to camp along the coast, and sleeping on the beaches is definitely no-go.

FOOD

If you're seriously into eating or follow a vegetarian diet, then you're not going to be too happy with the Kenyan cuisine. Meals consist mainly of meat (usually beef, goat and mutton) with potatoes, rice or *ugali* (maize cooked into porridge.) Travellers who take to *ugali* are rare – most non-Kenyans loathe the stuff. Cooked red kidney beans are the usual alternative to meat, so vegetarians have to learn to love them! Looking on the bright side, eating is cheap in Kenya, and the starchy diet is filling.

If you're on a tight budget, then you'll find yourself eating the above meat-and-stodge meals at a *hoteli*, Kenya's confusingly named cheap eateries. These are open only at lunchtimes – in Kenya, lunch is the main meal of the day. The mid- and top-range hotels have restaurants which provide better and less tedious meals, if you can afford the higher prices. After a few weeks of mutton and *ugali*, roast chicken in an upmarket restaurant can seem wildly exciting.

Fast food is widely available in Kenya – it's cheap but very greasy! Sausages, eggs, chicken and fish are popular, as are fried chips with tomato sauce. The most common Kenyan snack is the *sambusa*; a variant of the Indian samosa, it is a deep-fried pastry triangle stuffed with spiced mince meat. These are gorgeous when eaten fresh and hot, but vile if they're allowed to get cold and greasy.

Kenya does have one thing going for it foodwise: a wide variety of high-quality yet cheap home-grown fruit. Feast on whatever's in season locally: bananas, guavas, custard apples, coconuts, papaya, pineapples and mangoes.

Tea and coffee lovers will be as frustrated as the vegetarians. The Kenyans like their tea very milky, even more sugary, and preferably well-stewed. They use instant coffee in small quantities combined with vast amounts of milk and sugar. As for alcohol: the beer is warm, and the most common Kenyan wine – papaya wine – has the distinction of smelling as bad as it tastes. In short, you don't go to Kenya for its food and drink!

BUDGETING

Most people who travel to Kenya want to go on safari – and it's this which will eat up your budget. Three-day camping safaris cost from US$175 per day; the cost per day is less the longer you go, eg US$100 per day on a seven-day trip. Safaris which involve staying in lodges or tented camps will cost at least four times the above daily rate. Watch out for companies offering rock-bottom prices – you'll probably get what you pay for.

However, away from the game parks Kenya is a cheap country to travel. Public transport is reasonably priced, as is accommodation provided you're happy with just the basics. Food is very cheap (you can have an entire meal for the equivalent of 75p!), albeit monotonous.

Work opportunities are severely limited. The Kenyans believe that if an African can do the job, there's no need to hire a white person. Opportunities do exist in teaching and in working for the international aid agencies. Work and permits must be organized before you arrive in Kenya.

FURTHER INFORMATION

Kenya Tourist Office, 25 Brooks Mews, London W1Y 1LF (tel. 0171 355 3144) will provide tourist literature and information.

Kenya High Commission, 45 Portland Place, London W1N 3AG (tel. 0171 636 2371).

Background reading: Lonely Planet's *Kenya – Travel Survival Kit* (£8.95.) and *Africa on a Shoestring* (covers over 50 African countries). A list of Kenya's youth hostels can be found in the International Youth Hostels Association's Guide *Budget Accommodation: Africa, America, Asia and Australasia.*

The best-known book set in Kenya is undoubtedly *Out of Africa* by Karen Blixen, and it's better than the Meryl Streep movie. For up-to-date African literature, try something by the uncompromisingly radical Ngugi wa Thiong'o – his books include *Petals of Blood, Devil on the Cross* and *Weep Not Child.* These titles are all published by Heinemann.

Nairobi

AIRPORT FACILITIES

Jomo Kenyatta International Airport lies on the road to Mombasa, 15 km outside Nairobi. Tourist information is available 24 hours a day from the Hertz car rental desk, and the usual restaurants, shops, duty-free and post office facilities are on hand. The National Bank of Kenya is open 24 hours a day and Barclays from 6 a.m. to midnight. Make sure you confirm flights 48 hours prior to departure. Check-in times are 30 minutes before a domestic flight and one hour prior to an international flight. There is a departure tax of $20.

CITY LINKS

Bus: The cheapest – though not the safest – way of getting to Nairobi from the airport is by number 34 bus. The journey costs about US$0.25 and lasts around 45 minutes, but many tourists are separated from their valuables before the journey's end. A crowd forms, a bit of jostling takes place and hey presto! – your bag or money pouch has gone. Be suspicious of everyone. Sort yourself out and make sure your valuables are put away before going anywhere near the bus.

Airline bus: The Kenya Airways minibus costs US$1 and leaves at roughly hourly intervals from 7 a.m.–8 p.m. for the 30-minute journey into Nairobi. The bus will drop you off at any city centre hotel. To go back to the airport, pick up the bus from the airline's city terminal in Koinange Street.

Taxi: If you have a late night flight, this is the only way of getting into Nairobi. The standard fare is approximately US$8.

USEFUL ADDRESSES
Tourist office: Tourism Department, Box 54666, Nairobi (tel. 331030).
Main post office: Haile Selassie Avenue (though a new GPO is set to open in the near future), open Mon.–Fri. 8 a.m.–5 p.m. and Sat. 9 a.m.–12 p.m.
British Embassy: Bruce House, Standard Street. PO Box 30465 (tel. 335944).
US Embassy: Embassy Building, corner Haile Selassie Avenue & Moi Avenue. PO Box 30137 (tel. 334141).
British Airways: International Life House, Mama Ngina St (tel. 334362).
Emergency services: Police/ambulance 999.
Medical assistance: Try Dr Sheth, Bruce House, Standard Street or go to the Nairobi Hospital. But don't go to the Kenyatta Hospital, where the cure is rumoured to be worse than the ailment.

GETTING ABOUT
Nairobi is a compact city, so you can get around the main sights quite comfortably on foot. If you prefer to ride, then buses are the cheapest way of getting around, but are best tackled without a backpack as they're very crowded! Taxis can't be hailed on the street but there are taxi ranks at the railway station, outside the main hotels and at the museum. Only those with a death wish should attempt to cycle in Nairobi.

SIGHTS
To get yourself oriented head for the KENYATTA INTERNATIONAL CONFERENCE CENTRE (KICC) in City Square –. Nairobi's tallest building. The viewing level is on the 28th floor, though access is occasionally restricted if there's a conference taking place. Although viewing is free, you'll be expected to tip the guide!

The NATIONAL MUSEUM on Museum Road houses paintings by the late Joy Adamson, an exhibition of native birds and mammals, tribal crafts and a section on the culture and crafts of the coastal Swahili people. Over recent years, however, the displays have become shabby and many tourists therefore prefer to visit the free NATIONAL ARCHIVES rather than pay US$1 at the museum. The National Archives are on Moi Avenue, right opposite the Hilton, and include photographs of Kenyatta's and Moi's various state visits plus exhibitions of handicrafts and paintings. There's only one proper art gallery, the WATATU on the ground floor of Bruce House, Standard Street. It usually exhibits work by local artists and is worth a browse.

For an insight into Kenyan politics head for PARLIAMENT HOUSE on Parliament Road. You can get a permit for the public gallery – and if parliament is out of session you can arrange to take a tour of the buildings.

The RAILWAY MUSEUM on Station Road is not to be missed; in addition to its collection of rolling stock, it provides an excellent insight into Kenya's colonial history. It also exhibits the silverware from the 'Lunatic Express' – a train which once ran between Uganda and Mombasa despite lack of demand, lack of trade and lack of economic sense.

Reptile-lovers will enjoy a visit to the SNAKE PARK, (opposite the National Museum) which has living examples of most species of snake found in East Africa. If you really want to, you can watch the snakes being fed – with live frogs – and being milked for anti-venom serum. There's also a crocodile pit, and a collection of tortoises. Admission is US$1.

There are several large markets around the city centre, plus smaller ones in every residential area of Nairobi. Travellers flock to the CITY MARKET, right in the centre of town; it looks like a huge, yellow temple from the outside, but inside sells fruit, vegetables, flowers, African carvings, dog-baskets, local jewellery, bamboo chairs, fish, etc. It's pricier than the city's other markets, but then you're paying for its central location.

There are numerous craft shops, but it's important to look around before dipping in your pocket, as price and quality varies. Be warned: there are a lot of imitation goods designed especially for the tourist trade! If you get offered objects made from ostrich egg shell, ivory or elephant hair, do not accept them – they're either false or illegally imported from other parts of Africa. Should you want to buy a safari outfit, there are several good quality shops around Kimanti Street, Kenyatta Avenue, Biashara Street and Muindi Mbingu Street. They're on the expensive side, but worth it.

ACCOMMODATION
Youth hostel: You need to be a YHA member to stay at the hostel on Ralph Bunche Road (723012). It's clean, efficiently run by friendly wardens, and offers the luxury – in Kenyan budget accommodation! – of constant hot showers. A bed costs from US$4. Never try to walk back to the YHA from the city centre after dark – there have been reports of people doing so getting robbed.

Hotels: Nairobi boasts a good selection of budget accommodation but women travelling alone should avoid the Al Mansura Hotel on Munyu Road; there have been some complaints that the general atmosphere can make you feel uneasy.

Popular city centre hotels include:

New Kenya Lodge, River Road (tel. 222202). Very central and cheap (from US$6, depending on the number of beds per room). Basic but clean, it attracts interesting characters from all over the world! If the main lodge is full, you'll be put in the Annexe on Duruma Road. Travellers complain that though the prices are the same, the atmosphere isn't – and, more importantly, some of the rooms don't have windows.

Iqbal Hotel, Latema Road (220914). Tremendously popular city centre hotel. Beds cost from US$6 per night. Don't bother turning up to book a room after 9 a.m. – you simply won't get in. The Iqbal's noticeboard is *the* place to look for just about anything you want to know or buy! Get up very early if you don't want to wash with cold water!

Central YMCA, State House Road, PO Box 63063 (tel. 724066). Prices from US$12.

Cheap hotels outside the city centre:

Mrs Roche's, Parklands Avenue, opposite the Aga Khan hospital. A bed in a shared room of this legendary hotel costs from US$7 (but be warned: you might have to bed down on the floor on your first night, as the place is so popular!) or pitch your own tent for much less. The atmosphere at Mrs Roche's is terrific, almost carnival-like, and again the noticeboard is something of an oracle.

Dolat Hotel, Mfangano Street (222797). Slightly expensive, but quiet, friendly, immaculately clean and very secure. It costs from US$15 for a room with a bath and hot water.

The Green View Lodge, off Nyerere Road (720908). Wooden huts in a bush setting, with a restaurant and bar. Rooms from US$10, including breakfast.

FOOD

In Kenya, lunch is the main meal of the day and naturally, restaurants are geared towards this; indeed, many restaurants close in the evening, and if you do find one that's open, you'll be faced with a limited menu. Nairobi has restaurants from all over the globe – including Italian, Chinese, Indian and steak houses – which aren't too expensive, so it might be worth splurging on these rather than trying to survive on Kenya's own monotonous cuisine!

Dhaba Restaurant, Tom Mboya Street (tel. 334862): Indian food.

Panda Restaurant on the corner of Tom Mboya Street and Cabral Street: Chinese food.

Trattoria, corner of Wabera and Kaunda streets: Italian.

Carnivore, just past Wilson airport in Langata (tel. 501775): immensely popular, serves excellent steaks. All-you-can-eat for under $10.

Malindi Dishes, Gaborone Road: Kenyan cuisine. The food is livened up considerably by coastal coconut and spices.

Supreme Restaurant, River Road: Indian vegetarian food for from US$5. The fruit juices are excellent.

Blukat Restaurant, Muindi Mbingu Street: another good Indian vegetarian restaurant – meals cost from US$4.

African Heritage Café, through the African Heritage shop on Kenyatta Avenue (tel. 337507): very popular – the barbecue section has a choice of red meat, chicken or fish with chips and salad. Arrive early for lunch (served midday till 2 p.m.), or you'll end up waiting.

Illiki Café, ground floor, Ambassador Hotel, Moi Avenue: serves really good breakfasts: you can gorge cheaply on cereals, bacon, sausages, beans, egg, toast, fruit, cakes and fruit juice.

ENTERTAINMENT

You can see a good film for as little as US$1 in Nairobi – but if you don't want to watch scratched films, it's better to pay a little extra and head for one of the better cinemas, notably the Nairobi or the 20th Century in Mama Ngina Street. The cheaper ones, including the Odeon and Embassy are on Latema Road. Scan the newspapers to find out what's on.

There are some good discos in the centre of Nairobi: try the very popular Florida 2000 on Moi Avenue, which stays open until 6 a.m. Like most nightclubs, admission costs from US$2. Single men will either have to put up with or enjoy the attentions of unattached local women. The New Florida on the corner of Koinange and Banda streets is another favourite. Less popular but reputedly just as good is the Hollywood on Moktar Daddah Street. There aren't any strict codes of dress in Nairobi night spots: jeans, trainers and T-shirts are all acceptable.

For live music, try the African Heritage Café on Banda Street between 2 p.m. and 5 p.m. on Saturdays and Sundays. Entrance is US$0.25. The favourite spot with locals is the Bombax Club on Ngong Road, which has live bands every Thursday, Friday, Saturday and Sunday evenings. An absolute must to visit is the open-all-hours-all-year Modern 24-Hour Green Bar in Latema Road. There the jukebox is always blazing, and you'll see every form of life imaginable, including dope dealers, whores and hustlers. The bar is covered in wire mesh, with a tiny hole for your money and beer to pass through. For more genteel surroundings, try the Grosvenor Hotel in Ralph Bunche Road or the lawns of the Fairview Hotel, Bishops Road:

EXCURSIONS

NAIROBI NATIONAL PARK is only a few kilometres away from the city centre, and is the oldest game park in Kenya. You won't see an elephant here (the habitat's not suitable), but you will see lion, giraffe, zebra, cheetah and leopard – and it's one of the best places for spotting a rhino. As with all the game parks, you have to explore it in a vehicle – so you'll have to go on a tour, hire a car, or try to hitch a lift with other tourists at the main gate. If you decide on the third option, take bus 24 from Moi Avenue.

The BOMAS OF KENYA at Langata is a cultural centre near the National Park. On display are all aspects of traditional Kenyan life: dancing, music, crafts and food. The dancing displays take place in the main auditorium, and are timed so as to give you plenty of time to walk around the 'bomas' (homesteads) and compare the different styles of construction and the tribes' various crafts. Well worth the US$6 entry fee.

If you've read or seen *Out of Africa*, you'll want to visit the KAREN BLIXEN MUSEUM. When Kenya became independent, the farmhouse where Karen lived was presented by the Danes to the Kenyan government – along with the adjacent agricultural college. It's in Karen Road, Karen, is open daily from 9.30 a.m.–6 p.m. and costs US$2. To get there, take bus 27 from Kenyatta Avenue or 24 from Moi Avenue.

The NGONG HILLS to the west of Nairobi offer excellent views of the capital – but avoid going there alone as there have been several reports of muggings, especially at weekends. This area, incorporating the villages of Karen and Ngong, is where white settlers set up farms in the early colonial days, and you'll find the houses to be typically Home Counties English! LIMURU is another former 'old settlers' stamping-ground: take a look at the KENTMERE CLUB, Limuru Road, Tigoni (0154 41053) and see colonial England for yourself! If you're in Nairobi for Christmas and have the cash to spare, treat yourself to a Yuletide banquet at the Kentmere. While you're out there, it's worth taking in a tea farm, and seeing the whole process of tea production. Visits are organized by Mitchell's Kiambethu Tea Farm, Tigoni (0154 40756).

SOUTH AFRICA

VITAL STATISTICS
Red tape: A full passport is required, but there are no visa requirements for Australian, NZ, Canadian, US and UK (and some others – check with the nearest consulate) passport-holders for visits of up to 90 days.

An onward ticket and proof that you have sufficient funds to cover your stay are also required. People travelling overland who arrive without an onward ticket may be asked to place a deposit with the customs officials, the amount of which will be roughly the price of an air ticket home.

Customs: 400 cigarettes, 50 cigars and 250 g tobacco; 1 l spirits and 2 l wine; 50 ml perfume; 250 ml toiletwater; plus additional gifts to the value of R500.

Health: A yellow-fever vaccination certificate is required for those coming from infected areas. There is a malaria risk throughout the year in the Transvaal Lowveld, Kruger National Park and Zululand in Natal. Health insurance is required.

Language: Afrikaans and English are the two official languages. Zulu, Xhosa and other African languages are also spoken.

Population: 38 million.

Capital: There are three capitals: Pretoria (administrative), Cape Town (legislative), and Bloemfontein (judicial). These three are also the capitals of their respective provinces: the Transvaal, the Cape, and the Orange Free State. The fourth, and smallest, province is Natal, capital Pietermaritzburg. However, Johannesburg is the largest city in South Africa, and is regarded by many travellers as the unofficial capital.

Political system: Republic. South Africa rejoined the Commonwealth in July 1994 with Nelson Mandela as President.

Religion: Various Christian denominations.

Time: Two hours ahead of GMT from October to March, and one hour ahead April to September.

Money: The currency is the Rand (R), divided into 100 cents.

Coins: 1, 2, 5, 10, 20 and 50 cents and R1, R2. Notes: R2, R5, R10, R20 and R50. £1 = R5.57.

Tax: There is a value added tax of 14% on most goods and services.

Communications: South Africa's telephone system is efficient, and it's possible to dial direct to Europe and North America from public telephones (there's a minimum charge of R1 for international calls, and of 20 cents for internal calls).

The postal service is also fast and reliable. Airmail to the UK takes about one week. Internal mail takes two to five days. Poste restante should be sent to main post offices. To ensure that letters are filed correctly, advise friends to underline your surname (otherwise mail may get filed under your first name).

Electricity: 250v AC/50 Hz in Pretoria; 220–30v AC/50 Hz elsewhere.

Business hours: BANKS: Mon.–Fri. 9 a.m.–3.30 p.m.; Sat. 8 a.m.–11 a.m.

POST OFFICES: Most are open Mon.–Fri. 9 a.m.–4.30 p.m.; Sat. 8 a.m.–noon.

SHOPS: Mon.–Fri. 8.30 a.m.–5 p.m.; Sat. 8.30 a.m.–12.30 p.m.

OFFICES: Mon.–Fri. 8.30 a.m.–5 p.m.

Holidays: 1 and 2 January; 21 March (Human Rights Day); 27 April (Freedom Day); Good Friday and Easter Sunday; 1 May; 10 October; 16, 25 and 26 December.

Climate: South Africa has an agreeable climate: no matter when you visit, the weather is likely to be favourable. In summer (Oct.–Mar.) daytime temperatures range from 21–8°C, though the nights are cool once you move away from the humid eastern coast. In winter, days are mild to warm, but nights can get very cold – sometimes below freezing! The heaviest rains occur in summer, particularly in the east of the country.

DO'S AND DON'TS
Incidents of rape or murder of hitch-hikers in South Africa have increased, but it's still a lot safer to hitch there than it is in Europe or the USA, or even, apparently, Australia. If you do intend to hitch, keep your eye on the news for any troublespots – you don't want to end up trying to thumb a lift in a township that's just exploded into violence.

WHERE TO GO FOR WHAT
The game and nature reserves, hiking trails and superb coastline are what lure most people to South Africa – plus a desire to see

what life really *is* like out there compared with what we see on the news.

JOHANNESBURG (or Joburg) tends to be the primary South African destination for travellers, many of whom will find it a disappointment: the scenery is dull and the city itself seems lacking in character. There's plenty to do, but nothing you couldn't do in any other city! Just outside the city, however, there are some scenic and interesting places, and the KRUGER NATIONAL PARK, South Africa's major tourist venue, is but half a day's drive away. Covering an area the size of Wales, the Kruger contains more animal species than any other game reserve in Africa. In the course of a day's drive it's possible to spot elephant, rhino, buffalo, cheetah, hyenas, baboons, giraffes and even, if you're lucky, a lion. The bird life is equally varied, boasting vultures, yellow-billed hornbills and the secretary bird. Flora species include indigenous shrubs and trees such as the acacia, mopane, wild fig, and baobab.

Also popular with tourists is CAPE TOWN, with its spectacular backdrop of Table Mountain. The oldest city in South Africa (founded in 1652), it contains many places of historical interest. The surrounding Cape Peninsula offers wonderful beaches and scenic nature reserves which are a botanist's paradise – the Cape of Good Hope alone contains more indigenous floral species than the whole of the British Isles!

DURBAN's attractions include an excellent beach and a good range of budget accommodation. The beach is ideal for surfers, and also safe for swimming – which makes it a popular destination for South African families. There's also an amusement park, an aquarium, and a snake park. Just 20 km north of Durban is UMHLANGA ROCKS, a popular resort town with one of the best beaches in South Africa. If you can tear your self away from the coast, the Zululand game parks lie within easy reach of Durban. These include the MKUZI GAME RESERVE, which has more than 400 species of birdlife, and TEMBE ELEPHANT RESERVE, which opened in 1990, and protects a herd of elephant which once moved freely between South Africa and Mozambique, but now need to be protected from poachers.

Hikers are spoilt for choice in South Africa: DRAKENSBURG offers mountain wilderness, rock art and some game; the eastern and northern TRANSVAAL has mountains, forest, game and birds; and there's spectacular coastal scenery in the TRANSKEI.

And finally, if you want to visit the administrative capital, PRETORIA is at its best in spring-time, when the jacarandas are in bloom. Its NATIONAL ZOOLOGICAL GARDENS, with 3,500 animal species, is one of the largest zoos in the world. And while on the subject of world records: Church Street, at 26 km, is one of the longest straight streets in the world.

INTERNAL TRAVEL

Air: The major cities are linked by regular South African Airways flights. They're reasonably priced: a one-way ticket from Johannesburg to Cape Town, for example, will set you back about R661. Other airlines include Comair (who operate routes not covered by SAA, such as Johannesburg to Skakuza in the Kruger National Park), Airlink, Phoenix and Sun Air.

If you've limited time in the country and want to see as much of it as possible, it's worth taking up SAA's 'Africa Explorer' fare: you have to buy a minimum of four flight coupons, and the cost is dependent on your choice of routing.

Rail: Most of the major towns are served by rail, and there are also international routes to Zimbabwe, Botswana and Mozambique. Intercity and international fares often include sleeping arrangements. Three classes of cabin are available: first-class cabins have four bunks; second-class six; third-class cabins supposedly sleep six as well, though in reality they usually end up with rather more than six tenants! Fares are average by Western standards – for example, a second class trip from Johannesburg to Durban would cost about R108.

South Africa's most famous and luxurious train is the Blue Train, which runs regularly between Johannesburg and Cape Town. Tickets start at about R6,300 for 'A-Class' and R1,825 for 'D-Class', and you need to book well in advance.

Bus: Most of the major routes are serviced by coaches – the main operators include Greyhound, Translux and Intercape. Reservations should be made in advance, either through the operator or a travel agent. As a rule, the price of a one-way ticket costs about R10 less than it would to travel second class by train.

Minibuses: These are cheaper than coaches and cover some routes that the coach operators don't – and, as they still tend to be regarded as 'black' transport, they're an ideal place to meet South African blacks. They operate on a first-come, first-served basis, and leave as soon as they're full. Take care that you're on the right bus – it can be dangerous to find yourself in one of the townships.

Car hire: To hire a car, you need to be 23 years old, have a valid international drivers' licence, and you must take out insurance – this works out at about R6 per day. Petrol works out at roughly R15 per 100 km. This isn't too expensive, especially if you're travelling with a couple of other people and you plan to visit game reserves. The three main car hire companies are Avis, Budget and

Imperial (represented in the UK by Hertz), but there are smaller local operators which are considerably cheaper. Most offer an 'unlimited kilometres' deal in which you hire the car for a minimum of five to seven days at a flat daily rate with no extra charge per kilometre driven. If you're planning long-distance travel, this is the deal to opt for. Nationwide operators that compete favourably with the local outfits include the rapidly expanding Tempest Car Hire and Dolphin Car Hire. They have offices in most major towns, including Johannesburg, Cape Town and Durban.

Hitching: Hitching is a good way of getting around South Africa; the people are generally hospitable, and will often offer you a meal or even accommodation for the night as well as a lift. Off the main routes, it's the only way of getting about, if you don't have your own car.

Local transport: The major towns are served by buses, minibuses and taxis.

ACCOMMODATION

Youth hostels: There are YHAs in all major cities. Prices range from R17–27 per person per night. There are some private hostels, and YMCAs and YWCAs in some towns, but these are more expensive – about twice the cost of the YHA.

Hotels: South Africa's hotels are of a very high standard, but tend to be expensive. Your best bet is to go for a one- or two-star hotel – these tend to be family-run establishments, and perfectly comfortable. You'll pay from about R50 per night for a room in a two-star hotel. The three- and four-star hotels are luxurious, and five-star hotels rank alongside the best in the world.

Self-catering: On-site caravans, chalets, flats, huts . . . There's a good range of self-catering accommodation in South Africa, at varying prices. It's usually a cheaper option than a hotel room, especially in the game reserves.

Campsites: All South Africa's main tourist attractions have campsites nearby; indeed, it's the only form of accommodation in some of the reserves. Prices vary, but the average cost is about R15 per night. If you intend to do some camping – and it really is a perfect way of seeing South Africa – get a copy of the SATOUR (South African Tourism Board) pamphlet on caravan parks. This lists some 600 sites, with maps showing how to get to them. SATOUR has offices in all the major towns, and also in London (tel. 0181–944 8080).

FOOD

All the usual Western fare is available in South Africa; you'll find steak houses, hamburger joints, pizza parlours and fish and chip shops. It's all reasonably priced, too.

For traditional African fare, try *putupap* or *mieliemeal*, a maize porridge eaten with a meat or bean-based stew. It's a staple meal throughout southern and East Africa, and it's very tasty. There are a number of delicious traditional *potjiekos* (stews): try the tomato *bredie*, a lamb and tomato-based stew. Other dishes worth trying include *biltong* (dried sticks of spicy raw meat), and *koeksisters*, (plaited, sticky pastries oozing syrup). Venison is served at many restaurants, especially those around game reserves, the sea food and crayfish is particularly good in Cape Town and along the Atlantic coastline. The *braii* – Afrikaans for barbecue – is a regular weekend activity for white South Africans. Go along to one and try *boerreworst*, a yummy type of sausage.

If you want to save money and cook for yourself, you'll find meat is cheap and of good quality; a T-bone steak, for example, can be bought for as little as R7. South Africans are meat devotees, so vegetarians aren't well catered for. There are only a handful of health food shops, though in the major cities most good restaurants offer *some* vegetarian dishes. Supermarkets, however, are well stocked, and fresh goods such as fruit and vegetables are plentiful and cheap by European standards.

BUDGETING

By African standards, South Africa is expensive. By Western standards it's extremely good value: food is cheap, especially if you opt for self-catering and use the supermarkets. Beer (or rather, lager) and wine are both good and cheap – there's a thriving wine industry in South Africa, and connoisseurs rate it highly.

Accommodation doesn't have to be expensive, provided you stick to camping, self-catering or the hostels. Transport is average for Western countries, but hitching is easy and comparatively safe (though the usual rules do apply to lone female hitchers). Those on severely limited budgets will find that by hitching everywhere, cooking your own food and using youth hostels or campsites, it's possible to spend as little as R40 a day. And if you have cash to spare, it's possible to hire a car, eat out, and use two-star hotels on about R300 a day.

South Africa is suffering from high unemployment, and work opportunities for the round-the-worlder are scarce.

FURTHER INFORMATION

South African High Commission, Trafalgar Square, London WC2N 5DP (tel. 0171 930 4488).

The South African Tourism Board's main office is in Pretoria – write to Private Bag X164, Pretoria, 0001, South Africa (tel. 012 347 0600). SATOUR offices offer brochures covering accommodation, game reserves and hiking trails, as well as road maps and regional information. In London, try SATOUR, 5–6 Alt Grove, London SW19 4DZ (tel. 0181 944 8080).

Background reading: Specifically aimed at the budget traveller, Brandt Publications' *Guide to South Africa* (£9.95) contains lots of useful information and practical tips. To learn more about the history of South Africa, try T. Davenport's *South Africa: A Modern History* (Southern). Nelson Mandela's *The Struggle is My Life* and Steve Biko's *I Write What I Like* are the collected speeches and writings of two of South Africa's most prominent post-war political figures. Donald Woods' *Biko* is also worth reading for an insight into the appalling injustices of apartheid. Fiction lovers should enjoy A. Paton's *Cry the Beloved Country* and the novels of Nobel prize-winner Nadime Gordimer. Heinemann's publish works by black South Africans – contact them at Halley Court, Jordan Hill, Oxford OX2 8EJ.

Cape Town

AIRPORT FACILITIES

D. F. Malan Airport is about 22.5 km from the city centre. It has five terminals, an information desk, foreign exchange, and the usual restaurants, bars and duty-free facilities. Check-in times are 60 minutes prior to domestic departures, and 90 minutes before international departures.

CITY LINKS

A bus leaves the airport for Cape Town 30 minutes after every incoming flight. There's also a taxi rank at the airport; agree a price with the driver before taking a cab.

USEFUL ADDRESSES

Tourist office: Cape Tourist Board (CAPTOUR) have an office next to the railway station in Adderley Street (tel. 27 21418/5202). They produce an accommodation guide, a shopping and services guide, and the monthly *What's On In Cape Town*. They'll also ring around to find you somewhere to stay. SATOUR's Cape Town office is next to the Adderley Street railway station, in the Golden Acre Building (tel. 21 6274).

Main post office: on the corner of Parliament and Darling.

British Embassy: 91 Parliament Street (tel. 461 7220).

US Consulate: Broadway Industries Centre, Heerengracht, Foreshore (21 4283)

Emergency services: dial 10111 for police: 021 10177 for ambulance; 021 461 5555 for fire.

GETTING ABOUT

In some areas of the Cape, public transport is non-existent – hitching is easy, though, or it might be worth contacting a local car-hire firm so you can drive out to the various regions.

Bus: The main bus terminal is the Golden Acre bus terminal – phone 45 5450 for timetables and details. There's also a city hopper service around the centre of town.

Rail: Regular train services connect Cape Town to most Boland towns.

SIGHTS

The view from TABLE MOUNTAIN is one of the most breathtaking in the world: far below lies Cape Town city, the peak known as Lion's Head, and Table Bay. If you're feeling fit (or masochistic), climb to the top, but take care as the weather is extremely changeable and the mountain is reputed to claim an average of two lives per year. There are cable cars to take you to the top; catch a bus to the cableway from Adderley Street. On the eastern slopes of Table Mountain is the KIRSTENBOSCH BOTANICAL GARDEN, presented to the country by Cecil Rhodes, with a fine selection of South African plants in a superb natural setting. Birdwatchers will enjoy the RONDEVLEI BIRD SANCTUARY, about 4 km from Muizenberg.

Worth exploring in the city itself is the MALAY QUARTER, with its charming pastel-coloured houses and minarets, and the CASTLE OF GOOD HOPE, completed in 1679 and said to be the oldest remaining European-built building in Africa. It's now a naval base, but guided tours are available at weekends.

Cape Town's two most important museums are the CULTURAL MUSEUM and the NATURAL HISTORY MUSEUM, both situated in the botanical gardens in the city centre. The Cultural Museum focuses on South Africa's colonial history. The Natural History Museum has some impressive whale skeletons, and superb examples of rock art.

Ostriches, baboons, elands and springboks roam freely in the CAPE OF GOOD HOPE NATURE RESERVE, and over 1,500 plant and 150 bird species have been recorded there. There are hiking trails and game-viewing roads, plus a restaurant and shop. The highlight of this area is CAPE POINT, where you can stand at the foot of the 1860 lighthouse and watch the meeting of the Atlantic and Indian oceans. There's no public transport, so you'll have to hitch a lift or hire a car for the day.

As for the beaches: MUIZENBERG, east of the city, is among the most popular, while recommended ones to the west are CLIFTON and LLANDUDNO. Naturists should make for SANDY BAY, Cape Town's recognized, though unofficial, nudist beach, 2 km south of Llandudno.

ACCOMMODATION
Youth hostels: There are a few hostels on the Cape peninsula:

Stan's Halt, The Glen Camps Bay (tel. 438 1405) is situated on the lower slopes of Table Mountain and is generally regarded as the better of the two Cape Town IYHA hostels. Dormitory accommodation costs from R15 per person per night. Get off the bus at Kloofnek and follow the signs.

Abe Bailey Youth Hostel, 11 Maynard Road, Muizenburg (tel. 788 4283), not far from the station. IYHF hostel; same prices as Stan's Halt. Near main beaches. To get to the hostel from Muizenberg station, walk along Beach Road, then on to Maynard Road.

The Backpacker, 74 New Church Street (tel. 23 4530). This private hostel was opened in 1990 by two young travellers; it's of a high standard and free of the YHA rules. Costs R15 per person per night.

Belvedere YHA, Higgo Crescent (tel. 23 9811). More expensive (R27 per night) but much larger. This is off Bellevue Road.

Rolling Stones Youth Hostel, 94 Lower Main Road, Observatory (tel. 448 1124). This is a 10-minute train ride from Cape Town. R20 per night.

Zebra Crossing Travellers Lodge, 82 New Church Street (tel. 22 1265). Laundry service, mail holding. R20 per night. Take the Kloofnek bus from outside OK Bazaars on Adderley Street to stop no. 068.

Hotels: Check out CAPTOUR's *Accommodation Guide* for a comprehensive list of accommodation and prices.

Tudor Hotel, Greenmarket Square (tel. 24 1335). Singles from R90, doubles from R150.

Chalets and campsites: For self-catering, the Zandvlei Caravan Park (tel. 788 5215) has an excellent reputation – it's about 1k from Muizenberg station and just a five-minute walk from the beach. A four-berth chalet will only cost R55–140 per night. The caravan park also allows tents. Seaforth Beach Chalets, 2 km from Simonstown station, has basic chalets for a basic R55–100 per room. Their phone number is 786 1463.

FOOD
Cape Town is the gastronomic capital of South Africa. Gourmets should check out CAPTOUR's *Restaurant Guide* for a list of restaurants and prices. Some eateries worth trying include:

Hard Rock Café: branches at Main Road, Rondebosch, and Beach Road, Sea Point. Good burgers, fresh linefish and steaks; excellent salads. You'll need to queue if you arrive after 9 p.m.; there's live music on certain nights.

Blues, Victoria Road, Cape Town. Cajun, Californian and Mediterranean dishes. The Blues brownies are magnificent. Terrific views over Camps Bay; popular with the younger set, but a bit noisy for intimate conversation.

The Wharfside Grill, Mariner's Wharf, Hout Bay Harbour. Part of a thronging seafood and entertainment complex, usually besieged by tourists during high season. The food is superb and comes in sailor-sized portions.

The Round House, The Glen, Camps Bay. The place to go if you fancy a crocodile steak. It's a stylish restaurant in what was once the hunting lodge of Lord Charles Somerset. Scottish salmon is also on the menu. There are picnic baskets in summer.

Waterfront Café, Victoria and Alfred Waterfront. Cosmopolitan and classical dishes. The terrace overlooks Mountain Bay.

ENTERTAINMENT
The *braii* is a favourite activity, and if you have any South African friends, you're sure to be invited to one. Many hotels hold summer *braii* at the poolside where you can tuck into the *boerreworst*, have a few glasses of South African wine and enjoy yourself!

The Nico Malan Centre, D. F. Malan South Foreshore (tel. 21 5470) is Cape Town's main arts centre; the resident ballet and opera companies perform in the Nico Theatre and Opera House. Plays are performed in both English and Afrikaans, and there's an annual open-air Shakespeare season in January and February. The smaller Arena Theatre is where experimental work and lesser-known classics are performed. Blakes, the complex's restaurant, has a cabaret show.

Sea Point is a beach resort with a number of good taverns and pubs: try the popular Bertie's Landing, at Fish Quay, where you can watch the sunset, eat fish and chips and enjoy live music. The Pump House, Dock Road, still pumps water today and is great fun to visit – there's a lively atmosphere, bands play at the weekend, and Pump House Draft is a pretty good beer! For jazz, try Rosie's and All that Jazz, Quay 5, which has a bar, restaurant and dance floor. Finally, Ferryman's Tavern, alongside Victoria Wharf, was the first pub to open on the waterfront – it serves excellent pub lunches.

EXCURSIONS

BOLAND, about 60 km outside Cape Town, has been a wine-making region since 1688 when the French Huguenots arrived in the area and brought the craft with them. Today there are 24 wine farms and a number of wine routes, all nestling in beautiful Cape countryside. Notable wineries include the Nederberg Winery in the Paarl Valley and KWV Wine Cellars in Paarl, which welcomes visitors for tours and sampling four times every day. And you mustn't miss the Boschendal Estate, on the Helshoogte Road between Stellenbosch and Franschoek. This is one of the oldest wineries in the country – a restored Cape Dutch house on the premises has been turned into a museum containing period furniture. All the wineries charge a nominal fee, give you a tumbler, and allow you to try a specified number of wines. Getting to and around the Boland is easy – the main towns have railway stations, and thumbing a lift is no problem.

STELLENBOSCH with its old whitewashed buildings is the home of South Africa's foremost Afrikaans university. On Dorp Street there's a fascinating little shop, Oom Samie se Winkel, which sells toys, twig brooms, ostrich feathers and jars of pickled cauliflowers – among other things! There are a couple of hiking trails in the Boland area: the LIMIETBERG stretches 37 km from Hawequas state forest to Tweede Tol and takes two days to cover; the 55 km HOTTENTOTS HOLLAND starts at Sir Lowry Pass and finishes near Franschoek, and takes three days. The hikes are popular, especially over weekends, so you'll need to book. The Western Cape Forest Region, Private Bag 9005, Cape Town 8000 (tel. 402 3403) runs the trails, and you should contact them for details.

South of Cape Town, on Walker Bay, lies HERMANUS, one of the Cape's most popular resorts. It's a charming town, with cobbled alleyways and open-air restaurants. The only drawback is that it's so touristy. There are some good walking trails near Hermanus, especially those along the cliffs, which give you terrific views of Walker Bay.

The SALMONSDAM NATURE RESERVE has a variety of small mammals, antelope and bird life – look out for black harrier, and the orange-breasted and malachite sunbird. It's safe to walk freely here, and some three-day trails have been laid out. There's a small camp in the centre of the reserve where you can hire a hut or pitch your tent. Telephone the ranger on 0027283/770062 for more details and to make advance bookings (necessary at weekends).

Johannesburg

AIRPORT FACILITIES
Jan Smuts International Airport is 24 km west of Joburg. It has five terminals: international arrivals and departures; national arrivals and departures; and feeder services.

There is an information desk in both arrivals halls; and there are the usual banking, post office and duty-free facilities, along with restaurants, cafés and bars, facilities for disabled travellers, and facilities for babies and young children.

CITY LINKS
Bus: The cheapest way to town is on the SAA/Rotunda bus, which departs from the airport every half-hour and take 30 minutes to reach Joburg railway station.
Taxi: It takes about 25 minutes to reach the city centre, but it's expensive.
Car hire: The major firms are represented at the airport, but it's cheaper to travel downtown by bus and check out local car-hire prices.

USEFUL ADDRESSES
Tourist offices: Johannesburg Publicity Association, North State Building, corner Market and Kruis Streets (tel. 29 4961); SATOUR, Carlton Centre, PO Box 1094, Johannesburg 2000 (331 5241).
Emergency services: Police and fire 999; ambulance 402 4222.

GETTING ABOUT
There are regular buses throughout Joburg's three regions (the city centre or 'town'; Hillbrow; and Braamfontein), but everything

stops at night. Taxis are expensive. Your best option is car hire or to rely on your own two feet (the distances are walkable, as long as you're the energetic type).

SIGHTS

Joburg is a bit lacking in 'must-see' places, but if you've pre-booked a few days there, don't despair; there are lots of attractions within reach of the city (see **Excursions**, p. 252).

The AFRICANA MUSEUM in the public library on Bree Street will provide a good insight into African heritage; there are replicas of huts, displays of beadwork, plus ethnic clothing, hunting and domestic equipment. JOHANNESBURG ART GALLERY, Klein Street near Joubert Park, houses some good collections of South African, British, Dutch and French art. The ALDER MUSEUM OF THE HISTORY OF MEDICINE at the South African Institute for Medical Research, Hospital Hill, makes for a fascinating visit with its turn-of-the-century operating theatre, witch-doctor's home, and an African herbarium amongst other things! And train buffs will thoroughly enjoy a trip to the RAILWAY MUSEUM at the station.

Other than that, it's a matter of wandering around and taking in the atmosphere. There's a good flea market in MARY FITZGERALD SQUARE, where you'll be able to pick up local ethnic crafts and clothes. DIAGONAL STREET is also an interesting place to browse: a variety of African and Asian goods are offered for sale in the numerous shops and kiosks.

It's worth making the short 6 km trip to GOLD REEF CITY, which is a recreation of what life was like in the 1880s gold town – you'll be able to go down what was once the world's richest gold mine; watch a gold ingot being poured, fossick for gold, and see how the former inhabitants used to live (compare the worker's house with that of his boss).

ACCOMMODATION

There's really not an awful lot of budget accommodation to choose from.

Youth hostels: The YHA, 32 Main Street (tel. 436 2837) is the cheapest place to stay, with dormitory accommodation starting at about R20 per night. It tends to get full, so phone before making the long trek to get there. Take any bus going south from the railway station, get off at Eloff Square bus depot, and catch a number 47 bus. Get off at stop 24.

Twice the price, but the next cheapest you'll get, are the YMCA and YWCA. They're both in Rissik Street, about a five-minute walk north from the railway station. There's one telephone number for both hostels: 724 4541.

Hotels: Most of Joburg's budget hotels are in the Joubert Park/ Hillbrow area. Make your way to Joubert Park, about a ten-minute walk from the railway station, and check out the hotels along Smit Street:

Europa (tel. 724 5321). R50 per night.

Pads (28 5702). R50 per night.

Little Roseneath (724 3322). R50 per night.

For a similar price, try one of the following hotels in the Hillbrow/ Berea area:

Chelsea, Catherine Street (642 4541).

Statesman, 16 Joel Road (642 7165).

Ambassador, Pretoria Street (642 5051).

Campsites: Sadly, there aren't any campsites within reach of central Joburg.

FOOD

There's no way you can starve in Joburg. The number of restaurants, fast-food chains and street stalls is evidence that eating out is Joburg's favourite pastime. Hillbrow is a cosmopolitan area, and the range of cuisine reflects that. There's every type of food, including Mexican, Indian, Chinese and Italian.

If you want to eat out – and if you've been travelling overland through Africa, you'll find Joburg a gourmet paradise – then it's best to ask your hotel or the publicity office (or fellow travellers) about the best places to eat. If money is limited, the most reliable of the fast-food chains is Mike's Kitchen: at these steakhouses you can tuck into a main course for not much more than R20.

ENTERTAINMENT

Joburg has pretty good nightlife, especially compared with the rest of South Africa. Pick up a free copy of *Blake's Guide to Johannesburg* (most hotels will have it), which comes out monthly and lists everything that's happening in Joburg – not just theatre and cinema, but the latest art exhibitions and sporting fixtures, plus restaurants, hotels and excursions. The *Weekly Mail* also gives a comprehensive list of arts events.

The theatre scene (like so many other things in Joburg) is centred around the Market Theatre – you can't miss it on the map. It tends to concentrate on South African plays. Next to the Market Theatre is Kippie's, a popular club with live African jazz every night. If you fancy an all-night rave, head for The Junction on Bee Street. Those staying in the Hillbrow area won't have to walk very far to find a club or disco: most are situated along Pretoria Street and Kotze Street.

Be careful walking back to your hotel, there have been frequent muggings in the Hillbrow area. The other problem with nightlife in Joburg is the lack of late-night public transport and the scarcity of taxis. You really need your own transport.

EXCURSIONS

The chief reason most folk visit Joburg – and indeed South Africa – is because of its proximity to the KRUGER NATIONAL PARK. Covering an area the size of Wales, the park is divided into three main areas – the south (south of Sabie River), the central region (between Sabie and Olifants Rivers) and the north (north of Olifants River). Some 147 mammal, 507 bird, 114 reptile, 33 amphibian and 49 fish species have been recorded there. The southern region tends to attract the most tourists because the largest camp, Skakuza, is based there.

Hitching is forbidden in the park (though there's nothing to stop you hitching to it), so you'll either have to hire a car or join a tour. If you're travelling on your own, the cheapest option is a tour; there's less freedom, but the fact that you'll have an experienced guide means you're likely to see more animals. Tour operators include:

Drifters, PO Box 48434, Roosevelt Park, 2129, Johannesburg (tel. 673 7012), do a three-day camping tour at a fairly reasonable price.

Wildlife Safaris, PO Box 3134, Randburg, 2125 (886 4065).

Grosvenor Tours, PO Box 6932, Johannesburg 2000 (708 1777), are slightly more expensive. If you want to book your Kruger trip before you leave the UK, they have a branch at Richmond Bridge House, 419 Richmond Road, Twickenham (tel. 0181 892 3687).

If there's more than one of you, then the thing to do is hire a car with an unlimited kilometres deal. By camping and cooking your own food, you can spend a week in Kruger Park for as little as R500 per person. It costs about R10 to take a vehicle into the park, then there's an additional charge of R12 per person. Joburg's cheapest car hire company is Rent-a-Wreck (tel. 402 7043). Ask fellow hostellers at Joburg if they can recommend other car hire companies, perhaps running current special deals. The same goes for tours.

There are also five hiking trails in the park, which last three days and are led by armed rangers. These are often booked up at least a year in advance, so if you want to see Kruger that way, make arrangements early on while planning your round-the-world trip. They cost from about R250. Contact the National Parks Board, PO Box 787, Pretoria 0001 (tel. (012) 343 2007) for information on foot safaris and other details about Kruger Park. Advance bookings for overnight accommodation in huts or something more luxurious must be made via the National Parks Board. If you intend to camp, then it's probably better to reserve in advance as well. The campsites charge about R12 to pitch a tent, with R7 per person on top. Huts can cost anything from R35 to R200 depending on how basic or luxurious you want your accommodation to be.

To maximize your chance of seeing wildlife, it's best to stick to the dirt roads (a lot of tourists avoid them, so it's much quieter) and drive slowly. When planning your daily itinerary, allow for this, otherwise you'll find yourself missing out on wildlife because of having to cover the ground. If you have time, spend a week in the park – there's plenty to see, and the longer you stay and more slowly you travel, you'll have more chance of seeing the animal everyone goes to Kruger to see: the lion.

There are a number of private game reserves close to Kruger Park which are more expensive, but because rangers will be taking you on a game drive or leading you on foot, you're much more likely to encounter a lion or cheetah. The best-known private reserves are MALA-MALA, SABI-SABI, and LONDOLOZI; a night at one of these will set you back at least £150. To book, contact Game Lodge Reservations, PO Box 783968, Sandton 2146, Johannesburg (tel. 883 4345).

Just 40 km from Joburg lies PRETORIA, and it's worth a visit, not least because it's more attractive to look at than Joburg, especially in October when the jacarandas are in bloom. It's short on budget accommodation, however, so spend just a day there. Take in the impressive UNION BUILDINGS, the administrative headquarters of the South African government, and enjoy the panoramic views of Pretoria. There are statues of General Louis Botha, Field-Marshal J. C. Smuts, and General J. B. M. Hertzog too, along with the War Memorial, Garden of Remembrance and the Police Memorial.

There's a good nature reserve, the WONDERBOOM, 5 km from Pretoria. Among other fascinating flora, it has a 1,000-year-old fig tree, which has spread out over half a hectare. Only 6 km from Pretoria is the VOORTREKKER MONUMENT, which commemorates the Boer prisoners of the 1830s who trekked from the Cape to the Transvaal, which was at that time a new territory beyond the sphere of British rule. Climb 260 steps up to the dome, which has a brilliant panoramic view of Pretoria and its environs.

West of Joburg, *en route* to KRUGERSDORP are the STERKFONTEIN CAVES, with their impressive stalagmite and stalactite formations. In 1936 an almost complete female Australopithecus skull, estimated at more than two million years old, was found here.

You might also want to take a trip from Joburg to SUN CITY, the luxury resort complex which hosts, among other things, the world's richest golf tournament. As the homeland of Bophuthatswana, it has been possible for Sun City to stage pop concerts and other events which could not be held in South Africa because of the sanctions issue. It has a casino (gambling is banned in South Africa) and top-notch sporting facilities. Quicksilver run daily coaches from Joburg to Sun City – phone 403 1395 for times and prices.

BAHRAIN

VITAL STATISTICS
Red tape: To enter Bahrain, you need a valid passport, a return or onward ticket and, unless you're a British citizen born in the UK, a visa. One-month visas may be obtained at the airport for a fee of £3 – provided you can produce a letter from friends or relatives in Bahrain, a photo, and a 'No objections' certificate from the Immigration Office. If you book into a large hotel, they can arrange a visa in advance for you. Business visas cost £10 on production of a letter from your company, a photo and a 'No objections' certificate. Long-term business visas, of one to two years, are available if the company in Bahrain obtains a 'No objections' certificate on your behalf.

Customs: 400 cigarettes or 50 cigars or 225 g tobacco in opened packets; 50 ml perfume; 2 bottles wine or spirits (non-Muslims only); and gifts up to the value of BD50. Unpolished pearls produced outside the Gulf come under strict import regulations and some goods are boycotted by members of the Arab League.

Health: A yellow fever vaccination certificate must be produced if you are coming from an infected area. It's wise to take a course of anti-malaria tablets before entering Bahrain. The water is generally safe to drink. Travellers should take sensible precautions against the heat, and also make sure they have sufficient medical insurance to cover private treatment. Cholera and typhoid vaccinations are recommended but not required.

Language: Ninety per cent Arabic, with some local dialects. The official business language is English.

Population: Approx. 500,000.

Capital: Al Mamana, population about 130,000.

Political system: The country is governed by the Emir and a cabinet of appointed ministers.

Religion: 85% Muslim, with Christian, Bahai, Hindu and Parsi minorities.

Time: Three hours ahead of GMT.

Money: The currency is the dinar (BD), divided into 100 fils. Coins: 5, 10, 25, 50 and 100 fils. Notes: 500 fils, BD1, BD5, BD10, and BD20. £1 = BD0.58.

Communications: The phone network is one of the most modern in the Gulf. International direct dialling is available from all phones. The dialling code for Bahrain is 973. The postal service is reliable. Airmail service to the UK takes three or four days.

Electricity: Manama: 230v AC. Awali: 120v AC.

Business hours: BANKS: Sat.–Thurs. 7 a.m.–12 p.m.

SHOPS: Sat.–Thurs. 8 a.m.–12 p.m. and 3.30 p.m.–6 p.m.

OFFICES: Sat.–Wed. 7 a.m.–2.15 p.m.

Holidays: 1 January (New Year's Day) and 16 December (National Day) are annual public holidays. Muslim holidays are also celebrated, but these change every year. The main holidays are: Ramadan (21 Jan.–20 Feb.); Eid Al Fitr, the first day after Ramadan, when it can be difficult to travel or to find restaurants open during daylight hours; Eid-el-Adha (29 April); and Al Ashoura.

Climate: If you don't like the heat, don't go to Bahrain between June and September, as temperatures regularly hit 43°C. It's a lot cooler between December and March (winter), and there's usually some light rainfall at this time. It's pleasantly warm in spring and autumn. It's advisable to wear sunglasses all year round. November/December is the best time to visit.

DO'S AND DON'TS

Bahrain is a Muslim country and so to avoid giving offence you should follow the usual codes of behaviour for Islamic countries: use the right hand not the left for eating, greeting and gesturing; dress conservatively and try to behave with a degree of decorum. If you think you will find it difficult to abide by the rules of Ramadan (when, for example eating is prohibited during daylight hours), don't go during this time.

WHERE TO GO FOR WHAT

Bahrain comprises 34 islands, only a handful of which are of interest since most of the archipelago is uninhabited and barren. The chief island is BAHRAIN, its main attractions being the present capital, MANAMA; the ancient capital, BALAD AL-QUADIM; and the picturesque old town of RIFAA, with its impressive fort.

MUHARRAQ ISLAND is the site of Bahrain's modern international airport and the attractive town of HEDD, which has a number of preserved ancient houses. The most attractive island is probably NABI SALIH, with its little lakes and ponds and luxuriant vegetation. The northern coast of SITRA is also quite pleasant. The other islands are barren and virtually impossible to reach.

INTERNAL TRAVEL

With no internal airlines or railways, there's really only one way of getting around Bahrain and that's by road.

Bus: For the budget traveller, the cheapest way of getting around is by bus; most mainland towns and villages are on a bus route, and the standard fare is 50 fils. Taxi fares should always be agreed in advance, as drivers tend to pay little attention to government limits. Fares increase by 50% after midnight.

Taxi: You can hire a taxi by the hour if you want to have a quick tour. Bargaining is the rule. Expect to pay about BD9 per hour.

Car hire: All the usual international car-hire firms are out there, but you need to apply in person to the police in Isa Town for a permit to drive. If you hold a UK, US or Australian licence, you need only apply for the permit and take a sight test. Everyone else has to take a driving test. Driving is on the right.

Ferry: Bahrain's islands are connected by motorboat or dhow. A local travel agent in Bahrain will be able to give details of fares and timetables.

ACCOMMODATION

Bahrain's hotels are basically aimed at the business traveller and as such are nearly all out of the backpacker's price bracket. There are some second-class hotels and service flats around – for details of these, contact the Bahrain Tourist Office at the airport (tel. 21648). The cheapest hotel rooms go for about BD15–20. There are a couple of youth hostels, one in Manama and one in Muharraq; beds need to be booked 15 days in advance, and you can't stay longer than six nights. Preference is given to younger YHA members. For further information, contact the Bahrain Youth Hostels Society, PO Box 2455, Manama (tel: 973 727 170). Expect to pay about BD15 per night.

FOOD

Arabic food tends to be strongly flavoured and spicy. Lamb is a favourite dish, usually served with salads and dips. Arabic sweets are sweet and sickly – if you've an extremely sweet tooth, you'll love 'em! As in other Gulf states, dining out is a favourite pastime, and there are good restaurants aplenty, serving all types of international cuisine.

Alcohol is extremely expensive. The most common drinks available are beer and the Arab spirit *arak* (a grape spirit flavoured with aniseed). Tea is a common drink, and so is coffee – the Arabic variety, served in small cups and stewed at length for maximum flavour. It's strong!

BUDGETING

It's possible to find accommodation at less than BD20 per night, which is very reasonable for a Gulf state. If you do all your travelling by bus, it won't be all that expensive either. Restaurants tend to be pricey, but if you're willing to live off takeaways, you can be thrifty when it comes to food, too.

Any work opportunities – mainly nursing or TEFL teaching or working for a Bahrain company – would be long-term and would have to be arranged beforehand, with the company you'd be working for organizing your 'No objections' certificate.

FURTHER INFORMATION

Lonely Planet's *Arab Gulf States – Travel Survival Kit* is one of the few travel guides available for the budget traveller. *Looking for Dilmun* by Geoffrey Bibby gives an account of life in Bahrain through the eyes of an archaeologist in the 1960s.

Information can be had from the information office at the Embassy of the State of Bahrain, 98 Gloucester Road, London SW7 4AU (tel. 071 370 0092) or the Bahrain Tourism Company, PO Box 5831, Manama, Bahrain (tel. 530 530). They do not have a UK office.

Manama

AIRPORT FACILITIES

Bahrain's only airport is on the island of Muharraq, 6 km north-east of Manama. There's just one terminal, but it's served by 69 airlines, is open 24 hours a day, and has all the usual facilities: information desk, banks, foreign exchange, duty-free, car rental, snack bars, restaurants, etc. Check-in time is 90 minutes before departure, and departure tax is BD3.

CITY LINKS

Bus: Between 5.10 a.m. and 11 p.m., you can catch the number 4, 6 or 10 bus to Muharraq bus station, and from there pick up the number 1, 2 or 19 bus to Manama bus station. Buses leave the airport every 20–30 minutes, and the fare to Manama is about 100 fils. The journey takes about half an hour.

Taxi: The taxi fare from the airport to Manama is officially BD4, but it's best to agree that price before you go. The journey takes approximately ten minutes. Remember that taxi fares increase by 50% after midnight.

USEFUL ADDRESSES

Tourist office: Bahrain Airport (tel. 21648). Another source of leaflets and information is the Thomas Cook office at Unitag House, Government Road, Manama (tel. 258 000).

British Airways: Alkhalifa Road, Manama (tel. 253 503)

British Embassy: Al Mathaf Square, PO Box 114 (tel. 254 002/ 253 503)

US Embassy: Shaikh Isa Road, PO Box 431 (tel. 714 151)

Medical Assistance: American Mission Hospital (tel. 253 447) or International Hospital (tel. 591 666)

GETTING ABOUT

There's an efficient bus service around Manama, and to other destinations around the island. The standard fare within the city is 50 fils; to anywhere outside the city, 100 fils. Taxis are readily available, but make sure you agree the fare before setting off on your journey.

SIGHTS

Manama will be something of a disappointment to history buffs – it's a thriving modern city whose oldest relic is the tomb of Sheikh Ahmad Al-Khalifah, which dates back to the eighteenth century. The focal point of the town is SHEIKH SULMAN SQUARE, with JUMA MOSQUE close by. The historic BAZAAR starts here and extends the full length of Bab Al-Bahrain: here you can barter for an array of goods, including gold, pearls, jewellery, clothing, material, antiques, Persian carpets, brass and copper. Along the sea front, Government Road has some handsome buildings, in particular the National Bank and Government House. The PALACE, near Guadibiya Gardens, is a particularly impressive U-shaped structure, built in the 1930s; its huge dining-hall is used for state banquets. The NATIONAL MUSEUM, on the intersection of Muharraq Causeway and King Faisal Highway is well worth a look, as is the 16th-century ARAB FORT, close to the airport.

ACCOMMODATION
Accommodation in Manama is generally expensive as the nicer hotels are geared towards businessmen. Budget travellers should try:

Al-Jufayr Youth Hostel, No. 1105, Road 4225, Al-Jufayr (tel. 727 170). This lies south-east of the city centre, opposite the Bahrain School; accessible by taxi. Expect to pay BD15 per night.

Hotel, Al-Khalifa Avenue (tel. 211 549). Formerly known as the Al-Afrah Hotel, this offers singles/doubles for BD15/25.

Central Hotel, off Municipality Square (tel. 233 553). Private bath and TV. Singles/doubles: BD15/25.

Bahrain Hotel, Al-khalifa Avenue (tel. 253 478). Located near the intersection with Road 453. All rooms have private baths. Singles/doubles: BD20/30.

FOOD
Bahrain has all kinds of international restaurants: Italian, Greek, Chinese, Mexican, Indian — you name it, Bahrain's got it. The big hotels also have superb restaurants, many with fabulous views over the Gulf, though these can be expensive. There are, however, take-aways dotted all about the city representing every ethnic cuisine, so you won't have to starve.

ENTERTAINMENT
Oh, dear — the entertainment on offer isn't exactly thrilling. The beach at midday is reputed to be the real high spot of Manama. The nightclubs are all based at the top hotels, and are pretty sophis-ticated and expensive. Hotels such as the Sheraton run supper clubs where you can combine a meal with an evening's entertainment, such as a band or cabaret. The Alliance Française is a cultural organ-ization which organizes such social activities as dances, excursions and film-shows. Films in Arabic and English are shown at Bahrain's cinemas. You may find, after an excursion-packed day, you won't have much energy left for nightlife.

EXCURSIONS
The old town of RIFAA, 16 km south of Manama, is unquestionably the most picturesque in Bahrain. It is dominated by the old Amir's

fort, which dates back to the 18th century. The town is surrounded by lush countryside and the HANANI SPRING provides Rifaa with the finest water in the land.

Thousands of fascinating burial mounds, dating back to the third century BC, line the road from A'ALI to ZALLAQ, thus forming the largest Bronze Age cemetery in the world.

There are some excellent beaches and sports facilities along Bahrain's western coast: SHEIK'S BEACH, where the Amir has his country residence, is especially superb. You can enjoy wonderful views across to Saudi Arabia and Qatar from the top of the JEBEL DUKHAN – the 'Mountain of Smoke' – near Sheik's Beach. You need police permission to visit RAS AL-BARR at the southern tip of the island, but it's worth the hassle of getting it as there's fabulous wildlife there, including gazelle and pink flamingoes, and the seagull eggs which cover the shores at certain times of the year are a local delicacy. If you prefer an easy life, go and see the wildlife at nearby AL AREEN WILDLIFE PARK.

South-west of Manama, the 14th-century SUQ AL-KHAMIS MOSQUE is the most interesting and imposing of the three mosques in the former medieval capital of Bahrain, BALAD AL-QUADIM. Just under a kilometre outside the village is the Pool of the Virgin – AIN ADARI – which is a favourite haunt of the locals, thanks to its cool gardens and groves. The northern part of the island has several interesting archaeological sites, including the now dilapidated Portuguese fort of QUALAT AL-BAHRAIN near Budaiya, and the remains of the Bronze Age stronghold of DILMUN close by.

The only two islands worth a trip are NABI SALIH, which pilgrims used to swim to from Manama, and MUHARRAQ. The latter is the location of Bahrain's museum, where a few of the exhibits – including gold seals used by the merchants of the ancient town of Dilmun – date back some 4,000 years.

For tours of Bahrain and Muharraq, contact Bahrain Explored (tel. 246 266).

EGYPT

VITAL STATISTICS
Red tape: A full passport, valid for at least six months after your arrival date is required of all visitors. British, European, American, Australian and New Zealand tourists will also need a visa. Though visas can be obtained on arrival in Cairo, it is recommended that you apply to an Egyptian Embassy or Consulate in your country

of origin by post or in person. You'll need to complete an application form, present your passport, a passport photograph, and the fee (allow two to three weeks if applying by post).

Within seven days of arrival in Egypt all tourists must register their passport with the police. The tourist office or your hotel manager will tell you where to register, and often will do the paperwork for you (it's just a matter of filling in a form, but if you don't do it you'll be fined E£40).

Visa extensions are usually granted for up to one year – go to the Mugama Building in Cairo or to any police station. Again you'll need a passport photograph, a fee of about E£6, and proof that you have enough money to cover your stay.

Customs: The following goods can be imported into Egypt without incurring customs duty: 200 cigarettes or 25 cigars or 200g tobacco; 1 l spirits; a reasonable amount of perfume or eau de cologne; gifts up to the value of E£500. Note: all cash, traveller's cheques, credit cards and gold over the value of E£500 must be declared on arrival.

Health: Immunization is recommended against cholera, typhoid, tetanus, polio and hepatitis. Tap water is undrinkable outside Cairo (and I wouldn't risk it even there!). It's advisable to bring an AIDS pack (see **Medicine**, p. 99).

Language: Arabic. Colloquial Arabic is used in everyday life, while news broadcasts, political speeches and religious sermons are given in classical Arabic.

Population: 58 million.

Capital: Cairo, population 15 million.

Political system: 'Democratic socialist' according to the 1971 Constitution. While in practice the system is neither democratic nor particularly socialist, it's among the most liberal of the Arab nations. President Hosni Mubarak has been in power since 1981.

Religion: Predominantly Muslim. Other religions include Christian Orthodox of the Coptic and Egyptian Church.

Time: Two hours ahead of GMT.

Money: The currency is the Egyptian pound (E£), which is divided into 100 piasters (pt). Coins are virtually extinct. Notes: 5pt, 10pt, 25pt, 50pt, and E£1, E£5, E£10, E£20. £1 = E£4.74.

It's certainly not safe to carry large amounts of cash around as theft is all too common. Credit cards are not accepted by small hotels, restaurants and shops in Egypt, so traveller's cheques are the most convenient means of payment. Compare rates when changing money, as commission fees vary. Try to carry Egyptian money in small denominations, as street vendors, taxi drivers and bus drivers tend not to give any change.

Tax: There is a hotel tax, which is about 10% in most locations, though in Cairo it's 19%.

Communications: If you're not the patient type, you should avoid the Egyptian phone system – and perhaps forget about Egypt altogether! Long-distance and international calls can be made from one of the leading hotels, or prepare yourself for a very long wait and try the 'Centrale', a government telephone office (when you finally do get to the phone, you'll have to pay in advance for a specific amount of time).

Airmail letters and postcards to Europe and the States cost E£1. If you want to send a postcard, post it at a major hotel rather than the post office, that way it's more likely to reach it's destination. Poste restante is available in most of the major cities, but letters can take up to three weeks to arrive. Advise correspondents to make your surname clearly distinguishable on the envelope (there is a risk that it may otherwise be pigeonholed under your first name). ·

Electricity: Most areas 220v AC, 50 Hz. Certain rural parts still 110–380v AC.

Business hours: BANKS: Sun.–Thurs. 8.30 a.m.–2 p.m. money-changing facilities are also available from 4–8 p.m. on those days.

POST OFFICES: Sat.–Thurs. 9 a.m.–3 p.m.

SHOPS: Sat.–Thurs. 9 a.m.–2 p.m. and 5 p.m.–8 p.m. (9 p.m. in summer). Some also open on Friday, the Muslim day of communal prayer.

OFFICES: Sat.–Thurs. 9 a.m.–2 p.m.

Holidays: 21 Jan.–20 Feb. (Ramadan); 25 April (Sinai Day); 1 May (Labour Day); 23 July (Revolution Day); and 23 December (Victory Day). During the month of Ramadan, devout Muslims do not eat or drink during daylight hours and many restaurants and food stores are therefore closed. There are a number of other religious festivals celebrated in Egypt, but though offices and banks shut down, most tourist sites remain open.

Climate: There's only one word for it: *hot*. Summer temperatures can reach 54°C in the south of Egypt, though fortunately humidity is low in that part of the country. The temperature in Cairo reaches a mere 36°C in summer, but air pollution makes the atmosphere stifling. Alexandria's weather is temperate with high humidity. Winter temperatures are much more comfortable (in the low 20s). If, however, you can cope with the heat, you'll find summer a better time to travel – there are fewer tourists and cheaper prices.

DO'S AND DON'TS

The usual codes of behaviour for Islamic countries apply: use the right hand not the left for eating, greeting and gesturing; dress conservatively and try to behave with a degree of decorum. The Egyptian authorities regard living together outside marriage as immoral, and an openly gay lifestyle is completely taboo here (as it is throughout the Middle East).

There's recently been an upsurge in terrorist attacks carried out by Moslem Fundamentalists on Western targets. Contact the Foreign Office for advice before you plan your visit: their traveller's help line is 0171 270 4129.

There's often a ban on photography in holy places, and at archaeological sites and museums (and you will fall foul of the authorities if you take photos of border crossings, airfields, bridges or railway stations). When visiting mosques, remember to take your shoes off – and in the more touristy mosques, you'll possibly have to pay to get them back again. Women should be covered from head to foot when visiting a mosque.

Egyptians believe all Western women are like the ones they see in American movies – free with their money and their bodies. To reduce unwelcome attentions from Egyptian men, women should avoid wearing shorts, miniskirts or tight-fitting clothes. It's usual for female travellers to be groped on overcrowded buses, so if you're travelling alone and want to avoid harassment, it's better to go by train – preferably first class.

Tipping – *baksheesh* – the poor in return for a service or favour is an ancient Islamic tradition. Many Egyptians regard Westerners as not only wealthy but dumb enough to be conned. You're likely to meet beggars who'll perform some service, such as opening a door before you can get to it, and then demand *baksheesh*. Firmly refuse all such demands. On the other hand, it's the done thing to tip waiters and cab drivers – unless there's a service charge already on your bill.

WHERE TO GO FOR WHAT

CAIRO, the capital, is grimy, overpopulated, noisy and frustrating. People either love the colourful chaos or find the poverty, constant traffic and unrelenting sun too much to bear. Most tourists are drawn to Cairo by the urge to see one the Seven Wonders of the Ancient World: the PYRAMIDS OF GIZA. The Pyramids lie 14 km to the west of Cairo, where the city meets the desert. Again, if you're the solitary type, you won't enjoy Giza – the complex is full of tourists, beggars, touts and camel-owners.

Most of the places you'll want to see – pyramids, ancient temples and tombs – stand alongside the Nile. A river cruise sounds romantic – and it is. Unfortunately, it's also expensive. You'll need to make arrangements before leaving home, and prices start at about E£250 per night. It's cheaper to go by train, bus or service taxi to Aswan or Luxor, then transfer to a *felucca*. These boats sleep up to eight people, and you hire them and the captain for approx. E£70 per person per night for a four-day cruise between Aswan and Luxor.

The VALLEY OF THE KINGS, near Luxor, is another major tourist attraction. There are some 64 tombs in the valley; only nine of which are currently on public view. Each tomb costs E£7 to view, though combined tickets for three tombs are available (it's worth buying three combined tickets to see all nine tombs). It is here you'll find the renowned TOMB OF TUTANKHAMUN. In the same region, near West Thebes, are the magnificent temples of Hatshepsut, Ramses II, Seti I and Ramses III. And yet more ancient temples and tombs and museums can be found at ASWAN, which is also close to the Lake Nasser's dam (trigger of the 1956 Suez crisis).

ALEXANDRIA, once the domain of Cleopatra, is now frequented for its seashore. Since the beaches are overcrowded and polluted, you probably won't be tempted to join the sunbathers (in the unlikely event that you do decide to take a dip, and you're female, please note that in Egypt women are expected to keep their clothes on, even to swim!)

SINAI, a region handed back to Egypt under the 1979 peace treaty with Israel, is well worth a visit. Aside from being the one place in Egypt where you can expect to see orderly traffic, the big attraction is Mount Sinai, where God gave Moses the Ten Commandments. Mount Sinai is a tough climb and can be treacherous by night; if you're not used to climbing it's probably best not to attempt it.

An adventurous excursion is to follow the trail of the Western Desert Oases – Khaga, Dakhla, Farafra and Bahariya – through the SAHARA. This route is actually a prehistoric branch of the Nile. If you decide to make the trip, be warned: it's *very* hot (50°C by day, 20°C by night), very isolated, and the roads are poorly maintained.

INTERNAL TRAVEL
Air: Internal flights are serviced by Egyptair, while Air Sinai connects Cairo with the Sinai and Israel. An economy class one-way ticket for the hour-long flight between Cairo and Luxor costs about £50. There are no student discounts or special-rate youth fares.
Rail: If you're planning a long-distance journey within Egypt, then

train is probably the best way to go. (Moreover there is a 50% student reduction on major rail routes.) Trains are, however, very crowded, and because so many Egyptians use them, the government tries to discourage tourists – thus station signs and railway schedules are never in English. But Egyptian travellers are more than happy to point you in the direction of your platform and the ticket office – where you can expect a long wait. If the queue looks interminable, and you're desperate to board your train, the fine for not having a ticket is minimal.

Because of the overcrowding, it's best to book yourself into an air-conditioned second-class carriage – first-class travel is obviously more expensive and gives you only a little more room. However, women travelling alone should seriously consider paying the extra to avoid harassment from Egyptian men. Certainly, travelling third class is something a woman on her own should avoid. Carriage numbers are in Roman numerals.

There are second-class sleeper cars available on some lines, but these tend to get booked up very quickly. One word of warning – unmarried couples are not permitted to share a sleeper cabin. Sleepers can be reserved at wagon-lit offices in Cairo, Luxor, Aswan and Alexandria.

Five trains a day run from Cairo to Alexandria (E£15.30) and a sleeper train runs from Cairo to Luxor (E£395.95).

Bus: Intercity buses are very cheap but extremely overcrowded. They're good for short trips – where the train service can sometimes be a problem – and also service some areas where trains don't go – such as the Sinai, Abu Simbel and Hurghada. Buses between the major cities leave frequently throughout the day, while those to the Sinai and the oases tend to go only early in the morning. If possible, check departure times with the station the day before you travel.

Because of the overcrowding and heat, it's usually better to fork out a little extra to travel by air-conditioned bus (available on most major routes).

Service taxis: These are intercity taxis, linking Cairo with other destinations. The cab seats up to eight passengers, but they tend to pack in more. Fares should be agreed with the driver beforehand, and split equally between the passengers. Cars leave as soon as they're filled – which usually takes about 15 minutes. They depart from various locations around Cairo – ask at the tourist office or hotel. They're a cheap and flexible form of travelling – though some drivers are more competent (and some more reckless) than others.

Car hire: If you're travelling with a small group, this could be the most economical way of seeing Egypt. The cheapest rentals start at about £30 sterling per day with unlimited mileage. You'll need an international driver's permit, plus a variety of special permits to travel on secondary roads in the Delta; along the Suez Canal between Ismailiya and Suez; the Red Sea Coast between Suez and Hurghada; the coastal road to Libya beyond Marsa Matruuh; any area surrounding the Siwa Oasis; and all areas in the Sinai off the main roads and outside the Federation-Klingon neutral zone. Get permission from the Travel Permits Department of the Ministry of the Interior on the corner of Sheikh Ridan and Nuban Street, Cairo. Take your passport and photographs and be prepared for a lengthy wait.

Make sure you take out insurance, as any driving insurance you have at home won't cover you here – and no wonder! Driving in Egypt is a hellish experience and you'll need nerves of steel to cope with all the chaos.

Hitching: Hitching is fairly rare in Egypt, though travellers claim Egyptians are usually happy to pick up foreign hitchers – for a fee. Women should not attempt to hitch, especially if travelling alone.

Local transport: You'll never have a problem finding transport round the main towns and out to the tourist attractions. Towns are served by local buses – cheap, but hot and overcrowded – taxis and trams, plus, in Cairo's case, an efficient metro system.

Taxis: Cabbies frequently attempt to rip off tourists, so always bargain over the fare, making sure it's understood and agreed before setting off.

Bicycles: Only the brave and/or crazy need cycle here. Apart from the hazards posed by other road users, there have been many accounts of cyclists being bombarded with rocks thrown by villagers.

ACCOMMODATION
Youth hostels: There are 15 YHA hostels in Egypt, and if you're on a tight budget these are the places to stay, costing between E£7 and E£12 per night. However, they do vary greatly in quality. It's essential to keep a close watch on your passport, visa, cash, and any other valuables. Most of the hostels have kitchen facilities. For details contact the Egyptian Youth Hostel Association, 1 El-Ibrahimy Street, Garden City, Cairo.

Hotels: Egypt's accommodation varies from luxurious tourist resorts to cheap and squalid rooms in back alleys. Somewhere in the middle lie inexpensive and clean hotels – but you need to search for them. Always ask to see the room before you accept it.

Prices vary from E£12 to E£45 per night. There's also a hotel tax which is usually included in the price – again, check this out first. Prices also go up in high season.

Note that sometimes hotels won't allow unmarried couples to share a room, and that hot water and private baths are luxuries in Egypt. And take your own toilet paper as it won't always be provided.

FOOD
The eating comes cheaply – but it does have a tendency to play havoc with your digestive system. Few people escape upset tummies, so go prepared with the Dio-calm. Unless you have an absolutely iron constitution, it's best to avoid buying very cheap snacks from street vendors.

Egypt is one country where vegetarians won't have to starve or endure a boring diet. Meat is a luxury for the majority of Egyptians, so the most common food is *fuul*, black or brown beans with oil, salt and lemon juice – sometimes it's served with an egg or with small pieces of meat. A typical local dish is *molokhaya*, a spicy green stew made from a flat leaf and cooked either by itself or with pieces of chicken, lamb or rabbit.

For inexpensive food shopping, head for the *souk* (market), but select food carefully. Egyptian bakers produce some delicious pastries, including *baklava*, made from filo dough, honey syrup and nuts. Fruit and fruit juices are expensive for locals, but tourists will find them excellent value.

Egyptians are great tea and coffee drinkers – with a tendency to prefer their drinks syrupy-sweet. Tea is taken without milk, but is thick with sugar. The *ahwa* (Arabic coffee) comes with no sugar, with medium sugar, or with lots of sugar. It is possible, occasionally, to get Western-style coffee. For a refreshingly gorgeous drink on a hot day, try *kirkaday*. It's a red drink made from the flower of the fuchsia plant.

BUDGETING
Egypt is extremely cheap to visit – even the tourist attractions are easy on your pocket. A ticket to see the Tomb of Tutankhamun, for example, costs just E£6; entry to the Pyramid complex is E£10 with another E£10 to go inside the Pyramids (that's about £4 altogether, and students go in half-price). Food, accommodation and travel are also inexpensive, which compensates for the lack of luxury.

Work opportunities exist mainly in the field of teaching English as a foreign language. If you're familiar with Arabic, then you stand a good chance of finding work in one of the foreign companies in Egypt.

FURTHER INFORMATION

Egyptian Embassy, 2 Lowndes Street, London SW1X 9ET (tel. 0171 235 9777).

The Egyptian Tourist Authority at 170 Piccadilly, London W1V 9DE (tel. 0171 493 5282/3) can provide information and literature on travelling in Egypt.

Background reading: *Let's Go: Israel and Egypt* (Pan, £13.99) is crammed with useful information for anyone visiting either or both countries – there are also sections on Jordan and the West Bank. It includes a language glossary for Arabic and Hebrew. *Fodor's Egypt* is also a useful guide for the budget traveller.

For a taste of good modern Egyptian literature, dip into the novels of Naguib Mahfouz, winner of the Nobel Prize for Literature in 1988. His classic *Children of Gebelawi* – banned in Egypt – retells the stories of the Koran in a modern Cairo setting. He is published in Britain by Heinemann Press. Nawal El Saadawi is a feminist writer published by Zed Press; her best-known book is *The Hidden Face of Eve*, a moving account of what it's like to grow up as a woman in the Islamic Middle East. Huda Sha'rawi, another feminist, is the author of *Harem Years: The Memoirs of an Egyptian Feminist*, published by Virago. It's a fascinating account of the last generation of upper-class Egyptian women to spend their childhood and married life in the segregated world of the harem.

Western writers who've used Egypt as a setting for their books include Olivia Manning, whose Levant Trilogy follows Harriet and Guy Pringle to wartime Cairo; and Mark Twain recounts his adventures in Egypt in *The Innocents Abroad*.

For the writings of the ancient Egyptians, see The Book of the Dead, The Song of the Harper and The Tale of the Eloquent Peasant, all originally inscribed on stone and now classic folklore.

Cairo

AIRPORT FACILITIES

Cairo International Airport is situated 24 km north-east of the city. It has two terminals, each with a departure and arrival hall. You'll find tourist information, duty-free facilities, a post office and cafeterias in all the halls, but restaurants and bars are only in the departure halls. There's a shuttle bus service available 24 hours a day between the two terminals.

CITY LINKS
Bus: Services for central Cairo depart from the airport every hour: the number 400 bus goes to Tahrir Square, the number 410 to Ataban Square. The journey takes about an hour and costs approximately 75pt. There is also a taxi service.

USEFUL ADDRESSES
Tourist office: 5 Adly Street (tel. 391 34 54). It's actually marked 'Tourist Police'.
Post office: 55 Sarwat Street. Ataba Square (tel. 91 00 11). Poste restante facilities are round the corner, in Bidek Street.
British Embassy: 7 Ahmed Ragheb Street (tel. 354 08 50).
US Embassy: 5 Latin America Street (tel. 355 73 71).
Emergency services: dial 122 for police; 125 for fire; and 123 for ambulance services.
Medical emergencies: The major hotels have resident doctors who can issue prescriptions. Your Embassy will give you a list of doctors and hospitals equipped to handle foreigners. The Anglo-American Hospital is next to the Cairo Tower, in Botanical Garden Street, Gezira-Zamalek (tel. 340 61 62/3).
Pharmacy: First Aid Pharmacy, corner July 26 Street and Ramses Street (tel. 74 33 69) is open 24 hours a day. In Egypt, pharmacists are regarded as doctors and can give injections.

GETTING ABOUT
Metro: Completed in 1987, this is incredibly – for Cairo – efficient, air-conditioned and even clean. The trains run every few minutes between 6 a.m. and 1 a.m., and rides cost from 15–50pt. They get a bit crowded in the rush hour, before 9 a.m. and from 5–7 p.m., so try to avoid travelling then.
Bus: Cairo's frequent public buses are the cheapest way of getting around (apart from walking), but they do have a reputation for breaking down, and are hot, crowded and extremely uncomfortable. Most services run from 5.30 a.m. until after midnight, but during Ramadan there's a break between 6.30 p.m. and 7.30 p.m.
  Cairo's two main bus stations are located in Tahrir Square. The one in front of the Mugama is for services to Giza and the southern parts of Islamic Cairo. The station in front of the Nile Hilton serves northern areas and the rest of Islamic Cairo. Rides generally cost 10pt. Catching a bus at the station is easy; in the street it's a different

matter. Summon up your courage and leap on – it's rare for a bus to stop. The same applies when it's time to get off.

Minibus: The red-and-white minibuses cover most of the routes served by the normal buses. At 25–60pt they're more expensive than buses, but they are much more comfortable and far less crowded (most Cairenes can't afford them). They go from the Mugama Station and from the Arab League Building.

Taxi: Go for the black-and-white ones (the colourful Peugeots will rip you off). Acceptable fares are E£1 for the first kilometre, and 25pt for each additional kilometre. You're expected to pay for luggage. Make sure you can tell the driver where you want to go in Arabic, or have your destination written down (again, in Arabic).

Most of Cairo's main sights are in walking distance of Tahrir Square. Watch the traffic though – it's not going to stop for you!

SIGHTS

For panoramic views of Cairo – stretching right across to the Pyramids – head for the observation deck in CAIRO TOWER, on Zamalek Island, in New Cairo. The other main island, Roda, is home to one of Cairo's most noteworthy ancient monuments – the NILOMETER, built in 8 BCE to measure the height of the river and so predict the harvest yield.

The New City has an abundance of markets, including the weekly camel market at Imbaba. The animals are in a pitiful state, and if you're the type who gets upset by cruelty to animals, it's probably best not to go. For more traditional wares, try the markets in the TAHRIR area, where you'll also see the impressive STATUE OF RAMSES II in front of Ramses Station.

The EGYPTIAN MUSEUM in Tahrir Square is home to the contents of Tutankhamun's tomb as well as other treasures from the days of the pharaohs. Admission is E£10 (E£5 to students), plus a further E£10 if you want to take photographs. (Open Sat.–Thurs. 9 a.m.–4 p.m.; Fri. 9–11.15 a.m and 1.30–4 p.m.) Other interesting museums in New Cairo are the MUSEUM OF MODERN ART, Gezira Street, Zamalek, featuring Egyptian painting from 1940 to the present day; and the MANIAL PALACE MUSEUM, next to the YHA, which has an absorbing collection of Islamic furnishings.

Islamic Cairo is crowded and poverty-ridden; nevertheless it's worth visiting for the impressive palaces, mosques and museums. Avoid visiting mosques on Friday afternoons when the faithful gather for prayer. This part of the city is dominated by the CITADEL, begun in 1176 and continually built and rebuilt since then. The

MOSQUE OF MUHAMMAD ALI is inside the Citadel complex; it's in two parts, the courtyard and the House of Prayer, and depending on how much *baksheesh* you have to offer, you might be able to enter the Tomb of Muhammad Ali, with its giant candlestick holders. But if you've only time to visit one mosque in Cairo, go for the MOSQUE OF IBN TULUN, which is the largest and oldest one in the city, dating from 879 AD. It's extremely elegant, with a courtyard covering almost seven acres.

The MUSEUM OF ISLAMIC ART, off Ahmad Maher Square, has fabulous collections of Islamic pottery, calligraphy, carpets, wood-carvings and metalwork. There's also a collection of ancient Koranic scientific and philosophical manuscripts. (Open Sat.–Thurs. 9 a.m.–4 p.m., Fri. 9–11 a.m. and 1.30–4 p.m. Admission is E£8 (E£4 to students).

The CITIES OF THE DEAD is the name of the area to the north-east and south of the Citadel; it contains hundreds of tombs and mauso-lea from the Mamluk era. Cairenes still live there, and tombs often double up as public benches, or even goalposts. The Northern Cem-etery contains finer monuments than the Southern Cemetery, including the celebrated 15th-century MAUSOLEUM OF QAYTBAY built for a Mamluk slave who became leader of Egypt. The Southern Cemetery houses Egypt's largest Islamic mortuary – the MAUSO-LEUM OF IMAM ASH-SHAFI'I – erected in 1211.

OLD CAIRO is where the fascinating COPTIC MUSEUM is situated, opposite the Mar Girgis stop on the metro. The museum houses the world's finest collection of Coptic art, including a display of woodwork and frescoes, parts of which date back to the fourth century. There's also a collection of non-Biblical gospels, including that of Thomas, from the 13th and 14th centuries, along with Coptic church texts of various periods. Admission is E£8, E£4 to students, plus E£10 for taking photos. (Open Sat.–Thurs. 9 a.m.–4 p.m., Fri. 9–11 a.m. and 1–4 p.m.)

The ruins of the ROMAN BATTLEMENT, a first-century fortress, are directly in front of the museum. A short distance to the south is the CHURCH OF AL-MUALLAQA, the earliest known site of Christian worship in Egypt, originally erected towards the end of 3 AD. The 10th-century CHURCH OF ABU SERGA off Mari Girgis Street also merits a visit; well below sea level, it contains a crypt where the Mary, Joseph and Jesus are reputed to have rested on their journey into Egypt.

ACCOMMODATION
Youth Hostel: The IYHF hostel is at 135 Abd al-Aziz al-Saud Street, Roda Island (tel 84 07 29). It is clean and conveniently

located, but the bunk beds are wall-to-wall. There's an 11 p.m. curfew. A night's stay for YHA members costs E£7.

Finding a clean, comfortable, budget hotel room is something of a challenge. But they are there if you take time to look around. Never accept a room before inspecting it first. Always take your own loo roll.

Fontana Hotel, Ramses Square (tel. 91 58 10). Very good downtown accommodation. A double with bath costs E£75.

Pensione Roma, 169 Sharia Muhammad Farid (tel. 391 10 88). Excellent value for money: a double with bath costs approx. E£35 including breakfast – you must book ahead for this one!

Hotel Tee, 13 Adly Street (tel. 391 10 02). Clean, and it actually has hot water 24 hours a day. Rooms are single, and cost E£22–E£28 if you want *en suite*.

Tulip Hotel, 3 Tala'at Harb Square (tel. 393 94 33). Single rooms cost E£14, E£19 with shower and phone. Doubles are E£30. Breakfast included in the price.

Al-Nil Zamalek Hotel, 21 Maahad al-Swissry Street (tel. 340 18 46). A quiet place to stay. The rooms are modern, with air-conditioning, bath and fridge. Single rooms cost E£40 per night, doubles E£50 with breakfast included in the price.

El-Hussein Hotel, al-Hussein Square (tel. 91 80 89). In the centre of Khan-al-Khalili, this hotel offers excellent views of the al-Azhar Mosque, and the rooms are clean and spacious. Single rooms are E£38 (make sure you ask for a room with a bath).

FOOD
You can eat for next to nothing in Cairo. There's a wide choice of restaurants and cafés, as well as the ubiquitous street stalls.

Felfela, 15 Sharia Hoda Sharawy Street (tel. 392 27 51). One of the finest restaurants in Cairo, offering excellent Egyptian cuisine at very reasonable prices. Open daily 8 a.m.–12 p.m. Try the spiced *fuul* (E£2.50) and the *om ali*, a pastry baked with honey and raisins (E£2.50).

Al-Guesh, 32 Falaki Square (tel. 354 54 38). The place for a yummy shish kebab. It is open 9–12 a.m. There are also good steak dishes, costing between E£7–15.

El-Dahhan, al-Hussein Square, Khan-al-Khalili (tel. 93 93 25) also serves superb kebabs; it's packed out all the time, so it must be good.

Doumyati, on the north side of Falaki Square (tel. 392 22 93). One of the most popular (and least expensive) restaurants in Cairo. Tuck into lentil soup, potato sandwiches, and of course various varieties of *fuul*.

Prestige Pizza, Geziret-al-Arab (tel. 347 03 83). The best place to go for pizza. It's a bit upmarket, but the pizzas only cost E£7–12.

Don't miss out on Cairo's cafés – unless you're a lone woman, in which case the harassment may be too offputting. Two of the best cafés are Fishawi's Khan al-Khalili, al-Hussein Square and Groppi, in Tala'at Harb Square. The former is furnished in 19th-century European style, and offers such refreshing drinks as mint tea. Groppi is worth a visit for the delicious ice cream and pastries.

ENTERTAINMENT

Most tourists flock to the sound and light show at Giza; the three pyramids are illuminated and the story of the ancient pharoahs is told by the Sphinx in various languages (for the English narrative, go on Monday, Wednesday, Friday or Saturday – though apparently it's much funnier to go on a non-English night). Some say the show is over-rated and over-priced (tickets cost E£10, or E£25 for an organized tour).

The Rida troupe perform traditional Egyptian dances at the Balloon Theatre, al-Nil Street, Aguza. Admission costs E£8. Free entertainment can be had at the Mausoleum of al-Ghoury in al-Muizz Street, where members of the Sufi sect perform a traditional religious dance on Wednesday and Saturday nights.

Bars worth visiting include the El Patio, off Shagarat-ad-Durr Street, Zamalek, where imported beers, delicious cheesecake and Western-movie style swinging wooden doors attract tourists and foreigners living in Cairo. For something extremely upmarket, try Jackie's – Cairo's most exclusive night spot, in the Nile Hilton. It costs E£20 and formal dress is required.

Cairo's cinemas run foreign-language films (check the *Egyptian Gazette* for details) but watching a movie will drive you spare – the Egyptians read the subtitles out loud!

EXCURSIONS

Most visitors to Cairo come to see one of the Seven Wonders of the Ancient World: the PYRAMIDS OF GIZA. These are located 14 km to the west of the city, together with the inscrutable SPHINX (who has now lost most of her nose). The three main Pyramids were built for three pharoahs: Cheops, Chephren and Menkaure. Beware: the climb to and inside the Pyramids is arduous, and anyone who suffers from claustrophobia should *not* attempt to enter them! Some say that the Pyramids are disappointing, being much smaller than one would imagine. One thing you can be sure of, however, is that there'll be hordes of people there and you'll get no peace from the traders. To get to Giza, take the number 8 bus from the front of the Mugama Building, Tahrir Square; the last stop is right outside the entrance to the Pyramids. Minibus number 83 will give you a more comfortable ride there: pick it up outside the station, to the right of the Mugama Building.

If your nerves have been completely shattered by the mayhem of Cairo and you long for something calmer, head for WADI AL-NATRUN. A two-hour bus ride away from downtown Cairo, this town has been the home of the Coptic community in Egypt for 1,500 years, and the four remaining monasteries are still functional, soothing and impressive. Get there by the blue bus which leaves from the station behind the Egyptian Museum, north of Tahrir Square. There's nowhere to stay overnight, which is a pity – make the most of your day there!

The village of KARDASSA has become popular with tourists, due to its local crafts (much of what you see in Cairo's souvenir shops is made in Kardassa, and while it's cheaper to buy here, prices have increased along with the number of visitors). You'll find a Kardassa-bound minibus in Giza Square.

The world's oldest Pyramid, built in 2700 BC, is the principal attraction of SAQQARA, along with the burial ground of the pharaohs who ruled at nearby MEMPHIS. Getting to Saqqara is a hassle, as there are no direct buses: it's best to take a taxi, or perhaps fork out E£15 for one of Salah Muhammad's Luxor Tours – you'll find information on the tours on posters in budget hotels.

The most attractive place near Cairo is the NILE DELTA, a flat agricultural land once acclaimed as the most fertile region in the world. The picturesque NILE BARRAGES, constructed in the 19th century to regulate the flow of water into the Delta, are located 15 km north of Cairo.

UNITED ARAB EMIRATES

VITAL STATISTICS
Red tape: A full passport and a visa are necessary (though nationals of GCC status are exempt from the visa requirement). British citizens will be granted a 30-day visa at the airport; to avoid

lengthy interrogation, make sure you have an onward or return ticket. All other nationalities must apply for a visa through a Dubai-based sponsor or the hotel where they intend to stay. If you have an Israeli stamp on your passport you may be denied entry. It's best to check any changes and developments in the visa situation before you leave with the Ministry of the Interior, Department of Nationality, Passports and Residence, PO Box 228, Abu Dhabi.

Customs: The duty free allowances vary according to the airport. Passengers to Dubai are allowed 2,000 cigarettes or 400 cigars or 2 kg tobacco; 1 l toilet water; and 50 ml perfume. Apparently, non-Muslim visitors may import 2 l spirits or 2 l wine – but, to be honest, I wouldn't try it.

Passengers to Sharjah face no restrictions at all on tobacco or perfumes, but alcohol is forbidden. And passengers to Abu Dhabi are allowed 200 cigarettes or 50 cigars or 500 g tobacco, and gifts up to the value of Dh10. There are restrictions on alcohol, so it's best not to take any in.

In addition, the import of pornographic material is prohibited, so your books and magazines will be checked on arrival. What UAE officials see as pornography is mild to us and magazines like *Cosmo* could easily fall foul of their regulations.

Health: Vaccination against smallpox is essential, and there's a year-round risk of malaria except in the main cities. A yellow fever or cholera vaccination certificate must be produced by all travellers coming from infected areas.

Take care with water: although in the main cities it is purified, it's nevertheless a good idea to boil. It's vital to take out health insurance, for while medical facilities in the UAE are top notch, they don't come cheap.

Language: Arabic and Urdu. English is the language of commerce.

Population: Approx. 1.75 million.

Capital: Abu Dhabi, population around 500,000.

Political system: A Union Council of Ministers responsible to the Supreme Council has executive authority and implements Union laws.

Religion: Islam (mainly Sunni) with Christian, Hindu and Parsi minorities.

Time: Four hours ahead of GMT.

Money: The monetary unit is the Dirham (Dh), divided into 100 fils. Coins: 1, 5, 10, 25 and 50 fils and Dh1. Notes: Dh1, Dh5, Dh10, Dh50, Dh100, Dh500 and Dh1,000. The official exchange rates are £1 = Dh5.71; US$1 = Dh3.67, but there's no exchange control, so the Dirham is freely convertible depending on the bank you go to. Major credit cards are accepted in the big hotels and large shops.

Tax: On top of the cost of restaurant meals, you'll have to pay a 10% service charge and a 5% government tax.

Communications: Local telephone calls are free and direct dialling is available for international calls. Airmail letters and parcels take about five days to reach the UK.

Electricity: 220v AC (240v AC in Abu Dhabi).

Business hours: In the Islamic world, the 'weekend' runs from midday on Thursday through Friday.

BANKS: Sat.–Thurs. 8 a.m.–12 p.m. Airport banks are open longer and at weekends.

SHOPS: Sat.–Wed. 8 a.m.–1 p.m. and 4 p.m.–8 p.m.; Thurs. 8 a.m.–12 p.m.

OFFICES: Sat.–Wed. 7 a.m.–1 p.m. and 4p.m.–7.30 p.m.; Thurs. 7 a.m.–12 p.m.

Holidays: 1 January; 21 Jan.–20 Feb. (Ramadan); 30 May (Islamic New Year); 8 August (Prophet's Birthday); September/October (Ashoura); 2 and 25 December.

It can be difficult to travel or find restaurants open during the Holy Month of Ramadan. Note that Muslim holidays alter according to the lunar calendar: check with Islamic cultural centres before you go.

Climate: Summers are hot and humid; temperatures can reach 44°C in July and August. It's cooler during the winter. Probably the most comfortable time to go is either spring or autumn.

DO'S AND DON'TS

The main tourist season runs from November to February. Don't even consider going in July or August – you'll spend the whole time in an air-conditioned hotel.

It is advisable to modify your dress and behaviour in all Islamic countries so as not to cause offence. Locals wear a *dishdasha* (a long robe) and a *guttrah* (headdress). Flip-flops are not tolerated in many hotels and restaurants. Women especially should dress conservatively. Use the right hand not the left for eating, greeting and gesturing. It is illegal to eat, drink or smoke in public during Ramadan.

The UAE is considered the most liberal country in the Gulf, but when it comes to photography it is considered offensive to photograph people, especially women, without their permission. Don't even think about photographing anything vaguely military, including the airport.

WHERE TO GO FOR WHAT

The UAE isn't a tourist country in the traditional sense. It is made up of seven Emirates, of which DUBAI is the second largest. One of the most important commercial centres in the Middle East, its Jumirah Mosque is one of the loveliest in the region. The city is also a convenient base from which to take a day safari into the desert, or excursions to neighbouring towns such as SHARJAH, which has a wonderful new *souk*, and AJMAN with its impressive historic palace. The KHOR KALBA beach, famous for its shells, is within easy reach, too.

The UAE's capital city, ABU DHABI, has very few old buildings remaining – the Old Palace is one of the few which remains intact in this modern, commercial city. The standard of the modern architecture, however, is such that even Prince Charles would approve of it; the Trade Centre and the interior of Sheikh Mohammed's palatial residence are particularly attractive.

At AL-AIN, near to Abu Dhabi, there's an interesting camel market, plus parks and a zoo. The Omani village of BURAMI boasts a couple of interesting forts and the Gardens of Hilli.

INTERNAL TRAVEL

Air: Gulf Air links all the internal airports. The good news is that the flights provide a quick way of getting about; the bad news is they're very expensive. Definitely out of the budget traveller's reach. Note too that flights between the various Emirates are regarded as international, so if you're planning to travel throughout the Emirates, make sure you get a multi-entry visa.

Rail: The train-loving traveller is in for a big disappointment here. There aren't any railways!

Bus: There is no bus service between the Emirates, and only a limited service links Dubai's major towns. The Dubai Commerce and Tourism Promotion Board, PO Box 594, Dubai, UAE (tel. 511 600) can provide you with details of fares and timetables.

Taxi: Widely available, and as long as you don't use the ones waiting outside the main hotels, they're actually not all that expensive (especially by UAE standards). Long-distance trips can be arranged, but it's important to agree the fare in advance. Dh220 should be adequate for a taxi ride from Dubai to Abu Dhabi, so if there's a small group of you, it's worth it. 'Service Taxis' can work out cheaper. They usually leave when full and carry 7–9 passengers. Local governments organize taxi depots.

Car: The major international companies, plus a few local ones, hire out cars. However, it can be a complicated process: an international driving licence isn't acceptable, so you have to get a temporary licence from the traffic police. You'll need your current licence, passport and two passport photographs. There's a mass of bureaucracy involved, but hire firms are generally happy to help you wade through it. Rates vary – make a few comparison checks before taking the plunge.

ACCOMMODATION

The UAE isn't really geared towards tourism – and certainly not to the budget traveller. You'll be very lucky to find a hotel costing less than Dh200 per night. The international hotels are good value for what you get – especially compared with some London hotel prices – but starting at Dh300 per night, they're out of the budget traveller's league.

However, take heart – the YHA do operate here. There are only six hostels throughout the Emirates, and they're a bit spartan, but cost from only Dh10 per night, and they open between 7 a.m. and 11 p.m. Contact the United Arab Emirates Youth Hostel Association, PO Box 9536, Al Qusais Road, nr Al Ahli Club, Dubai (tel. 667 989) for details.

FOOD

Dining out is a major pastime in the UAE and both Dubai and Abu Dhabi have some excellent restaurants representing every ethnic variety, including Chinese, Japanese, Filipino and Thai. Arabic food is mainly derived from Lebanese cuisine. While the quality is excellent, you do have to pay for it. Remember that only hotel restaurants are licensed.

If there's no service charge included on your bill, then it's usual to leave a 10% tip. This, however, goes to the management and not the waiter. If you want to tip the waiter, give the money to him personally.

BUDGETING

This is far from being an on-a-shoestring country, but if you can manage to stay at the YHA, eat takeaways and travel with other folk to cut down on taxi or car hire costs, you needn't spend a great deal of money.

Work opportunities do exist, though they tend to be long-term, rather than the couple of months here and there variety generally preferred by the round-the-worlder. Nursing, nannying and TEFL teaching jobs are regularly advertised in the British papers; construction engineers are also in demand. The money is excellent – social life can be grim (especially if you're partial to the odd tipple).

FURTHER INFORMATION

Lonely Planet's *Arab Gulf States – Travel Survival Kit* is one of the few guides that covers this region. For further information, try the Embassy of the United Arab Emirates, 30 Prince's Gate, London SW7 1PT (tel. 0171 581 1281), the Consulate, 48 Prince's Gate (tel. 0171 589 3434) and Dubai Commerce and Tourism Promotion Board, 34 Buckingham Palace Road, London SW1 0RE (tel. 0171 828 3153).

Dubai

AIRPORT FACILITIES

Dubai International Airport is just 4 km from the city centre. It's extremely modern and regarded as one of the best in the Gulf. There are two terminals, one for departures, and a new one for arrivals. All the usual facilities are there, including an information desk, duty-free, foreign exchange and banks. There are even a couple of bars, but alcohol is only served to non-Muslims. Most facilities are open 24 hours a day.

Check-in times are 45 minutes before domestic flights; 120 minutes before international departures. Kill time by exploring the airport's Arab Heritage Museum, which highlights local culture and traditions, and has a good display of antiques and artefacts.

And finally the good news if you're down to your last fils: there's no airport departure tax!

CITY LINKS

The major hotels run courtesy coaches to and from the airport. The taxi fare into town is about Dh35. The number 4 bus goes to the Deira Bus Station every 30 minutes and costs about Dh2.

USEFUL ADDRESSES

Tourist office: Ministry of Information and Culture, PO Box 5053, Deira, Dubai (tel. 615 500)
British Airways: PO Box 1989 (tel. 314 141)
Main post office: Za'abeel Road, on the Dubai side.
British Embassy: Tariq bin Zayed Street, PO Box 248 (tel. 521 070)
US Consulate: PO Box 4009, Abu Dhabi (tel. 313 115).
Emergency services: Fire 222 222; police 221 111. You can't call an ambulance – if injured, alert reception at your hotel or hostel.

GETTING ABOUT

Taxi is the most efficient and inexpensive way of getting about the city. Fares around Dubai work out at approximately Dh7 for short journeys and Dh12 for trips over the Creek, but there are no meters – fares are by negotiation only.

The *abra* (water-taxi) runs from early morning to midnight. On the Deira side of the dock they stop at the junction of Al-Sabka and Beniyas Road. On the Dubai side the *abra* stop is located in front of the Captain's Stores. There is a flat fare of 25 fils which is collected on the boat as it leaves from the dock.

There are two bus stations: Deira and Dubai. Numbers and routes are posted in Arabic and English. The number 12 goes to the World Trade Centre.

SIGHTS

Dubai is divided into the old town of Dubai and the new business district of Deira, the two being separated by the lovely CREEK. One thing you must do is take an *abra* (water taxi) down the Creek and watch the bustle of life along its banks; you'll see traditional wind-tower houses and superb modern architecture. At the inland end of the Creek is a large lagoon where you'll see thousands of birds, including flamingoes.

Apart from the Creek, the main attraction of Dubai is its *souks* (markets). Mainly located in the old town, the *souks* are located in hundreds of minuscule shops, agleam with gold chains, bangles, necklaces and pendants. The best-known is the GOLD SOUK in Deira, where hundreds of shops offer an array of jewellery at bargain prices. Apparently 22, 21 and 18 carat gold is a fantastic buy, with prices calculated according to the weight and workmanship of each item. Then visit Deira's old SPICE SOUK for the heady aroma of fragrances from around the world. Dubai is virtually a tax-free city, so it's a good place to buy electrical goods, cameras, watches and leather, as well as gold. The duty-free shop at the airport is reputed to be among the best in the world, so you can keep shopping right until the last minute.

The DUBAI MUSEUM in Al Fahidi Street (tel. 531 8621) is housed in the 150-year-old AL FAHIDI FORT and has an excellent collection of Bedouin jewellery, antique costumes, pottery and tools. The elaborate JUMIRAH MOSQUE, towards the west of Dubai, is at its most beautiful at night when it's illuminated, making it the most photographed sight in Dubai. Another exquisite building worth taking a look at is the reconstructed, wind-towered PALACE OF SHAIKH SAEED, the grandfather of Dubai's present ruler.

ACCOMMODATION
Youth hostel: There's only one YHA hostel: the Dubai Hostel, Al Quasais Road, next to the Al Ahli Club on the eastern outskirts of the city (tel. 667 078). It has 50 beds and is rumoured to accept only men. Advance booking is essential. Dh70 per person. To get there, take the Al-Ittihad Road and turn right on to Al Quasais Road.

Hotels: Before your trip, either book the youth hostel or decide that this is one of the cities where you're going to have to splash out. The Ministry of Information and Tourism in Dubai can provide you with a list of hotels if you write to them in advance, but they probably won't tell you about these:

Mirage Hotel (tel. 271 666). In an alley just off Al-Sabkha Road. Tiny rooms with shared toilet facilities. Dh70 singles/Dh120 doubles.

Stars Hotel, Al-Buteen Street (tel. 235 000). Dirt cheap (Dh50 singles/Dh100 doubles) but no bath.

Imperial Palace Hotel, Naif South Street (tel. 211 344). Dh100 singles/Dh140 doubles, but worth the extra cash.

FOOD
Eating out is a favourite pastime in Dubai, and there's a superb selection of restaurants – unfortunately, they're all on the expensive side. If you want to fork out for a good restaurant, though, one of the best ones is the revolving Al Dawaar at the Hyatt Regency Hotel, which offers spectacular views over the city as well as superb Arabian and Indian cuisine. La Rotisserie at the Dubai Inter-Continental is a French restaurant with magnificent views of the Creek.

Indeed, most of the good restaurants are based in the hotels, and will certainly be outside your price range, unless you've won a fortune at the camel races. You won't have to starve, though, as there are a few reasonably priced takeaways around: especially recommended is an Indian takeaway, the Tandoor, opposite the Marine Hotel (tel. 436 098/216).

ENTERTAINMENT
As I've said, eating out is the great Dubai pastime. However, there are one or two other things to do, including going to one of Dubai's English-language cinemas. Most nightlife centres on the hotels, which offer dinner-dances, live bands and discos. Current popular haunts include Studio 7 at the International, the Music Room at the Inter-Continental, Aphrodites at the Chicago Beach and

Rumours at the Ramada. Many of the hotels have British-style bars, offering pub grub as well as drinks. Despite, or because of, its name, try Thatcher's at the Dubai Marine for a traditional British atmosphere. Biggles, at the Airport Hotel, is also very good. The Der Keller at the Chicago Beach serves traditional German fare. None of these venues are really within the price range of the budget traveller.

If you're only in Dubai for a few days and want a night out to remember, go to see a camel race. Race meets take place every Thursday or Friday during the winter months, either on desert tracks or on Dubai's official race circuit, Nadd Al Shibba (tel. 378 000 for details of meets). The locals take it all very seriously, and watching the spectators will no doubt be just as entertaining as the races themselves.

EXCURSIONS
Dubai is an excellent base for taking a safari into the desert; your hotel or the tourist board will be able to give you details of who to go with and how to book. Desert safaris are great fun and you'll see traditional Bedu villages, towering red dunes, camel camps and mountain wadis (dry stream beds).

A four-wheel drive desert safari can be as hazardous as it is elating: there have been occasions when the 4WDs have crashed on a sand dune, resulting in their passengers being hospitalized. At any rate, expect to return covered with bruises from the bumpy ride.

DNATA World Travel (tel. 220 217/21170) offers half-day tours of Dubai, plus trips to SHARJAH to see the attractive new *souk*, and to AJMAN for the old palace. You might also like to crash out for a day or so at one of the beach resorts, such as KHOR KALBA, where you'll find thousands of beautiful shells. East of Dubai is another beach resort, KHOR FAKHAN, and also the desert oasis of DHAYD. It's OK for women to wear swimwear on the beaches or by the hotel pool, but when walking around town it's advisable to wear shirts or light trousers with tops that leave something to the imagination.

For camel racing, check out the track on Za'abeel Road in Dubai. It's free on Fridays, but make sure you get there by 8 a.m.

ASIA

Asia can be divided roughly into two: the mostly affluent, industrialized north, and the more laid-back, more 'typically Asian' south. Within those generalizations, however, there lies a wonderfully varied continent to explore.

WHERE TO GO FOR WHAT

JAPAN has no one drawing-card. It's a country that you can take one of two approaches to: the first is to buzz round the main tourist destinations in a week or two, catch some temples and see Asia's economic miracle in action; the second is to look on it more as a place to dwell a while, to work, perhaps learn the language and slowly discover that it isn't as relentlessly Westernized as it appears at first glance.

Japan's near neighbour, CHINA, couldn't be more different. It's a country for the off-the-beaten-track traveller – not the $1-a-day, seat-of-the-pants type, but for those who are interested in people rather than places, and in a culture that couldn't be more different from their own. China is for travellers who have (or can cultivate) patience, tact, humour, insight and cultural sensitivity. The China of emperors, willow gardens and colourful festivals is gone (if it ever really existed), and if that is what you are interested in, you'd be better off visiting Taiwan, Hong Kong, or even Vancouver.

HONG KONG serves too often as a transit point for visitors either beginning their Asian travels or those who have had enough of Asia and need Big Macs for breakfast, lunch and dinner. That's rather a pity, as Hong Kong deserves to be considered as a destination in its own right with peaceful outlying islands and exotic villages to explore. Moreover it's an ideal place to explore on foot.

To most people THAILAND and the PHILIPPINES spell 'beach', in spite of the fact that Thailand also offers a profusion of magnificent temples, scenic treks and friendly people, while the Philippines has dramatic, volcanic landscapes that beckon the mountaineer, hiker, caver, canoeist and other adventurous spirits. Both countries are excellent for island-hopping, the Philippines particularly so.

MALAYSIA is the great undiscovered or overlooked Asian destination. It considers itself a notch above its immediate neighbours, more 'civilized' and better off. Its colonial legacy is interesting for students of history, and there are some amazing jungle hikes. It's ideal for a taste of the tropics without the hassle of, say, Indonesia.

INDONESIA is the last great wilderness, an island nation of vastly diverse scenery, peoples and cultures. Volcanoes, jagged mountains, impenetrable jungle, tribal villages, beautiful beaches, modern cities – Indonesia has all of these, and more. Lying as it does between Australia and Singapore, there is a well-marked tourist trail through the beaches and temples of Bali and the historical relics of Java, but the more intrepid can spend months getting away from the crowds, exploring jungles and small islands. If you think you won't be able to adjust to haggling and bargaining as a way of life, though, then Indonesia is not for you.

The latter caveat also applies to INDIA. Though it differs in almost every way from Japan, it, too, is a country that attracts many people who choose to spend a long time exploring it thoroughly and trying to get to know it well. The 'hippy trail' days are long gone and, although there are some leftovers from that era still hanging around, India tends now to attract more run-of-the-mill travellers. India's history and its varied cultures are what bring visitors because – with the possible exception of the Taj Mahal – there is no one reason to visit India, but then, who ever needed a reason to travel anyway?

TAKE HEED

Please be a good tourist. Read some of the books recommended below. Learn about the culture and customs of the countries you want to visit, and respect them. There are far too many Western travellers in Asia who spend their time riding roughshod over or criticizing local customs, causing great offence in the process. Such behaviour is sometimes the result of ignorance, but is more often arrogance. Resist the impulse to say: 'Back home, we . . .' You're not back home, and what you would or would not normally do is entirely irrelevant. In some of the countries mentioned in this section the welcome is now cooler than it has been in the past, and small wonder. So read up, educate yourself, and aim to be the model guest. If there is something in a particular country that really makes you unhappy, the best thing you can do is leave.

Another reason for researching your Asian trip thoroughly is to familiarize yourself with the risks involved in travelling to certain countries. In Thailand, the Philippines and Indonesia, cases of travellers being drugged and robbed are not uncommon, and a variety of cons and rip-offs are perpetrated on naïve tourists. Knowing about potential problems means that you can sidestep them for a hassle-free trip.

Do not get involved with drugs in Asia. Any locals who offer to sell them to you are more than likely to then turn you in to the police (for the reward), if they're not working for the police in the first place. The authorities throughout Asia take an extremely dim view of both trafficking and possession, and impose severe penalties on foreigners and their own people for such crimes. In most places the punishment is a lengthy jail sentence followed by deportation, but in Singapore and Malaysia the death penalty is imposed. Possession of or trafficking in so-called 'soft' drugs is considered to be just as serious a transgression as cases involving hard drugs. If you take any prescription medicines with you, make sure you carry the prescription, too, and don't *ever* transport items across borders for anyone.

EMPLOYMENT OPPORTUNITIES
Tight visa controls, a dearth of job opportunities, and low rates of pay mean that Asia is not an attractive proposition for those seeking work. Whereas in the past Japan and Hong Kong offered rich pickings, the world recession has taken its toll and unless you have contacts your chances of finding employment are slim.

INTRA-CONTINENTAL TRAVEL
There are no air or rail passes that cover the entire continent, or even parts of it. As travel in and out of most countries is cheap or reasonably priced (Japan being the notable exception), there is no need for them. Passes for individual countries are discussed in the relevant sections. Many travellers on round-the-world air tickets organize stopovers in Tokyo/Hong Kong and Bangkok, with an overland portion to Singapore, where they pick up air travel once more. This maximizes travel opportunities throughout the region and eliminates backtracking to Bangkok to catch flights out.

FURTHER INFORMATION
Between them, Lonely Planet's *North-East Asia on a Shoestring* and *South-East Asia on a Shoestring* will get you everywhere you would want to go in those regions. The *South-East Asia Handbook* from Moon Publications is pretty good, though it isn't particularly well laid out and doesn't include much in the way of cultural information. By way of contrast, Fodor's *South-East Asia* is extremely clear and informative. The drawback is that while it's more than helpful for pre-trip planning, it doesn't include listings of cheap accommodation. If you plan to travel extensively in the north, you might be better off with individual country guides, for details of which see the sections following.

On a more literary note, *The Great Railway Bazaar* by Paul Theroux was written in the seventies, yet this account of a train journey through Asia has lost none of its relevance. And well on its way to becoming a cult classic is Pico Iyer's *Video Night In Kathmandu*, which tells of travels through Asia and encounters with (amongst other oddities) backpackers clutching their Lonely Planet guides ... see if you can recognize yourself! Finally, for a taste of life in colonial days, look no further than Somerset Maugham's short stories, many of which are set in southern Asia.

CHINA

VITAL STATISTICS

Red tape: A full passport is required for all visitors to China, together with a visa. The visa can be obtained from any Chinese Embassy (or via your travel agent), and are also readily available in Hong Kong (allow 3 working days). Some towns/cities/areas in China are, however, closed to foreigners and even with a visa you will be denied entry. Though you must state your travel itinerary on the visa application, you can deviate from it during your stay. One- or two-month visas are available.

Customs: Visitors may bring in 400 cigarettes, 2 bottles of wine or 0.75 l of spirits (the allowances increase slightly if you are staying for more than six months). You have to declare all of your valuables – jewellery, watches, cameras, Walkmans, etc. – on a form upon entry to China. Declare *everything* of this nature, don't lose your copy of the form, and do not be caught leaving the country minus any of your declared possessions. Keep receipts for the souvenirs you buy in case they are asked for on departure. The export of antiques is restricted.

Health: No vaccinations are required unless arriving from an infected area. (If you plan to stay for over a year, though, a health certificate is necessary.) Should you be travelling in the south of the country, precautions against malaria would be sensible. The water is not safe to drink, and infectious hepatitis (hepatitis A) is a real possibility if you eat at places where standards of hygiene are low. The dry, dusty environment may cause sore throats.

It is advisable to take an AIDS pack (see **Medicine** p. 99).

Medical costs are minimal and the standard of care excellent, though Oriental rather than Western medicine is the norm.

Language: Mandarin is the most widely spoken Chinese dialect, with Cantonese being more common in the south. There are eight major dialects, but the written language is the same wherever you go.

Chinese is a tonal language, which means that the meaning of a word changes depending on the intonation. English is not widely spoken, though people working in the tourist industry generally have a working knowledge of it, and many others study it in their spare time. The Chinese are *very* good at sign language.

Population: Just over 1 billion.

Capital: Beijing

Political system: Communist.

Religion: Buddhism, Taoism and Confucianism are the traditional faiths. There are also Muslim and Christian minorities. All religious worship came under attack during the Cultural Revolution, but is now making a comeback.

Time: Eight hours ahead of GMT.

Money: The Chinese currency is called Renminbi. The standard unit is the Yuan (Y). A jiao is $^1/_{10}$ of a yuan. A fen is $^1/_{10}$ of a jiao. £1 = about Y13. Notes are in denominations of 1, 2, 5, 10 and 50 yuan, and coins in denominations of 1, 2, and 5 fen.

The FEC (Foreign Exchange Certificates) formerly issued to tourists no longer exist.

There are two prices for everything: the Chinese price and the tourist price, and tourists (naturally) pay more. At many tourist attractions, for example, there will be two ticket windows – and even if you approach the Chinese window speaking fluent Mandarin, you will be redirected to the other one.

You can exchange foreign currency and traveller's cheques at most hotels, and all of the hard currencies are readily accepted. You cannot buy or sell yuan outside China; make sure to keep all of your exchange receipts so that you can convert your yuan before leaving.

Communications: The phone system is not good. Tourist hotels have phones in every room, but public telephones are next to nonexistent. Long-distance and overseas calls must go through the operator; the majority either fail to go through at all or get cut off. Even local calls (which are free) tend to be a hassle. There are telex services available at the bigger hotels.

Post to and from China takes about a week and is reasonably reliable. You'll find postal facilities in the hotels and usually the Friendship Stores, too.

Media: The *China Daily* is a home-grown English-language daily newspaper, and the *South China Morning Post* (from Hong Kong) is often available also.

Electricity: 220v AC.

Business hours: POST OFFICES: 8.30 a.m.–8.30 p.m.

SHOPS: 9 a.m.–7 p.m., seven days a week.

OFFICES: Mon.–Fri. 8 a.m.–12 p.m. and 2p.m.–6 p.m.
Holidays: 1 January; February: lunar New Year (three days); 8
March; 1 and 4 May; 1 June; 1 July; 1 August; 1 October. Avoid
travelling during the lunar New Year period as everything closes.
Climate: Spring and autumn are the best times to visit China.
Winters in the north are cold and dry with temperatures generally
a few degrees below zero in Beijing, and much lower further north.
Summers (May–August) are hot (20–30°C) but not humid. You
can expect sandstorms in April and rainfall in July and August.

Central and southern China endure long hot and humid summers (around 30°C). Typhoons frequently occur around the
southern coastal regions from July to September. Winters are short
(December or January to March) and cold, but not so severe as in
the north.

DO'S AND DON'TS
Dress and behave modestly: with the exception of Guanzhou
(Canton), where they are used to foreigners and their decadent
Hong Kong neighbours, shorts and miniskirts are not a good idea,
and neither are bare shoulders. Chinese couples hold hands in
public, but that is about the only display of affection you will witness, and it is best not to indulge in the hugging, kissing or touching
that is acceptable in Western nations. (And Western men should
take particular care not to touch Chinese women.) Women
shouldn't smoke in public. As in Japan, take care not to stand
chopsticks upright in your rice bowl when eating, because of its
association with death rituals.

Handshaking is the usual form of greeting and, if invited to someone's home, a gift will be appreciated – particularly goods that
cannot be obtained easily in China, such as foreign-brand cigarettes
or alcohol; sweets or a souvenir from your country are also
welcome.

The Chinese government is keen to discourage tipping, and it is
not standard practice. If you feel that hotel staff or a tour guide,
for example, have given good service, a small gift (chocolate,
scented soap) is more appropriate.

There are a million photographic opportunities in China (but be
careful not to take snaps of anything that might be security-
sensitive); many Chinese are happy to pose for photos if asked,
and will be delighted if you offer to send them copies. Don't get
too hung up about trespassing on people's privacy, though: you
will often find yourself caught in the viewfinder, unasked, of a
Chinese person's camera.

Perhaps the most important thing when travelling in China is to keep a cool head and a sense of humour. This can sometimes be a tiring, frustrating and confusing place to travel in and, while ordinary people are usually kind and friendly to foreign visitors, officialdom – in the shape of the tourist authorities, railway ticket sellers, etc. – seems to exist solely to obstruct and annoy. You'll be told lies (often), but it may be that the person you're dealing with can't rather than won't give an answer, and would rather tell a lie than lose face by admitting that they don't know. Faced with this sort of situation, you may find yourself tempted to get into an argument, or to shout at someone who is being less than helpful. Try to avoid this: you will be causing them a loss of face, which in turn will make them even more unhelpful. However frustrating a situation gets, do your best to smile and be patient: it'll get you much further in the long run, not to mention saving you from an early death by apoplexy.

WHERE TO GO FOR WHAT

With 23 provinces and 56 different nationalities in its population of one billion, China is a vast and diverse country – the third largest in the world. most visitors other than the truly determined will see only selected parts of it: Beijing for its historical buildings and short hop to the Great Wall; Guanzhou because of its proximity to Hong Kong and as a stopping-off point on the way to Guilin (in Guanxi Province), famous for its lush vegetation, beautiful mountains and rivers of a million paintings; Shanghai, the seaport, for its 'colonial' heritage and sleazy 'Chinatown' image.

If you feel like branching out, Xian, in the central Shaanxi Province, was once the capital of China and is home to the Terracotta Warriors, thousands of which were buried with the Emperor Qui Shihuang and only recently excavated. They are an impressive sight.

In the east of the country is the Yangtse, which you can cruise down. Along its shores are Suzhou, a town thousands of years old, with a reputation for beauty, and Nanjing, another one-time capital of China. It's an industrialized city, but still contains many historic buildings. Shanghai is a good place to start a visit to this region.

In the south-west is Emei Shan, a mountain with temples and monasteries built on its slopes; a place well known to hikers and hillwalkers.

Out-of-the-way places are Hohhot in Inner Mongolia and Tibet, on the border with India. Tibet is remote and difficult to reach, but thoroughly fascinating if you can make it in.

China is *big* – it would take you several months to a year to explore it properly, and travelling there can often seem like an initiative test. Those interested purely in seeing the sights and not in meeting the people would be well advised to think seriously about taking an organized tour.

If you select one region, a month is about the right time to allow, and to see one city and its surrounding area, a couple of weeks would suffice.

INTERNAL TRAVEL

Air: If you plan to travel long distances within China but have limited time, you may have no choice but to fly. There are at least 8 different companies, including China Airways. Tickets are sometimes in short supply, the food is idiosyncratic, and the pilots don't believe in slowing down when they land. Unless you enjoy white-knuckle rides, take a train.

To go from one side of the country to the other (Shanghai to Urumqi) it will cost about £208. Shanghai to Xi'an costs about £78.

Rail: The rail network is extensive and well organized (except for ticket selling) and makes a great way to see the country. Train travel is about 25% cheaper than flying. Foreigners pay 75% more than the Chinese, so it's expensive, unless you opt for the lowest class of travel. Purchasing a ticket is a very complicated procedure: there is a separate ticket office for foreigners (in Beijing, it's in the Arrivals hall) or you should be able to buy tickets at the tourist office. It's not always easy to get a ticket out of a railway official – smile, have patience, and allow plenty of time. Some travellers suggest that purchasing a ticket on the black market is a better option. There are four classes, with prices to match: hard seat (cheap and uncomfortable), soft seat and, for overnight journeys, hard sleeper and soft sleeper. The soft sleeper is luxurious, hard sleeper berths are perfectly comfortable – but don't even *think* about a hard seat for overnighters. Take a picnic with you, and some bottled water, in case the train runs out/doesn't have any. One major annoyance that you'll have to contend with is thick clouds of cigarette smoke (technically, smoking is no longer permitted, but that doesn't seem to stop anyone).

Bus: The service is good, but there are no night buses, and luggage space is limited. Fares are comparable with those for hard seat travel on the trains. That the roads are often in a poor state is the drawback to long-distance travel, but if you are not going too far they are a viable alternative to the railway.

Taxi: There are a good number of taxis in most places, but taxi drivers usually don't speak English. Have your destination written down in Chinese. Taxis are supposed to be metered (though the drivers sometimes get around this) and fares are reasonable. You'll also have to put up with the driver's tapes of Taiwanese balladeers (pack a Walkman!). Taxis generally don't stop when flagged down, but try anyway, as they sometimes do. They can be picked up at hotels and official ranks, but don't leave it too late to ask for one if travelling from your hotel to the airport or station: there may be row upon row of taxis outside a hotel yet not a driver in sight.

Boat: You can cruise the Yangtse from Chongqing to Wuhan (three days) or use the coastal ferries to get to destinations such as Shanghai. It's a slow form of transport, though.

Bicycle: This is the way to travel in China. Just about all the locals cycle, and there is always a rental outlet in the centre of town (hotels can usually recommend a good local firm). You'll have to leave your passport or a hefty deposit with them, but the rates are low. Don't forget to pay whenever you park at a bicycle parking spot: if you don't, your bike will be towed.

Local transport: Buses are fun. They're sardine-can crowded (hopelessly so in the rush hour), but anyone who has ever experienced a Glasgow bar on a Saturday night will know how to use their elbows to good effect. Once on board, you'll be overcome by the mingled smells of garlic, sweat and tobacco. Fares start at around 5 fen and seldom exceed 10 fen, depending on distance. Pay the conductor, who has a booth near the doors. Carry a bilingual bus map (available from the tourist offices), point to your destination and the conductor will take the right fare (often they'll tell you when you've reached your stop). Buses stop running early, usually before 10 p.m.

Walking is not really an option for sightseeing as cities are large and very spaced out, and the sights are never close together. If someone says that something is 'only a few blocks away', don't believe it. A Chinese 'block' can be over a kilometre long. In Beijing particularly, walking is neither recommended nor really possible.

Car: Foreign visitors are forbidden to drive in China.

ACCOMMODATION

As solo travel for foreigners in China has only been possible for relatively few years, the hotel situation is still group-orientated – and the tourist authorities would seemingly prefer it to stay that way. The majority of foreign visitors are expected to stay in huge, Western-style hotels which are, almost without exception, very expensive. At the absolute rock-bottom are hotels/inns for native Chinese. Unless you are right off the beaten track and no alternative exists, you are unlikely to get into the latter.

A compromise of sorts (though still not in the budget league) are the hotels which take 'Overseas Chinese' and other foreigners.

However, as more and more unaccompanied travellers venture into the Middle Kingdom, dormitory-style accommodation is beginning to spring up, most commonly in cities such as Beijing, Guanzhou, Shanghai, and other places on the tourist trail, where hotels have simply turned a few rooms into multi-bedded dorms; these will sometimes be mixed, sometimes segregated, and are usually very comfortable, with flasks of hot water and jasmine tea provided. The same places may also offer reasonably priced doubles. Be warned that in the bigger, cheaper, more established dorms the bed linen isn't changed too often, so your own sleeping sheet or sleeping bag would be useful. For information on Youth Hostels (in Beijing only), contact CYTS, 23B Dong Ziao Min Xiang, Beijing 100006.

FOOD

You may think you know Chinese food, but what you get in China is nothing like what you're familiar with. If it moves, it gets eaten. A quick trip to a market will show you cats, dogs, snakes, frogs and other exotica for sale and being carted off by restaurateurs. If you choose to go to cheap, local eating places, you'll be dining on rice, egg soup, fried vegetables and fried meat and noodles. These restaurants are small and basic café-type places that are difficult to identify as restaurants until you get used to them. Nobody there will speak English: learn a few food words, take a phrase book, or point, nod and smile. It is a good idea to carry your own chopsticks in case those of street vendors and the cheaper cafés have not been properly cleaned.

In some places there will be tourist restaurants that will have English menus and average food for a reasonable price. Some restaurants have separate sections for Chinese and foreign diners, but you can eat wherever you like. The 'tourist' section will be more expensive, but the food will also be better. The large hotels have more pricey restaurants (but hardly likely to break the bank), with good food that's more like the 'Chinese' food Westerners are accustomed to. Some towns have fast-food or burger joints.

If you go to a casual restaurant that only has a Chinese menu, don't be afraid to go into the kitchen and point at what you want to eat.

Eating times are early: dinner is served at about 5 or 6 p.m., and most restaurants close by about 8 p.m., though more and more are staying open later. Jasmine tea is usually served with meals. Chinese bottled beer is good, and Coke and Fanta are available.

BUDGETING

A constantly changing price situation in China, plus a fluctuating exchange rate, makes it difficult to estimate daily expenditure. In the aftermath of the Tiananmen Square incident, for example, train fares increased about threefold, while hotel tariffs plummeted. However, the yuan was subsequently radically devalued, so things balanced out. As a rough guide, though, you should certainly be able to get by on £10–£20 a day (or less).

Don't count on there always being a cheap dorm available – demand now exceeds supply several times over – and allow for a bed in a shared room/dorm costing around Y15–20 or Y40 per night, while a twin room in a cheap hotel will be about Y45 per room. Food costs won't be too high if you eat in Chinese establishments: set lunches can sometimes be had for around Y10, and dinner will be usually only a few yuan more. Expect to pay around Y8 for food from stalls. Treble these prices (at least) if you choose to eat in the Western-style hotels. Look out for bakeries: snacking on their wonderful breads and pastries makes for a cheap, filling breakfast or lunch. Local transport costs only a few fen (10–20), and admission prices (with the exception of the outrageously priced Forbidden City) are usually under Y5. A major expense will be intercity travel by train or plane: prices will run into hundreds of yuan. Unfortunately, there are no passes available.

All of the above are city prices. The country is always cheaper, and Beijing is more expensive than elsewhere.

If you're working or studying in China, apply for foreign expert status. This will permit you to pay for purchases in RMB.

A word of warning – China is full of backpackers constantly complaining bitterly that they didn't get Chinese prices somewhere, sitting up all night on trains in hard seats to save a few yuan, and refusing to pay the 5-fen parks entrance charge. Simply face the fact that you are not going to get the Chinese price, make up your mind to overlook the odd yuan overcharge, budget accordingly, and don't become one of these bitter travellers who think their host country owes them a debt for travelling there. Remember you're the guest: if you don't like their customs, leave. At least you have that option!

FURTHER INFORMATION

China National Tourist Office, 4 Glentworth Street, London NW1 5PG (tel. 0171 935 9427).

Embassy of the People's Republic of China, 49–51 Portland Place,

London W1N 3AG (tel. 0171 636 1835). Write to the consular
Consular Section for visa information.

Background reading: Lonely Planet's *China – Travel Survival Kit*
is excellent if you plan to travel widely in China, but because it's
not annually updated the ever-changing nature of China means
that it tends to go out of date quite quickly. The *Insight City Guide:
Beijing* is also very good.

There have been many, many books written about China. If you
can stand the adjectival overload, Colin Thubron's *Behind the Wall*
is informative, while Paul Theroux's *Riding the Iron Rooster* will tell
you less about Chinese society but an awful lot about trains. The
Tibet chapter is simply marvellous. *Life and Death in Shanghai* by
Nien Cheng is the moving autobiographical account of one
woman's experience of the Cultural Revolution; *Wild Swans* by
Jung Chang is an extraordinarily powerful, life-changing, personal
history of a grandmother, mother and daughter, which gives a
woman's view of China from the time of concubines, through the
rise of Communism, the Cultural Revolution, up to the present
day. Going further back into the past, *The Puppet Emperor* by Brian
Power is about the life of Pu Yi, the 'last emperor'. *One's Company*
by Peter Fleming, a travelogue of the 1930s, remains astonishingly
relevant and highly amusing. *The Good Earth* by Pearl S. Buck is a
famous fictional account of China, while *The Joy Luck Club* is a
novel about first-generation Chinese-Americans learning about the
lives of their Chinese mothers.

Beijing

AIRPORT FACILITIES

Beijing Capital Airport is about 30 km north-east of the city. There
are shops, a couple of restaurants, an information desk, a post
office, and a currency exchange on the first floor, and a duty-free
shop. The airport is large and well run, but dimly lit and not terribly
well provided: not a place you would want to spend a lot of time
in. The satellite lounges have nothing apart from some uninspiring
gift counters.

Check-in time is 90 minutes prior to departure. You may find
that claiming baggage and clearing customs is a slow process. The
airport international departure tax is now Y60.

CITY LINKS
Bus: The aviation authority, China Airways (formerly CAAC), runs a bus linking the airport with their downtown office; departure times coincide with flight arrivals/departures. It costs only a few yuan, *but* you will probably find that it has left the airport before you, the foreigner, have cleared customs and exchanged some money.
Taxi: It costs around Y100 for a ride into the centre, which is not too bad, and obviously the best way to get to the CITS or a hotel without having to negotiate (complete with luggage) Beijing's initially confusing streets and buses.

USEFUL ADDRESSES
Tourist office: China International Travel Service (CITS), 28 Jianguomen Wai (tel. 515 2562). The Beijing Hotel branch, on Jianguomennei, is nearer to the railway station. CITS sell bilingual bus maps (an absolute necessity). Supposedly they make railway bookings, but don't count on it: they have a habit of sending you off to the railway station.
Beijing Tourist hotline: In Beijing tel. 513 0828 (24 hours).
Main post office: International Post & Telecommunications Building, Jianguomen Beidajie, near the Friendship Store (beside the Asia Pacific building). Poste restante mail should be sent here.
British Embassy: 11 Guanghua Lu (tel. 532 1961).
US Embassy: 3 Xiushui Beijie (tel. 532 3831). The US Consulate is at 2 Xiushui Dingjie.
Emergency services: dial 110 for the police, 09 for the fire brigade.
Medical assistance: The Capital Hospital will deal with foreigners and is located between Wangfujing and Dongdan, not far from the Beijing Hotel (tel. 55 3731, ext. 274 or 222 for home visits).
Friendship store: Jianguomen Beidajie (marked on most maps). Sells souvenirs, stamps, household goods and imported food. There's a post box outside.
Foreign language bookshop: Wangfujing Street, behind the Baihou Dalou department store.

GETTING ABOUT
Bus: Unless you have a lot of money for taxis, you'll have to use the bus for getting around — Beijing is *huge*. The system is very good, cheap (from 10 fen) and maps showing bus routes are available from the CITS. Try to avoid rush hour.
Subway: It is much less crowded than the bus, though its routes

are limited. There are, however, stops near many of the sights on the tourist trail. There is a flat fare of 50 fen. The subway operates from 5 a.m.–11 p.m.

Taxi: A common sight at some Beijing hotels is a forecourt full of driverless taxis! They are reasonably plentiful, however, and you'll always be able to pick one up at the Friendship Store or at the hotels, and they can sometimes be flagged down in the street.

Bicycle: One of the joys of Beijing is cycling round it, though aggressive use of the bell is recommended! There are rental outlets at the Qiao Yuan Hotel, the Mongolinginen Hotel, the CITS office on Jianguomen Wai (tel. 592391), and opposite the Friendship Store. Normal price Y3 a day with 100 FEC deposit. Take an extra padlock with you and secure it to an immovable object – theft is not unknown.

SIGHTS

Naturally, you have come to Beijing to see the FORBIDDEN CITY, former home of the Ming and Qing dynasty emperors. The buildings and courtyards, which date from the 15th century, are truly works of art, and many of the buildings contain historical artefacts. The entrance fee is Y60, and there is a 'Walkman tour' at no extra cost. *You do not have to pay for the Walkman tour*, though it may be presented as obligatory. On the other hand, anyone with a Walkman and tape gets free entry to certain courtyards and buildings for which there is otherwise a separate charge – and the tapes are certainly informative. (At one time, staff were offering copies of the tapes for a small fee, so there may be pirates around – ask about!) You'll need the best part of a day to see the Forbidden City, so don't rush it.

Nearby is TIANANMEN SQUARE, scene of many political rallies and proclamations, and home of statues depicting 'heroic' working people. It's an impressive square, large and open, with the massive History Museum on the east side and the Mao Mausoleum to the south. Nowadays, of course, it is principally associated with the bloody events of 4 June 1989.

Opposite the north side of the Forbidden City is JINGSHAN PARK (Coal Hill), which affords splendid hilltop views of the city. The red rooftops of the Forbidden City look lovely from here, particularly at sunset. There is a small charge for entrance to the park. If you feel like travelling out to the north-western suburbs of Beijing, another park that should be seen is the beautiful Yihuyuan, once the grounds of the SUMMER PALACE which the imperial family removed to in the hot summer months.

The 15th-century TEMPLE OF HEAVEN is located in the

Chongwen district: it's the purplish-coloured building that graces the tourist posters. Set in parkland, it's more than worth a visit. Finally, a beautifully tranquil place is the Tibetan LAMA TEMPLE (Yonghe Temple) in the north-east of the city. The entrance gate is perhaps its most stunning feature, and the gardens are very pretty – it's a good place to end a bike ride, but there are buses which go there. There is an entrance fee of Y4. Be mindful of the fact that the Lama Temple is a working temple, and behave respectfully.

For shopping, try WANGFUJING STREET, though you may not find too much to buy. The souvenirs that the Friendship Store sells can also be bought outside China.

ACCOMMODATION

The China International Travel Service (CITS) (see **Beijing: Useful Addresses**, p. 295) can help you find a room – provided they're in a helpful mood. As with CITS offices all over the country, the service varies from cheerful but maddeningly uninformative through grudgingly half-helpful to downright stubborn (they *are* improving, though). They prefer to deal with tours and internal travel arrangements rather than night-by-night beds. Most hotels have a CITS stall where you can buy bus maps etc.

Hotels: Beijing hotels are often full, and they have a disconcerting habit of being pulled down. The following places are (fairly) well established, and you should have luck at some of them, but be warned that prices often change, too (upwards as well as down-wards), so those given should be taken as a rough guide only:

Jingtai Hotel, 65 Yongwai Jingtaixi, near Tiantan Park. Dorms, for around Y20 per person. Doubles/triples cost Y50/60. Take bus number 45 or 25 to nearby Anlelin Lu. Same directions as Yongdingmen but turn first left after Jingtai Dept Store. Lovely hotel compared to some of the others.

Yongdingmen Hotel, 77 Anlelin Lu. Triples from Y60 and doubles from Y75. Take bus 39 from the station to the Pishuangyu stop (first after the canal) and walk back and left into Anlelin Lu. Take the number 9 bus from the station.

Long Tan Hotel. Opposite Long Tan Park at 15 Panjiayuan Nanli, it's a bit further out than the other hotels, but is very clean and comfortable, with friendly staff. A bed in a multi-bedded, mixed-sex room costs Y30. Take bus number 41 or 35 to the first stop after the flyover. Dorm beds Y20, doubles Y80. Great hotel.

Qiao Yuan, on Yongdingmen, near the railway station. Take a

number 20 bus from the centre. It's the backpacker's hangout, and at Y25 per dorm bed (doubles Y60–80 with shower), is undeniably one of the cheapest places in town. But the staff – probably fed up with the bitching, penny-pinching, bad-tempered travel types that tend to end up there – have a reputation for unfriendliness. You would do better spending a little extra cash elsewhere.

Beijing Youth Hostel, 22 Banchang Alley, Doncheng District (tel. 440436). Associated with the IYHF, but not actually affiliated with it.

Jinghua Hotel, Nansanhuan Xilu, in the southern part of the third ring road around Beijing. Doubles with bath Y55–65. Take bus no. 2 or 17 from Qianmen.

FOOD

Naturally, you'll want to eat Peking duck while in the capital: the Qianmen Quanjude restaurant at 32 Quanmen Dajie (tel. 75 1379) is highly recommended. The waitresses are helpful, and speak a little English. There are three set menus to choose from, and prices are around Y30 per person (drinks extra). The nearest subway stop is Qianmen. Meals will be served around 5/6 p.m.; arrive early.

For 'eating local' (and, more importantly, cheaply), Chongwenmen Dongdajie, the road which leads from the Chongwenmen intersection towards the station, has a few reasonable eating places scattered along it. Take your phrasebook or your best Chinese along and just give it a go.

For do-it-yourself lunches or breakfasts, there are market stalls around the Chongwenmen intersection during the day, and an indoor market close to the hotel. The Friendship Store sells imported foods, and, though pricey, it's a good place for fresh fruit.

There is now (unfortunately – is nowhere sacred?) a Kentucky Fried Chicken close to Tiananmen Square, and a Pizza Hut on Dongshimenwai Street, as well as a McDonald's at the corner of Wangfujing Street and East Changan Street, near Beijing Hotel: meals from Y12. Opposite the Beijing International Hotel on Jianguomennei are a couple of local restaurants with great, cheap bi-lingual menus for Y20 p.p. Hawker stalls can feed you for Y5, but don't be afraid to haggle, and avoid traders round the station who rip off tourists.

ENTERTAINMENT

There isn't much in the way of nightlife in Beijing; watching TV in your hotel room is about as wild as it gets. If you'd like to experience a night at the cinema (Chinese films, mostly), there are a number of cinemas scattered around Wangfujing and N. Dongdan. There are some discos in the Western-style hotels, but they are not worth going out of your way for. Hotels are also the places to go if you just want a quiet drink.

Performances of the Beijing Opera are worth seeing. Try the Capital Theatre on Wangfujing, or the Guanghe, off Qianmen Lu. The costumes are spectacular, but if you are unused to Chinese music, you may find that you can't sit out an entire show. If possible, try not to miss the acrobats. Their theatre is the Acrobat Rehearsal Hall on Dazhalan, off Qianmen Dajie (at the Qianmen duck restaurant end of the street).

A good source of information is the *China Daily* (don't leave the hotel without it!), and the CITS can also advise on performances. You can obtain theatre tickets either from them or at the venues (where you save commissions). Ticket prices are cheap, only a few yuan. Cinema and theatre performances will start early (6.30–7.30 p.m.) and finish early (around 9 p.m.), and even the bars and discos close not much later than that. Remember that public transport stops early, too.

EXCURSIONS

There is really only one day-trip from Beijing, and that is to the GREAT WALL at Badaling, 70 km north-west of the capital. You can book a bus tour at the CITS or at some hotels, but these are foreigners-only and consequently rather expensive (Y45 from the Qiao Yuan or the Long Tan hotels). Considerably cheaper are the Chinese tours (the guides usually speak English, too), and you can buy tickets for them at the office opposite the Chongwenmen Hotel. All of the bus tours, however, have one thing in common – they simply do not allow enough time at the wall. You'll get about an hour there, and when you arrive at the wall, turn left to escape the crowds (they tend to go right) and climb as far as you can. Great views. (If you decide on a D-I-Y trip, there is a train from Beijing to Badaling.)

Most tours will also stop in at JUYONG PASS and the MING TOMBS, both of which are interesting enough as diversions, but hardly worth going out of your way to see if you are travelling independently of a tour. Juyong Pass is a garrison town of the Mongol period, containing a rather lovely 14th-century marble and stone archway. As for the Tombs, the animal statues that guard the entrance are fascinating, and the gardens that contain them are lovely, but a Ming Tomb itself is best described as a hole, a very long way underground. If you want to travel to TIBET, you must get a separate visa.

The TRANS-SIBERIAN RAILWAY is an epic journey rather than a mere excursion. The Beijing offices of the CITS will make bookings for you should you decide to leave China by this route. You will need visas for countries the Trans-Siberian passes through: the Mongolian Embassy is on Jianwaixiushui Beijie, the Polish on Jianwai Ritan Lu and the CIS Embassy is located on Dongzhimen Beizhongjie.

HONG KONG

VITAL STATISTICS

Red tape: A full passport is required, but for tourist purposes a visa is not necessary. British citizens can stay for up to twelve months without a visa, while subjects of Commonwealth countries and British dependent territories are allowed a 90-day visa-free stay. Citizens of the US and many Western European countries get one month.

Those intending to work in the colony must apply for a work visa at any British Embassy or Consulate, or by contacting the Department of Immigration, Wanchai Tower, 7 Gloucester Road, Wanchai, Hong Kong. In the UK, enquire at the Hong Kong Government Office (see **Further Information**, p. 295). UK citizens who decide after arrival in Hong Kong to work should apply for an ID card. This will be issued with no problem, and will permit you to seek employment. While in Hong Kong, you should carry some form of identification (with photograph) at all times; if caught without it, you could face prosecution.

Customs: There is a duty-free allowance of 1 l alcohol, 200 cigarettes or 50 cigars or 250 g tobacco, plus 60 ml perfume and 250 ml toilet water.

Health: No immunizations are required, except in the case of those coming from an area infected with cholera. Requirements can change, however, so check before you leave. Hospital, dental and eye care are excellent. Health insurance is recommended. Though tap water is said to be safe to drink, most people drink boiled or bottled water.

Language: Chinese (Cantonese dialect, invariably) and English. Though not all Hong Kong residents are bilingual, street signs etc. are, and most Chinese that tourists have dealings with will speak English. English-speaking policemen wear a red flash on their shoulders.

Population: 6.1 million (98% Chinese).

Political system: Hong Kong is run by a British-appointed Governor, together with the Executive Council and the partially elected Legislative Council. The colony reverts to Chinese rule in 1997 and until then, the last-ever Governor will be former Tory MP Chris Patten. Lose an election, win a colony.

Religion: Buddhism, Confucianism and Taoism are the three main religions, with a Christian minority.

Time: Eight hours ahead of GMT in winter, nine hours ahead in summer (Apr.–Oct.).

Calendar: The Chinese New Year marks the start of the lunar calendar, and falls at the end of January/beginning of February. There are twelve years in the Chinese calendar, each named after an animal.

Money: The currency is the Hong Kong dollar (HK$1), divided into 100 cents. Coins: 10, 20, and 50 cents, HK$1, HK$2 and HK$5. Notes: HK$10, HK$20, HK$50, HK$100, HK$500 and HK$1,000. £1 = HK$12.

You can change money (European, Australian, US, and most South-east Asian currencies) at banks (the best option), hotels, shops or at moneychangers, which abound. Places displaying good rates may charge a big commission, so shop around and always check how many HK dollars you will get on a transaction.

Credit-card use is common, and encashing traveller's cheques presents no problems.

Communications: Local calls from private phones are free; from public phones there is a charge. You'll find public phones in hotel lobbies, shops, restaurants and post offices. Call 1081 for Directory Enquiries. You can direct-dial international calls from most hotels, some public phones and at the Hong Kong Telecom International company offices.

The postal system is good. Airmail letters to the UK and the US take 3–5 days.

Media: The *South China Morning Post* and the *Hong Kong Standard* are two English-language papers produced in Hong Kong, and the *Asian Wall Street Journal* and *International Herald Tribune* are also available. They cost from HK$4–HK$8. There are two TV channels broadcasting in English, from mid-afternoon each day.

Electricity: 200v AC/50Hz. Appliances designed for lower voltages may burn out, but many hotels have shaver adaptors.

Business hours: BANKS: Mon.–Fri. 9 a.m.–4.30 p.m.; Sat. 9 a.m.–12 p.m.

POST OFFICES: The main post offices are open Mon.–Fri. 8 a.m.–6 p.m.; Sat. 8 a.m.–2 p.m.

SHOPS: Shops are usually open seven days, except over the lunar New Year, when almost everything closes down. Opening hours vary from one area to the next: Hong Kong Island (Central and Western districts), 10 a.m.–6 p.m.; Hong Kong Island (Causeway Bay and Wanchai), 10 a.m.–9 p.m.; Kowloon (Tsim Sha Tsui, Yau Ma Tei and Mongkok), 10 a.m.–8 p.m.; Tsim Sha Tsui East 10 a.m.–7.30 p.m.

Holidays: 1 January; 19–21 February (lunar New Year); 4, 5, 6, 8 April; 8, 10, 20 June; the last Monday in August and the Saturday preceding; 28 September (mid-autumn Festival – one day); 21 October (Chung Yeung Festival – one day); 25 and 26 December. Check the exact dates with the Hong Kong Tourist Association.

Climate: Summers (June–September) are hot (30–32°C), wet and extremely humid. July to September is also the typhoon season: TV and radio warnings will be broadcast when a storm looks imminent. There are also lights and signals systems all over the colony. If a signal 8 goes out, stay indoors; in the unlikely event that a signal 9 or 10 is broadcast, batten down the hatches and stay put.

Spring (March–May) and autumn (October–December) tend to be milder and less humid, with cool evenings. January and February can be rather chilly, and you'll need winter clothing. Autumn is the best time to visit.

DO'S AND DON'TS

With so many different nationalities living in the colony, the chances are that you'll offend someone at some time. The majority group, however, is the Chinese: see the introduction to the **China** section for some points on Chinese etiquette.

The main religions in Hong Kong are Taoism, Buddhism and Confucianism, though there are also temples dedicated to particular gods or goddesses. When visiting a temple of any description, be respectful. Dress modestly, and remember that the building is a place of worship and not a photo opportunity.

Handshaking is the usual form of greeting upon meeting people, and in a business context cards are always exchanged. It might be as well to get some printed (they can be done with English on one side and Chinese on the other) as they are widely used, and the Chinese are wild about them.

If you are invited out to dinner, a return invitation is customary. You can tip taxi drivers and hairdressers 10%, though this is optional. Restaurants usually add a service charge to their bills, but a lot of customers leave a 5% tip for good service.

Bargaining for goods is the norm, except in the department stores, but don't expect an easy time of it from the trader. Don't start haggling until you have made up your mind to buy, having shopped around first to get an idea of prices. Make sure you take cash with you (rather than traveller's cheques or credit cards) when you are ready to buy.

Beware of fake goods. Counterfeit goods are not so much of a problem where clothing or music cassettes are concerned, but be cautious where jewellery, electronics and cameras are concerned. At the jade market in particular, much of what you see will be fake. The HKTA recommends that you shop at places displaying their 'red junk' logo: the proprietors in these cases have agreed to operate ethically, so there is less chance of being ripped off. A free shopping guide, listing the particulars of member shops, is available for travellers. Make sure that any guarantees which accompany goods are valid worldwide and, in general, use your common sense and think before you buy.

Women, beware of Chinese pimps trying to recruit you. Don't be fooled into going to a 'modelling shoot', especially in the Tsim Sha Tsui area – the pimps can be forceful.

Ivory jewellery and trinkets are still available in Hong Kong. If you value the elephant, and don't want to break the law, don't buy them.

WHERE TO GO FOR WHAT
If you are interested in hiking, or simply in getting away from it all, then the New Territories and the outer islands are the place for you. Though the distances involved are not great – no more than a few hours' travel usually – these outlying areas are a world away from Central in terms of atmosphere and pace of life, and a couple of weeks could easily be spent exploring them.

The NEW TERRITORIES has many interesting villages, industrial towns, monasteries and fishing hamlets; and there is also Castle Peak, a mountainous area. If you're short on time, you can do a circular day-trip.

Of the most visited islands, CHEUNG CHAU and LAMMA both have good beaches and pleasant walks; while LANTAU is more rugged and therefore ideal for the more ambitious hiker. The HKTA has good leaflets, maps, ferry timetables, etc. for island excursions. Avoid weekends. If you plan on hiking, the winter months and autumn are best, but make sure you're properly equipped.

Too many people zip through Hong Kong on a brief shopping expedition, or come just to pick up visas for China. Visitors from the US intent on shopping may find that most goods are not particularly cheap, but other nationalities (especially Europeans) should find a few bargains. TSIM SHA TSUI is as good a place to start as any – you'll find everything you could ever want, from cameras to clothing and cosmetics, in and around Nathan Road. The enormous Harbour City Shopping Centre (comprising the Ocean Terminal, Ocean Centre and Ocean Galleries) is also located in Tsim Sha Tsui (on Canton Road), and is good for electronic merchandise. For clothing, visit The Lanes (between Queens Road and Des Voeux Road, Central), or the streets around Nathan Road and Causeway Bay. Denim is a good buy. The Jade Market lies at the junction of Kansu Street and Reclamation Street, Kowloon. There is also a local market in the town of Stanley, on Hong Kong Island, which is good for clothes, household goods and foodstuffs.

INTERNAL TRAVEL
Air: There has been an increase in the helicopter service between Hong Kong and Macau. This trip takes twenty minutes and departs from helipads at Hong Kong's Shun Tak terminal and the wharf in Macau. There are hourly departures from Macau starting at 8.30 a.m. until 4.30 p.m. and from Hong Kong between 9 a.m. and 5 p.m.
Ferry: The Star Ferry (tel. 366 2576) travels the harbour from Tsim Sha Tsui (Kowloon side) to Central (Hong Kong Island) in eight minutes and costs HK$1.50 for a top-deck ride. You should take at least one night-time ferry trip during your stay – the views are marvellous. There are also services connecting Central and Hung Hom, and Tsim Sha Tsui and Wanchai.

Inter-island ferries, to Lantau, Cheung Chau and Lamma, for example, depart mostly from the Outlying District Services Pier or the Central Harbour Services Pier – try to avoid travelling on these ferries at weekends. Costs are from HK$6.50–HK$12, and the Hong Kong Information and Gift Centre can provide current schedules and fares.

It is also possible to take ferries to nearby Macau and Guanzhou (Canton).
Rail: The Kowloon-Canton Railway (tel. 602 7799) runs a through-train service from Kowloon to Guanzhou four times daily, and also operates a local stopping service, useful for getting around Kowloon for only a few dollars.

The Mass Transit Railway, or subway, is fast and clean, and runs along the northern side of Hong Kong Island, and across to various points on Kowloon. Vending machines (correct change only) dispense tickets which are valid for 90 minutes. They cost HK$3.50–HK$9 and are collected at your destination, retained by turnstiles that recycle them through the system. There is also a Stored Value Ticket, useful for multiple journeys, which can be used on the Kowloon–Canton Railway, too. For information, call 750 0170.

LRT (Light Rail Transit): This rail service runs between Yuen Long and Tuen Mun in the New Territories. Fares cost between HK$3–4.50 (tel. 468 77 88). This is much faster than the tram.

Bus: The buses will take you just about anywhere you want to go, though you are only likely to use them for longer journeys, such as to the New Territories (walking is better in Kowloon, for example). Fares cost from HK$2–22 and you'll need the exact money. Most buses run from about 6 a.m. until midnight, though there is a through-harbour service every 15 minutes (the no. 121) in the small hours.

Tram: The trams run only east–west along the northern side of Hong Kong Island, with a short detour to Happ Valley. There is a flat fare of HK$1.20, and although the trams are not fast, they are fun to ride and make an interesting sightseeing experience. For information, tel. 559 8918.

Bicycle: For traffic and parking reasons, cycling is not recommended in Central and Kowloon. Indeed, bicycle rental facilities are scarce in these places, though it is possible to rent bikes on Lantau or Cheung Chau, and from towns in the New Territories.

Car: Private ownership of cars is discouraged, as the parking and traffic situations are horrendous. Hence the vast amount of public transport. Car hire is available, but it's not worth the hassle.

Taxi: Taxis are red, and those with no roof sign are not metered. The flagfall is HK$11.50 for the first 2 km, and HK$1 for each additional 200m. There is a baggage charge of HK$5 per item, and a surcharge of HK$20 for a trip through the harbour tunnel (for the driver's outward and return toll). Drivers do not usually speak English.

Minibus and maxicab: Both operate a little like taxis in that you can hail them anywhere and get off anywhere. The former are small red and yellow buses which do not run regular routes; the latter are green and yellow, and run between the Peak and Central, Aberdeen and Causeway Bay, and Shouson Hill Road and Pedder Street. Fares are higher than those on the regular buses (HK$3–6).

Rickshaw: You'll find them near the Star Ferry pier in Central (or they'll find you) but they are more of a photo opportunity than a realistic mode of transport these days. The 'boys' will expect a fee (HK$50) for photos.

Consult the Hong Kong Tourist Association for excellent transport advice, particularly if you intend to travel outside Kowloon and Hong Kong Island.

ACCOMMODATION
Although there is a plethora of budget rooms and dorms, rents in the colony are so high that people working here generally stay in the guest houses instead of renting flats, which means that a lot of places are often full. Everything gets booked solid over the Chinese New Year period.

FOOD
You'll find food of every description and every national origin in Hong Kong, whether it be beans on toast or burritos. And you will find everything that your stomach desires in Tsim Sha Tsui, including Western fast-food. The information centre offers a free dining and entertainment guide.

BUDGETING
Because transport costs are so low (many visitors get around the centre on foot anyway), your expenses in that direction will be negligible. The major daily costs will therefore be accommodation and food. Hostels charge around HK$75 per night, and the cheaper guesthouses about HK$160 per person per night. If you do as the locals do and eat Chinese, you'll be able to dine in restaurants for HK$100 or less, though the usual cost-cutting exercises of eating at fast-food outlets or buying your own food at the markets or supermarkets (they are everywhere) will bring down costs considerably. Most people seem to get by on £20–£25 per day. (If you're in town to shop, adjust your budget accordingly!)

A night out in a pub will set you back about another HK$100 (though it varies from place to place), but be careful not to end up in a hostess bar, where you'll pay (and can end up with) a lot more. Discos and nightclubs will have a cover charge. Some bars have a Happy Hour somewhere between 5 p.m. and 9 p.m. Canned beer costs only a few dollars.

Hong Kong is full of travellers taking time out to replenish the coffers, and work opportunities do exist here. There is *always* English-teaching work, for which you won't necessarily need qualifications; the hourly rate should be around HK$40–50 (or you can go freelance and charge a little more). For women, there is also hostessing/waitressing work, but it is not particularly well paid. Men and women can sometimes pick up modelling or film-extra work, but don't rely on it for a living, and be careful if someone approaches you about this kind of work – you may end up in the sort of films your mother wouldn't like!

In general, work is best fixed up on the spot rather than before leaving home. Professionals can try registering with an agency or checking out the vacancies in the English-language papers. Now that the colony is being handed back to China and the long-term residents are leaving, there are some short-term contracts available.

FURTHER INFORMATION

The Hong Kong Tourist Association (HKTA), 125 Pall Mall, 5th Floor, London SW1Y 5EA (tel. 0171 930 4775).

Hong Kong Government Office, 6 Grafton Street, London W1X 3LB (tel. 0171 499 9821).

Background reading: *Hong Kong, Macau and Canton – Travel Survival Kit* from Lonely Planet is highly recommended. A good alternative is *Hong Kong and Macau: The Rough Guide* and the Fodor's guide, though aimed at the better-heeled traveller, is clearly laid out and exceptionally informative. Recent travelogues include *Hong Kong* by Jan Morris.

In the fictional field, Richard Mason's *The World of Suzie Wong* is possibly the most enduringly famous novel set in the colony. Though you may not like blockbusters, *Tai-Pan* by James Clavell was meticulously researched and offers an accurate picture of the beginnings of the colony. Also worth a look are *Dynasty* and *Mandarin*, both by Robert Elegant.

If you ever get the chance to see some of the films that come out of Hong Kong, do so. Nothing can beat the pace and excitement of Jackie Chan movies, while the ghost stories (part Kung Fu, part high comedy) give an insight into Chinese death rituals and superstitions of the past. *Rouge* (a ghost story) and *Painted Faces* (about the now defunct Beijing Opera School) both show aspects of a Hong Kong that is, sadly, gone forever.

Hong Kong Island and Kowloon

AIRPORT FACILITIES

The descent into Kai Tak Airport (tel. 769 7531) must rate as the most spectacularly hair-raising in the world: be sure to get a window seat. Arrivals enter on the ground floor of the terminal; departures leave from the first. Once through customs, you will find a HKTA desk, a currency exchange (not particularly good rates) and a Hong Kong Hotels Association desk, which will check room availability for you. There are several different exits from the terminal: the one on the left side will take you to the Airport Transportation Terminus.

On the departures level there is a post office, a Hong Kong Telecom Service office, currency exchange, a coffee shop/bar and restaurant and duty-free shops. Other facilities include an unaccompanied baggage service desk and a left-luggage counter. Once through to the Departures Hall, there are more shops, restaurants, etc. Shop prices are not cheap.

Check-in time is two hours prior to departure. Departure tax is HK$50 (children under 12 are exempt).

There are plans for another airport, to be built on Lantau, but it won't be finished for some years and certainly not until after the Chinese take control of Hong Kong.

CITY LINKS
Kai Tak, only 5 km north-east of Kowloon, is a 20-minute drive from Kowloon, 30–45 minutes from Hong Kong Central. There are four airport buses that stop at various hotels in Kowloon and on Hong Kong Island. The A1 goes to the Kowloon Star Ferry Terminal, calling at the Ambassador, the Peninsula and the Regent (this is the one to get for the YMCA and Chungking Mansions). The A2 goes on through the cross-harbour tunnel to hotels in Central, while the A3 runs to Causeway Bay; the Tai Koo area is served by the A5 bus. Fares cost between HK$9 and HK$12, and there are taped announcements to indicate the stops.

Taxis will cost around HK$40–45 to Kowloon, HK$80–105 (includes the tunnel fee) to Hong Kong Island. Fares to hotels and other places in Tsim Sha Tsui are listed by the airport taxi rank. Remember to add on the baggage charge to the fare.

USEFUL ADDRESSES
Tourist office: Hong Kong Tourist Association's Information Centre is in the basement of Jardine House, Central (tel. 801 7111). Open Mon.–Fri. 9 a.m.–6 p.m.; Sat. 9 a.m.–1 p.m. The Information & Gift Centre is also in the basement. The Kowloon branch is in the Star Ferry concourse, open Mon.–Fri. 8 a.m.–6 p.m. The HKTA has leaflets on everything from walking and tram tours to festivals and the outlying islands. Overall, their service is excellent.

A multi-lingual visitor hotline (tel. 801 7177) operates Mon.–Fri. 8 a.m.–6 p.m.; weekends and public holidays 9 a.m.–5 p.m.
Department of Immigration: Immigration Tower, 7 Gloucester

Road, Wanchai (tel. 824 6111). Deals with employment visas/visa extensions.

Hong Kong Student Travel Bureau: Room 1021, 10th floor, Star House, Tsim Sha Tsui, next to the ferry terminal (tel. 730 3269). Offers budget air and rail travel, plus visa service; can also organize tours, visas, etc. for China.

Traveller's Hostel: 16th floor, Chungking Mansions. Offers similar service to HK Student Travel Bureau. (There are many budget travel agents in Hong Kong, but be careful – not all are honest. Try the two listed here.)

Post office: On Hong Kong Island, the General Post Office is to the right of the star Ferry Terminal; on Kowloon, there is one at 10 Middle Road (behind the Ambassador hotel). Poste restante mail, unless otherwise specified, will go to the GPO on Hong Kong Island.

US Embassy: 26 Garden Road Central, Hong Kong (tel. 523 9011).

Medical assistance: Queen Mary Hospital, Pokfulam Road, Hong Kong Island (tel. 819 2111); Queen Elizabeth Hospital, Wylie Road, Kowloon (tel. 710 2111); Princess Margaret Hospital, 2–10 Lai King Road, Lai King (tel. 310 3111). Many hotels have duty doctors. If the problem is not too serious, you may want to try herbal medicine. A Chinese doctor can prescribe the herbs for you.

Bookshop: Swindon Books, 13–15 Lock Road, Tsim Sha Tsui. A really excellent bookshop, with a good stock of books (factual and fictional) on Hong Kong, China and Asia in general.

GETTING ABOUT
See **Internal Travel**, p. 304.

SIGHTS
A visit to Hong Kong Island would not be complete without a trip to the summit of the PEAK. As the famous harbour view gradually unfolds beneath you, you may begin to wonder why the tram seems to be travelling straight up instead of at an angle. Relax: it's been operating for over 100 years in perfect safety. The tram terminus is in Garden Road, behind the Hilton hotel, and the fare is HK$10, one way. There's also a scenic bus route: take the number 15 from the Central bus terminal. Or you can walk, if you're up to it. The view from the top – 397 metres above Hong Kong – is one of the best in the world. There is a viewing complex, complete with binoculars, restaurants and gift shops. To really get the best out of it, you should go up twice: once during the day for a view of the New Territories and a look at the aeroplanes taking off and landing, and once at night, for the lights.

You can hike (about 4 km) down the Peak to ABERDEEN, originally a fishing village and a ship-building port, now transformed into a tourist haunt by virtue of its floating restaurants. It's an interesting place to walk around, or to take a sampan tour. Not far away is OCEAN PARK, which contains an aquarium and the Middle Kingdom complex, highlighting 5,000 years of China's history and culture. Admission is HK$130, and it's open seven days (but avoid weekends). In the same area, on Robinson Road, are the Zoological and Botanical Gardens, which house over 300 species of bird. The best time to visit is in the early morning, when local people perform Tai Chi exercises there.

To the west of Central is SHEUNG WAN, where you will find 'the Lanes' (see **Where to Go for What**, p. 303) and, at the junction of Ladder Street and Hollywood Road, the Man Mo Temple, the oldest temple (*c.* 1847) in Hong Kong. The area around the temple was used for location shots in *Suzie Wong*, and Ladder Street (the flight of steps by the temple) is over a century old. Continuing westwards, the FUNG PING SHAN MUSEUM at Hong Kong University contains Chinese artefacts, and is open Monday to Saturday. Admission is free.

CAUSEWAY BAY is where the (in)famous Jardine Matheson company set up shop in the 1840s, and the area is littered with street names that recall those days. The typhoon shelter on the waterfront is home to a number of junks and sampans, and the noon-day gun (the one in the song 'Mad Dogs and Englishmen') is nearby.

Just off Tai Hang Road, within walking distance of Causeway Bay, are the Aw Boon Haw, or TIGER BALM GARDENS, famous for a collection of mythological statues in the worst possible taste. Worth a visit! Admission is free and the opening hours are 10 a.m.–4 p.m. daily.

The cheapest Hong Kong Island attraction is, of course, the trams. Get a seat on the top deck, at the front.

A stroll along the waterfront will lead you to most of the main attractions on KOWLOON. The golfball-shaped SPACE MUSEUM is here, as is the MUSEUM OF ART, and you can take tea in the impressively colonial PENINSULA HOTEL (but be properly dressed).

North of Tsim Sha Tsui is YAU MA TEI, a colourful district that is interesting to walk around; there are a few temples here, the Jade Market, the Temple Street night market (open 6.30 p.m.–midnight), and the typhoon shelter teeming with junks. Make sure to obtain the Yau Ma Tei walking leaflet from the HKTA.

ACCOMMODATION

Most budget accommodation is located in Tsim Sha Tsui, on or around Nathan Road, in the heart of Kowloon.

Hostels: Rooms cost about HK$100 (doubles HK$130), dorms from HK$35−40, and there is always a space to be found somewhere. The most popular places to stay are concentrated on Nathan Road: Chungking Mansions and Mirador Mansions. Both are high-rise complexes of guest houses with varying amenities. Prices range from HK$100 (doubles HK$130), with dorms at HK35−45.

Chungking Mansions, Nathan Road, Kowloon. (The entrance is a shopping arcade facing Nathan Road.) There are over 100 guest houses. Find the lifts A−E. The idea is to walk around and check out prices. Be sure to check that the air-conditioning works and the place is not too grubby before you hand over any cash. Blocks A and B have the most and the cheapest options. C, D and E have less guest houses but tend to be cleaner.

BLOCK A:

Traveller's Hostel, 16th floor (tel. 268 7710). A well-established hostel, but don't expect a quiet night. It has rooms and dorms, an information board, a travel agency, and is a good place to meet other travellers.

London Guest House, 6th floor. Good singles, all with phones.

Park Guest House, 15th floor (tel. 368 1689). Air-conditioned singles and doubles.

BLOCK B:

Traveller's Friendship House, 6th floor (tel. 311 2523). Cheap dorms.

BLOCK C:

Tom's Guest House, 16th Floor (tel. 367 9258). Clean and quiet.

BLOCK D:

Guangzhou Guest House, 13th Floor (tel. 724 1555).

BLOCK E:

Hometown Guest House, 10th Floor (tel. 723 8229). Carpeted rooms, one of nicest and most expensive in whole complex.

Mirador Mansions, 58 Nathan Road, Kowloon. (Enter from Moody Road.) Same set-up as at Chungking Mansions.

BLOCK A:

Welcome Guest House, 7th floor (tel. 721 7793). Friendly management. Laundry service. Can help arrange Chinese visa.

BLOCK D:

Kowloon Guest House, 10th floor (tel. 366 1090). Double rooms with private bath, TV, air-conditioning and possibly your own fridge!

Also worth trying:

International Youth Accommodation Centre (IYAC), 6th floor, 21A Lock Road, Kowloon (tel. 366 3419). Dorms HK$28. Features a coffeeshop and a restaurant.

YMCA, 41 Salisbury Road, Kowloon (tel. 369 2211). Dorms HK$80. Singles HK$280. Doubles HK$560.

The IYHF hostels are all a bit out of the way, with only one, Ma Wui Hall on Mt Davis, Hong Kong Island being anywhere near centrally situated – and even it takes a bit of getting to. The HKTA at the airport or in town can direct you there. Advance reservations for *all* IYHA hostels via Head Office are compulsory. The address is: Room 225–6, Block 19, Shek Kip Mei Estate, Shamshuipo, Kowloon, or ring 817 5715 if the office is closed. Hostels cost HK$15–40 per night.

For longer-term options, check out the adverts in the *South China Morning Post* or the *Hong Kong Standard*. Rents are, however, very high. A lot of people end up staying in Chungking Mansions for the duration.

FOOD
An eating must is dim sum, small delicacies such as dumplings, spring rolls, meatballs and buns. Tea is served with the food, and the cost is around HK$8 to HK$20 per dish. There are restaurants serving dim sum all over the place, but here are some names to try:

Luk Yu Tea House & Restaurant, 26 Stanley Street, Central (tel. 523 5464). This traditional restaurant is quite an experience. Dim sum hours are 7 a.m.–6 p.m.

Capital Restaurant, Chungking Mansions, 36–44 Nathan Road. Dim sum.

Pearl City Restaurant, 36 Paterson Street, Causeway Bay. Dim sum hours 11.30 a.m.–5 p.m.

Can Do Restaurant, 37 Cameron Road, Tsim Sha Tsui. A cheap café popular with visitors and restaurants (no dim sum, though).

South China Restaurant, 104 Austin Road. Cut-price Western breakfast available.

For pub food try:

Ned Kelly's Last Stand, 11a Ashley Road, Kowloon.

Blacksmith's Arms, 16 Minden Avenue, Kowloon.

Vegetarian eateries include:

Choi Kun Heung Vegetarian Restaurant, 219 E. Nathan Road.

Vegi Food Kitchen, 8 Cleveland Street, Causeway Bay.

Wishful Cottage, 336–40 Lockhart Road, Causeway Bay.

If you really want to eat cheaply, try the night markets, where numerous food vendors sell a variety of interesting dishes and you can simply wander and point. (It may be as well to take your own chopsticks, though, as the utensils are not always so clean.) Try the stalls on Temple Street, Kowloon.

The HKTA's *Dining & Entertainment Guide* can point you in the direction of many other restaurants of every nationality.

ENTERTAINMENT

It is still possible to see Chinese opera in Hong Kong, mostly during the festival periods, though there are sometimes performances in the street and elsewhere in the colony: consult the HKTA about upcoming events and festival dates. The music often grates on Western ears, but after a time you get used to it and realize its beauty. The costumes are colourful and quite fantastic.

For bars and clubs, head for the Wanchai area on Hong Kong Island: once the hangout of US servicemen on leave from Vietnam, things are decidedly quieter now. Lockhart Road is the main drag, but as some places are rather seedy, it is perhaps best avoided by unaccompanied women. Try the Old China Hand or the Horse & Groom.

In Central, the Lan Kwai Fong area (top of D'Aguilar Street) is where the expats and the 'chuppies' (Chinese yuppies) go to drink and dance. Check out Underground and 1997 for the disco scene; Mad Dogs, on Wyndham Street, is recommended for pubbing, as is the Bull & Bear on Chater Road.

On the Kowloon side, the aforementioned Blacksmith's Arms

and Ned Kelly's (see **Food**, p. 312) are friendly places, or try Someplace Else (in the Sheraton Hotel, Nathan Road). Rick's Café, 4 Hart Avenue, has live music and no cover charge.

The 'girlie' bars are mostly located in Wanchai and Tsim Sha Tsui. The best known is the Bottoms Up topless bar at 14—16 Hankow Road, Central, which featured in a James Bond movie. Actually, it's rather sedate. If you want heavier stuff, a taxi driver is the best source of information. WARNING! There's an exorbitant 'service charge' in these bars for ridiculous things (such as talking to the waitress)! If you refuse to pay, musclemen will take out your wallet for you. Advertisements for cheap drinks may lure you in, but they'll empty your wallet in the end.

Cinemas abound, a large number of them showing imported English-language films, the rest Kung Fu/Jackie Chan/Chinese melodramas. Many films are edited, though, to cram in as many showings as possible. Entrance fees are reasonable, and check the papers for details of daily screenings.

The publication *Hong Kong This Week*, available from HKTA Information & Gift Centres, gives up-to-date information on all kinds of entertainment.

EXCURSIONS
Besides excursions to the New Territories and the outlying islands (see **Where to Go for What**, p. 303), there are a number of side-trips you can take (too many, in fact, to list here: consult the HKTA for a complete guide to what's on offer). In New Kowloon (north of Kowloon proper) is the SUNG DYNASTY VILLAGE. Chinese history Disneyland-style, this re-created 1,000-year-old settlement comes complete with people in period costume. It's best to take a guided tour for this one, though you can go on your own (take the MTR to Mei Foo Stn.) Admission is HK$110 (weekdays) or HK$75 on weekends. Tours cost from HK$160 and include a meal. Also in new Kowloon is the 2,000-year-old HAN TOMB (also known as Lei Cheng UK), discovered in the 1950s. It has a small museum (both tomb and museum are a branch of the Museum of History) open Mon.–Fri. 10 a.m.–8.30 p.m.; Sat.–Sun. 12—5.30 p.m.

You'll need your passport for a day-trip to MACAU, the nearby Portuguese colony, which is also due to be handed back to China in the near future. Hong Kong's residents flock there at the weekends to gamble in the colony's many casinos, but Macau has other charms: churches, temples, ruins and crumbling colonial buildings. There are ferry, jetfoil and hydrofoil services from Hong Kong. Most nationalities do not need a visa, but if necessary they can be obtained on arrival. The Macau Tourist Information Centre in Hong

Kong is at 305 Shun Tak Centre, Room 3704, 200 Connaught Road, Central.

If you are feeling more adventurous, hop over the border to China. You could go for the day to GUANZHOU (Canton) – the train costs HK$183 one way – or take the overnight ferry and stay a little longer. China visas cost HK$150. Besides the agents mentioned in the **Hong Kong & Kowloon: Useful Addresses** section (p. 308), the two Chinese travel agencies which can organize tickets/visas, etc. are the China Travel Service, 77 Queen's Road, Central and the China International Travel Service, (CITS), South Seas Centre, 75 Mody Road, Tsim Sha Tsui East (tel. 525 2284). They can book you on an organized tour, but this works out considerably more expensive than going it alone.

INDIA

VITAL STATISTICS
Red tape: All visitors must have a full passport and a visa. There are different categories of visa – single, double and multiple entry; transit; tourist; business – and the fee varies according to the nationality of the applicant. A tourist visa is valid for six months, but can be extended for a further six months once you are inside India. Visas may be obtained from any Indian Consulate, Embassy or High Commission, but it is recommended that you get one before leaving home, rather than in another country.

Certain parts of India (politically sensitive ones) are restricted, and tourists require special travel permits to visit them.

Customs: There is a duty-free allowance of 200 cigarettes or 50 cigars or 250 g tobacco, plus 1 litre alcohol and a small quantity of perfume for personal use. Large amounts of cash (over US$10,000) should be declared. Cameras, video cameras, Walkmans, etc. should be entered on a special form upon entry to India; the form has to be shown again on departure, and all of the listed items accounted for.

There are restrictions on the export of antiquities (anything over 100 years old). Items made of ivory or animal skins may not be exported.

Health: No immunizations are required unless you are coming from an area where yellow fever has been reported. Many countries that you visit *after* India will ask for proof of cholera vaccination, and it is recommended that you have one in any case. Vaccinations against hepatitis A and typhoid are also advisable, and polio and tetanus boosters won't go amiss. You should take precautions against malaria, too. Tap water, ice in drinks, unpeeled fruit and raw vegetables are all unsafe.

There is both free and private health care in India, but you would be advised to take out insurance. You should opt for the private health care.

Language: Hindi is the official language, though there are over a thousand other languages and dialects. English is widely spoken and you will hardly ever be in a situation where there are no English-speakers about. The south of the country has the majority of English speakers.

Population: Around 810 million.

Capital: New Delhi, population 8.5 million.

Political system: Parliamentary democracy.

Religion: The Hindu religion is the main one, but the Muslim, Sikh and Christian religions are also followed.

Time: Five and a half hours ahead of GMT.

Money: The Rupee (Rs), divided into 100 paise, is the currency. Coins: 10, 20, 25 and 50 paise, Rs1, Rs2 and Rs5. Notes: Rs1 (slowly going out of circulation), Rs2, Rs5, Rs10, Rs20, Rs50, Rs100 and Rs1,000. £1 = Rs50.

Don't accept notes with a tear on the edge because you'll never get rid of them. Notes with holes through the middle, however, are fine (this is the result of the Indian practice of stapling money together).

As a foreign visitor, you must pay for flights, rail fares and hotel accommodation, etc. in hard currency, traveller's cheques or by credit card, unless you can produce an exchange certificate to show that you changed your foreign currency into rupees legally. If you wish to change your rupees back into hard currency when leaving, you will need to produce your exchange certificates. The import and export of rupees is forbidden. It is possible to change cash on the black market, which is illegal but ignored (usually); stick to small amounts. US dollars and sterling are the best currencies to travel with.

Traveller's cheques can be cashed at most banks, but make sure to carry well-known brands (American Express traveller's cheques, however, are now problematic because of recent cases of fraud). Credit cards are accepted in large city establishments, but the international VISA card is almost useless: on a recent trip to India the only bank where you could buy rupees with VISA cards was the Andhra Bank, and the transaction took over two hours – even though they call themselves the VISA Bank of India! (International banks tended to be faster.) Some hotels have VISA stickers on the door and at the counter but that only means that they accept cards with the inscription 'Valid in India and Nepal'. Only big tourist-oriented shops accept VISA.

Tax: Hotel services are liable to a 7% luxury tax and a 10% expenditure tax if the bill is paid in rupees (but since foreigners are expected to pay in foreign currency, the latter isn't a problem).

Communications: The telephone system is faulty, to say the least: bad connections, broken phones and calls that get cut off are a permanent feature. Large hotels in the big cities have international direct dialling, alternatively, overseas and long-distance calls can be made from privately run telephone boxes marked PCD-STD-ISN. If the phones defeat you, you can send telegrams instead.

The postal service can be reliable at times, but letters have been known to arrive at their destinations mangled, while others have simply failed to arrive. Never send valuables or cash through the post. If you want to send a package, set aside a whole day, because it involves having a tailor stitch it in cloth and seal the edges with wax – not to mention a great deal of queuing. Before you wrap it up yourself, check with the post office – they may require to see the contents of the package before you post it. Always wait to see your stamps franked, so that they can't be stolen.

Media: There are various English-language newspapers produced in India, such as the *Times of India*, the *Hindu*, and the *Indian Express*. Newspapers from overseas are available in large towns and cities.

Electricity: 220v AC/50 Hz.

Business hours: BANKS: Mon.–Fri. 10 a.m.–2 p.m., Sat. 10 a.m.–12.30 p.m. (later in Bombay).

POST OFFICES: Mon.–Fri. 10 a.m.–5 p.m.; Sat. 10 a.m.–1 p.m.

SHOPS: Mon.–Sat. 9.30 a.m.–6 p.m.

OFFICES: Mon.–Fri. 9.30 a.m.–5 p.m. Some offices open on Saturday mornings.

Holidays: 1 and 26 January; Good Friday; 15 August; 2 October; 10 November (Divali); 25 December. There are, in addition, a number of local holidays; the Indian Tourist Office can advise when these occur. Check about holidays periodically while you are in India.

Climate: There are roughly three seasons in India: the hot season (Feb.–May), the monsoon season (May–Oct.) and the cool season (Nov.–Feb.). The climate varies according to the region: Southern India is tropical all year round (warm clothing will, however, be required at any time of year for visits to hill areas); the monsoon season runs from April to July (and October to December, in some places). In the central plains, the hot season is arid and scorching (around 40°C); monsoon rains fall from June to September; during the cool season temperatures drop sharply at night. The north is chilly even in summer. Winters are cold, with heavy snowfall in high places. Warm clothes are necessary all year round.

The north aside, the best time to visit is between October and March, when temperatures don't exceed 32°C and there is low or no humidity.

DO'S AND DON'TS

India is a different world, so begin by throwing all your preconceptions and Western notions out of the window. Slow down and adjust to a different pace of life; there's no point in getting annoyed that it can take an entire morning to unravel the red tape involved in buying a train ticket – that's just the way things are, and getting angry won't do you the slightest bit of good. If you're the type who likes things to work, to run on time, and if you expect honest, accurate answers to questions, India may severely damage your health. Pop a few Valium or stay away. It *is* an incredibly frustrating country. But it's also one of *the* sights of the world and, in retrospect at least, your time will have been well spent.

Handshaking is often used as a form of greeting, but only amongst men (strict Muslims won't shake hands with women, so Indian women aren't familiar with the custom). The more usual greeting is to put your hands together, bow your head slightly and say 'namaste'. It would be a courtesy to learn to do this, but take your cue from the Indians you meet until you're sure which greeting is appropriate. 'Namaste' does not mean 'hello', as some locals might translate it. It is a semi-formal greeting used when meeting someone for the first time or seeing an acquaintance after some time apart. Don't toss it around like 'Hi' – it sounds ridiculous.

Perhaps the cultural difference that initially confounds visitors the most is the odd, Indian 'head-wag'. This is a sort of rolling of the head from side to side which is used as an affirmative (especially in the south), though it looks to Western eyes like a 'No'.

Another thing to remember is that Indians don't like to tell you something you won't want to hear. If you're asking for directions and they don't know the way, they'll make up an answer rather than disappoint you. Important information should be triple-checked.

Always remove footwear upon entering a place of worship (and even some private homes). If you are invited to someone's home, a small gift would be appreciated – preferably something from home, as imported items are expensive and prestigious. One thing to watch out for when eating, either in a person's home or in any other situation, is to use the right hand only, as the left hand is considered unclean. Cutlery is seldom used.

Insist on (and keep) exchange receipts. These are necessary if paying hotel bills in rupees.

Tipping is customary, and you should tip the usual people – taxi drivers, waiters, porters, guides, etc. The tip given is usually a few rupees or 5% of a bill. Another form of tipping is baksheesh, which is nothing short of bribery and a custom that many Western travellers have trouble with: adjust – it'll make life easier. Think of it as tipping someone *before* they do something for you instead of afterwards.

Something else that causes soul-searching amongst travellers is the profusion of beggars. One option is to seek out a local charity or aid agency that you would like to support, and make a donation to them instead of giving to the beggars themselves or only give in when it feels right. Whether you're comfortable with it or not, you *are* rich to most Indians, simply by virtue of being able to afford to travel there.

Always keep an eye on your luggage, especially at train stations. Do as the locals do: buy a small lock to chain up your bag while you're sleeping on a train.

Carry toilet roll with you at all times unless you want to 'go native', which involves the left hand and a dipper for water. On this note, always use your right hand for eating, handling food, touching other people, waving and pointing, and especially when offering something (like money). The left hand is (for obvious reasons) considered unclean.

At the time of going to press there were problems in Kashmir with backpackers being taken hostage and threatened with execution by Kashmiri rebels at war with the Indian authorities. Before planning your trip, call the Foreign Office advice line: 0171 270 4129.

WHERE TO GO FOR WHAT
India is a *big* country. If you plan on seeing all of it you'll easily use up your visa and will probably have to extend it. Many people visit only the 'Golden Triangle' of Delhi, Jaipur and Agra, for which a month or so will suffice.

The north's attractions include: VARANASI, the oldest city in India and a centre of Hindu pilgrimage where people come to purify themselves by washing in the River Ganges, and the dead are cremated by the riverbanks; SHIMLA, state capital of the tiny hill state of Himachal Pradesh, is a former summer capital of the British, and the colonial past of this pretty town is reflected in its streets and buildings; KASHMIR is India's northernmost state and a place of great natural beauty, with mountains, lakes and forests; the province of LADAKH is as far north as you can go – it's a remote place of barren mountains and hilltop Tibetan monasteries, a truly off-the-beaten-track destination (but see **Do's and Don'ts**, p. 318).

In the northwest, don't miss RAJASTHAN (Jaisalmer in particular). This looks like something right out of *Indiana Jones*.

In the west of the country are BOMBAY and GOA, and information about this region can be found in the Bombay section, below. To the east lies CALCUTTA, the largest city in India, with its beautiful Botanical Gardens and Marble Palace, plus the Victoria Memorial. Also in this region are DARJEELING, a wonderful hill resort where there are many tea gardens, and BHUBANESWAR, with its hundreds of temples. Darjeeling can offer you 'comfort' that's up to Western standards if you need a break. To get away from it all, you can fly from Calcutta to the ANDAMAN ISLANDS, known for the beautiful beaches and coral gardens.

In the south, there are Hindu temples in and around MADRAS, capital of Tamil Nadu. Or, for a taste of colonial days, there is PONDICHERRY, former French colony and now a pretty seaside resort. Travel down the 'spice coast', KERALA, where spices are grown on secluded plantations and the waterfront towns bear hallmarks of past trade with Europe and China. And lastly, don't miss MYSORE, a city of magnificent palaces and museums.

INTERNAL TRAVEL

Air: Indian Airlines and Vayudoot have now merged to form the major carrier on domestic routes. Fares are low, but buying a ticket involves as much red tape as buying a house would anywhere else! Though the level of service is good, safety and punctuality standards are not. Flying is therefore not the best way of getting around the country in a hurry – besides, you'd miss all of the scenery. Of course, it makes sense if you need to cover long distances quickly and aren't too bothered about seeing the bits in between. There are air passes available at US$400 (covering the whole country for 21 days) or US$200 (specific regions). In Delhi, details of departures can be obtained by dialling 144.

Rail: The train is *the* way to travel in India. It is cheap, an ideal way to experience the country, and there's never a dull moment. Rail enthusiasts will be delighted to find that there are a number of steam locomotives still in service. Buying a ticket, again, is a complicated procedure, but you'll soon get the hang of it.

There are various classes to choose from (first, air-con, sleeper, reserved, express, second . . .) with prices to match. Second class (wooden seats) is comfortable enough for short journeys, and second-class air-con is fine for long trips. It really isn't a good idea to travel without a reservation though, and on overnight journeys and popular routes, you'll have to make advance reservations anyway.

On many trains, there is a women-only carriage, which is less crowded than the others, and which foreign women travelling alone often find useful.

Foreign visitors may purchase an Indrail pass (either in India or from agents overseas) at £71 for 7 days, £80 for 15 days, £110 for 30 days, £165 for 60 days or £210 for 90 days (second class); these are worth it if you intend to cover a lot of ground in a short space of time. Though you don't have to pay sleeper supplements, etc. with the pass, you do still have to make advance reservations.

Bus: Usually not much cheaper than going by train, but you will have no choice but to use the bus in remote areas where there is no access by rail, e.g. the Himalayas. Buses break down a lot and are overcrowded, but the ones that cover the long-distance routes are generally of a better standard. Many buses don't have windows, so bring your all-weather gear. Keep an eye on your luggage and try to sit near the front, where it's more comfortable. Really, bus travel in India is only recommended for the hardy.

Driving: Car-hire firms such as Hertz have outlets in the big cities. Drive on the left. It is advisable to hire a driver with the car rather than drive yourself.

Hitching: Not recommended. It's a very, very slow way to get around such a vast country. Moreover, public transport is so cheap that there's no real need to hitch, not even to meet people – you'd meet more on a train.

Local transport: Each city has its own bus system. If you can master the buses (they can be confusing), they are a cheap way of getting about, as the fares are only a few rupees. Avoid them during the rush hour, and be on your guard for pickpockets.

Most people use bicycle or motorized rickshaws instead, as they cost not much more than the bus. There are regular taxis, too, and horse-drawn carts (*tongas*) in some places. Only taxis have meters, but the drivers probably won't use them. You'll have to agree the fare (based on your destination) beforehand, as you will with rickshaws, etc. Where drivers *do* use the meters, the rates are usually out of date and the revised rates are printed on a card. The drivers may ask two or three times the printed rate, though.

In the bigger towns and cities, walking can be difficult as the streets are so crowded. Wade into the experience cautiously – look out for your valuables. If you can't face the crowds, bicycle-rickshaws are best – and you won't have to look for them, as they'll come to you. Be sure to agree on a price beforehand, and don't worry about the 'I don't want to treat another human being like an animal' pangs of conscious. You are contributing to the local economy. Bicycle rental is also possible in many places – a great way to transport yourself about the sights.

ACCOMMODATION
There is accommodation to suit every pocket in India, from 5-star luxury hotels right down to dormitories. You can get a list of government-approved hotels from the tourist board before you leave home, although the hotels listed do not go below 1-star, for which you would pay Rs300–400. If you arrive somewhere late at night, just attach yourself to a rickshaw driver (or, more likely, he'll attach himself to you!), as they are a good source of hotel information and will take you somewhere suitable. The airports have hotel booking desks, too, though they deal only with the more upmarket establishments.

Youth hostels: Hostel accommodation is available in most parts of the country. Though they are not always conveniently placed, there is a hostel near most tourist destinations. Costs are between Rs15 and Rs25 per night. Privately run dormitories are rare.

Hotels and guest houses: Every town has a number of hotels that charge less than Rs200 per night for a perfectly comfortable (if basic) room. The low-priced hotels are often clustered together in one part of town, but it usually pays to look around a bit before settling on one in particular, as they are not always clean.

Alternative accommodation: Also available to foreign travellers are government rest houses and tourist bungalows. There are also railway retiring rooms for use by rail passengers in transit – they are for short stays only, but are cheap. In Kashmir, houseboats are where most people stay. Like hotels, there is a range of categories, with prices to match.

FOOD
India is the one country in Asia where vegetarians have no worries, as almost all of the dishes are meat-free – for a change, it's the carnivores who may face difficulties.

Some Indian food is already familiar to Westerners, though the quality *won't* always be what you're used to. An Indian meal in London, Edinburgh or Bradford tastes nothing like the food in India. The level of spiciness varies (generally hotter in the south). Better to nibble before digging in.

You can eat at streetside food stalls or bazaar cafés, and there are tourist restaurants in many places. Eating is generally cheap, though meat and Western dishes will be more expensive. European and Chinese food is available in the large hotels, and there are Western-style snack and fast-food eateries in the cities.

It's necessary to drink plenty of liquids to avoid dehydration, and there are a wide selection of soft drinks to choose from: *lassi*, a refreshing yogurt-based beverage, is a favourite with visitors; sugar-cane juice is deliciously different, and there are a variety of tropical fruit juices available in cans. Or try the locally made bottled fizzy drinks. Should you get tired of flavoured juices, etc., bottled mineral and soda water are widely available. Ensure that the seal on the bottle cap has not been broken or tampered with; it's not unknown for unscrupulous vendors to make up their own versions of Coca Cola using the local tap water. The results may fool you – until you hit the toilet a few hours later and have to stay there for the rest of the day!

You cannot buy alcohol on certain days in some states, and a few states are completely 'dry'. However it isn't usually a problem for foreigners to buy alcohol, and you can, if you wish, ask for an 'All India Liquor Permit' when you apply for your visa (or you can get one from the tourist offices in Delhi, Bombay, Calcutta and Madras). All of the major hotels and some restaurants are licensed to sell alcohol (even in Tamil Nadu, which is supposed to be a dry state). The whisky is good, as is the gin and rum, but Indian wine isn't so palatable. There are many brands of Indian beers and lagers, all of which are drinkable. If you are visiting Goa, try *feni*, the local brew made from cashews.

Coffee and tea are available, both automatically served with milk and sugar.

If you go to a restaurant offering 'meals ready' this usually means a platter of rice and bottomless side dishes for Rs10–15 – a great deal.

WARNING: Few visitors escape stomach troubles in India, even those who are quite careful. To reduce the likelihood of food poisoning, always peel fruit and don't eat salads or ice cream. Some travellers stay away from meat, particularly pork. Never drink tap water and avoid ice in drinks (some drinks are served with crushed ice – ask for yours to be made without). Until you've got used to the local food, it's best not to eat at stalls, and – obviously – never eat anywhere where standards of hygiene are suspect. India is simply one of those countries where conditions are unhygienic, and people can die from diarrhoea. You can never be too careful about what you eat and drink.

BUDGETING

India is a cheap country to travel in. You can get a good room for £3–4 or less (a lot less, if there's a dorm available), and a whole day's food won't come to more than a pound or so. Long-distance travel, local bus and rickshaw fares are cheap. Even accounting for snacks, postcards home, and entrance charges to museums, etc. you should easily be able to get by on £5 per day. In fact, the only thing that is really expensive (relatively speaking) is alcohol. Expect to pay the equivalent of your daily food expenses for a bottle of beer.

Forget about looking for work: you'd only be paid a pittance if you could land a job. One source of emergency cash is to sell your Walkman, camera, watch, etc. (though you can only do this if you haven't declared the items upon entering India). You will frequently be approached by people wanting to buy Western electronic goods, so there should be no problem in finding a buyer. Another way of making your finances stretch further is to change money on the black market – though the situation changes from time to time, and the premium isn't always favourable enough to make it worth your while. Check out the current state of play with other travellers, first.

FURTHER INFORMATION

Government of India Tourist Office, 7 Cork Street, London W1X 1PB (tel. 0171 437 3677).

India High Commission, India House, Aldwych, London WC2B 4NA (tel. 0171 836 8484). Apply to the consular section for visas, which will take several weeks by post or a couple of days if applying in person. There is also a consulate in Birmingham.

Background reading: The Lonely Planet guide to India and the *South Asian Handbook* (Trade and Travel Publications) are both excellent guides. If you intend to do a lot of travelling by train, *India by Rail* by Royston Ellis (Brandt Publications) will tell you everything you need to know about Indian railways and makes interesting reading. The *Insight City Guide* series features Delhi, Jaipur and Agra, for those interested in visiting only the Golden Triangle.

The days of the Raj have inspired a wealth of literature about the European in India. E. M. Forster's *A Passage To India* and Paul Scott's *The Raj Quartet* are both insightful works about the clash of two cultures, while Scott's *Staying On* is the poignant tale of an elderly couple who decide to remain in India after independence. *Heat and Dust* by Ruth Prawer Jhabvala is another story set in colonial days. *The Seekers*, by the same author, is a collection of short stories about modern-day India. Dominique Lapierre's *City of Joy* (about Calcutta) has won great critical acclaim and comes highly recommended, as does Christopher Portway's *Indian Odyssey*.

Bombay

AIRPORT FACILITIES
Bombay's airport is 26 km from the city. It has two terminals, which are several kilometres apart and linked by bus. Terminal 1, (Santa Cruz), handles domestic traffic, while Terminal 2 (Sahar) is the international terminal. In the latter, most facilities (including the restaurants and currency exchanges) operate round the clock. There is a tourist information desk in the arrivals hall, plus a couple of banks, and bus and taxi ticket counters. A restaurant and snack bar are located on the first floor, along with a duty-free shop and a 24-hour post office.

The baggage claiming process can be unbelievably slow, but clearing customs is usually uncomplicated for foreigners. Check-in time is at least 90 minutes prior to departure (though most airlines recommend 2–3 hours) and the departure tax is Rs300 for all international flights except those to neighbouring countries, where the tax is Rs150. Domestic departure tax is 10% of the fare, except where the fare has been paid in foreign currency, in which case the tax is waived.

CITY LINKS
Bus: Airport buses connect the domestic and international terminals with one another and with the Air India/Indian Airlines office at Nariman Point, downtown. The journey from Sahar takes about 90 minutes and costs Rs35. Tickets should be bought at the counter in the arrivals hall or on the bus itself. The buses run from early morning until about midnight. Alternatively, there is a public bus, the number 321, which links the city and the airport at a cost of Rs3.50.
Taxi: There is a pre-paid taxi scheme in operation. The price varies according to destination, but will be around Rs120, and vouchers can be bought at the police booth in the arrivals hall. Or you could try negotiating a cheaper price with one of the waiting taxi drivers outside the terminal. The journey to the centre of town takes approximately one hour.

USEFUL ADDRESSES

Tourist office: Government of India Tourist Office, 123 Maharshi Karve Road, near Churchgate Station (tel. 29 3144). Open Mon.–Fri. 9.30 a.m.–6 p.m.; Sat. 9.30 a.m.–1 p.m. Good maps and leaflets available here.

Foreigner's registration office: Office of the Commissioner of Police, Dababhoy Naoroji Road (tel. 26 8111). Visas can be extended here.

UK High Commission: 2nd Floor, Mercantile Bank Building, Mahatma Gandhi Road (tel. 27 4874).

US Consulate: Lincoln House, 78 Bhulabhai Desai Road (tel. 82 3611).

Post office: The GPO from which poste restante mail can be collected is on Nagar Chowk, near the Victoria Terminus Station. It's open 7 days.

Emergency services: Ambulance 102 and Police 100.

Medical assistance: Bombay Hospital, New Marine Lines (tel. 286 3234); St George's Hospital, near the GPO (tel. 415 0246).

GETTING ABOUT

Rail: Trains mostly carry commuters to and from the suburbs, but can be useful for some city centre journeys. Trains run frequently between 5 a.m. and midnight, but it is highly recommended that you avoid travelling during the rush hour. There are both first- and second-class carriages.

Bus: The bus system is good (certainly the best organized in India), making Bombay an easy city to get around (except in rush hour, when things get extremely crowded). The bus service is run by BEST (Bombay Electrical Supply & Transport Co.) and you can buy an outline of their routes at kiosks in the city centre.

Taxi: There are plenty of taxis and motorized rickshaws around. Make sure to agree an acceptable fare rate before you move off.

On foot: Walking is a viable way of getting around certain parts of the city, as it is quite a compact place – in the Fort area, for example, there are many hotels and attractions within easy reach of each other.

SIGHTS

In the Colaba district of Bombay, you'll find the GATEWAY OF INDIA, a splendid Muslim-style arch that is a famous city landmark. From the nearby waterfront, you can take a boat out to the ELEPHANTA CAVES ISLAND 100 km away. Worth it for the boat trip alone, the island is notable for its temple cave, which is dedicated to Shiva.

Back in the city, the HANGING GARDENS, built high above the centre, on top of Bombay's reservoirs, are the place to go for excellent views. Right next door are the TOWERS OF SILENCE, where the Parsi dead are laid out for their bones to be picked clean by vultures. Needless to say, sightseers are not permitted to enter here.

A must-see is the PRINCE OF WALES MUSEUM, which houses natural history exhibits, art and archaeological artefacts. It is set in beautifully serene, landscaped gardens. There are also a couple of interesting temples to visit: the WALKESWAR TEMPLE on Malabar Hill and the MAHALAXMI TEMPLE, the oldest in Bombay.

For a touch of local colour, take a stroll at CHOWPATTY BEACH of an evening, and mingle with some of the weird and wonderful characters (snake charmers, sadhus, monkey-trainers . . .) who gather there. But don't go swimming there, as the water is polluted.

ACCOMMODATION

There is often an accommodation shortage in Bombay, so it's best to start your room hunt as early in the day as possible. Most of the cheap accommodation centres around the Taj Mahal Hotel, in the Colaba district. Ormiston Road in particular is a good place to go in search of rooms (try the Rex, 8 Ormiston Road, tel. 23 1518), but shop around – some of the cheaper hotels aren't so good. There are a few places on Mereweather Road (all in the under-Rs200 range) worth staying at:

Salvation Army Hostel, 30 Mereweather Road (tel. 24 1824). Clean and well organized, offers dorms as well as rooms. Bed and breakfast Rs65.

Whalley's Guest House, 41 Mereweather Road (tel. 22 1802). A little more expensive than others listed here, but breakfast is included in the price.

Carlton, 12 Mereweather Road (tel. 23 0642). Rs130 for a single.

Apollo Guest House, 1st Floor, Mathuradas Estate Building, Colaba Causeway (tel. 204 5540). Singles/doubles: Rs170/190.

Hotel Prosser's, Corner of Henry Road and PJ Ramchandani Marg (tel. 24 1715). Singles/doubles: Rs190/260.

FOOD

You'll find a lot of food stalls selling snacks at Chowpatty Beach and there are a number of cheap restaurants around Colaba. Restaurants worth trying include:

Berry's, Vir Nariman Road (tel. 204 6041). Tandoori food at reasonable prices.

Copper Chimney, Annie Besant Road (tel. 22 513). Tandoori.

Britannia and Goa Restaurant, Wakefield House, Sprott Road. Family-run Parsi restaurant.

Satkar, Indian Express Building, Churchgate. Vegetarian restaurant.

Pizza King, 245 Annie Besant Road (tel. 493 9757).

Waikiki, 16 Murzban Road (tel. 204 4112). A burger and fast-food joint.

Maharajah Cafe, four doors down from the British Bank of the Middle East at Elphinstone Circle.

ENTERTAINMENT

There are regular performances of Indian music and dance at many venues throughout the city, such as the National Centre for Performing Arts and the Little Theatre, both at Nariman Point. There are also a good number of cinemas about (Bombay being the film capital of India), some of which show English-language movies. You can check film, theatre and cultural events listings in a free fortnightly publication produced by and available from the tourist office.

There are bars and discos in the big hotels. The Cellar in the Oberoi Towers Hotel and Studio 29 at the Bombay International are both discos open to non-residents.

Horse-racing meets are held at the Mahalaxmi Racecourse.

EXCURSIONS

None of the suggestions listed below are suitable for day-trips from Bombay, as they all take a few hours (all night, in the case of Goa) to get to by train or bus, but all are nevertheless worth the effort.

South-east of Bombay lies MATHERAN, a scenic hill station whose main attraction is the toy-train ride up to it. There are good views and walks, and the atmosphere is relaxed – truly an escape from the city. Also out in hilly country is PUNE (Poona), which is actually a large city, but cooler and less frenetic than Bombay. It has some lovely gardens and palaces, and there is a good bus tour of the city that visitors can take.

North-east of Bombay are the towns of ELLORA and AJANTA, both of which have impressive temple-caves decorated with Buddhist paintings and sculptures. Nearby GOA is a powerful magnet for tourists. Once a Portuguese colony, it became a hippy colony in the 1960s and 1970s, but is now attracting package tourists to its beautiful beaches. The streets and buildings of PANAJI, the capital of Goa, reflect a heavy European influence. It's the beaches, however, that most people come for; those in the north are flooded with package tourists, so head south to avoid the crowds. COLVA and BENANLIM are both quiet and unspoilt.

Delhi

AIRPORT FACILITIES
Indira Gandhi International Airport has two terminals: the international terminal (Terminal 2) is 20 km south-west of the city, Terminal 1 (domestic flights) lies 10 km from the centre. The two terminals are linked by a courtesy shuttle bus.

Flights arrive and depart from Terminal 2 around the clock, so all facilities are open 24 hours. There is an information desk, a tourist information counter, a foreign exchange and snack bars in the arrivals hall; duty-free shops, restaurant, bar, bank and post office in the departures hall. Terminal 1 has some cheap 'retiring rooms' for rent, which may be useful if you are arriving or departing at odd hours. Contact the Airport Manager (tel. 39 1351) for details.

Check-in time is 120 minutes prior to departure for international flights. Departure tax is Rs300 for international destinations other than to neighbouring countries, for which it is Rs150.

CITY LINKS:
Bus: There is a bus service run by the Ex-Airman's Transport Association (EATS) (tel. 331 6530). It goes to and from Connaught Place in the city and costs Rs15. The journey takes around 45 minutes, and buses run until about 11 p.m.
Taxi: As a lot of flights arrive at strange hours, you will probably have to use a taxi to get downtown. The airport taxi rank is just outside the arrivals hall, and it is unlikely that the drivers will use their meters. There is a pre-paid voucher scheme in operation, and the fare to Connaught Place is Rs190. There is a small charge for baggage.

USEFUL ADDRESSES
Tourist office: Government of India Tourist Office, 88 Janpath (tel. 332 0005). Open Mon.–Fri. 9.30 a.m.–6 p.m.; Sat. 9.30 a.m.–1 p.m. There is also a Students Travel Information Centre at the Imperial Hotel, Janpath (tel. 332 8512).
Foreigner's registration office: 1st Floor, Hans Bhawan, Bahadur Shah, Zafor Marg (tel. 27 2790 or 331 8179). You can extend tourist visas here.

Post office: There are many post offices in the city, but post restante mail should be collected at the GPO at Baba Kharak Singh Marg. Make sure that poste restante mail is addressed to the GPO at *New* Delhi, 110001, otherwise it'll end up in Old Delhi.
British High Commission: 8 Shantipath, Chanakyapuri (tel. 60 1371).
US Embassy: Shantipath, Chanakyapuri (tel. 60 0651).
Emergency services: Ambulance 102 and Police 100.
Medical assistance: All India Institute of Medical Sciences: Sri Aurobindo Marg (tel. 66 1123); Safdarjang General Hospital: Sri Aurobindo Marg (tel. 66 5060).

GETTING ABOUT
Rail: There is a suburban train service, but it isn't of much use to the tourist.
Bus: The service is quite good, though the buses are crowded at most times of the day. Get a bus map from the Delhi Transport Corporation office in Scindia House, Janpath, as it will help you sort out the routes. Bus information is also available at the DTC booths throughout the city. Telephone enquiries are dealt with on 331 9847. Watch out for pickpockets on crowded buses.
Taxi and rickshaw: Bicycle rickshaws are rare, but there are motorized trishaws and taxis for hire. There are also some *tongas* in Old Delhi. Taxi drivers might use their meters if you insist, but you'll have to negotiate a fare for the other forms of private hire transport.
Bicycle: There are bicycle rental shops on Pahar Ganj and near Minto Bridge. Rentals cost around Rs25 per day.

SIGHTS
Delhi is divided into two parts: Old Delhi and New Delhi. The new section of the city is spacious with wide streets, parks, and grand buildings that incorporate elements of Indian design into an essentially Western classical style. New Delhi was designed in the 1920s by Sir Edwin Lutyens, the British architect, after the decision was taken to move India's capital from Calcutta to New Delhi. It is ironic that the British found themselves having to leave India not many years later, thus preventing them from enjoying their symbol of British India.

Within New Delhi, tourists tend to gravitate towards CONNAUGHT PLACE, where there are shops, eating places, travel agencies and the Embassy area. It's near Connaught Place, on Janpath, that you will find the excellent NATIONAL MUSEUM, which houses Indian art, artefacts and textiles. It also contains an anthropological section, which is dedicated to tribal art and antiquities, and there is a fascinating musical instruments' gallery. A daily film show takes place at 2.30 p.m., and you can buy books of Indian art on the ground floor. The museum is closed on Mondays. Admission is free.

Old Delhi was built by the moghuls in the 17th century. It is here that you'll find the RED FORT (Lal Qila), which was modelled on the red sandstone fort at Agra and completed in 1648. Entrance to the fort is via the Lahore Gate (which leads to the CHATTA CHOWK, or covered bazaar – once full of stores selling silks and jewellery, it now contains souvenir shops). Inside the fort you'll find landscaped gardens, pavilions and marble palaces. The chief attractions are the PEARL MOSQUE (Moti Masjid) and the museum. The mosque is tiny and ornate, with three marble cupolas. The museum is situated in the former harem quarters, the Palace of Jewels, and now contains precious stones, artworks, weaponry and textiles – it's a must-see.

Just a kilometre away from the Red Fort is the JAMA MASJID, a marble-and-sandstone mosque which, like the Red Fort, was the work of the Shah Jahan (who also built the Taj Mahal). It's the biggest mosque in India, and its name means 'the Friday mosque' (that being the day that the Shah would use it for midday worship). There are three gateways to the mosque, the eastern one once having been reserved for use by royalty alone. It is a quite beautiful building that should not be missed.

Another fascinating mosque is the QUTAB MINAR, dating from the end of the 12th century and located in the south of Delhi. The massive tower for which it is famous was intended to dominate the locality and to remind people of the power of both God and their ruler. The building is five storeys high, topped with a beautiful cupola and decorated with calligraphic inscriptions and other ornate details. Right next door is the QUWWAT-UL-ISLAM, which predates the Qutab Minar by a few years and is the oldest mosque in India.

Once you've had your fill of buildings, take a pleasant stroll along the banks of the Yamuna, where you'll find memorials to India's past leaders, of which the one to Mahatma Gandhi is the most prominent. Alternatively you can go shopping around Connaught Place, or in the more colourful bazaars of CHANDI CHOWK in the old city, where there are silk traders, gold and silversmiths and embroiderers.

ACCOMMODATION

Hotels: The cheap areas of Delhi are Janpath and Paharganj, both very central. The following accommodations all charge around Rs100 per person or less:

Sunny Guest House, 152 Scindia House, Janpath (tel. 331 2909). Single and double rooms.

Ringo Guest House, 17 Scindia House, Janpath (tel. 331 0605). Rooms and dorms.

Royal Guest House, 44 Janpath (tel. 332 9485).

White House Tourist Lodge, 8177 Pahar Ganj.

Venus Hotel, 1566 Pahar Ganj.

Tourist Camp, J. L. Nehru Marg (tel. 27 2898), near Connaught Place. Very popular with Western visitors.

Youth Hostel, 5 Nyaya Marg, Chanakyapuri (tel. 301 6285). Has a bank and a travel agency, and breakfast is available.

Hotel Bright, 1089−90 Main Bazaar (tel. 752 5852). Good value for money.

Hotel Namaskar, 917 Chandiwalan (tel. 572 1234). A little bit more expensive, but worth it. Many extras you won't find in other hotels.

Hotel Vivek, 1541−50 Main Bazaar (tel. 52 1948). Popular place with restaurant on the ground floor.

You can get information about other cheap places at the Tourist Office or Student's Travel Office, both on Janpath (see **Useful Addresses**, p. 326). You could also stay with a local family as a paying guest − ask at the tourist office for details.

FOOD
You'll find plenty of grocery shops, stalls and restaurants serving Indian and foreign food on Connaught Place and Pahar Ganj. Just look around, or try the following:

Sona Rupa, 46 Janpath. Vegetarian Indian food.

Nirula's, L-Block, Connaught Place. Fast food and snacks are served. Good for breakfasts, and a long-time favourite with overseas visitors.

El Arab, Regal Building, Connaught Place. Lebanese food. Dishes in the Rs45−70 range.

Mughlai, M-17 Connaught Place. Indian food.

Berco's, L-Block, Connaught Place. Chinese.

ENTERTAINMENT
There is a Son et Lumière at the Red Fort which may interest you; it operates daily at six p.m., except during the rainy season, and the admission fee is minimal. For details of this, and of cultural

events such as classical dance shows, and other entertainments, check in the free *Delhi Diary*, available from hotels and many shops.

Drinking will have to be done in hotel bars, as will dancing the night away; the Hyatt Regency and the Taj Mahal both have popular discos which open at 10 p.m.

EXCURSIONS
Two hundred kilometres from Delhi lie AGRA and the TAJ MAHAL. Begun in 1630, the Taj took 20 years to complete; the beautiful building and gardens remain one of the most famous sights in the world. Also at Agra is a splendid fort, containing examples of both Hindu and Muslim architecture. It was here that the Taj's creator was imprisoned by his son. Since Agra can be reached in a couple of hours by express train from Delhi, a day-trip is possible, but it's better to stay overnight and get an early start to avoid the hordes that descend daily upon the Taj. An interesting side-trip from Agra is to FATEHPUR SIKRI, only 40 km away. It was briefly the capital during the 16th century, and palaces and tombs from that time remain.

A little further away is JAIPUR, the 'pink city' and capital of the state of Rajasthan. It takes its nickname from the sandstone palace buildings, which now contain museums and an observatory. Jaipur is too far from Delhi for a day-trip − if you can spare the time, spend a few days enjoying the city, its markets and the nearby hill forts. That way you can also visit UDAIPUR, the 'lake city' of parks, serene lakes and island palaces.

INDONESIA

VITAL STATISTICS
Red tape: A visa is not required provided you have a passport with at least six months' validity, plus an onward ticket (you *will* be asked to produce it), and so long as you enter and leave via any of the following approved gateways:

Jakarta:	Sukarno Hatta airport, Tanjung Priok seaport
Sumatra:	Polonia airport, Belawan seaport
Batam Island:	Patu Besar airport, Batu Ampar seaport
North Sulawesi:	Sam Ratu Langi airport, Bitung seaport
Ambon:	Patimura airport, Ambon seaport
Bali:	Ngura Rai airport, Benoa or Padang Bai seaports
Surabaya:	Tanjung Perak seaport
Biak:	Frans Kaisiepo airport

The list of approved gateways changes frequently, so you should check before buying your air or sea ticket that your destination is so designated. A 60-day, non-extendable visa will be granted on arrival. If you plan to enter or leave somewhere other than a gateway port, you will have to apply for a visa at an Indonesian Embassy in advance of your trip.

Customs: There is a duty-free allowance of 200 cigarettes or 50 cigars or 100 g tobacco and 2 l spirits. The import of pornography is prohibited, as is any literature containing Chinese characters. Attempting to bring in non-prescription drugs is punishable by life imprisonment. You may not export antiques or products made from the shell of the sea turtle or Indonesian currency exceeding Rp50,000.

Health: No immunizations are required except yellow fever, if you are coming from or have recently passed through an infected area. Typhoid, polio, hepatitis A, and cholera vaccinations are strongly advised, as are precautions against malaria. The water is not safe to drink.

Language: Bahasa Indonesia, a Malay variant, is the national language, though several hundred local languages and dialects are spoken throughout the islands. Indonesian is considered to be an easy language to pick up, as both grammar and pronunciation are simple. Some English is spoken, particularly by younger people, while many older Indonesians speak Dutch.

Population: Around 180 million.

Capital: Jakarta, with a population of over 7 million.

Political system: Basically, power rests with the president, though there is a form of party political system and what is known as 'consensus democracy'. President Suharto has been the head of government since 1965.

Religion: The majority are Muslim, with Buddhist, Christian and Hindu minorities. Animist faiths and belief in magic are still important, particularly in remote areas.

Time: There are three time zones. Java and Sumatra are seven hours ahead of GMT; Bali, Lombok, Sulawesi and Timor are eight hours ahead; and Irian Jaya and Maluku are nine hours ahead.

Money: The currency is the Rupiah (Rp). Coins: Rp5, Rp10, Rp25, Rp50 and Rp100. Notes: Rp100, Rp500, Rp1,000, Rp5,000 and Rp10,000. £1 = Rp2,930.

Changing money and traveller's cheques in the main cities and at the Balinese resorts is no problem, though it's best to carry US dollars and dollar traveller's cheques from a major bank or company, such as American Express. All the Indonesian branches of Standard Chartered Bank (a British international bank which operates throughout Asia) are happy to exchange foreign currency traveller's cheques in all major currencies, including US, Australian and NZ dollars, UK sterling, German marks, French and Swiss francs, Dutch guilders, and Japanese yen. It will also exchange regional Asian currencies such as Singapore, Malaysian and Hong Kong dollars (but not Thai Baht or Philippine pesos). Standard Chartered has offices in Bandung, Medan, Surabaya and Semarang, and there are two branches in Jakarta; all are under British management and the staff are fluent in English. They can also arrange inward money transfers.

Once you leave the main centres, you'll have to carry sufficient rupiah (in small denominations) for the duration, as changing money in remote areas can be difficult, if not impossible.

Communications: There is an international direct dialling service to main cities abroad, but it's best to put such calls through from hotels or large post offices. Public call boxes are unusual – again, try the hotels, which often have pay phones in the lobby. You can send telexes and telegrams from telegraphic offices.

Internal mail services, except to remote islands, are fast. Letters overseas can take up to ten days to reach Europe. Poste restante mail usually arrives safely, if not always rapidly.

Media: There are several English-language newspapers, such as the *Jakarta Post*, the *Indonesian Observer* and the *Indonesia Times*. The Singaporean *Straits Times* is also available, as are Western publications such as *Time* and *Newsweek*.

Electricity: 110 AC/50 Hz, and often 220v AC/50 Hz. Plugs are the two-pin variety.

Business hours: BANKS: Mon.–Fri. 8 a.m.–2 p.m., and Sat. 8–11 a.m.

POST OFFICES: Mon.–Fri. 8 a.m.–12 or 2 p.m., and Sat. 8–11 a.m.

SHOPS: Mon.–Sat. 8.30 a.m.–8 or 9 p.m. Some shops open on Sundays.

OFFICES: Mon.–Fri. 9 a.m.–5 p.m. (government offices: 8 a.m.–3 p.m.).

Holidays: 1 January; 21 January–21 February (Ramadan); 4 March; Good Friday; 29 April; 1 May; 17 August; 9 October; 25 and 26 December.

Climate: The climate is tropical, with a year-round temperature of 21–33°C and high humidity. There are two seasons, 'dry' and 'rain', and though the climate differs from place to place, most areas are dry from May until September or October. The temperature may fall dramatically at night and in and hilly areas, so in

addition to lightweight clothes (preferably made of natural fibres)
you'll need some warm clothing if you intend to visit the
mountains.

CULTURAL DOS AND DON'TS

Indonesians are known for being incredibly friendly people. You'll
probably be asked a lot of questions about yourself, and you may
be followed about – that's just their way of reaching out to you,
so try not to get irritated about it. On the other hand, if you detect
an air of insolence or if you are being harassed (women travellers
sometimes find this a problem, particularly in Sumatra), the best
thing to do is ignore it and quietly disappear from the scene. Don't
get angry or answer back.

A handshake is the common form of greeting, but that aside be
cautious about touching members of the opposite sex. Touching
anyone on the head is a serious breach of etiquette. When eating
(or handing something to someone), use the right hand only, as the
left is considered unclean. In Muslim areas, it would be offensive for
you to be seen consuming food or drink in the daytime during
Ramadan. It's best to stick to eating at your hotel or *losmen* at
this time.

Despite the hot climate, dressing in skimpy clothes is not acceptable. Shorts are not appropriate for either men or women, and bare
shoulders and flip-flops are similarly frowned upon. Remember
that even though people are quite relaxed about it, Indonesia *is* a
Muslim country. Modesty and conservative dressing are *very* important. The way that people will react to you depends a lot on how
you present yourself. The only places where you can get away with
a minimum of clothing are Kuta beach and similar resorts geared
to overseas holidaymakers – but even in these places it might be
as well to consider that just because the locals are *used* to something
it doesn't mean that they like it.

Tipping is not an Indonesian custom, so please don't do it. Expensive hotels levy a service charge, and you can leave your small
change with taxi drivers.

WHERE TO GO FOR WHAT

The vast majority of visitors to Indonesia follow a well-worn path
through Java and Bali. This is because most of the other islands
are difficult to get to, or to travel through, or both, and have thus
escaped being developed for tourism – which is precisely what
makes Indonesia one of the most exciting destinations in Asia. If
you do plan to follow the tourist trail, allow around a month in

one country. If you're branching out a bit, you'll find yourself staying up to the 60-day limit – and probably having to leave the country and re-enter it in order to extend your visa.

On Java, YOGYAKARTA is a major draw for visitors. It's a university city, famous for its preservation of traditional culture, with dance schools, wayang (shadow puppet) theatres and a great poetic tradition. The craftworks are excellent here, too, especially batik items. The city also provides an excellent base for touring the cultural sites of central Java, including its ancient Buddhist temples – such as the one at BOROBUDUN. There are also volcanoes within easy reach of the city. For other Javanese attractions, see the **Jakarta** section, p. 342.

From Java, it's a relatively short hop to BALI. There are a number of reasons why Bali has become such a popular destination – the one which immediately springs to mind is the beach resorts. However, it is in addition 'the island of a thousand temples', climbers will be unable to resist its dramatic mountains, and the friendliness of the people is legendary. If you *are* going there for the beach scene, avoid KUTA BEACH, which is nothing more than an Australian Benidorm. SANUR BEACH (near the capital, Denpasar) is less developed and much quieter. Some travellers avoid Bali's resorts altogether and go to the nearby island of LOMBOK instead. The pace of life is altogether more relaxed there, and some of the beaches you'll have all to yourself.

Continuing down the chain of islands that stretch to the east of Bali, KOMODO is home to the famous 'dragons' – 3-metre long lizards – which are found only here and on two other Indonesian islands. FLORES is a tranquil, unspoilt island whose towns still show signs of the days of Portuguese rule.

Off-the-beaten-track destinations begin with SUMATRA, which has notoriously bad roads that are difficult to travel. Tourists come here primarily for LAKE TOBA, though many now consider the lake over-visited and therefore disappointing. There are also some fine national parks. It is a wild, jungle landscape that you will either love or hate – there seems to be no in between. The island is very strictly Islamic, and some women travellers have reported being harassed here. It may not be wise for women to travel alone.

KALIMANTAN, part of the island of BORNEO, is another out-of-the-way spot, where most of the travelling is along rivers by boat. The people here (the Dyaks) still live a tribal life and dwell in stilt houses. If you visit villages in Kalimantan, don't expect a free ride: take gifts with you in exchange for hospitality.

North-east of Bali is SULAWESI, probably best known for its 'undertaking' business. TORAJALAND's funerals are elaborate affairs that last for days and involve animal sacrifice. They have become a major tourist attraction – though this is now beginning to create its own problems, as families sometimes beggar themselves in order to put on a good show for visitors. There are also some marvellous coral reefs off the north coast of the island.

Adventurers might try MALUKU (the Moluccas) east of Sulawesi. These are the 'spice islands': expect dense jungles, beaches with good snorkelling, coral gardens, and some tough travelling. Tougher yet, and only for the truly determined traveller, is IRIAN JAYA, which is jungly, rough and mountainous, and inhabited by people living a traditional tribal lifestyle. Getting around is difficult because of the terrain, so you might have to take a lot of flights. Certain parts of Irian Jaya are closed to foreigners, and there is usually some paperwork to complete before you can even get there from other regions of Indonesia.

The Indonesian islands are so many and so varied that it is impossible to give more than the briefest overview of them here. For anyone planning to travel outside Java and Bali, further background reading and an in-depth guidebook are essential.

INTERNAL TRAVEL
Air: Indonesia has an extensive air network linking its many islands. The major carrier (and the most expensive) is Garuda (London office: tel. 0171 409 1091). Other airlines include Merpati (owned by Garuda), Bouraq, Madala, Senpati and Bali Air (owned by Bouraq). Between them, they offer a comprehensive selection of routings – and aircraft, from modern planes through turboprops to small aeroplanes with no doors! Air travel is cheap by international standards, but will cost several times the price of travelling by ferry, train or bus. You'll get cheaper deals on tickets by buying from travel agents rather than the airlines. *Always* reconfirm your flight a day or so before departure, as the airlines overbook as a matter of routine.
Rail: Train travel is only possible on Java and Sumatra, though there is a rail/ferry connection between Java and Bali. The network on Sumatra is not up to much, but that on Java is quite useful for getting around. Some routes offer comfortable, air-conditioned carriages, other services are slow, overcrowded and hot. Prices vary, too, to match the standard of the trains, but are not too expensive in any case.
Ferry: The network is extensive, but the service varies wildly from air-conditioned comfort to hot and crowded with an interesting array of vermin as travelling companions. Basically, the more popular a route, the better the facilities.

There are a number of classes to choose from on most boats, from first to deck class. If the route you are taking is one of the off-the-beaten-track variety, it's probably best to shell out for first-class berths: ferries are cheap, so it won't bankrupt you. Take a picnic, too. On some services, however, deck class is perfectly okay, providing it's not the rainy season.

Pelni, the state-owned shipping company, has passenger vessels serving all main ports. The head office in Jakarta is at Jl. Gajah Mada 14 (tel. 343 307).

Bus: This is the main form of transport, both local and long distance, and it's very cheap. Most buses are air-conditioned. On Java and Bali, most roads are surfaced, making road travel reasonably quick and comfortable. In other places, roads can be bumpy and potholed dirt-tracks, or nothing but mud. Sumatra's roads are notoriously uncomfortable. Watch out for bag-slashers and pick-pockets on the buses.

Bemo: An amazing collection of vehicles carry passengers on the roads. In addition to buses and minibuses, there are trucks and pick-up trucks (*bemos*) with bench-seats in the back, and sometimes long-distance taxis. The trucks and *bemos* are the most crowded and uncomfortable forms of transport, but also the cheapest. If there's a group of you and you want to go somewhere off the beaten track, it may be worth chartering a *bemo*.

Besides doing the long-distance routes, *bemos* are also a popular form of public transport within towns. Fares – a couple of hundred rupiah or so – are paid to the driver. Foreigners are overcharged as a matter of course.

Car hire: An international driving licence is necessary, and driving is on the left.

Bicycle: In some places (mostly the tourist centres), you can hire bicycles for only a pound or so per day. Motorbikes may also be hired. There are a lot of motorcycle accidents on Bali every year, so take care.

Hitching: It's just about feasible to hitch, but there aren't too many private vehicles around. Count on long waits between lifts.

Local transport: There are a number of private hire vehicles around, such as taxis, *becaks* (cycle rickshaws) and *bajajs* (three-wheeled motorized vehicles). You'll also find horse-drawn carts with space for passengers in some places. Except in Jakarta, where taxi drivers use their meters, you'll have to bargain your fare in advance, as you will with *becaks* and *bajajs*. Becaks are the cheapest (it is possible to charter a *becak* plus driver for the day at low cost).

ACCOMMODATION

Finding a place to stay is rarely a problem. Wherever there are taxis or *becaks*, the drivers will be able to take you to a cheap lodging house. In many cases, they'll know where Western travellers usually go and automatically take you there. In really out-of-the-way places, try asking the local policeman or community headman where you can stay. You'll find that outside the main centres the cheaper alternatives either do not exist or don't take foreigners. Be prepared to have to pay more, the further off the tourist trail you go.

Hotels and pensions: There are a variety of cheap lodging and guest houses about. Cheapest are *penginapan*, which have a bare minimum of furniture in the rooms and *very* thin walls. Slightly more expensive are *losmen* and *wisma*: these family-run places tend to have more in the way of comforts and may include breakfast in the price of the room. In practice, there's often little distinction between the three. Facilities are basic: the toilet is usually a hole in the ground, and the 'bath' is a tank from which you scoop water over yourself. Most places are, however, perfectly comfortable. Some *losmen* offer dormitory accommodation as well as rooms, but this is unusual, and there are no official youth hostels on Indonesia.

If you can't live without comfort, there are mid-range hotels for under £20 per person per night. The rooms will have air-conditioning or a fan, a shower or bathroom attached, and there will be other extras such as a restaurant or a swimming pool in the hotel. There are also top-end hotels in the cities, for which you'll have to pay the same prices as anywhere else.

FOOD

Rice is the staple of most Indonesian dishes, with a variety of accompaniments such as fried vegetables, bean porridge, prawns or hot, spicy curries. Satay is a well-known Indonesian favourite, the fish dishes are good, and you can if you wish sample such delicacies as frog and dragonfly. Indonesian food is very spicy (each area has its own favourite spice), though restaurants catering for tourists often tone down the spice content.

The cheapest places to eat are food stalls or *warungs*, which are very basic, makeshift restaurants. The food at such places is often extremely good, but if you are prone to stomach problems when travelling, they're perhaps best avoided until you have built up some resistance to the local food.

Chinese food is widely available (though it's more expensive than Indonesian) and other cuisines, such as Japanese, Mexican, Korean and Indian, can be found in Jakarta. Western fast-food has made inroads into Java and Bali, and wherever the tourists go.

There's a wonderful selection of tropical fruits and juices to choose from (see the **Malaysia** section, p. 368 for examples of some of the fruits you can expect to find). You might want to give *durian* a miss though (it smells like a mixture of Egyptian sewers and vomit, and is so awful that it's been banned from aeroplanes and hotels). Despite local assurances that it tastes wonderful, I'd give it the body-swerve. Drinks that you should try include: *tulak* (palm wine); *brem* (rice wine); and the very potent *arak* (distilled rice wine). Coke and other fizzy beverages are much in evidence, but the fruit drinks are better. Tea and coffee are served very sweet.

You'll eat very well in Indonesia. There are street stalls everywhere, and you'll pick up food words very quickly. However, most travellers, no matter how careful they are, seem to experience stomach problems at some point during their travels. As a precautionary measure, many people avoid shellfish, raw vegetables (the water they're washed in isn't always clean) and dairy products. Don't drink tap water (stick to bottled), and don't take ice in drinks. In general, use your common sense when looking for places to eat, and don't patronize stalls or restaurants where hygiene is suspect.

BUDGETING
It is rather difficult to give estimates of daily expenditure in terms of Indonesian currency, as the rupiah is currently unstable, with a fluctuating exchange rate and a constant inflation problem. Prices quoted in rupiah in this section will very probably be out of date by the time you get to Indonesia. However, even as costs go up, the rupiah continues to be devalued against foreign currencies, so daily expenditure for the visitor remains more or less the same and £8 (or less) per day should be enough to get by on if you stick to the main tourist areas. A room in a *wisma* or *losmen* costs about £2 at most (though if you want extra comforts such as air-conditioning, you'll pay a little more). There are few dorms, and they are not much cheaper, anyway. A good meal in a tourist restaurant, with beer, would cost about the same again, but a meal from a stall or *warung* will come to well under a pound. Outside the main centres, however, expect to pay more for food and lodging.

Local transport is cheap. At the moment, it costs no more than a few hundred rupiah for bus journeys around town. Entrance charges to temples are also usually a few hundred rupiah, with museums, etc. costing a little more. Combine the two and you'll still be hard put to spend more than a pound a day on sightseeing.

Indonesia is not a particularly good place to supplement your money by working. There are quite a lot of English teaching opportunities, but the pay is low and you will require a work visa.

FURTHER INFORMATION

Embassy of the Republic of Indonesia, 127 Edgware Road, London W2 2HR (tel. 0171 499 7661).

Indonesia Tourist Board, 3/4 Hanover Street, London W1R 9HH (tel. 0171 493 0030). Open 9 a.m.–5 p.m. Mon.–Fri.

Background reading: Since Indonesian tourist offices abroad are a bit thin on the ground, you'll have to rely primarily on guidebooks (or ask the nearest Indonesian Embassy for any information they can supply). For the budget traveller, there's not much to choose between Lonely Planet's *Indonesia – Travel Survival Kit* or Moon publication's *Indonesia*, except that the latter is geared towards American travellers. Either will tell you all you need to know about travelling in Indonesia. (Lonely Planet also has a guide to Bali and Lombok, for those not travelling so widely.)

Unfortunately, the majority of the travelogues on Indonesia are the product of another era, like Robin Hanbury-Tenison's *A Pattern of Peoples* (a portrayal of Indonesian people and society that was written in the 1970s) and a more recent title by the same author, *Worlds Apart* (which contains some chapters on Indonesia and Malaysia). *Culture Shock! Indonesia* is an in-depth study of Indonesian culture, written by two long-term residents of the country, Cathie Draine and Barbara Hall. Finally, there is a very amusing piece on the Komodo dragons in Douglas Adams' *Last Chance To See*.

Fictional works by present-day Indonesian authors tend to get stuck on the banned list, so you'll have to settle for Conrad's *Lord Jim*, which takes place partly in Sumatra, and Christopher Koch's *The Year of Living Dangerously*.

Jakarta

AIRPORT FACILITIES

Sukarno Hatta International Airport, opened in 1985, is situated 35 km from Jakarta. The currency exchange, post office and shop are open at times which coincide with departing/arriving flights, but the first-aid post is operational 24 hours. The information desk and coffee shop are open when they feel like it.

There are three terminals: Terminal A for international flights,

Terminal B for Garuda's domestic flights, and Terminal C for all other domestic services. Check-in time for international flights is 90 minutes prior to departure, and the departure tax is Rp21,000. The domestic departure tax varies, but is about one-third of the international tax, and is usually included in the cost of the ticket.

CITY LINKS

Bus: The journey to the city takes about one hour, or less if the traffic allows. There is an airport bus every 30 minutes, which costs Rp3,000. It goes to various points downtown, one of them being Gambir station, not too far from the Jalan Jaksa area, where much of the budget accommodation is located.

Taxi: In addition to the Rp15,000–20,000 fare to the centre, you will have to pay a Rp3,000 road toll. Use the Bluebird taxis (which are blue), as they are reckoned to be the safest and the drivers will almost certainly use the meters.

USEFUL ADDRESSES

Tourist office: Visitor's Information Centre, Jalan M H Thamrin 9. Provides city maps, details of tourist attractions, accommodation lists and bus, train and air schedules. Open Mon.–Thurs. 8 a.m.–5 p.m.; Fri. 8 a.m.–3 p.m., and Sat. 8 a.m.–12.30 p.m.

Main post office: Jalan Pos Utara 2, near the Istiqlal Mosque. There is a small charge for each item collected from the poste restante.

British Embassy: Jalan M H Thamrin 75 (tel. 33–0904).

US Embassy: Jalan Merdeka Selatan 5.

Emergency services: Telephone 110 for Police and 119 for ambulance.

Medical emergencies: The SOS Medika Vayasan clinic on Jalan Prapanca Raya 32–4 (tel. 77–1575) has English-speaking staff available and is open 24 hours.

GETTING ABOUT

Bus: Jakarta has a good bus network. There are regular city buses which cost Rp200, and Patas express buses which cost Rp450. The latter are less crowded. Additionally, there are small orange-and-blue minibuses that supplement the main services. Watch out for pickpockets on the regular buses and keep luggage, daysacks, etc. close to you in case of bag-slashers. You can buy a bus map at the tourist office.

Bajaj: These motorized rickshaws have seating for two people. You can flag them down on the street, and will have to negotiate a fare.

A short trip should cost well under a pound. They are not allowed on the major thoroughfares.

Becak: Because they are not allowed into the centre of Jakarta until late at night, *becaks* tend to be confined to the side streets and smaller neighbourhoods. Very cheap.

Taxi: Taxis are plentiful and metered. Prices start at Rp800 and most trips around town will cost no more than a few thousand rupiah. Bluebird cabs are the most reliable, but there are other good companies around. Licensed taxis have yellow plates.

SIGHTS
Many travellers think of Jakarta as a rather dull, nondescript modern city and try to give it a miss. If, however, it's your gateway to Indonesia (and most likely it will be, if you arrive by air), you'll find a few sights to hold your interest.

KOTA, formerly known as Batavia, was once the capital and a Dutch trading port. Though many of the buildings in this, the old part of town, have been demolished, some have been restored and either remain in everyday use or have been preserved as museums. The centre of Kota/Batavia is Taman Fatihillah Square, where you'll find three museums: the JAKARTA HISTORY MUSEUM, the WAYANG MUSEUM and the ART MUSEUM. The first of these is housed in the former city hall, a 17th-century building which also served as a prison. It now contains Dutch artefacts and memorabilia. The Wayang Museum holds a marvellous collection of traditional shadow puppets, and you can see performances there on Sunday mornings. The Art Museum contains Indonesian paintings and ceramics. All three museums are open every day except Monday, and close around lunchtime.

Another museum to look out for in the area is the MARITIME MUSEUM by the Sunda Kelapa port. However, the docks themselves – with the fish market outside and wonderful old sailing ships inside – are more interesting than the museum. There's a small entrance fee to the docks, and you can take a boat trip around the ships. For detailed information on the Kota district, there's a booklet on Old Batavia that you can buy at the National Museum.

Not far from Kota is GLODOK, the city's Chinatown and commercial centre. It is predominantly modern, but a small area retains the old winding streets and cramped buildings, and it's worth exploring the markets and the 17th-century Dharma Jaya Temple.

You won't be able to miss the NATIONAL MONUMENT in the ultra-modern Merdeka Square. The tower is 132 metres high and is a useful landmark in the city. You can join a long queue to ascend to the top of the monument and look at the view, or visit the small museum at the bottom – though the latter is generally considered to be a waste of time and money. Far better is the NATIONAL MUSEUM on the west side of the square. It's reckoned to be one of the best museums in South-east Asia, and it houses many exhibits pertaining to the everyday lives and culture of Indonesia's various peoples. It also has a display of Chinese ceramics and a treasure room that you can view on Sundays. If you visit only one museum in Indonesia, this should be it. The National Museum, too, is closed on Mondays and keeps short opening hours.

Jakarta has its own Indonesia-in-miniature. Known as TAMAN MINI, it's about 9 km from the city centre and should be treated as a half-day trip at least. It has museums, traditional Indonesian houses, gardens, a lagoon, an audio-visual show and cultural performances on Sunday mornings. It's a great way to get an overview of the country. You can get there by public transport or with an organized tour.

ACCOMMODATION
Jalan Jaksa and the surrounding streets are where most of the budget accommodation is. It's very central – not far from Merdeka Square – and some places offer dorm beds. The standard of the facilities varies greatly from place to place, so shop around if you have time.

Hostels: The Wisma Delima at Jalan Jaksa 5 (tel. 33–7026) is a favourite traveller's haunt, and also the cheapest. It has dorm beds for Rp3,000, though they'll give a discount to IYHF card-holders. Single/double rooms cost Rp10,000/11,000. The rooms are small and airless, but it's as good a place as any to start a room search, as they can direct you to other possibilities if full.

The Djody Hostel at number 27 (tel 34–6600) offers rooms from Rp15,000–18,000 and dorms at Rp7,500. It has shower facilities and is clean. The Norbek Hostel at number 14 (tel. 33–0392) comes well recommended. Prices start at Rp9,000. Some of the rooms are air-conditioned.

Off Jalan Jaksa, at Jalan Wahid Hasyim 168 is the Wisma ISE Guesthouse. It's a bit further than the other places, but worth the walk. It's friendly and clean and there aren't so many foreign visitors there, so you can avoid the 'traveller's ghetto' scene if that's something you're not too keen on. They have single and double rooms and prices range from Rp11,500–Rp15,000. You can also get breakfast for Rp2,500.

The Borneo Hostel at No.35 on Kebon Sirih Barat Dalam, just off Jalan Jaksa (tel. 320 095) has dorm beds for Rp4,000 and rooms starting at Rp12,000.

FOOD

You could do worse than to stay on Jalan Jaksa for cheap food. Many of the guest houses have good, inexpensive cafés and there are plenty of food stalls around, too. There are also a few restaurants serving Western food (Angie's at Jalan Jaksa 16 is popular).

They serve good satay at the Senayan Satay House, Jalan Kebon Sirih 31, not far from Jalan Jaksa. It's a little more expensive than some places, but worth it for the air-conditioning. For cheaper satay, Jalan H A Salim is lined with many excellent stalls.

You can also eat Chinese, Japanese, Indian, etc. in Jakarta, but if you've been travelling in Asia for some time and have had enough of the food, there is always the George & Dragon at Jalan Teluk Betung 32, a British-style pub serving fish and chips and steak pie. Western fast food is available from a number of outlets (Kentucky Fried Chicken, A & W, etc.) on Jalan H A Salim and Jalan Wahid Hasyim.

ENTERTAINMENT

There are regular cultural performances of music, dance, puppet theatre and so on at various venues in the city. The Taman Ismail Marzuki arts centre on Jalan Cikini Raya stages a performance every night. They sometimes have Western films as well as the native arts. The Bharata Theatre on Jalan Kalilio has dance or theatre most nights and the Jakarta Hotel offers weekly dance shows. Check performance listings in the *Jakarta Post* or enquire at the Visitor's Information Centre.

The *Post* is also the place to look for cinema schedules. There are a good number of cinemas in Jakarta, some of which occasionally show English-language films, though Asian action/adventure movies are the regular fare.

Big hotels are the best places for discos or bars. The Jaya Pub at Jalan M H Thamrin 12 has long been a popular bar with both foreigners and local people, and has live music in the evenings. Music is also found at the Hotel Sari Pacific's Pitstop, a popular nightclub.

EXCURSIONS

One hour by train from Jakarta is BOGOR, famous for its 19th-century Botanical Gardens which contain around 15,000 plant species from all over the world. As Bogor is in the hills, it can be used as a base for hill-walking. You can also take a bus trip through the beautiful Puncak region, which is full of tea plantations, hill resorts, waterfalls, lakes and valleys, to BANDUNG, Indonesia's second largest city. Once a Dutch garrison town, little of its colonial past remains and the city is now renowned as the home of traditional performing arts and as an educational centre. It, too, is a good base for hill walks: you can visit the nearby TANGKUBAN PRAHU VOLCANO, though the volcano's very accessibility has led to excessive tourism.

Also accessible from Jakarta are the THOUSAND ISLANDS. A few of the islands have been developed as resorts, but many are sparsely populated or completely deserted. Some (such as Pulau Bidadan and nearby islands) can be visited on day-trips, while others are for longer trips. Pulau Putri, Pulau Perak, Pulau Penlangi and Pulau Papa Theo, collectively known as Jakarta's 'tropical paradise' have good swimming and scuba diving.

A few hours west of Jakarta is the CARITA BEACH resort. Many people use it as a base for visiting the volcanic island of KRAKATAU in the Sunda Straits. Krakatau erupted violently and spectacularly in 1883, killing thousands of people and creating huge *tsunamis* in the region, strange sunsets around the world, and finally blowing itself out in the process. The 'son' of Krakatau is taking up where its parent left off and is periodically active. It is possible to take a boat out to the island and to climb the volcano. The seas can be rough, so make sure you pick a *good* boat and don't try it during the rainy season.

JAPAN

VITAL STATISTICS
Red tape: A full passport is required, plus a return or onward ticket and sufficient funds for your stay. Visas are not necessary for UK citizens intending to stay less than six months, nor for citizens of Canada, New Zealand or the USA staying for less than three months. Australians, however, do need a visa.

All foreign nationals (even tourists) staying more than 90 days must obtain an Alien Registration Card from the ward office nearest to where they live. It must be carried at all times: failure to produce one when asked will result in a long visit to the police station. Those intending to work must obtain the relevant visa (and the job) before entering Japan. Australians, New Zealanders and Canadians aged 18–25 can apply for a working holiday visa.

Customs: The duty-free allowance is 400 cigarettes or 100 cigars or 500g tobacco, three bottles of spirits (760ml each), and a small quantity of perfume for personal use. You should declare all medicines that you have with you, even aspirin.

Health: No mandatory immunizations, unless you are coming from an infected area. Private health insurance is essential.

Language: Japanese. The writing system is complex, but the language is, mercifully, non-tonal. Most numerals are arabic, and there is enough English around for you to identify buildings, labels in the supermarket, etc. The Japanese are not great sign-linguists and their English is for the most part dreadful, so be prepared to have a bash at the basics of the language if you intend to travel outside the main cities.

Population: 123 million.

Capital: Tokyo, population 13 million.

Political system: Democracy. Until the 1993 elections, when bribery scandals caused disillusioned voters to desert the party, the Liberal Democratic Party (LDP) had ruled unchallenged since 1955. There is an Emperor, Akihito, but his role is a purely constitutional one.

Religion: Buddhism and Shinto, with a Christian minority.

Time: Nine hours ahead of GMT.

Calendar: Though years AD are frequently used, the Japanese system is to count in Emperor years. There were 64 years in the last era, Showa, which ended with the death of Hirohito in January 1989. The current era is known as Heisei. Dates are written year, month, day.

Money: The currency is the mighty Yen (Y). Coins: Y1, Y5, Y10, Y50, Y100, Y500. Notes: Y1,000, Y5,000, Y10,000. £1 = Y132.

It is easiest to carry money in traveller's cheques – preferably in yen, with US dollars the second choice. Beware, though, sometimes even yen traveller's cheques are not accepted outside main cities. Currency exchanges can be found in the larger banks and hotels. Credit cards are still relatively unusual, and therefore unlikely to be accepted outside the big cities. Theft is uncommon, so it is safe to carry large amounts of cash with you.

Tax: Since 1989, a 3% consumption tax has been levied on most goods and services. Sometimes included in the stated price, sometimes added on at the till, it always involves piles of fiddly Y1 coins. If it is any consolation, the Japanese hate it as much as you surely will.

Communications: The telephone system is excellent, and you will never have to look far for a public telephone. The blue and red varieties take Y10 coins only, as do the pink ones (found in bars, restaurants, etc.). Yellow and green ones accept Y10 and Y100 coins; the green ones have an indicator that shows how much money you have left, and most of them take prepaid phonecards, available in department stores. (They're prettier than picture postcards, and make good souvenirs.) Numbers starting with '0120' are free of charge to the caller.

You can make direct overseas calls from green phones that are marked 'International and Domestic' (dial 001, then the country code, etc.), but there aren't too many of them around – try the railway stations and the big hotels. A three-minute call to the UK costs about Y2,160. Calls are cheaper off peak: there is a 20% discount Mon.–Fri. 7–11 p.m. and Sat.–Sun. 8 a.m.–11 p.m.; and a 40% discount on calls made from 11 p.m.–8 a.m. Alternatively, dial 0051 for the international operators, all of whom speak English.

Post offices are marked with a red 'T' with a bar across the top. The postal service is very efficient, and overseas mail takes around seven days to reach its destination. Poste restante mail is best sent only to city post offices.

Electricity: 100v AC. Plugs are flat two-pin.

Business hours: BANKS: Mon.–Fri. 9 a.m.–3 p.m.

POST OFFICES: Mon.–Fri. 9 a.m.–5 p.m., and in some cases on Saturday mornings.

SHOPS: Large stores open from 10 a.m.–6 p.m., six or seven days a week; small local shops stay open longer, seven days a week.

OFFICES: Business hours are Mon.–Fri. 9 a.m.–5 p.m.; *working* hours are until the boss says you can go home.

Holidays: 1, 2, 3, 15 January; 12 February; 20 March (Vernal Equinox); 29 April; 3, 4, 6 May; 16, 23 September; 10 October; 4 and 23 November; 23, 30, 31 December. Try to avoid travelling over New Year and Golden Week (the April/May holidays), as trains are booked solid. If a national holiday falls on a Sunday, the following Monday will also be treated as a holiday.

Climate: Hokkaido and northern Honshu have Siberian winters and pleasantly warm, if short, summers; from Kyushu island south-wards the climate is subtropical; in the rest of Japan winters are not unlike those in Europe and summers are hot (in excess of 33°C) and humid. The humidity gets worse after the rainy season (June/July). There are frequent short-lived typhoons in September. Spring (March/April) and autumn (Oct.–mid-Nov.) are pleasant and mild.

DO'S AND DON'TS
The potential for unwitting transgressions of etiquette is almost endless (for example, nose-blowing in public is not acceptable – sniff instead). Although foreigners are usually excused their various rudenesses, a little cultural sensitivity goes a long way. You may

think some conventions silly, pointlessly archaic, or even sexist, but try to remember whose country it is. Above all, no matter how frustrating everything gets, never lose your temper with another person, as it causes them a tremendous loss of face. They will simply become silent and stubborn and you will lose whatever argument you were trying to have.

You'll see a lot of bowing, but don't go overboard about it and risk looking obsequious. When meeting someone you know, or when being introduced, incline your head and bend slightly from the waist. Some Japanese, aware of Western customs, will shake hands, but take your cue from them.

Gift-giving can be a complicated business, dictated as it is by matters of obligation and indebtedness. However, if you visit someone's house it is polite to bring a small present: chocolates, cake, or the inevitable tea-towel from home is about right. The presentation of gifts is not done in a casual manner: use both hands and give a slight bow (this applies to the exchange of business cards also). If presented with a gift, don't open it in front of the giver but save it for later.

Remove your shoes in the entryway before stepping into a house – failure to do so will not be forgiven. Outdoor shoes are also taken off and exchanged for plastic slippers in Japanese-style hotels and some public buildings. In certain places even slippers have to be exchanged for 'toilet slippers' when you go to the bathroom. A Japanese toilet is a very interesting experience: you don't sit on it but squat facing the hooded end. You'll soon get the hang of it. Japanese bathrooms all have tiled floors, because you wash *before* getting into the bathtub, using a basinful of water to rinse off with. It would be a major *faux pas* to take soap into the tub, as everyone uses the same water and it is purely for relaxing in.

It is customary for men to sit cross-legged on the floor but this is considered impolite for women, who should arrange themselves with their legs tucked beneath them. If it all becomes too much, stretching the legs out is perfectly acceptable.

Should you be invited out to a restaurant or bar, your host will want to foot the bill – nevertheless you should offer your share. Beware: if you do the inviting, you pay! Never stand your chopsticks up in a rice bowl or pass food from your chopsticks to another's: both are reminiscent of death rituals. Refill your neighbour's glass with drink, but never your own. You can cover your glass with your hand if you don't want any more. Pouring soy sauce over rice is not done, slurping noodles is. It's advisable to bring your own handkerchief or paper tissues as most restaurants don't provide napkins (and most public toilets don't have toilet roll).

Tipping is not a Japanese custom. Don't do it.

WHERE TO GO FOR WHAT

If temples are what you want, KYOTO is definitely the place to go. It can easily take a week or more to explore the city and surrounding area, but if time is short it's possible to get round the main sights in two or three days. Kyoto is also famous for its cherry blossoms (April) and autumn leaves (October/November), and it's a good place to shop for traditional arts and crafts.

You could spend forever in TOKYO, which has a little bit of everything – temples, museums, shrines, McDonald's – and which is a good base for a number of excellent day trips (see **Tokyo** section, p. 357). If it's your first stop in Japan, you'll probably want to spend some time organizing yourself, and most overseas visitors seem to stay for a week or two.

Palm trees, volcanoes and hot springs can be found on the small island of KYUSHU, whose compact size makes it possible to travel around and get a feel for the island very quickly. Hot spring lovers should not miss BEPPU, a resort town in the north-east.

Western Honshu is where you will find HIROSHIMA, plus the island-dotted Seto Inland Sea (on the Pacific side) and the more rugged SAN-IN COAST (Japan Sea side). One day is sufficient to explore Hiroshima, as there is little more than the Peace Park to see. There are a couple of nice excursions from the city (see **Hiroshima** section, p. 364), and two out of the three sights the Japanese rate as 'must-sees' are also located in this area: the floating shrine gate at MIYAJIMA island and the AMANOHASHIDATE (Bridge to Heaven) sandspit. A number of towns of historical interest are dotted around the region, but they are rather spread out and travel on the San-in coast is slow.

For the great outdoors, HOKKAIDO is the place. Some visitors zip in and out of SAPPORO, the prefectural capital, in a few days, but the lakes, mountains and rivers require at least a week or two of serious attention. Hikers won't want to leave.

Anywhere in cherry-blossom time (March/April) is pretty, and autumn is also pleasant. Unfortunately everyone knows it and crowds ensue. Avoid beauty spots at weekends during this time.

INTERNAL TRAVEL

Air: Flying is expensive, there are no passes and few discount bargains around. JAL, ANA and Japan Air System are the major carriers on domestic routes. In Tokyo, Haneda is the airport for internal flights.

Rail: Most visitors travel intercity by train, as the rail service is extensive and efficiently run. The national company (now privatized) is Japan Railways (JR); smaller private lines operate on some of the commuter and holiday routes. The faster the train, the higher the fare, and you have to state which type of train you are taking when buying tickets: the *Shinkansen* ('bullet' train) is the fastest, covering long-distance routes; the *tokkyu* (limited express) is slightly slower; and the local *futsu* services, which stop at every lamppost are slowest of all.

The Japanese Railway (JR) pass, available only at travel agents outside Japan and not for use by foreign residents of the country, costs Y27,800 for 7 days, Y44,200 for 14 days and Y56,600 for 21 days. The 7-day pass compares favourably with return fares from Tokyo to Kyoto (around Y26,000). The pass can be used on JR trains, buses and ferry services, but not on private railways; it is therefore not worth using it for travelling around Tokyo, only once you are ready to move on.

Bus: There is a long-distance bus network, with fares comparable to those of the cheapest trains – though Japan's traffic jams ensure that they are much slower than even the slowest train. Nevertheless, overnight services between the main cities (such as those connecting Tokyo with Nagoya, Kyoto, Osaka, Hiroshima, or linking Tokyo with Sendai and points north) are quite popular. Book at Japan Travel Bureau (JTB) offices.

However, watch out for the Japanese peak travel season: there's a mass exodus of people heading for the coast or countryside from 27 Dec.–4 Jan., 29 Apr.–5 May and the week around 15 August, and trains are always booked solid at these times.

Ferry: As one would expect with an island nation, there are a great many ferry routes linking the four main islands to each other and to hundreds of smaller ones. For long-distance journeys (e.g. to Hokkaido or Kyushu), they are a very cheap, if slow, form of transport. The ferries which travel the Seto Inland Sea pass the prettiest scenery.

Hitching: This is uncommon, but nevertheless a possibility (even though not all Japanese drivers understand the meaning of the outstretched thumb! – it helps if you write your destination in Japanese on a cardboard sign). Many are the tales of extraordinarily kind motorists, and they will be more inclined to go out of their way if you are prepared to make some effort to speak to them in their own language. The usual rules for women hitchers apply.

Local transport: Several cities have their own local rail networks and many have a subway system. Tickets are bought from coin-operated machines – hang on to them, as they are collected at the other end. Fares usually start at around Y120–150 and rise according to the distance travelled. If you can't calculate the price from the network diagrams, either ask the ticket collector or buy the cheapest ticket and pay the excess at the fare adjustment window when you arrive at your destination. Station signs are usually written in both Roman and Japanese characters, and network maps in English are normally available from tourist information offices.

Bus travel is easy – provided you understand Japanese – as taped messages announce each stop in advance. Take a numbered ticket when you board the bus (by the rear doors) and a panel near the driver will indicate the fare (sometimes it's a flat fare). Pay when you get off. Some cities also have tram systems – a useful cross between buses and trains. Tariffs are similar to those of the trains.

Taxis: Don't expect much change from Y1,000, even for short trips. A red light indicates that the taxi is available; don't whistle for one (just wave), and don't tip the driver. All taxis are metered. Doors open automatically, so stand clear! Because few drivers speak English, it's best to have your destination written down in Japanese or, better still, carry a map. Giving an address in any town is a complicated business, as only the major streets have names: addresses consist of the name of an area and a string of numbers denoting blocks and streets within that area. The numbers are seldom logical or sequential, and most people navigate by landmarks or maps that someone has drawn for them. Taxi drivers are no exception.

ACCOMMODATION

The Tourist Information Centres at Narita Airport in Tokyo and in Kyoto can book budget accommodation for visitors through the Welcome Inn Reservation Service and will provide lists. Most train stations have an information office, often with someone who can speak a little English, and they usually offer a booking service for *ryokan* and *minshuku*.

Youth hostels: There is no age limit for 'youth' hostels, but you will need a membership card to stay at most of them. Prices vary; expect to pay Y1,900–3,500 per person per night, thus bringing them within the price range of those on a tight budget. You should *always* book in advance; even a phone call from the station will suffice, but never turn up unannounced. Computer booking is possible from Tokyo: ask how to go about it at either of the hostels there, or at the YH Association offices at Hoken Kaikan, 1–2 Sadohara-cho, Ichigaya, Shinjuku-ku, Tokyo 182 (tel. 3269 5831).

As in every country, standards vary from place to place, but they are always well run. Most hostels do not have a members' kitchen, instead they provide cheap meals (but unless you delight in cold pork cutlets and salad these are best avoided). Curfew is usually 10 p.m.

Hotels: The budget traveller has a choice between *ryokan* (Japanese inns), *minshuku* (small, family-run B&B establishments), and business hotels. At a *ryokan* you'll take your shoes off at the door, sleep on a futon, have dinner in your room and bathe in the communal (but segregated) bath. You will usually be expected to take breakfast and dinner there. Prices can be as low as Y4,200 per person, occasionally less, but Y5,200–8,200 is more common. *Minshuku* are smaller versions of *ryokan*, with prices from around Y5,000 per person.

Business hotels offer no-frills accommodation aimed at businessmen and single travellers. Clean, comfortable, Western-style, you'll always find them around railway stations as well as in the town centres. Some start at around Y4,200 a night, but Y6,200–7,200 is the norm. A few twin rooms are available. The Green, Tokyu Inn and Hokke Club chains are among the cheapest.

Private accommodation: For longer-term options, you'll probably want to get into a *gaijin* house (*gaijin* being an overused word loosely meaning 'foreigner'), at least to start off with. These are either basic dorms or shared-room places, and they are mostly located in Tokyo and Kyoto – the TICs in those cities can give you information about them. For apartment-hunting, you will need a Japanese guarantor, an estate agent, a lot of cash, and most probably a Japanese go-between to help you negotiate the various complexities that are involved. Good employers will often assist.

If possible, take a tent with you to Japan. You can put it up in almost any park or sports field, as long as you arrive between 9 p.m. and 10 p.m. and leave before 8 a.m., so you are not in anyone's way. The police do not mind and most parks have clean toilets. You can also sleep inside most railway stations.

FOOD

You will never starve in Japan, even if you cannot speak a word of the language. Most coffee shops and restaurants display plastic models of the food on offer, or have menus with pictures, so you can at least point. Look out for coffee shops offering Japanese and Western-style fixed-menu breakfasts at around Y500. Branches of Mr Donut do good, cheap breakfasts, too. Almost all restaurants offer set lunches – officially known as *teishoku*, but unofficially referred to in Janglish as *ranchi setto* – where magnificently large portions cost anything from Y520–1,200. Fastfood has taken off in a big way, with branches of McDonald's in even the smallest towns, and Wendy's and Kentucky Fried Chicken in the cities, where you can eat the food you know so well for not much more than Y520.

But why eat Western food when you can sample Japanese cuisine? Sushi bars abound, and most have a conveyor belt from which you choose the dishes that appeal (around Y100–500 a throw). The ubiquitous noodle is a cheaper option sold from specialist stalls and shops: be adventurous and try *ramen* (noodles in chicken stock with various meat and vegetable options); *soba* (buckwheat noodles in a fish-based soup); or *udon* (thick, white noodles). *Izakaya* or *robatayaki* restaurants are cheap, cheerful and noisy places, where you can eat an evening meal for around Y1,000. You'll know them by the noise. Try *yakitori* (chicken on a stick); *sashimi* (raw fish); *nikijaga* (meat and potatoes) or *onigiri* (rice balls with fish or vegetable fillings).

Vegetarians will find themselves in difficulty, as a meat-free diet is a concept that the Japanese have yet to grasp. You can master the art of saying *niku nashi* ('no meat'), but this is by no means infallible as ham, for example, is not considered to be meat. Learn to love rice, pickles and salad.

There are always restaurants around the railway stations or on the top floor of large department stores; if you become desperately short of cash, trawl their food halls for the free samples always on offer.

You can help save a tree or two by bringing your own chopsticks instead of using the wooden disposable ones in every eating place. A statistic from a few years back said that the Japanese got through 11 billion pairs of them in one year alone!

Sake, Japanese native rice wine, can be drunk hot or cold. Don't forget to say 'Kampai' ('Cheers')!

BUDGETING
Many budget travellers are put off visiting Japan because of its reputation as an expensive country. While it certainly ain't cheap, visitors need not spend exorbitant amounts: prices are often comparable with northern Europe. If you plan to stay mostly in hostels, expect to spend around £35–40 on daily expenses (and it's possible to get by on less).

You can eat for around Y1,500–2,000 per day, providing you ditch the coffee habit (Y400!) and take full advantage of the many *ranchi setto* deals around (see **Food**). If you can't live without caffeine, stick to Mr Donut or the Doutour chain (Y150–200). Bars are not cheap: beer is around Y500 and upwards, *sake* or *shochu* a little less, other spirits Y800 and more. Beer from vending machines costs around Y300. For bus/subway fares, entrance fees, etc., allow another Y1,000 or so.

Job opportunities exist for the round-the-worlder, but are now in limited supply. Travellers can no longer expect to breeze into Tokyo on a 90-day tourist visa, pick up well-paid English teaching jobs and leave town richer by several hundred thousand yen. Changes to the immigration laws mean that anyone giving work to a foreigner not possessing a proper visa faces prosecution, while foreigners working on a tourist visa are routinely deported after returning from 'visa runs' to neighbouring Korea. A huge influx of foreigners – many of them New Zealanders, Australians and Canadians on working holiday visas – have flooded the market, which is considerably smaller now that the world recession has finally hit Japan. Nowadays you must be prepared to put a considerable amount of time, effort and money into looking for work (two months and well over £1,000 are current estimates!)

The classified ads of the *Japan Times*, particularly on a Monday, are the best place to look for English-teaching posts. The legal minimum wage for full-time teaching is Y250,000 per month, while part-time and freelance private teaching pays around Y2,000–3,000 per hour. Another option open to women is hostessing (which is perfectly respectable in Japan and does not involve prostitution), for which you should get around Y2,500–3,000 per hour. Occasional 'event' work comes up, which involves nothing more than mingling with guests at large functions (it lends an international feel to the proceedings) and being paid upwards of Y10,000 for a night is a good sweetener to help you smile broadly and make polite conversation.

Besides the *Japan Times*, the monthly *Kansai Time Out* (which covers the Kyoto/Osaka/Kobe area) also advertises jobs, and the Kimi Ryokan in Tokyo (see **Accommodation**, p. 353) has an information centre which may be of help.

FURTHER INFORMATION

Japanese Embassy, 101–4 Piccadilly, London W1V 9FN (tel. 0171 465 6500).

The Japan National Tourist Organization (JNTO), Heathcoat House, 20 Savile Row, London W1X 1AE (tel. 0171 734 9638) will provide useful tourist literature and information. You should be able to get a listing of Japanese youth hostels from them.

Background reading: The recently updated Lonely Planet guide, *Japan – Travel Survival Kit*, is full of useful information for the budget traveller intending to spend some time in Japan. Those intending to work should study *Jobs in Japan* by John Wharton (Global Press, £9.95).

Guidebooks aside, there are few books about modern Japan, fictional or otherwise, available in this country. Of the travelogues, *Unbeaten Tracks in Japan* by Isabella Bird (Virago), an account by a Victorian of the intrepid variety, is still in print and worth reading. *The Roads to Sata* by Alan Booth (Penguin) is reasonably interesting, though it helps to have some knowledge of Japan before you start it.

The best place to obtain books about Japan is in the English-language section of a Japanese bookshop, such as Kinokuniya or Maruzen. Yukio Mishima, perhaps the most famous of Japan's authors, is considered unrepresentative either of Japanese writers or of Japan. Other (better) classical authors worth reading include Tanizaki and Kawabat. Avoid novels of the 'mutant ninja' genre unless you want to get a totally false impression of modern Japan. If you see *I Am a Cat* by Soseki Natsume, buy it: it's guaranteed to make you laugh.

Tokyo

AIRPORT FACILITIES

All international flights bar one land at Narita Airport, 66 km from Tokyo. There are two passenger terminals and the airlines are divided between them as follows: Terminal 1 handles British Airways, Virgin Atlantic, SAS, Korean Airlines, Finnair, Air France and Lufthansa; Terminal 2 handles Japan Airlines, All Nippon Airways, and all other airlines including Thai Airways, Qantas, Aeroflot, KLM and China Airlines. A free shuttle service connects Terminals 1 and 2; buses run every 10–15 mins with a journey time of 10 mins. Departure tax is Y2,000, and check-in time is usually one hour prior to departure.

Both terminals have the usual restaurants, post offices, duty-free shops, currency exchange facilities, etc. To the right as you exit customs in Terminal 1 you will see a Tourist Information Centre (Mon.–Fri. 9 a.m.–8 p.m.; Sat. 9 a.m.–12 p.m.), where you can pick up transport and tourist maps. A second Tourist Information Centre (tel. 0476 34 6251) is located on the first floor of Terminal 2 (open daily 9 a.m.–8 p.m.). Terminal 1 also houses a Japanese Railway office, where you can validate your JR pass if you plan to start travelling straight away, while the Welcome Inn Reservation

Center (Mon.–Fri. 9 a.m.–8 p.m.) in the TIC will book inexpensive accommodation in the city for you. There is even a clinic at basement level.

Domestic flights generally leave from Haneda Airport, an 80-minute journey from Narita.

There are some curiosities to be noted at the airport. In the main building (3rd floor) you'll find an audio-video room with personal TVs or booths for 2–3 people; open 7 a.m.–10 p.m. It costs Y400 per two hours for an individual, Y800 for a group booking. The 'Refresh Room' (same location) offers shower booths costing Y600 for the first hour and a napping space for Y2,000 for the first four hours.

CITY LINKS
Haneda Airport is only 12 km from Tokyo and well served by monorail to the centre. From Narita, the modes of transport are as follows:

Rail: There are two train companies running to Tokyo from stations beneath the terminals. All trains leave first from Terminal 1, stopping at Terminal 2 before proceeding to Tokyo. Trains to the airport stop first at Passenger Terminal 2 before proceeding to Terminal 1.

The JR Narita line offers services of varying speeds (journey time 50–90 mins) and prices (around Y1,260–4,000) to Tokyo, Ikebukuro, Shinjuku and Yokohama stations. You can make subway connections at the first three of these stations.

The private Keisei line runs to Keisei Ueno station, where, again, there is a subway station very close by. There are express, limited express and non-stop services. Travel times are 60–90 minutes, prices from Y940–1,740.

Limousine bus: The buses run from Narita to various hotels and central points such as Shinjuku and Ginza; to Haneda Airport; to Tokyo City Air Terminal (TCAT); and to Yokohama. Tickets cost upwards of Y2,500, depending on destination, and should be purchased at Limousine ticket counters in the arrivals wing of the airport or adjoining city departure points. Being so far from the city, travel time is usually around 1½–2 hours, but may be more if the traffic is bad.

Taxi: Don't even consider it.

USEFUL ADDRESSES
Tourist office: Tourist Information Centre (TIC), 1–6-6 Yuraku-cho (tel. 3502 1461). Take exit A2 from Hibiya station (on the Hibiya, Chiyoda and TOEI Mita lines), the TIC is opposite. Open Mon.–Fri. 9 a.m.–5 p.m.; Sat. 9 a.m.–12 p.m.

Main post office: Next to Tokyo station in the station plaza. Poste restante mail should be addressed to: Central Post Office, Tokyo, Japan, where it will be held for thirty days.
British Embassy: 1 Ichiban-cho, Chiyoda-ku (tel. 3265 5511).
US Embassy: 1–10-5 Akasaka, Minato-ku (tel. 3224 5000).
Emergency services: Dial 110 for police, 119 for fire or ambulance.
Medical assistance: American Pharmacy, 1–8-1 Yurakucho, Chiyoda-ku – just around the corner from the TIC, near Yurakucho and Hibiya subway station (tel. 3271 4034). International Clinic, 5–9 Azabudai 1-chome, Minato-ku (tel. 3583 7831 from 9 a.m.–12 p.m. and 2.30–5 p.m.).
Emergency help in English: Tokyo English lifeline (TELL) tel. 5481 4347.
Bookshops: Maruzen, Nihonbashi (opposite the Takashimaya department store exit from Nihonbashi subway station). Closed on Sundays. The Kinokuniya is at Shinjuku-dori, diagonally opposite Mitsukoshi department store. Nearest subway station is Shinjuku-sanchome.

GETTING ABOUT
Rail: There's a comprehensive JR and private rail network covering the city and suburbs. It can be a bit confusing at first, but many of the lines you are most likely to use interconnect with subway stations, and are marked on the subway maps. Morning rush hour on both trains and subways is best avoided – though this is when you might see the 'pushers' in action. A 'one-day open ticket' can be purchased giving unlimited rail travel. The 'Tokyo combination ticket' covers bus, tram and subway.
Subway: This offers an excellent system that really couldn't be easier to navigate, and is the mode of transport that you are most likely to use for getting about. There are wonderfully clear, bilingual, colour-coded network maps available from the TIC, but you should find diagrams somewhere in the stations.
Bus: Not recommended: the bus system is confusing even to the Japanese and beset by constant traffic jams.
Taxi: Rates start at Y600. A taxi ride will work out very expensive because of the traffic, and during cab shortages on Friday and Saturday nights, you will see people holding up two or three fingers, indicating how many times the meter price they are willing to pay to get home.

SIGHTS
The IMPERIAL PALACE is only open to the public two days a year – 2 January and 23 December – but you can walk round the

outside, and visit the gardens, which afford a good view of the palace. Nearest stations are Tokyo or Hibiya.

The MEIJI SHRINE is a beautiful Shinto shrine dedicated to the memory of the Emperor Meiji and Empress Shoken. It was completed in 1920 but, like so many of Japan's treasures, was destroyed (it's usually by fire, flood or earthquake, but in this case it was World War II) and rebuilt in the 1950s. The neighbouring park (entry Y400) has some beautifully peaceful walks. Nearest station is Harajuku.

Dedicated to Kannon, goddess of mercy, the SENSOJI TEMPLE (yet another post-war reconstruction) stands in the Asakusa area. Asakusa was once the site of Tokyo's 'water trade' (all things pertaining to the pursuit of pleasure), but the red lights and the bright lights have now moved elsewhere (Kabuki-cho; Shinjuku).

UENO PARK is lovely in its own right, but if that's not incentive enough, it's also home to the TOKYO NATIONAL MUSEUM (Y400), which holds the world's biggest collection of Japanese art, the METROPOLITAN MUSEUM OF ART (contemporary art, no admission fee except to special exhibitions), the SHITAMACHI HISTORY MUSEUM, a recreation of Tokyo's working-class district of the old days (Y200), and the TOSHOGU SHRINE, dating from the 17th century (Y100). All museums are closed on Mondays. Also in the park is UENO ZOO, which has good conditions by Japanese standards but, unless you want to see the pandas, there's no compelling reason to visit it. Nearest station is Ueno.

For shopping (strictly *window* shopping; you can't afford it), the GINZA district is where the fashionable people go, and it's worth a wander. There are also a number of small (free) galleries in the area, and, for all things technological, the Sony building. It's a short walk from the Imperial Palace, or take the subway to Ginza station. Serious shoppers should not neglect the massive department stores such as Isetan, Seibu and Mitsukoshi (you'll be able to buy cheap souvenirs in them – purses and the like) which often hold art exhibitions on their top floors. Akihabara is the place for cheap(ish) state-of-the-art electrical goods.

HARAJUKU and SHIBUYA are where the young-and-trendies go, and both have a vibrant atmosphere. Outside Shibuya station is a small statue of Hachiko, the Greyfriar's Bobby of Japan: a faithful dog who, even after his master had died, continued to go to the station where they used to meet every day. It's not worth going there just to see Hachiko, but look out for it. The tale is told to all Japanese schoolchildren as an example of the virtue of loyalty.

The venue on a Sunday afternoon is YOYOGI PARK, the place to see Japanese (or perhaps it's just Tokyo's) youth culture at its most abandoned, outlandish and noisy. Everyone is here, from the original rockers in their shades and leather jackets, through roller skaters and glam rock bands to crusading Mormon missionaries. In recent years, the bands have tended mostly towards punk, but other kinds of music are represented, and there are some good dance acts. Take your camera and your earplugs, travel the subway to Harajuku station and just follow the noise.

Finally, if you've had enough of temples and Tokyo trendies, there's a Disneyland on the outskirts of the city. Buy a 'passport' ticket for around Y4,800, and you won't know you're not in California.

ACCOMMODATION

Japanese addresses being so confusing/uninformative, telephone numbers only are given for the following, so you can ring ahead and ask for directions.

Youth hostels: It's a good idea to make advance reservations if you can.

Tokyo Kokusai YH (tel. 3235 1107): near Iidabashi station. (Sometimes known as Tokyo International Hostel). On leaving the station, look for the tall, glass-fronted building – the YH is on the 18th floor. It's air-conditioned, and the facilities are excellent, but it is often booked out, and reservations well in advance are almost always essential.

Yoyogi YH (tel. 3467 9163): this is the more user-friendly of the two IYHF hostels. There are usually vacancies, the staff will often let you stay beyond the three-day limit, there is a large, well-provided kitchen and, though the dorms are closed during the day, the day-room is left open. Take the private Odakyu line from Shinjuku station to Sangubashi. Head towards a tower that looks like an onion on a spire, over a level crossing and the expressway. The YH is in the former Olympic compound, building number 4.

Tokyo YWCA Sadohara Hostel (tel. 3268 4451). Couples are permitted. Nearest subway station is Ichigaya; take the Ichigaya exit. Prices from Y6,200.

Hotels: You can book *ryokan*, hotels, etc. at Narita airport (see **Airport Facilities**, p. 357).

Ryokan Katsutaro (tel. 3821 9808). A ten-minute walk from Ueno station, along Shinobazu Pond. From Y3,900 per person.

Kimi Ryokan (tel. 3971 3766). Currently flavour of the month with foreign visitors. It's near Ikebukuro station (you can ask directions at the nearby police box), and costs upwards of Y2,600 per person, but you'll have to book a few weeks in advance. It has an information centre, and is a good place to get into if you plan to stay on for a while, or to start job-hunting.

Hokke Club Ueno (tel. 3823 3111). A business hotel ten minutes from Ueno station. Prices from Y5,360.

Shinjuku Park Hotel (tel. 3356 0241). Not far from Shinjuku station. Y6,000 and up.

FOOD
Tokyo restaurants are simply too numerous and various to even begin listing here. See **Japan: Food**, p. 354, for the lowdown, and just look around for the type of restaurant you want. The Shinjuku and Roppongi districts are good hunting grounds; you should find reasonably priced sukiyaki restaurants in the former. In any event, you will never be far from a Kentucky Fried Chicken or a noodle shop, and if you hanker for the Indian, Thai, Cambodian, French, etc. gastronomic experience, Tokyo is the place to be.

Should you prefer to buy your own food, you may have difficulty finding a supermarket in the city; however, most department stores have a food section. Japan is one of the few places where it is almost as cheap to eat out as in. Fresh fruit and meat are particularly expensive.

ENTERTAINMENT
So far as traditional spectacles go, a few hotels hold tea ceremonies that you can watch or join in with, and regular performances of Noh and Kabuki theatre take place in the city. There are even occasional Bunraku (puppet theatre) shows, and sumo wrestling tournaments are staged in January, May and September. Consult the TIC about venues and ticket prices (which can be as low as Y1,000–2,000).

Many cinemas show English-language films, which are subtitled, not dubbed. Tickets cost around Y1,600. Unfortunately, the cinemas often become very crowded and patrons sometimes have to stand: avoid weekends for this reason. Check the English-language *Tokyo Journal* or *Tokyo City Guide* for listings.

If night-clubbing is your scene, Roppongi is *the* place to be. Venues that don't have an entrance charge (Y2,000 upwards) may have a cover charge instead. You'll find everything from reggae clubs to acid house. There's also a Hard Rock Café. Point yourself towards Roppongi Crossing and just take it from there.

If you just want to go pubbing, get someone who knows their way about to lead you to their watering-holes so you don't end up in expensive hostess or karaoke bars by mistake. Alternatively, drink where you eat or seek out an *aka-chochin* (red lantern) bar, where working men drink.

Looking at the bright lights is free!

EXCURSIONS
'Don't say "kekko" [wonderful] until you've seen NIKKO', goes the saying. Sensory overload is the order of the day – not least on the terrifying hairpin bends on the mountain road up to LAKE CHUZENJI and the KEGON WATERFALL. Even better than the scenery is the truly stupendous TOSHO-GU SHRINE and the RINNOJI TEMPLE; it's worth spending the night in Nikko so you can devote more time to all the sights. Take the Tobu Nikko line from Asakusa station (the rapid train is cheaper than the limited express and takes only an hour and a quarter), and stop off at the tourist office in Nikko for essential sightseeing information.

A commuter train ride from Tokyo is YOKOHAMA, the port to which foreigners were admitted in the 19th century when Japan re-opened its doors to outside trade after a long isolation. Today, it is a modern city with only a few attractions for the visitor. Japan's only real Chinatown is here; the SANKEI-EN GARDEN is pretty; the FOREIGNER'S GRAVEYARD quite fascinating; and the SILK MUSEUM is located near the harbour front.

Only a little further along the same train line lies KAMAKURA, former capital of Japan. There are a large number of interesting temples in the town, and a beautifully serene GREAT BUDDHA which should not be missed. Not far from the Buddha, the HASE KANNON TEMPLE contains a poignant sight: row upon row of small statues of the god Jizo, all commemorating the souls of dead children. From Kamakura station, take the private Enoden line to the third stop, which is near the Hase Kannon Temple. Most of the other temples are within walking distance of Kita-Kamakura station.

Last but not least, there's FUJISAN (not Fuji*yama*!) and the Fuji Five Lakes, about two hours by bus from Tokyo. The Fuji climbing season is in July and August (the mountain is closed at other times); start at midnight and reach the summit in time for the sunrise. Climb it once and you're a wise man, twice and you're a fool – so they say. Be warned, though, however many times you climb it, Fuji will never look as pretty from the summit as it does from a distance. There are six climbing trails, ranging from 15–25 km. The most popular starts from Lake Kawaguchi.

The Tokyo TIC will provide information on these and other excursions.

Hiroshima

Just two hours by *Shinkansen* from Kyoto and five hours from Tokyo by train is Hiroshima, the city whose name is synonymous with the atom bomb.

The information office at the station (on the south side, not the *Shinkansen* side) will make bookings for you, and will supply a map in English with tram routes and tourist sights marked on it. The trams are the easiest way of getting about.

SIGHTS
The focal point for visitors is, of course, PEACE PARK; its museum and memorials stand as a reminder of the events of 6 August 1945. If you are in the city on the anniversary, you will experience the full force of Peace Day, when anti-nuclear campaigners from Japan and the rest of the world converge on Hiroshima (and the locals stay away). It's all a little over the top, but at night there is a beautiful ceremony at the Otagawa River, when lighted lanterns are floated on the water. The park is lovely, and the museum manages to tell the story without being horrifically graphic. A visit there is not a depressing experience, but it will be a profoundly moving one.

If you have time, the SHUKKEI-EN GARDEN is worth a look; the Castle, on the inside at least, is not. Kinokuniya (sixth floor of Sogo department store) and Maruzen (in the Hondori) both have good books about Hiroshima, and there's a good international reading room in the park, right next to the museum.

ACCOMMODATION
There's a good YH in Hiroshima (tel. (082) 221 5343), where a swimming pool goes some way towards compensating for the early wake-up call. Several business hotels are located near the station and in the centre.

FOOD
Don't miss eating at Mi-chan, spiritual home of *Okonomiyaki*, a speciality of Hiroshima. It has been described as a cross between a Japanese crêpe and a Japanese pizza – try it and see. Mi-chan is on the same street as Tenmaya department store, Hatchobori.

ENTERTAINMENT
Hondori is the main shopping street, and there are plenty of eating places nearby. The bars and bright lights are in Nagarekawa.

EXCURSIONS
Twenty-five minutes by train from Hiroshima is the 'floating' *torii* (shrine gate) of MIYAJIMA ISLAND. Take the ferry to the island, buy crackers for the tame deer, wade out to the *torii*, and climb Mt Misen, if you're feeling energetic.

Another twenty-five minutes down the same train line is IWAKUNI, whose main attraction is the KINTAIKYO, an unusual wooden bridge – originally built in 1673, destroyed by flood, rebuilt in 1953 – which sits in a wooded valley overlooked by a hilltop castle. It costs Y210 to cross the bridge, and on the other side is KIKKO PARK, Japan's answer to the English village green, with a cable car or woodland walk leading to the castle, and a white snake sanctuary.

Lastly, if you really want to get away from it all, consider a day at SANDANKYO GORGE. There is a hiking trail which follows a lively river through the woods. The gorge is cool in summer, spectacular in autumn and pristine in winter. It takes a few hours to get there, by bus (2 hours and 10 minutes from Hiroshima), or by train from Yokogawa station.

Kyoto

Kyoto was the imperial capital of Japan for over 1,000 years. Today it is an often confusing urban sprawl with an unattractive centre that leaves the visitor wondering where all the history is. It's there – shrines, temples, gardens, castles – you just have to go looking. The city is at its most attractive during the cherry-blossom and autumn leaves periods and is, consequently, packed out at these times. November, school-trip season, should be avoided completely: all you'll see is an ocean of school uniforms. From Tokyo, it's about 3–4 hours by train.

USEFUL ADDRESSES
Tourist office: The TIC is a short walk (in a northerly direction) from the station. Open Mon.–Fri. 9 a.m.–5 p.m.; Sat. 9 a.m.–12 noon. There are limits put on the time that the staff spend on each enquiry (to cope with the flood of visitors to the city), so it's best to have a specific idea of what you want to know before you go

in. They have leaflets on everything from walking tours of Kyoto and nearby Nara through shopping for traditional crafts to finding inexpensive accommodation. They can arrange volunteer guides for you, given reasonable notice.

Japan Travel-Phone: A seven-day service providing travel-related information in English. In Eastern Japan dial 0088 222800 for info.; in Western Japan dial 0088 224800; in Tokyo dial 3503 4400; in Kyoto dial 371 5649.

Teletourist Service: 24-hour taped information on events in the city. Tel. 361 2911.

LOCAL TRANSPORT

There is a subway, but it is of limited use. Buses are the best way to get around – network maps are available from the TIC. A 'Trafica Kyo Card' is available for both buses and subway for about Y1,000.

SIGHTS

There are far too many sights to list all of them here, but the following are ones that you will certainly want to consider.

In the city centre, NIJO CASTLE, built in 1603, is well known for its 'nightingale floor', which squeaks as you walk on it (the original intention was to warn inhabitants of the presence of intruders). There is also a beautiful garden right next to the castle. An explanatory leaflet in English is provided; admission costs Y500.

On top of a hill in the east of the city is KIYOMIZU TEMPLE, a truly magnificent place that should not be missed. There has been a temple on the site since the 8th century, but the present buildings date from the 17th century onwards. Admission Y300, and watch out for the steep uphill climb! It's an enjoyable walk from the temple to nearby Maruyama park. Also on the east side, the 15th-century GINKAKU-JI (Temple of the Silver Pavilion) started life as a nobleman's villa. Within its peaceful grounds are gardens and mountainside walks to follow. Admission Y400.

To the north of the city, the KINKAKU-JI (Temple of the Golden Pavilion) is another converted villa, immortalized in a book of the same name by Yukio Mishima, who based his story on a true event of 1950, when a young monk burned the building to the ground. Reconstructed in 1955, the temple is a favourite with visitors; all over town, you'll see postcards of it – in the snow, in autumn, etc. Admission Y400.

Not far from the Golden Temple is RYOANJI TEMPLE, which is famous for its rock and gravel garden. The gravel is raked into different formations each day, and looking at it is curiously relaxing. Admission Y400.

Visiting the IMPERIAL PALACE requires a special pass. This can be applied for (you'll need to show your passport) 20 minutes before the 10 a.m. or 2 p.m. tour. Admission free.

ACCOMMODATION
There are many hostels and dorms in the city – consult the TIC. Two of the most conveniently situated are:

Uno House (tel. 231 7763). The ultimate foreigner's crash pad; central, cramped, but clean (though you might want to avoid the kitchen). Dorms Y1,500, rooms Y1,600 per person. Take bus number 205 from the station to the Kawaramachi-marutamachi-mae stop.

Higashiyama YH (tel. 761 8135). Mega-clean, air-conditioned and a convenient base for sightseeing, *but* it's regimented, not particularly friendly, and they'll make you pay for evening and morning meals whether you like it or not.

FOOD
There are many options for food, both Western and oriental. The Tourist Information Centre will supply lists of restaurants.

ENTERTAINMENT
For traditional entertainment, go along to a hotel tea ceremony that you can watch or join in with. Also, there are regular performances of Noh and Kabuki theatre in the city. There are even occasional Bunraku (puppet theatre) shows, and sumo takes place in January, May and September. Consult the TIC about venues and ticket prices (which can be as low as Y1,000–2,000).

There are plenty of cinemas showing English-language films, which are subtitled, not dubbed. Tickets cost around Y1,600. Unfortunately, the cinemas often become very crowded, and patrons sometimes have to stand; avoid weekends for this reason. Check the English-language *Tokyo Journal* or *Tokyo Time Out* for listings.

If night-clubbing is your scene, Roppongi is *the* place to be. Places that don't have an entrance charge (Y2,000 may have a cover charge instead. You'll find everything from reggae clubs to acid house. There's also a Hard Rock Café. Orientate yourself towards Roppongi Crossing and just take it from there.

If you just want to go pubbing, get someone who knows their way about to lead you to their watering-holes so that you don't end up in expensive hostess or karaoke bars by mistake. Alternatively, drink where you eat or seek out an *aka-chochin* (red lantern) bar, where working men drink.

Looking at the bright lights is free!

EXCURSIONS
A popular day-trip from Kyoto is NARA PARK. Feed the tame deer, visit the Great Buddha and stroll through the trees.

MALAYSIA

VITAL STATISTICS
Red tape: Technically, most visitors require nothing more than a full passport to enter Malaysia for tourist or business purposes. You may, however, be asked to show return on onward tickets and adequate funds for your stay. Malaysian immigration officials are none too keen on the 'hippy' look or scruffiness in general, and deny entry to anyone they don't like the look of. Men with long hair can expect a hard time.

A pass with the granted length of stay will be issued upon entry – the duration will be at the discretion of the immigration officials, but is likely to be three months (one month for French nationals). Notable exceptions are Commonwealth passport holders from India and Sri Lanka, who will have to apply for a visa in advance.

You will need your passport to travel between peninsular Malaysia and Sabah and Sarawak, as they have separate entry formalities.

Customs: You may bring in 200 cigarettes or 225 g tobacco, plus 1 l wine or spirits duty-free. A deposit (refundable on departure) may be levied on items such as video cameras: make sure to get a receipt if this happens. There are restrictions on the export of antiquities.

Though it is well known that the Malaysians hang convicted drug traffickers, it is worth reiterating here. Whereas in Thailand foreigners are exempt from the death penalty, no such exceptions are made in Malaysia. Don't carry things across borders for anyone, and keep an eye on your luggage at all times when entering or exiting the country. Thief-proof your bags so that nothing can be added which should not be there; traffickers have been known to use unsuspecting travellers in this way, and ignorance will not be considered a valid defence. If you are carrying prescription drugs with you, make sure you carry the prescription, too. You have been warned.

Health: No vaccinations are required, except for yellow fever, if arriving from infected and endemic zones. You are advised to take precautions against malaria and dengue fever, both spread by mosquitoes. Avoid tap water outside the cities. Health insurance is necessary. Pharmacies dispense both Western and Chinese medicines, there are private clinics everywhere, and a visit to a doctor will cost about M$20.

Language: Bahasa Malaysia (Malay) is the national language. Other languages used are Mandarin and Tamil. English is widely spoken (it is compulsory in schools).

Population: 18 million.

Capital: Kuala Lumpur, population around 1 million.

Political system: Parliamentary democracy. There is a constitutional monarchy in place.

Religion: Islam is the official religion, but Malaysia is multi-racial, so Buddhism, Taoism, Hinduism and Christianity exist alongside the muslim faith.

Time: Eight hours ahead of GMT.

Money: The currency is the ringgit, also known as the Malaysian dollar (M$), which is divided into 100 sen. Coins: 1, 5, 10 and 50 sen. Notes: M$1, M$5, M$20, M$50, M$100 and M$1,000. £1 = M$3.79.

You can change money and traveller's cheques at banks and hotels or at unofficial moneychangers, but shop around, as rates vary. Credit cards are accepted at most large establishments in Malaysia. There are no restrictions on the import or export of currency.

Tax: Hotels carry a 5% government tax and sometimes a 10% service charge.

Communications: Public telephones are available in most towns: you'll find coin-operated phones in supermarkets and post offices, and there are also card-operated phones. You'll need 10-sen coins for local calls, while phonecards (costing M$3–50) can be bought at airports, petrol stations and 7–11 stores. International direct dialling is possible from most cities, but the calls are best made from the hotels.

Overseas postage is cheap, and mail will take about a week to Europe or N. America.

Media: There are quite a few English language papers, the main ones being the *New Straits Times* and *The Star*. Foreign publications are available from the main newsstands and bookstalls.

Electricity: 220v AC. Plugs are usually square 3-pin.

Business hours: BANKS: Mon.–Fri. 10 a.m.–3 p.m., Sat. 9.30 a.m.–11.30 a.m.

POST OFFICES: Mon.–Sat. 8 a.m.–5 p.m.

SHOPS: Mon.–Sat. 8.30 a.m.–6.30 p.m. Supermarkets and department stores are open 10 a.m.–10 p.m.

OFFICES: Mon.–Thurs. 8 a.m.–12.45 p.m. and 2 p.m.–4.15 p.m.; Fri. 8 a.m.–12.15 p.m. and 2.45 p.m.–4.15 p.m.; Sat. 8 a.m.–12.45 p.m.

Sunday is a day off for all of the above, except in Johor, Kedah, Perlis, Kelantan and Terengganu, where Friday is the day of rest, with early closing on Thursdays.

Holidays: 21 Jan.–20 Feb. (Ramadan); 18 February (Chinese New Year); 1 May, plus two other festival days; June (King's Birthday – one day); July (one day); 31 August, plus one other day; October/November (two days); 25 December. There are also various regional public holidays, contact the tourist board for details.

Climate: There are no distinct seasons in Malaysia, which is hot and humid all year round. It is, however, a little cooler than other tropical countries, with temperatures ranging from 21–32°C. The hill resorts are even cooler.

Sabah, Sarawak and the east coast of peninsular Malaysia experience monsoons from November to February. The west coast's rainy season is from May to September, but the rains are short-lived and not very heavy.

Bring warm clothes if you plan to visit the hill resorts, and remember that temperatures in the tropics drop at night.

DO'S AND DON'TS

Both women and men should dress conservatively in Malaysia, as it is a predominantly Muslim country and scanty clothing may give offence. Shorts are considered odd, even for men, and going shirtless is not acceptable. Visitors should give especial consideration to their appearance when visiting a temple or mosque, and shoes will more often than not have to be removed before entering such places.

You'll probably have to take off your shoes inside Malaysian homes as well. If, when visiting someone, you are offered food that does not involve the use of cutlery, remember that Malays and Indians use the right hand to eat with, as the left hand is considered unclean.

Pointing at people and things is bad manners so far as the Malays are concerned, and you should never pat anyone – not even a child – on the head (the head is considered sacred). Don't point your feet at anyone either, or do something like put them up on a chair or table (feet being the lowest part of the body, in every sense of the word).

You can be fined for littering or spitting, and cigarette smoking is banned in a lot of public places.

Tipping is not a Malaysian custom and, though tips may not be refused if offered, they are certainly unnecessary.

WHERE TO GO FOR WHAT

A lot of people whizz through Malaysia overnight on the train from Thailand to Singapore. It's not a big country, but it deserves a little more attention than that. Spend a couple of weeks at least – or better still a month or so – and go trekking in the rainforests and the national parks.

The main national park is TAMAN NEGARA, on the eastern side of Malaysia, to the north-east of Kuala Lumpur. The park's headquarters and accommodations are located at KUALA TAHAN, which is reached by river boat. From here you can go trekking, fishing, swimming, shooting the rapids, or wildlife-watching.

There are a couple of other parks and reserves not far from Kuala Lumpur (ask at the tourist office), but the major parks are in Sabah and Sarawak, on the island of BORNEO. In fact, Sabah's main attraction is the KINABALU NATIONAL PARK, where you can climb Mount Kinabalu (a two-day trip), or simply look at the birds, plants and animals, and visit the hot spring. The view from the top of the mountain is phenomenal. Arrangements for visiting the park can be made in Kota Kinabalu, about two hours away.

SARAWAK has the ancient NIAH CAVES, discovery site of a 40,000-year-old skull, home of rock paintings, bats and edible bird's nests (as in bird's nest soup, but don't get too excited: the chief ingredient is bird saliva). Visitors can walk in the forests around the caves and look out for birds, squirrels, monkeys and butterflies.

Besides the Niah National Park, there is also BAKO NATIONAL PARK – a rainforest with good walking trails – and GUNUNG MULU NATIONAL PARK, which has limestone caves and a variety of plant and fungus species. Both Sabah and Sarawak are home to a range of tribal peoples, and each has a number of good beaches and some interesting architecture.

Less intrepid travellers can content themselves with trips to the hill stations (see **Kuala Lumpur: Excursions**, p. 379), or to PENANG and LANGHAWI, holiday islands just off the coast. The area has some popular beach resorts (though, like all resorts, they're not that great if you're not into touristy places), as well as some marvellous temples, sites of historical interest and a good museum in Georgetown. MELAKA, on the west coast, is a fascinating town: it has been under the colonial rule of each successive invading power, and this has left it with a hybrid architectural and historical legacy. It's a marvellous place to stroll around.

In complete contrast, KUALA LUMPUR is a modern, commercial city. Though it has its charms (see the **Kuala Lumpur** section, p. 375), there's little reason (other than stocking up on leaflets at the tourist office) to spend an extended period there. Every state in Malaysia has something to recommend it – so get out there and enjoy. If possible, obtain the Malaysian tourist authority's range of leaflets on each state before leaving home – they're a bit on the glossy side, but are a good guide to the country's many attractions.

INTERNAL TRAVEL

Air: Malaysia Airlines (MAS) is the principal domestic operator. Fares are (roughly) two or three times those of the equivalent train journey, but still reasonable.

Rail: Trains are comfortable and reliable. There are really only two lines: one running from Singapore along the west coast through Kuala Lumpur, Butterworth and on to Thailand; the other branches off at Gemas and goes up to the north-east near Kota Baru, also linking with Thailand. There are some minor branch lines here and there.

Express trains have two 'classes' – with or without air-conditioning – all other trains (express and local) have three classes. Prices vary accordingly, and you'll have to pay extra for a berth on overnight trains. Seats can be booked in advance.

There are a couple of rail passes available only to foreign visitors (enquire at main railway stations), though they are not worth it if you do not plan to use the train a great deal. The 'Visit Malaysia' rail pass allows unlimited domestic rail travel: US$55 for 10 days, US$120 for 30 days.

Bus: There are three types of bus: non air-conditioned interstate, non air-conditioned state, and air-conditioned expresses connecting major towns (the air-conditioning on these is fierce). The services are cheap, fast and comfortable, though (as the tourist board puts it) on occasions the buses 'do not adhere strictly to schedule'.

Town and city buses can be confusing, but fares are cheap (amounting to sens rather than M$). It's best to have the correct change before boarding.

Car: Self-drive is hassle-free in Malaysia and there are many rental operators around. Daily rates vary from M$240 to M$350, with weekly rates also available. Petrol costs just over M$1 per litre. Driving is on the left, and you'll need an International Driving Licence.

Taxi: Outstation taxis offer a long-distance interstate service on a shared-cost basis. There are ranks in most main towns, with taxis bound for different destinations. They leave as soon as they have their full complement of four passengers, and the fare is a fixed price per person. (You can charter a taxi by paying four times the per capita fare.) The roads are good and it's a wonderful way to travel, even if the drivers are a bit manic at times.

Local taxis are theoretically metered, but you'll often have to haggle the price out of the driver before moving off.

Bicycle rickshaw: Trishaws are on the wane, but in those towns where a service still operates they are often the best way of getting about. Fares are about M$1 per kilometre, though you should always agree the price beforehand.

Hitching: The hitching is good, though, as in Japan, only foreigners do it. It's a good way to meet the local people and resident foreigners who pick up hitchers.

ACCOMMODATION

There is plenty of budget accommodation in Malaysia.

Youth hostels: There is a limited network of hostels, but most of the main tourist destinations − Kuala Lumpur, Penang, Melaka (Malacca), the Cameron Highlands, etc. − are covered. They usually cost around M$10 or less, though the Kuala Lumpur hostels and the one in Melaka are more expensive. Sometimes rooms are available in addition to dorms. There are also some privately run dormitories around, particularly in the beach resorts. Advance booking is recommended during school holidays (roughly: April, August, November, December).

Hotels: Chinese hotels offer basic but generally clean rooms for around M$10−25. They are often noisy, though, and are sometimes located in bad areas, so it's wise to check them out before taking a room. Couples can save a bit of money by renting a single room (most singles have a double bed); you won't be charged extra if two share. BEWARE: some hotels are also brothels. Look out for peep-holes in the walls.

There is no shortage of expensive international hotel chains in the cities. Costs are: singles − from M$140; doubles − from M$180. Mid-range and cheaper hotels are also plentiful, though. A 'budget' hotel (defined by the tourist authorities as 'a 20 to 50 room hotel') will cost from M$40 for a single, and from M$50 for a double. Not a bad deal. Prices at the cheaper hotels are usually quoted inclusive of taxes, the more expensive hotels without.

Government rest houses: These throwbacks to colonial days can be found in most main towns and at the hill stations. Primarily intended for travelling government officials, others may stay in them if space is available. They get packed to the rafters during the school holidays, and unfortunately you can't make advance reservations. Prices range from M$20–50.

FOOD
A number of different cuisines may be sampled in multi-racial Malaysia, though the range is more limited in remote places. You'll find Cantonese restaurants and food stalls, as well as Sichuan, Shanghai and Beijing restaurants, plus some places serving lesser-known types of Chinese cuisine. In fact, Chinese food is more common than Malay! Indian food is widely available and very good, which is good news for vegetarians. Western food can be found in the restaurants of large hotels and in the ubiquitous fast-food chains.

Malay food is hard to come by outside the cities, so make the most of it while in Kuala Lumpur. *Satay* (barbecued beef or chicken served with peanut sauce) is the best-known dish, but experiment with *nasi lemak* (rice cooked in coconut milk and served with fish, egg, peanuts and cucumber), *laksa johor* (noodles in a fish curry gravy with vegetables), *soto ayam* (spicy chicken soup with rice and vegetables) and *laksa lemak* (noodle soup with a coconut base).

There is a wide range of restaurants to suit the large, moderate or low budget, but use your sense if eating at the cheaper places, and don't patronize anywhere where standards of cleanliness are in doubt. Food stalls are, however, safe to eat at on the whole.

One of the gastronomic delights of Malaysia is its wide range of tropical fruits. Apart from the more familiar pineapples, bananas, mangoes and guava fruit, here are just a few of the tropical fruits you can try: *mangosteen*, a slightly acidic sour-sweet fruit that tastes a little like a mixture of grapes and strawberries; the *pomelo*, a citrus fruit; the *rambutan*, a lychee-like spiny fruit; and the *cempedak* (jackfruit), which has a sweet-tasting yellow flesh.

WARNING: Seafood may present a health risk, and you should avoid tapwater and ice outside the cities. It is possible to contract hepatitis A in Malaysia.

BUDGETING
Malaysia, like Hong Kong, is one of those places where you can spend as little or as much as you want. Dormitory-style accommodation can be as low as M$8 per night, and even if you go upmarket and stay in a hotel, the cheaper establishments cost from M$10–40. Many family-run hotels offer free drinks, snacks or breakfast,

too. On the other hand, if money's no object there are a number of international hotel chains with European prices.

A meal in a hotel restaurant costs M$20–22, but a mid-priced local restaurant will charge M$10–12 and, at the other end of the scale, lunch or an evening meal at a food stall will set you back only M$4 or so. The bad news is that – in relative terms – alcohol is expensive. A bottle of locally brewed beer will cost about M$3. Soft drinks are a lot cheaper.

Getting around, however, is cheap: bus fares cost less than M$1, and even taxi rates are reasonable. Long-distance travel may seem more expensive than in some other countries, but there is such a vast range of options that whatever your budget you'll find something affordable (and there's always hitching, if you're really broke).

All in all, it should be more than possible to get by on less than £12 a day for everyday expenses – and you won't even be roughing it. In Malaysia, living cheaply is quite painless.

FURTHER INFORMATION

High Commission of the Federation of Malaysia, 45 Belgrave Square, London SW1X 8QT (tel. 0171 235 8033).

Malaysia Tourism Promotion Board, 57 Trafalgar Square, London, WC2N 5DU (tel. 0171 930 7932).

Background reading: Lonely Planet publish an excellent guide combining *Malaysia, Singapore & Brunei*. Insight's guide to Malaysia and Trav Bugs' *Malaysia* are also good pre-trip reading.

On the travel literature front (and if you can understand what he's on about), there is Redmond O'Hanlon's *Into the Heart of Borneo*, a story of jungle adventuring. Fictional accounts of Malaysia include Joseph Conrad's *Lord Jim*, and the short stories of Somerset Maugham. A more contemporary work is *Turtle Beach* by Blanche d'Alpuget (recently made into a film), which deals with the harsh treatment suffered by Vietnamese boat people arriving in Malaysia in the sixties.

On arrival, check out the MPH and Berita bookshops for a wide range of books on Malaysia.

Kuala Lumpur

AIRPORT FACILITIES

Subang Kuala Lumpur International Airport is Malaysia's principal airport, and is 20 km from the city. It has two terminals: one for international arrivals, the other for domestic flights. There is a tourist information centre (open until 11 p.m.) in the arrivals terminal. Both terminals have the usual bars, restaurants, shops, post offices, currency exchanges and car rental desks.

Check-in time is 90 minutes prior to departure for international flights and 45 minutes prior to departure for domestic. Departure taxes are roughly as follows: domestic flights M$3; to Singapore & Brunei M$5; all other flights M$15.

CITY LINKS

Taxi-Limousine: This is the main mode of transport to and from the airport. Services operate on a coupon basis: you purchase a coupon from the desk inside the terminal, and it is then given to the driver in payment. There are 13 coupon 'zones', with prices from M$12.20 to M$25.20. Beware of touts, who try to buck the system.

Bus: Public bus number 47 links the airport with the Kelang bus terminal downtown and costs only a few ringgit.

USEFUL ADDRESSES

Tourist office: Malaysia Tourist Information, 109 Jalan Ampang (tel. 243 3929). This complex has everything: a bus-booking centre, phone and fax facilities, currency exchange, daily audio-visual and cultural shows, not forgetting the tourist information counter. Smaller branches are located at Jalan Sultan Hishamuddin, near the railway station, and inside the station itself. There is also the Kuala Lumpur TIC on Jalan Parlimen.

Immigration office: Block 1, Pusat Bandar Damansara (tel. 255 5077). You can extend your visa here.

MSL Travel, the youth and student travel operator, is in the Asia Hotel on Jalan Haji Hussein (tel. 298 9722).

Main post office: Jalan Hishamuddin, central district, near the Dayabumi building and Central Market. Open Mon.–Sat. 9 a.m.–6 p.m., and you can collect poste restante mail here.

British High Commission: 13th Floor, Wisma Damansara, 5 Jalan Semantan (tel. 248 2122).

US Embassy: 376 Jalan Tun Razak (tel. 261 6277).

Medical assistance: The General Hospital is in the north of the city, situated between Jalan Pahang and Jalan Doktor Latiff.

Emergency services: Dial 999.

Libraries: The British Council has a library on Jalan Bukit Aman (tel. 298 7555) and there is also an Australian Information Library on Jalan Yap Kwan Seng (tel. 242 3122). The New Zealand Library is on Jalan Tun Razak (tel. 248 6422).

GETTING ABOUT

Most of Kuala Lumpur's sights are within reasonable distance of each other and the downtown area is compact, so walking is the best way to get around. (It's a bit like Glasgow or Sheffield in places, though, with massive great roads between you and the place you want to get to.)

Bus and minibus: There are a number of bus companies and also minibuses operating in the city. Fares depend on distance, and start at 20 sen (50 sen flat fare for the minibuses); make sure you have the correct change. The system is confusing, however, so it's far better to walk around town and use taxis for un-walkable journeys. Minibuses are faster and cost a fixed 60 sen.

Taxi: The taxis are cheap, and you shouldn't pay more than a few ringgit per short trip, though prices go up 50% between midnight and 6 a.m. Licensed taxis are yellow. There is a complaints number to ring if you have problems with a particular taxi: call 293–5188, quoting the taxi's licence number.

SIGHTS

It's worth a wander round the city centre to look at the buildings. There are a number of different architectural styles, from Islamic to colonial. Look out for the OLD POST OFFICE and the RAILWAY STATION: both are a mixture of colonial and Moorish, more like mosques than is the National Mosque itself. Beside MERDEKA SQUARE (a cricket ground) is the mock-Tudor ROYAL SELANGOR CLUB building and other mementoes of colonial days.

CHINATOWN is another historical place and nearby is CENTRAL MARKET, a Malaysian-style shopping mall housed in an art-deco building. There are temples of all descriptions everywhere you go; a visit to the beautiful JAME MOSQUE is a rewarding experience. There are few museums in Kuala Lumpur. The main one is the MUZIUM NEGARA (National Museum), situated by the pretty Lake Gardens, which has displays on Malaysian history, indigenous peoples, native crafts, etc. It is a good museum, and entrance is free. Not far away are PARLIAMENT HOUSE and the NATIONAL MONUMENT, a memorial of the post-war 'Emergency' period.

ACCOMMODATION

Hostels: There are a number of good cheap places in Kuala Lumpur. Jalan Raja Laut and Jalan Tuanka Abdul Rahman are good places to look, though some streets around them are more than a little seedy.

International Youth Centre Foundation, Jalan Tenteram Vandar

Tun Razak (tel. 971 9204). Has 57 rooms costing from M$15–70.

Meridian International Youth Hostel, 36 Jalan Hang Kasturi (tel. 232 5819). Very centrally situated (close to Central Market). Dorm beds cost M$7.50–10.00, and there are some double rooms for around M$20. Very popular with travellers.

Kuala Lumpur International Youth Hostel, 21 Jalan Kampung Attap (tel. 230 6870). It has 84 beds and costs M$10 per night.

YMCA, Jalan Tun Sambanthan (tel. 274 1439). Has 60 rooms from M$24–77.

YWCA, 12 Jalan Jang Jebat (tel. 238 3225). It takes women, couples and families. Rooms from M$30–80.

Hotels: Chinatown – right in the centre of town – has a lot of cheap hotels. A lot of them are brothels, though, so check them out carefully.

Colonial Hotel, 29–45 Jalan Sultan (tel. 238 0336). 36 rooms from M$19–27.

Kawana Tourist Inn, 68 Jalan Pudu (tel. 238 6714). 20 rooms from M$12–45.

Leng Nam Hotel, 165–167 Jalan Bandar (tel. 230 1489). 22 rooms from M$18.

B&B: Paradise Bed & Breakfast, 319 Jalan Tuanka Abdul Rahman (tel. 293 2322). Rooms M$25–37. Small and friendly.

Diamond City Lodge, 74B,C,D Jalan Masjid India (tel. 293 2245). Dorms M$10, rooms from M$26.

Madras Hotel and Restaurant, 343 Jalan Ipoh (tel. 441 7689). Dorms from M$10–25, rooms from M$15–25. Quite small.

FOOD

Kuala Lumpur has Malay, Thai, Indian, Chinese, Japanese, Indonesian and Western restaurants – and far too many of them to begin recommending any in particular. The Jalan Tuanku Abdul Rahman, home of budget accommodation, is also a good place to look for reasonably priced Malaysian and Indian restaurants, plus foodstalls of various kinds. Chinatown is another good hunting-ground: the second floor of the Central Market has a vast range of stalls and restaurants. There's also a variety of fast-food chains in the city – though with so much else on offer, it would be a pity to frequent them. For *the* eating experience in Kuala Lumpur, head for one of the night markets, such as Jalan Petaling in Chinatown, and pig out!

Steak gourmets shouldn't miss the restaurant in the Coliseum Hotel on Jalan Tuanka Abdul Rahman. It costs a little more than other places, but it's worth it for the food and the atmosphere.

ENTERTAINMENT
There are free dance and cultural shows held daily at the main tourist information centre (see **Kuala Lumpur: Useful Addresses**, p. 376), but not much else in the way of regular displays of Malaysian culture. Be sure to ask at the tourist office for details of performances. The best places for local colour and atmosphere are the night markets.

Cinema-going is a popular activity, and there are a number of places that show English-language films: keep an eye on the English press for details of showings. The best cinemas are in Central Square. Ten-pin bowling is a popular activity among young Malaysians, so there are a number of bowling alleys.

Pubs, discos and karaoke bars abound. The Betelnut disco on Jalan Pinang (opposite the Holiday Inn) has no cover charge, and attracts big crowds. Other discos to try are the Tin Mine in the Hilton Hotel and Club Oz in the Shangri-la. For karaoke, there is Lai-Lai Karaoke in the Sungai Wang Plaza or Tapagayo on Jalan Bukit Bintang. All of the big hotels have bars, and the Kai Peng district is the upwardly-mobile area of wine bars, trendy discos and other such places of entertainment.

EXCURSIONS
Less than an hour from Kuala Lumpur are the BATU CAVES. These huge limestone grottoes are a site of Hindu pilgrimage during the Thaipusan Festival (February). Because of their popularity (they attract thousands of visitors every year), they are rather touristy and best avoided at weekends and holidays.

Two places to see Malaysia's nature without having to venture too close to the real thing are the NATIONAL ZOO AND AQUARIUM and TEMPLER PARK. The former, 13 km from the city, displays species of fish and wildlife native to Malaysia, while the latter is a kind of 'jungle park' with hiking trails, butterflies, birds and animals. It lies 22 km north of Kuala Lumpur and is easily reached by bus.

Further afield are the hill stations — the GENTING HIGHLANDS, FRASER'S HILL and the CAMERON HIGHLANDS. The first is the only place in Malaysia where it is legal to gamble, so Malaysians flock there to do just that. There are also a golf course, other sports facilities and a cable car. It's more of a low-key Las Vegas than a place to escape the city crowds. In complete contrast, Fraser's Hill is a quiet, cool place with jungle walks, swimming at the Jurian Waterfalls, golf, tennis and plant farms and nurseries. The Cameron Highlands are probably the best known of the hill resorts – the quintessential colonial retreat from the heat. Originally a vegetable and tea-producing area (signs of the ex-pats' presence still remain), it is now a resort with good jungle trails, a tea factory to visit, and butterflies to go looking for. Because of longish travel times, the hill stations are more suited to 2–3 days visits rather than day-trips from the capital.

NEPAL

VITAL STATISTICS
Red tape: All visitors require a full passport and (with the exception of Indian nationals) a visa. The 30-day visa costs US$40 and can be applied for either in advance, on arrival in Kathmandu, or at road borders. The maximum stay allowed on a tourist visa is 120 days. This involves extending the 30-day visa at US$2 per day for the second and third months and US$3 per day for the fourth month. If you plan to trek, bear in mind that you have to apply for a trekking permit, complete with the time and course of the proposed trek if you plan to venture outside of the Kathmandu Valley, Pokhara and Chitwan National Park. Permits usually cost US$5 per week for the first four weeks, then US$10 per week. To obtain visa extensions and trekking permits, go to the central immigration office in Kathmandu on Tridevi Marg (tel. 418 573).
Customs: The duty-free allowance permits 200 cigarettes, 20 cigars and one bottle of alcohol. Travellers cheques over US$5,000 should be declared. There are special restrictions on firearms, large amounts of film and photographic equipment. No gold is allowed.

No antiques, silver, precious stones, wild animals or non-prescription drugs may be exported.
Health: No immunizations are required unless you are coming from an infected area. Vaccinations against cholera, meningitis, polio, hepatitis A and typhoid are recommended, and tetanus boosters are also advisable. Malaria is a risk which is generally restricted to the area adjoining India.
Language: The official language is Nepali. Various ethnic groups use their own language but also understand Nepali.
Population: 19 million.
Capital: Kathmandu, population 800,000.

Political system: Communist.
Religion: Officially Hindu, but Buddhism is also practised.
Time: Five and three-quarter hours ahead of GMT.
Money: The Nepal rupee (R) is divided into 100 paisa (p). Coins: 5, 10, 25 and 50 paisa. Notes: R1, R2, R5, R10, R20, R50, R100, R500 and R1,000.

Traveller's cheques are difficult to cash outside Kathmandu and Pokhara. It's best to carry US dollars (especially for visas). Most hotels quote the prices in US dollars, and airline tickets must be paid for in foreign currency. Try not to carry US$100 bills – they will be hard to cash and are not accepted for visas.

Communications: There are few public telephones in Nepal. Hotels and shops may allow you to use theirs for a small fee for domestic calls. In remote parts of the country there is no telephone service. For international calls, use the Central Telegraph Office, open 24-hours and located just south of the GPO on Sundhara in Kathmandu.

The postal service to and from Nepal is not reliable. Anything larger than an envelope has little or no chance of reaching you in Nepal. If you must send a package, post it from outside Nepal. If you need to receive mail, it is best to have it sent to American Express in Kathmandu or have it held at your embassy.

Electricity: 220v AC/50 Hz. Plugs tend to be the Indian round-pin variety.

Business hours: BANKS AND OFFICES: Sun.–Fri. 10 a.m.–5 p.m.

POST OFFICES: Sun.–Fri. 10 a.m.–5 p.m.

SHOPS: Sun.–Fri. 9.30 a.m.–7.30 p.m. (but some shops only open for a half-day on Friday).

Climate: The main tourist season in Nepal is Sept.–Nov. With cool, clear days, this is the ideal trekking season. It follows the monsoon season and comes before the cold winter months. Feb.–Apr. is also popular with tourists. Average temperatures in Kathmandu: January around 10°C); July around 25°C.

DO'S AND DON'TS

Kathmandu and Pokhara are very touristy cities. The Thamel area of Kathmandu is known as the travellers' centre and is full of locals hassling the new arrivals to buy virtually useless items. The rickshaw drivers are notorious for overcharging for their services, especially during September and October. Travellers are advised to bargain hard, because at the end of the journey the price will eventually work its way up a bit. Though prices may seem significantly lower than in Western Countries, it must be understood that Nepal is operating on a different economic scale.

Religion is an integral part of Nepali life. If you visit a temple or shrine, you will usually be expected to take off your shoes. Leather articles should not be taken in. When you walk around a temple or stupa, go clockwise.

WHERE TO GO FOR WHAT

Many travellers spend only a couple of weeks in Nepal, passing through on their way to India. This is a mistake! Nepal may be relatively small, but for the adventurous there are months of fun to be had.

KATHMANDU is an exciting, bustling city. It is quite easy to spend several days wandering around its narrow streets. Go in search of bargains, explore the various temples and monuments, or simply watch the locals rushing about the markets. DURBAR SQUARE and the Hindu temple at PASUPATINTH with its burning ghats are not to be missed.

NAGARKOT is a village in the foothills outside Kathmandu where, on a clear morning you can get a stunning view of Everest and the surrounding mountains. This is an ideal way to see the peaks if you are just passing through and do not intend to go trekking.

POKHARA is a more peaceful lakeside retreat. There is certainly less pollution than in Kathmandu and a lot less hassle. Here you can just sit and gaze at the ANNAPURNA MOUNTAIN RANGE across the lake. Alternatively, Pokhara is the gateway to the KALI GANDAKI and SETI rivers, as well as treks around ANNAPURNA.

TREKKING

This is what most people come to Nepal for. Without a doubt, the views of the peaks and the feeling of achievement you get from a hard trek through the mountains is simply unforgettable. Treks can vary from a single day to several months. Obviously the best views and greatest satisfaction are afforded to those who trek for a few days at least.

There are different ways to arrange a trek. Nepal isn't the right place to exercise typical 'backpacking'. You can arrange your own trek by leaving the tent and the stove behind and relying on local food and accommodation. This way, you will be contributing to the local economy. It's also probably the cheapest way to trek, but it means that you will have to stick to inhabited regions. If you are trekking with a small group of friends, you could organize – with the help of a trekking company – hired porters to carry the equipment and sherpas to set up camp and prepare the food. This could take up to a week to organize. The easiest, and costliest (about US$100 per day), way is to go on an organized trek with a Western guide. Though expensive, it is a stress-free way to experience the Himalayas. All food, equipment and organization, including trekking permits, is taken care of by the company.

The most talked about treks are:

The Annapurna Circuit – a tough trek lasting 3 weeks

The Annapurna Base Camp Trek – tough, lasts 10–12 days

The Everest Base Camp Trek – a 3–4 week trek which can be shortened by flying part of the way.

Trekking can be organized with UK companies, but they invariably charge more than you would pay in Nepal. There are 150 Nepal-based trekking companies. A complete list is available from the Trekking Agents Association of Nepal (TAAN) PO Box 3612, Kathmandu (tel. 225 875). It's worth going there personally to ask questions. It's located on Kantipath, next to the Hotel Yellow Pagoda. If you want unbiased advice on trekking, try talking to Western-owned rafting companies.

RAFTING AND CANOEING

Other than trekking, the adventurous come to Nepal to run the rivers. The Himalayas are the world's highest mountains and hence they feed the largest of rivers. It is possible to access these rivers with Western-standard equipment and excellent guides for prices much lower than you would find anywhere else. Most companies have offices in both Kathmandu and Pokhara.

The favourites are:

The Trisuli, a grade 3–4 high-volume river about 2 hours from Kathmandu. Trips can last 1–4 days, depending on your needs, and can end at the Royal Chitwan National Park. This is not a true 'wilderness river' as part of it runs along a major road. For the canoeist, this is an ideal introduction to large-volume rivers. Companies usually charge about US$35 per day.

The Sun Kosi: a world-famous rafting river. The grade is also 3–4 but the trips usually last 8–10 days. The 'River of Gold' provides a fantastic wildlife adventure through the Nepalese countryside. Huge rapids and stunning scenery make this a real trip to remember. As the rapids tend to start small and get progressively more difficult down the river, it is ideal for the canoeist who feels he/she needs some practice before entering the hardest rapids. Companies usually charge around US$45 per day.

The Karnali: a trip on this, Nepal's largest river, is a real expedition. To reach it you must go on an exhausting bus ride, followed by a 2-day trek. Porters are hired to carry the rafts, canoes, food and other equipment during the trek. Very few tourists/trekkers come here – this is the real Nepal! The river is not rafted as much as the others, so it is very unlikely that you will see another group. The grade 3–4 rapids run through the most beautiful and untouched areas of Nepal, with abundant wildlife. You can end your trip with a visit to the Royal Bardia National Park. This 12-day trip will cost about US$600, but is worth every cent.

Recommended for rafting and canoeing are the following four companies:

Equator Expeditions, PO Box 8404, Kathmandu (tel. 416 596/694). Located next to Kathmandu Guest House, Thamel, Kathmandu.

Himalayan Encounters, Kathmandu Guest House, Thamel, Kathmandu (tel. 432 632/417 426).

Himalayan River Exploration (HRE), PO Box 170, Lazimpat, Kathmandu (tel. 414 073).

Ultimate Descents, Him Thai Plaza, PO Box 6720, Kathmandu (tel. 229 389).

A UK-based company that can organize and/or offer information about rafting:

Splash Whitewater Rafting, Lamas Buildings, 20 Market Square, Aberfeldy, Perthshire, PH15 2RD (tel. 01887 829 706).

INTERNAL TRAVEL
Air: The prices for domestic air travel have become inflated in recent years. Royal Nepal Airlines run most of these flights but share the sky with Nepal Airways, Everest Air, Necon Air, Dynasty Aviation and Asian Airlines Helicopter. All tickets must be purchased in foreign currency, preferably US dollars. Nepal is notorious for flight delays and cancellations due to bad weather and overbooked passenger lists. Don't confirm a flight only once, confirm it as many times as you can up until the flight time.
Rail: There are no railways in Nepal.
Bus: The bus is the main form of transport, however slow it may be. Prices for privately operated and public buses are determined by the time it takes to get to the destination, rather than by distance. Tickets go on sale a day before departure at the bus station. Seat reservations are also made when you purchase the ticket. Try to avoid being above the back wheel. A front seat, or one near the door, will offer the most room. As a rule, the bus doesn't leave

until it's full, and that includes the aisle. Timetables are virtually non-existent. Patience is the only way to get through this experience.

Taxi: You probably won't find a taxi outside of Kathmandu and Pokhara. They are metered and rather inexpensive, but hard to find at night.

Car: Cars and Land Rovers are available for rent but it's not advisable to drive. If you are involved in an accident, the driver will be put in jail until the case is sorted out. Avis and Hertz extend their services to include a free driver with every rental.

Hitching: This is non-existent in Nepal. In the event that someone picks you up, you are expected to pay something.

Bicycle: If you can endure the chaos on the roads, rent a one-speed Chinese or Indian-made bicycle. Mountain bikes can be rented in the touristy-areas of Kathmandu.

Rickshaw: These are fun, but the drivers are renowned for trying to rip off tourists. Be firm with your price.

ACCOMMODATION

In Kathmandu you'll find a range of hotels. The international hotel chains are represented here as well as small, cheap guest houses. In the hills and along the trekking routes, you'll find 'bhattis', which are small bamboo houses close to the trail, and inns. Expect to pay at least US$5—7 per night in Kathmandu.

FOOD

Strictly speaking, Nepalese food is bland-tasting. A typical meal may be made up of *dhal bhat tarkar*: lentil soup, rice and vegetables. Other local grub includes *tama*, a dried bamboo-shoot soup; *gurr*, a large potato pancake with cheese and spices; *buff*, water-buffalo; and *tsampa*, grain mixed with tea or milk. A lot of meals are vegetarian. If you stay at trailside inns, you may find *chang*, which is basically Himalaya moonshine, though it is only mildly alcoholic.

Indian food has had an impact here and can be easy to find in the cities. In Kathmandu you can find an assortment of restaurants offering everything from traditional Nepalese fare to Indian or European food.

BUDGETING

Kathmandu and Pokhara will be your most expensive stops in Nepal, unless you have arranged an organized trek with a Western company. If you are staying in the cheapest accommodation and living on local, Nepalese food, expect to spend US$8—10 a day. With a few extras, like taxis and restaurants in Kathmandu, expect about US$12–15 a day. On the trail, your budget will depend on the style of travel. The cheapest way to go is independently on the popular routes, staying in inns along the way. This should run to about US$5–8 a day.

FURTHER INFORMATION

Nepalese Embassy, 12A Kensington Palace Gardens, London W8 4QU (tel. 0171 229 6231/1574).

Background reading: *The Waiting Land* by Dervla Murphy tells of travels in Nepal during a time of transition. Peter Matthiessen's *The Snow Leopard* is a tale of a trek through the Himalayas that brings up serious thoughts about life and spirituality. *White Water Nepal* by Peter Knowles and Dave Allardice is an excellent guide book for rafting and kayaking in Nepal. Both Lonely Planet's *Nepal: Travel Survival Kit* and *Trekking in the Nepal Himalaya* are excellent guides.

Kathmandu

AIRPORT FACILITIES
All international flights land at Tribhuwam Airport, 5 km east of the city centre.

CITY LINKS
Bus: The Blue (Sajha) Bus runs daily 8 a.m.–10 p.m. from the front of the terminal and drops you off on Kantipath. There's another, local bus that drops you off at Ratna Park. This is a fraction of the Blue Bus price, but can be difficult.
Taxi: Usually these charge semi-fixed fares of US$1.20–2.00.

USEFUL ADDRESSES
Tourist office: Ganga Path, Kathmandu (tel. 2 11203).
Immigration office: Tridevi Marg (tel. 418573).
Main post office: Kantipath, Kathmandu.
British Embassy: Lainchaur (tel. 4 11789/14588)
US Embassy: Panipokhari (tel. 4 11179/12718)
Medical assistance: Bir Hospital (tel. 2 21119); Nepal International Clinic (tel. 4 12842).

GETTING ABOUT
Bus: Buses are cheap but very crowded. The bus stations are chaotic. If you are determined, ask the tourist office for advice, but

it will be much easier to get around the city on foot or bicycle.

Taxi: Licensed taxis have black licence plates. Most are metered, but agree on a price anyway. The prices are reasonable, though after 8 p.m. they go up by 50%.

Cycle rickshaws: These can be found almost anywhere. It is important to establish where you are going and set a price before you start. At the end of the trip, most drivers will try to get you to pay more than the agreed price. Be firm.

Bicycle: These can be hired from outlets all over the Thamel and Freak Street areas for about US$0.50 per day. If you want to rent long-term, you can bargain for a cheaper rate.

SIGHTS

DURBAR SQUARE holds the OLD ROYAL PALACE (open Sun.–Thurs. 10.30 a.m.–4.15 p.m., Fri. 10.30 a.m.–2.15 p.m.). This building has been added to over the years and used to be the home of the Nepalese Royal Family until 1956. Only a small part of the palace is open to the public, but be sure to see the BASANTAPUR TOWER. The square is full of free-standing temples and statues that you can spend hours looking at. Don't miss the KASTHAMANDAP (or 'House of Wood'). It is believed to have been constructed in the twelfth century.

North of Durbar Square you'll find INDRACHOWK and KEL TOL, two streets that contain numerous temples. But for amazing views of the city and the surrounding valley, head for SWAYAMBHU, perched on a hill west of Thamel. This temple complex has a 2,000-year-old stupa which is the most important symbol of Buddhism in Nepal. Swayambhu is more than just a tourist site, a visit there is an experience. The NATIONAL MUSEUM (open Sun.–Thurs. 10.30 a.m.–4.30 p.m., Fri. 10.30 a.m.–2.30 p.m.) is just 1 km south of Swayambhu and is worth a visit.

For the city's largest fruit and vegetable market, go to ASAN TOL. Kathmandu's most famous street is FREAK STREET; it's real name is in fact Jochne Street, but it was nicknamed Freak Street in the hippy days of the Sixties and Seventies. Though today its freakiness has faded a bit, it is still one of the main gathering places for travellers in the city.

ACCOMMODATION

The Thamel area is the centre for budget accommodation in Kathmandu. Simply walking around this area and investigating your options should secure you a place to stay. Freak Street (Jhochhen Tol) is somewhat run-down, but has cheap prices. Try to get there by 9 a.m. for the biggest selection. Longer stays can usually warrant a lower price.

A few well-known places are:

Kathmandu Guest House, Thamel (tel. 4 13632). This is the place to stay. Offers many services including currency exchange, luggage storage, phone office, etc. Newer rooms cost US$14/19 for singles/doubles. Older rooms go for US$4–9.

Tukche Peak Guest House, Thamel (tel. 2 15739). Next to the Kathmandu Guest House. Singles/doubles: US$4/8.

Earth House Lodge, Thamel (tel. 4 10050). Clean rooms for US$4–7.

Annapurna Lodge, Freak Street (tel. 4 213684). One of the nicer places in the area. Singles/doubles from US$4/7.

Century Lodge, Freak Street (tel. 4 214341). A bit run-down. Singles/doubles: US$3/6.

ENTERTAINMENT

If you're interested in learning about meditation, yoga or massage, you've come to the right place. The Himalayan Yogic Institute, Baluwatar (tel. 413094) offers a wide range of meditation courses, workshops on massage, and keeps up a library. The Patanjali Yoga Centre, Chhauni (tel. 272321) offers meditation and yoga courses.

If you're looking for bars, Thamel is the only area open late at night. The Pumori Cultural Centre, Jyatha Thamel, puts on a dancing/singing show and offers a Nepalese meal. Most cinemas only show movies in Hindi.

EXCURSIONS

See **Trekking** and **Rafting and Canoeing** p. 382.

THE PHILIPPINES

VITAL STATISTICS

Red tape: A full passport is obligatory, but visas are unnecessary for most nationalities (business travellers and tourists alike) provided the intended stay is less than 21 days and a return or onward ticket can be produced. Visas for longer stays (up to 59 days) are available from Consulates or Embassies of the Philippines at a cost of around £10. You must apply in person if you are a first-time visitor to the country. Employment visas cost around £200.

Customs: Visitors may bring in 400 cigarettes or two tins of tobacco and two bottles of alcohol not exceeding 1 l each, plus a small quantity of perfume and clothing for personal use. Firearms, pornography, and drugs unaccompanied by a medical prescription are prohibited from entry. Currency exceeding US$3,000 must be declared, and the import or export of more than 5,000 Philippine pesos is prohibited.

Health: No immunizations are required, unless you are arriving from an infected area. Do check as your time of departure approaches, however, as requirements change. There is a malaria risk in remote areas below 600 m. Tap water is safe in and around Manila and other cities. Standards of health care are excellent, but be aware that AIDS is becoming a problem in the Philippines and it is advisable to carry an AIDS kit (see p. 98). There are special precautions advised for cholera, malaria, typhoid and polio.

Language: Filipino, based on Tagalog, is the national language, though it has only relatively recently become so, and is not understood by everyone. There are many diverse cultural groups in the Phillipines, each with their own dialects. English is widely spoken, and a small percentage of the population speak Spanish as their mother tongue.

Population: 62 million.

Capital: Manila, population 10 million plus.

Political system: Liberal democracy.

Religion: Predominantly Roman Catholic (80%), with Protestant and Muslim minorities.

Time: Eight hours ahead of GMT.

Money: The currency is the Peso (P), divided into 100 centavos. Coins: 1, 5, 10, 25, and 50 centavos, and P1. Notes: P5, P10, P20, P100, P500 & P1,000. £1 = around P38.

For convenience, carry US dollars either in cash or small-denomination traveller's cheques which you can exchange at banks or licensed moneychangers. Outside Manila, you will probably only be able to change money at hotels. The black market is not worth getting involved in: the rates are not particularly favourable, and fraud is common.

Tax: Hotel prices are subject to a 10% service charge and 13.7% government tax.

Communications: In remote areas of the Philippines telephones may not always be available. Domestic calls often involve bad connections and long waiting times. Overseas calls, however, can be dialled direct from most hotels, though calls to smaller towns overseas will have to go through the operator. You can also send telexes or telegrams abroad.

The postal system is reasonably efficient and airmail letters overseas take around 7–10 days. Take your letters to the post office and watch them get stamped so that the stamps can't be stolen for re-use.

Media: There are numerous English language daily newspapers available in major towns.

Electricity: 220v AC/60 Hz, though 110v is available in most hotels. Plugs may be two or three-pin, round or flat.

Business hours: BANKS: Mon.–Fri. 9 a.m.–4 p.m.

POST OFFICES: Opening times vary, but Mon.–Fri. 9 a.m.–5 p.m. and Sat. 8 a.m.–1 p.m. is roughly standard. They sometimes close for lunch.

SHOPS: Mon.–Sat. 9 a.m.–7 p.m. Large stores and tourist shops may also open on Sundays.

OFFICES: Mon.–Fri. 8 a.m.–5 p.m.; Sat. 9 a.m.–12 p.m.

Holidays: 1 January; Maundy Thursday and Good Friday; 9 April; 1 May; 12 June (Independence Day); 1 and 30 November; 25 and 30 December.

Climate: Tropical. The dry season is from November to June. The rainy season is July to October, when you can expect monsoons. Daytime temperatures average 27°C year-round (though it gets hotter still from March to May), but the evenings (and the winter months – November to February) are cooler. The best time to visit is during the dry season.

DO'S AND DON'TS

Filipinos are friendly, open people who will want to get to know you. Take care not to repay their friendliness and hospitality with stand-offishness or condescension. Asia is too full of Westerners who think they are on a personal mission to tell the locals 'how we do it at home' – don't be one of them.

With their Spanish names and American English, Filipinos (particularly in Manila) may appear very Westernized, and it is sometimes hard to remember that they are Asians, with an Asian way of doing things. For instance, the million questions they ask about you, your family and your home country are not intended as nosiness but as signs of a friendly and genuine interest. There is also the question of 'face': as in other Asian countries, if you lose your temper with someone (or with those millions of questions), you will make them very unhappy, uncomfortable and morose. So keep your temper. The same wish not to lose face will lead people to answer questions with 'yes' even when the answer should be 'no' or 'I don't know'. They don't do it to annoy or mislead, they just don't want you to be disappointed.

You can repay any hospitality that you receive with small gifts and trinkets, such as pens, lighters or souvenirs from home. Anything imported will go down well, particularly if it has a well-known brand name.

Dress is casual most of the time, but you should dress a little more formally in a business setting and modestly when visiting churches or other places of worship – no expanses of flesh, in other words. Women can, generally speaking, get away with shorter skirts than in many other parts of Asia, but if you plan to visit Muslim areas, dress accordingly.

Tipping is not necessary in the Philippines, though hotels will always add a service charge to their bills.

WHERE TO GO FOR WHAT
There are over 7,000 islands in the Philippines. Manila is on LUZON, the main island and the one that most visitors see first. A few hours north-west of Manila is LUCAP and the beautiful beaches of the HUNDRED ISLANDS, where a lot of tourists stop off for a spot of sunbathing or snorkelling before heading further north into the CORDILLERA MOUNTAINS.

In the mountains, you'll find BAGUIO, Luzon's summer capital (the year-round average temperature is 20°C), with its lovely parks and excellent opportunities for souvenir shopping. The main reason for visiting the region, however, are the famous rice terraces of BANAUE, carved out of the mountains by the Ifugao tribe several thousand years ago, and dubbed the 'eighth wonder of the world'. A side trip to SAGADA (lakes, waterfalls, caves) is recommended. Other attractions in the north include the Spanish-style architecture of the towns, golf courses (if that's what amuses you), and yet more beaches and scenery. Allow at least a couple of weeks for touring the area.

The southern part of Luzon is best known for the MAYON VOL-CANO, said to be the most symmetrical volcano cone in the world. It can be climbed, though it's a strenuous expedition to undertake over several days (with the aid of a guide) – not an afternoon stroll in your Reeboks. A little north of Mayon is TIWI, which offers hot springs and some rather interesting ruins.

MINDORO, south of Luzon, is becoming more popular with tourists because of its good beaches, which are quiet (for now) and relaxed. PUERTO GALERA, on the north coast (beaches, coral reefs), is a popular resort. Also lying roughly to the south of Luzon (and less than an hour by air from Manila) is the island of PALAWAN, often called 'the last frontier'. There are beaches here, too, and it's a tranquil, sparsely populated island where jungles and wildlife are the main attractions. There are beautiful lakes and rivers, archaeological sites, and the more adventurous traveller can try caving, diving, trekking and other such activities. Accommodation is thin on the ground, and it is a place most suited to those who are determined to escape the crowds. Take precautions against malaria if visiting the island.

Lying between Luzon and Mindanao to the south are the group of islands known as the VISAYAS. The main centre for ferry services is CEBU, the second city of the Philippines and the best embarkation point for island-hopping. Allow plenty of time if you plan to flit from island to island: ferries are often slow and, from some islands, infrequent. Cebu itself is historically significant (it's the oldest city in the archipelago – Magellan landed here) and it has many (expensive) beach resorts, but you'll find quieter places on the other islands: of the alternatives, BORACAY is the most beautiful. Do not miss BOHOL (only a short distance from Cebu City), with its intriguing Chocolate Hills. ILOILO, in the western Visayas, is worth a look, architecturally speaking, as it contains many examples of Spanish colonial buildings.

The Visayas has one of the main diving areas. BATANGAS, MINDORO and PALAWAN are considered the best spots. For more information, contact the Philippine Commission on Sports Scuba Diving, Dept. of Tourism Building, Tm Kalaw Street, Rizal Park, Manila (tel. 503 735).

Finally there is MINDANAO, the second largest island group. This is where the greatest concentration of Muslims is to be found. There has been an independence movement here (involving armed struggle) for some years and certain areas are reckoned to be unsafe, so you should enquire about potential trouble-spots (which will be country rather than urban areas) before visiting. Some tourist destinations (such as the Sulu Islands) are affected by the troubles.

South-west of the main island is ZAMBOANGA, which the brochures will tell you is 'exotic' – a moot point, but it has a fort and a market, and is the jumping-off point for the SULU ISLANDS. DAVAO on the south coast is a much more interesting destination. It has a Chinatown, a large Buddhist temple and the DABAW MUSEUM of ethnic artefacts. There are also numerous orchid farms in the area. Nearby is MOUNT APO, the highest peak in the country and home of the endangered Philippine eagle. The trek to the top will take you four to six days, and there is an annual 'mass climb' around Easter. Consult the Davao tourist office about treks.

INTERNAL TRAVEL
Air: Philippine Airlines (PAL) (UK office: tel. 0171 499 9496/9536) is the national carrier. Until recently they enjoyed a virtual monopoly, but PAL now face competition from charter companies Aerolift and Pacific Air. Flying is many more times expensive than other forms of transport, but the services are frequent and comprehensive. Airport security is strict. There is a domestic departure tax of P50 and an international departure tax of P500.
Ferry: Fleets of ferries link the various parts of this island nation. However, as several recent and disastrous sinkings bear witness, the quality of service is far from consistent; while some ships are perfectly safe and comfortable, others are perilously overcrowded or downright dangerous. Avoid travelling by sea at Christmastime as tickets sell out and boats are crowded. Tickets cost only a few hundred pesos, but those who wish to island-hop should be warned that it's a slow way to travel.
Rail: There is only one railway line, on Luzon island, operating north and south out of Manila. The route is Legarpi–San Fernando, which runs three times per day, with one overnight service.
Bus: Long-distance bus fares are *very* cheap (a few pounds, usually) and departures are frequent. If they're full, buses sometimes leave earlier than scheduled. There are many competing companies, and prices vary according to such factors as whether the bus is air-conditioned or not, the distance to be travelled and the type of road-surface (gravel or covered). Fares are collected on the bus. Two warnings: the roads are bumpy, and you'll need to keep an eye on your luggage.
Car: Avis, Hertz and a number of local firms in Manila and other cities will rent a car to you, but it doesn't come cheap. You'll need an international driving licence.
Local transport: The most colourful (and the most popular) form of local transport is the brightly painted 'jeepney'. The original jeepneys were left behind by the US army after WWII, but the ones

you will see now are up-to-date models. They are supposed to carry only twelve passengers, but actually take many more. Their routes are fixed, with the main stops written up somewhere (though this may not be any help until you know your way around) and the fare will be only a few pesos. Just yell out when you want to get off. Outside the cities, jeepneys are used for long-distance journeys (most wait until they are full before setting off).

There are regular buses, too. They display only their end destination and, like the jeepneys, will be a little difficult to negotiate at first. Prices are similar to those of jeepneys, and you pay when you get on. Air-conditioned buses cost much more (three or four times as much), but are less crowded.

Taxi: There's no shortage of taxis in the cities, but if you use them, make sure that the meter is switched on and stays on.

ACCOMMODATION

Youth hostels: There are a good number of youth hostels in the Philippines. They cost from P100 per person per night, and you'll find them on the islands and out in the country, as well as in the cities. They don't usually have member's kitchens, but provide meals at a cost of P35 instead. There is also privately owned dorm accommodation in Manila, for about the same price.

Pensions: Cheap rooms (and sometimes dormitories), from around P100–300 for a single room. The price depends on whether the room has a private bathroom and a fan or air-conditioning. A single room often has a double bed in it, so two people can share at no extra cost; double rooms usually have two double beds in them and cost a little more.

Hotels: Medium-priced city hotels cost from P350 upwards (rooms are cheaper at the beach resorts and out in the country). Before you take a room in a cheap hotel, check the fire escapes and fire exits: Filipino hotels have a nasty habit of burning down. At the beach resorts, cheap accommodation will be very basic.

FOOD

The burger, pizza, fried chicken, etc. have made inroads in the Philippines, so you need not pine for home. There are also plenty of Chinese restaurants. Alternatively, the native cuisine is a mixture of Chinese, Malay and European food and is (mostly) not very spicy. A typical Filipino meal consists of rice and a selection of dishes served together. Seafood figures prominently in the diet. Try *adobo*, a typical dish made of chicken, pork and octopus stewed in vinegar, garlic and soy sauce; *sinigang*, sour vegetable soup with meat or fish; or *kare-kare*, a meat-and-vegetable stew in peanut sauce. Though it's a delicacy, you might want to give *balut* a miss: it's a lightly boiled duck egg – with a partially formed duck embryo inside.

As you can see from the above, vegetarians are not particularly well catered for, though there should always be some vegetable dishes on offer (fish-eaters will have no problems). Some restaurants do not have menus, you just choose from the displayed dishes instead.

For drinks, don't miss San Miguel beer, which is widely available. As is Coca-Cola. Try to stick to bottled drinks, and avoid ice cubes in anything – the tap water from which they are made is not safe, except in Manila.

BUDGETING

Inflation has been a problem in the Philippines over the past few years, which means that prices given in this guide should be taken as a rough indication only. However, an almost simultaneous devaluation of the peso means that you get more pesos to your pound or dollar, so it's still a cheap place to visit.

If you stay in hostels or cheap hotels, your accommodation costs won't amount to much more than £8–10 a night (frequently less). At current prices you can get a good restaurant meal for P150 or less, and even the nightlife is not too expensive, with cinemas charging only a few pesos and disco/club/music lounge entrance charges costing between P50 and P100. Drinks are cheap, too, except in hostess bars, where male customers will have to pay about P200 for the girl's drinks as well as their own bar tab.

The other day-to-day expenditure will be bus fares, which are negligible. Adding it all up, and excluding long-distance travel costs, the budget traveller should be able to get by quite comfortably on around £10 a day (or less), and will probably not spend even that much once out of the cities.

FURTHER INFORMATION

Embassy of the Republic of the Philippines, 9a Palace Green, London W8 4QE (tel. 0171 937 1600). Visa applications should be made to the consular office at the above address. There are also consulates in Glasgow, Edinburgh and Liverpool (Wirral).

Philippine Department of Tourism, 17 Albemarle Street, London W1X 4LX (tel. 0171 499 5443). This very helpful office should be able to supply you with all the information you need.

Background reading: Lonely Planet's *Philippines* guide, though not so well laid out as other titles in the series, is excellently informed, particularly on the cultural and personal safety aspects of travelling in the country. The *South-East Asia Handbook* from Moon Publications contains a good section on the Philippines.

Unfortunately, there are not many books that deal with the Philippines. You'll find coffee-table books in Manila, otherwise try *Travels in the Philippines* by Fedor Jagor (if you can find it) before you go.

Manila

AIRPORT FACILITIES
Manila is served by the Ninoy Aquino International Airport (NAIA), 7 km from the centre, and by the Manila Domestic Airport. The NAIA has all the usual services: duty-free shops, restaurants, exchange facilities, left-luggage, etc. There are tourist information counters in the arrivals lobby, and at the hotel desk you can organize rooms in all price ranges. Car rental firms are well represented, and there is a clinic (open 24 hours) on level 2.

Arrivals is on level 2, departures on level 3. Check-in time for international flights is 120 minutes prior to departure (60 minutes for domestic flights), the departure tax is P250 (international) or P10 (domestic). Even if you are simply transferring flights, you will have to pay the relevant tax.

CITY LINKS
Bus: There should be a bus service operating between the airport and the main hotels and guest houses in Manila, though the situation is somewhat changeable. Tickets may be purchased at the Shuttle Bus counter next to the Hotels & Tours Assistance desk. The journey takes 30 minutes.

Alternatively, you can get downtown on one of the yellow public buses that leave from the stop located to the right of the terminal's exit doors. The fare is only a few pesos.

Some of the hotels offer free a transport service for their guests, and it might be worth using the hotels desk to book into one of them for a night, if you can afford it. There is also a shuttle bus service to the Manila Domestic Airport.

Taxi: The only accredited taxi service at the airport is run by G & S Transport Corporation, part of Avis. There is a fixed-fare system to different downtown locations, with prices from US$15. This is expensive, but other (supposedly metered) cabs can also be very dear. The trip downtown should work out at about P50; however, cab drivers often charge many times more than the meter price – or don't use the meter at all, claiming that it's broken. Insist that the meter be switched on before the taxi moves off.

Beware of people posing as tourist officials. They will take you to pirate cabs, where the fare charged is likely to be US$50 rather than P50.

USEFUL ADDRESSES
Main tourist office: Department of Tourism, near the junction of Rizal Park and Taft Avenue in the Ermita district (tel. 599 031/502 928). There are also offices at the airport and in the Nayong Pilipino.
Tour operators: YSTAPHIL, the youth and student travel information service, can help you with travel information. Their office is in the United Condominium, 1656 Taft Avenue (tel. 581 314).
Main post office: The General Post Office is in the Intramuros district, alongside the river. It has a poste restante counter.
US Embassy: 1201 Roxas Boulevard, Ermita, Manila (tel. 521 7116).
British Embassy: 15th & 16th Floors, LV Locsin Building, 6752 Ayal Avenue, corner Makati Avenue, Makati, Manila (tel. 816 7116).
Tourist hotline: 24-hour information tel. 501 728/660.
Emergency services: Call 599–0111 (police – all of whom understand English) and 561–176 (fire brigade).
Medical assistance: You can call ambulances on the following numbers:

Philippine General Hospital	576 061
North General	471 081
Manila Medical Centre	591 661
Makati Medical Centre	855 9111

Shops: National Book Store, 701 Rizal Avenue, Santa Cruz, Manila. There are many other good bookshops around, but the National has the biggest selection.

GETTING ABOUT
Rail: The Light Rail Transit (LRT) runs from north to south Manila, crossing the busiest districts. It's fast, but of limited use for sightseeing.
Bus and jeepney: There doesn't seem to be such a thing as a bus map of Manila, so you'll have learn to recognize the major place names that are displayed on the front and sides of jeepneys and buses. Both are extremely crowded in Manila, but you also have the option of travelling by the picturesquely named Love Buses – more expensive than the opposition, but roomier and

air-conditioned. The Ayala Medical Center Love Bus is useful for travelling between the tourist area of Ermita and Makati, another sightseeing/shopping area.

Taxi: Plentiful and cheap, but the usual warnings about meter use apply. Golden Cabs (if you can find one) are reckoned to be the most honest and reliable.

Car hire: There are many car rental agencies in the city, but due to mad motorists and traffic congestion, driving is not recommended.

Bicycle: Not recommended.

SIGHTS

Without doubt, RIZAL PARK (also known as the LUNETA) is Manila's most obvious tourist attraction. It's huge, and a good place for a stroll and for people-watching. Rizal Park tourist office can give you a walking-tour map. The park has (amongst other things) Chinese and Japanese gardens, a skating rink, a chess plaza, various historical monuments and memorials, free concerts, and lots of people just meeting together.

The other main point of interest is INTRAMUROS, the walled city built by the Spanish in the 16th century, though it was largely destroyed by bombing during World War II. The SAN AGUSTIN CHURCH survived, however, and houses a museum. FORT SANTIAGO — used by the Japanese as a centre for imprisonment and execution during the war — also remains, but MANILA CATHEDRAL was rebuilt after the war. The CASA MANILA is a period house (19th century) which merits a place on your itinerary.

There are a great many excellent museums in Manila. Indeed, too numerous to list here (consult the tourist office), but the AYALA MUSEUM is recommended for its depiction of Philippine history, and the NAYONG PILIPINO (Philippine Village) near the airport houses a good museum of ethnology. The MALACANANG PALACE (former home of President Marcos) is the place to go to see Imelda's shoes. Try to avoid Saturdays, though.

For shopping, there is the Harrison Plaza in Malate, the Makati Commercial Center, and the sprawling, busy main streets of Ermita and Malate. The Pistang Pilipino is a touristy market on Pedro Gil and M H del Pilar streets; other markets are dotted throughout the city. Good buys include woodcarvings and shellcrafts. The department stores aside, a little haggling is expected when shopping.

Lastly, don't miss the CHINESE CEMETERY in the suburbs of Santa Cruz: some of the graves are built like houses, complete with kitchens and air-conditioning. You can take the LRT there.

ACCOMMODATION
Youth hostels: Manila has three hostels:

The CFA Hostel, Old Station Mesa. Caters for groups only.

Youth Hostel Philippines, 1572 Leon Guinto Street (tel. 521 3078).

Manila International Youth Hostel, 4227 Tomas Claudio Street (tel. 832 0680). Comfortable, quiet, and centrally located. It is also the location of the student travel office. YHA members P75.
Hotels and pensions: The tourist office in Manila can help you find a pension (and more expensive rooms), as can the airport tourist office. Be sure to check out the rooms first before taking them though, particularly in the cheaper establishments.

Malate Pension, 1771 Adriatico Street, Malate (tel. 596 671). This is the traveller's hangout, with dorm beds from around P105, rooms from P315–350, a coffee shop and a noticeboard. There will probably be a waiting list to get in, but it's a good place to start an accommodation hunt.

Casa Dalco, 1910 Mabini Street, Malate (tel. 508 855). There is another Casa Dalco a little further out, at 1318 F. Agoncillo Street (tel. 598 522). Both are lovely houses, clean and quiet, with rooms from P250–550. The more central one of Mabini Street fills up quickly, though.

Lucky Pension: 1726 Adriatico Street, Malate. Small, clean rooms for under P250.

FOOD
Manila's restaurants rival Hong Kong's in terms of variety. Whatever you're looking for (Filipino, Chinese, Indonesian, Mexican, Japanese, Swiss . . .), you'll find it in Manila. Adriatico Street, in the Malate district, Makati Avenue, Del Pilar Street and Mabini Street are probably the best hunting grounds, as they offer the greatest diversity. For reasonably priced Filipino food, try the Barrio Fiesta chain: there's one at 110 Bocobo Street, Ermita, and another on Makati Avenue. Alternatively, there's the Aristocrat, located at the junction of Roxas Boulevard and San Andres Street, open 24 hours.

Fast-food junkies will find a Kentucky Fried Chicken and a Pizza Hut in Harrison Plaza, Malate, and Shakey's outlets on Mabini Street and Makati Avenue. There's also a Mr Donut (good for cheap breakfasts) on Mabini Street. Don't miss Rosie's Diner at 1427 Del Pilar Street for cheap burgers etc. and a slice of American 1950s snack-bar nostalgia.

ENTERTAINMENT

Performances of Filipino theatre, dance and music do take place, but not regularly. Check the local papers or with the tourist office for upcoming shows. The main centre for these activities is the Cultural Centre of the Philippines on Roxas Boulevard. There is also a popular musical and dance revue held every evening at Pistang Pilipino at the junction of Del Pilar Street and Pedro Gil Street. There'll usually be more than one show, so check times in advance (the earlier show(s) are usually free of charge). Many of the big hotels and restaurants put on dinner shows which can cost anything up to P400. Try the Zamboanga restaurant in Adriatico Street or the Philippine Plaza Hotel (highly recommended). For music lovers, there is also a free concert in Rizal Park every Sunday. There are many cinemas in the city – check the papers for programme listings.

Manila also has an active bar and nightclub scene: all of the big hotels have them, and Makati Avenue is lined with discos and live/video music bars. Try the Billboard, the Metro, or the Stargazer in the Silahis Hotel, Roxas Boulevard, for dancing. There should be good music at the Café Adriatico in Adriatico Street, and at the Hard Rock Café in the same street. Filipino musicians really are excellent, so take advantage of the chance to listen to a live band whenever you can. Most entertainment spots will have a cover/entrance charge, so check first – but it's unlikely to amount to more than P100.

Manila's nightlife is not without its notorious side. Ermita, the tourist district, doubles as the red-light district, with M H del Pilar Street and Mabini Street being the main hotspots. Some of the bars are perfectly innocuous, others not. The Kangaroo Club, 1430 Mabini Street, might prove to be a quiet(ish) port in a storm, and the Boomerang Club and Birdwatcher's Bar in the same street are ordinary pubs, as are the Lili Marleen, the Weinstube, and Edelweiss on M H del Pilar Street.

Naturally, most of the people wandering the street at night are Western males, but there are some sightseers, too. Men intending to get involved in the 'hostess' scene should be aware that AIDS is a growing problem in Manila.

EXCURSIONS

A popular day-trip from Manila is to the island of CORREGIDOR – the 'uninvadable' Corregidor, which was overrun by the Japanese during World War II. It is now a war memorial, where visitors can wander round a museum or the deserted bunkers and look at rusting hulks. There are organized tours from Manila (which are rather expensive) or you could do it under your own steam by getting to Mariveles and chartering a boat from there. This takes longer but is cheaper. Should you wish to stay overnight, there is a rest-house on the island but it's very basic.

Another good excursion is to the town of TAGAYTAY, which offers prime views of LAKE TAAL and its active volcano (a second lake is situated inside the volcano's crater). You can hire a boat to take you out to the volcano (but fix a price first to avoid being ripped off) and it is possible to climb it, though you should obtain permission first. *En route* to the lake, a lot of people stop off at LAS PINAS to look at the bamboo organ in the San José church, and at the jeepney factory.

If shooting the rapids takes your fancy, then PAGSANJAN is the place. The river trip up (and back down) the gorge is what most tourists come for (waterfalls, flowers, wildlife), though there are also good swimming and a number of marvellous photo opportunities, not to mention the mild fame that Pagsanjan enjoys as a result of standing in for Vietnam in many a war movie. The boat trips *should* cost a couple of hundred pesos, but rip-offs are many, with huge tips often being demanded by the boat operators. The town has several guest houses and a youth hostel, and an overnight stay will permit an early start to avoid the crowds which gather from late morning onwards. Weekends are impossible.

For walking and hiking, the area around SAN PABLO is relaxed and pretty, with springs, waterfalls, lakes and a volcano that can be climbed. San Pablo lies a couple of hours from Manila; the nearest youth hostel is at Sampaloc Lake.

If you are interested in organized tours, try the Philippine Travel Agencies Association, S-326 Secretariat Building PICC, CCP Complex, Roxas Boulevard. There are a number of special-interest tour programmes on offer (scuba diving, golf, film-making, educational tours, etc.) that visitors may like to enquire about, and they should be able to put you in touch with the relevant operators.

SINGAPORE

VITAL STATISTICS
Red tape: All visitors require a full passport. EC, US, Canadian and Australian nationals do not need a visa; a stay of at least 14 days will be granted on arrival and this is extendable upon application to the immigration authorities in Singapore. You may be asked to show return or onward tickets plus sufficient funds for your stay.

As in Malaysia, men with long hair or of a scruffy appearance will be given a hard time at entry points. Foreign nationals may not work without an employment pass.

Customs: There are no duty-free allowances when entering from Malaysia, and cigarettes can no longer be brought in duty-free from anywhere. These exclusions aside, visitors' allowances are: 1 l port or wine, 1 l of spirits and a limited amount of excise goods for personal use. Pornography (that includes *Playboy*) will be confiscated.

As in Malaysia, the death sentence is mandatory for drug-smuggling. This will be the punishment for the trafficking of heroin or morphine, and probably for other drugs as well – it *is* enforced. If found guilty of possession or using drugs, all you will see of Singapore is the inside of a jail cell.

Health: No immunizations are required except for yellow fever, if arriving from or having recently passed through an infected country. Malaria is not a danger here, and a cholera vaccination is unnecessary. However, precautions against typhoid and hepatitis A are recommended. Tap water is safe to drink. Medical care in Singapore is of a high standard. Health insurance is recommended.

Language: Singapore has four languages: Chinese (Mandarin), English, Tamil and Malay. English is taught in schools and is the language of business and administration; most Singaporeans speak it well.

Population: 2.7 million.

Political system: Parliamentary democracy. The head of state is the president, elected by parliament every four years. From 1959 until 1990, the Prime Minister was Lee Kuan Yew (known as 'Harry' Lee or 'PM'), under whose strict rule Singapore prospered economically, became spotlessly clean and achieved an amazingly low crime rate. Though no longer Prime Minister, Lee's influence lives on. Voting is compulsory in Singapore.

Religion: Buddhism, Taoism, Islam, Hinduism and Christianity are the main religions, but there are many others besides. Freedom of worship is constitutionally guaranteed.

Time: Eight hours ahead of GMT.

Money: The currency is the Singapore dollar (S$), divided into 100 cents. Coins: 5, 10, 20 and 50 cents, and S$1. Notes: S$1, S$5, S$10, S$50, S$100, S$500, S$1,000 and S$10,000. The currency of Brunei is completely interchangeable with that of Singapore. £1 = S$2.16.

You can change money and traveller's cheques at banks or at moneychangers (the latter may offer better rates). Traveller's cheques are accepted for payment in hotels, department stores and some smaller shops, and get a better exchange rate than cash. Credit card use is widespread. There is no restriction on the import or export of any currency.

Communications: There are public telephones everywhere, phonecards are widely used, and credit-card calls are also possible. Local calls cost 10 cents (time limit: 3 minutes) from payphones, but are free from private phones (which includes most hotel room phones). A full international direct-dialling service is available. It is cheapest to phone abroad from the GPO or the telephone company (Telecom) customer centre at Exeter Road.

The postal service is efficient and offers express as well as regular services for both local and international mail. Overseas mail takes about one week.

Media: Local English-language newspapers are the *Straits Times* and the *Business Times*.

Electricity: 220–240v AC/50 Hz. Many hotels have 110v outlets. Plugs are square 3-pin.

Business hours: BANKS: Mon.–Fri. 10 a.m.–3 p.m.; Sat. 9.30 a.m.–1 p.m.

POST OFFICES: Mon.–Fri. 9 a.m.–5 p.m. (until 9 p.m. on Wednesdays).

SHOPS: Mon.–Sat. 10 a.m.–9 p.m. Most department stores stay open much later, and many are also open on Sundays.

OFFICES: Mon.–Fri. 8.30 a.m.–4.30 p.m. (5 p.m. for non-government offices). Some people work on Saturday mornings.

Holidays: 1 January; February (Chinese New Year – three days); Good Friday; 1 May, plus one other day; June/July (one day); 9 August; October/November (one day); 25 December.

'Floating' holidays are: Hari Raya Puasa (one day in April/May) and Hari Raya Haji (one day in July/Aug).

Climate: The year-round average is 28°C, and the temperature rarely drops below 25°C. Being so close to the equator, Singapore is also humid, and it rains frequently. The monsoon period is between November and January. Bring warm clothes to wear *indoors* – the air-conditioning is vicious!

DO'S AND DON'TS

The largest racial group in multi-ethnic Singapore is the Chinese (the two other main groups are Indians – mostly Tamils – and Malaysians).

Fines for 'anti-social behaviour' can run to hundreds of dollars (S$1,000 for littering, for example), and punishable offences include jaywalking; eating, drinking or smoking on the underground; failing to flush toilets; and violating parking restrictions (if you can work out what they are in the first place). For certain offences, a hefty fine could be the least of your problems: an American teenager was recently flogged for vandalizing cars. Smoking is prohibited in all air-conditioned public places, and men with long hair are still frowned upon.

Tipping is not a Singaporean custom, and it is actually prohibited in hotels which levy a service charge. As in the rest of Asia, dress modestly when visiting temples.

WHERE TO GO FOR WHAT
As Singapore is so small, all of its major attractions are covered in the **Sights** and **Excursions** sections, pp. 407, 411.

INTERNAL TRAVEL
See **Getting About**, p. 406.

ACCOMMODATION
There is no official youth hostel in Singapore, but there are a fair number of private hostels with prices from S$10 per night. Cheap rooms cost from around S$15/20 to S$30/40; from there, it's a jump in price to about S$80−100 and upwards. Singapore also has a YMCA and a YWCA with accommodation in private rooms. The cheapest eating is at the 'hawker centres', where you can put together an excellent meal from the various food stalls for less than S$5 (buying and preparing your own food won't work out much cheaper).

BUDGETING
Singapore is not one of the cheaper Asian countries, but the wide range of accommodation and food options means that you really can spend as much or as little as you like. A sensible daily minimum to budget for would be about £15; allow a little more if you plan to stay in cheaper hotels rather than dorms, and a lot more if you go wild in the electronics stores!

Transport is cheap, so getting around isn't going to cost you more than a few Singapore dollars per day. A night on the town will be expensive, though, with beer in most bars costing S$8 or more, and most discos having a cover charge (averaging S$20). Those bars and discos without a cover charge have more expensive drinks to compensate.

There are job opportunities in Singapore, but not of the on-the-road variety. Most jobs have to be fixed up before leaving home, and you'll need either to have excellent qualifications or to be transferred out by a company with a base in Singapore. The usual standby of teaching English doesn't apply here, as English is a kind of lingua franca of the various ethnic groups, and most Singaporeans speak it well.

FURTHER INFORMATION

Singapore Tourist Promotion Board, 1st Floor, Carrington House, 126–30 Regent Street, London W1R 5FE (tel. 0171 437 0033).
Background reading: Lonely Planet's *Malaysia, Singapore & Brunei* is good, or there is their *Singapore City Guide*, for those who plan on visiting only Singapore. The *Insight* guide to Singapore is also useful, and *Introduction to Singapore* by Irene Hoe (Odyssey Guides), though not so helpful to the budget traveller, contains some fascinating excerpts from books about Singapore, and essays on life in the country; excellent pre-trip reading.

There isn't much on the travel literature front (most travel writers consider modern-day Singapore too boring). Look out for books by Alex Josey, once Lee Kuan Yew's press secretary, on politics and history. Two books on the founding of Singapore are: Maurice Collins' *Raffles* and Raymond Flowers' *Raffles: The Story of Singapore*. For fiction (based on fact), try *King Rat* by James Clavell, a story of internment during World War II, and the *Singapore Grip* by J. G. Farrell, a truly hilarious off-the-wall tale of colonial life just prior to the Japanese invasion. Look around the bookshops in Singapore for other good books.

Singapore City

AIRPORT FACILITIES

Changi International Airport, 20 km from downtown Singapore, rates as one of the best – if not *the* best – in the world. It has two terminals, but at present most arrivals and departures operate out of Terminal 1, which has wall-to-wall restaurants and snack bars, the usual duty-free shops, left-luggage facilities, car-hire desks, post offices and banks. The foreign exchange counters are open virtually all of the time, and there are information desks in the arrival and departure halls, plus a free hotel reservation service that stays open until 11.30 p.m. There are also two medical centres and, in the transit/departure hall, a play area, a hairdressing salon, a theatre with an audio-visual show about Singapore, along with a number of day rooms which you can rent if you need a shower or a snooze. Terminal 2 has all of the above, plus a business centre and a gym. Most of the facilities are open until 11 p.m., some 24 hours.

Terminals 1 and 2 are connected by monorail. Check-in time is two hours prior to departure (international flights) and 45 minutes prior to departure (domestic flights). Departure tax is S$15.

CITY LINKS

Bus: Public buses run from the basement of the airport into the city. The most convenient is the number 390 bus which will take you to the Orchard Road area, where most budget accommodation is to be found. The journey takes less than an hour and costs from S$1.50. The bus runs until midnight.

Taxi: Taxis are plentiful, and are metered, there are various surcharges (for baggage, etc.) including a S$3 charge that applies to taxis leaving the airport (but not going *to* it). The fare downtown should work out at around S$20, all told.

USEFUL ADDRESSES

Tourist office: Raffles Hotel Arcade, Nos.2–34, 328 North Bridge Road (tel. 1 800 334 1335/6 – freephone). Open Mon.–Fri. 8.30 a.m.–5 p.m.; Sat. 8.30 a.m.–1 p.m.

Immigration department: South Bridge Centre, 95 South Bridge Road (tel. 532–2877). This is where you should go for visa extensions.

Main post office: Fullerton Street. The GPO has an excellent poste restante service.

British High Commission: Tanglin Road (tel. 474–9333).

US Embassy: 30 Hill Street (tel. 338–0251).

Emergency services: Dial 999 for police, 995 for fire/ambulance.

Medical assistance: Singapore General Hospital is on Outram Road (tel. 222–3322).

GETTING ABOUT

MRT: The MRT (Mass Rapid Transit) train system is cheap and easy to use, though it is geared towards commuters rather than tourists. The city stations are underground, the suburban ones above ground, and some of the stations have been decorated with works by commissioned artists. Fares start at S$0.60; tickets are bought at coin-operated machines and inserted into automatic turnstiles. There's an S$10 'stored-value' ticket which you can buy from the manned ticket offices, which avoids the necessity of queuing at machines. There is a S$2 fine for under-paying.

Bus: The bus system is very good and easy to use. Be sure to pick up the pocket guide produced by the bus company (available from newsstands or bookstores) or information from the tourist office on the city's sights and relevant bus routes. Fares start at S$0.50 and don't go much higher than a dollar. You'll need exact change, which you drop into the box by the driver. Alternatively, you can buy an Explorer ticket, which gives unlimited travel for one day (S$7) or three days (S$15). These can be purchased at major hotels and SBS Travelcentres. There is also a 'Farecard' which can be used on both buses and trains; these cost S$12 or S$22 (a fare for each trip is deducted from the total amount on the card) and can be bought from MRT stations. A free bus map comes with the passes.

Taxi: There are a number of taxi firms operating in Singapore. All cabs have meters, service is usually good and the fares are reasonable. Rates start at S$2.20, but there are a number of confusing surcharges: the after-midnight charge, the airport departure charge, charges for entering or leaving the Central Business District at certain times, the baggage (if placed in the boot) charge and the telephone and advance booking charges. None of the above amounts to more than a few dollars, but if you incur several of them at once, it can make your taxi ride somewhat more expensive than expected! At least you don't have to tip the driver.

Trishaw: There are still some bicycle trishaws around, mostly in Chinatown and around some tourist spots. You'll have to agree the fare beforehand. The best place to get this is in the square in front of the National Museum.

Car hire: Driving is not recommended in the centre, mainly because of the traffic congestion and complicated coupon-parking systems in the Central Business District. If you want to hire a car for longer excursions, though, all the major car hire firms are represented in the city. Driving is on the left, and you'll need an international driving licence.

Bicycle: You can hire bicycles at a few places, but they are not a good idea for transporting yourself around the sights, again because of the traffic. You'd be better sticking to the buses.

Ferry: There are ferries to the nearby islands of Sentosa, Kusu and St John's. These leave from the World Trade Centre on weekdays at 10 a.m. or 1.30 p.m. There are extra sailings on Sundays.

SIGHTS

Although Singapore is predominantly a modern city of concrete and glass, you'll find evidence of its colonial past and ethnic diversity in certain areas and buildings. Join the coachloads of tourists drinking bucketloads of Singapore Sling cocktails at the RAFFLES HOTEL; or opt out of that and, for a real taste of the long-gone days of the British Empire, take afternoon tea in the garden instead.

Not far away is the PADANG, a cherished green space in front of the City Hall, where cricket was – and still is – played at weekends during the season (Mar.–Sept.). The clubhouses remain: the Singapore Cricket Club (for the Europeans) at one end of the green and the Singapore Recreation club (for Eurasians) at the other. Another survivor of those days is the waterfront GPO building: worth a second look when you go to pick up your mail. You'll see other colonial leftovers in the city centre.

Two areas ideal for a leisurely stroll are CHINATOWN and LITTLE INDIA. Many of the former's original buildings have been torn down, but others were saved and some of these have been restored. You'll find traditional Chinese businesses in operation (fortune-tellers, mask-makers, herbalists, etc.), some good food and souvenirs, and a number of temples, including the mid-18th-century THIAN HOCK KENG TEMPLE, which was used by the sailors who cruised in and out of Singapore. Little India is smaller than Chinatown, but no less evocative. There is some excellent eating to be done, a lot of atmosphere to soak up, and the Buddhist TEMPLE OF 1,000 LIGHTS to visit (the thousand lights sit at the foot of one of the Buddha statues).

Finally, if you are interested in the unique Peranakan culture (i.e. that of the Malay-speaking, Straits-born Chinese), don't miss PERANAKAN PLACE. More of a museum than an ethnic neighbourhood, it is a collection of old houses which have been converted into a kind of folk museum. It's a bit touristy, but fascinating nevertheless, and the entrance charge is only a few dollars. Other museums worth visiting include the NATIONAL MUSEUM AND ART GALLERY, for which we must thank the ubiquitous Stamford Raffles, founder of Singapore. It displays Asian (particularly Chinese, Indian and Mongolian) artefacts and craftwork, contemporary Asian art, a jade collection, and some Raffles memorabilia. The EMPRESS PLACE MUSEUM is dedicated to Chinese culture and history, while the SINGAPORE SCIENCE CENTRE is a hands-on, button-pushing, fun type of place, with a planetarium as just one of its attractions. CHANGI MURALS, painted by sick POWs are worth visiting at St Luke's Chapel, 151 Martlesham Road, Changi Camp.

If the great outdoors appeals, Singapore is full of parks and gardens. Give the Tiger Balm Gardens a miss (stiffish entrance charge, and not particularly worth it) and head a little way out of town to BUKIT TIMAH, a nature reserve where you can hike in the rainforest and do some wildlife spotting. It's about a half-hour from the centre, and there is a bus – but avoid it at weekends.

The JURONG BIRD PARK, also out of town, is another place not to be missed. It has just under 4,000 birds – many of them flying free – and a large walk-in aviary. Nearer the centre of town are the BOTANIC GARDENS (admission is free) and the adjoining CHINESE and JAPANESE GARDENS. For details of the other green areas and parks in Singapore, including a good zoo (offering a night safari), crocodile parks, and orchid gardens, ask at the tourist office.

If you are a shopaholic, Singapore has been described as one big shopping mall – and it's true. You can't walk far along Orchid Road without tripping over a mall or a department store, and there are many shops in other locations. Try Chinatown or Little India for more interesting shopping. CHANGE ALLEY in the Central Business District, the bargaining and haggling centre, has (somehow) escaped total modernization. Outside the department stores, haggling is expected. Make sure to get *international* guarantees on any electronic goods that you buy.

ACCOMMODATION
Hostels: Singapore has no official youth hostels. It does have a number of YM and YWCAs, though they are priced like mid-range hotels.

Metropolitan YMCA, 60 Stevens Road (tel. 737 7755). Takes men, women and couples. S$55–130.

YWCA, International House, 1 Orchard Street (tel. 337 3444). Singles/doubles S$60/S$70. Dorms S$20.

Hotels: Bencoolen Street, and the streets around it, are the traditional site of cheap accommodation. It's within walking distance of the city centre and Orchard Road, and if you just head there and wander around, you're sure to find somewhere to stay. There are a lot of dormitories and cheap guest houses where the rooms are small but clean. The following places offer dorm beds at S$10 or less, and rooms for around S$20/30.

Hong Guan Building, 173 Bencoolen Street. (There is no sign on the building, so you'll have to ask directions.) There are a number of guesthouses at this address, including:

Goh's Homestay, 6th floor (tel. 339 6561). Some travellers have been able to work here in exchange for room/board. They offer rooms, dorms, an eating area and a good atmosphere.

Why Not Homestay, 127 Bencoolen Street (tel. 338 0612). Next to the Sahib Restaurant.

Airmaster Travel Centre, 36B Prinsep Street (tel. 338 3942), just off Bencoolen Street. Offers dorm beds or rooms. Good reputation.

Traveller's Club, 41 Bencoolen Street (tel. 339 7848). Very cramped and crowded, but a good place to meet other travellers. Beds in large dorms or six-bed rooms.

Sandy's Place, Goodwill Mansion, 355 Balestier Road (tel. 252 6711). Rooms or dorms. Clean and friendly.

Nature Traveller House, Pulau Ubin (an island off the NE coast). Take the ferry from Changi Village. Located near the police station on the island. This is an off-beat, quiet hotel offering dorms, singles and doubles.

FOOD

Singapore is your chance to put on some of the weight you lost in other, less well-fed parts of Asia. It's a glutton's paradise, with a large variety of national cuisines to choose from. There are prices to suit every budget and an eating-place in evidence every time you turn around.

The cheapest places to eat (only a few S$) are the hawker centres which, in concept, are a bit like the food plazas in North American malls in that you can buy food from any stall and sit at any of the tables that are set out. The stalls are open at lunchtime and in the evenings, and you'll find Indian, Chinese and Indonesian food – and even fish and chips. Though it's cheap, the food is perfectly safe to eat, as the centres have to be licensed and to comply with strict health regulations in order to operate. You'll find them everywhere, but the following are popular:

Newton Circus on Scotts Road, near the Newton MRT station. Known for its good seafood and trendy atmosphere.

The Cuppage Centre on Cuppage Road (off the southern end of Orchard Road). Also has a produce market.

The Satay Club (only open at night). Open-air food centre just off Stamford Road, near Raffles City – it's *the* place for satay, as the name suggests. Be sure to tell them how many 'sticks' you want.

As for restaurants, there are several leaflets available from the tourist office that can point you in the direction of good food, from hawker centres right up to the most expensive restaurants. Some inexpensive restaurants (expect to pay a few dollars more than in the hawker centres) that you might like to try are:

Fatty's, Albert Complex on Albert Street (tel. 338–1087). They serve cheap Cantonese food, and a visit here while in Singapore is practically obligatory.

Banana Leaf Apolo, 56 Race Course Road (tel. 293–8682). Famous
for its spicy fish head curry. It's in the area known as Little India
(around Serangoon Road), and there are many other Indian restaurants in the locality, some of them vegetarian.

Kwan Yim, Located in the South-east Asia Hotel on Waterloo Street
(tel. 338–2394). Serves Chinese vegetarian dishes.

You'll find Malay restaurants in the Central Business District and
on Orchard Road. And with Shakey's Pizza, McDonald's, Dunkin'
Donuts, etc. anywhere you care to look, Western fast food is well
represented.

ENTERTAINMENT

The best cultural shows take place during the festivals: check with
the Singapore Tourist board for dates. At other times, a few of the
hotels have cultural nights, which consist of Chinese, Indian or
Malaysian music and dance shows, and optional dinner. The Mandarin Hotel and the Hyatt Regency are the two with established
shows, but others offer similar entertainment: check with the tourist office for exact days and times. Costs will be about S$20 for the
show alone, S$40/50 with dinner.

Cinemas are inexpensive (about S$3.50 or S$4) and the ones
around Orchard Road are where you'll find English-language
movies. Check the *Straits Times* for listings.

There are any number of bars, karaoke bars and discos in Singapore and, again, the Orchard Road area is the best hunting ground.
Check before you go into any bar whether or not there is a cover
charge, how much the drinks are, and that you're not going into
a hostess establishment, where there will be a charge for the conversation.

For live music with your drinks, try the very expensive Top Ten
in Orchard Towers, 400 Orchard Road, or the ever-popular Saxo-
phone Bar on Cuppage Terrace (no cover charge). There are many
other bars in Orchard Towers, and there is a Hard Rock Café at
Orchard Place. A popular disco is The Warehouse at 332 Havelock
Road, next to the River View Hotel, or The Library in the Mandarin
Hotel, Orchard Road.

In all nightspots (including bars), the dress code is 'smart casual'.
In many places, jeans are *not* acceptable.

EXCURSIONS

Singapore is small, so there aren't too many short excursions to be
made. A few islands nearby are popular with day-trippers, foremost
of these being SENTOSA. Once a military base, it is now a large

fun park, with beaches, sports facilities, a butterfly park and other attractions. Weekends should definitely be avoided. Cycling around the island is fun, and you can camp there overnight in pre-erected tents. Two slightly quieter islands are ST JOHN'S ISLAND and PALAU KUSU. They are better for uncrowded swimming (except at weekends), and the latter has a Chinese temple and a hermit's shrine to visit.

For those interested in wartime history, it's only a short trip to CHANGI VILLAGE on the east coast. It's a quiet place, with some reasonable swimming, good restaurants, and ferry connections to a couple of islands. A trip to Changi can be combined with a visit to the CHANGI PRISON MUSEUM, where Allied prisoners were interned during the war and subjected to horrendous treatment. Murals painted by sick POWs can be seen at St Luke's Chapel, 151 Martlesham Road, Changi Camp.

Singapore also has ferry links with Indonesia and Malaysia (and a train to the latter), both of which are very close.

THAILAND

VITAL STATISTICS
Red tape: All visitors need a full passport and a visa. Travellers staying 30 days or less and with a confirmed return or onward flight will be granted a transit visa on arrival. Travellers from New Zealand are granted a 90-day transit visa. No extensions are possible with these visas. Alternatively, you can apply to a Thai Embassy or Consulate outside Thailand for a transit visa, a 60-day tourist visa or a 90-day non-immigrant visa (the latter includes business visits). Extensions to these visas are available from immigration offices in Bangkok, Pattaya, Hat Yai or Chiang Mai. A fine is levied for every day that you overstay your visa.
Customs: 200 cigarettes or 250 g tobacco, plus 1 l each of wines and spirits are allowed duty-free. You need a licence to export antiques, and there are restrictions on the export of Buddha images.
Health: No immunizations are required, except for yellow fever for travellers arriving from an infected area. Malaria is a serious risk in hilly, forested and rural areas, and precautions against typhoid, polio, cholera and hepatitis A would also be sensible. Be aware that, because of the country's sex industry, the incidence of AIDS is now reaching crisis proportions. It is not safe to drink tap water (avoid ice in drinks, too): carry water-purifying tablets or drink bottled water. Medical facilities in Bangkok and other large

cities and towns are good. Health insurance is recommended.

Language: The national language is Thai, which is tonal. English is widely spoken in Bangkok, but don't expect to find any English speakers outside the main tourist centres.

Population: 58 million.

Capital: Bangkok, population around 5.8 million.

Political system: There is a House of Representatives, elected by the people, and a Senate which is nominated by the King on the advice of the Prime Minister. The monarch's role is constitutional.

Religion: Buddhism, with Muslim and Christian minorities.

Time: Seven hours ahead of GMT.

Money: The currency is the Baht (B), divided into 100 stang. Coins: 10, 25 and 50 stang, B1, B2 and B5. Notes: B10, B20, B50, B100 and B500. £1 = B36.

Cash and traveller's cheques can be changed at most banks, moneychangers or in hotels. Ask for small-denomination notes when changing money. Credit cards will be accepted in large stores, hotels and restaurants. You cannot take more than B50,000 out of the country.

Communications: Overseas calls can be dialled direct from telephones in Bangkok. Elsewhere, you will have to go through the operator (dial 100). There are many public telephones available: use the red ones for local calls, blue for long-distance. Telex, and telegram facilities are also available at any telegraph office, and there are some fax services in Bangkok.

The postal service is efficient and generally reliable, particularly poste restante services. Airmail letters to Europe take about one week.

Media: The home-grown English language newspapers are the *Bangkok Post*, the *Nation* and the *Bangkok World*. They and the imported newspapers are available in Bangkok and other main centres.

Electricity: 220v AC/50 Hz.

Business hours: BANKS: Mon.–Fri. 8.30 a.m.–3.30 p.m.

POST OFFICES: Generally, Mon.–Fri. 8 a.m.–6 p.m.; Sat. 9.30 a.m.–3 p.m.

SHOPS: Mon.–Sat. 10 a.m.–8 p.m.

OFFICES: Mon.–Fri. 8.30 a.m. – 4.30 p.m.

Holidays: 1 January; February (one day); 6 and 13 April; 5 May, plus one other day; July (two days); 12 August; 23 October; 5, 10 and 31 December.

Climate: The climate is tropical, with average daytime

temperatures in the upper 20s. It is humid all year round, but conditions are generally hottest from March to May, and cooler than average from November to February. During the rainy season, June to October, flooding may occur.

DO'S AND DON'TS

The Thai people have long had a reputation for friendliness towards strangers. However, it has been noted by some visitors that the welcome is less warm these days, particularly in Bangkok and the 'Golden Triangle' region. No doubt this has more than a little to do with a combination of the sex tourists, the recent influx of lager louts on package deals, and all the usual problems that mass tourism generates. Fortunately, the Thais are taking positive action, and have embarked on a campaign of education. At the airport, you may be handed a leaflet explaining the customs of the country and asking you to observe them. Read it.

One very important point is *never* to show disrespect towards the Royal Family. Don't make jokes about them, because they won't be taken as such. If you ever hear the national anthem played, do as the Thais do and stand still until it comes to an end. Respect should also be shown towards the Buddhist religion, and to images of Buddha.

The common form of greeting is the *wai*: a nod of the head with the hands placed together, as if praying. Some people, keen to welcome you in Western style, will shake hands, but leave it up to them to decide. Thais don't *wai* to their social inferiors, such as children.

It would be a major *faux pas* to touch anyone on the head, even a child, as the head is considered sacred. Avoid using your feet to point at things or people, as the feet are thought to be base.

When visiting temples (and private homes), shoes are removed. Shorts, sleeveless T-shirts and flip-flops are totally unacceptable dress if you plan to enter a temple or holy site. In fact, shorts are not a good idea for either men or women, except at beach resorts. Men should not walk around shirtless either. Western women have imported the custom of topless sunbathing to the beach resorts and hotel pools, but to do this is to offend the Thai sense of modesty. That they put up with it at all is only because they are generally very tolerant of other people's ways.

Thais are, in fact, very easy-going people. Their flexible ideas where time is concerned may infuriate, but don't ever lose your temper about that or anything else – impatience and personal criticism of any kind cause loss of face and will therefore only make things worse.

Tipping is becoming more common, particularly in hotels and restaurants. Taxi drivers do not expect to be tipped, though.

WHERE TO GO FOR WHAT

There is no single 'must-see' in Thailand. People come for the beaches, the trekking, the people, or just because it's a cheap country to travel in. Everyone agrees that BANGKOK is a sprawling, noisy mess, but most visitors end up there sooner or later. You'll either love it or hate it: allow yourself a week there and find out which category you fall into. Avoid it during the rainy season though; the city is invariably flooded.

In the north of the country is CHIANG MAI. Long used as a base by trekkers, there are also a number of impressive temples, some waterfalls and an elephant camp in the vicinity. Treks can last from a few days to a week but, unfortunately for keen walkers, the trekking scene has been ruined by tourism: there are now too many trekkers on most routes, and the countryside is suffering the consequences. There are still some quiet trails left – hire an expert guide to help you find them.

Further north still is CHIANG RAI, another trekking centre. It's located in the area known as the 'Golden Triangle', where Burma, Laos and Thailand meet and where people grow opium. The drug trade brings its own problems, and you should never trek alone in this area because of the possibility of attacks. That said, because the area is more remote the trekking is better. As in Chiang Mai, hire a good guide.

Northern places of interest for the less hardy include the ruins of SUKHOTHAI, first capital of Thailand and a centre of Buddhist civilization; the town of LAMPANG, known for its temples and festivals; and LAMPHUN, whose centrepiece is the ancient WAT PHRA-THAT HARIPUNCHAI, which was built partly in Burmese style.

If you are interested in architecture (and in getting well away from tourists), consider visiting the north-east of the country, known as the ISAN REGION. It borders Cambodia and Laos, and a number of places have Cambodian-style buildings. There is an ancient Khmer site at PHRASAT PHANOM KUNG and, on the Mekong river, the towns of NONGKKHAI and CHIANG KHAN contain a number of stunning and unique Buddhist temples. Also in the region is the PHU KRADUNG NATIONAL PARK, a flat-topped mountain that provides a habitat for elephants, tigers and deer and a variety of plantlife. The pace of travel in Isan is slow, so allow quite a bit of time for a visit.

For more conventional pursuits, the main beaches lie along the eastern seaboard and in the south. PATTAYA and KOH SAMET are very popular and best avoided, though the latter is not too crowded outside the peak season (December to January). The small island of KOH SI CHANG is not so heavily populated, with some good swimming and snorkelling. Further south is KOH SAMUI, another popular resort island which still manages to have some quiet beaches. PHANGAN ISLAND, nearby, is less developed; Surat Thani (on the mainland) is the jumping-off point for Phangan and the other smaller islands near Koh Samui. PHUKET, on the west coast, is one holiday island that should definitely be given a miss.

INTERNAL TRAVEL

Air: Thai International provides almost all domestic flights. The service is good, and flights from Bangkok to other towns and cities operate daily in most cases. Plane fares are expensive when compared to bus or train travel, but if you are island-hopping and can't take forever about it, flying will get you there in a matter of hours as opposed to an overnight journey by bus/train and ferry.

Rail: Although trains are slow, they're comfortable, inexpensive, reliable, and safer than the bus. Advance bookings are advisable on all routes, and it's vital to book if travelling at weekends or during the holidays. Almost all trains have three classes; rapid and express trains carry surcharges of B20 and B30 respectively, and there are further supplements for air-conditioned carriages and sleepers. Even with these surcharges, train travel is extremely cheap. There are a few passes for unlimited rail travel: the 'Red Pass' (B3,000 2nd class/B2,000 3rd class) includes all the supplements; the 'Blue Pass' (B1,500/B1,100) doesn't include supplements. If you plan to travel almost everyday and want less hassle, the Red Pass may be worth it. The 'Explorer Pass' (for under-30s) doesn't include any supplements and runs for 7 days (B560 2nd class/B440 3rd class), 14 days (B680/B520), and 21 days (B800/B600). The Eastern and Oriental Express runs between Bangkok and Singapore, part of the original Oriental Express route. There are regular departures from Bangkok on Wednesday or from Singapore on Sunday. The two-day trip lasts about 41 hours and costs about £700 one-way or £1,130 round-trip. In Bangkok tel. 227 2068 or 251 4862; in London tel. 0171 928 6000.

Bus: Long-distance buses travel at such a speed that unless you possess nerves of steel and enjoy white-knuckle rides, you may be better off taking the train! They're clean and well-run, but theft can be a problem, so keep an eye on your belongings. Another (more serious) worry is the occasional armed hold-up of buses which run through remote areas on major tourist routes.

Two classes of bus operate: air-conditioned and non

air-conditioned. The former is about 50% more expensive and all
seats must be reserved in advance. Overnight services are popular,
with refreshments and movies on offer on some routes.
Ferry: There are numerous ferry services from mainland Thailand
to the offshore islands. It is often possible to travel by 'long-tail'
fishing boat.
Hitching: The authorities discourage hitching, with the result that
although it is not illegal, hitch-hikers are seldom seen. Do not
attempt it in the north, which can be a hazardous place at the best
of times because of armed robbery and drug running. If you do
take lifts, no matter how friendly the driver, *never* accept offers of
drink or food: the drugging of tourists is, unfortunately, all too
common.
Local transport: Bus travel is cheap (a few baht) but crowded,
and the local bus networks are usually good. Air-conditioned buses,
where they exist, will be a little more pricey, but correspondingly
more comfortable.

Taxis, bicycle rickshaws and *tuk-tuks* (motorized bicycle rickshaws) are always plentiful, but meters are never used so be sure
to negotiate fares in advance. Drivers rarely speak English.

It is possible to rent bicycles and motorbikes in many tourist
destinations. Cycling is a good way of getting about, but think
carefully before you hire a motorbike: accidents involving
foreigners occur in large numbers every year (particularly at the
beach resorts), and several deaths have resulted. Only experienced
motorcyclists should attempt it, and helmets and protective clothing
should be worn at all times. Also, you'll usually be held responsible
for repairs if anything breaks.

ACCOMMODATION
You can get up-to-date listings of accommodation in the various
regions from Tourist Authority of Thailand offices in the main tourist areas within the country, or from one of the overseas branches.
Though a lot of Thai accommodation is very reasonably priced, it
doesn't mean that the rooms are inferior. Never leave valuables in
your room, though, as theft is a problem – and it isn't always the
locals.
Youth hostels: There are only a handful of hostels; Bangkok has
four and Chiang Mai two. Most offer rooms as well as dorms. Expect
a dorm bed to cost B50–100.
Guest houses: Dormitories are few and far between in Thailand,
but there are plenty of cheap guest houses around which are clean,
quiet and well run, and some of them have dorm beds for around
B60. A double room in a cheap guest house should cost from B120,

a single room B75. For these prices, don't expect air-conditioning or a swimming pool; such extras would bump the price of a room up to B300−400 (although it is possible to find some for not much more than B200).

Hotels: There are plenty of luxury hotels waiting to relieve you of your money (B3,000−4,000 per night at the Hilton, Interconti-nental, etc.), which makes a mid-range hotel sound like a bargain at around B1,000. Chinese-Thai hotels can be found throughout the country. They usually come in one of three classes: 'hâwng AE' (with air-conditioning) B250−500, 'hâwng phát lom' (with fan) B100−250, or 'hâwng thammà daa' (no fan, no bath) B60−100.

Beach bungalows: At the beach resorts, many people rent bunga-lows. They are usually very basic wooden structures raised off the ground, and they cost about the same as a cheap guest house.

FOOD

Unusually for Asia, Thai people eat with spoons and forks rather than chopsticks. Thai food is hot and spicy − watch out for those chillies! − though it has been toned down a bit in some tourist restaurants to cater for Western tastes. Curries, rice, stir-fried veg-etables and noodles are the usual fare, and a typical Thai meal consists of a number of such dishes − though the tourist restaurants have got it down to just one main dish. Thailand is known for its delicious seafood, but if you are one of those people who experience stomach problems when travelling, shellfish are perhaps best avoided.

Food stalls and cheap local restaurants abound, so you won't starve. Wherever there are stalls, you can put together a meal for under B50 by wandering down a street picking out a number of dishes. In Bangkok, every kind of cuisine can be found − there are even German and Hungarian restaurants! Outside the main tourist areas, however, there will be communication problems unless you speak Thai, so it's a good idea to learn the names of a few dishes before venturing away from the hordes.

Vegetarians can expect a fairly lean time of it, as most dishes have meat in them. Some noodle dishes are meat-free, though, and there are always stir-fried vegetables and rice.

In restaurants, tea will usually be served with meals, and soft drinks are widely available. Coffee is sometimes on the menu, but it's awful. Tap water is unsafe, and ice is usually suspect, so stay away from both.

BUDGETING

Thailand is cheap by anybody's standards. Assuming that you stay in dormitories or the cheapest hotels, your accommodation costs will average B60 per night. Food is also a bargain – you'd be hard put to spend much over B150 in a restaurant, and the average cost of a substantial meal at a local restaurant or from foodstalls is B60.

Using ordinary, non air-conditioned buses to get about, transport costs shouldn't exceed B20 per day. Entrance fees really only apply in and around Bangkok and perhaps Chiang Mai; some temples charge B2–3, while admission to some of the big museums can be as high as B50, or even B100. Lying on a beach, however, is free. Add these estimates together and you have a basic daily budget of around B350 (about £7).

For night-time entertainment, beer in most bars (even in 'hostess' bars) costs B50–100. In discos, drinks prices jump to B200, and you can also expect a cover charge.

Remember to budget for long-distance transport costs, though – unless you are flying – even long journeys won't cost more than a few hundred baht.

FURTHER INFORMATION

Tourist Authority of Thailand, 49 Albemarle Street, London W1X 3FE (tel. 0171 499 7679).

Royal Thai Embassy, 29–30 Queen's Gate, London SW7 5JB (tel. 0171 589 0173/2944). There are Royal Thai Consulates in Birmingham, Liverpool, Cardiff, Hull, Dublin and Glasgow.

Background reading: Lonely Planet's *Thailand* is the best guidebook as far as the budget traveller is concerned. Trav Bugs' *Thailand* makes excellent reading, and will tell you a lot about the country before your trip.

The Paradise Eaters by John Ralston Saul is not only an extremely good novel, but one that will give you a better profile of Bangkok than any travelogue could. Set against a background of the city's sex-and-sin industry, it features some real-life Thai characters and has a lot to say about the Westerner in Asia. Carol Hollinger's *Mai Pen Rai* is a humorous account of a foreigner's experience of living in Thailand. It is available from bookshops in Bangkok.

Bangkok

AIRPORT FACILITIES
Don Muang International Airport (tel. 535 1254) is 25 km from Bangkok. It is a large, busy, well-organized place with two terminals, one for domestic flights and one for international. When arriving or departing, your luggage may be searched for drugs: make sure you're not carrying any, knowingly or unknowingly.

There are a couple of duty-free shops at the airport (and one in town, on Silom Road). They accept a wide range of currencies. There is also a restaurant and a foreign exchange in each of the terminals, and an accommodation desk in the arrivals area. Departures has an information desk, left-luggage facilities, a 24-hour bank, a post office, and a medical centre. You can even get your hair cut.

Check-in time is 90 minutes prior to departure for all flights. If you are leaving the country, there is a departure tax of B200. Domestic departure tax is B20.

CITY LINKS
Bus: You'll have to leave the airport and go out on to the highway in order to catch the public buses. The fare downtown varies, but shouldn't be more than B25. The last buses leave early to mid-evening. Buses 29, 59, 95, and air-conditioned buses 4, 13 and 29 go to town. The 13 goes to Sukhumvit Road and the 59 to Banglamphu, both common destinations.

Rail: You have to cross the main road outside the airport to reach the train station, from which there is an erratic but fairly frequent service into Bangkok. It costs about the same as the bus. You could also go straight to Chiang Mai, though you would most probably need an advance reservation.

Limousine: Thai International run a kind of pre-paid taxi service to the city. You buy coupons (costing B300) from a counter in the arrivals area before boarding the vehicles. Though expensive, this is the hassle-free way of getting downtown. The same company also runs a minibus to downtown hotels, but it's generally considered neither convenient (it's slow) nor a great bargain pricewise (B100).

Taxi: The cabs that leave from just outside the airport terminal won't take you to the city for much less than B300, and you'll have to bargain the drivers down to that. In any case, don't pay more than the limousine service. If you go out on the highway, you might be able to get a cheaper fare.

Use licensed taxis only (yellow plates, with rooftop signs). Tourists using unlicensed cabs have been known to disappear for a while, only to turn up robbed, beaten up – and sometimes dead. If in doubt, ask the airport staff which taxis are all right to use.

Road journeys from the airport to Bangkok can take anywhere from 30 minutes to two hours, depending on traffic.

USEFUL ADDRESSES
Tourist office: Tourism Authority of Thailand (TAT), 372 Bamrung Muang Road, Bangkok 10100 (tel. 226 0060/0072). Open 8.30 a.m.–4.30 p.m. daily, with friendly staff and good information. You can get a bus map here, and a bilingual street map.
Tourist police centre: 509 Worachak Road (tel. 221 6206 ext. 5). They deal with tourist complaints and security matters.
Main post office: Charoen Krung Road (tel. 234 9530). You can pick up poste restante mail here.
British Embassy: 1031 Ploenchit Road (tel. 253 0191).
US Embassy: 95 Witthayu (Wireless) Road (tel. 252 5040).
Emergency services: for all emergencies, contact the tourist police (tel. 221 6206/10).
Medical assistance: British Dispensary, 109 Sukhumvit Road (tel. 252 8056); Bangkok Christian Hospital, 124 Silom Road (tel. 233 6981); Bangkok Nursing Home, Convent Road.

GETTING ABOUT
Bus: Buses are frequent and the system is comprehensive, if confused. Get a bus map from the tourist office, bookstores or newsstands, but don't bank on its accuracy. Fares are B3–5 on ordinary buses or minibuses, though they go up later at night. Air-con buses cost B5–15. Pay the conductor on the bus.
Taxi: Taxis and *tuk-tuks* are plentiful. When you're bargaining your fare with taxi drivers, the minimum you can expect to pay will be B50. For trips across town, B100–150 is about right. Don't pay more than B200 for any journey, except to the airport. Drivers don't speak English, so have your destination written down in Thai, and use your fingers for price negotiations (four fingers is B40, five fingers B50, etc). *Tuk-tuks* cost between B30–150. Metered taxis are cheaper than non-metered ones, but are harder to find.
Bicycle: Bangkok traffic is absolutely horrendous, so you won't want to be hiring a bicycle.
On foot: Walking is something that the Bangkok resident does not do a lot of, and you'll soon find out why! The city is far too big to allow from getting from A to B on foot, and it's also too hot. You'll find yourself using public transport or taxis a lot of the time.

SIGHTS

There are several hundred temples (*wats*) in Bangkok, but the one that you should not miss is the WAT PHRA KEO (Temple of the Emerald Buddha). It is part of the GRAND PALACE complex, which is situated alongside the Chao Phya River. The buildings date from the late 18th century and are a collection of traditional spires, elaborate rooftops, pagodas and pavilions. The Emerald Buddha (made from jasper) dates from the fifteenth century. (Open 9 a.m.–5 p.m. daily, admission B100.)

On the other side of the river is the WAT ARUN, which has an 82-metre high tower decorated with Chinese porcelain that is best viewed at sunset. The other temple 'must-see' is the WAT PO, south of the Wat Phra Keo. It is Bangkok's oldest temple and a one-time educational centre. It's known for its 46-metre long reclining statue of Buddha. Consult the tourist office for details of Bangkok's other temples.

The NATIONAL MUSEUM (tel. 224 1396) is good for an overview of Thai culture and art. Aside from its huge collection of classical Thai art, it also contains exhibitions of art from other South-east Asian countries. (Open 9 a.m.–12 p.m. and 1–4 p.m. except Mondays and Fridays when it is closed all day.) There are free English-language tours (at 9.30 a.m.) that well worth joining: Thai Art and Culture is on Tuesdays, Buddhism on Wednesdays and pre-Thai Art on Thursdays. Not far away is the NATIONAL GALLERY (same opening hours), which holds exhibitions of contemporary Thai art.

JIM THOMPSON'S HOUSE, off Rama IV Road at Soi Kasem San 2, was the house of an American probably more famous for going missing in Malaysia's Cameron Highlands in the 1960s than anything else. The house (consisting of several old wooden houses joined together) is full of Thai and other Asian furnishings and artefacts. The house itself is a delight, and the gardens are lovely.

If you're into folk art, the KAMTHUNG HOUSE at 131 Soi Asoke is devoted to Thai history and is full of native crafts. Other attractions include: CHINATOWN, for a stroll around the traditional Chinese shops, businesses and temples; LUMPINI PARK, with its lakes, trees, paths and early morning Tai-chi; VIMARNEK PALACE, once a 19th-century royal country retreat, but now part of the metropolis. A less soothing spectacle is the SNAKE FARM on Rama IV Road, where you can watch venom being milked (for medical use).

The FLOATING MARKET should be avoided at all costs, as there are more pleasure craft than market boats. There is no one main shopping area in Bangkok – shops and market stalls appear everywhere. The weekend market at Chatuchak Park is a big draw, and you're sure to find absolutely everything there, from handicrafts to kitchenware.

ACCOMMODATION

Budget travellers mostly head for the Banglamphu district of Bangkok, as it offers something for everyone: cheap guest houses, dorms, and reasonably priced hotels with air-conditioning and swimming pools. The cheaper rooms tend to fill up early, but you are bound to find somewhere to stay whatever the time of day. Try to avoid guest houses on Khao San Road, though, as it is very noisy – go for the side-streets instead. Also, try the area north of Banglamphu, near the National Library. The following suggestions are all in the budget price range (see **Thailand: Accommodation**, p. 417):

Hostels: Not far from Banglamphu:

Bangkok International Youth Hostel: 25 Phitsanuklok Road (tel. 282 0950/281 0361). Quiet and clean, this comes well recommended. It has rooms as well as dorms. From B50 per night.

Banglamphu Youth Hostel: 105 Chakkraphong Road (tel. 282 7454).

Hotels: The hotel desk at the airport will find you a room in a reasonably-priced hotel – worth thinking about if you arrive late on in the day. A few possibilities in the Banglamphu vicinity are:

Privacy Guest House: 69 Tanao Road (tel. 282 7028).

Hello Guest House: 63 Khaosan Road (tel. 281 8579). From B70.

James's Guest House: 116 Prachatiphatai Road (tel. 280 0326).

Backpacker's Lodge: 85 Sri Ayutthaya Road (tel. 282 3231).

Shanti Lodge: 37 Sri Ayutthaya Road (tel. 281 2497). From B150.

Sawatdee Guest House: 71 Soi, 3 Sri Ayutthaya Road (tel. 281 0757/282 5349). From B50.

If you want to get away from the Banglamphu and surrounding areas altogether, try:

Miami, Soi 13, 2 Sukhumvit Road (tel. 25 5611). Singles at under B200 and doubles at just over that.

World, 1996 New Petchaburi Road (tel. 314 4340). Rooms at around B300.

Swan, 31 Custom House Lane (tel. 234 8594). Rooms at around B300.

FOOD

Restaurants serving both Western and Thai food are dotted all along Khao San Road in Banglamphu, and there are food stalls everywhere. The Petchaburi Road is a good place for street food. The shopping centres and department stores are the best places for fastfood, Western and Thai; and the restaurants in the big hotels will provide you with a taste of home.

Tumnak Thai, 131 Rajdapisek Road (tel. 277 3828). Perhaps the best-known restaurant in Bangkok: a 3,000-seater where the staff get about on roller skates, and there is Thai dancing and entertainment. The food is average, but the prices are reasonable.

Whole Earth Restaurant, 93 Soi Lang Suan, Ploenchit Road. Thai vegetarian food at prices a little more expensive than other restaurants.

Cabbages and Condoms, Soi 12, Sukhumvit Road (tel. 251 5552) Worth visiting for the name alone, it is a nonprofit-making restaurant (with very good food) run by 'The Condom King', Dr Mechai, an energetic advocate of birth control.

Sara Jane's, 36 Soi Lang Suan, Ploenchit Road (tel. 252 6572). Cheap, local cuisine.

The Royal India, 392/1 Chakraphret Road in Pahurat (tel. 221 6565) is a reasonably priced option for authentic north Indian cuisine.

Cholas, downstairs in the air-conditioned Woodlands Inn on soi Charoen Krung 32, near the post office, also serves decent north Indian food at a slightly higher price than the Royal India.

The Bussaracum at 35 Soi Phipat off Convent Road, which is in the east of Silom Road, is thoroughly recommended for Thai food. It specializes in Royal Thai cuisine, the standard of which is excellent. Rather a fancy place, reflected in the price, it has very attentive waiting staff and menus with pictures so that you can see what the dishes are actually supposed to look like.

ENTERTAINMENT

There are a couple of venues that host performances of traditional Thai arts: the Centre of Traditional Performing Arts on Rajadamnoen Road holds weekly displays of dance and music, and the National Theatre on Na Phra That Road has outdoor classical dance performances from November to May. In both cases, check with the TAT office for exact times and days. If there are any performances scheduled while you are in town, don't miss them.

Some restaurants and hotels have dinner/dance shows which feature dance, music and displays of Thai martial arts (plus dinner!). They're a little touristy, but pretty good. The nightly show at the Baan Thai Restaurant, Sukhumvit Soi 32, is recommended, and other regulars are the Chao Phraya Restaurant, the Dusit Thani Hotel and the Oriental Hotel.

If you'd like to watch people violently (but skilfully) beating each other up, there is Thai kick boxing at the Lumpini Stadium on Rama IV Road. Fights start at 6 p.m., earlier on Saturdays.

More conventional nights out can be had at discos in the luxury hotels: try Diana's at the Oriental Hotel, or the Flamingo at the Ambassador. Nasa at 999 Ramkamhaeng Road is also very popular: the décor is futuristic, and it's said to be the biggest disco in the world. The Rome Club in Patpong III is a gay disco patronized by both gay and straight young people.

'Jazz' bars (not all of them play jazz!) are popular with those who want a laid-back, relaxed drink with good music and informal surroundings. Brown Sugar on Soi Sarasin is a favourite spot. Nearby, on Soi Lang Suan, is Round Midnight. Sukhumvit Road is a hunting ground for bars: Witch's Tavern on Soi 55 is a British-style place, and the Blues Jazz Pub, Soi 53, is known for its exceptionally good resident band.

Even in the infamous Patpong area, there are a few quiet(ish) bars (such as the Crown Royal or Bobby's Arms on Patpong Road). It's okay for foreign women to drink in the Hostess or go-go bars in this district (though whether they'd want to is another matter) and there are usually some couples out and about having a look at Sin City. The clientèle is mostly male, however, and the atmosphere is definitely sleazy. Patpong I has market stalls along it, while Patpong III is the gay area. Patpong II is mostly hard core. There are many rip-off places in this area – not surprisingly. One to avoid is the 'Lucky Bar'. Gunpoint requests for exhorbitant sums of money for drinks are not unheard of.

Men thinking of getting involved with prostitutes should consider that the incidence of HIV infection amongst them is high – and getting higher. Moreover, the 'girls' sometimes turn out to be transvestites. The women get little (if any) of the fee paid to the bars for taking them out. Avoid the hard-core 'upstairs bars', where hefty charges will be demanded before you leave, and violence threatened if you don't pay up.

EXCURSIONS

A must for anybody who ever saw the film *Bridge on the River Kwai* is a trip to KANCHABURI (you can take a train or a bus there from Bangkok – the train goes over the bridge). A lot of people do it as a day-trip, but it is well worth staying longer as there is a lot to see in the town, the scenery is great, and there are some excursions from Kanchaburi to be done (the ERAWAN FALLS and ERAWAN

NATIONAL PARK are nearby). The bridge itself — reconstructed in part, because of bomb damage — looks nothing like the one in the film, but the train ride across it is spectacular, and you can walk across when there are no trains around. Elsewhere in town, the JEATH MUSEUM, a reconstruction of a POW camp, is a sobering and moving experience, and there is a war cemetery on the outskirts of town.

North of Bangkok lies AYUTTHAYA, one-time capital of Thailand and now a historical site of ruined temples and palaces. There are also three excellent museums, the best of which is undoubtedly the Ayutthaya Historical Study Centre. It has audio-visual presentations and reconstructions of the one-time splendour of the town prior to its destruction by the Burmese in 1767. You could visit Ayutthaya in one day from the capital, or stop over for a little longer on your way north. Not far away is BANG PA-IN, a 19th-century summer retreat of the royal family. It has buildings in a mixture of Thai, Chinese and Italian styles, and makes a good boat trip from Ayutthaya.

The tallest Buddhist monument in the world is at NAKHON PATHOM, and the town itself is thought to be the oldest settlement in the country. It's a pleasant place, and the hour-long train ride from Bangkok is relaxing and scenic. The floating market at DAMOEN SADUAK lies 60 km south of Nakhon Pathom. It has become an alternative to the floating market in Bangkok (though it, too, can be a bit touristy).

There are a few purpose-built tourist attractions within easy reach of the capital. They are: the ANCIENT CITY (a sort of Thailand-in-miniature); the ROSE GARDEN and parks; and the CROCODILE FARM. They're all rather artificial, but ask at the TAT for details if you're interested. The beach resort nearest to Bangkok is PATTAYA, some two hours away. It's certainly not one of Thailand's best, but if you're in need of some R&R, it's worth considering.

AUSTRALASIA & OCEANIA

Australasia is an essential destination on most travellers' itineraries. Australia and New Zealand offer both breathtaking and contrasting scenery, moreover – so it seems from the outside, at any rate – there's no problem with either language or culture. And the Pacific Islands are a great place to relax after a few months' hectic travelling.

WHERE TO GO FOR WHAT

Outdoor types will love AUSTRALIA: there are national parks galore offering fabulous scenery, light to strenuous walking from short trails to week-long hikes. Lovers of flora and fauna will be enthralled by the profusion of native plants and the kangaroos, koalas, kookaburras, wallabies, wombats, dingoes, etc. which are peculiar to Australia. The deep ochre of the Outback, set against the strong, clear, blue sky is a phenomenon not found anywhere else in the world. In many ways, Australia is truly unique. Its best beaches (both for 'sunbaking' and surfing) are centred around Sydney, Queensland and Perth. Divers should head for the Barrier Reef or for the coral reefs off Perth. Any non-swimmers planning to visit Australasia should learn to swim before they go if they don't want to miss out on a lot of fun, not to mention the unforgettable experience of snorkelling among the fantastic coral reefs.

The Opera House may have put Sydney on the world map as far as the arts are concerned, but Melbourne is Australia's culture capital, with several theatres and cinemas, and there's usually an opera, ballet, or a concert being staged. For a taste of the real Australia, though, you need to head for the Outback – immerse yourself in the Aboriginal rock art at Kakadu, and in the legends of Ayers Rock. Swelter in the humid heat of the desert or the 'top end' around Darwin. When you're in Sydney or Melbourne you could be in any city in the world – but when you've finally hauled yourself to the top of Ayers Rock, you'll know for sure that you're in the Australia you once dreamed about.

Many travellers cram in a trip to NEW ZEALAND at the end of their Antipodean sojourn before flying off to Asia or the States, only to find they haven't allowed enough time to make the most of this incredibly beautiful country. Don't make that mistake. Leave yourself at least six weeks to explore New Zealand. It's a great country for outdoor pursuits. There are several tough hiking trails and any visitor to New Zealand should try to fit in at least one of these. There's also climbing (including the Fox and Franz Joseph glaciers), skiing, sailing, fishing, riding, white-water rafting and, of course, bungy-jumping. Less intrepid travellers will still find much to appreciate: the scenery is stunning, and there's amazing wildlife to enjoy – spot one of New Zealand's native birds, go whale-watching at Kaikoura . . . Or for a taste of Maori culture head for the North Island. Those with an interest in colonial history will enjoy a visit to the Bay of Islands (the best spot for sunbathing, too) and no one can fail to be fascinated by the boiling mud and fizzing volcanoes of Rotorua. However, should you be the type who thinks museums, art galleries and trips to the ballet are all-important, New Zealand may prove a disappointment; apart from the occasional open-air appearance by Dame Kiri Te Kanawa, there's very little in the way of culture.

The PACIFIC ISLANDS, with their fabulous scenery, blissful climate and exotic cultural traditions are well worth a visit. FIJI in particular is a great favourite with travellers. The 300 volcanic islands which make up the Fiji archipelago offer natural delights in the way of beaches, coral and scenery, and the Fijians themselves enjoy the reputation of being among the friendliest people on earth. Tourism has suffered from the coups of the early 1990s, but Fiji appears to be stable now. Spend some time there – you won't regret it!

TAKE HEED
Because we share a common language, there's a tendency to assume that Australia and New Zealand are just like home. They're not. (For that matter, they're nothing like *Neighbours* either!) To many Australians, the 'old country' is no longer Britain – it may be Greece or Yugoslavia, or even part of Asia. This new Australia is on its way to becoming a republic, and visitors may find the fierce patriotism of the would-be republicans irritating.

As for New Zealand: well, there are times you'll think you're sitting in your living room in Britain: all the news seems to be British news, and peak-time TV viewing features *Coronation Street* (three months behind the UK), *Emmerdale* and *The Bill*. But again, it's a totally different country and culture: they are passionate about the outdoor life, environmental issues are important to them and are taken very seriously. Don't, whatever you do, admire the gorse: pretty as it may be, this unstoppable plant (introduced by the Poms, of course) has wiped out some of the native flora and the Kiwis loathe it.

Both the Australians and New Zealanders are tremendously hos-pitable people – always ready to offer you a bed for the night or a lift. Don't abuse their hospitality by outstaying your welcome. This applies especially to staying with the 'rellies' everybody seems to have out there. They'll welcome you with open arms but, naturally enough, won't want you staying with them for weeks on end, eating their food, drinking their plonk, and doing little or nothing in return. Antipodeans have developed an antipathy towards 'bludgers'.

If you want to visit a Pacific island during your travels, you need to exercise some caution. Certain islands, like Fiji, can be politically unstable; others, like Tahiti, have been so taken over by the tourist industry that they've lost a lot of their original charm. Papua New Guinea is considered extremely unsafe for women (it's not even safe for men after nightfall). It's difficult to generalize about the safety aspects, but it's fair to say that those who take sensible security precautions and respect local customs are unlikely to come to harm.

EMPLOYMENT OPPORTUNITIES
Australia has long enjoyed the reputation of being a land of opportunity. For travellers, it has been a great place to pick up well-paid work before moving on again. Sadly, the recession has bitten Australia hard, and the government has cracked down on granting work permits to foreign visitors. It's important, then, to make sure that you have enough money to get you around Australia and don't bank on making extra cash there.

INTRA-CONTINENTAL TRAVEL
The new 'G'Day Air Pass' is available to non-residents of Australia and New Zealand. This breaks the area into four zones (**1** West and Central Australia, **2** East Australia, **3** Hayman Island, and **4** New Zealand). You must purchase a minimum of two coupons, and the maximum allowed is eight. Each coupon is £80 if you travel in a single zone or £105 for a multi-zone coupon. Unfortunately, travel between Australia and New Zealand is not covered by this pass.

Many travellers on round-the-world tickets organize stopovers in a couple of Australian destinations plus Auckland. If New Zealand's not one of your stopovers, then the cheapest option is to book a flight from either Sydney or Melbourne to Auckland, or from Hobart to Christchurch. Cairns and Darwin are good sources for cheap flights to Fiji and other Pacific Islands. Since the deregulation of Australia's airlines in 1990 fares have varied considerably, so it's best to shop around before booking a flight. Fellow travellers are often the best source of information on the latest bargains to be had. Make sure you have a multi-entry visa for Australia so that you can take advantage of these flights.

FURTHER INFORMATION

There are no travel guides covering Australasia as a whole; see the individual country sections for guidebooks on the places you're planning to visit. *Australia and New Zealand, a Traveller's Survival Kit* (Vacation Work) is an excellent guide for those who intend to visit both countries. It covers all the sights and essential things to do, plus tips on where to stay, where to eat out and where to find the best local night-life.

AUSTRALIA

VITAL STATISTICS

Red tape: A full passport is required, and all visitors (with the exception of New Zealand passport holders) need visas. For those who don't plan to seek work in Australia, there are two categories of visitor's visas: one for up to three months, which is free; and one for over three to six months, which costs £16. A working-holiday visa costs £71 and is valid for one year. Although it is reputedly valid only for 18- to 25-year-olds, it is still possible to get one if you're over 25; all you have to do is fill in a lengthy form, submit to an interview, and provide evidence of your ability to support yourself while in Australia. Applications for all types of visa should be made to the Visa Section, Australian High Commission, Australia House, Strand, London WC2B 4LA (tel. 0171 379 4334); Australian Embassy, 1601 Massachusetts Avenue NW, Washington DC 20036 (tel. 202 797 3000) or in person to your nearest Australian Consulate.

Customs: 250 cigarettes or 250 g tobacco or 50 cigars. 1 l alcohol. You are also allowed gifts up to the value of A$400 (A$200 for people under 18). There are strict regulations against the import of foodstuffs and other potential sources of disease and pestilence.

Health: A yellow fever vaccination certificate is required if you're coming from an infected area (including former endemic areas). Carriers of the disease are responsible for the isolation expenses of all fellow travellers who have not been vaccinated.

UK residents are entitled to treatment under the Medicare system (the Australian equivalent of the NHS); when you arrive in Australia, register at the nearest Medicare office, producing your passport and visa. You will be given a Medicare number, though it can take a couple of weeks or so for your actual card to be issued. Under Medicare, in- and out-patient treatment at a public hospital is free, apart from drugs and dressings for which a charge is made. Note that Medicare doesn't cover dental fees (which are expensive), ambulance charges, treatment for any pre-existing conditions, and any jabs you might need for the next stage of your trip. US and Canadian visitors receive free health treatment only for emergencies; insurance is advisable.

The biggest concern health-wise is the strength of the sun and the attendant risk of skin cancer. Hence the SLIP SLAP SLOP campaign: slip on a hat, slap on protective sun lotion, slop down plenty of drinking fluids if you're going out in the sun.

Language: English. Aborigines have their own languages.

Population: Around 17 million.

Capital: Canberra (Australian Capital Territory), population 286,000.

Political system: A democracy, with federal and state governments, and – for the time being at least – the Queen as nominal head of state. The Labour party has been in federal office since 1983, and the current Prime Minister is Paul Keating. State government leaders are known as state premiers.

Religion: Anglican, Roman Catholic and other Christian groups, including the Seventh Day Adventists.

Time: The three time zones are Eastern (ten hours ahead of GMT); Central (nine and a half hours ahead of GMT); and Western (eight hours ahead of GMT). All states except Western Australia and Queensland switch to daylight savings time Oct.–Mar.

Money: The currency is the Australian dollar (A$), divided into 100 cents. Coins: 5, 10, 20 and 50 cents, A$1 and A$2. Notes: A$5, A$10, A$20, A$50, and A$100. £1 = A$2.15.

Carrying large amounts of cash isn't a good idea; opt for sterling or US traveller's cheques instead. Credit cards are widely accepted in Australia, apart from some remote parts of Tasmania. If you plan to work in Australia, or are staying for a few months, it is easy to open a bank account once you're there.

Communications: Operated by Telecom, Australia's telephone system is efficient and cheap. Local calls cost just 20 cents from private telephones and 30 cents from payphones, and you can chat for as long as you like. Card-operated phones have appeared in the major cities over the past few years; phonecards are available (from post offices) in units of A$2, A$5, A$10, A$20 or A$50, and are handy for international or interstate calls.

Post offices are more like shops, with an array of stationery, boxes and stamps for sale, plus the usual poste restante, telex and fax facilities. Mail to the UK is swift, often taking just four days. Parcels and Christmas cards can be sent economy air, which is cheaper than normal airmail and only takes about a week longer to arrive (surface mail takes about six weeks).

Electricity: 240–50v. Plugs are flat three-pin, but they differ from the UK variety.

Business hours: BANKS: Mon.–Thurs. 9.30 a.m.–4 p.m.; Fri. 9.30 a.m.–5 p.m. Some city-centre branches open Mon.–Thurs. from 8 a.m.–6 p.m. and Fri. 8 a.m.–8 p.m. Rural areas may have just one bank that is open only one or two days per week.

POST OFFICES: Mon.–Fri. 9 a.m.–5 p.m., with main post offices open on Saturday morning.

SHOPS: Mon.–Fri. 9 a.m.–5.30 p.m., with late-night shopping until 9 p.m. on Thursdays and/or Fridays. Many city-centre shops open on Sundays as well as Saturdays.

OFFICES: Mon.–Fri. 9 a.m.–5 p.m.

Holidays: 1, 26 January; Good Friday, Easter Saturday, Easter Monday and Christmas Day are all national holidays. There are in addition a number of state holidays, and when you're travelling around the country these seem to occur all too frequently. For an up-to-date list, it's best to contact each state's tourist office before going out to Australia.

Climate: Queensland, the Northern Territory and the north of Western Australia have two seasons: dry (from April to October) and wet (from November to March). During the wet season, torrential rain often causes severe flooding, and cyclones are common.

Sydney, Adelaide, Melbourne and Perth all have temperate winters and hot summers (temperatures can reach 40°C). Tasmania has a temperate climate. The only snow falls in the mountainous regions of south-east mainland Australia and in Tasmania.

DO'S AND DON'TS

Australians regard theirs as the best country in the world, its cities as the best, its sports people as the best, etc. etc. They like nothing better than a bit of Pom-bashing (the Scots, Welsh and Irish, however, are generally considered OK) and they really dish it out when England loses a cricket match (but try not to tease them when Allan Border's out for a duck — they won't take kindly to it!). However, Australians on the whole are very positive people (wouldn't you be if you saw that much sun?).

When travelling, remember that distances are vast — it's 25 times the size of the UK. If you're driving, remember to carry a sufficient supply of water and food.

WHERE TO GO FOR WHAT

New South Wales: Travellers usually head straight for SYDNEY, Australia's most populous and vibrant city, built around a magnificent harbour incorporating the HARBOUR BRIDGE and the OPERA HOUSE. But Sydney isn't typical of New South Wales any more than it is typical of Australia. The state encompasses a range of climatic zones from the sub-tropical north to the SNOWY MOUNTAINS of the south (which offer superb winter skiing). Closer to Sydney are the beautiful BLUE MOUNTAINS — fabulous for bushwalking. BYRON BAY, to the north, is a popular beach resort situated on Cape Byron, Australia's most easterly point. TAMWORTH, in the heart of farmland, is the country-and-western capital of Australia. For a taste of the outback, the mining town of BROKEN HILL, 1.161 km from Sydney, continues to yield a wealth of zinc, lead and silver. CANBERRA, Australia's capital city, is a well-planned and scrupulously clean city with a somewhat artificial air, but should you want to see the Federal Parliament in action, this is the place. It's also the home of the Australian Institute of Sport, where the country's future sporting superstars enjoy outstanding training facilities.

Victoria: MELBOURNE, the state capital, is very much the cultural and sporting centre of Australia, with plenty of theatres and major sporting events. Victoria may be the smallest of the mainland states, but has lots going for it, from superb surfing beaches to the haunting beauty of the VICTORIAN ALPS. North of Melbourne is the ancient rock formation, HANGING ROCK, setting of the film *Picnic at Hanging Rock* and one of the most incredible sights in Australia. There are several gold towns worth a visit, including BENDIGO and BEECHWORTH.

Queensland: Although BRISBANE is the state capital, travellers are more likely to head for CAIRNS, with its tropical climate and unparalleled access to the GREAT BARRIER REEF. It's a state which has something for everyone: commercial resorts like SURFERS PARADISE and the GOLD COAST, unspoilt beaches to the north of Cairns, rainforest, sugar plantations, and uninhabited desert. BUNDABERG is famous for its rum distillery, and there are seasonal whale-watching tours and a turtle rookery. ROCKHAMPTON lies on the Tropic of Capricorn, with the popular but touristy GREAT KEPPEL ISLAND offshore. The WHITSUNDAY ISLANDS are becoming increasingly popular with divers and snorkellers and are reached from the quiet coastal town of PROSPERINE. Inland, MOUNT ISA provides a brief stopping-off point for travellers *en route* to or from the Northern Territory. There's no mountain at 'the Isa', but it does have the world's largest silver-lead mine, with daily tours available.

Northern Territory: This, most travellers agree, is the *real* Australia – miles of uninhabited desert in the centre, and swamps, gorges and crocodiles at the 'Top End'. AYERS ROCK, Australia's biggest tourist attraction. It's awesome to look at, especially at sunset. The climb is a hard one – and the noonday sun will only make it harder, so start out early. Nearby are the dome-shaped OLGAS, with their superb gorges. The Ayers Rock Resort is the place to stay for access to the Rock and the Olgas. ALICE SPRINGS is a stopover point *en route* to Ayers Rock Resort. South Australia or the Top End; features include the dry Todd River, the puddle-sized spring from which the Alice got its name, and the world-famous Flying Doctor service and telegraph station. Way up north, DARWIN is an extremely modern city; much of it had to be rebuilt after the destruction caused by Cyclone Tracy on Christmas Day 1974. There's not much to see, but it does provide a good base for tours to KAKADU NATIONAL PARK (where *Crocodile Dundee* was filmed). Kakadu has swamps and a host of wildlife (including crocodiles), spectacular waterfalls and ancient Aboriginal rock art. LITCHFIELD PARK is closer to Darwin and less touristy, with termite mounds, hot springs and waterfalls, and the scenic backdrop of Tabletop Range. KATHERINE GORGE is a spectacular place for canoeing, and offers good walking tracks, plus the Cutta Cutta Caves.

Western Australia: PERTH is the capital, with its port of FREMANTLE – which secured a place on the world map when it staged the America's Cup in 1987. Perth has fabulous beaches and some fine museums and art galleries. ROTTNEST ISLAND is not far away and many are lured there by the beautiful coral and to see the 'quokka', Australia's smallest marsupial. MONKEY MIA, north of Perth, is the place to go if you want to swim with dolphins. BROOME is a pearl-diving town. KALGOORLIE, east of Perth, still thrives as a gold-mining town.

South Australia: ADELAIDE is undoubtedly the most charming of Australia's state capitals. It has a tranquil atmosphere, beautiful beaches, lots of churches, a casino, and the annual grand prix. Its wineries are based in the Barossa Valley, Southern Vales and the Clare Valley. KANGAROO ISLAND is excellent for wildlife and the FLINDERS RANGES have fabulous gorges and canyons, and an array of wildlife. COOBER PEDY, an opal-mining town, is curious in that most of its residents live underground. It has two subterranean churches, one Catholic and one Protestant (the latter is decorated with a particularly beautiful simplicity).

TASMANIA: Too many travellers neglect 'Tassie', either due to lack of funds or because they aren't aware of what it has to offer. It is more like the South Island of New Zealand than mainland

Australia in terms of climate, terrain and pace of life. The stunningly scenic CRADLE MOUNTAIN AND LAKE ST CLAIR national park has a host of walking tracks, including the 80 km Overland Track, which takes about five days. HOBART is the capital, with the former penal colony of PORT ARTHUR (where the Tolpuddle martyr George Lovelace was sent) close by. There are some good beaches on the east coast, though much of the west coast is inaccessible. The mining towns of QUEENSTOWN, STRAHAN and ZEEHAN are worth a visit.

INTERNAL TRAVEL

Air: If you are short of time, this is the most efficient way to travel this vast country. Unfortunately, despite deregulation of the airlines in 1990, internal air fares are not cheap. A one-way ticket from Melbourne to Perth, for example, will cost about A$300. With the Australian aviation industry in a state of flux, it is best to check newspaper ads, or ask travel agents and airlines for the best current deals. Each airline has a toll-free reservations number within Australia: for Ansett, call 008 131353 (or 008 131355 for its discount fare information service), East-west 008 366 1300 and Australian Airlines 008 922 5122.

There are two air passes available. The 'Explorer Pass' is available regardless of whether or not you fly to Australia with Qantas. You must buy a minimum of two coupons but no more than eight. The price is A$300 per coupon in one sector and additional sectors are available from A$150, which can be bought once you arrive. This pass is only available for non-residents of Australia and must be purchased outside Australia. The 'G'Day Pass' is similar to the 'Explorer', but additional sectors cannot be added once you arrive. For more details, see **Intra-Continental Travel** p. 429).

Rail: Australia's railway network basically consists of the following routes: Sydney to Perth via Adelaide; Adelaide to Alice Springs; Adelaide to Sydney via Melbourne; and Sydney to Cairns. The Indian-Pacific line from Sydney across the Nullarbor Plain to Perth takes 64 hours and offers the longest straight stretch of railway in the world.

Rail passes available include:

The Austrailpass, which is only available outside Australia, allows unlimited travel on all rail services except for Adelaide suburban services and special excursion trains. Prices for the economy pass start at A$460 for 14 days, A$595 for 21 days; A$720 for 30 days, A$1,030 for 60 days, and A$1,180 for 90 days.

The Austrail Flexipass gives unlimited budget travel for 8, 15, 22 or 29 days over a 6-month period. The prices are A$360, A$520, A$735 and A$945 respectively. The pass must be purchased outside Australia.

The NSW Discovery Pass costs A$249 and is valid for unlimited travel in New South Wales for a month.

The East Coast Discovery Pass costs A$199 and offers unlimited stops to Brisbane and the Gold Coast or Brisbane and Cairns.

Bus: For those with enough time to spare, this is one of the best ways of travelling around the mainland. The major carriers – Australian Coachlines (formerly two separate operators, Greyhound and Pioneer) and Bus Australia – cover almost every conceivable destination, and the buses are equipped with air-conditioning, toilets, reclining seats and videos. Bus Australia tends to be a little cheaper than its rival.

There are three round-Australia passes on offer, combining bus travel and YHA accommodation. The Explorer Passes include four different routes (The All-Australian, Aussie Highlights, Best of the West and Best of the East). All of these passes are valid for 12 months. Each route has different prices and you can choose whether you want 15, 20, 40 or 60 nights' accommodation. The prices range from A$725 for 15 nights with the Best of the East Pass, to A$2,010 for 60 nights with the All-Australian pass. The Aussie Pass has no fixed route and is valid for travel for 7–90 days within a period of 30–180 days, plus YHA accommodation. Prices range from 7 days' travel within 30 days, plus 15 nights' accommodation for A$540, to 90 days' travel within 180 days plus 60 nights' accommodation for A$2,795. In addition, there is a Sunseeker Pass which includes two routes, both with various stops up the east coast. The pass is valid for 6 months with 15–60 nights' accommodation. Prices range from A$375 for 15 nights' accommodation to A$1,025 for 60 nights.

Tasmania isn't covered by Bus Australia or Australian Coachlines. Its local carriers, Tasmanian Redline Coaches and Hobart Coaches, both offer travel passes which cost up to A$100, depending how long you want to travel. Be warned: buses don't run on Sundays.

Car hire: Drive on the left. Your national driving licence is valid for three months; an international driving permit (issued in your home country) for a year. The minimum age for car hire is 20.

If you're planning to travel Australia with friends, it can be worthwhile to buy a second-hand car or campervan and sell it at the end of your travels. Hostel noticeboards are a good place to find details of cars and vans for sale, as are the classified ads sections of the main newspapers. If you are a member of the AA, RAC or another foreign motoring organization, the state motoring organization for the Australian Automobile Association (AAA), 212 Northbourne Avenue, Canberra, ACT 2601 (tel. 06 247 7311) will check the car or van over for about A$100.

Hitching: If you're planning to hitch, an important thing to remember is that Australians don't 'thumb' a lift, they simply point a finger down at the road. Tasmania is great for hitching: the motorists are friendly and, as with New Zealand, you're likely to be offered overnight accommodation or a meal in addition to a lift. Mainland Australia is generally safe – though women should avoid hitching alone through the chauvinistic Outback – and relatively easy over short distances. Long distances, however, can be a problem – especially across the Nullabor! If you can afford it, buses are a much more reliable option.

Local transport: Sydney, Melbourne, Perth, Adelaide, Brisbane and Darwin all have cheap and efficient local buses and trains (and, in Melbourne's case, trams). Most other towns, if they don't have good public transport, are small enough to explore by foot. Canberra is excellent for cycling.

ACCOMMODATION
Hostelling is popular with Australians as well as overseas visitors, and the intense competition between individual hostels and hostel chains means many of them offer a range of perks, such as courtesy pick-up, tour agency facilities, and information on places to visit in the area and how to continue your travels around the country.

Youth hostels: Australia has 152 YHA hostels, with beds costing between A$8 and A$20, depending on the location and whether you want a single room, double room or dormitory accommodation. The hostels are listed in the Australian *YHA Accommodation Guide*, available from YHA offices within Australia. If you want to hostel in Tasmania, bear in mind that outside Hobart the YHA is the only option; YHA membership is therefore essential if you're planning a trip across the Bass Strait. As in Europe and North America, you must carry a regulation sleep sheet rather than a sleeping bag. Contact the AYHA on 02 565 1699.

Backpackers' hostels: A popular alternative to the YHA, especially among those who dislike compulsory morning duties, segregation of the sexes, and the no-alcohol rule. Prices are roughly the same as the YHA. Backpackers Resorts of Australia, 116 Jonson Street, PO Box 1000, Byron Bay, NSW 2481, (tel. 018 666888) publish a booklet listing some 100 backpackers hostels; it's free within Australia, or there's a A$5 charge if ordered by post from overseas. Membership of Backpackers Resorts of Australia costs around A$10, and offers discounts on bus lines and at various hostels.

Motels: Motels are popular among Australian families, and are comfortable and inexpensive (about A$25 per night). Friends travelling together may find that a family room in a motel is cheaper than staying in a youth hostel.

Hotels: What Aussies (and New Zealanders) term a 'hotel' is in fact a tavern. Many do offer comfortable accommodation as well, and you will meet the locals in the bar, but noise levels can be high, and women sometimes feel uncomfortable requesting a bed at the bar. (There is usually no reception desk.)

Homestays and farmstays: These are becoming increasingly popular with tourists wanting to sample typical Australian life – especially in the Outback. Farmstays tend to be more expensive, from about A$70 per day. Some outbuildings have been converted to backpacker accommodation, which costs from about A$7–15 per day. Town and Country Hosts, 110 Alfred Street, Milsons Point, NSW 2061 (tel. 02 955 0536) act as agents for about 200 farms and homes throughout Australia. Or try Stephanie Savage, Houseguest, PO Box 16, Glenoye, NSW 2157.

Private accommodation: If you're planning to work in one particular place for a few months, check hostel noticeboards for flatshares. The cost of one-bedroom 'units' or flats varies from about A$80 a week in Adelaide to about A$135 in Sydney. Units tend to be let unfurnished, and the minimum leasing period is normally three months. Bonds of several hundred dollars are required by the landlord/lady, and a reference from a previous landlord/lady helps.

Campsites: Accommodation is often in short supply in the more remote areas, so a tent is a cheap and handy option. It's possible to camp in rest areas (most of which have water, toilets, tables and barbecue stands) as well as bona fide campsites.

FOOD

Food in Australia is excellent – and reasonably cheap. Aside from beef, lamb, poultry, fish and fruit and vegetables, you can sample peculiar 'delights' such as kangaroo, buffalo, crocodile steaks or burgers, and emu. The Aboriginal delicacy of witchetty grubs – the white larvae of certain beetles – can be savoured in restaurants which specialize in bush tucker.

The big cities offer a full range of ethnic restaurants where the portions are usually larger and the costs cheaper than you would find in their British equivalents. There is no sales tax, though at weekends and on public holidays there may be a surcharge for the higher cost of staff. Most restaurants are Bring Your Own (BYO) with corkage costing from about A$2. Outside the big cities, eating places are often restricted to the local pub and the fish-and-chip shop.

BUDGETING

Australia is no longer 'the land of opportunity' for the traveller seeking work. It is becoming increasingly difficult to pick up casual labour between spells of travelling. Unemployment is currently at around 10% and it can take time to find a job. Everyone working in Australia is required to apply for a tax file number. You can apply at the nearest post office or tax office and will normally have to produce your passport to show that it bears a working-holiday visa. Non-residents of Australia earning up to A$20,600 are taxed at 29%.

The best way of finding work is often to walk in and ask – at city restaurants, bars and shops, or at farms and ranches. Alternatively, look in the Situations Vacant columns of the newspapers. The Commonwealth Employment Service (CES) – a chain of job-centres with branches in all cities and towns – advertise current vacancies, and also produce the *Harvest Table*, a guide to the fruit-picking seasons in the various states. Queensland, especially around Bundaberg, is perhaps the best place for fruit-picking. Payment is either by the bucket or by the hour (men are often paid A$1 more per hour than women). If you're good on horseback and have some experience of farm labour, you might find work on stations in the Northern Territory, Queensland or Western Australia.

The main tourist resorts (especially those in Queensland and the ski centres in the Australian Alps), are good places to find work in catering, bars or hotels. Hostels sometimes offer a free bed in exchange for cleaning duties or doing a late shift on the reception desk. And travelling hairdressers will be able to earn some cash by giving their fellow hostellers' hair a trim.

And finally, if you can't find a job and are starved of food and cash, you could try the local blood donor centre – your blood in exchange for a sandwich and a cup of tea!

FURTHER INFORMATION

Australian Tourist Commission, Gemini House, 10–18 Putney Hill, London SW15 6AA (tel. 0181 780 2227).

Victoria and Tasmania are represented by the Southern Tourism Promotion section of the Australian Tourist Commission.

Background reading: The traveller's bible, *Australia – Travel Survival Kit* (Lonely Planet), is crammed with helpful information. Other useful guides are: *Australia & New Zealand, Travellers' Survival Kit* from Vacation Work, and *Fodor's Australia*.

If you're going to Ayers Rock, you might want to read Lindy Chamberlain's *Through My Eyes*, the story of her daughter's disappearance at Ayers Rock and Lindy's subsequent imprisonment. Miles Franklin's *My Brilliant Career* and *My Career Goes Bung* provide a brilliant insight into women's lives in Australia during the last century. For a taste of modern Australian writing, check out Peter Carey.

Cairns

AIRPORT FACILITIES

Officially opened as an international airport in 1984, Cairns couldn't be more conveniently situated – just over 5 km from the city centre. It has two passenger terminals – one for international arrivals and departures, one for domestic arrivals and departures.

Airport facilities include an information desk, currency exchange, car hire and duty-free outlets. Check-in times are 90 minutes prior to international departure times and 30 minutes before domestic departures. The departure tax is A$25.

CITY LINKS

The airport shuttlebus (tel. 359555) runs between the city and the airport, and costs about A$4. Regular local buses and taxis can be found outside the terminal. Australian Coachlines, Bus Australia and McCafferty's also stop at the airport.

USEFUL ADDRESSES

Tourist office: Far North Queensland Promotion Bureau at the corner of Hartley and Wharf Streets (tel. 513588).
Australian Coachlines: Trinity Wharf (tel. 513388). Part of the Greyhound group.
YHA Travel: 20–24 McLeod Street (tel. 313158).
Post office: on the corner of Grafton Street and Harley Street (tel. 514200).
Cairns area code: 070.
Emergency services: police fire ambulance, dial 000.

GETTING ABOUT

It couldn't be easier: most of the hostels run courtesy buses into the centre, even those which are only a five-minute walk away. The main attractions are all in the city centre, as are the best places to eat.

SIGHTS

The attraction of Cairns is undoubtedly the GREAT BARRIER REEF, and the town's massive tourist industry is totally geared towards taking you, the visitor, out there – whether to dive, snorkel or to view the coral from a glass-bottomed boat. Your hostel or hotel will have information on all the options, and will be able to make the booking for you. Competition is fierce; all the companies are pretty good and provide similar options.

Most travellers recommend taking a diving course as the best way to see the coral; there are several of these on offer, costing from A\$100, depending on the length of the course. Diving schools operate from Green Island, Fitzroy Island and Michaelmas Cay, and courses can last anything from half a day to a week.

Snorkellers can book a trip to Green Island with the tour operator Great Adventures; the A\$40 return fare includes rental of snorkelling gear, and you'll get at least two hours' snorkelling time. Those who prefer to see the reef from the safety of the glass-bottomed boats can also go on these cruises – but should prepare themselves for a disappointment. The boat trips are very short, only 10 minutes, and although you can see that the coral's beautiful, you don't actually feel you're *there*. Non-swimmers should take the plunge and learn to swim before heading for Cairns and the Reef – it's worth it!

The town itself doesn't offer much in the way of sightseeing, but it's a lively and friendly place – always packed with travellers, and with lots of cheap eats, drinks, entertainment and accommodation. For panoramic views of the city, climb MOUNT WHITFIELD, close to the impressive BOTANICAL GARDENS. Other places worth a visit include the HISTORICAL MUSEUM on the corner of Lake and Shields Streets, with its display of Aboriginal arts, and the LAROC CORAL JEWELLERY FACTORY (tel. 516924), on the corner of Amuller and Comport Streets.

ACCOMMODATION

Hostels: Cairns is easy on the budget traveller, with numerous backpackers' hostels, many of them along the esplanade. Unless you specifically want to stay at the YHA or at a hostel someone has recommended, there is no need to book ahead; representatives from all the hostels meet incoming buses and trains. Accommodation is cheap: a dormitory bed will cost somewhere between A$9 and A$13 per night, with many hostels offering discounts during the wet season.

McLeod Street Hostel, 20–24 McLeod Street (tel. 510772).

Gone Walkabout Hostel, 274 Draper Street, (tel. 516160).

Tracks Hostel, 149 Grafton Street, (tel. 311474).

You'll be able to book trips to the Reef and other attractions through the hostels, and most of them lay on nightly entertainment, such as barbies or discos. Many more hostels on the esplanade.

FOOD
Cairns is an inexpensive gourmet paradise – so make the most of it! Grafton Street is the place to head if you're looking for vegetarian, steak, Chinese or Italian restaurants. Especially recommended are Ricardo's, at number 89 and also Milliways (a.k.a. 'The Restaurant at the End of the Universe') at number 142. And if you're homesick for British food, try the Cock and Bull on the corner of Grove and Digger Streets, where you'll also be able to enjoy a pint of (warm?) British beer! Rusty's pub, at the corner of Sheridon and Spence Streets, serves excellent breakfasts between 6 and 9 a.m.

Several restaurants and discos offer meals of the all-you-can-eat-for-five-dollars variety and, not surprisingly, they are packed out every night:

Backpackers' Restaurant in Shield Street Mall. Top of the bill with travellers because of its selection of all-you-can-fit-on-the-plate main courses plus salad. It's very busy, so prepare to queue!

Brumbys, corner of Grove and Digger Streets (tel. 517483). Another popular backpackers' restaurant.

Playpen Backpackers' Dance Club, corner of Lake and Hartley Streets. Serves a range of tasty, cheap meals.

ENTERTAINMENT
The drinking comes as cheaply as the eating in Cairns, and there are numerous pubs and hotel bars to choose from. The free weekly entertainment guide *Barfly* – found in all hostels – has the latest information on local action, including any live bands appearing in the clubs and pubs. Hostel staff will be able to tell you which venues are currently most popular.

Cairns has five cinemas, including the Coral Drive-In on Bruce Highway, and two small theatres.

EXCURSIONS

The Reef isn't the only place worth visiting from Cairns. Don't miss a trip to the ATHERTON TABLELANDS, a lush dairy farming area; the pretty town of KURANDA is a popular destination which can be reached by a special daily tourist train from Cairns, costing A$23 one-way or A$33 return. The KURANDA RAINFOREST RESORT has backpackers' accommodation starting at A$15, with free transfers from Cairns. Other attractions on the Tablelands include Lake Eacham and the Curtain Fig Tree (a tree which was eventually killed by a parasite vine).

PORT DOUGLAS, north of Cairns, used to be a quiet coastal town, but is now the home of a booming tourist resort called the Mirage. It's a good base for exploring the northern part of the Reef, and there are also some beautiful coastal walks. Further north lies COOKTOWN, site of Captain Cook's 1770 landing to repair the *Endeavour*, and subsequently an 1880s gold-mining town.

The final frontier of Australia is CAPE YORK. It's primarily Aboriginal land, with thick jungle, deserted beaches and crocodile-infested creeks. You'll need to join a tour to get into this wilderness: contact tour operators AAT King's, 107 Draper Street, Portsmith, Cairns (311155).

Melbourne

AIRPORT FACILITIES

Situated 22 km north-west of the city, Melbourne Airport has become quite a tourist attraction by virtue of its extensive garden display and art gallery. The terminal is a three-storey building, with a central international section and two domestic sections. It has all the usual airport facilities, including information and accommodation desks, post office, medical services and duty-free outlets.

Check-in times are 120 minutes prior to international departures, and 30 minutes before domestic departures.

CITY LINKS

Bus: Skybus (tel. 335 3066) operates a regular service linking airport and city from 6 a.m.–10.45 p.m. The journey takes about 30 minutes and the one-way fare is A$8.50. It stops on request anywhere along the route, including the two main youth hostels.

There are other regular airport buses serving various Melbourne suburbs, including Dandenong, Frankston and Knox, as well as the

towns of Geelong and Ballarat. Timetables and fares for all airport buses are available at the airport information desk.
Taxi: Taxis are available, but not usually worth the expense.

USEFUL ADDRESSES
Tourist office: Victorian Tourist Commission, World Trade Centre, corner of Flinders and Spencer Streets (tel. 650 1522).
Australian Coachlines: 58 Franklin Street (tel. 664 7888).
YHA Travel Centre: 205 King Street (tel. 670 7991).
Main post office: Corner of Bourke and Elizabeth Streets (tel. 660 1343). Open Mon.–Fri. 8 a.m.–6 p.m.; Sat. 8 a.m.–1 p.m.
British Consulate General: 17th Floor, 90 Collins Street (tel. 650 4155).
US Consulate General: 553 St Kilda Road (tel. 526 5900).
Emergency services: police, fire, ambulance, dial 000.
Medical assistance: Royal Melbourne Hospital, Parkville (tel. 342 7000).

GETTING ABOUT
Melbourne's public transport system – known as the 'Met' – is cheap and efficient. Information is available from the Met Shop, 103 Elizabeth Street (tel. 617 0900). Fares are calculated according to the number of zones travelled, and tickets are valid for trams, buses and suburban trains. Tickets can be bought from the Met Shop, certain newsagents, 7–11 Stores, and some milk bars (tel. 131638 for details). An all-day ticket for Zone One is A$3.80. A weekly ticket costs A$16.10.
Tram: The quickest way of getting around the city and inner suburbs is by tram. If you don't already have a ticket when you board the tram, you can buy one from the conductor.
Rail: Areas not covered by tram have a suburban train service. The city centre part of the train network is known as 'The Loop': all suburban trains call at these central stations (Spencer Street, Parliament, Museum, Flagstaff and Flinders Street), so you can go anywhere from the Loop.
Bus: Services operate mainly in the inner and outer suburbs. The double-decker City Explorer bus runs from 10 a.m.–4 p.m. daily, departing on the hour from Flinders Street Station. Tickets cost A$15.
Taxi: These can be hailed in the street or hired at one of the many ranks around the city. The standing charge is about A$2.60 and there is a per kilometre charge on top, which varies depending on the time of day. Note that because of Victoria's strict drink-driving laws, it can be a problem finding a taxi after the pubs close.

Bicycle: Melbourne is fairly flat, has acres of parks and gardens and more than 500 km of cycle trails. Information and maps for cyclists can be obtained from Bicycle Victoria at 29 Somerset Place, Melbourne 3001 (tel. 670 9911).

SIGHTS

For those who like gruesome history, a visit to OLD MELBOURNE JAIL in Russell Street is a must. Bushranger Ned Kelly was hanged there in 1880, and today you'll see refurbished cells, the whipping post, and the death masks of former inmates. Well worth the A$5 admission fee.

The NATIONAL GALLERY OF VICTORIA, next to the Arts Centre in St Kilda Road, contains some outstanding Aboriginal and early settlers' art. Admission starts from A$3, which includes a guided tour, but parts of the gallery are free on Mondays.

Sports lovers will find plenty to see and do in Melbourne. The AUSTRALIAN GALLERY OF SPORT & OLYMPIC MUSEUM in Jolimont Terrace contains memorabilia from the Melbourne Olympics and Australian sport in general. There's also a wheelchair in which you can pit your strength and speed against the world's leading disabled athletes – you'll go out admiring them, as three minutes seems a very long time for your tired arms! The entrance fee is A$5. On the same site are the MELBOURNE CRICKET GROUND (MCG) and FLINDERS PARK NATIONAL TENNIS CENTRE, home of the Australian Open.

Over a quarter of the inner Melbourne area is covered by parkland. The KINGS DOMAIN alone stretches from St Kilda Road to South Yarra *but* is interrupted by some busy roads! The ROYAL BOTANIC GARDENS on the south bank of the Yarra River have 36 hectares of international flora.

Shopaholics are well catered for with a choice ranging from the expensive stores such as Myers, David Jones and Georges in the city centre and the boutiques of upmarket Toorak, to the brilliant Queen Victoria covered market in the north-west of the city. The market offers fresh food, bargain clothing, household goods, and souvenirs; worth a morning's browsing.

Melbourne can't rival Sydney for surfing beaches, but it does have some good swimming beaches at ST KILDA, HALF MOON BAY, ALBERT PARK and MIDDLE PARK. The Mornington Peninsula also offers excellent beaches, including a surfing one at ROSEBUD and a nudist one at SOMERS.

ACCOMMODATION

Hostels: Melbourne has two YHA hostels:

Queensberry Hill Hostel, 78 Howard Street, North Melbourne (329 8599). The newest and most luxurious YHA hostel in Victoria, the Queensberry Hill opened in 1991. It costs from A$18 per night, and has 348 beds in various room sizes. Facilities include a cafeteria and travel agency.

Youth Hostel, 76 Chapman Street (tel. 328 3595). This city-centre YHA hostel costs from A$16.

There are a number of private backpacker hostels, mainly in the trendy St Kilda area (prices start from about A$11 per night):

The Coffee Palace, 24 Grey Street.

The Ritz, 169 Fitzroy Street (tel. 525 3501).

Leopard House, 27 Grey Street (tel. 534 1200).

Melbourne Travellers Hostel, 28 Grey Street (tel. 534 8995). Provides useful tips and help with job-hunting, as well as rooms.

Backpackers by the Beach, 24 Mitford Street (tel. 525 4355).

The Nunnery, 116 Nicholson Street, Carlton. An appealing hostel.

YWCA, 489 Elizabeth Street (329 5188). City-centre location close to the Australia Coachlines terminal. From about A$18 per person per night (sharing a four-bed room) to about A$45 (for a single room).

Student residences: The University of Melbourne offers accommodation during student vacations, and while it is more expensive than the hostels (from about A$38 per night for non-students), the quality of accommodation and food is very good. Telephone Ormond College (348 1688), Queens College (347 4837) or St Hilda's College (347 2258) for details.

Hotels and motels: If you're after a hotel or motel, avoid those opposite Spencer Street station, as they tend to attract local weirdos. St Kilda is Melbourne's red-light district, but the higher quality hotels there, such as the Diplomat, 12 Acland Street (tel. 534 0422), are safe enough. The Miami Motor Inn at 13 Hawke Street, West Melbourne (329 3003) offers bed and breakfast for about A$30 per person in a double room.

Private accommodation: Melbourne is cheaper than Sydney for long-term accommodation. See hostel noticeboards, or take a look at the noticeboard in Readings Bookstore, 338 Lygon Street, Carlton. The *Melbourne Age* classified section is another good starting-point.

Camping: Melbourne has quite a few camping sites, although none of them are very close to the centre and seem to be more caravan sites than actual camping with tents. The Coburg East site (10 km north) and the Footscray site (9 km west) are probably the closest. The Footscray site has only on-site vans but the Coburg one seems to be better equipped. The following are sites which take campers as well as caravanners: Northside Caravan Park, 158 Kororat Creek Road, Williamstown (17 km south), camping A$15, cabins and vans A$30 (tel. 397 2395); Melbourne Caravan Park, 265 Elizabeth Street, Coburg East (10 km north), camping A$12, on-site vans A$30, flats A$45 (tel. 354 3533).

FOOD
Melbourne boasts more than 2,000 restaurants representing every ethnic variety and suiting every pocket (four out of every five are BYO); it's simply impossible to list them all here. If you're a foodie, it's a good idea to invest in the *Melbourne Age*'s annual gastronomic guide to the city, *Cheap Eats in Melbourne*. It costs about A$11.55 and is available from newsagents and bookstores. Alternatively, word of mouth will guide you to the value-for-money restaurants.

Ethnic cuisine tends to be concentrated in individual areas or streets: if you want Italian food, for example, head for Lygon Street, Carlton, where you'll find plenty of restaurants and cafés to choose from (you can't miss this street, just follow the smell of garlic and baking dough!). Toto's at 101 claims to have been Australia's first pizzeria, and its speciality is a spaghetti ice cream, which looks like spaghetti bolognese.

Swan Street in Richmond is the place to head for Greek restaurants, while Little Bourke Street in the city centre offers Chinese food. The home of Spanish cuisine is Johnston Street in Fitzroy, and Vietnamese food-lovers should head for Victoria Street, North Richmond. Melbourne's Chinatown centres around the Spring Street end of the city, and has a brilliant Chinese food market on Sundays. Mariners, at 9 Fitzroy Street, St Kilda (tel. 534 5630) offers excellent seafood and pasta dishes. Next door, at number 7, the same owners run an equally brilliant pizza parlour.

For good pub food, try the Waterside Hotel, 508 Flinders Street; the Golden Age Hotel, 287 King Street; the Lemon Tree, 10 Grattan Street, Carlton; and the Met, 42 Courtney Street, North Melbourne.

Fitzroy is becoming an increasingly trendy area to eat, especially the restaurants and cafés on Brunswick and Rathdowne Streets. Charmaine's ice cream parlour at 370 Brunswick Street boasts 25 flavours of the 'best ice cream in the world'.

ENTERTAINMENT

Melbourne has a lively arts scene, much of which centres around the Victorian Arts Centre, on St Kilda Road, south of the Yarra River. It houses a concert hall, the State Theatre, the Playhouse and the George Fairfax Studio. Tickets for all events can be booked through the BASS ticket agency (tel. 11500).

The city's theatres offer a variety of entertainment; the major theatres are Her Majesty's at 219 Exhibition Street; the Comedy Theatre at 240 Exhibition Street; the Russell Theatre, 19 Russell Street; the Princess Theatre, 163 Spring Street; and the Athenaeum Theatre at 188 Collins Street. There are also various fringe theatres. Listings appear daily in the *Age*.

Melbourne has a number of independent cinemas as well as the chain ones like Hoyts and Greater Union – again the *Age* offers comprehensive listings of what's on and where. For music, most major concerts are held at the Sports and Entertainment Centre on the banks of the Yarra. Other venues include Flinders Park, in Batman Avenue, and in summer, outdoors at the Sidney Myer Music Bowl.

It may surprise you to learn that Melbourne boasts more than twice as many nightclubs as Manhattan. King Street is lined with them, one of the most popular being the Shout Rock Café on the northern end. All nightclubs insist on a reasonable standard of dress, so no thongs or shorts! Popular nightclubs in other areas include Stringfellows in Lygon Street, Carlton and the Chevron on the corner of St Kilda and Commercial Roads.

Sports lovers will think they've found paradise: Melbourne is the home of Aussie Rules football (clubs all over the city) during the winter; the Australian Open Tennis at Flinders Park every January; and the Melbourne Cup horse race on the first Tuesday of November at Flemington racecourse. (This race is so important to Melbournites that the day is a public holiday in Victoria.) The Melbourne Cricket Ground (MCG) is near the tennis centre and houses 100,000 fans for Test matches.

There are numerous pubs around Melbourne, mostly open from 10 a.m.–12 p.m. The best range of beers can arguably be found in the Loaded Dog at 324 St Georges Road, North Fitzroy (tel. 489 8222).

For up-to-the-minute information on entertainment, see Friday's edition of the *Age*.

EXCURSIONS

PHILLIP ISLAND'S fairy penguin parade attracts virtually as many tourists as the Great Barrier Reef and Ayers Rock. At dusk the diminutive birds – just one foot high – emerge from the sea and waddle along the beach to their nests among the sand dunes. Tickets cost approx. A$5 and are sold at the Phillip Island Information Centre in Newhaven (tel. 059 567447). Alternatively, trips to the Penguin Parade can be booked through YHA or backpacker hostels in Melbourne.

The DANDENONG RANGES, 40 km east of the city, make an excellent day out. Attractions include the Puffing Billy Steam train between Belgrave and Emerald Lake (tel. 03 870 8411 for a talking timetable); the William Ricketts Sanctuary at Mount Dandenong (a sculpture park celebrating the relationship between the Aboriginal people and the land); and the Healesville Wildlife Sanctuary, a walk-through park with hundreds of Australian fauna bred at Healesville. Take the train from Melbourne to Belgrave, or see the hostel noticeboards for details of day-trips.

Further afield, there's excellent hiking and wildlife-spotting at WILSONS PROMONTORY, a national park 200 km east of Melbourne. The headquarters are at Tidal River (056 808538) and both camping and cabin accommodation are available.

BALLARAT lies west of Melbourne, and its principal attraction is SOVEREIGN HILL, a recreated goldmining township, complete with a tour of the mine. Other 1850s mining towns worth a visit are BENDIGO and BEECHWORTH, which have preserved hotels, houses and townhalls from the Gold Rush era.

HANGING ROCK is an awesome rock formation – and an extremely arduous climb. Unfortunately, it's impossible to reach without a car, so if you can't afford to hire one for the day, try talking nicely to someone who owns a car. It's one of the few places where you'll see koalas in their natural environment.

West of Melbourne, the GREAT OCEAN ROAD is extremely scenic, passing through the pretty coastal town of LORNE and the lush forest of the OTWAY RANGES to the spectacular sandstone formations of the Twelve Apostles, London Bridge, The Arch and The Blowhole. Again, details of tours of the area can be found at the YHA offices or on hostel noticeboards.

Perth

AIRPORT FACILITIES

Perth International Airport is 16 km east of the city. There are two terminals (one domestic, the other international) on opposite sides of the runway. The usual airport facilities, including an information desk, bank, restaurants and bars, shops, duty-free and car rental facilities are available. There is a 24-hour accommodation desk in the international terminal. Check-in times are 120 minutes prior to international departures, and 40 minutes before a domestic flight.

CITY LINKS
Airport bus: This runs hourly to the city centre from 5 a.m.–9.20 p.m., takes 40 minutes and costs about A$7. The bus picks up from the Ansett offices on the corner of Irwin Street and St George's Terrace, from the Australian Airlines office at 55 St George's Terrace, and from major hotels. For information, dial 250 2838 or 479 4131.
Bus: For about A$1.20 you can travel on the number 338 bus to the city centre from outside the arrivals hall of the domestic terminal.
Taxi: These cost about A$18 to the city centre. There is an official sharing scheme at the airport; ask at the information desk in the domestic arrivals hall for details.

USEFUL ADDRESSES
Tourist office: Western Australia Tourist Centre, Albert Facey House, Forrest Place (tel. 483 1111).
Australian Coachlines: 26 St George's Terrace (tel. 221 3411).
Main post office: 3 Forrest Place (tel. 326 5211).
British Consulate-General: Prudential Building, 95 St George's Terrace, Perth (tel. 321 5611).
Perth area telephone code: 09.
Emergency services: dial 000.

GETTING ABOUT
Rail: Train services run from Perth to Fremantle, Midland and Armadale. A new line to Burns north of Perth was due to be completed by 1993. Purchase tickets from vending machines on the station prior to boarding the train. Fares operate on a zonal system and tend to be within the same price range as the buses, see below. Daytripper tickets cost A$4.80 and give one-day's unlimited travel for two adults on bus and rail.
Bus: All travel within the inner city is free! Otherwise, fares operate on a zonal system and prices range from A$0.65–A$3.30, depending on how many zones you travel through.
Taxi: Taxi ranks can be found throughout the city and in Fremantle, but flagging down taxis can be a problem because of Perth's wide streets and the vast amount of traffic. To book a cab, phone 221211. The standing charge varies between A$1.70

and A$2.90 depending on the time of day, plus about A$0.75 per kilometre.

SIGHTS
Perth has some beautiful white beaches including SCARBOROUGH, COTTOSLOE, TRIGG, CITY BEACH and the nudist beach at SWANBOURNE. If you've been travelling around a lot, these provide are an excellent place to crash out and make the most of the Perth sunshine.

For the avid sightseer, Perth also offers good museums and galleries, most notably the ART GALLERY OF WESTERN AUSTRALIA in James Street, with its ever-changing exhibitions of contemporary art, and the WESTERN AUSTRALIA MUSEUM in Francis Street, which has an Aboriginal gallery, veteran and vintage cars, and mammal and wildlife displays.

Parkland includes Hyde Park, Stirling Gardens, the Supreme Court Gardens and the Alan Green Conservatory. KINGS PARK is among Australia's finest, affording panoramic views of the city centre and the Swan River.

The main shopping areas are around Hay Street Mall and Forrest Place, and tourists are usually steered towards Ye Olde London Court, a historic-looking arcade with a host of souvenir shops. The suburb of Claremont has some classy designer shops. For Aboriginal arts and crafts, try Creative Native in King Street.

Perth's port of FREMANTLE hit the headlines by staging the 1985 America's Cup yachting series, and its places of interest include the ROUND HOUSE, a former jail, in High Street, with poky cells in which up to 15 prisoners at a time could be held.

ACCOMMODATION
Hostels: Perth's three YHA hostels are all in Northbridge and charge from A$11 per night. They all get busy in summer, so it's best to book ahead. Western Australia is the only Australian state in which sleeping bags are allowed in youth hostels.

60 Newcastle Street (tel. 328 1135).

46 Francis Street (tel. 328 7794).

For non-YHA hostels, head for Aberdeen Street in Northbridge:

Perth Travellers Lodge, 156 Aberdeen Street (tel. 328 6667).

Top Notch Hotel, 194 Aberdeen Street (see Perth Travellers Lodge for tel. no.).

Aberdeen Lodge, 79–81 Aberdeen Street (tel. 227 6137). Beds cost from about A$10 per night

Cheviot Lodge, 30 Bulwer Street, Northbridge (tel. 227 6817). From A$10 per night.

YWCA (tel. 998212). From A$18 per night.

In Fremantle, the Bundi Kudja YHA is at 96 Hampton Road (335 3467) and there's a backpackers' hostel called Port Lodge at 28 Marine Terrace (335 3032.)
Hotels: If you want a hotel, you'll find many of them were built for the America's Cup and are decidedly upmarket (i.e. not budget).

The Grosvenor Hotel, 339 Hay Street (tel. 325 3799) is among the cheapest: prices start at about A$35 per night for a single room.

The Grand Central Hotel, 379 Wellington Street (tel. 325 5638) is in the same price range.

The Australia Tavern, 4 Edward Street, Fremantle (tel. 335 2542) is good, and costs about A$40 for a double room.
Homestays and farmstays: Homestay of WA, 40 Union Road, Carmel, WA 6076 (tel. 293 5347) organizes a range of home and farm accommodation, bed and breakfast or self-catering units. If you're visiting Fremantle, contact Fremantle Homestay, 14 Herbert Street, Fremantle (tel. 430 4000) where B&B costs from A$35 per person.
Camping: Much like any other major city, Perth does not have a huge selection of campsites at a convenient distance from its centre. There is camping available, though, at the following sites: Careniup Caravan Park, (14 km north): 467 Beach Road, Gwelup, camping is A$15 for two, on-site vans from A$30 (tel. 447 6665); Central Caravan Park (7 km east), 34 Central Avenue, Redcliffe, camping is A$15 for two, on-site vans from A$130 per week (tel. 227 5696); Kenlorn Caravan Park, (9 km south-east), 229 Welshpool Road, Queens Park, camping A$15 for two (weekly rates available), on-site vans from A$130 per week (tel. 458 2604).

FOOD
Perth has a good range of international restaurants, roughly a quarter of which are Thai, Malaysian, Chinese or Vietnamese. The Sun-market Centre, down an alley off the corner of Murray and Barrack Streets, has a good reputation for Asian food. Prices are reasonable: only around A$8 for a meal.

In addition to being the prime hostel location, Northbridge has numerous inexpensive restaurants representing virtually every nationality. Especially popular are:

Fishy Affair, 121 James Street: seafood restaurant.

Los Gallos, 276 William Street: Mexican.

L'Alba, 100 Lake Street (tel. 328 3750): late night café serving cheap and tasty pasta meals – so you know where to go after you've been to the pub or out dancing.

Granary Wholefoods, 37 Barrack Street: a good place to go for lunch (a vegetarian meal followed by delicious home-made ice cream costs about A$10).

If you want to splash out, there are some excellent upmarket restaurants in the city centre. Hilite 33 on Level 33 of Martin Tower, St George's Terrace, is a revolving French restaurant – the panoramic views are amazing, though the food's not really all that brilliant!

Fremantle has a host of good restaurants and cafés. Old Papas on South Terrace is the trendiest eating spot and serves excellent *focaccia* sandwiches and desserts. Another good place to try is the Sail and Anchor pub at 64 South Terrace, opposite the markets: its bar snacks and meals are as good its beer!

Those who enjoy eating out regularly should buy a copy of *Cheap Eats in Perth*, available from bookshops and newsagents.

ENTERTAINMENT
Perth's main theatre is His Majesty's, on the corner of King and Hay Streets (tel. 322 2929). The Regal Theatre has an innovative 'Crying Room' which enables those with noisy children to watch the play or concert without disturbing everybody else.

There are scores of cinemas, including several city centre complexes (Hoyts, Greater Union, Lumière, etc.) and some excellent suburban screens showing first releases. In the suburbs there are also several drive-ins. Listings can be found in the *West Australian* newspaper (or tel. 0055 14632).

For nightclubs, make for the city centre or – where else? – Northbridge. Popular clubs include Gobbles at 613 Wellington Street, Havana at 69 Lake Street, Northbridge, and the Exit Nightclub at 187 Stirling Street. If you want to see how the yachting fraternity rave, try Christies in Fremantle. The Nedlands Park Hotel – a.k.a. Steve's – at 171 Broadway, Nedlands is a very popular university pub with regular live bands. The Ocean Beach Hotel at Cottosloe and the Lookout Bar at Scarborough Beach offer good drinking with a sea view.

FESTIVALS AND EVENTS
The Festival of Perth takes place in February and March each year, and offers an extensive performing arts programme including theatre, music and an outdoor film festival.

EXCURSIONS

ROTTNEST ISLAND, a two-hour ferry ride from Perth, offers a stunningly rugged coastline, a beautiful coral reef, a notorious history as an Aboriginal prison, and Australia's tiniest marsupial: the quokka. The quokkas know when it's feeding time and come out to meet the coachloads of tourists. Beware though – if you try to stroke them without offering food, they bite! Daily ferry services to 'Rotto' operate from Barrack Street Jetty, Perth and East Street Jetty, Fremantle; it costs about A$35 for a return trip. For an extra A$10, you can take the Underwater Explorer from the Island jetty: a 50-minute submarine cruise of the reef, to view the coral and a couple of old shipwrecks. You get a much better view of reef life this way than you do by glass-bottomed boat up at the Great Barrier Reef. There are plenty of opportunities for snorkelling and diving and it's cheaper than up at the Great Barrier Reef (telephone the Rottnest Island Authority on 372 9729 for details; tourist information or the staff at the jetty will also be able to direct you).

YANCHEP and NAMBURG NATIONAL PARKS lie north of Perth. Yanchep boasts native animals, limestone caves, wildflowers, black swans and a koala colony. Namburg is the home of the curious ancient limestone formations known as the Pinnacles. Tours of both national parks can often be booked via the hostels, as well as through the Western Australia Tourist Centre.

Some 19 km east of Perth, the DARLING RANGES offer scenic Australian bushland; visitors in springtime will see fabulous wildflowers in bloom. A hundred kilometres further east lies the rich agricultural land of the AVON VALLEY, with the historic towns of NORTHAM, YORK and TOODYHAY in its midst.

ARMADALE, 26 km south of Perth, is the place to go to see how people lived a century ago. The recreated Pioneer Village is open Mon.–Fri. 10 a.m.–5 p.m.; Sat. 12–5 p.m.

Sydney

AIRPORT FACILITIES

Kingsford-Smith International Airport, named after an Australian aviator, is 12 km south of the city centre. It has four terminals: one international and three for domestic flights. All the usual airport facilities, including information desk, bank, duty-free and shops, plus a nursery, are available. Check-in times are 60–90 minutes prior to an international flight, and 30 minutes before domestic flights.

CITY LINKS
Bus: The Airport Express bus stops outside both the international and domestic terminals and charges A$5 for a one-way trip to the city centre. The journey to Circular Quay takes approximately half an hour. Two companies provide transfers to the city and King's Cross hostels for A$5.50.
Taxi: Taxis can be found outside the terminals, and cost from about A$18 into downtown Sydney.

USEFUL ADDRESSES
Tourist office: Travel Centre of New South Wales, 19 Castlereagh Street (tel. 231 4444).
British Airways: 64 Castlereagh Street (tel. 258 3300).
Greyhound Pioneer: Oxford Square (tel. 286 8666/8688) and Corner Hay and Castlereagh Streets (tel. 281 2266, or toll-free 132323).
Main post office: Pitt Street, between King Street and Martin Place. Open Mon.–Fri. 8.15 a.m.–5.30 p.m. and Sat. 8.30 a.m.–12 p.m. The poste restante is always busy, so expect to queue (or, if possible, have mail sent to the suburb where you're staying).
British Consulate-General: 116 The Gateway, 1 Magaurie Place, Sydney (tel. 27 7521).
US Consulate: 39 Castlereagh St., Sydney (tel. 373 9200; fax. 373 9184).
Sydney area telephone code: 02.
World Travellers Centre: Travellers' Contact Point, 428 George St., Sydney (tel. 221 8744).
Emergency services: police, fire, ambulance, dial 000.
Medical assistance: Sydney Hospital (tel. 228 2111).

GETTING ABOUT
Separate daily bus and train passes are available (from stations and some newsagents), and there is also a weekly 'red pass' which, for about A$16 entitles you to travel on buses, trains and ferries in the very large central zone. For travel information tel. 131500.
Rail: The network covers both city centre and suburbs, with fares ranging from A$1.20 upwards depending on distance travelled.
Bus: Sydney has a good bus service, with fares calculated on a zone basis. Information on buses, timetables and fares is available from the inspectors' offices along Circular Quay or in the Queen Victoria Building on York Street. A Bus Tripper ticket for A$7.30 gives unlimited bus travel for one day.

Buses with three-digit numbers beginning with 1 and 2 leave from Wynyard Park and head north; buses beginning 3 head east from Circular Quay; and 4 and 5 buses go south and west, also from Circular Quay.

There are two free buses: the 666 runs between Wynyard Station and the Art Gallery of New South Wales; the 777 runs between the Domain Parking Station and Wynyard Station.

The Sydney Explorer sightseeing bus runs continuously and charges about A$15 for a tour of 22 places of interest. A Sydney Explorer pass (which allows you to hop on and off) is good value for money at A$20.

Ferry: A trip across the harbour is not to be missed: downtown Sydney is at its most attractive from the water. The main commuter destinations from the harbour are Manly, Taronga Zoo, Mosman, Balmain, Kirribilli, Neutral Bay and Cremorne. Services are frequent during rush hour, and half-hourly the rest of the day. For prices, telephone the Ferry Information Service on 247 4738. Consider investing in a travel pass if you're likely to be using both ferries and buses.

SIGHTS

Sydney's HARBOUR BRIDGE and OPERA HOUSE are two of the most famous sights in the world, let alone Australia – and they really are as impressive as you've always imagined they'd be. The 134-metre high bridge offers excellent views of the waterfront from its pylon lookout – climb up for a token fee. The Opera House is a fantastic building, and contains four theatres, a performing arts library and three restaurants. However, the best views of Sydney are from SYDNEY TOWER, in the shopping centre on the corner of Market and Pitt Streets. The observation deck is open from 9.30 a.m.–9.30 p.m. (11.30 p.m. on Saturdays) and costs about A$6.

The futuristic DARLING HARBOUR has become a major tourist attraction, and is home to the POWERHOUSE MUSEUM (tel. 271 0111). The Museum combines a science centre with displays of social history and decorative arts. Admission is free, and it's open daily from 10 a.m.–5 p.m. The AUSTRALIAN MUSEUM in College Street, near Hyde Park is also free (open 10 a.m.–5 p.m. daily); it specializes in natural history, and has some excellent Aboriginal displays. The ART GALLERY OF NEW SOUTH WALES (tel. 225 1700) exhibits paintings by many of Australia's premier artists, plus Aboriginal works.

The ROYAL BOTANIC GARDENS (tel. 231 8125) in Macquarie Street are open daily from 8 a.m. to sunset, and feature rainforest flora, enormous Moreton Bay fig trees and a cactus collection. TARONGA ZOO (tel. 969 2777) is home to such Australian native fauna as koalas, kangaroos and snakes, as well as the usual lions, elephants, giraffes, etc. A ticket covering return ferry, admission and the chairlift up to the zoo can be bought from Circular Quay for about A$20. Maps are available at the entrance and included in the cost, A$14.00 per adult.

Sydney's most famous beach is BONDI. It gets crowded, but it's excellent for people-watching and surfing. To get there, take the number 380, 382 or 389 bus from Circular Quay or from Bondi Junction railway station. The authorities have spent some A$350m on cleaning up Bondi, which was badly affected by sewage pollution during the 1980s. Other good beaches include COOGEE, which is only a few kilometres south of Bondi and can be reached by buses 372, 373 and 374 from Circular Quay. MANLY BEACH is accessible by ferry, and is crowded with 'sun-bakers' and surfers.

For shopping, the Queen Victoria Building on the corner of Market and George Streets contains several levels of shops linked by ornate passages and staircases. Darling Harbour has an outstanding shopping complex which can be reached by the famous monorail. Sydney's largest department stores are David Jones and Grace Brothers (don't bother cracking the 'Are you free, Mr Humphries?' jokes – they've heard them all before) which are both connected to the Centrepoint Complex. There are a number of good markets, including Paddington Market on Saturdays and Paddy's Market in Redfern at weekends.

ACCOMMODATION
Youth hostels: There are four YHA Hostels in Sydney – three of them in Glebe.

Hereford YHA Lodge, 51 Hereford Street (tel. 660 5577). Beds from A$13 per night. Rooftop pool and a sauna.

Glebe Point Hostel, 256 Glebe Road (tel. 660 8878). From A$13 per night.

Glebe YHA, 262 Glebe Road (tel. 692 8418).

Forest Lodge Hostel, 28 Ross Street (tel. 692 0747). Caters mainly for longer-term travellers. From about A$90 weekly.

Dulwich Hill Hostel, 407 Marrickville Road (tel. 569 0272). Also caters for long-term travellers. From about A$90 weekly.

Most of the private hostels are situated in the Kings Cross district, which is very lively – and very seedy. The price of a bed ranges from about A$13 to A$20 per night. Since the fire at the Downunder backpackers' in Kings Cross in 1989, fire precautions and security have been stepped up at all hostels.

The Downunder, 25 Hughes Street (tel. 358 1433). Now completely rebuilt after the fire, and fairly popular.

Original Backpackers, 162 Victoria Street (tel. 356 3232).

Pink House, Barncleuth Square (tel. 358 1689).

Rucksack Rest, MacDonald Street, Pitts Point (tel. 358 2348).

Wattle House Hostel, 44 Hereford Street, Glebe (tel. 692 0879).

Coogee Beach Backpackers Hostel, 94 Beach Street, Coogee (tel. 665 7735).

Lamrock Hostel, 7 Lamrock Avenue, Bondi (tel. 365 0221). One of a number of popular Bondi hostels.

Hotels: Many hotels and guest houses offer backpackers' accommodation, though this apparently tends to be inferior to that offered by hostels, and usually costs twice as much. And if you're looking for something a bit more upmarket than backpackers' accommodation, you'll find that many of the hotels and guest houses are a bit dingy, and usually complete with a noisy bar. Among the places recommended by travellers are:

Neutral Bay Lodge, 45 Kurraba Road, Kirribilli (tel. 953 4199). Single rooms with a TV and fridge from A$180 per week.

Pension Albergo, 5 Day Street, Leichhardt (tel. 560 0179). Charges A$30 per person for a double room, including breakfast.

Private accommodation: Travellers intending to spend a few months working in Sydney should check the hostel noticeboards and the *Sydney Morning Herald* for flats. Renting a flat is expensive, and you usually have to pay four or six weeks' rent in advance as a 'bond'. Most flats are unfurnished and you may be asked to sign a six-month lease.

FOOD

Sydney is crammed with excellent restaurants – cheap and expensive, and of every ethnic variety – there simply isn't room to list them all. But if you're feeling hungry and aren't sure where to head, the The Rocks is a good place to start; it has salad bars, hamburger joints, steakhouses, and crêperies. Other areas with a number of good eateries include the city centre, Kings Cross, Glebe, Surry Hills, Bondi and Paddington. Sydney's Chinatown is based in the area around Dixon and Hay Streets.

For snacks, try the international food hall at Darling Harbour or the one at Manly Wharf Complex. The city centre has numerous sandwich bars, kebab stalls, and bakeries, where you can sample the ubiquitous Australian meat pie.

Wherever you walk in Sydney, you'll find a number of inviting places to eat, so if you intend to spend a few weeks there and enjoy eating out, it's worth investing in a copy of *Cheap Eats in Sydney* (available from newsagents), which will outline the best places to go.

Budget restaurants include:

Geronimo's, 106 Curlewis Street, Bondi. Indian cuisine. A$10 all you can eat.

University of Technology, Tower Building, Level 3, Broadway. Prices set with students in mind.

Bill and Toni's, 74 Stanley Street, East Sydney. Italian eatery. BYO.

ENTERTAINMENT
It's impossible to get bored in Sydney – there's always something going on. The Opera House is expensive, but it's worth attending a concert just to say you've been there. The box office number is 250 7777, but tickets can be booked in advance from abroad through Qantas offices.

The *Sydney Morning Herald* runs theatre and cinema listings and also publishes a Friday Metro Guide, which includes information on half-price previews, pub theatres and fringe theatre as well as music venues.

Popular nightspots include Selina's in the Coogee Bay Hotel and the Colosseum in Kings Cross. And Kings Cross, with its red-light district and selection of weird and wonderful people, is a great place to wander around for an evening's entertainment – but if you're female, it's better not to wander about there alone.

FESTIVALS AND EVENTS
The Festival of Sydney runs from New Year's Eve to February and offers numerous free events, including jazz, folk, rock and classical concerts in the Domain. At other times of year, there's often free entertainment at the Rocks and around Circular Quay, including music and street theatre.

EXCURSIONS
A two-hour train ride from Sydney, the BLUE MOUNTAINS (named after a blue haze which hangs over the hills and valleys) are often a visitor's first experience of the Australian bush. KATOOMBA is the area's main tourist centre, and offers splendid views over the

mountains, including the Three Sisters rock formation. The Giant Stairway is the arduous way of descending to the valley, or you can take the heartstoppingly fast funicular railway, which costs from A$2. The scenic skyway is a short but scary cable-car ride across one of the valleys; it costs about A$3. Those with little time to spare can book a day tour of the region through tourist information or the hostels.

CANBERRA is a five-hour bus trip from Sydney. You won't need more than a couple of days to cover the sights: the PARLIAMENT BUILDING opened in 1988; it's extremely ornate with a glass roof – you'll either love it or hate it. When Parliament is in session, it's worth booking a ticket (tel. 277 4890) to see Mr Keating *et al* in action at Question Time – the exchanges tend to be rather more colourful than the British ones! The WAR MEMORIAL is a much more dignified building, and claims to be Australia's second most visited attraction after the Opera House. Sports lovers will enjoy a visit to the AUSTRALIAN INSTITUTE OF SPORT, behind the YHA hostel. A budding sports star will take you on a tour of the facilities and tell you about life and training at the school. When you've been there, you'll know why Australia wins more Olympic gold medals than the Brits do.

COOMA, 427 km south of Sydney, is the principal town in the Snowy Mountains. The ski season is from July to September, and during this time accommodation can be expensive. To economize, stay in a sub-alpine town like BERRIDALE rather than main resorts like Thredbo, and commute by bus to the slopes.

BYRON BAY, north of Sydney *en route* to Queensland used to be a wonderful place to relax on an unspoilt beach. These days it's much more touristy.

FIJI

VITAL STATISTICS
Red tape: A full passport is required, plus a return or onward plane ticket and adequate funds to cover your stay. Visas aren't required by citizens of Commonwealth countries, most European countries and the USA. It is necessary to obtain a permit before your arrival in Fiji if you intend to stay for more than one month (UK nationals intending to stay less than a month do not require a permit). Once there, it's possible to extend the permit for a further six months, provided you have sufficient funds.
Customs: 500 cigarettes or 500 g tobacco, plus 2 l spirits or 4 l

wine or beer. Goods to the value of F$400 may also be brought in. Fruit and plants may not be imported.

Health: It's advisable to take precautions against typhoid. No vaccination certificates are needed. Health insurance is recommended.

Language: English, Fijian, and Hindi.

Population: Just over 750,000.

Capital: Suva, on the island of Viti Levu, population around 80,000.

Political system: Democracy.

Religion: Methodist and Hindu, with Muslim and Roman Catholic minorities.

Time: Twelve hours ahead of GMT.

Money: The currency is the Fijian dollar (F$), divided into 100 cents. Coins: 1, 2, 5, 10, 20 and 50 cents. Notes: F$1, F$2, F$5, F$10 and F$20. £1 = about F$2.07.

It's a good idea to carry small-denomination notes and a few coins around, as you'll find a strange lack of change at the markets and from taxi drivers! Traveller's cheques and major credit cards are widely used. Crime is pretty low on Fiji – the locals may disagree, but compared to Western countries it's safe and you can carry cash around.

Communications: Phone boxes are now easily available. Calls can also be made from hotels.

Letters take about a week to reach the USA and Europe. Poste restante facilities are available at main post offices; letters should be marked 'General Delivery'.

Electricity: 240v AC/50 Hz.

Business hours: BANKS: Mon.–Thurs. 9.30 a.m.–3 p.m.; Fri. 9.30 a.m.–4 p.m. The Bank of New Zealand at Nadi International Airport is open 24 hours a day.

POST OFFICES: Mon.–Fri. 8 a.m.–4.30 p.m., Sat. 8 a.m.–12 p.m.

SHOPS: Mon.–Fri. 8 a.m.–4.30 p.m. (some shops close on Wednesday afternoons); Sat. 8 a.m.–1 p.m.

OFFICES: Mon.–Thurs. 8 a.m.–4.30 p.m. and Fri. 8 a.m.–4 p.m.

Holidays: 1 January; Easter (three-day holiday); April (Ratu Sir Lata Subluna Day); first Monday in June (Queen's birthday); August (Bank Holiday); October (Fiji Day – closest Monday to 10 October) and Diwali Festival; 25 and 26 December (Prophet Mohammed's birthday).

Climate: Tropical, with a dry season between April and November and a wet season from December to March. Maximum temperatures can reach 33°C between December and February, while minimum temperatures of around 17°C may occur between June and August.

DO'S AND DON'TS
Tourism is a major income industry since the coup of the early 1990s. The situation now seems to have stabilized and the authorities are eager to regain tourists' confidence; you should be quite safe.

WHERE TO GO FOR WHAT
The Fiji archipelago consists of some three hundred islands, of which only a hundred or so are inhabited. The two main islands are Viti Levu and Vanua Levu. Most of the islands are actually volcanic peaks of a now submerged continent – the surrounding coral reefs are among the most fantastic in the world.

Fiji's capital, SUVA, is on Viti Levu. It's a cosmopolitan city, but not a very exciting one. Don't spend too long there, the best beaches are all on the other side of the island. NADI, Fiji's best-known city, is hardly a thrill-a-minute place either, but nearby there are some good beaches (see the section on **Nadi**, p. 465). For diving and snorkelling opportunities, some beautiful island resorts lie offshore, accessible from both Nadi and the nearby town of LAUTOKA.

Vanua Levu has some beautiful scenery and is the quieter of the two islands. The main towns, SAVUSAVU in the south and LABASA to the north, are divided by an expanse of mountain tableland dotted with coconut plantations. Around the island are secluded beaches from which you can explore the coral reefs.

To escape the tourist trail, try Fiji's third island: TAVEUNI. Its rural village remains unchanged from a century ago. High in the mountains, cradled in an old volcanic crater, lies LAKE TAGIMAU-CIA, its surface covered by a floating mass of fuchsia-like tagimaucia flowers. These red-and-white flowers are beautiful – but contrary to what the locals and some guidebooks will tell you, the plant *does* grow elsewhere!

INTERNAL TRAVEL
Air: Regular inter-island services are provided by Air Fiji, Sunflower Airlines, Turtle Airways and Air Wakaya. Fares are reasonable – a one-way flight from Nadi to Suva costs about F$60. Of particular interest to travellers is Fiji Air's special package, by which you can fly to the islands of Vanua Levu, Ovalau, Taveuni and Kadavu within 30 days for around F$200. The package can only be bought in Fiji; contact Air Fiji on 313 666 (Suva) and 722521 (Nadi).

Departure tax is F$20.

Boat: Inter-island ferries operate between Viti Levu, Vanua Levu and Ovalau. Economy fares are cheap, but schedules are subject to alteration. It's best to check times and fares with the ferry companies: the Patterson Brothers, Epworth House, Nina Street, Suva and the Consort Shipping Company, Dominion Arcade, Suva.

One of the best forms of transport for meeting the locals are the (extremely basic) copra boats, which go to most of the islands. Again, you'll need to check out schedules and fares with the companies who run them (Patterson Brothers and Consort Shipping Company, as above).

Bus: Several companies operate air-conditioned buses between Suva and Nadi, and Lautoka and Suva. Queens Coach (tel. 722 036 in Suva and 722 036 in Nadi) runs between Suva and Nadi Airport, and a one-way fare is about F$12. The Fiji Express does virtually the same route for F$6 more (tel. 25 637 in Suva and 722 821 in Nadi). Sunbeam Transport operates the Lautoka–Suva trip; for times and fares, contact them on tel. 382 122 (Suva).

Car hire: Not really an enticing option, as rates can be quite high, there's often a problem with maintenance, and the roads themselves are very poor. Expect to pay at least F$50 per day for unlimited travel. All the hotel chains have car rental desks – your national driving licence is acceptable. Driving is on the left.

Taxi: An inexpensive way of getting about. The fare between Nadi and Suva is around F$42, so if there are a few of you, it works out cheaper than the bus. Finding a cab can prove difficult on Sundays, and sometimes of an evening.

Hitching: It's frowned upon for locals to do it, no matter how poor they might be, yet no one seems to object to foreigners thumbing a lift. Hitchers report that getting a lift is fairly easy.

ACCOMMODATION

Youth hostels: Four privately owned establishments in Fiji have been approved by New Zealand YHA, so all YHA members are entitled to a 20% discount on dormitory accommodation. The three hostels in the Nadi area are listed below (see **Nadi: Accommodation**, p. 466), the fourth hostel is the Hide-A-Way Resort, Queen's Road, Coral Coast, PO Box 233, Sigatoka (tel. 50 177). Prices start at about F$10–12 per night.

Hotels and guest houses: Cheap establishments range in quality from basic-but-clean to ·downright shabby. Prices start at about F$12 per night for a bunk, around F$22 for a single room. If however you're willing to fork out between F$50 and F$75 per night for a single room, you'll find yourself with a wide choice of hotels, many with additional facilities such as air-conditioning, swimming pool, and good restaurants and bars.

FOOD
Fiji may be made up of more than 300 paradise islands, but if you're hoping for a gastronomic heaven, you'll be extremely disappointed. Though the quality and quantity of food has improved during recent years, there's nothing much to thrill the tastebuds.

The four main cuisines on offer are Fijian, European, Chinese and Indian. Fijian fare includes fish, shellfish, pork, beef, chicken, yams, rice, coconut milk, taro, cassava, tropical fruits, and such greens as ferns and taro leaves. Chinese and Indian restaurants serve excellent meals (beware, though, Indian food here tends to be spicier than in Britain). European cuisine is of the steak, potatoes and veg variety. The typical price for a full meal in a restaurant would be approx. F$7.

Markets and supermarkets sell a range of cheap, good quality fruits and vegetables, but make sure you wash foods thoroughly before tucking in. You'll find meat, poultry and dairy products are cheap, but tinned foods tend to be imported and therefore on the expensive side.

While you're there, you should try the Fijian male population's favourite drink, *yaqona*. It's made from the root of the pepper plant and used to be drunk in traditional ceremonies appointing a new chief or launching a canoe. It's now a social drink, passed around in coconut shells. Westerners who've tried it claim it tastes like watery mud, nevertheless the Fijians seem to thrive on it.

BUDGETING
Fiji is cheap to visit, and its beaches are a good place to flop if you're short of cash after seeing all there is to see in Australia and New Zealand. Accommodation and food are inexpensive, as is transport. What *will* eat up your budget though, if you want to see the coral, is a diving course (cost: around F$300). There are 22 dive operators in Fiji, so shop around for the best rates.

In the face of high unemployment, your chances of picking up work here are extremely remote. Work permits are like gold dust: the government will only issue them to people whose skills it considers worth having. If, for some reason, you're determined to work in Fiji, write to the Permanent Secretary for Home Affairs, Government Buildings, Suva (or to the Fijian Embassy in your country of origin) before you set off on your trip.

FURTHER INFORMATION

Embassy of Fiji, 34 Hyde Park Gate, London SW7 5BN (tel. 0171 584 3661).

Fiji Visitors' Bureau, Suite 433, High Holborn House, London WC1V 6RB (tel. 0171 242 3131).

Background reading: *Fiji – Travel Survival Kit* (Lonely Planet) is extremely informative, and Fodor's *South Pacific* has a good chapter on Fiji and is especially useful if you're planning to see other Pacific islands, such as Papua New Guinea, Tonga and Western Samoa in your trip.

The great novel set in Fiji has yet to be written. So any would-be Booker Prize winners should have their pens at the ready!

Nadi

AIRPORT FACILITIES

Nadi International Airport, just 8 km north of the city, is open 24 hours a day. It has two terminals: one for domestic flights; one for international. The usual facilities, including an information desk, hotel reservations desk, medical centre, restaurant, postal and duty-free outlets are available. Check-in times are 45 minutes before domestic flights; 90 minutes before international flights. Departure tax is F$10.

CITY LINKS

Queens Coach and Fiji Express operate between Nadi International Airport and the city itself (see **Fiji: Internal Travel**, p. 462). Most of the hotels run courtesy coaches to and from the airport. It's only a ten-minute trip.

USEFUL ADDRESSES

Tourist office: Fiji Visitors' Bureau is at the airport (tel. 72 433).
Embassies: British Embassy, PO Box 1355 Victoria House, Suva, Fiji (tel. 311 033); United States Embassy, PO Box 2181, 31 Loftus Street, Suva, Fiji (tel. 314 466).

GETTING ABOUT

Regular buses run between Nadi and Lautoka and Nadi and Suva. See **Fiji: Internal Travel**, p. 462 for information about buses, taxis and car hire. Various tour companies operate trips to areas around Nadi not covered by public transport; contact the tourist information desk at the airport, or at your hotel for details and costs.

SIGHTS

There's not much to see in Nadi itself: it's basically one long, main street — Queen's Road — which is lined with duty-free shops. (If you're a shopaholic, you'll love the place!) But it's a good base for exploring the rest of Viti Levu, and it does have some good beaches: spend some time soaking up the sun on Walloaloa, Newtown and Regent beaches. They're good for jogging or picnics too.

On Queen's Road, just 2.5 kilometres outside Nadi is WAQADRA GARDEN, crammed with the most fabulous fauna and flora. The F$5 admission fee also includes tropical fruits and a refreshing drink. Another destination on your itinerary should be the GARDEN OF THE SLEEPING GIANT, 5 km from Nadi airport in the direction of Lautoka, once the private garden of actor Raymond Burr (he of *Perry Mason* and *Ironside* fame). Lying in the shadow of the Sabeto mountains, which are supposed to resemble a sleeping giant, it boasts some 40 varieties of Asian orchids and Cattleya hybrids. Admission is F$6 for one person, $10 for two.

ACCOMMODATION

Youth hostels: Three Nadi motels have been approved as backpacker accommodation by the YHA of New Zealand:

Nadi Bay Motel, Wailoaloa Beach Road, PO Box 1102, Nadi (tel. 723 599).

Seashell Cove Resort, Momi Bay, PO Box 9530, Nadi Airport (tel. 50 309).

All are clean and comfortable, and prices start at about F$8−10 per night.

Hotels/motels: The Nadi Sunseekers Hotel on Narewa Road, near the Regent and Sheraton Hotels (tel. 700 400), is among the best of the cheaper hotels. It has air-conditioning, a swimming pool, dormitory accommodation, and is very clean. It costs about F$8 for a dormitory bed. Singles F$20.

If you want to be by the beach, then pay the F$3 cab fare to the Traveller's Beach Resort, Newtown Beach (tel. 723 322). Prices start at F$15. It's clean and comfortable, in a lovely setting. Definitely the cheapest beachside accommodation on offer.

FOOD
Eating is usually done in hotel restaurants; you'll find that hotels and motels with budget accommodation will also offer inexpensive meals. But if you prefer to eat out, there are a few eateries worth a visit:

Mama's Pizza, Queens Road, next to the Dominion International hotel. Popular with the locals; the pizza's quite good and cheap – from about F$7.

Curry Restaurant, Clay Street. Serves really good, hot Indian curries. Expect to pay about F$5.

Maharaj, Namaka, on the main highway between Nadi and the airport. Easily one of the finest restaurants in Fiji – and it's a cheap one too! For prices starting at about F$6, you can tuck into excellent seafood, curries and Chinese food. A must.

ENTERTAINMENT
If you want night life, then Fiji isn't the best place to be. Saturday evening fun ends at midnight because there's a strict Sunday curfew. What action there is centres on the main hotels: for live bands try the Travelodge (tel. 722 227) or the Mocambo (tel. 722 000). Entertainment more usually takes the form of traditional dancing and firewalking exhibitions (brilliant to watch). Locals will be able to tell you which hotel is the current flavour of the month for entertainment.

The *Fiji Times* gives listings for Nadi's four cinemas; films are in English or Indian.

FESTIVALS AND EVENTS
The Bula Festival takes place in Nadi every July, and the Fijians celebrate with dancing and food. 'Bula' means 'welcome', and welcome is just what you'll be, so join in!

EXCURSIONS
North of Nadi, on the west coast of Viti Levu, lies LAUTOKA. Fiji's second largest city (Suva is third; Nadi first) and its second port, Lautoka is the centre of the sugar industry, so make sure you visit the SUGAR MILL. Contact the Fiji Sugar Corporation (tel. 60 800) for details of tours and prices.

From Lautoka you'll be able to visit some beautiful island resorts. If you're young, free and single and looking for someone special, head for BEACHCOMBER ISLAND. You can walk around it in ten minutes, but there's plenty of nightlife, plus snorkelling. The boat ride there takes only 45 minutes. Other, larger islands, with beautiful beaches, diving and snorkelling facilities can also be reached from Lautoka – check out Malolo Lallai, Malolo Island, Mana Island, Tacarua Island, Matamanoa Island and the extremely touristy (what else with a name like this?) Treasure Island.

A pretty village reputed to be the oldest settlement in Fiji, VISELSEL lies between Nadi and Lautoka, and is definitely worth exploring. It was the first landing point of Christian missionaries to Fiji and there's a large Methodist church commemorating their arrival in the centre of the village.

It's fun to take a trip on the CORAL COAST RAILWAY which leaves the Fijian Resort complex on tiny nearby Yanuca Island at 9.45 a.m. daily, and takes you through rainforest and canefields to NATA-DOLA BEACH. You can then spend the day snorkelling, diving, windsurfing or relaxing before making the journey back at 4 p.m. The journey takes 90 minutes each way, and the trip costs F$61. Tickets are available from any tourist desk in hotels, resorts or at the airport.

NEW ZEALAND

Red tape: A full ten-year passport is required. Visitors must have onward or return tickets, and be able to support themselves financially while in New Zealand. British passport holders do not require visas for visits of up to six months (but the passport must be valid for three months beyond the intended date of departure from New Zealand); other nationalities can stay for up to three months. Australians do not require visas and are exempt from permit requirements.

Anyone with a firm offer of employment in New Zealand before leaving the UK can apply for a temporary work visa. Young people who are given a written offer of casual work during their holiday can apply to one of the Immigration Service offices (Auckland, Manukau, Hamilton, Palmerston North, Wellington and Christchurch) for a work permit.

Customs: 200 cigarettes or 50 cigars or 250 g tobacco, 4.5 l wine plus 1.125 l spirits. No fruit or plants can be brought into the country.

Health: No vaccination certificates are required. Health insurance is advisable.

Language: English, with Maori spoken by the Maori people.

Population: 3,300,000.

Capital: Wellington, population 318,600.

Political system: Parliamentary democracy, with the Queen as nominal head of state. The National party has been in power since 1990, and the current Prime Minister is Jim Bolger.

Religion: Church of England, Presbyterian, Roman Catholic, Methodist, Baptist. There is a Christian radio station, Radio Rhema, 'the public conscience of New Zealand'.

Time: Twelve hours ahead of GMT (thirteen hours ahead Oct.–Mar.).

Money: The New Zealand dollar (NZ$), divided into 100 cents. Coins: 5, 10, 20 and 50 cents. Notes: NZ$5, NZ$10, NZ$20, NZ$50, NZ$100. £1 = NZ$2.33.

As with most countries, the easiest way of carrying money is in either sterling or US dollar traveller's cheques. Credit cards are widely accepted.

Communications: New Zealand has an excellent telephone system. The new card-operated phones enable you to dial direct to anywhere in the world. Cards – priced at NZ$5, NZ$10, NZ$20 and NZ$50 – can be bought from post offices, local 'dairies' (corner shops) and from some YHA hostels. Local calls are free from private telephones, and cost 20 cents from phone booths. At the time of going to press New Zealand was in the process of updating her telephone system and changing all six digit numbers to seven digits. The changeover should be completed during 1995.

The usual postal, cable, telegram, telex and telephone facilities are available from post offices. Airmail to the UK takes between five and seven days.

Electricity: 230v AC/50Hz. Most hotels and motels provide 110v AC sockets for electric razors. The majority of power sockets accept 3-pin flat plugs, though it's worth taking an adaptor (often required) just in case.

Business hours: BANKS: Mon.–Fri. 9 a.m.–5 p.m.

POST OFFICES: Mon.–Fri. 9 a.m.–5 p.m.

SHOPS: Mon.–Fri. 9 a.m.–5 p.m. (department stores may open for late-night shopping until 9 p.m. on Thursdays); Sat. 9 a.m.–12 p.m. Many supermarkets are open on Sunday.

OFFICES: Mon.–Fri. 8 a.m.–4 p.m. or 9 a.m.–5 p.m.

Holidays: 1 and 2 January; 6 February; Good Friday and Easter Monday; 25 April (Anzac Day); 1 May; 6, 10 June (Queen's Birthday); 15 August; 5 October (Labour Day); 25 and 26 December.

Climate: New Zealand has a moderate climate, with the exception of the mountain regions which have enough snow in the winter (July/August) for good skiing, and the area to the north of Auckland, which is sub-tropical. The average summer (December to February) temperature for Auckland is 23°C; Christchurch is usually a couple of degrees lower. Average winter temperatures for Auckland and Christchurch are 15°C and 11°C respectively. The best time to go is Feb.–Mar. as this is the driest time of the year.

WHERE TO GO FOR WHAT

The South Island is where New Zealand's famous fiords and glaciers are situated, and it is undeniably the most beautiful of the country's three islands. The North Island, however, has a fascinating geological history to offer: Auckland, New Zealand's largest city, is built around extinct or dormant volcanic cones, and at the centre of the North Island lies ROTORUA, famous for its boiling mud, geysers and hot springs (and one of the best places in New Zealand to experience Maori culture). Rotorua information office is on 07 348 5179. Northland's most popular resort area is the BAY OF ISLANDS with its sub-tropical climate, peaceful beaches and rainforests. It was in WAITANGI that the Maori chiefs gathered in 1840 and ceded New Zealand to Queen Victoria. Two popular tourist destinations are situated at the tip of Northland: CAPE REINGA, the northernmost point of New Zealand, and 90 MILE BEACH.

Heading down towards Wellington, TONGARIRO NATIONAL PARK is a popular place for skiing and hiking, and LAKE TAUPO is world famous for its rainbow trout. WELLINGTON has the deserved reputation of being the windiest capital city in the world, and is also susceptible to earth tremors, being situated on twelve active faultlines. It is also the home of New Zealand's House of Parliament, known as 'the Beehive' because of its shape.

From Wellington, ferries run to PICTON on the South Island, via the stunning MARLBOROUGH SOUNDS. The South Island's main city is CHRISTCHURCH, with beautifully maintained parks and a terribly English aura. North of Christchurch is KAIKOURA, where tourists flock in increasing numbers for early morning whale-watching trips. To the west, the stunning FOX and FRANZ JOSEF GLACIERS are located in the WESTLAND NATIONAL PARK. In the heart of the Alpine region lies MOUNT COOK, and scenic flights over the entire region can be taken from TEKAPO, where the Church of the Good Shepherd overlooks a breathtakingly beautiful lake.

DUNEDIN is known as 'the Edinburgh of the South' as the architecture is somewhat similar in style to Scotland's capital. The similarity is reinforced by the street names being the same, and Dunedin is steeped in Scottish history. The nearby OTAGO PENINSULA offers fabulous wildlife, including penguins and albatross. The southernmost city, INVERCARGILL, also has a definite Scottish flavour and is the gateway to New Zealand's third island, STEWART ISLAND. Wildlife is in abundance here, and you can spot kiwis in the wild. But take care when walking – the tracks are very tough.

The real tourists' mecca of New Zealand is QUEENSTOWN, the place to go for skiing, bungy-jumping and rafting. There are numerous coach trips and scenic flights to Milford Sound and the fiords available from Queenstown. If the Milford Track is fully booked, then New Zealand's second most well-trodden track, the Routeburn, is accessible from Queenstown as are other popular routes, the Greenstone, Hollyford and Kepler.

INTERNAL TRAVEL

Getting around New Zealand is easy, and special passes are available for domestic travel by air, train and bus, or for a combination of all three (check with the YHA or tourist information for details of current deals). However, with various companies and routes offering special single fares (always publicized at the local hostels and tourist information), it is often cheaper to buy tickets as you go along, opting for the cheapest deal each time – especially if you're not in a hurry.

Air: Internal flights within New Zealand are not cheap, unless you manage to get a special discount flight. Both Air New Zealand and Ansett New Zealand offer discounts on some one-way flights between Auckland, Wellington and Christchurch, which are worth considering if you don't want to do the Cook Strait ferry crossing twice. There are special passes such as Ansett NZ's 60-day Airpass, and Mount Cook Airline's Kiwi Air Pass (only available outside New Zealand) which offers a one-way trip on each of their routes within 30 days.

The Freedom Pass can be used along with Air New Zealand or Qantas tickets on Air New Zealand's domestic routes or Mount Cook Airlines. This pass allows you four domestic flights for around £150 or six flights for around £190. This pass must also be purchased outside New Zealand.

The new 'G'Day Air Pass' is available to non-residents of Australia and New Zealand. This breaks the area into four zones (1 West and Central Australia, 2 East Australia, 3 Hayman Island, and 4 New Zealand). You must purchase a minimum of two coupons, and the maximum allowed is eight. Each coupon is £80 if you travel in a single zone or £105 for a multi-zone coupon. Unfortunately, travel between Australia and New Zealand is not covered by this pass.

Rail: There are only eight routes in New Zealand, the best-known and most luxurious being the Overlander Tranz Alpine service between Auckland and Wellington. There is an extremely scenic route between Christchurch and Greymouth. InterCity's Travelpass, in addition to rail travel, covers bus services and the inter-island ferry. In egalitarian New Zealand, there's no first-class train travel. There's a nationwide Central Reservations Centre (tel. 0800 80 2802) open 7 a.m.–9 p.m.

Bus: The three main services are InterCity, Newmans and Mount Cook, all of which offer their own passes, valid for travel over a fixed period. YHA members often get a 30% discount on both passes and individual tickets.

During the past few years, special buses geared towards backpackers have been introduced. The Kiwi Experience takes you from Auckland to Wellington in two or four days, Nelson to Queenstown in six days and Queenstown to Christchurch in three days on a variety of passes. The trips allow you to stopover anywhere you like and then pick up the next bus – there are daily departures. You'll find leaflets listing prices and schedules for all these services at the YHA and at backpacker hostels.

Travelpool: A service only recently introduced in New Zealand, this system of car-sharing/car-pooling has operated successfully in many other countries. Travelpool has widened the existing range of options for getting about in New Zealand, enabling visitors to travel cheaply and to make contact with 'Kiwis' at the same time. Car owners register with Travelpool their name, address and phone number, their proposed destination, date and time of departure, type of car and registration number (this can all be done over the phone). Travellers looking for a ride ring the Travelpool and if there's something they want, they can call in to the Travelpool shop and pay a commission fee in exchange for the driver's phone number. It is then up to the traveller and the car owner to arrange the details of the journey including the cost sharing.

Obviously, the more people in a car, the cheaper the trip. For example, a driver might use NZ$32 worth of petrol to get to New Plymouth. If three travellers are taken in the car, this will be shared four ways so that everyone pays NZ$8 for petrol. The driver saves NZ$24 and the travellers pay NZ$19 (NZ$8 plus NZ$11 commission fee) each for the trip.

Boat: There are four ferry sailings daily between Wellington and Picton, in each direction. The cost depends on the season, and the journey lasts three hours and twenty minutes.

Hitching: This is fairly easy, since New Zealanders are used to hitch-hikers and happy to offer lifts – the South Island is also probably one of the safest hitching places in the world. The real problem is the lack of traffic, especially in the more remote parts of the country, but you should still remember to take care.

Local transport: Local bus services have been subject to deregulation, and in some areas have ceased to exist at all. There are reduced bus fares and day-rovers in some cities during off-peak hours. In some areas, such as Wanganui, taxis have replaced buses as a form of public transport because their rates are more competitive. You can flag down a taxi, or go to a rank, and you don't have to tip in New Zealand, another boon for the budget traveller.

ACCOMMODATION

Finding accommodation is easy: all the visitor information offices have details of places to stay, and other travellers soon will fill you in on which places to head for and which to avoid. In general, New Zealand's budget accommodation is excellent, so you can't go far wrong.

Youth hostels: The YHA network in New Zealand is brilliant: hostels are open all day, they've virtually abolished chores, and there is no age limit. Non-members are permitted to stay (for a higher fee), but it is advisable to become a member if you're travelling during the busy season. For a fee of one dollar, the hostel manager will book your bed at the next hostel. The Youth Hostels Association of New Zealand, PO Box 436, Christchurch, (tel. 03 799 970) will provide you with an accommodation guide as well as details of discounts on travel passes.

Backpackers' inns: Wherever there's a Youth Hostel, there will usually be one or more Backpackers' Inns (they also cover places where the YHA don't have accommodation). These inns tend to be of a very high standard and with similar prices to the YHA. Dorms are not segregated and alcohol is usually allowed. The Pavlova Backpackers chain – easily recognizable by the lurid purple and green decor – is proving increasingly popular, perhaps because some of its hostels offer a free piece of Pavlova on arrival! Backpackers Marketing, 34 Auckland Street, Picton (tel. 03 573 6598) and Budget Backpackers Hostels NZ Ltd, Foley Towers, 208 Kilmore Street, Christchurch, can provide details of backpackers' hostels.

Hotels: In New Zealand the term 'hotel' refers to a tavern (a 'private hotel' is a hotel without a bar). Some New Zealand hotels offer cheaper rooms or dormitory accommodation aimed at backpackers.

Motels: These exist in abundance, and are usually equipped with kitchens. Designed for families, the rooms are suitable for groups of friends as well.

Guest houses: These cost about the same as motels, but the price includes breakfast, and there is a much more homely atmosphere.

Motorcamps: These offer a choice of cabins, flats, motel units or on-site caravans. If a group of you are travelling together, a motorcamp can prove the cheapest option. Some offer bunk-style accommodation at a cheaper rate than Youth Hostels.

Campsites: There are numerous roadside campsites in New Zealand, with kitchens and showers provided – but if you're planning to cook, take your own utensils. Tent sites usually cost NZ$9 per person.

Farmstays: There are several companies which arrange for tourists to sample life on a typical New Zealand farm – some of the farms even allow you to try your hand at sheepshearing. Prices are relatively expensive, but breakfast and dinner are included. Those willing to earn their keep on a farm can try Willing Workers on Organic Farms, PO Box 10–037, Palmerston North, North Island. They can provide you – at a fee – with a list of farms which take on helpers in exchange for food and accommodation.

FOOD

Food is very good and very cheap in New Zealand, not to mention plentiful: outside the main cities, you can buy an entire sheep for as little as NZ$20. New Zealanders are great meat-eaters, and lamb, steaks and meat pies are all worth sampling. Their fish and shellfish is excellent, too.

Some hotels in Rotorua offer Mauri 'hangi' evenings, where you can eat traditional fare such as vegetables and fish steamed in a pit in the ground. These evenings are expensive, and are geared towards tourists on coach tours. But some fish shops sell *paua patties* (green abalone burgers) and you can try smoked eel (the Maori word for this being *tuna*!)

In the cities, restaurants have become more cosmopolitan. BYO (bring-your-own bottle) places are the best value; most charge for corkage. Fruit and vegetables are cheap and excellent eating; kiwi fruit in particular are absurdly inexpensive. Try *kumara* (Maori sweet potato), it's wonderful.

There's a no-tipping tradition in New Zealand, and it is rare for a menu to show prices exclusive of Goods and Sales Tax (GST).

BUDGETING

New Zealand is, overall, a cheap country. Beware of overspending, though: everything seems like a bargain when you convert it back to sterling, and it's easy to find yourself going on every tour, eating out regularly – and suddenly out of pocket! The dollar is currently strong.

Working opportunities for the round-the-worlder are limited – most people opt simply to travel in New Zealand and seek work in

Australia. There is some fruit-picking (see hostel noticeboards for details, or approach farmers directly), mainly in the orchards around Kerikeri, Motueka and the Bay of Plenty. Willing Workers on Organic Farms (see p. 474) will send details of farmers offering food and accommodation in exchange for work, and anyone with sheep-farming or dairy experience should have little difficulty finding work on the land.

Queenstown, as an extremely popular year-round tourist resort, is where most travellers head for waiter/waitressing jobs, bartending, etc. Japanese tourists flock here and some of the hotels, restaurants and souvenir shops are Japanese-owned. The youth hostel noticeboard has details of vacancies. Experienced skiers might find seasonal work on one of the ski fields.

Staying in hostels and eating moderately, expect to spend NZ$18–20 per day.

FURTHER INFORMATION

New Zealand High Commission, New Zealand House, 80 Haymarket, London SW1Y 4TQ (tel. 0171 930 8422).

Tourist Office – address as above (tel. 0839 300 900).

New Zealand Immigration Service for work visa enquiries: tel. 071 973 0368.

Air New Zealand, Elsinore House, 77 Fulham Palace Road, London W6 8JA (tel. 0181 846 9595).

Background reading: *Australia and New Zealand: Travel Survival Kit* (Vacation Work) contains an excellent section on New Zealand. Other guides worth studying include Fodor's *New Zealand* and, what seems to be the backpacker's bible in New Zealand, Lonely Planet's *New Zealand – Travel Survival Kit*. For specific information about the outdoors, see Lonely Planet's *Tramping in New Zealand*.

Ngaio Marsh, creator of the Roderick Alleyn detective novels is probably New Zealand's best-known writer – though there are better ones. Try one of Katherine Mansfield's novels, or read Booker Prize-winning author Keri Hulme's *The Bone People*. And if you enjoy children's books, you'll love anything by Margaret Mahy.

Auckland

AIRPORT FACILITIES

Auckland International Airport is 22 km south of the city. There are three passenger terminals: the international terminal deals with arrivals on the ground floor, and departures on the first floor. The domestic terminals has arrivals and departures on the ground floor.

Auckland offers all the usual airport facilities: shops, information desk, duty-free and post office. Check-in times are 90 minutes prior to international flight departure times and 30 minutes before domestic flight departure times. The departure tax is NZ$20. An inter-terminal bus runs every 30 minutes.

CITY LINKS
Bus: The Airporter bus departs on the hour and at half past the hour, heading downtown. It costs NZ$10 one-way. Door to door Supershuttles depart on request and cost from NZ$14 single.
Taxi: Cab fare costs roughly four times the bus fare. You'll find taxis waiting outside the terminals. NZ$40 to city centre.

USEFUL ADDRESSES
Tourist office: There are visitor information offices throughout the city.
British Airways: Dilworth Building, corner of Queen and Customs Streets, Auckland (tel. 367 7500).
Main post office: Mail Service Centre, 167–91 Victoria Street W (tel. 792 200).
British Consulate General: 17th Floor, 151 Queen Street (tel. 303 2971/3).
Emergency services: Dial 111 for fire, police or ambulance.
Medical assistance: Auckland Hospital, Park Road, Grafton City (tel. 797 440).

GETTING ABOUT
Bus: Most of Auckland's buses are run by the Auckland Regional Council (ARC) and fares are calculated on a zonal system. The ARC offers a NZ$10 Busabout one-day pass, valid on all routes after 9 a.m. City buses stop running at 5 p.m. on Saturdays and Sundays.

United Airlines operates a NZ$10 tourist Explorer Bus, which runs once an hour from 10 a.m.–5 p.m. daily and stops at the main tourist attractions.

SIGHTS
Nobody goes to New Zealand for its cities, and although AUCKLAND is the country's fastest-growing metropolis, it's not a terribly exciting one and it has no world-famous tourist attractions. However, the fact that it's built around volcanoes makes it interesting geographically, and it's a good base for exploring the North Island. It has

a cosmopolitan, multicultural flavour, thanks to its South Pacific and Asian immigrants.

MOUNT EDEN is one of the extinct volcanic cones, which is worth climbing for the view of the city, ocean and other craters; this natural viewing deck affords a much better view than that from the BNZ OBSERVATION DECK in Queen Street.

The Auckland DOMAIN is a large park incorporating sportsfields, the WINTER GARDENS and the AUCKLAND MUSEUM. The museum houses a collection of Maori and South Pacific artefacts. It's also the place to see a model of the moa, the huge New Zealand bird which is now extinct.

Kelly Tarlton's UNDERWATER WORLD, opposite Orakei Wharf, takes you on a conveyor-belt trip through an underwater tunnel, while sharks, stingrays and other fish swim along on the other side of the acrylic tunnels. The admission charge is NZ$10. There is a new Antarctic attraction. The AUCKLAND ZOO merits a detour if you're interested in New Zealand native fauna; in the nocturnal house you can see a kiwi. The zoo is situated at Western Springs, near the MUSEUM OF TRANSPORT AND TECHNOLOGY (MOTAT) and the two are connected by tram – or you can walk through a very pretty park. The MOTAT is a lot more interesting than it sounds, with old trains and trams and a sci-fi playground. Admission is NZ$9, but YHA members get a 20% discount. Admission for the zoo is also NZ$9, with no discount. Auckland's MARITIME MUSEUM has recently opened.

If you're in Auckland in November, then visit PARNELL ROSE GARDEN to enjoy the roses in full bloom. ONE TREE HILL, once the site of a fortified Maori village, really does have just the one tree, along with an observatory offering spectacular views.

Shoppers and browsers will enjoy VICTORIA PARK MARKET on Victoria Street West with its foodstalls and buskers, not to mention the clothing, jewellery and handicrafts stalls. The CHINESE MARKET on Quay Street near the bus station is worth a look, even if many of the goods for sale don't seem to be remotely Chinese! There are plenty of craft shops in downtown Auckland and in the upmarket shopping districts of Parnell and Ponsonby. If you want any films developed while you're in New Zealand, the Camera House chain is probably the best of the bunch.

Those brave enough for bungy-jumping – and who don't have time for a trip to Queenstown – can leap into the harbour courtesy of BUNGEE BATS in Halsey Street (it costs about NZ$85). If you like the water, the beaches of MISSION BAY, ST HELIERS and JUDGES BAY offer a variety of watersports. For those who are happier watching, there's rugby or cricket at EDEN PARK, trotting club meetings at ALEXANDRA PARK RACEWAY in Epsom, with flat racing at ELLERSLIE and AVONDALE.

ACCOMMODATION
Hostels: There are two YHA hostels – one downtown and one in Parnell – and some 16 private hostels:

Auckland International Hostel, corner of City Road and Liverpool Street (tel. 309 2801). A mere 200m from Queen Street, this central hostel has mostly twin rooms with some singles and triples, a restaurant, a food shop and a domestic travel service. It costs from NZ$18 a night.

Parnell Hostel, 2 Churton Street (tel. 379 3731). Only a few minutes from downtown Auckland. Costs from NZ$16 a night. It is best to book if planning a stay between December and March, as many travellers prefer the village atmosphere of Parnell to staying in the heart of the city.

YWCA, corner of Grays Avenue and Pitt Street. Accommodation for men and women at NZ$32 a night or NZ$200 a week, including all meals.

Georgia Backpackers' Hostel, 189 Park Road, Grafton (tel. 309 9560). Popular at around NZ$16 per night (with a reduction of NZ$2 for those staying more than three nights).

Eden Lodge Tourist Hotel, 22 View Road, Mount Eden. From NZ$16 per night.

Kiwi Hilton, 430 Queen Street (tel. 358 0188). From NZ$16 per night.

Downtown Backpackers, corner of Queen and Fort Streets (tel. 373 3471). From NZ$16 per night.

Auckland Central Backpackers, 9 Fort Street (tel. 4358 4877). From NZ$15 per night. Open 24 hours

Some of the hostels have courtesy phones at the information desk at the airport and run their own shuttle buses.

Hotels and motels: If you want to be near the airport, Skylodge International Motel at 144 McKenzie Road, Mangere (tel. 275 1005) has a budget hostel from around NZ$25 a night and the Auckland Airport Skyway Lodge, 30 Kirkbride Road, Mangere (tel. 275 4443) has four-bedded rooms from about NZ$28 per person. Downtown, the Grande Vue Tourist Hotel at the corner of Princes Street and Eden Crescent (tel. 303 3017) charges around NZ$25 for a single room and NZ$40 for a twin room.

FOOD

Auckland is New Zealand's most cosmopolitan city as far as food is concerned. Arguably the best place to dine out is along the Ponsonby Road, which has numerous BYO restaurants offering Indian, Spanish and Korean food as well as traditional New Zealand fare.

Parnell isn't out of the budget traveller's range when it comes to eating – there are plenty of menus at affordable prices, with lots of Italian restaurants and Californian-style bars to choose from. The Karangahape Road is where you'll find South American food, and the Khyber Pass Road has some good Asian restaurants.

Vegetarians tend to get a raw deal in meat-eating New Zealand, but there's cheap vegetarian food to be found at Badgers in the High Street or Domino's in Lorne Street.

The Chinese Market has about 14 stalls selling international main dishes and the Plaza Shopping Centre in Queen Street has ethnic food stalls.

ENTERTAINMENT

There's more late-night entertainment in Auckland than you'll find in the rest of New Zealand. The Aotea Centre near the corner of Queen and Wellesley Streets is the main arts centre, offering a variety of shows, ballet, opera and plays.

If you want live music, *the* venue is the Gluepot in the Ponsonby Club Hotel, on the corner of Jervois and Ponsonby Roads. The main venue for international bands is the Western Springs Stadium. At weekends, a number of Auckland's hotels offer live jazz.

There are plenty of cinemas in Auckland, showing the latest, experimental, and old Hollywood films. They still have intermissions! During the summer, there's free open-air theatre (often Shakespeare) in the university grounds.

Pubs include the Backpackers Pub on the corner of Hobson and Victoria streets. The Kiwi in Symonds Street is popular with students, while the Shakespeare Tavern in Albert Street offers a wide range of ales, stouts and lagers.

FESTIVALS AND EVENTS

An annual folk festival is held in late January at Oratia.

EXCURSIONS

There are several islands which can be reached by ferry or catamaran – run by Fullers and Pacifica (the latter are usually the cheaper of the two) – from Waitemata Harbour. The most unusual of these is the volcanic RANGITOTO ISLAND. It takes about an hour to walk up to the summit. WAIHEKE ISLAND is only 35 minutes away from Auckland by the Quickcat Express – and if you don't like cities and have some time to spare, it's worth staying at the YHA there rather than in Auckland. There are special offers combining YHA accommodation on the island with transport there and back. The beaches are uncrowded and superb. GREAT BARRIER ISLAND offers hiking, fishing, surfing, scuba diving and bird watching (several rare New Zealand birds may be sighted here). Fullers and Pacifica have introduced fast services to the island, and it's also possible to travel there with the Great Barrier Islands Co.

The rugged WAIKAKERE RANGES are within an hour's drive from downtown Auckland, and the four roads which branch off from the Scenic Drive will each lead you to a beautiful beach: Whatipu, Kerikeri, Anawhata and Piha (dominated by the majestic Lion Rock).

Further afield, NORTHLAND and the BAY OF ISLANDS are easily accessible from Auckland, with youth hostels and backpackers inns offering overnight accommodation. CAPE REINGA is the northern-most point of New Zealand and you can walk up the headland to the lighthouse to see where the Pacific Ocean meets the Tasman Sea. In KAITAIA, a number of tour operators offer trips to the Cape and along 90 Mile Beach (it's actually 64 miles – 103 km – long) but individuals are discouraged from driving along the beach because of soft sand and tides. In addition to a wide array of watersports, the Bay of Islands has much to offer in the way of historical interest, including the Waitangi Treaty House, just a short walk from Paihia. Fullers offer a variety of cruises, including a four-hour trip to CAPE BRETT sailing through the Hole-in-the-Rock, and the 'cream trip' (so called because it was originally patronized by dairy farmers).

The rugged COROMANDEL PENINSULA, south-east of Auckland, is good for hiking and beaches. And both the WAITOMO CAVES (where glow-worms can be seen from the black-water raft trips) and the geysers and boiling mud of ROTORUA are accessible from Auckland. It's a good idea to go for a two- or three-day trip there if you have a little time to spare.

Christchurch

AIRPORT FACILITIES

Christchurch is a small airport by international standards, with just two terminals: one domestic, one international. It is equipped with a bank, post office, restaurant, bar and duty-free, as well as an information desk. Check-in times are 90 minutes before an international flight departure, and 30 minutes before a domestic flight.

CITY LINKS
Bus: The Christchurch Transport Board operates a regular service, taking in Worcester Street, Cashel Street, Riccarton Avenue, Riccarton Road, Ilam Road and Memorial Avenue. It costs roughly NZ$2.40.
Taxi: These are quite expensive, costing about ten times the price of the buses, NZ$20 to NZ$30.

USEFUL ADDRESSES
Tourist office: There are visitor information offices throughout the city.
British Airways: 1st Floor, National Mutual Arcade, Hereford Street (tel. 792 503).
British High Commission: Christchurch Trade Office, The Dome, Regent Theatre Building, Cathedral Square (tel. 379 6100).
Main post office: Cathedral Square (tel. 353 1899).
Emergency services: dial 111 for fire, police, ambulance.

GETTING ABOUT
Christchurch is a city you can easily walk or cycle around (the Rolleston House Youth Hostel hires out bikes) which is just as well. The railway station is more than 1.5 km outside the city centre, on Moorhouse Avenue and national deregulation in 1991 left the Christchurch bus system in chaos.

SIGHTS
Christchurch is known as the most English of New Zealand's cities, and its neat parks and gardens certainly lend it a dignified atmosphere. CATHEDRAL SQUARE lies at the centre of the city; its tower affords a good view of Christchurch. Cathedral Square offers a variety of free entertainment by way of buskers and jugglers, and the infamous Wizard makes a daily appearance at 1 p.m. each day to hold forth on a variety of controversial topics (including the inferiority of women). The Information Centre has a selection of city walk brochures, which you can follow on your own. The Punting-on-the-Avon Company on the corner of Worcester Street and Oxford Terrace will take you down the AVON RIVER :the trips are priced to the number of punting minutes, from about NZ$8 for 20 minutes.

The BOTANIC GARDENS, in addition to native New Zealand plants, boasts a rose garden, and it's a good place for walking or relaxing. On Sunday afternoons there's sometimes live music.

Within the Gardens is situated the CANTERBURY MUSEUM, a reconstruction of 1850s nostalgia, comprising shop fronts and period cottages. The ROBERT MCDOUGALL ART GALLERY next door to the museum has paintings of the Maori people and various Maori artefacts. Both the museum and art gallery are free. The Antarctic Centre is near the airport.

There are dozens of places in downtown Christchurch where you can buy sheepskin and souvenirs, as well as craft shops selling Maori artefacts. At weekends, the open-air market outside the Arts Centre is a good place to hunt for jewellery, pottery and other arts and crafts. The city mall and the shopping area of COLOMBO STREET have all the usual stores.

ACCOMMODATION
Hostels: There are two YHA hostels:

Rolleston House, Worcester Street (tel. 366 6564). Conveniently situated near the Botanic Gardens and opposite the Arts Centre. From NZ$16 per night.

Cora Wilding hostel, Eveleyn Cousins Avenue (tel. 389 9199). A 10-minute bus ride (on the number 10 bus) from the city centre. Named after the founder of the New Zealand YHA movement, this hostel is in a lovely, quiet location and often has beds when the downtown YHA is full. From NZ$14 per night.

Non-YHA hostels include:

Pavlova Backpackers, Cathedral Square (tel. 366 5158). From NZ$14.

Foley Towers, Kilmore Street (tel. 366 9720). Very popular among backpackers.

Hotels: Some downtown hotels offer cheap backpacker accommodation, including the Hereford Private Hotel in Hereford Street (tel. 379 9536) and the Ambassadors Hotel in Manchester Street (tel. 366 7808).

Campsites: There are a few motorcamps around the Addington Racecourse area, including Meadow Park, Meadow Street (352 9176) which charges around NZ$30 for two in a cabin, and around NZ$18 for two people pitching a tent.

FOOD
There are roughly 100 BYO (bring your own bottle) restaurants in Christchurch, including a reasonable range of ethnic food. Dux de Lux in the Arts Centre is highly popular, partly because it's over the road from the city youth hostel, but also because it has an

excellent range of vegetarian meals. Ethnic food stalls throng the area around Cathedral Square, and there are several Mexican restaurants in the city, including the Mexican Cantina on the corner of Worcester and Manchester Streets. The Oxford Victualling Co., by the river, has traditional roasts at low prices.

For those who prefer to do their own cooking, be warned – groceries are difficult to find in central Christchurch, so it's best to arrive with a few provisions, and ask a local where the nearest dairy or supermarket is.

ENTERTAINMENT

Not surprisingly, the Arts Centre is the cultural focal point of Christchurch, with plays, films, dance, concerts, recitals and experimental theatre. The main venue for both classical and rock music is the Town Hall on Kilmore Street. Pubs include Warner's Hotel in Cathedral Square which has live Irish music and draught Guinness. The public bar of the Bush Hill Hotel in Riccarton Road is popular with students.

FESTIVALS AND EVENTS

There is an annual three-day folk festival at Whitecliffs, 80 km inland from Christchurch, in February. There's also a summer festival in Haghey Park.

EXCURSIONS

The BANKS PENINSULA, south-east of Christchurch, remains unspoilt and is worth a visit. AKAROA, where the French settled in 1840 only days after Britain had laid claim to the country, is the major town in the area. In addition to its French heritage, Akaroa is of interest for its whaling history.

KAIKOURA, north of Christchurch, has grown increasingly popular over recent years thanks to the attraction of whales. Two companies run whale-watching trips (as well as trips to swim with dolphins). One is run by Maori people (Kaikoura Tours: tel. 319 5045) and the other by 'pakeha' (New Zealand Nature Watch: tel. 319 5662.) The three-hour trips cost about NZ$75 and sperm whales, dolphins, seals and albatross usually put in an appearance. There's a local YHA and a Kaikoura Backpackers Hostel; both will book trips for you.

The Tranzalpine Express train offers cheap day-returns to Greymouth, taking you through some stunning South Island scenery. The same train runs through ARTHUR'S PASS :stopover for the excellent hiking opportunites, plus shorter day and half-day walks and a good visitors' centre. There's a Youth Hostel in Arthur's Pass Village.

It is possible to travel from Christchurch to TEKAPO in a day, enabling you to take a scenic flight over MOUNT COOK and the glaciers.

QUEENSTOWN is undoubtedly *the* place to go in New Zealand if you're into skiing, hiking, or the latest adventure sports like bungy-jumping, whitewater rafting and jetboating. Once you're there, there's considerable temptation to do something adventurous, just as there is to climb Ayers Rock at Yulara. The town itself is beautiful, built around LAKE WAKATIPU and flanked by the REMARKABLES and CORONET PEAK. Coronet Peak is best for advanced skiers, while the Remarkables offer excellent packages for beginners: three-day beginners' courses can cost as little as NZ$75.

Whitewater rafting and jetboating take place along the SHOTOVER and KAWARAU rivers, while there is bungy-jumping from the Kawarau Bridge or – for those who've conquered Kawarau and want something more daring – from the 70 m SKIPPER'S CANYON BRIDGE. Once you've decided to throw yourself off a bridge, you'll definitely want the photos and video to prove it to your friends back home, and a bungy-jump can end up costing you more than NZ$100. But jumpers agree it's worth it for the thrill! There are several hostels, including a YHA, but it's best to book in advance as this is a busy year-round resort. Hostel noticeboards have details of special offers comprising two or more adventure sports, trips to MILFORD SOUND, and skiing deals.

Both the MILFORD TRACK and the ROUTEBURN are accessible from Queenstown, but remember that for these walks, as for any other hikes in New Zealand, you have to register with the Department of Conservation (tel. 379 9758) before departing, and then de-register when you finish.

LATIN AMERICA

Delightful but too dodgy is a label commonly applied to Latin America. True enough, parts of the continent are dangerous, but don't let this issue – no matter how persuasive – sway you from experiencing the place for yourself.

The New World discovered by Columbus spawned the Spanish- and Portuguese-speaking nations that have become known as Latin America, which incorporates Mexico and everything south of it.

WHERE TO GO FOR WHAT
The three countries highlighted here – Mexico, Peru and Brazil – have distinctive characteristics and each merits a visit in its own right. MEXICO has key attractions like the Mayan ruins on the Yucatán peninsula, and the complex of pyramids at Teotihuacán, while towns like San Miguel Allende and Taxco are steeped in colonial history. Baja California, to the north-east, is the place to relax and kick back for a while – it's also a famed spot for whale watching.

PERU packs a punch from the mountainous Inca Trail and the lost city of Machu Picchu to Lake Titicaca (the world's highest navigable lake) and the Andes themselves. For those in search of civilization, Cuzco, with its ancient Inca ruins, is the oldest continuously inhabited city in the Americas. Those seeking escape from civilization might prefer the dense Amazonian jungles of north-eastern Peru.

BRAZIL is enormous; its bulk accounts for nearly half of South America. As befits a country of this size, it has one of the most stunning of capital cities in Rio de Janeiro. Its famous beaches, Copacabana and Ipanema, are more than matched by the majesty of Sugar Loaf Mountain and Corcovado Mountain, on which stands the 36-metre statue of Christ the Redeemer. Natural splendour to equal this man-made achievement can be found at the spectacular Iquassu Falls, or in the Pantanal swamplands of Mato Grosso. Brazil's colonial past awaits in the mining town of Ouro Preto. And, of course, a trip up the Amazon is an unmissable experience.

Crowded, sprawling cities are a feature of Latin America. There's no need to avoid them completely, but you may find yourself glad to get away after just a few days. That said, the other rumour – that Latin American cities are some of the liveliest places on earth – is also true.

TAKE HEED

Vigilance when travelling is important the world over, but particularly in Latin America with its high level of street crime in the cities. Thankfully stealth rather than aggression is the usual tactic, but you must be on your guard the whole time. Why are things so bad? The raging inflation and debt hangovers from the 1980s haven't helped to build stable societies, the more so since large numbers of people (many of them indigenous Indians) have been pushed onto the streets. Ostentatious Gringos flaunting expensive possessions in the face of this poverty are far from welcome.

Even in liberal-minded Brazil, outside the modern centres such as Rio, local people will not thank you for dressing provocatively (or scruffily) and flouting conventions of modesty. The wearing of army-surplus clothing can get you into all sorts of trouble in South America, where military fatigues are not a fashion statement.

Swigging beer all day and ending up raucously drunk adds to the negative stereotype – and weakens your judgement when it comes to weighing up dodgy situations. The use of or trafficking in drugs is a serious offence and heavy penalties are imposed. People offering to sell you drugs on the street may be police agents: don't take the chance. The authorities are automatically suspicious of anyone rolling their own cigarettes; unless you enjoy being body-searched it's best to switch to commercial brands.

In Peru, discontent has spilled over into terrorist violence. Since the Shining Path generally attacks strategic targets, foreign visitors should not be directly at risk (see **Peru: Do's and Don'ts**, p. 511).

EMPLOYMENT OPPORTUNITIES

Employment laws in Latin America expressly prohibit visiting foreign nationals from looking for work. Despite this, teaching is the main unofficial occupation open to travellers spending time in the region. English is a popular language because it opens up tourist industry job opportunities for the locals. Most teaching work is therefore found in the cities. At roughly US$3 an hour the pay isn't great, but with private lessons on top you'll probably be making just about enough to get by. Word of mouth will be as good a way of finding work as any, but check the local English-language press for possible openings. Wherever you end up teaching, don't get so engrossed in the job that you forget to renew your tourist card or permit. For further advice, read Susan Griffith's *Work Your Way Round the World* (Vacation Work).

BUDGETING

A comfortable average daily budget in Latin America is US$30. You'll spend at least this in the cities; considerably less in the countryside. Peru is especially cheap, not least because of the fall off in tourism due to terrorist violence. Brazil, however, is less affordable than its neighbours.

If you want to maintain a decent standard of living, you should allow US$15–20 for accommodation, with dinner accounting for a further US$5 or more. Beer costs US$1–2. Public transport (buses are your best bet) is very cheap, and consequently very crowded. To cut costs eat where and what the locals do, and turn a blind eye to some of the grubbier corners of your hotel bedroom. Because spiralling inflation is forever devaluing local currencies, change as little of your hard currency as possible at any one time. You'll be able to pay for costs like accommodation in US dollars anyway.

INTRA-CONTINENTAL TRAVEL

There is a range of air passes available which will permit you to circle the entire continent or to visit specific regions or individual countries (for details of the latter, see the country sections below). Remember, however, that a pass must be bought in advance for hard currency from outside the country for which it is to be used. Some airlines offer tokens which can be exchanged for flights, others issue passes for a specific itinerary. At the time of going to press, itineraries on offer include: London–Rio–Lima–La Paz–Rio–London, fixed-date pass with three-month validity for approx. £1,000; and a flexible six-month pass covering London–Cartegena–Bogota–Rio–Quito–Lima–La Paz–Santiago–Buenos Aires–Rio–Caracas–London for approx. £1,300.

Mercosur air pass: the fare for this pass is set according to the distance flown. Linking the Mercosur Common Market countries of Brazil, Argentina, Uruguay and Paraguay, the pass is valid for up to 30 days (from a minimum of 10 days), and is good for travel in two or more countries. You must buy it before travelling, and because the fare is set according to your route you'll need to have a definite itinerary in mind before setting off. The price is determined by how far you travel; 1,900 miles costs US$225, or 2,500 miles costs US$285. To arrange a Mercosur Pass – which is a joint project offered by Varig Brazilian Airlines and Aerolineas Argentinas, in conjunction with seven other airlines – speak to your travel agent or contact Varig (0171 629 9408), or Aerolineas (0171 494 1001).

Condor air pass: at a cost of about £1,400, this pass carries you from the UK to South America and back again via eight capitals in the region, as well as Rio, Cartagena and Cuzco. For up-to-the-minute details, contact the Colombian airline Avianca (tel. 0171 408 1889).

A number of specialist Latin American travel agencies operate in the UK, including:

Journey Latin America (tel. 0181 747 8315).

Passage to South America (tel. 0171 602 9889).

Steamond International (tel. 0171 978 5500).

Exodus Expeditions (tel. 0181 675 5550).

Explore Worldwide (tel. 01252 319448).

FURTHER INFORMATION
In addition to the various tourist boards listed in the individual country sections below, there is a Latin American Tourist Board (LATA) at 10 Hanover Street, Mayfair, London W1R 9HF (tel. 0171 493 2214).

The best of the regional guidebooks are Vacation Work's *South America: Travel Survival Kit*, Emily Hatchwell and Simon Calder; *Mexico and Central America Handbook*, ed. Ben Box (Trade and Travel Publications); and *The South America Handbook* (Trade and Travel Publications). Those planning to seek employment should consult *Work Your Way Round the World*, Susan Griffith (Vacation Work).

BRAZIL

VITAL STATISTICS
Red tape: A full passport is required, and should be valid for at least six months from the intended date of your arrival in Brazil. British nationals do not need a visa. However, Americans, Canadians, New Zealanders and Australians should apply for a visa from the nearest Brazilian consulate before leaving home. They usually take two days to process and you'll need to show your air ticket when applying. Tourist visas are valid for 90 days, transit visas for 10 days.

Customs: There is a duty-free allowance of 600 cigarettes, 2 l spirits and 3 l wine. A limited quantity of excise goods – items such as cameras, radios and tape recorders – can be brought in for personal use, provided there is only one of each. Tourists are entitled to buy up to US$500-worth of goods in duty-free shops.

Health: There are no compulsory vaccinations, but jabs against hepatitis A, typhoid and meningitis are recommended, as are anti-malarial tablets and a polio booster. Inoculation against yellow fever is strongly advised for trips to the Amazon region. Health insurance is recommended.

Language: Portuguese is the national language. English is widely understood.

Population: approx. 156 million.

Capital: Brasilia, population 1.6 million.

Political system: Civil government; the country is ruled by presidential decree.

Religion: Roman Catholic.

Time: Three hours behind GMT in the east, four hours behind in central and western regions, and five hours behind GMT in the far west. Daylight savings time operates March to October, when clocks go back an hour.

Money: The currency is the Real (R$), which is divided into 100 centavos. Coins: 10, 20 and 50 cents. Notes: R$50, R$100, R$200, R$500, R$1,000, R$5,000. £ = around R$1.45.

Communications: Public telephones are widely available in public places. They accept coin-like metal tokens called *fichas*, which can be bought at newsstands and in shops. There is an extensive internal direct dialling system, and it's possible to dial direct to North America, Japan and most of Europe. However, international calls are prohibitively expensive and some public phones are fitted with a blocking device. A 40% tax is added to all calls made from hotels.

Post: The Brazilian postal service has developed considerably over recent years. The same extortionate price is charged for letters and postcards.

Electricity: Rio de Janeiro and São Paulo: 110v AC, 60Hz. Recife and Brasília: 220–40v AC/60Hz.

Business hours: BANKS: Mon.–Fri. 10 a.m.–4.30 p.m.

POST OFFICES: Mon.–Sat. 9 a.m.–1 p.m.

SHOPS: Mon.–Fri. 9 a.m.–6.30 p.m.; Sat. 9 a.m.–1 p.m.

OFFICES: Government offices are open to the public Mon.–Fri. 9 a.m.–6 p.m.

Holidays: 1 January; February (Carnival/Mardis Gras – begins the Saturday before Ash Wednesday); Good Friday; 21 April (Tiradentes Day); 1 May; June (Corpus Christi – date varies); 7 September (Independence Day); 12 October (Our Lady of Aparecida Day); 2 November (All Souls' Day); 15 November (Proclamation of the Republic); 25 December.

Climate: Because the bulk of the country lies just south of the equator, the Brazilian climate is pretty much the same year round. With temperatures ranging from 18–30°C, it's comfortable in most of the states. Coastal towns benefit from a refreshing sea breeze.

Light clothing is suitable for almost every region at any time of the year.

DO'S AND DON'TS
Crime is a problem in the cities: purse snatching is rife, and any valuables left unattended for even a minute will disappear. Be on your guard at all times, but especially if you should be in Rio at carnival time.

Polite conversation should be just that – drop in plenty of greetings: 'Bom dia' in the morning, 'Boa tarde' after lunch, and 'Boa noite' after dark. For this reason alone a working knowledge of Portuguese is all but essential.

Outside the big modern cities and tourist resorts you should avoid causing offence by flouting conventions of modesty. Dress conservatively, particularly when visiting churches.

WHERE TO GO FOR WHAT
An area which shouldn't be missed is the AMAZON RAINFOREST, in north-eastern Brazil. Trees up to 45 metres in height cover what is one of the world's largest natural forest reserves; a place where the fauna, flora, animal and plant life is as exotic as it is unique. Various trips into the forest are available from the city of MANAUS: it's possible to take a trip in a long-boat up small rivers, and stay in basic hotels in the middle of the jungle; take a canoe through the jungle marshes; or cut your way through the forest with a machete under the guidance of an experienced leader, sampling an enormous range of natural delights on the way.

The two largest urban centres in the north-east both offer a number of unique attractions and are well worth visiting. SALVADOR with its innumerable churches and fine beaches is one of Brazil's more exotic cities, a place packed with mysticism and folklore. One local tradition is the *capoeira* (once a fight but now a dance), another is the local spicy cuisine (try *vatapa*, *acaraje*, and chicken *xinxim*) sold on the streets by locals (Baianas) in long white skirts with decorative necklaces. The city of RECIFE was originally founded by the Dutch, and as well as being beautiful (it's known as the 'city of bridges and rivers'), it's a good base from which to explore nearby historical landmarks such as Olinda, Igaracu and the island of Itamaraca to the north.

SÃO PAULO, the most prosperous city in south-eastern Brazil, is one of the country's most worthwhile places to visit. An active cultural centre with three major universities and a range of interesting museums, it has an intriguing history (the city was founded in 1554 as a mission station by two Jesuit priests) and its heritage is reflected in the architecture of the 19th-century Opera House and in the charming residential areas. Aside from its cultural attractions, São Paulo is one of Brazil's liveliest after-dark cities, with an enormous selection of restaurants, nightclubs, and different entertainments.

The national capital, BRASÍLIA, lies to the west of the central region. There are a host of reasons to include it in your itinerary: its cultural significance (it's home to the national theatre); its political importance (it's the seat of government); and its academic reputation (there are four universities here). Architecturally, Brasília is interesting because of its modern, futuristic style. Through this part of Brazil runs the Araguaia River, and from the little town of ARU-ANA it's possible to sail down it on 'boatels' (floating motels), to the Indian villages on the island of BANANAL. The river also has excellent beaches.

FOZ DO IGUACU, near the southern border town of Iguacu – where Brazil, Argentina and Paraguay meet – boasts a spectacular array of 275 waterfalls, some almost 100 metres high. Still in the south, the Gramado and Canela Mountains (around 145 km from Porto Alegre) are part of the scenic GAUCHO MOUNTAIN range. Both make for excellent sightseeing, not least because of the tiny settlements of Alpine-style cottages which lend the area a Bavarian air.

These are just some of the worthwhile sights and places around Brazil, each reflecting either the immense natural beauty, vast culture, fascinating history or radical modernity of the country.

INTERNAL TRAVEL
Air: Between them the three major Brazilian carriers (Varig/Cruzeiro, Vasp, Transbrasil) fly to all the major cities and regions. Varig offers a five-flight, 21-day air pass for US$440 which can only be purchased outside Brazil; you will be required to show your international ticket, and only one pass per ticket is allowed. For details contact your travel agent or Varig Brazilian Airlines, 16–17 Hanover Street, London W1 (reservations tel. 0171 629 5824; information tel. 0171 629 9408).
Rail: The level of comfort is so poor that it's not advisable to travel long distances by train. In any case, Brazil has few rail routes apart from a strip along the eastern region connecting Rio, São Paulo and other large cities in the area.
Bus: This is the primary means of public transportation. Bus services linking Brazilian cities are fast and comfortable, the next most convenient way to travel after flying. There are plenty of longhaul services to choose from.

Car hire: The road and highway networks in Brazil are good. To hire a car you'll need an international driving licence and third-party insurance. There are plenty of car hire firms in the main cities, especially near airports. Traffic travels on the right side of the road.

Hitching: Hitching is difficult in Brazil (perhaps with the exception of the Amazon and Panatal) and due to several assaults by hitchers recently, the government has begun to discourage giving lifts to strangers. The Portuguese for hitching is *carona*, so 'Pode dar carona?' is 'Can you give me a lift?' Practically the only way to hitch a ride is to hang about the petrol stations and truck stops so you can talk to the drivers.

Local transport: Rio and São Paulo have limited underground networks. There are three classes of taxi: common, special or radio taxi, and luxury taxi; those in Rio and São Paulo are fitted with meters; elsewhere negotiate a price in advance.

ACCOMMODATION

Accommodation in Brazil, while affordable in comparison to other more developed counties, is not so cheap by South American standards. The Brazilian YHA (Rua Assembleia 10, Rio de Janeiro) operates some youth hostels in the cities. Budget hotels vary in price and quality, but there are plenty of decent places where you can get a bed for around US$12. Camping continues to grow in popularity; the main sites are in the tourist areas, but a tent will also prove handy in the more out of the way parts of the country. In the Amazon there are a variety of jungle lodges and huts. It is essential to book accommodation in advance during the carnival period (February).

FOOD

Traditional Brazilian menus are well worth exploring, and some of the national dishes come highly recommended: among the most popular is *feijoada* (black beans and rice — *feijoada completa*, the Saturday version, includes sausage and pork); *siri* (spicy stuffed crab); *frango con arroz* (chicken and rice); *vatapa* (shrimps or fish in coconut milk); *churrasco* (meat grilled over an open fire in true gaucho fashion); and *xinxim de galinha* (pieces of chicken in a white sauce). Any Bahian dishes will have been cooked in palm oil.

Local drinks to sample include *batida* (a cocktail made with a strong cane liquor), and *guarana*, the national soft drink, which is made with the seeds of an Amazonian fruit. And, of course, coffee: delicious, rich Brazilian coffee, served in tiny cups with vast quantities of sugar.

BUDGETING

Living costs in Brazil are less than half those in North America. Bargaining is a way of life out here and you can expect your money to go a long way if you avoid the tourist traps and act like the seasoned traveller you now are!

As far as employment opportunities are concerned, there is not much scope for different kinds of work. There is no need to attract foreigners into the country to take on unskilled jobs as there are several natives who would be only too willing to do them. Perhaps the best opportunity is for teachers of English. Experience is by no means essential to land yourself a teaching job on the spot. For more details, obtain the general leaflet 'Latin America: A Guide to Work and Opportunities for Young People' by sending £2 to Canning House, 2 Belgrave Square, London SW1X 8PJ.

FURTHER INFORMATION

Brazilian Embassy, 32 Green Street, London W1Y 4AT (tel. 0171 499 0877).

Brazilian Consulate, 6 St Albans Street, London SW1Y 4SG (tel. 0171 930 9055).

The Anglo-Brazilian Society, 32 Green Street, London W1Y 4AT (tel. 0171 493 8493).

Brazilian Information Office, 32 Green Street, London W1Y 4AT (tel. 0171 499 0877).

Background reading: There are a number of excellent guides for the budget traveller, including: *Brazil – a Travel Survival Kit*, by A. Draffen, R. Strauss, D. Swaney (Lonely Planet), *South America: A Travel Survival Kit*, by Emily Hatchwell and Simon Calder (Vacation Work), and *South American Handbook* (Trade and Travel Publications).

The novels of Jorge Amado, Brazil's greatest living writer, will provide an insight into this chaotic, colourful land which no guidebook can hope to match. His most famous works are *Dona Flor and Her Two Husbands* and *Gabriela, Clove and Cinnamon*.

Rio de Janeiro

AIRPORT FACILITIES

Galeão International Airport is 16 km north-west of the city. Its single terminal handles all international and many domestic flights.

The terminal is divided into three sectors: A handles domestic flights; sectors B and C are for international traffic.

The following services are open 24 hours a day: information desk (tel. 398 5050/398 6060), bank/currency exchange facilities, post office, car rental, restaurants and buffets, medical centre. Among the other standard services there's a duty-free shop for arrivals, and a hotel reservation counter (tel. 398 3256) which is open 8 a.m.–8 p.m. daily.

Check-in time is usually 90 minutes before international flights, 30 for domestic journeys. Airport departure tax is about US$16.

CITY LINKS
Bus: For transfers to the airport there is a bus service which runs from Sector B roughly every 15 minutes from 6 a.m.–8 p.m. This doubles as a service downtown. The journey takes about 40 minutes and it costs $2.60.
Taxi: Tickets for airport taxis can be bought at company desks on the arrivals level of the airport terminal. Metered taxis are also available. As with buses, the journey takes 40 minutes.

USEFUL ADDRESSES
Tourist information: Riotour, R. Assembleia 10, 8th Floor, 814 Rio de Janeiro (tel. 297 7117/232 5819).
British Consulate: Praia do Flamengo 284, Rio de Janeiro (tel. 552 1422).
American Express: Kontik-Franstur, Avenida Atlantica 2316, Copacabana.
Main post office: Rua Primeiro de Marco (corner of Rua do Rosario), Rio de Janeiro.
Emergency services: 24 hr pharmacy at Avenida Ataulfo de Paiva 1238 (tel. 274 8448).

GETTING ABOUT
Bus and tram: The cheapest way to get round town is by bus, so not surprisingly they're often crowded. Drivers like to go as fast as they can, unless they're jammed up in the rush-hour traffic. There are trams in operation in some parts of the city, mostly in Santa Teresa. The Central Station (tel. 291 5151) is located in the São Cristóvãs district of Zona Norte. Both buses and trams are popular with pickpockets, so be careful.
Metro: Squeaky clean in comparison to the other transport options. Two lines traverse the city. Runs 6 a.m.–11 p.m. Cost $0.75. Faster than buses, less bother than taxis.
Taxi: Affordable if there's a few of you. Fares are calculated by the

use of a meter and (because of inflation) a conversion chart – both are open to interpretation by imaginative drivers. If the meter isn't working, agree on a price or get out. Also make sure that the meter's been turned back to zero. The worst culprits are the drivers who haunt tourist spots and hotels, so avoid taking a cab in these areas. There's a 40% surcharge between 11 p.m. and 6 a.m. on Sundays.

Car hire: International and local hire companies are available, most notably at the airport and Copacabana. Expect to pay upwards of US$50 a day. Hertz can be contacted on tel. 275 4996/398 3162, Avis on tel. 398 3083/542 4249.

SIGHTS

RIO DE JANEIRO means 'river of January'; the name was given in 1502 when a Portuguese expedition landed on Brazil's east coast. Until 1882, when Brazilian independence was declared, Rio came alternatively under the control of the Portuguese and French. In 1960 Rio lost its status as Brazil's capital city, but to this day it remains the nation's cultural centre and one of its most powerful commercial and industrial hubs.

Rio is also a very beautiful city; not only is it blessed with a location on the western banks of the GUANABARA BAY, it's near to the TIJUCA MOUNTAINS and natural national monuments like Sugarloaf Mountain and CORCOVADO MOUNTAIN (complete with its famous statue CHRIST THE REDEEMER). The city's year-round summer climate further enhances its appeal, and helps account for the large influx of visitors every year which swell the ranks of the five million inhabitants.

SUGARLOAF MOUNTAIN, or Pão de Açúcar as it's known locally, towers above the sea at the entrance to Guanabara Bay. It stands at a height of some 396 metres, so not surprisingly its peak offers breathtaking views of Rio and the city's environs – though they're a fair distance off. Visitors are able to reach the top of the mountain and a sister peak in glass-enclosed cable cars. The ride takes 5 minutes and is in itself quite an exhilarating experience. Hop on at Praia Vermelha station, 25 minutes from the city centre.

The city centre has a multitude of tourist attractions. Downtown, interesting areas to stroll through include the PRACA MAUA (Maua Plaza) and the PRACA XV: the former is intriguing for the aged, elegant architecture of the streets and the ocean liners which anchor there; the latter because it's Rio's oldest square, and is surrounded by quaint buildings in different colours, as well as 16th-century churches. LARGO DA CARIOCA (Carioca Square), near the main shopping area, is another interesting spot, full of faith healers and shoe-shiners. Nearby is the CONVENTO E IGREJA DE SANTO ANTONIO (San Antonio convent and church), one of Rio's oldest buildings, dating back to the early 17th century, of interest for its architecture and for the paintings inside. Other churches to visit include the IGREJA DE SAO FRANCISCO DA PENITENCIA (Church of St Francis of the Penitence), which houses carved altars and roof paintings by Jose de Oliveira, one of Brazil's most celebrated artists. Elsewhere, the new CATEDRAL (Cathedral) on the Avenida Chile is famed for its avant-garde structure.

PARQUE FLAMENGO, which stretches along the shore of Rio's Flamengo area has much of interest. In its grounds can be found the NATIONAL WAR MEMORIAL, which consists of two pillars 45 metres high, on top of which is a curved bowl with an eternal flame; beneath the memorial a crypt houses the tomb of the unknown soldier and the remains of Brazilian soldiers who fought with the Allies in World War II. The nearby MILITARY MUSEUM contains World War II memorabilia, including weapons, photographs and murals. The MUSEUM OF MODERN ART, which is regarded by many as Rio's finest, is also situated in Flamengo Park, and contains works by famous artists both from Brazil and around the world. The ceramic and metal sculptures are particularly impressive. Elsewhere in the park are: children's playgrounds, sports fields, an old DC-3 aeroplane used as a children's climbing frame, bandstands hosting musical displays, and a small train which carries visitors from place to place within the grounds.

Aside from those in the park, other Rio museums you should try to see are the MUSEUM OF THE REPUBLIC at Rua do Catete 179, a historical museum which used to be the home of Brazil's presidents; the PHARMACY MUSEUM at Rua Santa Luzia 206, which contains a variety of old pharmaceutical equipment, and the POLICE ACADEMY MUSEUM at Rua Frei Caneca 162, which has a range of exhibits on fingerprinting, ballistics and other crime-cracking techniques and equipment.

Rest assured that there are several beaches in the Rio area: FLAMENGO and BOTAFOGO are the nearest to downtown; and there's LEGLON, GAVEA and BARRA DA TIJUCA. The most popular – and infamous – beach communities are, however, found at Copacabana and Ipanema. COPACABANA boasts the longest and widest beach area in Rio, and it's a major attraction most weekends, both at night and during the day; the beach front is packed with hotels, shops, pavement cafés and restaurants. Away from the beach, on the tree-lined streets leading towards the city, are antique shops, art galleries and cinemas – and maybe the occasional sighting of Barry Manilow humming his hit tune. IPANEMA is narrower but less crowded than Copacabana – and has been the inspiration for at least as many famous songs. The area is noted for its HIPPIE MARKET which takes place every Sunday in the Praca General Osorio. Although it's an area with a selection of good hotels and restaurants, Ipanema is primarily residential.

ACCOMMODATION

Hotels: The major budget accommodation centres are Gloria, Catete and Flamengo. The centre of town is empty at night and so not a good bet for accommodation. Prices, which generally include breakfast, start at US$15. The most popular haunts are always busy, and hotels across the city will be full at Carnival time in February.

Turistico, Ladeira da Gloria 30 (tel. 225 9388). Singles/doubles start at US$15–20. This well established backpackers' stop fills quickly. It's close to Gloria metro station.

Florida, Rua Ferreira Viani 81, Flamengo (tel. 245 8160). A comfortable place well looked after by the friendly staff. Near to Catete station. Again often busy. Singles/doubles start at US$25–30.

Novo Mundo, Praia do Flamengo 20, Flamengo (tel. 205 3355). A clean place noted for its outstanding views of Guanabara Bay and Pao de Acucar. Double rooms from US$50.

Rio Copa, Av. Princesa Isabel, Copocabana (tel. 275 6644). Singles start at US$50, doubles from US$65.

FOOD

Eating out is very popular among Brazilians and Rio has a thriving restaurant scene with many international establishments – Chinese, German, French, English and Italian among them. But there are also plenty of authentic Brazilian places, too.

Most restaurants serve lunch from 12–3 p.m., and dinner after 9 p.m. Cover charges are common, as is a complimentary side dish of bread and butter, quail eggs and a cold vegetable platter. If thinking of trying a particularly popular sit-down place, reserve a table. Alternatively, stroll through the streets until you find somewhere that takes your fancy. Fun, affordable places are found in the same areas as the cheap hotels, namely Catete and Largo do Machado, and Botafogo and Flamengo. Copacabana and Ipanema are 'I've had a coffee there' places – they can be very expensive.

Restaurant Amazonia, Rua do Catete 311 (tel. 285 7347). A meat eater's paradise with plenty of steak and chicken.

Café Lamas, Rua Marques de Abrates 18, Flamengo (tel. 205 0198). Highly recommended.

Garota de Ipanema, Rua Montenegro 39, Ipanema. An attractive pavement café. Not cheap, but soak up the very same atmosphere that inspired the song 'The Girl from Ipanema'.

ENTERTAINMENT
You'll never be stuck for something to do in Rio, its renowned after-dark scene caters for every conceivable taste, from quiet piano bars and English pubs to German beer halls and seedy cabaret shows. Most places come alive around midnight, once all those late evening dinners have been downed. As a rule, Brazilian nightclubs only admit couples, but this regulation has been relaxed over recent years, especially when it comes to tourists. You should stay clear of tourist hives like parts of Copacabana if you want a real night out in Rio. Dancing, Samba and jazz are popular options across the city. Check out *Program Ristour* from the Tourist Office for the full range of options.

Roda Vive, at the base of Sugarloaf Mountain, adjacent to the cable car station. Live dancing and music Brazilian *gafieras* style.

Jazzmania, Rua Rainha Elizabete (tel. 287 0085). A venue for local and international jazz greats. Not the cheapest place in town, but it's open till late – and it's one of the best.

Help (tel. 521 1296). If it's outrageousness you're looking for, this is the place. Cover charge $5.

Alternatively, try open-air drinking and dining spots such as the Cinelandia and Baixo Leblon. Wherever you are, keep an eye out for backstreet places away from the main thoroughfares.

That several cinemas around town show obscure English-language 'Art House' movies is a measure of how seriously Rio takes the business of entertainment. Where culture is concerned, Rio's Municipal Theatre (Teatro Municipal) is the main attraction for opera, ballet and concerts.

FESTIVALS AND EVENTS
Carnival time overtakes the city each February. Traditionally a final blow out before a month of abstinence during Lent, it rocks Rio like nothing else – either that or it's a tourist trap par excellence. You won't know for sure unless you experience it, but Carnival time is celebrated throughout Brazil, so you can easily stumble across more authentic provincial events.

EXCURSIONS

CORCOVADO (Hunchback Mountain) is one of Rio's most popular attractions. The imposing statue of Christ the Redeemer can be reached by riding on an open-sided cog railway which leaves from Cosme Velho station. The mountain itself has other attractions besides its more publicized features: along the road leading to the peak are numerous look-out points and picnic spots; there's also LARGO DO BOTICARIO, a collection of colonial houses.

FLORESTA DE TIJUCA is a tropical woodland full of interesting plantlife just a short drive from downtown Rio. Take a stroll through the woods and stumble across some of the small waterfalls and other natural delights. Close by, if less well hidden, is the 900-metre mountain, PICO DA TIJUCA. There are several picnic spots in the forest, but whatever your excuse for coming you'll have successfully escaped the hustle and bustle of the city.

ILHA PAQUETA is a small island in Guanabara Bay. An attractive place to explore, it's worth visiting for the boat trip alone because of the harbour view it affords of Rio. Once the summer residence of the imperial Brazilian family, Paqueta Island's population of something over 5,000 consists mainly of fishermen, and any activity to do with the sea is a favourite pastime of the locals. No cars are allowed on the island, and the methods of transport available to tourists are rented bicycles or horse-drawn carriages. Having spent some time relaxing on the beach, enjoy the first-rate seafood that's readily available.

SANTA TERESA is in the suburbs of Rio. This beautiful area provides a glimpse of what the old colonial city must have looked like. Narrow, tree-lined streets are lined with 19th-century houses – in stark contrast to the architecture of modern Rio. There's also a tram service in operation, Rio's last.

MEXICO

VITAL STATISTICS

Red tape: Most European citizens require only a valid passport and a tourist card (issued free by Mexican Consulates and authorized airlines) for a stay up to 90 days – except for nationals of Luxembourg and Portugal, who may only stay for up to 30 days, and French citizens, who require a visa. Passports are not required by citizens of Canada and the USA holding proof of citizenship and a tourist card. All visitors must produce onward tickets and sufficient funds for their stay in Mexico.

Customs: Visitors may bring in 400 cigarettes or 50 cigars or 250 g pipe tobacco, plus 3 l wine or liquor duty-free. In addition, personal items to the value of US$500 are permitted. Officially only one camera (photo/movie/video – not professional) and twelve rolls of film are allowed. Drug smuggling carries serious penalties: don't even consider it.

Health: There are no compulsory vaccinations for Mexico, but several inoculations are recommended, among them hepatitis, typhoid, tetanus and polio; anti-malarial tablets are also a good idea. All water should be sterilized, vegetables cooked and fruit peeled. Keep all wounds, no matter how minor, clean and covered. Visitors to Mexico City should allow time to acclimatize to the high altitude. Health insurance is strongly recommended. Take an AIDS kit (see p. 98).

Language: Spanish. Native pre-Columbian languages are spoken in rural areas. English is widely spoken, especially in tourist areas.

Population: 81 million.

Capital: Mexico City, population 20 million.

Political system: Democratic republic.

Religion: Roman Catholic (90%). The remainder are Muslims, Jews, and other denominations.

Time: Six hours behind GMT.

Money: The currency is the Mexican Peso ($), divided into 100 centavos. Coins: 5c, 10c, 20c, 50c, $1, $2, $5, $10, $20. Notes: $10, $20, $50, $100 and $500. The Peso is sometimes indicated by the symbol N$. This means 'New Peso' but has the same value as the Peso. £1 = about $8.72.

Communications: International direct dialling is available. Long-distance domestic calls are cheap, but international ones are expensive because of taxes. You'll find most public call boxes are out of order, but those that are working are easy to spot: just look for the queue! You can always find phones at shopping malls or big supermarkets.

Send letters by airmail; surface mail is slow. Within Mexico City there is an immediate delivery service (Entrega Immediata), which takes two or three days.

Electricity: 110v/AC in most places. Power sockets accept American plugs, so take an adaptor.

Business hours: BANKS: Mon.–Fri. 9 a.m.–2.30 p.m. Some banks are open on Sat. afternoons.

POST OFFICES: Main Mexico City office open Mon.– Sat. 8 a.m.–midnight, Sunday 8 a.m.–4 p.m.

SHOPS: In Mexico City: Mon.–Sat. 9 a.m.–8 p.m. Elsewhere: Mon.–Fri. 9 a.m.–2 p.m. and 4 p.m.–8 p.m.

OFFICES: Mon.–Fri. 9 a.m.–3 p.m., though this varies considerably.
Holidays: 1 and 6 January; 5 February; 21 March; Maundy Thursday and Good Friday; 1 and 5 May; 15 or 16 September (Independence Day); 12 October (Columbus Day); 20 November (Anniversary of the Revolution); 25 December.
Climate: Temperatures vary with altitude. The coastal and lowland areas are hot and humid, while Mexico City and the central plateau region have a temperate climate. The highlands tend to be fairly mild, but temperatures can drop dramatically at night. The best time to visit Mexico is between November and February, when it is generally dry and warm, though chilly at night. It's very hot during the summer (June to September). This is also the wet season, and there are usually showers at the end of the day.

DO'S AND DON'TS
As in most Latin American countries, street crime in the cities is a major problem and you should guard your valuables at all times. Don't go out bedecked with jewels and laden down with more expensive photographic equipment than you can carry: you will just be asking for trouble.

Though easy-going by nature, the people are very conservative in their attitudes. There is a prejudice against scruffy-looking travellers, and women will find they are hassled less if they dress modestly (in Mexico City the same applies to men). Treat officials with courtesy, don't allow yourself to be provoked or to display anger – and don't make the mistake of assuming that they won't understand offensive remarks made in English. A basic knowledge of Spanish and a little courtesy will go a long way in Mexico. At the very least, learn to greet people with 'Buenos días' or 'Buenas tardes' and say your pleases and thank yous.

Chiapas, a southern state on the Guatamalan border, has many guerrillas. It's advisable to check the situation through the Embassy before going anywhere near this area.

WHERE TO GO FOR WHAT
Among Mexico's most celebrated attractions are the great Mayan ruins in the state of Yucatan. The gateway to the Mayan world is VILLAHERMOSA, a beautiful city with a remarkable open-air archaeological museum. Mayan sites to visit include CHICHEN ITZA – don't miss the ball court arena and the inner area of the main pyramid – and the pyramids of UXMAL, for the spectacle of the

evening Light and Sound show. Nearer to Mexico City, the pyramids at TEOTIHUACAN, 'city of the gods', are similar marvels of human achievement.

North of Mexico City is the historic Bajio, the Mexican heartland. It is here in the mining towns, along the so-called Independence Route, that you will find the strongest sense of Mexico's colonial heritage. The picturesque SAN MIGUEL DE ALLENDE brims with colonial art and architecture, and is a classified national monument. Tucked away betwixt high mountains, GUANAJUATO is considered by many as the pearl of colonial towns. You'll find mummies here.

GUADALAJARA, Mexico's second largest city, has also maintained an old-fashioned romantic feeling. Its 16th-century architecture, Victorian wrought-iron kiosks and flower-lined streets and plazas reflect days gone by. Yet at the same time it's a sophisticated, modern metropolis with luxury boutiques as well as one of the largest open-air markets in the western hemisphere. The route from Mexico City to Guadalajara passes through MORELIA (noted for its fine baroque cathedral) and some spectacular mountains dotted with Indian villages, lakes and forests.

The beaches and resorts of Mexico are rightly famous. The best known are those on the Pacific coast, such as ACAPULCO – one of the largest and most vibrant cities in the country, though it has become very Americanized. But for pure tranquillity, go instead to the BAJA CALIFORNIA peninsula in the north-west. Although it passes through arid desert, the region's single highway, Route One, will take you to some of the country's most charming seaports. It gets cheaper the further south you go; drop in on seaside towns like SAN FELIPE and ENSENADE for fine food and long lazy days.

In the south there are a still a few relatively undeveloped stretches of coastline, although they're rapidly being 'discovered' by developers, and hotels are springing up all the time. Visit the villages of PUERTO ANGEL and HUATULCO now, before it's too late. The most popular of the Caribbean resorts is CANCUN, which has the added attraction of the nearby Mayan ruins at TULUM. A few kilometres off Cancun's shores lies the ISLA MUJERES, 'island of women', which has glorious beaches and is a water wonderland with excellent snorkelling opportunities on the coral reef.

INTERNAL TRAVEL
Air: The majority of flights go via Mexico City. There is a good service to all the big resorts, and to Morelia, Leon, San Luis Potosí, Guadalajara, Veracruz, Villahermosa, Merida, Tuxtla Gutierrez and Chihauhua. One-way fares available at the time of writing

included: Acapulco US$65; Guadalajara US$64, Veracruz US$58, Villahermosa US$96.

Mexicana Airlines offers an air pass called the Mexi Pass. This includes seven domestic zones plus international sectors. The pass is in the form of coupons which are exchanged for flights. A minimum of two coupons must be purchased; international sectors may only be purchased in addition to domestic coupons. Within the seven domestic zones, the coupons range in price from US$30–130 and the international sectors start at US$112 for the Miami–Cancun flight. NYC–Mexico City goes for US$217 one-way. For details, contact Mexicana Airlines' UK office (tel. 0171 930 9935).
Rail: The service is limited and tends to be slow. Trains are not really a practical option for touring the country, but there is a good (if far from rapid) service connecting Mexico City to Veracruz, Guadalajara, Queretaro, San Miguel de Allende and Nuevo Laredo.
Road: The pick of the bus services is the first class (*primera clase*) direct service (*directo*). As is the case across South America, buses go to the remotest towns and villages, but don't expect too efficient a service when it comes to time keeping. On the other hand, it's cheap: first class from Mexico City to Tijuana costs $55.
Car hire: It is possible to rent a car in any of the major cities. An international driving licence will be required. Traffic travels on the right-hand side of the road. Outside large cities, driving by night is not recommended.

ACCOMMODATION
Accommodation options in Mexico are wide ranging. There are hotels, converted haciendas, colonial-style hotels, motels, bungalows, boarding houses and hostels (though the latter are few and far between). Prices start at about US$8, but expect to pay an average of US$12 a night (more in cities).

FOOD
Though relatively new to European tastebuds, Mexican food is rated highly around the world. It has a Spanish and French heritage, but is made with South American ingredients. There's much more to it than tacos and burritos. As with the other culinary greats – French, Italian, Chinese and Indian – it has a distinctive taste, but it needn't be blisteringly spicy. Most flavours are smooth, mild blends of exotic ingredients. Even basic dishes like maize pancakes and chilli beans are cooked in a wide variety ways and forms, so a budget-conscious diet needn't be (too) monotonous. Many dishes combine savoury and sweet ingredients: chicken or turkey with

chocolate, for example. There are plenty of vegetarian delights in store, too.

For a decent meal in a reasonable restaurant you can pay as little as US$5. Street stalls are cheaper still. There are more than fifty types of chilli, so there'll be a different flavour to your *tacos, enchilados* and *crêpes* as you travel the country.

Fruit juices are popular and beer is cheap and plentiful. Wine is a speciality on the Baja California peninsula.

BUDGETING

In Mexico, living costs are much lower than those in North America. In fact, they are less than half of what you'd expect to find in the USA. Bargaining is a way of life here and so you will find that your money will stretch much further if you avoid the tourist traps and act like the streetwise traveller you now are! With bargaining, expect to pay at least 30% of the intial price.

There are few opportunities to find unskilled work in Mexico, as there are only too many locals willing to do this kind of work. However, there is a huge demand in Mexico for teachers of English. For more details, get hold of 'Latin America: A Guide to Work and Opportunities for Young People', by sending £2 to Canning House, 2 Belgrave Square, London SW1X 8PJ.

FURTHER INFORMATION

The Mexican Consulate, 8 Halkin Street, SW1X 7DW. (tel. 0171 235 6393)

Mexican Tourist Office, 60−61 Trafalgar Square, London WC2N 5DS (tel. 0171 734 1058).

Latin American Tourist Association (LATA), 10 Hanover Street, Mayfair, London W1R 9HF (tel. 0171 493 2214)

Mexicana Airlines, Aztec House, 61 High Street, Barnet, Herts EN5 5UR.

Background reading: Budget travellers are recommended to read Lonely Planet's two guides to the area *Mexico − Travel Survival Kit* and *Baja California − Travel Survival Kit*. Those planning to combine a visit to Mexico with trips to neighbouring countries should try *Mexico & Central American Handbook* (Trade and Travel Publications).

Fictional accounts of life in Mexico from the days of the Aztecs to modern times are thick on the ground, but Malcolm Lowry's *Under the Volcano* remains one of the best modern accounts.

Mexico City

AIRPORT FACILITIES
Benito Juarez International Airport lies 6 km east of Mexico City. It handles all flights to and from the area. The following facilities are available 24 hours a day: bank and foreign exchange services, restaurants and buffets, left-luggage lockers (US$1.50 per day), medical services. There's also a post office, a range of shops and duty-free outlets, a pharmacy, and several car rental desks. The airport is of linear design with terminals A through F. International arrivals come in to terminal E, departures terminal D.

Check-in time is 90 minutes before an international flight, 60 minutes prior to a domestic trip. An airport tax of US$8 is levied. For airport and tourist information, call 784 2040 (between 6 a.m.–11 p.m.), 571 3469/3492 (between 7 a.m.–2 a.m.).

CITY LINKS
Bus: There is a bus service to the city centre every 15 minutes.
Subway system: Follow signs for the Terminal Area Station which is located near terminal A. This is always overcrowded. Beware of pickpockets.
Taxis: Follow the TAXI signs out of the airport for the official (yellow) taxi service. The journey to the city centre costs US$7. Pay in the booth in advance, ignore all offers of help.

USEFUL ADDRESSES
Tourist office: Secretario de Turismo, Mexico City. (Tourism Hotline: tel. 250 0120.)
Main post office: Correo Central, Avenidas Tacuba.
British Embassy: Lerma 71, Colon Cuauhtemoc (tel. 207 0089).
US Embassy: Paseo de la Reforma 305 (tel. 211 0042).
Emergency services: Contact the tourist police on 625 8668.
Medical assistance: see above.
Travellers' hotline: In Mexico city 250 0123. Elsewhere dial 91 800 90932. Operates 24-hour service 365 days a year.

GETTING ABOUT
Metro: Buy ten tickets at a go to save time, and use the automatic barriers. Trains run every few minutes. It's a well signposted system, and easy-to-read maps are available. Services run from 5 a.m.–midnight.
Bus and minibus: At 100 centavos and 350–500 centavos respect-

ively, buses and minibuses (pesero) are relatively good value but are still up to ten times more expensive than the metro. Check windscreens for destinations. Services available roughly 5 a.m.–midnight.

Taxis: Stick to the yellow cabs and agree on a price when you get in. Expect to pay higher fares after 10 p.m.

Car hire: Expensive and impractical in congested Mexico City, but okay for travel elsewhere. Look out for cheap local firms; expect to pay US$50-plus a day, US$300-plus a week.

SIGHTS

Mexico City was originally built on a lake; when the Spaniards first saw it from the surrounding hills they thought they were about to take a prize as rich as Venice. Today much of the lake, and the city's beauty, has evaporated. But don't be discouraged because the Mexican capital is once again the 'true land of discovery': tough new anti-pollution laws have been introduced and, as the smog gradually lifts, the two volcanoes (Popocatepetl and Iztlacihuatl) which tower to the east of the city are slowly coming back into view. Not that it's a tranquil place – far from it. This, the world's largest city, shovels irritations and attractions upon the visitor in equal, heaped quantities. For a start there's the cacophony of old and new as ornate colonial buildings jostle with skyscrapers, as thousands of metro commuters shuttle past an ancient Aztec pyramid to reach the office, and motorists fight a losing battle to maintain traditional Mexican traits of courtesy and kindness as the congestion on the streets reaches fever pitch during the three-times a day rush hour (7.00–9.00 a.m., 1.30–3.00 p.m., 6.00–8.00 p.m.).

At the heart of the old city is the ZOCALO, one of the largest and most majestic plazas in the world. It is surrounded by a host of sights, among them the METROPOLITAN CATHEDRAL, which took 249 years to complete and is the largest in Latin America. There's also the PALACIO NACIONAL, which houses the presidential offices and contains murals by Diego Rivera. Opposite is the MONTE DE PIEDAD (the National Pawnshop), dating from 1777. From here you can stroll around the ALAMEDA PARK, and the PLAZA DE SANTA DOMINGO, where public scribes still offer their services, and CALLE MADERO, an old silversmiths' street. Behind the cathedral is the excavated Aztec TEMPLO MAYOR where the main Tenochtitlan pyramid once stood. Parts of the temple are still there, as is a good plan of the old city.

CHAPULTEPEC PARK is a large and attractive park, containing some very fine, old trees as well as a number of museums and galleries. In addition to the NATIONAL MUSEUM OF MODERN ART, it has the NATIONAL MUSEUM OF ANTHROPOLOGY, where the famous Aztec Calendar Stone is on display, along with many other pre-Columbian treasures. Nearby, in Chapultepec Castle (one of the few castles in Mexico) is the NATIONAL MUSEUM OF HISTORY. The imperial apartments that were once the residence of Emperor Maximilian are on view, together with a collection of carriages and other period pieces that span centuries of Mexican history. It was Emperor Maximilian who planned the majestic Paseo de la Reforma to take him from Chapultepec Castle to the Zocalo. In the centre of the boulevard is the dramatic COLUMNA DE LA INDEPENDENCIA, surrounded by statues of Mexican heroes and topped by a Winged Victory. The BAXILICA DE GUADALUPE contains a venerated shrine where the virgin is said to have appeared to the Indian, Juan Diego, in 1531. The SALUBRIDAD is an ultra-modern building with beautiful stained-glass windows by Diego Rivera.

In the Pedregal Quarter lies University City. Established in 1555 (it was the first university in the American continent) and subsequently rebuilt in the 1950s, it is a striking example of modern Mexican architecture. In sharp contrast is the Coyoacan area (which means 'place of coyotes'), a mellow, unspoilt oasis filled with colonial buildings and gardens. Take in the Franciscan monastery and the 16th-century Church of San Juan Bautista, while you're there. The fashionable Zona Rosa is the place for dedicated spendthrifts and window-shoppers alike. Many of the streets are pedestrianized and lined with cafés with parasol-shaded tables. The ice cream is a must here. Try the *cazota* flavour (similar to butterscotch).

There are several museums worth looking out for around Mexico City. The ACADEMIC DE SAN CARLO MUSEUM houses a fine collection of Old Masters, such as El Greco, Van Dyke and Titian. The other museum in Mexico City worth taking in is the FRIDA KAHLO MUSEUM in the Coyoacan section. On the site of her former house and studio, the home of this much-vaunted artist has been meticulously preserved. Close by is the spot where Trotsky was assassinated.

ACCOMMODATION
Youth hostel: The YHA is at Madero 6. It's not possible to book in advance, but for information write to: Association Mexicana de Albergues de la Juventud, Madero 6, Of. 314, Mexico 1. Expect to pay upwards of US$7.
Hotels: The cheap hotels are mostly in the old town, around Plaza Republica, Zocala and Almeda. Expect to pay upwards of US$12 for a double room. A 15% government tax is added to hotel bills. Recommended places include:

Monte Carlo, Uruguay 69 (tel. 521 2559). Comfortable and very clean. Zocalo is nearby.

Hotel Leon, Republica de Brasil S (tel. 512 9031). Grubby but cheap.

The University area is also worth a look; ask around for student lodgings. Try the hotels on Tlalpan Avenue.

FOOD
In addition to a wide range of international cuisines, you can sample regional and national specialities. Affordable restaurants can be found, but street vendors and cafés offer the best value. In a decent restaurant you can pay as little as US$8. Imported wines are expensive but most places will have a local list. You can feast in style in former haciendas which evoke Mexico's colonial past or eat more informally in the city's *fondas*. Watch out! Restaurants are extremely busy on Sundays from 2–6 p.m.

Good, reasonably priced eating places in Mexico City can be found on the Av. 5 de Mayo. These include Cafe 5 de Mayo, Cafe Popular and Cafe Blanca – all two minutes from the Zocalo. Other possibilities include the Parilla Suiza and La Tablita chains, which have branches all over the city.

The Vips restaurant chain has branches dotted across the city offering reasonable food at fair prices.

ENTERTAINMENT
Mexico City may not be the world's noisiest capital, but it still lights up after dark and certainly doesn't lack atmosphere. The Zona Rosa bubbles with nightlife in the evenings, while the old city centre is the place for more traditional Mexican entertainment: the Plaza Garibaldi's Mariachi bands attract tourists and locals alike; the latter come to request favourite songs of the bands – it's a bit touristy but go anyway.

Mexicans eat late, and many bars and dining halls combine food with entertainment. Places to look out for include Santa Cecilia, Tanampa and Mexico Tipico. Ask the staff in your hotel to recommend their favourite venues, as there are plenty of places off the tourist track.

Nightclubs are scattered across the city, particularly on Av. Insurgentes and Av. Paseo de la Reforma. Some well-known ones are:

El Marrakesh, Calle Florencia 36. Actually four clubs in one.

Cero Cero, Camino Real. A popular disco which pulses to impressive psychedelic lighting.

Gitanerias, Calle Oaxaca 15. A long-time favourite of flamenco aficionados.

On a more cultural note, the Bellas Artes (National Palace of Fine Arts) stages opera and dance performances (including the colourful Ballet Folklorico) amid a fine marble and art deco interior. Poetry is also popular.

EXCURSIONS
Just beyond the city are the fabled floating gardens of XOCHIMILCO, where you can rent a flower-bedecked boat and glide through the canals. TEOTIHUACAN, city of gods, lies 48 km north-east of Mexico City (take the bus from del Norte terminus): the ruins cover several square kilometres and are dominated by the majestic Pyramids of the Sun and Moon (the former was built between AD 0 and AD 300, as both a religious monument and solar symbol). The TEMPLE OF QUETZALCOATL is an impressive pyramid of superimposed layers. The site museum contains a rich collection of objects discovered during the excavations.

The road from Mexico City to Cuernavaca passes through spectacular mountain scenery. Once a winter refuge of Aztec and imperial nobles, CUERNAVACA itself is now a sprawling industrial town, but it's worth continuing on to see the ruins of XOCHICALCO, set in beautiful, rolling country. The site's most significant building is the TEMPLE OF THE PLUMED SERPENT, with its superb relief sculpture. There is also one of the finest ancient ball courts in Mexico.

Peace and tranquillity will be yours in DESIERTO DE LOS LEONES, a wooded national park 24 km out of Mexico City. Tula, 65 km away, has pyramids and sculptures, a fascinating museum, and a the church built in 1553. The Spanish-influenced city of PUEBLO, is one of the five largest cities in the Mexico. Its markets make an interesting stroll; keep an eye out for handicrafts made from onyx. For silver, travel to the colonial town of TAXCO, a two and a half hour journey away. Alternatively, an authentic city-dwellers' weekend-break can be had by travelling the 97 km to CUERNAVACA. Far away from the hassles of town life you can relax here while lapping up some of the region's year-round spring weather.

PERU

VITAL STATISTICS
Red tape: A full passport, valid for at least six months is all that is required of visitors from the EC, the States and Canada. Australians and New Zealanders need visas and should apply to their nearest Peruvian Embassy. Foreigners are usually given a tourist

card permitting them to stay for 60 days. Carry your tourist card at all times.

Customs: Visitors are allowed to bring in 400 cigarettes or 50 cigars or 50 g tobacco, and two bottles of spirits.

Health: There are no compulsory vaccinations, although inoculation against typhoid, polio and yellow fever and hepatitis are recommended, as are anti-malaria tablets, especially if visiting the rainforest. It is advisable to take an AIDS kit (see p. 98).

Language: Spanish is the official language, but Quechua is widely spoken, especially among the Indian population.

Population: Approximately 22 million.

Capital: Lima, population approx. 8 million.

Political system: Democratic republic.

Religion: Roman Catholic.

Time: Five hours behind GMT.

Money: The currency is the Nuevo Sol (NS), which is divided into 100 centavos. Coins: 1, 5, 10, 20 and 50 centavos. Notes: NS10, NS20, NS50 and NS100. The old currency, the Inti, is no longer in circulation. As ever, the US dollar is widely accepted. £1 = about NS3.60.

Communications: Pay phones in the cities accept tokens, but don't bank on many opportunities to use your tokens in the countryside.

The domestic postal service is at best unreliable. Because of inflation mail must be franked according to the current rate, not stamped – but at least that limits the attraction of pilfering stamps so they can be resold.

Electricity: Lima: 220v AC/60 Hz. Arequipa: 220v AC/50Hz. Iquitos: 110v AC.

Business hours: BANKS: Jan.–Mar. open Mon.–Fri. 8.15 a.m.–11.30 a.m.; Apr.–Dec. 9.15 a.m.–12.45 p.m.

POST OFFICES: Mon.–Fri. 9 a.m.–7 p.m., Sat. 9 a.m.–12 p.m.

SHOPS: Mon.–Fri. 10.30 a.m.–1.00 p.m. and 4–7 p.m.

OFFICES: January to March open Mon.–Sat. 9.30–11 a.m.; April to December open Mon.–Fri. 9.30–11 a.m. and 3 p.m.–5 p.m.; Sat. 9.30 a.m.–11.30 a.m.

Holidays: 1 January; Maundy Thursday and Good Friday; 1 May (Labour Day); 29 June (St Peter and St Paul Day); 28/29 July (Independence Day); 30 August (Santa Rosa de Lima); 1 November (All Saint's Day); 8 December (Immaculate Conception); 25 December.

Climate: In Peru's coastal regions, the climate is fairly cool from

June to November; there's virtually no rain, but humidity is high and there is little sunshine. The eastern Sierra region has heavy rains between October and April, and there is considerable variation between day and night temperatures. The Montana region, east of the Sierra, and the Selva – a jungle area of the Amazonian basin – both have tropical climates.

DO'S AND DON'TS
At the time of writing the Sendero Luminoso ('Shining Path') terrorist organization was continuing its offensive against the government, despite the fact of its leader having been arrested. They do not target tourists, but British citizens are nevertheless recommended to call the Foreign Office advice line (tel. 0171 270 4129) before booking anything (other nationals should contact an equivalent government ministry in their own country). Don't take the dangers lightly. Take precautions to find out the current situation and avoid any potentially dangerous areas.

Theft is a major problem. Fortunately thieves tend to rely on stealth rather than violence, so guard against opportunist pickpockets and bag-snatchers by travelling in pairs and being vigilant.

Peru has strict laws against the possession of, use of, and dealing in drugs. Violators are jailed and tried under Peruvian law. Sentences range from 15 years to life, and the process (from arrest to sentencing) can take from 9 months to 2 years.

WHERE TO GO FOR WHAT
One of Peru's most celebrated attractions for visitors is the EL TREN DE LA SIERRA railway journey from Lima north into the mountains of the Andes. This unforgettable trip takes passengers through 65 tunnels, across 61 bridges and climbs 4,800 m above sea level to a mountain pass – you may suffer the effects of altitude sickness on the way up, but you'll see the famed Jauja Valley and enjoy a glimpse of the mountain world of the old Inca tribes, a world which is impressive both in beauty and character. *En route*, the train stops at HUANCAYO, an important market centre in the central Andes. The town has a unique flavour – it was here that the native Huanca tribe fought the Incas in the 15th century, and the cultural legacy lives on in the colourful costumes and traditional dances of the region. The train also provides a link to civilization for MACHU PICCHU. Although its location was mentioned in various records, Machu Picchu remained 'lost' until 1911, when it was rediscovered by an American professor and proclaimed as the 'Lost City of the Incas'. Thousands of feet above sea level and atop one of the highest peaks in the Andes, a trip along what has become known as the

INCA TRAIL not only presents an opportunity to sample the Inca-controlled Peru of centuries ago, but the chance to soak up some of the most stunning scenery you'll ever encounter.

On your way to Machu Picchu you'll pass through CUZCO. Once the seat of the Inca Empire, it is commonly recognized as the archaeological capital of the Americas. The highlight of all the wonders on view is a fortress a couple of kilometres outside town known as SACSAYWAMAN. Built of interlocking curved rocks, each weighing an estimated 140 tons, its existence is made all the more astounding when you discover that it was constructed without the use of mortar. In the imperial city itself there are many churches and two cathedrals.

In southern Peru, on the border with Bolivia, lies LAKE TITICACA. Covering an area of 5,200 sq. km, it's the highest navigable waterway in the world, some 3,750 metres above sea level. A fascinating feature of the lake is the resident Urus tribe, who live on thick carpets of reeds scattered on the water's surface: a visit to these floating islands is highly recommended, not just for the spectacle, but for the chance to examine the lifestyle and culture of the Urus, one of the oldest tribes in this ancient country.

TRUJILLO, Peru's second largest city with a population of 400,000, is in the northern part of the country. Set against the brown foothills of the Andes, it has a jaded colonial character: old churches, monasteries and homes are much in evidence around its squares and streets. There are a number of interesting places to visit, among them the Archaeological Museum (Calle Bolivar 446) which is noted for its exhibits of Chimu and Mochica pottery, and the 18th-century house which was inhabited by General Iturregui when he pronounced Trujillo's freedom from Spain in 1820.

CHAN-CHAN, the imperial city of the Chimu civilization, is a short drive from Trujillo. Now a crumbling ruin, its citadels and sacred enclosures still provide a tangible insight into the culture and traditions of the Chimus as they were centuries ago. Not long ago a burial mound was excavated to reveal the skeletons of 13 young girls who'd sacrificed their lives to be buried alongside a Chimu king.

The third largest city in Peru is AREQUIPA. Situated at the foot of the El Misti volcano, the city is known for its Spanish-style buildings and old churches made of sillar, a pearl-white volcanic substance. The city grew with the Incas, and among its points of interest is the Santa Catalina convent; opened in 1970 and covering an area of 2 hectares it is almost a city within a city, housing a collection of furnishings and paintings.

INTERNAL TRAVEL

Air: Aeroperu and the Compania de Aviacion Faucett are the principal operators. Domestic air travel is comprehensive, and what's more, fares are relatively inexpensive. That said, Aeroperu and the Compania de Aviacio Faucett are notorious for overbooking their flights and it's therefore a good idea to re-confirm your flight 24 hours in advance. It's also advisable to re-confirm international flights 72 hours in advance.

Rail: The Central and Southern Railway operates into inland Peru from the coast. There is a service from Lima to Aoroya, with connections available to Cerro de Pasco in the north and Huancayo in the south. Arequipa and Puno are linked by rail, with a connecting line to Cuzco via Juliaca. Beware of pickpockets at railway stations and in carriages. There are no train connections between Lima and Cuzco.

Bus: Regular bus services are available from Lima to the major coastal towns as well as to many places inland. Travel is primarily overnight.

Taxi: There are taxis all over Peru. Agree on a fare in advance, especially in Lima. Also popular are *colectivos* – vehicles which will take you almost anywhere in the country; they can be booked in advance and a pick-up point arranged. Whatever form of transport you opt for, don't expect anything too extravagant, most vehicles are old and quite battered.

Car hire: All the major cities are served by car hire firms (chauffeur-driven cars are also available). An international driving licence is required, and traffic travels on the right-hand side of the road. The major road in Peru is the Pan-American highway which runs north from Lima along the coast to Ecuador, and south to Arequipa and Chile. Elsewhere, very few roads are paved.

ACCOMMODATION

Over the past few years hotels of every type and price have sprung up in Peru's major cities. Standards vary widely, and the cheapest of places can be very basic indeed, with erratic water supplies. But this, after all, is the lot of the budget backpacker across much of the developing world, and cheap and cheerful places can be found. Family-run guest houses are a safe bet, as are hostels. There is some camping, but beware of theft.

FOOD

Peruvian cuisine, called *criolla*, combines Spanish and Indian cooking with a mix of native spices and vegetables. Restaurants selling traditional Peruvian food are not difficult to find in Lima. Street stalls are good for light meals and quick snacks, but make sure the food is hot and fresh.

Look out for filling soups-cum-casseroles. Fried rice, chips and grilled chicken are common too. On the coast, fresh fish will make a welcome change, try the syrupy fish stew called *chilcano*. Another popular and tasty dish is *lomo saltado*, which throws together beef, potatoes, tomatoes and onions in a spicy fry-up. As with most Peruvian food it's generally served with rice. For variety's sake, spicy rice balls and deep-fried mashed potatoes are worth trying when available. A good introduction to the native cuisine can be had by tucking into a *piqueo* – a selection local dishes such as *ceviche* (marinated seafood) and *anticucho* (brochette) which is often served as a starter. Keep an eye out too for places offering *almuerzo* and *merienda*: these are value for money set meals served at lunch and dinner respectively.

Wash all this down with affordable local beer and wine, or try a *pisco* brandy. A variety of soft drinks is also available, from fizzy pop with the aftertaste of a thousand sugar cubes to refreshing herbal concoctions. Drink only bottled or boiled water.

FURTHER INFORMATION

Peruvian Embassy, 52 Sloane Street, London SW1X 9SP (tel. 0171 235 6867).

Faucett, Suite 163, 4th Floor, 27 Cockspur Street, London SW1 5BN (tel. 0171 930 1136).

Background reading: Lonely Planet's *Peru – Travel Survival Kit* will tell you all you need to know about where to go and what to do there. Peru's greatest living writer is Mario Vargas Llosa; his novels, including *Aunt Julia & the Scriptwriter*, have been translated into English. But if it's ancient history you want, look no further than John Hemming's *The Conquest of the Incas*.

Lima

AIRPORT FACILITIES

Jorge Chavez International Airport lies 16 km north-west of Lima. It has one terminal which handles all flights to and from the area – both domestic and international. Facilities include an information desk, bank and foreign exchange facilities, a hotel reservations counter, a bar and restaurant, a left-luggage counter, and car rental desks. Check-in times are 120 minutes prior to international flights,

45 minutes before domestic ones. International departure tax is US$17.50.

CITY LINKS
Bus: An airport link to the city runs roughly every quarter of an hour round the clock. The journey takes about an hour.
Coaches: Coaches run every five minutes to the city. Journey time is about 30 minutes.
Taxi: Readily available at the airport. Ticket touts are everywhere. Average fare to the city centre works out at US$10.
Colectivos: These lumbering cars also offer lifts to the city.

USEFUL ADDRESSES
Tourist office: ENTERPERU, Portal de Zela 965, Plaza San Martin (tel. 274077).
Main post office: Jiron Junin (west of Plaza de Armas). Open Mon.–Fri. 8 a.m.–7.15 p.m.; weekends 8 a.m.–12 p.m.
British Consulate: Edificio El Pacifico Washington, 12th floor, Natalio Sanchez 125, Plaza Washington (tel. 282 830).
US Embassy: Grimaldo del Solar, Miraflores (tel. 444 3621).
Medical assistance: Clinica Anglo-Americana, Av. Salazar (San Isidro) (tel. 440 3570). They speak English here, but you pay for it.

GETTING ABOUT
Bus: The bus service in Lima is quite extensive and reaches all the major parts of the city. There are both public and private buses in operation; both are okay, although the public services are more extensive.
Taxi and colectivo: Taxis are perhaps the safest method of travel (in terms of not getting lost) for those who don't speak Spanish. Can be hired easily, but taxis don't have meters, so the price should be agreed beforehand. *Colectivos* operate along much the same lines as taxis; they can be reserved in advance (pick-up points can be arranged) and will take you anywhere in the country, as well as on short trips around town.
Car hire: Firms operate in all the major hotels and at various points around the city. International firms include Avis, Hertz, Budget and National. Car rental can be expensive in Lima.

SIGHTS
First established by Spanish conquistador Francisco Pizarro as the 'City of Kings', Lima was the capital of Spain's South American empire right up until it gained independence at the start of the

19th century. The city got its name quite by accident – it was situated along a river and valley which the Indians knew as 'Rimac'; this was understood by the Spanish as 'Limac', and was subsequently shortened to Lima. Today it is very much the political and cultural focus of Peru: from government and industry to education and the media, everything is centralized here, including all international flights into the country – a fact that has prompted a population boom in the capital (8 million live here today compared with 500,000 in 1940).

For the visitor, the city has its own unique appeal that owes much to the mixture of South American and colonial architecture, the scenic resorts along the Pacific coast and the mountains in the distance which combine to make Lima one of South American's most attractive cities. At the same time the people, their life-style, customs and traditions give Lima a unique and fascinating cultural flavour reflecting the area's past as much as its present. But don't go there expecting a relaxing beach holiday – it doesn't have the best seaside resorts in South America, and it certainly isn't the most contented of nations. Terrorism, while not rife, is persistent – at the time of writing an offensive continues to be waged by the Shining Path organization. At the same time, a teetering economy has pushed many people onto the streets and into crime. Although this is not a reason to avoid Peru – bombs in Britain make the world headlines, too – it does mean extra care is needed: don't go out alone after dark, and listen for details of the latest dodgy areas to avoid.

As regards the more traditional travellers' pastime of sightseeing, a suitable place to begin a city tour is Lima's main square, the PLAZA DE ARMAS in the heart of town; its sights include the PRESIDENTIAL PALACE, the ARCHBISHOP'S PALACE, and the city hall. A good time to arrive here is at 12.45 p.m., when it's possible to view the changing of the presidential guard. The CATHEDRAL is also here; it dates back to the mid-18th century and its architecture repays careful examination, as do the carved choir stalls (a gift of Charles V to Peru); the remains of Pizarro, the Plaza's architect, are kept in a glass case here.

There are a number of interesting colonial churches within walking distance of the Plaza, among them the IGLESIA Y MONASTERIO DE SANTO DOMINGO (Church and Monastery of Santo Domingo) at Jiron Camana 170, Plazuela Santo Domingo; this was built in 1549, and today belongs to Dominican friars. Its architecture is typically colonial, and the building is also noteworthy for being the site of the founding of South America's oldest university, SAN MARCOS, in 1551. Another sight close by to the Plaza de Armas at

Jiron Ica 225 is the IGLESIA DE SAN AGUSTIN (Church of Saint Augustine), a beautiful building with a finely carved stone façade. Other Lima churches worth a visit both for their beauty and historical significance are the IGLESIA DE SAN PEDRO at Jiron Ucayali 300, the IGLESIA Y MONASTERIO DE SAN FRANCISCO at Jiron Ancash 300 and the IGLESIA DE LA MERCED at Jiron Ica 621.

The PLAZA DE TOROS DE ACHO (Acho Bullring) in the Plaza de Acho north of Balta Bridge, is an unmissable attraction in Lima – and not just for its status as focal point for the intense national passion for bullfighting. Built in the mid-18th century, it was restored in 1945 and the original façade, preserved and protected, remains intact. The bullfighting season takes place during October and November, and big names from around the world come to fight here on Sundays and public holidays.

At the PALACIO DE GOBIERNO in the Rimac district is LA ALAMEDA DE LOS DESCALZOS (the Promenade of the Barefoot Friars). This was inaugurated at the start of the 17th century by the viceroy, Marquis de Montesclaro, and was a fashionable spot where elegantly attired upper-class ladies and eligible gentlemen would come to meet. It's also the location of the Los Descalzos church, which is run by Carmelite friars; the monastery is closed to visitors, but its typical 17th-century beauty can be sampled from the outside.

There are several museums worth looking out for around Lima, including the MUSEO DE ANTROPOLOGIA Y ARQUEOLOGIA at the Plaza Bolivar in Puelo Libre, which houses various exhibitions and displays including rare weavings, pottery and mummies, and tapestries from Paracas and Nazca. Similar displays can be found at the MUSEO DE ARTE at Paseo Colon 125, where Peru's culture through the pre-Inca, Inca, colonial and republican periods is illuminated with the help of a wide range of exhibits. The MUSEO DE LA INQUISICION at Jiron Junin 548 (Plaza Bolivar), once the torture chamber of the Inquisition, nowadays houses one of the best collections of wood carvings in the city. It's also possible to visit prisoners' galleries and cells. The MUSEO ARQUEOLOGICO LARCO HERRERA at the Avenida Bolivar 1515 houses the famous Larco Herrera collection of pottery, which reflects an era of Peruvian culture (called the 'fluorescent era') from AD 200–600. The ceramics on show are mainly from mini-cultures along Peru's northern coast. Finally, take in the MUSEO DEL ORO (the Gold Museum) at the Avenida Alonso de Molina 1100, Monterrico, which houses some 7,000 pieces of worked gold including cups, images and ceremonial objects.

A good place for a pleasant stroll is CHINATOWN. Though not as exotic as it once was, this area around the Plaza de Armas still retains its oriental charms, and some tasty restaurants. Do, however, be careful after dark. Try not to go out alone; and no matter who you're with, the town centre is a place to avoid at night.

ACCOMMODATION

Hostels: These are on the increase. Some are better than others, but the YHA hostel accepts non-members (see below). Expect to pay US$9.

Youth Hostel Albergue Juvenile Internacional, Ave Casimiro, Ulloa 328 (tel. 465488). Half an hour by taxi from town centre. Beds at US$6.

Hostal San Sebastian, Jircon Ica 712 (tel. 232740). Clean and comfortable with friendly staff who speak English. There's a restaurant and laundry facilities are available – noisy at times though. Expect to pay US$5–10.

Hostel Mont Blanc, Emilio Fernandex 640, Santa Beatriz (tel. 338 055). Singles for US$15, doubles for US$20.

Hostel Accord Miraflores, Canturias 398 396 Miraflores (tel. 442 688/468 523). Singles for US$20, doubles for US$28.

Hotels: Prices start at US$8 per person; for a bit of luxury move up to the US$20–30 bracket (for a double room).

Hotel Continental, Jr. Puno 196 (tel. 275 890). Singles for US$20, doubles for US$30.

Hotel Concorde, Prolongacion Ricardo Palma 120 (tel. 479 235/476 486). Singles for US$22, doubles for US$30.

Family guest houses: Atmosphere and friendliness needn't come expensive in Lima, and well-run family guest houses are increasingly popular – most notably those away from the town centre in the more upmarket areas of Miraflores and San Isidro. The Caso Escobar, Domingo Elias 230 (tel. 457565) is a pleasant family-run place. Rooms cost US$10–15.

Camping: Basic facilities are available, but beware of theft.

FOOD

Where the choice of restaurants is concerned, Lima ranks up there with the most cosmopolitan of South American cities. Among the international cuisines to be found are Chinese, French, Spanish, Italian, German, Arab, Argentinian, Mexican, Swiss, Jewish and Japanese, and there are also numerous vegetarian restaurants.

Eating out is a popular pastime, and the city's restaurants are crowded places. Though it's possible to eat a lot cheaper, pleasant mid-range places charge in the region of US$15–20 per person. Lively yet safe places are scattered across the city, but are most likely to be found near to the new budget hotel areas like Miraflores.

Bircher Brenner, Schell 598, Miraflores (tel. 477118). A quaint place which offers some of the best vegetarian food in the city, as well as fresh juices and herb teas. Closed on Sundays.

Brenchley Arms, Atahualpa 174. A pub and a little bit of England – though not necessarily a place for Little Englanders. Tasty pub grub and beer.

Googies, Plaza San Martin. Good place for coffee and sandwiches.

ENTERTAINMENT

As is the case with every national capital, the nightlife in Lima is lively and varied. For something authentically Peruvian, search out a *peñas*, where you'll enjoy folklore and *criolla* – traditional music from the Highlands or the coastal regions. Las Guitarras is a *peñas* spot worth trying, but there are several others in Barranco, Miraflores, and each has been praised for its live entertainment.

For a night out strolling from bars to restaurants and cafés and back to bars, head for the Parque Diagonal in Miraflores, where there are a cluster of places to hang out. To take in a film or play, check out what's on offer at the Cine Pacifico in Miraflores, and Cabaña in the Parque de la Explosicion. But whatever you do, stick to the safe parts of town after dark. Women especially should not go out alone.

EXCURSIONS

The towns of CHACLACAYO and CHOSICA are situated close to each other around 30 km from Lima and provide a worthwhile day-trip from the city – mostly for reasons of climate and character. Some 80 years ago, Chosica was the top holiday resort in winter for the people of Lima, a fact reflected in the Victorian houses here. In time, it was superseded as the select resort by nearby Chaclacayo, where the higher altitude renders the climate even better. Today, Chosica counts among its attractions not only the pleasant climate but charming architecture, including a central plaza fringed with palm trees. Chaclacayo's points of interest include its traditional public market, which is a genuine example of mountain markets throughout Peru.

PARQUE DE LAS LEYENDAS (Park of the Legends) at Avenida de la Marina in SAN MIGUEL, a suburb of Lima, is a relatively small zoological park which offers a clear picture of the geography of the country through its various displays and exhibits, live and otherwise. The three principal geographical regions of Peru – the desert coast, the Andes and the Amazon jungle – are all represented, so it's a good snapshot of the country.

The town of BARRANCO, 3 km south of Miraflores, is a very beautiful place where the architecture and character are reminiscent of the Victorian era. A stroll will take you past splendid old mansions through quiet, leafy parks, and (in the summer) to a slightly cooler climate thanks to the proximity of the ocean.

LA HERRADURA BEACH, just south of the popular Costa Verde, is just as attractive, and less crowded than its more celebrated neighbour. A horseshoe-shaped bay, it's an ideal spot for watersports or simply relaxing after the grind of Lima. Along the shore there are various food stalls and restaurants selling a range of local delicacies.

NORTH AMERICA AND THE CARIBBEAN

The slave trade and immigration from the Old World threw together Europeans, Africans and Indians, thus transforming the colonial outposts into multicultural melting pots. What Canada, the USA and the Caribbean lack in relics of ancient history they more than make up for in their rich cultural heritage and spectacular scenery.

WHERE TO GO FOR WHAT

If you are looking for a city holiday, don't waste your money on a trip to the Caribbean. North America, and the UNITED STATES in particular, have some of the most vibrant and exciting cities in the world: New York, San Francisco, Chicago, New Orleans . . . But when you've had your fill of city life, escape to one of the national parks such as Yosemite, Yellowstone, or the Grand Canyon for some restorative hiking and camping. And don't neglect the state of Hawaii: with its volcanoes, beaches, abundant coconut trees, coral reefs and lush green valleys, Hawaii is well worth a detour.

Visitors to CANADA are often surprised to realize how huge it is. With the population concentrated in a relatively small region, the vast majority of the country remains uninhabited and unspoiled, offering the wilderness at its best with lakes, forests and mountains. It's the perfect country for outdoor pursuits such as canoeing, camping, hiking, whitewater rafting and skiing.

The Greater and Lesser Antilles – a chain of islands stretching 2,800 km between Florida and South America – go by a number of aliases: the Caribbean, after the indigenous Carib Indians who met the early settlers; the West Indies, because Columbus took a right instead of a left when he went in search of India; and the Antilles, after a mythical Atlantic continent. The region's common heritage of plantation slavery and colonial rule masks a rich diversity of distinctive countries and cultures. Although included here, Bermuda is not part of this flotilla of a continent; very much alone, it resides some 1,600 km further north.

Famed as it is for its winter sun, there's a great deal more to the Caribbean than beaches and barbecues, so by all means work on your suntan, but don't forget to explore. The few remaining isolated islands are those that have yet to be paved with an air-strip, and these uninhabited places are ideal for day-trips – some are little more than sand banks. Long, lazy days are assured and the locals are welcoming.

You can lap up the atmosphere and sunshine wherever you go, but each island has its own special attraction: for beaches and developed island life, head to BARBADOS; for a twisting coastline and elegant harbours, opt for ANTIGUA; for a sun-dried taste of old England – from red pillar boxes to 'bangers and mash' – set your course for BERMUDA.

TAKE HEED
Travellers must be vigilant to avoid crime in North America, just as in the rest of the world. The usual rules about keeping your eyes on your luggage and steering clear of the downtown areas of large cities like Los Angeles and Miami still apply. There have been various instances of attacks on tourists in the United States in recent months. Miami has been about the worst with some serious and fatal attacks. The best way to avoid trouble like this is to make sure you have a good map of the city you are visiting and are sure to stay out of the downtown areas. If hiring a car, then ask the hire company for a good map and if you are arriving in the city at night, get a taxi to your hotel and pick up your hire car in daylight.

EMPLOYMENT OPPORTUNITIES
Beware of falling foul of strict immigration laws. A number of publications provide details of jobs on offer and the legal requirements involved: The *How to . . .* series now includes *How to Live & Work in America*. Vacation Work publish a number of relevant titles, such as *Summer Jobs USA* and *Summer Jobs Abroad*, which contain ideas for short-term employment; full-time students may find *Internships: USA* useful; and Susan Griffith's *Work Your Way Around the World* is also very good. The Central Bureau publishes *Working Holidays*, a guide to paid and voluntary work in 70 countries; and *Volunteer Work*, which offers information on voluntary organizations in over 120 countries.

The marinas and docks of the Caribbean are among the few places where you'll find temporary work. Jobs are scarce, and Caribbean governments do not permit foreign visitors to take jobs which local islanders could do – so working as a deckhand or behind the bar of a visiting cruise liner is one of the few remaining opportunities. Chance your luck when you get out there – and risk being exploited as low-cost, illegal labour – or line up a job in advance (the main British agency for Caribbean shipping personnel is Lawson Marine Services Ltd, Royale House, 2 Palmyra Place, Newport, Gwent NP9 4EJ). The pay isn't magnificent, but beggars can't be choosers and you'll need all the money you can get your hands on if you want to hang out in the Caribbean.

INTRA-CONTINENTAL TRAVEL

If you plan to travel widely by air within North America, airpasses can offer generous concessions. To purchase an airpass, you must live outside the US and Canada and buy it prior to arrival. Though you cannot change your routing once the ticket is purchased – at least not without incurring some financial penalty – you may be able to alter your dates. In most cases you must also purchase your transatlantic ticket with the same airline from which you are buying your airpass. Where this is not compulsory, it usually works out cheaper. The usual requirements stipulate that you must make a minimum of three stopovers and complete your travel within 60 days. Major US airlines with Canadian routes will often include Canadian stopovers (and vice versa). Some airlines also offer extensions to Caribbean destinations at special rates if you buy an airpass with them (United Airlines, for example, offer reduced rate flights to San Juan and Barbados to their airpass holders). It is even possible to obtain a standby airpass: North-west Airlines have a 30-day pass ($449) and Delta issues passes for 30 ($499) or 60 days ($799).

Caribbean island-hopping is done mainly by plane. Services tend to connect specific regions within the Caribbean. Islands in the Lesser Antilles are a short half hour flight apart, and the East Caribbean block is well catered for by scheduled services. Local national airlines such as BWIA and LIAT offer 1-month passes. Prices for a 21-day pass start at US$170.

Ferries also commute around specific regions: the Virgin Islands, the Grenadines, and Gaudalupe and its French environs, are the main ones.

There are no coach or rail passes linking America and Canada, though each has its own internal passes. See individual country sections below for further information.

FURTHER INFORMATION

The publishers of *Let's Go* (Pan Books) and the *Rough Guide* series (Harrap Colombus) provide budget overviews of both Canada and the United States, along with a range of individual state and city guides. Lonely Planet's *Canada – Travel Survival Kit* is a thorough and readable budget guide to Canada, as is *The Traveller's Survival Kit: USA and Canada,* from Vacation Work. *Culture Shock! USA* (Kuperard) examines America's customs, characteristics and lifestyle. Comprehensive guides to the Caribbean include James Henderson's *The Caribbean,* (Cadogan Guides) and *The Caribbean Islands Handbook,* ed. Ben Box and Sarah Cameron (Trade and Travel Publications).

Most of the great North American writers are household names the world over, but Caribbean literature is less well known. Derek Walcott, a Nobel Prize winner for Poetry in 1992, has written several plays on the state of the region. Look out for performances of *Viva Detroit*, which tackles the thorny subject of tourism in the Caribbean, and *The Last Carnival*, which is one of a trilogy of plays looking at political developments in the post-colonial West Indies.

CANADA

VITAL STATISTICS

Red tape: Visitors need a full passport and an onward ticket. Citizens of the UK and Ireland, Australia and New Zealand do not require a visa. American citizens need only produce a driver's licence or other proof of identity. Other nationalities should check with the Canadian Embassy. Anyone planning to stay longer than three months or take up employment will need special permits.

Customs: 200 cigarettes, 50 cigars and 1 kg tobacco; 1.14 litres liquor; 1 litre wine or 8 litres beer. Gifts valued at not more than $40 may be imported.

Health: No vaccinations are required. It is essential to take out health insurance as medical treatment is expensive and even emergency care is not free.

Language: Officially Canada is bilingual: French and English. But don't rely on people in French-speaking areas speaking English, or vice versa.

Population: Approx. 27 million.

Capital: Ottawa, population over 300,000.

Political system: Parliamentary democracy with the Queen as Head of State.

Religion: The largest single group is Roman Catholic (around 46%). Other significant religions include the United Church of Canada and the Anglican Church.

Time: There are six time zones across Canada:

Newfoundland Standard Time:	three and a half hours behind GMT
Atlantic Standard Time:	four hours behind GMT
Eastern Standard Time:	five hours behind GMT
Central Standard Time:	six hours behind GMT
Mountain Standard Time:	seven hours behind GMT
Pacific Standard Time:	eight hours behind GMT

(Daylight saving time operates Apr.–Oct. except in Saskatchewan, and clocks go forward an hour.)

Money: The Canadian dollar is divided into 100 cents. Coins: 5c, 10c, 25c, $1. Notes: $2, $5, $10, $50, $100, $500 and $1,000. (All prices quoted in this section are in *Canadian* dollars.) £1 = $2.14.

Canadian dollar traveller's cheques in are the best way to carry the bulk of your money around. The major credit cards are widely accepted.

Tax: Since January 1991, there has been a new goods and service tax (GST) in Canada. The current rate is 7%. Foreign visitors may claim a full rebate of GST paid on goods which they take out of the country as well as on short-term accommodation. For a rebate application form, contact your Canadian Embassy.

Communications: The telephone system is very efficient. Public coin-operated telephones are found countrywide. Local and long-distance calls can be dialled direct from anywhere in Canada and in some areas international direct-dialling facilities are also available (elsewhere, dial '0' for the operator). The number of credit-card operated pay phones is on the increase; step by step instructions in their use are displayed by the phone and are like the US ones.

International letters are automatically sent airmail. Stamps can be bought in any post office or from vending machines in hotels, banks, railway stations and chemists. Poste restante mail can be sent to any post office, where it will generally be held for 15 days.

Electricity: 110v AC.

Business hours: BANKS: Mon.–Thurs. 10 a.m.–3 p.m.; Fri. 10 a.m.–6 p.m. Some banks are also open on Saturday mornings.

POST OFFICES: Mon.–Fri. 9 a.m.–5 p.m., Sat. 9 a.m.–noon.

SHOPS: Mon.–Sat. 9 a.m.–5.30 p.m.; many shops have late-night closing Thurs. and Fri.

OFFICES: Mon.–Fri. 9 a.m.–5 p.m.

Holidays: 1 January; Good Friday; Easter Monday; 20 May (Victoria Day); 1 July (Canada Day); 2 September (Labour Day); 14 October (Thanksgiving Day); 11 November (Remembrance Day); 25 and 26 December.

Climate: The climate in Canada varies between regions. In general, spring is warm with cool nights; summers are sunny and hot everywhere; autumn is cool with frost in most regions; from December to February, the weather is wintry with heavy snowfall in most provinces. The most extreme temperatures occur in the eastern and central provinces: Montréal, for example, drops to around 6°C in winter and 26°C in summer; Winnipeg reaches around 14°C in winter and 25°C in summer. By contrast, British Colombia has a more temperate climate, with average temperatures of 5°C in winter and 22°C in summer.

DO'S AND DON'TS
Don't commit the cardinal sin of assuming that Canadians are just the same as Americans. Your hosts will get extremely cheesed off. Canadians tend to be very conscious of the fact that America is considered the dominant partner; they worry about being smothered by American culture and can feel somewhat antagonistic towards their southern neighbour. Canadians are very proud of their history and roots and are keen to project their own identity. A disproportionate number of Canadian backpackers seem to have the Maple Leaf on their backpack or be carrying 'pins' from their provincial government. Bear this in mind if you hear a North American accent outside Canada – don't assume its owner is an American!

Canadians are very courteous and far more service-oriented than the British. Conversation invariably starts with 'Hi how're you doing?' and finishes with the obligatory 'You're welcome' with a smattering of pleases and thank yous in between. If you meet someone casually, it will be considered rude if you don't say hello.

The legal drinking age is 18 or 19, depending on the province. Canadian police are very strict about drugs – don't risk it.

WHERE TO GO FOR WHAT
Canada's sheer size – it's the second largest country on earth – and consequent vast distances between points of interest mean that sightseeing round the country inevitably involves a fair amount of travel. The major cities of TORONTO, MONTREAL and VANCOUVER are perennially popular with tourists for their abundance of things to see and do. Away from these centres, however, Canada has a wide and diverse range of attractions.

NIAGARA FALLS is one of the world's outstanding natural wonders, located on the US border between Lake Erie and Lake Ontario. Their 56-metre high booming white chutes of water not only possess a unique visual splendour – especially at night when illuminated – but the power of the water fills the atmosphere with a roar which can make a visit quite awe-inspiring.

The magnificent ROCKY MOUNTAINS of Alberta and British Columbia in Western Canada are conveniently accessible by road via four national parks. BANFF, JASPER, KOOTENAY and YOHO NATIONAL PARKS are all renowned for their dramatic scenery:

fantastic snow-capped peaks, forests, crystal-clear lakes and vast glaciers. Visitors can stay overnight in any of the parks (there is no indoor accommodation in Kootenay), but all accommodation must be booked well in advance. You can tour the parks by bus, bike or car. Alternatively the Rocky Mountain Railtour is a popular two-day rail trip through 950 km of spectacular scenery (see **Internal Travel**, p. 528).

CALGARY, on the east side of the Rockies, is an energetic city and popular stopping-off point on the way to the mountains. Surrounded by cattle ranches it also hosts the Calgary Stampede, a ten-day rodeo extravaganza which attracts cowboys and tourists alike.

QUÉBEC CITY, the capital of Québec province, is about two and a half hours' drive from Montréal. The city is Canada's focal point for French culture and is divided into two main sections, each possessing a distinct flavour more French than North American. The cliff-top 'Vieux Québec' with the grand architecture of its castle and cathedral dominates the historical lower town, where the narrow streets and buildings from the past evoke a quaint charm. Ninety-five per cent of locals speak French, although most are bilingual and communication is usually quite easy.

In keeping with Nova Scotia's Scottish ancestry, the picturesque island of CAPE BRETON has a distinctive Celtic character with its rugged highland scenery, old fishing villages, and inland 'bras d'Or' lakes. Scottish tradition is kept alive here by many of the local residents who still speak Gaelic and often indulge in bagpipe-playing or highland dancing. You can get there by air, rail or road.

Between Nova Scotia and New Brunswick, in the Gulf of St Lawrence, lies PRINCE EDWARD ISLAND, Canada's smallest province. Originally inhabited by the Micmac Indians — represented today on four reservations — Prince Edward Island is noted for its rich natural beauty. Its south shore is made up of flourishing green fields and trees atop red sandstone cliffs, while the north shore is renowned for its white silken sand.

Travellers with a real taste for adventure will revel in Canada's North-west and Yukon Territories, where temperatures drop as low as 33°C in winter (the summer average can reach 21°C). The tourist trade is still in its infancy here, enabling visitors to sample the provincial lifestyle on a more authentic, if slightly less comfortable, basis. The North-west Territories are divided into three districts: the DISTRICT OF FRANKLIN is renowned for Baffin Island, where there is good hiking, fishing, winter sports, mountaineering and superb scenery to enjoy; the DISTRICT OF MACKENZIE has excellent hunting and fishing as well as the mighty MacKenzie River for canoeists and cabin-cruisers alike; while embracing the great Hudson Bay is the DISTRICT OF KEEWATIN, where there are fewer activities on offer but dramatically scenic country to compensate. Almost uninhabited, the Keewatin is spectacular because of the tundra that sweeps over it, where the rock and low willows are home to vast caribou herds and the countless lakes are teeming with fish and waterfowl. Beautiful sunsets and the Northern Lights also provide spectacular displays in Keewatin's clear skies.

The YUKON TERRITORY boasts its own wide range of natural rugged delights. Its winters are long, dark and bitterly cold, but in summer the sun shines on picturesque jagged mountains, streams and a large variety of wildlife from mink to moose. Travel to the Northwest and Yukon Territories is by road (weather permitting), sea and air. Numerous package tours of the Territories are available, and these are the most comfortable way of getting to know the region.

INTERNAL TRAVEL

Air: Domestic air travel is expensive, though some passes are available:

Air Canada's airpass is valid for both Canadian and US cities. The price depends on how many cities you wish to visit and whether or not you book your transatlantic flight with Air Canada. The minimum number of cities is three (C$461 low season, C$500 high season) and the maximum is eight (C$761 low season, C$850 high). These prices apply only if you cross the Atlantic with Air Canada; if you fly with another carrier the airpass will cost more.

The Western Canada Airpass from Air BC offers unlimited flying in Western Canada – from Winnipeg as far as Vancouver – on a 'space available' basis for one, two or three weeks. The Airpass must be purchased outside North America and is not available to Canadian or US citizens. The 1995 prices are £119 for one week, £169 for two weeks and £219 for three. The UK sales office is at 7 Sandy Lane, Kingswood, Surrey KT20 6NQ (tel. 01737 832525).

The Eastern Canada Airpass from Air Ontario offers the same unlimited flying scheme as Air BC. You can go as far west as Winnipeg and as far east as Hartford, Connecticut, USA. The prices are £99 for one week, £149 for two weeks and £198 for three.

Rail: Canada's national rail network is VIA Rail. Rail travel in Canada can be an enjoyable experience but the network is geared to freight rather than people, so passenger services are limited and inefficient. VIA offers discounts of up to 40% on coach-class fares on off-peak days. These days differ according to the region in which you are travelling and tickets must usually be purchased about a week in advance. VIA also offers a 30-day railpass valid for 12 days of travel within that period. In peak season (1 June to the end of September) it costs $550; off-peak it costs $385, plus 7% tax. Under-24s pay $495 high season and $349 low season.

In addition to VIA, there are a number of private railway companies offering journeys through some of Canada's more inaccessible regions. The most famous of these is the Rocky Mountaineer Railtour: a two-day journey through 950 km of spectacular scenery in western Canada, including the Canadian Rockies. A one-way trip costs $425 for two people (rising to $479 between 6 June and 23 September). Prices include light meals and one night's accommodation.

Bus: Buses are the cheapest way for independent travellers to get around. The national bus network is Greyhound Lines of Canada, which operates services from Toronto to the west. Regional carriers operate in eastern Canada.

Greyhound issue two types of pass giving unlimited travel on all scheduled Greyhound routes: the Greyhound Canada Pass allows 7, 15, 30 or 60 days' unlimited travel on routes throughout Canada between British Columbia and Ontario with connections to Québec and several American gateway cities. Prices are £87, £115, £160 and £205. The All Canada Pass is available for 15, 30 or 60 days and includes interline coach routes to the Maritime provinces as well. It costs £145, £190 or £240. Both passes must be purchased overseas. Daily extensions are £10 per day and must be purchased at the same time as the pass. The UK agent is Greyhound International, Sussex House, London Road, East Grinstead, West Sussex RH19 1LD (tel. 0342 317317).

Car: UK citizens need only their UK driving licence to drive in Canada. Minimum age for car hire with most companies is 21, and you will normally need to produce a credit card. Front and rear seatbelts are compulsory. Drive on the right.

Hitching: Illegal on highways but legal on slip-roads.

Bicycle: Cyclists are well looked after in Canada. Most towns have cycling lanes and you can normally transport your bike on trains for a small charge.

ACCOMMODATION

Canada has a reasonable range of accommodation. Hostels tend to get booked up quickly, but hotel rooms are affordable when two people share. It's always advisable to book ahead, especially in the summer months. Most tourist offices will try to help, but they do not have specific bed-booking services. The Canadian government operates overseas tourist offices for the various provinces, and these are very helpful in providing accommodation lists.

IYHF hostels: The Canadian Hostelling Association has a network of hostels across Canada which are open to all ages. If you are not an IYHF member you will have to pay a small supplement. Hostels are graded according to their facilities; all have cooking facilities and separate dorms and bathrooms for men and women. Many close during the day and have a night curfew. Prices range from $10–$20 (expect to pay $15 on average).

Student residences: Many universities open their residences to tourists during the summer vacation (May–August). Check with the local tourist office.

Hotels: The cheaper hotel rates start at around $38 for a single and $48 for a double. Check what facilities are available before you book. Motels tend to offer smarter facilities at reasonable prices but are further out of town.

B&B: Bed and breakfast is becoming increasingly popular in Canada. To book this type of accommodation you have to go through an agency, and each region has a number of agencies to choose from. Standards in most B&Bs are very high. Prices start from around $35 for a single and $45 for a double. An enjoyable variation is to stay on a working farm. Ask the local tourist office for information.

Campsites: Canada is wonderfully set up for campers. Nearly every tourist spot, be it urban or rural, will have a campsite. Standards vary according to who runs the site. Those in national parks have excellent facilities. Prices range from $10–20, according to facilities and time of year. Unfortunately, some campsites are open to RVs (recreational vehicles) only; check before you set out.

FOOD

Canadian cuisine is as varied as the country itself and the nationalities that have settled in it. On the coast the speciality is seafood, fresh from the ocean. Typical Canadian seafood dishes include king crab, oysters, shrimp and other shellfish, cod, haddock and salmon. In the central plains, beef and agricultural products are the favoured dishes. Traditional dishes which come highly recommended include first-class beef, partridge, prairie chicken, wild duck and goose. In the major cities (particularly in Ontario) you can eat food of just about any nationality thanks to the multicultural make-up of the cities' populations. Québec, not surprisingly, has many restaurants which specialize in French cuisine. Montréal is a gourmet's delight.

In general, restaurants are reasonably priced: expect to pay $18–30 for an evening meal. (Tipping is a fact of life: give at least 15%, or expect a lot of rude looks and poor service if you dare to show your face in there again). Set-lunch menus are good value at under $10. Self-service restaurants and the various fast-food outlets offer decent meals at low prices, as do chain restaurants like Pizza Hut. For a cheap snack, pick up a sandwich from a deli for around $6. Or save money by skipping lunch and indulging in a delicious and extremely filling Canadian breakfast instead. For around $5 you can get eggs, bacon, hash browns, pancakes, waffles with maple syrup, etc – and it's usually served till quite late.

Alcohol is sold in nearly all hotels in Canada as well as in restaurants and bars. Provincial government-run liquor stores are the only places permitted to sell alcohol directly over the counter. The major Canadian brewers are Molson and Labatt but international beers are also sold, particularly Heineken. Restaurants allowed to serve alcohol display the sign 'licensed premises', since a lot of establishments allow customers to bring their own bottle.

Canadian bars tend not to be anything like the cosy pubs that Brits are used to; on the whole they're rather cold, anonymous places. Beer costs $2–4 a bottle but is cheaper on tap. Under-18s are not permitted in bars (in some provinces the age limit is 19).

BUDGETING

Canada is not a particularly cheap country, but neither are prices exorbitant. If anything, food is cheaper than in Britain. Some costs rise in high season, particularly travel. On the whole, bus is the cheapest form of travel year-round. If you manage to find beds in hostels, expect to pay around $18 per night. You can eat for $20–30 a day and beer is not expensive at around $3 per bottle, cheaper on tap. Entrance fees to tourist attractions tend to be dearer at $6. Because Canada attracts so many festivals, you can enjoy a lot of free outdoor entertainment. Nightlife need not be expensive – many clubs have no cover charge – but watch out for the drinks.

Unfortunately, working legally in Canada is extremely difficult; moreover regulations are strictly enforced and you are liable to get deported if found working illegally. To obtain legal employment you must apply for a working visa before you enter Canada. Students in full-time education can apply for a summer working visa through the Canadian High Commission or through BUNAC (tel. 0171 251 3472) which operates a Work Canada scheme enabling students to work in Canada for up to six months. BUNAC helps its members by producing a directory of jobs in Canada – most are in hotels and tourist resorts or in children's summer camps. Nannies and au pairs can also qualify for a work permit if they have either sufficient experience or relevant qualifications. Usually you will have to commit yourself to at least a year.

FURTHER INFORMATION

Canadian Tourist Office, Tourism Section, Canadian High Commission, Canada House, Trafalgar Square, London SW1Y 5BJ (tel. 0171 839 2299). Provides a bounty of helpful tourist literature on accommodation, internal travel, etc.

Québec Tourism, Quebec House, 59 Pall Mall, London SW1Y 5JH (tel. 0171 930 8314).

Alberta Tourism, Alberta House, 1 Mount Street, London W1Y 5AA (tel. 0171 491 3430).

Tourism British Colombia, British Colombia House, 1 Regent Street, London SW1Y 4NS (tel. 0171 930 6857).

Background reading: Good budget overviews include *Canada – Travel Survival Kit* (Lonely Planet) and *Canada, The Rough Guide* (Rough Guides Ltd).

Margaret Attwood is a popular Canadian author; *The Handmaid's Tale* and *Cat's Eye* are two of her best-known novels.

Montréal

AIRPORT FACILITIES

Montréal has two airports: Dorval deals with flights from Canada and the USA, while Mirabel Airport handles all other international flights.

Dorval Airport lies about 21 km west of the city and has one passenger terminal which is 8 storeys high. Most facilities are on the ground and first floors, including information desks, currency exchange, bars, restaurants and duty-free. For flight information call 514 633 3105.

Mirabel Airport is further out: 55 km north-west of Montréal. Its single passenger terminal has three levels. The main level contains tourist information, currency exchange, eating facilities, and duty-free. Flight information is available on 514 476 3010.

CITY LINKS

From Dorval, Aéroplus runs a bus service which drops off at various downtown hotels. The fare is $9 and the journey takes 20–30 minutes. A taxi will set you back $20.

From Mirabel the Greyline service runs every 30 minutes connecting the airport and downtown Montréal. Journey time is around 45 minutes at a cost of $13. A taxi to the city costs about $55.

There is also a bus service between the two airports which runs every 20 minutes and costs $9.65.

USEFUL ADDRESSES

Tourist office: Centre Infotouriste, 1001 rue du Square-Dorchester (tel. 873 2015).

Main post offices: 1025 rue Saint-Jacques; 1250 rue Université; 1250 rue Sainte Catherine Ouest (tel. 846 8390).

British Consulate, 1155 rue Université, Bureau 901 (tel. 866 5863).

US Consulate-General, 455 boul. René-Lévesque, C.P. 65, Station Desjardins (tel. 398 0973).

Emergency services: Dial 911 for police, fire and ambulance.

Pharmacy: 901 rue Sainte Catherine Est; open 24-hours.

GETTING ABOUT

Bus and metro: Montréal has an excellent mass-transit system which makes travel around the city quick and convenient. The ultra-modern metro runs from 5.30–1 a.m. Lines are colour-coded; tickets cost $1.75 (or $7 for a strip of six) and can be bought in the stations. Metro tickets are also valid for travel on buses (if you buy a ticket on the bus exact change is required). You can transfer between bus and metro to complete your journey, provided you pick up a transfer ticket from your first means of transport. For further information call 288 6287.

Taxi: Taxis can be hailed in the street or booked by phone.

Bicycle: There are several hire shops in the city: La Cordée is at 2159 rue Sainte Catherine Street Est (tel. 524 1515); Cyclo-Touriste is at Centre Infotouriste, 1001 Dorchester Square Street (tel. 393 1528). Bikes can be taken on the metro.

Car hire: All the major hire firms have branches at the airports, Central Station and in the city's main hotels, as well as their own central offices.

SIGHTS

Originally an Indian village by the name of 'Hochelaga', Montréal was discovered by the French explorer Jacques Cartier in 1535. Today this bilingual city has grown to become one of Canada's most important industrial centres as well as one of the country's major intellectual and artistic capitals. The name Montréal is derived from Mont Royal, the mountain at the heart of the metropolis, which dates back around 350 million years.

The rich history of this more French than Canadian metropolis can be sampled in the OLD MONTRÉAL (Vieux Montréal) district: cobbled streets, renovated old buildings and market-places from the 17th, 18th and 19th centuries – not to mention fine street and indoor entertainment – all make for a charming old-world atmosphere coupled with a lively streetlife.

One of Old Montréal's major attractions is PLACE JACQUES-CARTIER: opened in 1804, it is one of the city's oldest markets and a popular meeting place, complete with sidewalk cafés, flower stalls and period architecture, as well as street musicians and other assorted performers. Another enjoyable area is SAINT-AMABLE LANE, where artists draw portraits for passing visitors, and a variety of craftsmen have created an open-air gallery of sorts.

CHÂTEAU RAMEZAY in Old Montréal is a restored house which dates back to Montréal's days under French colonial rule and contains exhibits depicting life during that period. The NOTRE-DAME DE BON SECOURS church is a chapel formerly used by sailors, while the NOTRE-DAME BASILICA is a splendid building in neo-gothic style dating back to the last century.

Like most cities, Montréal has benefited from a growing cultural diversity as various ethnic groups have merged into metropolitan life. SAINT-LAURENT BOULEVARD, stretching from Old Montréal across to the north of the city, was settled by Jewish merchants in the early 20th century. More recently, Greeks, Slavs, Portuguese and Latin Americans have turned the area north of Sherbrooke into a genuine bazaar with many international restaurants and speciality stores selling imports from all over the world. Take your pick from a plethora of shops dealing in smoked meat, bagels and Kosher food, Hungarian, German, Greek, Portuguese and Spanish stores and vegetarian eateries.

West of Saint-Laurent Boulevard is DE LA GAUCHETIERE STREET, in and around which is the main hub of the city's Chinatown. This area really buzzes at the weekends as the restaurants and shops fill up with Chinese and other visitors. The pedestrianized PRINCE-ARTHUR STREET is one of the city's liveliest, lined with Greek and Vietnamese restaurants where diners can bring their own booze. In summer it's a magnet for street performers – clowns, magicians and musicians.

In JEAN-TALON STREET, the heart of Montréal's Italian district, the year-round Jean-Talon Market is very popular among Montréalers for its wide selection of fresh produce, meat, fish, pastries and handicrafts, and the outdoor stalls and noisy vendors create a true market atmosphere. Other markets worth browsing around are ATWATER MARKET, which deals in meat, cheeses and speciality foods, and GREATER MONTRÉAL CENTRAL MARKET which caters largely to the wholesale trade but nevertheless welcomes all shoppers.

Rising from the heart of Montréal is MONT ROYAL PARK, known locally as 'the mountain', a year-round playground with slopes providing facilities for skiing, cycling, skating and other activities. There's also a fine view of the city from its summit. Other green spaces include LAFONTAINE PARK, which contains a fairyland children's zoo and a lagoon for various water activities, and the BOTANICAL GARDENS, housing more than 25,000 different varieties of plants.

SAINT-DENIS STREET, known as the Latin Quarter, has become the main focus for nightlife; it contains the city's heaviest concentration of bars, restaurants, antique shops, art galleries and handicraft stores. ST-LOUIS SQUARE is surrounded by a beautiful array of houses whose architecture make the square one of the prettiest public gardens in town.

A unique feature of Montréal is its large number of underground complexes, linked together by pedestrian walkways and by the metro. Between them, these make up quite a sizable 'underground city'. Not only does this city beneath a city provide weatherproof access to hotels, offices, etc., but it also houses an extensive range of shops, boutiques, bars, cinemas and various other attractions.

The museums and art galleries exhibit a diverse range of culture. The MONTRÉAL MUSEUM OF FINE ARTS in Sherbrooke Street West houses world-class exhibitions, including a superb collection of pre-Colombian figures and another of Eskimo sculpture. The MUSEUM OF MODERN ART, in the Cité-du-Havre, displays contemporary art from both Canada and around the world. SAINT-JOSEPH'S ORATORY MUSEUM inside the main building of Saint-Joseph's Oratory on Mont Royal houses a collection of stained-glass windows, bronzes and mosaics; and LE MUSÉE D'ART SAINT-LAURENT on the Boulevard Sainte-Croix boasts some fine works reflecting the cultural heritage of the Québec province.

Among the many other museums, those worth visiting include LE MUSÉE DES ARTS DECORATIFS on Sherbrooke Street opposite the Botanical Gardens (decorative arts from the mid-19th century to the present day); the SAIDYE BRONFMAN CENTRE on the Chemin Côte Sainte-Catherine (contemporary works by national and international artists); and the MUSÉE DU CINEMA on the Boulevard de Maisonneuve East, which includes a display of film-making equipment dating back to the last century.

ACCOMMODATION

Montréal has a vast number of places to stay, many of which fall into the budget category. Even hotel rooms can be found fairly cheaply. The only disappointments are the campgrounds which are miles out of town.

Hostels and student residences:

Auberge de Montréal (IYHF), 3541 rue Aylmer, Montréal (tel. 843 3317). Members $17, non-members $20. Open 9.30 a.m.–2 a.m.

Collège Français, 5155 rue de Gaspé (tel. 495 2581). Prices start from $12.50 for dorms; rooms start at $15.

Collège Jean de Brébeuf, 5625 rue Decelles (tel. 342 1320). Dorms $15 per day or $70 per week. Singles $24 or $120 per week; doubles $20 or $100 per week.

YMCA, 1450 rue Stanley (tel. 849 8393). Singles $35; doubles $50. Men and women.

Université de Montréal, 2350 rue Edouard Montpetit (tel. 343 6531). Students $24; others $31.

McGill University, 3935 rue University (tel. 398 6367). Students $28; others $38. Open 15 May–15 Aug.

YWCA, 1355 boulevard René-Lévesque Ouest (tel. 866 9941). Singles from $40; doubles from $55. Women only.

Hotels:

Hôtel Castel Saint-Denis, 2099 rue Saint-Denis (tel. 842 9719). Singles and doubles from $33.

Hôtel le Breton, 1609 rue Saint-Hubert (tel. 524 7273). Singles from $33; doubles from $45.

Hôtel Viger Centre-Ville, 1001–1005 rue Saint Hubert (tel. 845 6058). Singles from $38; doubles from $43.

Hôtel Americain, 1042 rue Saint-Denis (tel. 849 0616). Singles from $38; doubles from $48.

Hôtel Louisbourg, 1649 rue Saint-Hubert (tel. 598 8544). Singles from $38; doubles from $43.

B&B agencies: A variety of agencies will fix you up with a room at prices starting from $30:

Downtown B&B Network, 3458 Laval Avenue, Montréal H2X 3C8 (tel. 514 269 9749/or toll-free on 1 800 267 5180)

Montréal Bed & Breakfast, 4912 Victoria, Montréal H3W 2N1 (tel. 514 738 9410).

Bed & Breakfast de Chez-nous, 3717 Sainte-Famille, Montréal H2X 2L7 (tel. 514 845 7711).

Montréal Oasis, 3000 chemin de Breslay, Montréal H3Y 2G7 (tel. 514 935 2312).

Campsites:

Koa Montréal Sud, 130 boulevard Monette, Saint-Philippe (tel. 659 8626). Exit 38 off Highway 15. $17–22.50.

Parc Mont Laval, 675 boulevard St Martin Ouest, Sainte-Dorothée (tel. 689 1150). $20.

FOOD

Montréal is renowned as one of North America's centres of culinary delight, since its 2,000-odd restaurants boast not only the best in authentic French and French-Canadian cuisine, but also a range of ethnic gastronomy from some 30 nationalities. Among the Québec specialities are Matane shrimp, Gaspe salmon, maple syrup and lobster from the Magdalen Islands. Good hunting areas include Sainte-Catherine and the Latin Quarter. Chinatown's De La Gauchetière Street, Prince Arthur Street's Greek and Vietnamese restaurants, and Sainte-Laurent Boulevard, north of Sherbrooke are just some of the best known locales for ethnic eateries.

Because of the large student population, finding a good cheap eatery isn't difficult. As well as restaurants, Montréal has a wide selection of cafés and delis which are usually cheaper – you should be able to get a decent feed for under $15. Restaurants in Duluth Street and Prince Arthur Street are also handy for budget travellers as you can bring your own booze. Remember tipping is expected – usually an extra 12–15%.

Beauty's, 93 Mont-Royal Ouest. Popular cheap eatery.

La Brasserie Holder, 3616 boulevard St Laurent. Excellent value French food in lively restaurant with artistic clientèle.

Café Ciné Lumière, 5163 boulevard St Laurent. Cheap French bistro with movies thrown in.

Le Gourmet de Szechuan, 862 Mount-Royal Street East. Genuine Chinese food.

La Mer à Boire, 429 St Vincent Street. Excellent French food in intimate cosy atmosphere.

Once Upon a Time, 600 Youville Street. American burgers and sodas in comfortable atmosphere.

La Pizzaiolle, 5100 Hutchinson Street. Delicious wood-burning oven pizza.

Hard Rock Café, 1458 rue Crescent (tel. 987 1420). Get your T-shirts and burgers here.

ENTERTAINMENT

Montréal has an enormous range of bars, discos and nightclubs to suit every taste and budget. Two of the city's liveliest areas for nightlife are Old Montréal and Saint-Denis Street – the Latin Quarter – a favoured student area. L'Air du Temps at 194 St Paul (Old Montréal) and Blue Dog, the popular free student club, at 3556 St Laurent, are just two good venues. The English-language newspaper, *The Montréal Gazette*, carries full listings, as does the free English weekly newspaper, *The Mirror*.

The most important centre for the performing arts – dance, opera, theatre, music – is the five-hall Place des Arts at 260 boulevard De Maisonneuve West (tel. 842 2112). The Montréal Symphony Orchestra and the Metropolitan Orchestra of Montréal both perform there regularly, as well as at the Notre-Dame Basilica. The Opéra de Montréal (tel. 985 2222) puts on five shows a year and the city has several ballet companies including the internationally renowned Les Grands Ballets Canadiens (tel. 849 8681). There's also plenty of theatre on offer. The Théâtre de Verdure stages free outdoor concerts – theatre, music, ballet – in Lafontaine Park (tel. 872 2644). The Saidye Bronfman Centre at 5170 Chemin de la Côte-Sainte-Catherine (tel. 739 2301) has a 300-seat theatre for plays, dance and music.

FESTIVALS AND EVENTS

Like most Canadian cities, Montréal has a busy calendar of festivals and events. June 10–20 sees the Montréal International Rock Festival, followed in July by the International Jazz Festival, with hundreds of venues both indoors and out. If it's comedy you want, the Just for Laughs Festival takes place in early August, while late August and early September is the time for the city's international film festival.

EXCURSIONS

The LAURENTIDES (Laurentians) are a range of mountains an hour's drive north of Montréal. To visit here is to sample some of Canada's most spectacular scenery – the mountains, lakes and valleys were carved out by the last glacial age. Today the area's natural beauty is complemented by excellent sports facilities (swimming, boating, golf, skiing, riding). Also worth visiting in the area is the Trappist monastery at OKA, which produces the famous Oka cheese, and the artists' colony at Val-David.

RICHELIEU-RIVE SUD, 30 minutes drive south of Montréal, is a valley steeped in history. The Richelieu River running through the valley has been witness to many a colonial battle and Indian wars.

Today the area is very tranquil and there are a number of historic sites and forts to visit. You can also take a pleasure cruise up the river and walk round the elegant old residences or country churches, particularly in CHAMBLY.

Half an hour's drive north-east of the city is LE LANAUDIERE. Centuries ago the region lay under water and this is evinced by the countless lakes, rivers and waterfalls which provide a wealth of natural beauty and make for superb sightseeing, as well as offering facilities for sports such as fishing and windsurfing. In the regional capital of JOLIETTE, the art museum contains medieval sculptures, Renaissance works and traditional Québec carvings.

Just across the Jacques-Cartier Bridge from Montréal is ÎLE SAINTE-HELENE, where you can enjoy a picnic or swimming in summer and snow-shoeing and cross-country skiing in winter. Other attractions on the island include the Alcan Aquarium, the Old Fort and La Ronde, an amusement park which offers craft workshops, restaurants and boutiques as well as amusement rides.

Toronto

AIRPORT FACILITIES
The Toronto-Lester B. Pearson International Airport is 24 km north-west of the city. Its three terminals handle domestic and international airlines. All terminals have banks, restaurants, duty-free and information counters. Airport information for Terminals 1 and 2 is on 247 7678 and for Terminal 3 on 612 5100.

CITY LINKS
Gray Coach Lines runs regular services every 20 minutes between Pearson International Airport and major downtown hotels. Journey time is around 80 minutes and a one-way fare costs $11. There are also frequent services to Islington, York Mills and Yorkdale subway stations. Metered taxis are available, too.

USEFUL ADDRESSES
Tourist office: Travel Information Center, Eaton Center, Level 2. Provides information on places to stay, where to eat, visitor attractions, etc.
Main post office, 20 Bay Street.
British Consulate-General, 777 Bay Street (tel. 593 1290).
US Consulate-General, 360 University Avenue (tel. 595 0228/ 1770).

Emergency services: Dial 911 for police, ambulance and fire.

GETTING ABOUT
Getting around Toronto is quick and easy.

Bus, tram and subway: The Toronto Transit Commission (TTC) (tel. 393 4636) operates bus, streetcar (tram) and subway services. The subway is the hub of the system and runs Mon.–Sat. 6–1.30 a.m. and Sun. 9–1.30 a.m. (though some lines operate round the clock). A single fare entitles you to a complete journey using whatever combination of services is necessary. If you transfer from one service to another, you must get a transfer ticket when you pay your fare. Buses and trams sell tickets; in subways you'll get tokens. Fares are $2 each; a two-journey ticket costs $3; you can also buy ten tickets and tokens for $13. On buses and trams you must have the exact change. TTC day passes costing $5 are also available.

Taxi: Taxis are widely available and can be booked by phone (tel. 364 7111) or hailed in the streets. Fares are metered and start at $2.40, with an extra $1 for every additional kilometre.

Car hire: All the major car-hire companies have offices in Toronto as do many smaller – and usually cheaper – local firms. Be careful where you park: your car is likely to be towed away if it is parked in a prohibited zone.

Bicycles: You can rent cycles from McBridge Cycle, 180 Queen's Quay West at Harbourfront (tel. 367 5651) or numerous other outlets throughout the city.

SIGHTS
Situated on the north-west shore of Lake Ontario, Toronto is a major commercial and industrial port on the St Lawrence Seaway system. It is the capital of Ontario province and is Canada's largest city. The contrast between past and present in Toronto is very striking indeed. While the downtown area is packed with tall buildings and bustling commercial districts, a great deal of Victorian architecture together with tree-lined streets survive in other parts of the city, helping to evoke a charming historical flavour. It's a 'city of neighbourhoods', each with its own characteristics and atmosphere, making a bit of legwork an enjoyable – and free – way to enjoy Toronto.

The city's main street (and the world's longest) is YONGE STREET, a good place to sit and gaze, and home to just about everything you could ever want to buy. Along BLOOR STREET is the southern boundary of the ANNEX, where writers, artists and students are concentrated and where a plethora of budget bookshops and cafés have sprung up. QUEEN STREET WEST is where many of Toronto's more Bohemian characters hang out, with outdoor vendors selling an assortment of off-beat items. Queen Street West is generally home to the 'in' bars, clubs and cafés.

Toronto's ethnic communities have each established their own areas: CHINATOWN stretches from Spadina Avenue to Bay Street; LITTLE ITALY is in the north-west of the city; and the Greek community is in the north-east. Each is worth a wander for its distinctive cuisine, its markets, and clothing outlets. At the corner of King and Jarvis Streets is the ST LAWRENCE HALL, a popular meeting place for Torontonians of the late 19th century which has been restored to its former elegance. If you explore behind it you'll find a typically raucous market which dates back to 1890 and sells meat, fish, cheese, bread and more.

Beside the lake at Queen's Quay West is the HARBOURFRONT – a recreational complex spanning some 90 acres. Harbourfront caters for a wide range of activities from watersports to theatre and dance, and also contains some fine restaurants and shops. In summer it's a lovely place to wander or to spend your lunchbreak. Recreation is also the name of the game at ONTARIO PLACE, a collection of three man-made islands rising out of Lake Ontario on which are built theatres, amusement rides, gift shops, boutiques and numerous other cultural and entertaining attractions.

For a taste of old Toronto, there are several places worth visiting. BLACK CREEK PIONEER VILLAGE, at the junction of Jane Street and Steeles Avenue, is an authentic reflection of life in the mid-19th century, complete with costumed villagers, restored buildings, animals and gardens. FORT YORK in Garrison Road off Fleet Street was built in 1793, destroyed in the war of 1812 and subsequently rebuilt. Today its role in that war is recreated through tours, displays and demonstrations by the Fort York Guard, dressed in the British army uniform of that era.

Where museums and art galleries are concerned, Toronto is home to some of Canada's most important. Among those of particular interest are the ROYAL ONTARIO MUSEUM at the junction of Avenue Road and Bloor Street; exhibits include Chinese art and artefacts, as well as an extensive depiction of the evolution of civilization. The ART GALLERY OF TORONTO is famous as the home of works by many Canadian artists together with paintings by Rembrandt, Van Gogh, Renoir, Picasso, and a notable collection of Henry Moore sculptures. Also worth a visit is the ONTARIO SCIENCE CENTRE in Don Mills Road. The centre has innumerable scientific and technological displays, many of which can be operated by visitors.

For a taste of the great outdoors, there are several parks in Toronto where you can pursue sports activities or just relax. EDWARDS GARDENS and JAMES GARDENS are tranquil and scenic. HIGH PARK has a boating, fishing and skating pond as well as the old farm property, COLBORNE LODGE. The three TORONTO ISLANDS have facilities for swimming and boating and are just 10 minutes by ferry from downtown. For botanical enthusiasts, ALLAN GARDENS has a giant greenhouse dating back to 1909 and crammed with tropical and semi-tropical trees and plants.

For an overall view of the city, take a trip up the CN CANADIAN NATIONAL TOWER. At a height of 544 metres, it's the highest free-standing structure in the world. It has two observation decks which provide panoramic views of up to 120 km on a clear day.

ACCOMMODATION

Toronto has a wealth of accommodation options, though it is never-theless advisable to book ahead in summer. The campsites are a long way out of town but if you have your own tent they're cheap. Accommodation Toronto operates a free hotel-reservation service (tel. 629 3800).

Hostels:

Toronto International Hostel (IYHF), 223 Church Street, Toronto (tel. 368 0207). From $18.

Leslieville Home Hostel, 185 Leslie Street, Toronto (tel. 461 7258). From $18.

Marigold International Hostel, 2011 Dundas Street West (tel. 536 8824). Take College Street or Dundas Street tram from downtown. Dorm beds start at $20.

B&B agencies:

Bed and Breakfast Homes of Toronto, PO Box 46093, College Park Post Office, 444 Yonge Street, Toronto, Ontario, M5B 2LS (tel. 363 6362). Suburban and downtown homes.

Downtown Toronto Assoc, B&B Guesthouses, PO Box 190, Station B, Toronto, Ontario, M5T 2W1 (tel. 977 6841). Singles from $48, doubles from $60. High-quality downtown B&Bs. Non-smoking.

Metropolitan Toronto B&B Registry, Suite 269, 615 Mount Pleasant Road, Toronto, Ontario M4S 3C5 (tel. 964 2566). Singles from $48, doubles from $60.

Toronto Bed and Breakfast Inc., Box 269, 253 College Street, Toronto, Ontario M5T 1R5 (tel. 588 8800). Singles from $42, doubles from $50.

Craig House in the Beach, 78 Spruce Hill Road, Toronto, Ontario, M4E 3G3 (tel. 698 3916). Singles from $45, doubles from $60.

College/university residences:

The Admiral House, 32–4 Admiral Road, Toronto (tel. 923 9233). Kitchen facilities available.

Hospitality Glendon, York University, 2275 Bayview Avenue, Toronto. Singles from $35, doubles from $60.

Neill-Wycik College Hotel, 96 Gerrard Street East, Toronto (tel. 977 2320). Singles from $40, doubles from $45.

Victoria University, 140 Charles Street West, Toronto (tel. 585 4524). Singles from $45, doubles from $60. Excellent downtown location.

Guesthouses:

Casa Loma Inn, 21 Walmer Road, Toronto (tel. 924 4540). 20-room inn. Singles from $45, doubles from $60. Non-smoking.

Grayona Tourist Home, 1546 King Street West, Toronto (tel. 535 5443). 6-room guest home. Singles from $40, doubles from $50.

Homewood Lodge, 65 Homewood Avenue, Toronto (tel. 920 7944). Singles from $38, doubles from $50.

Hotels:

Executive Inn, 621 King Street West, Toronto (tel. 362 7441). Well located in downtown Toronto. From $80 for doubles.

Hotel Selby, 592 Sherbourne Street, Toronto (tel. 921 3142). Singles from $50, doubles from $80.

Camping:

Indian Line Tourist Camp Ground, 7625 Finch Avenue West, off Highway 427 (tel. 678 1233). This is the closest campsite to Toronto. Open mid-May until mid-October. Electrical hook-ups, showers and laundry facilities. $22 including hook-up.

Milton Heights Campground, RR3 Milton (tel. 878 6781). Highway 401, west at Highway 25 (exit 320), north to Campbellville Road, west to town line. Open all year round. $20 plus hook-up.

FOOD

Like most of Canada's large cities, Toronto has undergone an influx of immigrants in the last decade so that it now offers a cosmopolitan choice of cuisine – so much so that it's now considered one of the best cities for dining on the American continent. It also has the largest number of restaurants of any city in Canada.

For the most enjoyable food, seek out one of the city's ethnic areas. Chinatown boasts a rich variety of restaurants and street vendors, and encompasses the small enclave of Kensington Market, whose narrow streets were once home to Toronto's Jewish community. Today you can buy Portuguese, West Indian, Kosher and other varieties of food from this cosmopolitan market. In the northwest of the city, Little Italy (Corso Italia) is a lively area of trattorias and sidewalk cafés – Toronto has the largest Italian population of any city outside Italy. North-east is Danforth Avenue which Toronto's Greek community has made its own. Some suggestions:

Astoria, 390 Danforth Avenue. Cheap Greek food in the heart of Toronto's Greek community.

Muddy York, 5 Church Street. Good food and friendly service.

Bellair café, 100 Cumberland Street, Yorkville. Good pasta.

King's Noodle House, 296 Spadina. Cheap Chinese food.

The big shopping malls such as Eatons are good for fast-food chain restaurants.

ENTERTAINMENT

Toronto regards itself as the cultural centre of Canada and the performing arts are represented on a grand scale, with over a hundred professional companies staging plays, opera, dance, etc. in the city. The Canadian Opera Company and the National Ballet of Canada share a home at the O'Keefe Centre at 1 Front Street East (tel. 872 2262). For classical music, the Toronto Philharmonic Orchestra performs at the splendid Massey Hall at 178 Victoria Street (tel. 971 9111), while the Toronto Symphony is based at the Roy Thomson Hall at 60 Simcoe Street (tel. 872 4255). There are also numerous theatres presenting a variety of shows, contemporary and classic – about fifty productions play in the city each month. Information and ticket reservations can be obtained by calling the venues direct. Prices range from $10–40. However, half-price tickets to many shows, opera, music, theatre or dance, can be purchased at the Five-Star ticket booth at the corner of Yonge and Dundas Streets on the day of the performance (Tues.–Sat. 12–7.30 p.m. and Sun. 11 a.m.–3 p.m.).

Toronto is a good training ground for bands and there are a number of excellent live venues in the city. Meyer's Deli at 69 Yorkville Avenue is a lively and usually crowded nightspot featuring live jazz of all kinds well into the early hours, while El Mocambo at 464 Spadina Avenue is a well-known live venue especially popular with blues fans. The Forum (Ontario Place) plays host to the big-name rock artists, as well as ballet and theatre troupes. To see what's on and where, check out the free newspapers, *Metropolis* and *Now*.

Sport is a great participant and spectator pastime in Canada. The 'national' sport is ice hockey, which children from the age of nine upwards learn to play. Ice hockey is a fast, exciting, and easy-to-follow sport and is excellent entertainment. Baseball is also taking off in Canada, especially since the Toronto Blue Jays have beaten the Americans at their own game.

FESTIVALS AND EVENTS
In late June the Metro International Caravan festival sets up around 40 'pavilions' across the city featuring the food, drink, music and dance of the different nationalities that have contributed to Toronto's development. The Caribana in August is a Caribbean festival which takes over the Toronto islands for a weekend of steel bands and reggae. Toronto is also a major movie town and the autumn Festival of Festivals extravaganza attracts visitors from far and wide.

EXCURSIONS
One of the delights of Toronto is that it doesn't take long to get out beyond the city limits, making day-trips a popular pursuit among Torontonians and visitors alike.

PARKWOOD in Oshawa, on the eastern bank of Lake Ontario, is a magnificent 55-room heritage mansion which is the estate of the founder of General Motors of Canada. The estate contains some of the country's most splendid art galleries, gardens and greenhouses, as well as a fascinating collection of antiques.

Around 33 km north-east of Toronto in Whitby, CULLEN GARDENS contains a wealth of natural beauty on its 50 acres. Along with the gardens' trees and flowers, there's a miniature village which features over a hundred buildings and a country fair, all of which provide a pleasant setting for a relaxing afternoon.

On a different note altogether is Canada's WONDERLAND, 33 km north-west of Toronto. This is Toronto's answer to Disneyland: a vast theme park containing fantastic delights. There's a wealth of amusement rides on offer which cater for adult visitors as well as children. Wonderland also provides an enormous range of live entertainment and visitors are frequently treated to elaborate Broadway-like shows.

Vancouver

AIRPORT FACILITIES
Vancouver International Airport is situated 11 km south-west of the city on Sea Island. The airport building has three levels: Level 1 handles international and trans-border arrivals; Level 2 handles domestic arrivals and US departures; Level 3 deals with domestic and international departures.

Banks are available for currency exchange on all levels, together with restaurants and snack shops, a post office on Level 3, and duty-free. Tourist information is available on tel. 276 6101.

CITY LINKS
Bus: A bus service linking the airport to many of the major downtown hotels runs every 15 minutes. This service also calls at the bus, Seabus and Skytrain terminals. The journey costs $9 one-way.
Taxi: The journey to the city centre costs around $25 and takes 30 minutes.

USEFUL ADDRESSES
Tourist office: Vancouver Travel InfoCentre, Pavilion Plaza, Four Bentall Centre, 1055 Dunsmuir Street (tel. 683 2000). Offers hotel reservations, travel information and currency exchange.
Main post office, 349 West Georgia.
Rail information: tel. 631 3500.
BC Rail: tel. 984 5246.
British Consulate General: 80–111 Melville Street (tel. 683 4421).
US Consulate General: 1075 West Georgia, 21st Floor (tel. 685 4311).
Emergency services: Dial 911.
Medical/dental emergencies: Dial 733 7758 to get the name of a local doctor; 736 3621 for a dentist.

GETTING ABOUT
Bus, skytrain and seabus ferries: Getting about in Vancouver is quick and convenient. The average single fare is $1.50 and tickets can be used on the buses, skytrain and seabus. A one-day pass is available for $4.50 which entitles you to unlimited travel on all of these systems. Tickets can be purchased from stations and from shops displaying the BC Transit sticker. The *BC Transit Guide* is also available from these shops and from the Vancouver Travel InfoCentre (tel. 261 5100).

Bicycle: There are several bike-hire shops round the city. Try Robson Cycles at 1463 Robson (tel. 687 2777), or Stanley Park Rentals at 676 Chilco & Alberni (tel. 681 5581).

SIGHTS

Cultured, cosmopolitan and with a touch of class, Vancouver is fronted by the Burrard Inlet and backed by the snow-capped Coast Mountains, making it one of the world's most attractive cities. The town itself is the commercial/industrial hub of British Columbia and its fine weather, breathtaking surroundings and varied menu of things to see and do make it a city to suit most tastes.

To sample the spirit of early Vancouver, take a wander through the old GASTOWN, site of the original settlement. As well as its restored buildings, shops and boutiques dealing in everything from leatherwork to antiques, Gastown has numerous cafés, restaurants and pubs. There's also an antique market and a weekend flea market.

Spread over several blocks in the city's east central area is CHINATOWN. Vancouver's Chinese community is Canada's largest and one of the biggest outside China. It offers a wide range of food markets, restaurants and curiosity shops selling oriental imports. The DR SUN YAT-SEN ORIENTAL GARDEN is the only authentic classical Chinese garden outside China. Designed in the Ming Dynasty style, it has typical oriental scenery and an atmosphere of peace and tranquillity.

In the city's West End is ROBSONSTRASSE. Originally Robson Street, its name was changed in the 1950s following an influx of several thousand German immigrants. The street has now developed into a shoppers' paradise and boasts dozens of international restaurants, boutiques, speciality shops and hotels.

There are 115 parks within Vancouver's boundaries. One of the largest is STANLEY PARK, just five minutes from downtown, situated next to the sea. Its 1,000 acres incorporate picnic and playground sites, sportsfields, a zoo, beaches, and the popular Vancouver aquarium, complete with whales. Among the city's other green spaces is EXHIBITION PARK, host to the Pacific National Exhibition (an agricultural fair, loggers' festival, rodeo, etc.) in late August each year, and QUEEN ELIZABETH PARK, which accommodates a conservatory with tropical plants, fish and birds. The FORT LANGLEY NATIONAL HISTORICAL PARK is a partially reconstructed Hudson's Bay Company post of the 1840s.

To real nature enthusiasts, the BOTANICAL GARDENS at the University of British Columbia are well known for their alpine flora from every continent. The VAN DUSEN BOTANICAL DISPLAY

GARDEN, which features Macmillan Bloedel's conceptual pavilion 'A Walk in the Forest', is also well worth a visit.

Vancouver's sporting attractions are many and varied. Probably best known is the covered stadium, BC PLACE, home to the Canadian Football League's BC Lions. Among the sporting events which usually provide a good day's entertainment are the auto-racing at Westwood circuit; harness-racing at Ladner; an annual rodeo at Cloverdale; and the BC Salmon Derby each July at Horseshoe Bay. If you want to partake yourself, Vancouver's mild year-round climate allows visitors to take full advantage of some superb outdoor facilities – everything from golf to alpine skiing is catered for within minutes of the downtown area.

There's a very large selection of museums and art galleries: the VANCOUVER ART GALLERY at 750 Hornby Street is noted for its works of the famous West-Coast painter Emily Carr, including her depictions of the British Columbia forests and Indian life. Northwest-Coastal Indian culture from the Stone Age to totemic art is featured in the CENTENNIAL MUSEUM in Vanier Park, where there is also an exhibition on the history of the province. More Indian culture can be found at the University of British Columbia's MUSEUM OF ANTHROPOLOGY, which contains one of the world's greatest collections of North-western Indian arts, including replicas of Haida long houses.

Next door to the Centennial Museum is the PLANETARIUM with a stars, light and sound show. The adjoining MARITIME MUSEUM displays the historic schooner *St Roch*, the first ship to navigate the North-west Passage in both directions and to circumnavigate the continent.

ACCOMMODATION

Hostels: Vancouver has a relatively small number of hostels:

Vancouver International Hostel (IYHF), 1515 Discovery Street (tel. 224 3208). Huge, well-located hostel. $15 members. Small supplement for non-members. Open 24 hours.

YMCA Hotel, 955 Burrard Street (tel. 681 0221). Comfortable with good facilities and centrally located. Singles/doubles $35/$60.

YWCA Hotel, 580 Burrard Street (tel. 662 8111). Great facilities including TV lounges, pool and fitness centre. Singles from $48, doubles from $68.

Downtown Vancouver Hostel, 144 West Hastings Street (tel. 669 8832). Centrally located. Dorms start at $12, singles at $22, doubles at $30. Breakfast included.

University of British Colombia, Conference Centre, Gage Towers, 5961 Student Union Blvd (tel. 822 1010). Open May–August. Singles/doubles: $20/$38.

Hotels: There are a large number of cheap hotels; here are just a few:

Kingston Hotel, 757 Richards Street (tel. 684 9024). Budget hotel with basic facilities. Breakfast included. Singles from $38, doubles from $48.

Budget Inn–Patricia Hotel, 403 East Hastings Street (tel. 255 4301). Cheap but rather a long way out. Singles from $38, doubles from $55.

Austin Hotel, 1221 Granville Street (tel. 685 7235). Singles from $45, doubles from $52.

Nelson Place Hotel, 1006 Granville Street (tel. 681 6341). Singles from $42, doubles from $48.

West End Guesthouse, 1362 Haro Street (tel. 681 2889). Singles from $65, doubles from $110.

B&B: agencies Accommodation is available but must be booked through agencies.

AAA Home Away from Home, 1441 Howard Avenue, Vancouver V5B 3S2 (tel. 294 1760). Offers singles from $35, doubles from $48.

AB & C Bed and Breakfast of Vancouver, 4390 Frances Street, Vancouver V5C 2R3 (tel. 298 8815). Offers singles from $38, doubles from $45.

Best Canadian (tel. 738 2074).

Town and Country Bed and Breakfast, Box 46566, Station G, Vancouver V6R 4GB (tel. 731 5942). Singles from $45, doubles from $65.

Campsites: Camping facilities for budget travellers are limited as most campsites expect you to have an RV.

Timberland Motel & Campground, 3418 King George Highway (Highway 99A) (tel. 531 1033). Half-hour drive from Vancouver. Tent sites $15.

FOOD

Vancouver takes great pride in its wide and cosmopolitan range of restaurants. Whatever the nationality, whatever the dish, it's bound to be served in Vancouver. Beef and fish are favourites among Vancouverites – seafood fresh from the Pacific is a speciality in many restaurants. Other options include German, Lebanese,

Indian, Vietnamese, Italian, Japanese, Danish and French cuisine. There are also the usual fast-food chains and supermarkets for those who want to make their own picnics. Vegetarians are well catered for. Not all restaurants take credit cards so check first, and many are shut on Sundays.

Chinatown is perhaps the best place for decent cheap food. Downtown Vancouver is also a happy hunting ground. Some budget suggestions:

Orestes, 3116 West Broadway. Authentic Greek cuisine with good service.

The Noodle Makers, 122 Powell Street. First-rate Chinese restaurant.

Only Fish and Oyster Café, 20 East Hastings Street. A Vancouver tradition famous for fresh seafood and fish'n'chips.

On-On Tea Garden, 214 Keefer Street. Excellent Cantonese cuisine.

Old Spaghetti Factory, 53 Water Street. Lively atmosphere and good Italian food.

The Naam, 2724 W 4th Avenue (tel. 738 7151). Popular veggie restaurant open 24 hours.

ENTERTAINMENT

Vancouver is one of the livelier West Coast cities and more adventurous entertainment-wise than most Canadian towns, particularly around the more off-beat areas of Gastown and Chinatown.

Vancouver has a healthy assortment of clubs, many of which put on regular live music. The Railway Club at 579 Dunsmuir and the Roxy at 932 Granville are two easy-going favourites. Jazz is the current 'in' sound, and the Hot Jazz Club at 2120 Main Street has a good dance floor and bar, and is one of the liveliest clubs in town. Genuine pubs are a find for the traveller weary of tacky American bars. One popular watering hole is the English Bay Café at 1795 Beach Avenue, a charming place where you can take in the ocean views until your glass is empty.

Vancouver also has a healthy cultural scene and prides itself on its receptiveness to 'alternative' culture. The major arts venue is the Queen Elizabeth Theatre at 649 Cambie Street (tel. 284 4444), which houses alternately theatre, opera and dance. Vancouver is also well served by its many cinemas which show the latest Hollywood blockbusters, the offerings of the 'independent' sector, along with re-runs of old classics.

The free weekly listings magazine *Georgia Straight* is a reliable guide to what's going on in the city. For tickets to events, TicketMaster is a dependable outlet and has numerous concessions around the city.

FESTIVALS AND EVENTS
Vancouver's welcoming climate makes the city a festival hot-spot. The International Jazz Festival comes to Vancouver in June, the Folk Music Festival in July and the International Film Festival in September.

EXCURSIONS
For a memorable trip aboard a legendary train, take the ROYAL HUDSON STEAM TRAIN along the coast. Starting in North Vancouver, the engine winds its way along the edge of the spectacular Howe Sound to its destination of SQUAMISH – a port and forestry town – 130 km away. You can have lunch in Squamish, then reboard the train for the return journey to Vancouver. It's also possible to travel one way by sea on the MV *Britannia*. Contact the Travel Infocentre for details.

GRANVILLE ISLAND in Vancouver is famous for its public market where an old warehouse neighbourhood has been restored to house shops and restaurants. Be sure to try the market's bread and doughnuts, home-made pasta and wide selection of fish and seafoods.

A 15-minute ride from downtown, GROUSE MOUNTAIN is packed with the delights of nature in summer and is one of Canada's most popular ski areas in winter, with slopes for everyone. A major attraction on the mountains is the 'Skyride', which covers the journey from the lower terminal to the 1,230-metre summit in five minutes, giving the riders a fantastic view. There's also a restaurant on the top half of the mountain, where the views are as good as the food.

British Columbia ferries offer a day-long cruise aboard their *Queen of the North* ferry through the Inside Passage, which takes you in great comfort through some of the world's most beautiful scenery. The trip is a very popular one and it's a good idea to book in advance.

VANCOUVER ISLAND is worth exploring, especially if you enjoy backpacking. The island is a 300-mile wilderness of appealing beauty. There is a stunning 7-day coastal trail at the Pacific Rim National Park where hikers can be lucky enough to see spouting whales and sea lions, heron and humming birds. Cape Scott is perhaps the most isolated destination, at the northern tip of the island. You can also visit the Hot Springs, north of Tofino by either boat or plane. For the active types, the Cowichan valley offers fishing and canoeing.

A great advantage of Vancouver's location is its close proximity to the ROCKY MOUNTAINS, which stretch through some of Canada's most scenic National Parks. To get to the Rockies from Vancouver, a commonly used and recommended route is via the city of CALGARY – renowned as much for its ranching and farming as for its oil industry. Air Canada operates several flights daily between the two cities. A good time to be in Calgary is early July for the world-famous CALGARY EXHIBITION AND STAMPEDE, a stirring 10-day celebration of the Wild West with everything from bacon breakfasts to bucking broncos and chuckwagon races. Within Calgary itself, there's tons to see and do. For outdoor activity, the city has 2,000-hectares of parkland to enjoy, notably First Creek Park for its fishing, horse-riding and cross-country skiing, and Glenmore Park for its sailing. Calaway Park corners the market on amusement rides – less greenery here but plenty of thrills and spills.

More sedate fresh-air pursuits can be enjoyed in Heritage Park, where the original buildings and vehicles recreate the West of long ago – they even sell penny candy in the general store. Also worth visiting is the Calgary Zoo and Prehistoric Park, where the life-size models of pre-historic creatures are as intriguing as the 1,400 live exhibits.

For a complete vista of Calgary and its surrounding beauty, a jaunt up the Calgary tower is recommended – its 188 metres afford a spectacular panoramic view.

USA

VITAL STATISTICS
Red tape: British citizens intending to stay less than 90 days do not require a visa but must have a full 10-year passport (the one-year British Visitors passport is not acceptable) and a return ticket. Most other nationalities will need a visa – check with your local US Embassy, or call the 'Visa Info' line on 0891 200 290.
Customs: 200 cigarettes or 50 cigars or 2 kg of tobacco, plus 1 l alcoholic beverage (if aged over 21). Gifts or articles up to a value of US$100. Make sure you have a prescription or written doctor's note if you are bringing in any prescribed drugs. Certain foodstuffs – particularly fruit and vegetables – are prohibited.
Health: Most visitors to the US do not need a vaccination certifi-

cate, though vaccinations may be required if you are coming from an infected area. Check with the nearest American Consulate or Embassy if in doubt. Health care in America is expensive: a simple visit to the doctor can cost around £50. As there is no reciprocal health-care agreement between the US and the UK, it is essential to take out adequate private insurance – at least £250,000 per person is recommended.

Language: English. Spanish is widely spoken in some southern areas (eg Texas, California) and among many immigrant communities in the cities.

Population: Around 245 million.

Capital: Washington DC, population 700,000.

Political system: Constitutional democracy. The Democrats regained the presidency from the Republican Party in the 1992 elections. The President is Bill Clinton.

Religion: Predominantly Protestant, but with a number of sizeable minority religions, notably Roman Catholic.

Time: The US spans four major time zones:

Eastern Standard Time	five hours behind GMT
Central Standard Time	six hours behind GMT
Mountain Standard Time	seven hours behind GMT
Pacific Standard Time	eight hours behind GMT
Alaska	nine hours behind GMT
Hawaii	ten hours behind GMT

(Daylight saving time operates Apr.–Oct. except in Hawaii, and clocks go forward an hour.)

Money: The currency is the dollar ($), divided into 100 cents. Coins: 1 cent (penny), 5 cents (nickel), 10 cents (dime), 25 cents (quarter), 50 cents (half dollar). Notes: $1, $5, $10, $20, $50, $100 and $500. £1 = 1.56.

It is easiest and safest to carry the bulk of your money in dollar traveller's cheques, which are accepted in many shops and restaurants as cash. Remember that you will usually need your passport when cashing cheques. Most major credit cards are accepted by hotels, airlines, large restaurants and stores; indeed, plastic is sometimes essential – in car hire, for example. You can change money at most major banks, but hotels do not as a rule exchange foreign currency.

Tax: A sales tax is levied on most goods in most states but it is not usually included in the price of items. The tax ranges from 3–15%. Many stores in New Hampshire are tax free.

Communications: The telephone system is efficient and public telephones are widespread. Long-distance and many international calls can be dialled direct. Coin-operated phones take 5, 10 or 25c coins. Some also take a telephone credit card. Local calls usually cost 25c. For long-distance calls you will need a hoard of coins; be ready to insert them according to the operator's instructions. For international calls dial '0' for the operator and ask how to call your country.

International mail is automatically sent by airmail unless otherwise specified. Stamps can be bought from post offices and vending machines. Mail boxes are blue. Poste restante is called 'general delivery'. Make sure you include the zip code in addresses.

Electricity: 110–120v AC/60 Hz. Sockets take flat two-pin plugs.

Business hours: BANKS: Mon.–Fri. 9 a.m.–3 p.m.

POST OFFICES: Mon.–Fri. 9 a.m.–5 p.m.; Sat 9 a.m.–12 p.m.

SHOPS: Mon.–Sat. 9.30 a.m.–6 p.m. Most major department stores have one late-night closing per week, usually on a Thursday or Friday, until 9.30 p.m.

OFFICES: Mon.–Fri. 9 a.m.–5.30 p.m.

Holidays: 1 January; third Monday in January (Martin Luther King Day); third Monday in February (President's Day); last Monday in May (Memorial Day); 4 July (Independence Day); first Monday in September (Labour Day); second Monday in October (Columbus Day); fourth Thursday in November (Thanksgiving); 11 November (Veteran's Day); 25 December.

Climate: Excluding Hawaii, Alaska and other outlying territories, the US can be divided into five climatic zones. The North Pacific area is the wettest part of the country and in winter there is a considerable amount of snowfall; summers here are fairly hot, with temperatures rising to 32°C. The mid-Pacific and Rockies are dry and very sunny for most of the year, with temperatures varying according to altitude – as high as 46°C in some places, as low as −20°C in others. The south-west region is the hottest and the driest in the US, with summer temperatures of 43°C and crisp winters with scattered frost. The mid-west is fairly dry with hot summers and very cold winters, while the eastern sector of the country has an average amount of rain, usually pleasant though often humid summers and snow in winter.

DO'S AND DON'TS

Shaking hands is the usual form of greeting. A relaxed and informal atmosphere generally prevails so as long as the fundamental rules of courtesy are observed, there is no need to fear offending people. Gifts are appreciated if invited to a private house where, as a rule, dress is casual. Smart hotels, restaurants and clubs insist on suits and ties or long dresses. Smoking is often restricted, especially in public buildings and on city transport, but signs will be displayed if this is the case. Tipping is widely practised and not included in the bill. Waiters will expect 15%, as will taxi drivers and hairdressers. Porters usually expect $1 per bag.

WHERE TO GO FOR WHAT
In a country as vast as the USA, it's difficult to know where to start. In true American style, the US offers all things to all men. If you want attractive cities (in the 'historical' European mould), head for Boston, New York, New Orleans or San Francisco. Beaches are wonderful over in the west. California doesn't have a monopoly on where to beach bum, but it's a good place to start. Florida too is popular, and enjoys a good year-round climate, though the tourists have moved in *en masse*.

The National Parks are worth familiarizing yourself with early on if you're into the Great Outdoors: Yosemite, Yellowstone . . . they're all wonderful places and there are Parks spread throughout the country.

For the 'wow' factor, the Grand Canyon in Arizona is an amazing sight. And from the drama of nature to the pinnacle of the man-made attractions – Las Vegas, where gambling, showbiz and wacky wedding chapels live side by side in a unique cocktail of kitsch.

Heritage trails through Virginia, Georgia and the Carolinas are a must for American history buffs: great scenery and a totally different side to the USA.

For skiing and superb Alpine scenery, Colorado is hard to beat, though Washington State and Oregon are less touristy and great places to head with a pair of walking boots and a rucksack. As are Wyoming and Texas, with a saddle and a spirit of adventure.

Quite frankly, there is not a state, or even a county in the USA which is not of interest. It is a wonderful country. Go. Oh, and have a nice stay!

INTERNAL TRAVEL
Air: Because of the huge distances involved, America is one of the few countries where air travel is a viable means of transport for the budget traveller. You may be tempted by a 7-hour plane journey from New York to California when the alternative is a 3-day bus ride. Most domestic airlines within the US offer discounted fares for non-US residents, provided bookings are made outside the US. These are known as VUSA (Visit USA) fares and often save you 25–30% on normal economy fares.

Many airlines also offer air passes, and these too must be purchased outside the USA. It is best to check with your travel agent for the pass most suited to your needs. The majority operate on a coupon basis: you purchase a number of coupons, each of which is valid for a flight of any length in the US. You must, however, use that airline to make your transatlantic journey. At the time of writing, for example, Continental Airlines was offering its transatlantic passengers a three-coupon pass for £260 and an eight-coupon pass for £460 for travel within a two-month period. US Air was offering a similar pass (£251 and £308 respectively). Like most passes of this kind, these must be purchased outside the USA. Air fares and offers are subject to constant change, so check with your travel agent for the most up-to-date information.

Please note that since 1990 smoking has been banned on all domestic flights lasting less than six hours.

Rail: The national railway is Amtrak. The rail network is geared to freight rather than passengers, but the trains are very comfortable and some of the routes afford fantastic scenery. Long delays are, however, common.

Amtrak offers regional and national passes which must be purchased outside the US. Prices vary according to the season: peak season runs from 28 May–29 August; other times are off-peak. The National Rail Pass gives unlimited travel throughout the country for 15 or 30 days. Prices for 15 days are $315 peak and $215 off-peak; for 30 days it costs $399 peak and $315 off-peak. In addition, there are four regional passes: the Far West, the West, the East and the Coastal pass. Prices range from $239 for a 15-day peak West Pass to $189 for a 15-day peak East Pass. It's best to book your seats in advance (this can be done in the US). Amtrak's UK agent is Destination Marketing Ltd, 2 Cinnamon Row, Plantation Wharf, York Place, London SW11 3TW (tel. 0171 978 5212).

Bus: Certainly the cheapest means of travel across America, if not the most comfortable. The largest carrier is Greyhound; their Ameripass (which is much cheaper when purchased outside the US) offers unlimited travel for 4 days (£55), 7 days (£90), 15 days (£135) or 30 days (£180). There is also a 4-day Ameripass for £50 which is valid Mon.–Thurs. only. Reservations are not necessary – seats are allocated on a first-come-first-served basis. The UK agent is Greyhound International, Sussex House, London Road, East Grinstead, West Sussex RH19 1LD (tel. 01342 317317).

If you travel continuously, it will take 3½ days to travel by bus from coast to coast.

Car hire: Because of the vast distances involved, hiring or even purchasing a car – far cheaper in the US than the UK – is a good way of seeing America. All car hire firms will require you to be over

21 (some insist on a minimum age of 26) and to be in possession of a full UK driving licence (which is valid for up to a year in the US). Car hire firms are obliged to provide at least third-party insurance.

Fly-drive packages are becoming increasingly popular, whereby your air ticket and car hire are arranged at the same time for a package price. This generally works out much cheaper than hiring a car on arrival. Alternatively you can rent an RV (recreational vehicle) which is a camper or motor home equipped with some form of sleeping and kitchen facilities.

Remember that in America cars drive on the right. Speed limits are strictly enforced and are much lower than in the UK: the limit on highways varies between 55–65 miles per hour, depending on the state.

Hitching: A cheap but potentially dangerous way to travel, especially in the big cities. The risks are far greater than in Europe: consider carefully before you raise your thumb. Note that it is illegal to hitch on freeways.

ACCOMMODATION
Hostels are less common here than in Europe, thus you are likely to have to stay in hotels or B&Bs, so be prepared to budget accordingly.

Youth hostels: The majority of US hostels are IYHF-affiliated. Those in the most popular tourist areas, such as New York and San Francisco, have to be booked well in advance and tend to restrict stays to 3 nights. A dorm bed costs $10–25 per night (more for non-members). Some cities also have YMCA/YWCAs, known as 'Y's, which have dorm beds plus single and double rooms at $30–45.

Hotels and motels: It is relatively easy to find a budget hotel or motel room in the USA, although the cheapest places are usually in the worst neighbourhoods. Singles start at around $30, doubles from $45. Even cheap rooms generally have a TV and bathroom.

B&Bs: Bed and breakfasts are private homes which let out spare rooms to tourists. Most have a friendly, homely atmosphere, and a generous breakfast is included in the price. As in Canada, many regions now have B&B associations which act as agents. On average expect to pay around $50–80 a night for a double.

Campsites: Camping is one of the cheapest and most popular forms of accommodation among travellers in the US, and can enable you to spend many of your nights amidst gorgeous scenery. There is a vast array of camping facilities across the country – National Parks, State Parks and forests provide public campgrounds, and elsewhere private sites are common. All are inexpensive: even the dearest sites probably won't cost you more than $15. RVs (recreational vehicles or motorhomes) are well catered for in all campgrounds. National Park sites in particular fill up quickly in summer, so aim to get there early.

FOOD

Americans love to eat. If food is your first love, this is the country for you. Cities large and small have an endless variety of coffee shops, cafeterias, delis, diners, fast-food outlets and restaurants. That's not forgetting the street vendors selling hot dogs, burgers, pizza slices, etc. You can eat just about anything, at any time of the day, anywhere.

Besides being the home of fast food and the mega salad, this nation of immigrants offers a truly cosmopolitan range of food – Chinese, Japanese, Italian, Greek, Mexican, Thai – and the portions are huge. Prepare to get fat. Breakfast alone can fill you up for the rest of the day. Usually served from 7–11 a.m., you can take your pick from ham, eggs, sausages, chips, hash browns, waffles and pancakes soaked in maple syrup. Lunch is usually from 11 a.m.–2.30 p.m. and many restaurants have lunchtime set menus which are excellent value. Dinner runs from 5 or 6 p.m. to around 9.30 p.m. Many restaurants offer an 'all you can eat' set menu one evening a week. On Sundays, brunch is served from 11 a.m.–3 p.m.

As you travel around the country, you'll notice that the local food that is offered will change from region to region. If you're in the Northwest, freshly caught salmon is the standard local fare. California boasts some of the country's best fruit and vegetables. The Mountain States (Wyoming, Colorado and Montana) will serve local game such as venison, moose, wild duck and even buffalo. Southwestern menus are influenced by Spanish and Mexican cuisine – watch out for the chili peppers! The Midwest is known for its hearty, home-cooked meals. In Louisiana, Creole cuisine abounds with dishes such as gumbo and jambalaya. Southern cooking features lots of barbecued meat and fried foods. On the East coast, seafood is everywhere; New England, especially, is known for its clam chowder.

The concept of service in America has gone well beyond that in the UK – but you are expected to pay for it. Tips should usually be 15–20%.

Alcohol cannot be sold to anyone under 21. In many states it's essential to carry ID with you, as establishments tend to enforce the rules rigorously. Bars are not as cosy as pubs, but generally stay open a lot longer. American beer is of the weak lager variety, though imports are available. Beers, spirits and wines may be bought in supermarkets and liquor stores and all are far cheaper than in the UK.

BUDGETING

Your biggest expense in America will be accommodation. If you are lucky enough to stay in hostels throughout, you could get by on $10–15 a day. At some point, however, it is probable that you will have to pay for hotel or motel rooms, which may set you back $30 or $40 per night. You can eat cheaply yet enjoyably, mixing fast-food stalls, delis and diners with the occasional slap-up meal in a restaurant – $15 a day should suffice. Booze is cheaper than in the UK, particularly if you shop in supermarkets. Transport costs are reduced if you buy some kind of pass, though the huge distances involved mean that transport will still take a fair chunk out of your budget.

Unfortunately, working legally in America is difficult. Strictly speaking, if you are on a tourist visa you are not permitted to seek paid employment and working illegally is grounds for deportation. However, there are a number of special cases. Students may also find success in applying for an internship in America – a period of work experience in line with your academic course. *Internships*, distributed by Vacation Work, is the best source of information on this option. BUNAC runs a summer Work America programme for students between the ages of 18 and 30 with sufficient funds (16 Bowling Green Lane, London EC1R 0BD, tel. 0171 251 3472).

A major source of employment are the famous US summer camps, which employ young people to teach or 'counsel' American kids sent away to camp in their summer holidays. The major organizations are BUNACAMP (see BUNAC, above) and Camp America (37a Queen's Gate, London SW7 5HR tel. 0171 581 7373). People with childcare experience can also apply to the au pair programme based at the same address. If you want to be an au pair, there are several UK agencies that handle placements.

FURTHER INFORMATION

United States Embassy, Grosvenor Square, London W1A 1AE (tel. 0171 499 9000).

United States Travel and Tourism Administration (USTTA), PO Box 1EN, London W1A 1EN provides some handy literature, though individual state tourist offices in the USA itself are much more helpful (tel. 0891 616 000, Mon.–Fri. 10 a.m.–4 p.m.).

Background reading: Of the hundreds of guides to choose from, three of the most useful are *Let's Go: The Budget Guide to the USA*

(Pan Books), an annually updated guide for the budget traveller; *Work Your Way Around the World* by Susan Griffiths (Vacation Work); and *How to Get a Job in America* by Roger Jones (How to Books).

Boston

AIRPORT FACILITIES
Logan International Airport lies 7 km north-east of Boston. It has five terminals: A, B, C, D and E. All have eating facilities and shops. Currency exchange and duty-free are available in terminals C and E. For airport information call (617) 567 1830.

CITY LINKS
Rail: A Rapid Transit Train runs to the city every 15 minutes from 5.30–12.30 a.m. Board the train at the airport subway station, which can be reached by taking the free Massport inter-terminal shuttle bus. Train fare is $0.90.
Coach: The Bus Airways Transportation Company (tel. 267 2981) runs a coach service to and from the airport every 30 minutes, making pick-ups at major downtown hotels.
Taxi: A taxi to the city costs around $15 and takes about 20 minutes.

USEFUL ADDRESSES
Tourist offices: Visitors Information Center, Tremont Street, near Park Street subway (tel. 267 6466). Massachusetts Office of Travel and Tourism, 100 Cambridge Street, 13th Floor (tel. 727 3201).
Post office: McCormack Station, Post Office Square.
Emergency services: Dial 911 for police, fire or ambulance.

GETTING ABOUT
Public transport in Boston consists of a subway system and a bus network. Both are quick, efficient and extensive.
Subway: Trains operate around the clock and fares are moderate; tokens bought in the stations are inserted into the turnstiles. Route maps are on display in every station. It's called the 'T'.
Bus: Tickets for the city's buses are bought on the bus. Regular services run throughout the city and its surrounding areas during the day, while a skeleton service operates after midnight.
Taxis: Taxis can be hailed in the street or booked by phone.
Car hire: All the major car hire firms operate in Boston, as

well as many smaller ones. Contact the Tourist Information office.

SIGHTS

Boston is the city where 18th-century Americans staged their fight against British rule to gain independence, and the city is immensely proud of its role in that struggle. From the BOSTON TEA PARTY SHIP where the war began, to the OLD STATE HOUSE where independence was first declared, all the sites from the days of colonialism and revolution are here, preserved just as they were in their finest hour.

Since its rebellious heyday, Boston has blossomed to become the bustling capital of New England. While it retains its old world charm and is considered one of America's more conservative cities, it is also a lively and cosmopolitan centre. Apart from the Anglo-Saxon descendants of its original settlers, the city's population is made up of large Italian, black and Irish communities, as well as the students of some 70 colleges.

Boston is clustered around the harbour, making its sights fairly easy to negotiate. Consequently it's ideal for touring on foot and the FREEDOM TRAIL – a red line painted on the city's pavement – will guide you along a 3-kilometre route taking in sixteen of Boston's most famous colonial and revolutionary landmarks. The trail starts at the Freedom Trail Information Center on Tremont Street. First stop is the PARK STREET CHURCH of 1809, where 'America' was sung for the first time on 4 July 1831. Subsequent stops include the OLD SOUTH MEETING HOUSE where the colonists plotted revolution; the Boston Tea Party Ship and Museum, a replica of the ship where the revolt was sparked; and the Old State House from where the Declaration of Independence was first read in 1776. Other points of interest connected with the fight for American independence are the PAUL REVERE HOUSE, the OLD NORTH CHURCH, FANEUIL HALL and the GRANARY BURYING GROUND which contains the remains of revolutionaries John Hancock, Paul Revere, Samuel Adams and Robert Paine, as well as the parents of Benjamin Franklin.

For a sense of 19th-century Boston, visit the city's BEACON HILL area with its gas-lit streets, cobbled roads and Victorian terraced houses. At the edge of Beacon Hill on Beacon Street is the golden-domed NEW STATE HOUSE, built in 1798 and the seat of the current Massachusetts State Government. The house was designed by Charles Bullfinch and boasts a beautiful interior design. Of more recent historical significance is the JOHN F. KENNEDY NATIONAL HISTORIC SITE at 83 Beals Street, where you can tour the house where President Kennedy was born; it has been left much as it was in his day.

Amid all this historic splendour, Boston isn't without its modern attractions. FANEUIL HALL MARKETPLACE offers excellent shopping, stalls, restaurants and bars, complete with street entertainment. NEWBURY STREET is Boston's exclusive shopping district. There's also a wide range of museums, including the MUSEUM OF FINE ARTS at 465 Huntington Avenue and the MUSEUM OF SCIENCE, whose exhibits include a space capsule and giant dinosaur. Next to this museum is the CHARLES HAYDEN PLANETARIUM, which puts on elaborate shows.

For a bird's-eye view of Boston and its environs, go up either the JOHN HANCOCK TOWER (New England's tallest building) or the PRUDENTIAL BUILDING. Both have observation levels near their summits and each affords a spectacular panoramic view. Across the Charles River from Boston is the city of CAMBRIDGE, worth the subway ride if only to visit Harvard Square, focal point of the celebrated Harvard University.

To relax from all this sightseeing, visit the BOSTON COMMON in the middle of the downtown area. The adjoining Public Garden is also very pleasant with its willow trees, lakes and swanboat rides, as is the CHARLES RIVER EMBANKMENT, the stretch of river between Science Park and the Boston University bridge, where there is parkland, fishing, and the famous concert shell where the Boston Pops Orchestra gives its summer concerts.

ACCOMMODATION
Accommodation in Boston is expensive. Book ahead to maximize your chances of getting a cheap deal.

Hostels:
Boston International Youth Hostel (IYHF), 12 Hemenway Street (tel. 536 9455). Book ahead. From $16.

Greater Boston YMCA, 316 Huntington Avenue (tel. 536 7800). A short trip from downtown by subway. Men and women welcome. From $38.

Berkley Residence Club (YWCA), 40 Berkeley Street (tel. 482 8850). Good facilities with comfortable clean rooms and not far from downtown. Women only. From $36.

Garden Halls Residence, 164 Marlborough Street (tel. 267 0079). Students only. Open in summer only. From $33.

Hotels/motels:
Suisse Chalet Motor Lodge, 800 Morrisey Boulevard, Dorchester (tel. 287 9100). Basic but comfortable. Doubles from $52.

Longwood Inn, 123 Longwood Avenue (tel. 566 8615). Quiet and friendly. From $42.

Beacon Inn, 1087 or 1750 Beacon Street, Brookline (tel. 566 0088). Small hotel in a quiet area.

B&Bs: There are a couple of UK agencies through which you can book B&B in Boston: Colby International, 139 Round Hey, Liverpool L28 (tel. 051 220 5848) and New England Inns and Resorts, 1 Farm Way, Northwood, Middx HA6 3EG (tel. 0923 821469).

FOOD
Eating out in Boston is a very popular pursuit among Bostonians and visitors alike and this is reflected in the city's wide selection of restaurants. Seafood is the local speciality – New England delicacies include freshly boiled lobster, swordfish steaks, clam chowder, oysters and cheese-gilded scallops. The food of old Boston is represented by the popular Boston baked beans and Indian pudding. Cambridge, just a subway ride across the Charles River, has a varied selection of international restaurants to choose from. The North End area of the city is renowned for its food, particularly Italian dishes. For cheap eats, Quincy Market is the place for a great assortment of takeaways. Faneuil Hall Marketplace is also popular.

Durgin Park, 340 Faneuil Hall Marketplace (tel. 227 2038). Seating is long tables where diners sit elbow to elbow. Seafood is a speciality.

The Union Oyster House, near Fanueil Hall (look for the big, red letters on top of the building). This is the oldest continuously-operating restaurant in the USA. The best clam chowder in the city!

Bangkok Cuisine, 177a Massachusetts Avenue. The best Thai restaurant in Boston.

Kebab-N-Kurry, 30 Massachusetts Avenue (tel. 536 9835). Fine Indian cuisine.

Oh! Calcutta!, 468 Massachusetts Avenue (tel. 576 2111). Large portions of Indian food.

ENTERTAINMENT
Boston offers a lot in the way of after-dark entertainment and between what goes on in the city and in Cambridge, there is enough scope to suit every taste. From jazz clubs to discos to quiet cafés, it's all here. The Bull & Finch on Beacon street has become one of Boston's most popular and well-known nightspots because it is the bar where the TV series *Cheers* was based. Joe's at 279 Dartmouth

Street is a current 'in-place'. Ryle's and the 1369 Club, both on Inman Square, Cambridge, play good jazz. Quincy market, a lunch-spot by the day, makes for a relaxing evening's entertainment with its quiet intimate restaurants and outdoor piano bars. There's also a thriving theatre – Boston's Theater District is centred around Tremont Street – and classical music scene in the city. The Boston Symphony Orchestra is based at the Symphony Hall, 301 Huntington Avenue (tel. 266 1492). Bostix, a ticket outlet in Faneuil Hall, sells half-price tickets for same-day events. For full details of what's on, look in the *Boston Phoenix*.

EXCURSIONS

LEXINGTON, a 19 km subway ride to the north-west of Boston, played an important role in the American War of Independence. Paul Revere rode through Lexington on the night of 18 April 1775 to warn the American revolutionary leaders of a British offensive, and it was on Lexington Green that minutemen spilled blood for the first time. Visitors can look back to revolutionary America in the Visitors' Center, which has a diorama depicting the battle. The HANCOCK-CLARKE HOUSE at 3 Hancock Street is where celebrated rebels John Hancock and Samuel Adams slept the night of 18 April. The MUSEUM OF NATIONAL HERITAGE at 33 Marriett Road features exhibits from all periods of American history.

During the summer, Baystate-Spray and Provincetown Steam-ship Company operate very pleasant harbour cruises from the city's docks. Stops during the cruise can be made at either GEORGE'S ISLAND STATE PARK, where there are good beaches for swimming, or at the picturesque PROVINCETOWN on the tip of Cape Cod.

CONCORD, easily accessible from Boston, has a wealth of historical connections. Besides its War of Independence relics, such as the Minute Man National Historical Park, Concord has a host of other bygone and present-day attractions, including the homes of writers Nathaniel Hawthorne and Louisa May Alcott, and Ralph Waldo Emerson House. WALDEN POND in Concord is the site of Henry Thoreau's famous 'return-to-nature' hermitage.

For a taste of the brighter and darker sides of New England history, take a trip to the town of SALEM. Famous for its beautiful architecture, Salem is equally well known for its controversial 17th-century witch trials, vividly recreated at the SALEM WITCH MUSEUM. The Essex Institute is an intriguing complex of houses dating back to the late 17th century, while Chestnut Street contains some of America's most beautiful old-world architecture.

Dallas

AIRPORT FACILITIES
Dallas—Fort Worth International Airport is one of the world's largest and busiest airports. The airport is 31 km north-west of Dallas and 31 km north-east of Fort Worth. There are four terminals. Currency exchange is available at terminals 2E, 4E and 2W. Duty-free shops are located in terminals 2 and 4; and there are catering facilities in all terminals. For airport information call (214) 574 8888.

CITY LINKS
There are a number of shuttle buses running between the airport and downtown Dallas and major hotels at a cost of around $10. The 'T' bus operates on a regular basis to Fort Worth. Taxis cost around $25 to downtown. The shuttles are much better value and no less efficient.

USEFUL ADDRESSES
Tourist office: Dallas Convention and Visitors' Bureau, 1201 Elm Street, Suite 2000 (tel. 746 6677). Visitors' centre: 1303 Commerce Street (tel. 746 6603).
Post office: 400 North Ervay Street, Dallas, 75201.
British Consulate-General: 813 Stemmons Tower West, 2730 Stemmons Freeway (tel. 637 3600).
Emergency services: Dial 911 for police, fire or ambulance.

GETTING ABOUT
Public transport in Dallas is quick and cheap. The Dallas Area Rapid Transit (DART) operates a reliable service which covers all areas of the city as well as most suburbs. The service runs from 5 a.m. till midnight and the downtown fare is 75c. Maps of DART routes are available at Main and Akard Streets. DART's Hop-a-Buses operate downtown on a park and ride system.

Taxis are widely available around Dallas and can be phoned for or hailed in the street. All the major car hire firms operate in Dallas.

SIGHTS
Next to Houston, Dallas is the second biggest city in Texas. Built on a flat prairie and situated in the north-east of the state, Dallas was originally a trading post. Rapid development over the years has made it one of the world's major commercial centres, counting

oil, banking and fashion among its important moneyspinners. A distinct Southern identity gives the city a character of its own. Stetson hats and cowboy boots are very much the order of the day.

Dallas is probably best known today as the site of the assassination of President John F. Kennedy. The JOHN F. KENNEDY MEMORIAL PLAZA on the corner of Main and Market Streets is an unprepossessing 9-metre high concrete structure, built in remembrance of JFK, whose assassination in Dallas on 22 November 1963 shocked the world and left a lasting imprint on the psyche of America. There's also a plaque at the corner of Houston and Main Streets which describes the route of President Kennedy's motorcade on the day of the shooting. The TEXAS SCHOOL BOOK DEPOSITORY, from where assassin Lee Harvey Oswald fired the fateful shots – according to the official version of events declared by the Warren Commission – is open to visitors. The SIXTH FLOOR EXHIBIT commemorates JFK's life, death and legacy. Some witnesses also claimed to have heard shots from the now famous grassy knoll, but these reports were never substantiated.

One of the most popular places with visitors is the STATE FAIR PARK at Parry and Second Avenue. Among its attractions is the Dallas Garden Center, which boasts a tropical garden, a solarium, a rose garden and other plant exhibits. The Aquarium features various freshwater, tropical and coldwater fish. There's also a harbour seal on show. Museums in the State Fair Park include the DALLAS HEALTH AND SCIENCE MUSEUM AND PLANETARIUM; the DALLAS MUSEUM OF NATURAL HISTORY, which has exhibitions of Texan animals and birds in their natural habitat; and the TEXAS HALL OF STATE, built in 1936 as a celebration of Texan independence. Fair Park also plays host to the State Fair of Texas which is the largest state fair in the US and takes place throughout October.

DALLAS CITY HALL on Akard Street is worth a visit for its sheer size, rising 168 metres in the air. For panoramic views of the city, go to the First National Bank at the corner of Elm and Akard Streets, or the 50-storey Reunion Tower on Houston Street which has a top-floor observation deck.

Another excellent museum in Dallas renowned for its architecture as much as for its exhibits is the DALLAS MUSEUM OF ART at 1717 North Harwood Street. Pre-Columbian art is heavily featured; the outdoor sculpture garden provides an ideal spot for lunch. If you have an interest in architecture, you might like to visit the DALLAS THEATER CENTER, designed by Frank Lloyd Wright.

The JOHN NEELY BRYAN CABIN was the first ever log cabin to be built in Dallas (in 1841). The first log cabin school in Dallas is in Old City Park at St Paul and Ervay Streets. The park also contains a southern mansion from 1885, complete with white columns. DALLAS ZOO at 621 East Clarendon Drive is one of America's top zoological parks. The BIBLICAL ARTS CENTER at 8909 Boedecker and Park Lane is noted for its popular light and sound presentations of 'Miracle at Pentecost'.

ACCOMMODATION
Budget accommodation is hard to come by. The cheaper motels all tend to be beyond the downtown area.

Youth hostel: IYHF, 1451 East Northgate Street, Irving (tel. 438 6061). Inconveniently located out in the suburbs. $16.

Hotels and motels:

Econolodge, 9386 LBJ Freeway (tel. 690 1220). Good facilities including a fine restaurant. From $38.

Rodeway Inn Central, 4150 North Central Expressway (tel. 231 5181). Handy downtown location.

Dallas Budget Inn, 4001 Live Oak Street (tel. 826 7110). Downmarket but cheap and close to downtown. From $27.

Delux Inn, 3111 Stemmons Highway (tel. 637 0060). Take the number 39 bus. From $27.

Ranch stays: If you fancy a ranch holiday, there are a couple of agencies you can book through in the UK:

Ranch America, 250 Imperial Drive, Rayners Lane, Harrow, Middx HA2 7HJ (tel. 0181 868 2910).

American Round Up, PO Box 126, Hemel Hempstead, Herts HP3 OAZ (tel. 0442 214621).

FOOD
Here in the heart of American cattle country, beef dishes are a popular feature of Dallas dining. As well as steaks and hamburgers, look out for spicy barbecued Texan beef and the local speciality, 'Texas Fried' – a breaded deep-fried cut of beef. Mexican restaurants are plentiful and there's a wide selection of European and oriental establishments. Greenville Avenue is one of Dallas' main dining centres and caters for all budgets, as do Deep Ellum and McKinney Avenue.

Deep Ellum Café, 2706 Elm Street (tel. 741 9012). Serves all-American dishes.

Aw Shucks, 3601 Greenville Avenue (tel. 821 9449). Outdoor seafood bar very popular with the locals.

Stuart Anderson Cattle Co, 7102 Greenville Avenue. Excellent steaks.

Old Spaghetti Warehouse, 1815 North Market (tel. 651 8475).
  Popular pasta joint.

ENTERTAINMENT
The nightlife scene in Dallas is a lively one. Clubs, corner pubs,
cabarets, live music, singles bars – there's no shortage around the
city. Greenville Avenue is where the largest choice of nightspots is
to be found. McKinney Avenue is also lively and the developing
warehouse district of Deep Ellum offers a selection of innovative
theatre and music. Dallas' most popular venues include Aw Shucks
at 3601 Greenville Avenue, an outdoor seafood bar very popular
with the locals and the ideal spot for raw oysters and a cold beer
on a warm evening. Dick's Last Resort at 1701 North Market Street
is an informal club which plays Dixieland jazz and has no cover
charge.
  For details of what's going on around town, consult the *Dallas
Observer*.

FESTIVALS AND EVENTS
Dallas hosts a wide range of cultural attractions encompassing
theatre, music and the arts. Because of the large number of festivals
that take place in the city, many such cultural events can be enjoyed
for free. The Montage festival in the downtown Dallas Arts District
is an outdoor family festival that showcases Dallas' performing arts
in early September. The Shakespeare Festival is one of the city's
most popular events, offering free productions in Samuel Grand
Park throughout June and July (tel. 699 2778). For music lovers,
the International Summer Music Festival takes place in the Morton
Meyerson Symphony Center (tel. 692 0203) from June to July.

EXCURSIONS
SIX FLAGS OVER TEXAS is a vast amusement park in Arlington,
24 km from downtown Dallas. As the name suggests, Texas and its
history come under the spotlight and the park's six sections reflect
six different state-ruling governments. Incorporated in these sections are a wide variety of amusement rides, shops, restaurants and
entertainment theatres.
  INTERNATIONAL WILDLIFE PARK, near to Six Flags, is home to
hundreds of wild animals roaming free in their natural habitat.
Visitors can drive through the park and observe them at close quarters. The 41-acre SOUTHFORK RANCH, home of the popular American soap opera *Dallas*, is a short drive north-east of downtown
Dallas and is now open to the public. Tours include a guided tour
of the Ewing Mansion and a tram ride round the ranch.

Los Angeles

AIRPORT FACILITIES
Los Angeles International Airport (or LAX as it's known), is one of the busiest travel centres in the world. The airport is 27 km southwest of the city and has nine terminals. The Tom Bradley International Terminal (TBIT) handles most international departures and arrivals, and has an information centre and a post office. Currency exchange and catering facilities are available at all terminals, as is duty-free. For airport information call 310 646 5252.

CITY LINKS
Bus: There are a number of shuttle buses which operate from the airport to downtown Los Angeles and other areas in the vicinity. Buses should be boarded on the lower level islands in front of each terminal; information and tickets for many lines are available at booths directly in front of the terminals. Otherwise you pay the bus driver. Tickets are around $15. There are also shuttle buses which will drop you at the LAX Transit Centre where you can catch local buses to take you into town; these are much cheaper but very slow as they make numerous stops *en route*.
Taxi: Taxis are readily available and cost around $25 for the ride downtown.

USEFUL ADDRESSES
Tourist offices: Downtown Los Angeles Visitor Information Center, 685 South Figueroa Street, between Wilshire Boulevard and Seventh Street (tel. 689 8822). Open Mon.–Sat. 8 a.m.–5 p.m. The Hollywood Visitor Information Center is at The Janes House, Janes Square, 6541 Hollywood Boulevard (tel. 461 4213). Mon.–Sat. 9 a.m.–5 p.m.
Main post office: 901 South Broadway at 9th Street (tel. 617 4413).
British Consulate-General , 3701 Wilshire Boulevard (tel. 477 3322).
Emergency services: Dial 911 for police, fire or ambulance.

GETTING ABOUT
Getting around Los Angeles if you don't have a car can be a major inconvenience. The city is not built for walkers.
Bus: The Southern California Rapid Transit District (RTD) bus service covers a wide area but the system can be complex. Buses are

not expensive – basic one-way fare is $1.10. They are quite fre-
quent, particularly on busy routes, and cover all the tourist areas.
However they do take a long time to get anywhere, since they stop
at virtually every corner. Pick up a timetable from one of RTD's
information offices (their main downtown office is at Areo Plaza,
505 South Flower Street, Level B). There is also a useful free 7-day
telephone information service which will tell you how to get from
A to B: dial I-800 252 7433.

A shuttle system (DASH) operates downtown Mon.–Sat. Have
the exact fare – 25 cents – ready.

Rail: Los Angeles is building a light rail system that will link downtown LA with outlying districts. Already in service is the Metro
Blue Line rail service between Downtown and Long Beach. For
information call 213 626 4455.

SIGHTS

Known as the 'City of Angels', Los Angeles has come a long way
since its days as a late-18th century settlement of some 50 people.
Today it stretches over an area of around 755 sq. km and is home
to a population of over 7 million. Most recently in the news because
of the 1992 riots which hit hardest in the east of the city, Los
Angeles, like New York, has its no-go areas – and East Los Angeles
is one of them.

Touring the sights requires some form of transport, if only
because they are spread out from downtown to outlying suburbs
such as Beverly Hills and Hollywood. It is one of the few places
where taking a tour might be worthwhile. Downtown Los Angeles
is where the history of the city is most evident. EL PUEBLO DE
LOS ANGELES STATE HISTORIC PARK along Main Street, contains
a number of buildings which have been preserved from the city's
Spanish and Mexican beginnings. You can sample the atmosphere
of those days in the park's Merced Theater, where 'Spectrum' is a
photographic documentary on the history of Los Angeles from 1860
to 1940. Other attractions in the park include the OLD PLAZA and
the former gambling and opium dens of the old Chinese immigrants
in the catacombs – these are usually included in walking tours of
the park, which start from the nearby visitors' centre at 130 Paseo
de la Plaza.

CHINATOWN is mainly centred around Hill and North Broadway
Streets and is full of typical Eastern charm – the people, the street
sounds, the food markets and the restaurants are straight out of
the Orient. LITTLE TOKYO, between 1st and 3rd and Main and
Central Streets, not only contains more than fifty excellent restaurants but also the JAPANESE VILLAGE PLAZA on East 2nd Street

– an America-goes-Japanese shopping mall where the stores sell all sorts of exotic jewellery, gifts and cookware. The JAPANESE-AMERICAN CULTURAL & COMMUNITY CENTER is at 244 South San Pedro Street, while the MUSEUM OF NEON ART at 704 Traction Avenue provides some interesting exhibitions, as do other smaller art galleries on the eastern edge of Little Tokyo.

Los Angeles, however, is really famous for two things: its beaches and Hollywood. The city's celebrated coastline has some of the world's biggest waves and most golden sand. If you can handle exposing yourself alongside the body-conscious Los Angelenos, ZUMA BEACH is the largest sandiest public beach in Malibu; SANTA MONICA is long, sandy and busy; VENICE BEACH is a fantastic place for people-watching at weekends – one of its main attractions is the body-building equipment which is open for use by the public; MANHATTAN BEACH is excellent for surfing and sunning. (See **Excursions**, p. 574 for further details.)

Hollywood, of course, is still the mecca of movies and television, albeit somewhat faded now. Some of the area's sparkle is captured in HOLLYWOOD BOULEVARD, where you can traverse the Walk of Fame with its concrete and bronze stars commemorating around 1,700 famous names; there's also Grauman's CHINESE THEATER at 6925 Hollywood Boulevard, where cinema personalities first started leaving their foot and palm prints in 1927. Many of these stars were laid to rest in HOLLYWOOD MEMORIAL CEMETERY on Santa Monica Boulevard, including Valentino and Fairbanks.

BEVERLY HILLS, west of Hollywood, is home not only to stars of stage and screen but also to some of America's most magnificent architecture and expensive shops. RODEO DRIVE has a bit of all three: a stroll along this famous thoroughfare offers excellent window-shopping. They say that if you have to think about how much you can afford, you can't afford it. The famous SUNSET STRIP BOULEVARD to the west of Hollywood has become a byword for tackiness and sleaze. It's still worth a visit, even though it's not the glamorous spot it used to be.

UNIVERSAL STUDIOS gives you a glimpse of how illusions are created for film, particularly those spectacular images such as earth-quakes and shark attacks. Universal is a day's trip on its own and includes live shows and movie-stunt exhibitions. WARNER BROS BURBANK STUDIOS offer tours on which you are more likely to see an actual film in progress. Tours are by reservation only (tel. 818 954 1744). If you like theme parks, Los Angeles also has its own DISNEYLAND, and WILD RIVERS in Laguna Hills has around forty water rides.

To take a break from the smog, head towards Hollywood's GRIF-

FITH PARK which covers an area of more than 4,000 acres and boasts several attractions, among them the LOS ANGELES ZOO and the outdoor GREEK THEATER, which has concerts year-round and the GRIFFITH OBSERVATORY AND PLANETARIUM. There's also a bird sanctuary and hiking trails among the park's mountains.

ACCOMMODATION
Budget accommodation is not easy to come by in Los Angeles and the problem is compounded by the difficulties of travelling round the city. Book your accommodation as far ahead as possible. Note that the Tourist Office will not make bookings for you.

Hostels:
Bill Baker International Youth Hostel (IYHF), 8015 South Sepulveda Boulevard (tel. 776 0922). Summer only. $11 for members. Supplement for non-members.

Hollywood Hostel (IYHF), 1553 North Hudson Avenue (tel. 467 4161). $10 for dorms; $30 for singles; $40 for doubles.

Los Angeles International Hostel (IYHF), 3601 South Gaffey Street (tel. 831 8109). $12 for members; another couple of dollars for non-members.

Huntington Beach Colonial Hostel (IYHF), 421 Eighth Street, Huntington Beach (tel. 714 536 3315). Near the beach. $9 for members; $10 for non-members.

Hollywood International Hostel, 7038 1/2 Hollywood Blvd (tel. 850 6287). Dorms start at $11, doubles at $30.

Banana Bungalow, 2775 Cahuenga Blvd (tel. 1-800-4HO-STEL or 851 1129). Located near Universal Studios. Free airport pick-up. Dorms start at $13.35 and rooms at $40.

Hotels/motels: Downtown has the best of the city's cheap hotels. Hollywood Boulevard is also a good area for budget motels. Rates in all areas tend to drop at the weekends as business travellers leave town.

Jerrys Motel, 285 South Lucas Avenue (tel. 481 0921). $42.

Academy Hotel, 1621 North McCadden Place (tel. 465 1918). $42.

Figueroa Hotel, 939 South Figueroa Street (tel. 421 9092). Conveniently located with good facilities. $72.

Park Plaza Hotel, 607 South Park View Street (tel. 384 5281). Former grand hotel which used to entertain some of Hollywood's stars. $48.

Orchid Hotel, 819 South Flower Street (tel. 624 5855). Clean and handily located. $38.

Hollywood Roosevelt, 7000 Hollywood Boulevard (tel. 466 7000). 1927 hotel loaded with Hollywood history. $72.

Travelodge Vermont Sunset, 1401 North Vermont Avenue, Hollywood (tel. 665 5735). Close to sights including Manns Chinese Theatre and Universal Studios. $42.

Hollywood Plaza Inn, 2011 North Highland Avenue, Hollywood (tel. 851 1800). Within walking distance of Hollywood Boulevard. $62.

B&B: You may be able to book B&B from England through Colby International at 139 Round Hey, Liverpool L28 (tel. 051 220 5848).

Campsites: Forget about camping as all the campgrounds are miles out of town.

FOOD

Like many of America's major cities, Los Angeles' food scene benefits from the range of different nationalities that live there. Mexican restaurants are centred mainly in the east of the city; Jewish and Eastern European food is most easily found in the Fairfax area; and Thai, Japanese, Chinese and Vietnamese restaurants are located, not surprisingly, in Chinatown and Little Tokyo. Fastfood, of course, is never more than a stone's throw away. If you're bored with hamburgers, shopping malls all have communal eating areas with a variety of cheap but decent fast-food outlets selling Mexican, Chinese, Italian, etc.

Gorky's, 536 East 8th Street (tel. 627 4060). Russian/American cuisine served round the clock in the city's Soho district. Lively atmosphere.

Mon Kee, 679 North Spring Street (tel. 628 6717). One of the best Chinese restaurants in LA and a local favourite.

El Cholo, 1121 South Western Avenue (tel. 734 2773). Excellent Mexican food.

Cliftons' Cafeteria, 648 South Broadway (tel. 485 1726). Home cooking in a 1930s setting.

Philippe, 1001 North Alameda Street (tel. 628 3781). An LA institution good for breakfast, lunch or dinner.

Musso & Frank Grill, 6667 Hollywood Boulevard (tel. 467 7788). Oldest restaurant in Hollywood.

Mario's, 1001 Broxton Avenue, Westwood (tel. 310 208 7077). Great Italian food.

Café 50's, 838 Lincoln Boulevard, Venice (tel. 310 399 1955). Fifties café with the works including jukebox and movie memorabilia.

ENTERTAINMENT

Los Angeles has a thriving after-dark scene. On any given evening, you can enjoy live pop, jazz, rock and country and western entertainers. For jazz, try the Palace at 1735 North Vine Street (tel. 462 3000). The Palomino at 6907 Lankershim Boulevard (tel. 818 764 4010) puts on live country and western shows. Mayan in downtown LA at 1038 South Hill Street (tel. 746 4674) is one of the hottest dance clubs in town.

Comedy clubs are something of an LA speciality. The Comedy Store at 8433 Sunset Boulevard (tel. 656 6225) is popular. You could also try the Comedy & Magic Club at 1018 Hermosa Avenue, Hermosa Beach (tel. 310 372 1193) which puts on comedians and magicians, or Igby's at 11637 Tennessee Place (tel. 310 477 3553) where big-name comics occasionally turn up in place of the regular stand-up comedians.

Of course, Los Angeles is the place to see movies. There are cinemas on just about every corner, the most famous being the Mann's Chinese Theatre at 6925 Hollywood Boulevard (tel. 464 8111) which has regular first nights. Westwood cinemas have a very studenty crowd. You can also get a ticket to watch a television show being taped before a live audience. You can write to the studio in advance or queue up on the day of the show, when tickets are allocated on a first-come first-served basis. Try ABC-TV, 4151 Prospect Avenue, Hollywood, CA 90027 (tel. 520 1ABC), CBS-TV, 7800 Beverly Blvd, Los Angeles, CA 90036 (tel. 852 2458), NBC-TV, 3000 W. Alameda Ave, Burbank, CA 91523 (tel. 840 3537 for recorded ticket information or 840 3538 for the ticket office), Paramount Pictures, 860 N. Gower Street, Hollywood, CA 90038 (tel. 956 5575), or Audiences Unlimited (tel. 506 0043).

The Hollywood Bowl is world-renown for its huge popular concerts and also hosts regular open-air concerts by the LA Philharmonic in the summer months. There is no one major cultural venue but the Music Center plays host periodically to several companies including the Civic Light Opera, the Joffrey Ballet and the Los Angeles Philharmonic Theater Group. Los Angeles has a very active theatre circuit and there are theatres scattered all over the city, including in Universal City, Hollywood, Santa Monica.

For up-to-date details of events and entertainment consult the calendar section of the *Los Angeles Times* or the free *LA Weekly* and *LA Reader*.

EXCURSIONS

There was once an unsuccessful attempt to turn VENICE, up the coast from Los Angeles, into a second Venezia. Today it is a bustling focal point for the most eccentric Angelinos. The grand hotels and buildings that it was hoped would turn the town into a high-class tourist resort have made way for health-food shops, pavement cafés and juice bars. OCEAN FRONT WALK is worth strolling along to see the bodybuilders on Muscle Beach and the army of rollerskaters, cyclists and joggers. All contribute towards the atmosphere that makes Venice Beach tick.

SANTA MONICA, a short drive north of Los Angeles, is an area of great charm. The beach is much frequented, as is the Old Santa Monica Mall, an outdoor shopping centre which is noted for its bargain-priced clothes and cheap ethnic foods. The more up-market Santa Monica Place is much the same only on a higher price scale.

MALIBU, a narrow stretch of coastline just north of Santa Monica, is a region of scenic cliffs and beautiful beaches. On a cliff above the ocean, just east of Malibu Beach, is the famed J. PAUL GETTY MUSEUM. Built as a replica of a first-century villa at Herculaneum, the plants and gardens are done in the style of the Romans. Inside are paintings, tapestries and furniture from the Renaissance period, as well as Greek and Roman sculpture. The MALIBU CREEK STATE PARK is 4,000 acres in size and has some 24 km of trails to wander along.

The suburb of PASADENA, 16 km from downtown, is home to the world-famous HUNTINGTON LIBRARY, ART GALLERY and BOTANICAL GARDENS. The library houses treasured collections of English and American literature; the gallery is noted for its centuries-old British paintings; and the gardens contain some of the world's rarest and most beautiful plants. New Year's Day in Pasadena is renowned for the TOURNAMENT OF ROSES PARADE and the ROSE BOWL.

Miami

AIRPORT FACILITIES
Miami International Airport is 11 km north-west of downtown Miami. It has one terminal with an information desk and currency exchange together with catering facilities, shops and a post office. Flight information is on 876 7000.

CITY LINKS
There is a bus service to downtown Miami and Miami Beach, which takes about half an hour and costs $1.25. There is also a shuttle service to Miami Airport TriRail station. A taxi downtown takes

around 20 minutes and costs $12–15. To Miami Beach it will take you 5 minutes more and cost around $22.

USEFUL ADDRESSES
Tourist office: Greater Miami Convention and Visitors' Bureau, 701 Brickell Avenue, Suite 2700, Miami (tel. 283 2707).
Post offices: 500 NW 2nd Avenue, Miami, or 1300 Washington Avenue, Miami Beach.
Emergency services: Dial 911 for police, fire or ambulance.

GETTING ABOUT
Public transport in Greater Miami is fairly good and getting from one place to another can be managed easily and quickly.
Bus: There is an extensive Metrobus system which links downtown with various municipalities. The fare is $1.25 each way and exact change is required. Bus-rail transfers cost 25 cents.
Metrorail: Metrorail is an elevated rail system which operates downtown. Useful stops include the Cultural Centre. Trains run every 15 minutes, more often in peak hours, and connect to Metromover, Metrobus and Tri-Rail. The fare is $1.25 each way and exact change is required.
Metromover: The Metromover is an amusement-park-style network of moving platforms, linked to Metrorail, which provides relaxing elevated transport around downtown. The fare is 25 cents.
Taxi: Taxis are widely available and can be hailed in the street or booked by phone. Rates are $1.40 per mile.
Car hire: All major car rental firms have offices in the Miami metropolitan area.

SIGHTS
Gateway to the state of Florida, the Greater Miami area is divided into two cities: Miami and Miami Beach. Separated from each other by Biscayne Bay but linked by virtue of several causeways and bridges, these two sunshine cities of hot temperatures, swaying palm trees and golden beaches were originally favourite winter haunts with tourists. Today, however, the area's 800-plus hotels accommodate visitors from the world over all year round, making Miami one of the world's foremost tourist centres.

The city's image over the years has been somewhat tarnished by a relatively high incidence of organized crime, more often than not drugs-related. The streets, however, tend to be no more dangerous than in other American cities and visitors are reasonably safe to enjoy what is not only an ideal spot for sun and relaxation, but also an exciting and cosmopolitan city.

One of the success stories in recent years has been the so-called ART DECO DISTRICT at the southern end of Miami Beach. The roots of the district stem from the 1930s when Miami was the East Coast's main winter playground and the era's progressive tone was translated into the building of hotels with bright colours and flamboyant structures. After years of decline, the area has been pronounced a National Historic District and restored to its former glory. The southern end of the Beach has once again become the hotspot of the East Coast with a string of famous names buying property there, including Madonna, Mickey Rourke, Kevin Costner and Matt Dillon. The Art Deco hotels have become popular backdrops for TV and films, commercial and fashion shoots; entertainment and nightlife is booming; and there is a plethora of people-watching pavement cafés. Despite its rejuvenation, the Beach remains a casual informal place, though the area's popularity with the media means you will probably notice an above average proportion of 'beautiful people' – aspiring models and the like.

The focal streets of the Art Deco district are OCEAN DRIVE and its environs, particularly Collins and Washington Avenue. Everything worth seeing is within walking distance and it is a thoroughly enjoyable experience with architectural delights round every corner, most of them functioning hotels, such as the Cardozo, the Cavalier, Park Central, Waldorf Towers, the Marlin and the Imperial. It's always worth going into the hotels because the lobbies are often classic examples of the style of the era. The ART DECO PRESERVATION LEAGUE WELCOME CENTRE in the Leslie Hotel, 1244 Ocean Drive (11 a.m.–6 p.m. daily) has a stack of literature on the district and conducts walking tours from 10 a.m.–2 p.m. on Saturdays.

Miami's heaviest ethnic influences are Caribbean and Latin American (the city is sometimes known as the capital of the Caribbean). The most prominent ethnic group, following the influx of refugees in the 1960s when Fidel Castro came to power, are the Cubans. LITTLE HAVANA is the enclave of Miami's Cuban community and is filled with the sights and sounds of their country of origin. South West 8th Street, CALLE OCHO, is the neighbourhood's main thoroughfare. The BAY OF PIGS MONUMENT at the Cuban Memorial Plaza is a reminder of an unfortunate episode in Cuban-American relations, and the Plaza itself is a popular meeting place.

Formerly known as Lemon City, LITTLE HAITI has become the heart of the Haitian community since the 1980s when Haitian refugees began settling here. The Creole language still filters through the neighbourhood, while restaurants serve Creole specialities and local clubs hum to the beat of Latin music. The CARIBBEAN

MARKETPLACE is a colourful arena housing nearly two dozen shops offering everything from Caribbean arts and crafts, books, records and clothes to tropical ice creams.

Other interesting districts include CORAL GABLES, the 'City Beautiful', a charming Spanish-style neighbourhood with huge poinciana and palm trees, ideal for cycling through. COCONUT GROVE, once home to Miami's bohemians, has become a fashionable upmarket district but still retains some of its old flavour.

An unusual museum but fitting to Miami is the AMERICAN POLICE HALL OF FAME at 3801 Biscayne Boulevard. Opened recently, it's a history of law enforcement and shows how police officers approach crimes in their efforts to solve them. Among the exhibits are a jail cell, electric chair and a 400-ton marble memorial honouring over 3,000 police officers killed on duty.

BISCAYNE NATIONAL PARK is mostly underwater and is marvellous for scuba divers who want to explore its coral reefs. EVERGLADES NATIONAL PARK contains a huge marsh and swamp rich in wildlife including alligators, deer, turtles and the manatee, a rare aquatic mammal. You can follow nature trails, take boat tours and rent canoes, or even camp out overnight.

ACCOMMODATION
Hostel: There is only one: Clay Hotel and Miami Beach International Hostel, 1438 Washington Avenue, Miami Beach (tel. 534 2988). A 100-room hostel with good facilities including TV, laundry, restaurant and kitchen. Dorm beds $10. Singles from $18. Doubles from $25.

Hotels/motels: For budget beds the best source is Miami Beach. Miami Airways Motel, 5001 North-west 36th Street (tel. 883 4700). Near the airport.

Park Central, 640 Ocean Drive, Miami Beach (tel. 538 1611). A striking blue and green building with its own pool. From $82.

Surfcomber Hotel, 1717 Collins Avenue, Miami Beach (tel. 532 7715). Comfortable hotel with pool. From $52.

Sasson Hotel, 2001 Collins Avenue, Miami Beach (tel. 531 0761). Comfortable hotel in the heart of Miami Beach. From $50.

Sagamore Hotel, 1671 Collins Avenue, Miami Beach (tel. 538 7211). Family atmosphere hotel close to the Miami Beach Convention Centre. From $55.

The Tropics, 1550 Collins Avenue (tel. 531 0361). Across from the beach. From $14.

Campsites: There is no camping in Miami.

FOOD

Miami is famous for its Cuban cuisine, courtesy of the immigrant population. Restaurants in Little Havana are genuine and inexpensive. Cuban *media noche* sandwiches and *mamey* ice cream are good for lunch; *café cubano* is also delicious, particularly with *churros*, deep-fried sweet dough you can dip in sugar. Recommended for dinner are *ropa vieja* (shredded beef in a light tomato sauce) or *masas de puerco* (fried pork). Little Haiti also has its own specialities serving up Creole tasters such as *griot* (fried pork) and *tassot* (fried goat).

Miami boasts excellent seafood, too. Local specialities include stone crabs, Florida lobster and crawfish. In addition there is a variety of Italian, Chinese, German, French, Vietnamese and other international places serving their own traditional fare – not forgetting traditional American cuisine.

News Café, 800 Ocean Drive, Miami Beach. Open 24 hours, this popular café has a newsstand inside and serves basic American fare.

Sierra's Café, 600 Brickell Avenue. Downtown family atmosphere restaurant serving homemade Latin cuisine.

Puerto Sagua, 700 Collins. Popular Cuban restaurant on Miami Beach.

Versailles, 3555 SW 8th street. Popular easy-going Cuban restaurant in Little Havana.

Guayacan Restaurant, 1933 S W 8th Street. Casual restaurant in Little Havana serving typical Nicaraguan food.

Seaside Café and Raw Bar, Sagamore Resort Hotel, 1671 Collins Avenue. Outdoor restaurant overlooking the Ocean in Art Deco district.

Joe's Stone Crab, 227 Biscayne Street. Famous crab restaurant which closes in the summer when crabs are out of season.

Wolfie's, 2038 Collins Avenue. Popular 24-hour deli on Miami Beach.

ENTERTAINMENT

Miami is the 'in' spot for nightlife on the East Coast with a good selection of clubs, discos and bars. Popular bars on Miami Beach include Whiskey at 1250 Ocean Drive and the Spot at 218 Espanola Way. There are several clubs on Washington such as Van Dome (1532 Washington) and The Paragon (1235 Washington). The Peacock Café (2977 McFarlane Road, Coconut Grove) is good for jazz and blues. Little Havana puts on authentic Spanish flamenco and its clubs beat to Latin music.

If you're starved of culture, the Gusman Cultural Center at 174 East Flagler Street (tel. 226 1812) plays host to the New World Symphony and Florida Philharmonic Orchestra. The Dade County Auditorium at 2901 West Flagler Street (tel. 532 4880) entertains both the Miami City Ballet and the Greater Miami Opera. PACE (Performing Arts for Community and Education) puts on musical, dance and theatrical events throughout the city, many of which are free (tel. 681 1470).

Check out the free weeklies *New Times* and the *South Beach Antenna* as well as the Friday issue of the *Miami Herald* for listings.

FESTIVALS AND EVENTS

Carnival Miami in March is the largest Hispanic festival in the US and is a week-long festival of dance, food and entertainment. Also in the spring is the Haitian Festival with arts and crafts, music and dance and an explosion of Haiitian cooking. In February the Gusman Cultural Center at 174 East Flagler Street hosts the annual Miami Film Festival. In August the Miami Reggae Festival is a two-day celebration of music and culture.

EXCURSIONS

KEY BISCAYNE, 10 km from downtown Miami across the Rickenbacker Causeway, is an ideal spot for any number of pursuits, relaxing or active. CRANDON PARK on the Key contains fine and often deserted beaches, together with a zoo, cabanas and bathhouses. To the south of the Key is BILL BAGGS CAPE FLORIDA PARK, which provides the perfect setting and facilities for fishing, boating, swimming and picnicking.

MONKEY JUNGLE, around 32 km south of Miami is a 10-hectare tropical rainforest which offers you the chance to see monkeys in their natural environment. The monkeys, mostly from Asia and South America, are all wild and roam free while visitors walk along routes through the park which are covered by cages.

The SERPENTARIUM, 18 km south of Miami at 12655 South Dixie Highway, puts on show a wide variety of reptilian life from the most harmless to the most deadly. Among its attractions are snakes, tortoise, iguanas and crocodiles. A favourite with visitors is the 'milking' of snake venom which is demonstrated during every tour.

New York

AIRPORT FACILITIES
New York has three airports: John F. Kennedy International, Newark International and La Guardia.

JOHN F. KENNEDY INTERNATIONAL AIRPORT
JFK International Airport is located in the borough of Queens, some 24 km south-east of Manhattan. JFK has nine terminals and handles domestic as well as international flights. There is a free bus service linking all terminals. The International Arrivals Building handles international arrivals. All terminals have an information desk, post boxes, eating facilities, currency exchanges and duty-free. For flight information call 718 656 4520.

Bus: The Carey Bus Service (tel. 718 632 0500) runs every 30 minutes from all terminals to Grand Central Station (railways) and the Port Authority Terminal (buses). Journey time is around an hour and costs $13 one way. Gray Line operates an Air Shuttle between all JFK terminal and mid-Manhattan hotels between 23rd and 63rd Streets and costs $18 one-way.

There are also coach services to La Guardia and Newark Airports. The service to La Guardia runs every 30 minutes and costs $11. Journey time is 60 minutes. The coach can be boarded on the arrivals level of each terminal. The coach service to Newark runs every 60 minutes and takes around 90 minutes. Fare is $12. Reservations should be made at the service desk in the main lobby of the International Arrivals Building.

Subway: The long-term parking bus operates from all terminals to the Howard Beach-JFK subway station, from where you can take the 'A' train to mid-Manhattan. Journey time is around 70 minutes. A token costs $1.25.

Taxi: Taxis are available outside every terminal. During peak hours, there are uniformed taxi dispatchers outside the International Arrivals Building. Fare is usually around $40. A taxi to La Guardia takes around 30 minutes and costs about $20. A taxi to Newark takes around 75 minutes and costs about $50.

NEWARK INTERNATIONAL AIRPORT
Newark is in New Jersey, 26 km from Manhattan and deals with both international and domestic flights. Each of the three terminals has an information desk, currency exchange, eating facilities and duty free.

Rail: There is a train service to Manhattan which leaves from Penn Station in Newark. To board it, passengers can take the Airlink minibus from all terminals every 30 minutes. Fare for the minibus is $4 and for the train $1.75.

Bus: The New Jersey Transit operates a 24-hour service to the Port Authority Terminal in Manhattan every 15 minutes. The fare is $7. Olympia Trails Coach also runs between Newark and Grand Central, Penn Station, or the World Trade Centre for the same cost. Gray Line runs a shuttle bus from Newark to all mid-Manhattan hotels between 23rd and 63rd Streets at a cost of $19.

Taxi: Fares to midtown Manhattan range from $35–40 plus tolls.

LA GUARDIA AIRPORT
La Guardia is located on the East River in the borough of Queens, 13 km north-east of Manhattan. All five terminals have an information desk, eating facilities and duty-free. A post office and currency exchange facility are available in the main terminal.

Bus: Carey bus service operates every 30 minutes to Port Authority Bus Terminal in Manhattan. Journey time is around 40 minutes and the fare is about $10 one way. Gray Line's shuttle bus departs from all terminals to hotels between 23rd and 63rd Streets. Fare is $12.

Taxi: Taxis are available outside each terminal. Fare to Manhattan is around $20.

There are also regular bus services to JFK and Newark.

USEFUL ADDRESSES

Tourist offices: New York Convention and Visitors' Bureau, Two Columbus Circle (tel. 397 8222). Information on events around town, accommodation and city transport. The State Division of Tourism, 51st Floor, 1515 Broadway (tel. 827 6250).

British Consulate: 845 Third Avenue (tel. 745 0202).

Main post office: 421 Eighth Avenue between W 31 and 33 Streets.

Emergency services: Dial 911 for fire, police and ambulance.

GETTING ABOUT

New York's roads are laid out on a grid system. All numbered streets go in one direction and the avenues run at 90° to them.

Subway: The subway is the quickest method of travel if you're travelling up and down Manhattan as opposed to across. There's a flat fare of $1.25, regardless of how far you travel. For this you'll receive a token which you insert into the gate at the beginning of your journey. You can buy tokens from kiosks in each station. Maps are posted inside the stations, though they are pretty incomprehensible. The subway runs 24 hours and serves all boroughs, except Staten Island. It's quite safe in the daytime but it's probably best to avoid the subway late at night.

Bus: Buses also have a flat fare of $1.25. While they are safer and cleaner than the subway, they take longer to reach their destination, especially during rush hour. A full service runs till midnight and a reduced service after that. Exact change is required on the buses. The tokens you use on the subway are also valid.

Taxi: New York's famous yellow taxis are widely available round the city but difficult to get in bad weather or during the rush hour. Taxis are metered – the fare starts at around $1.50 with an extra $0.25 charged for every fifth of a mile. It's also a good idea to carry a map since not all of New York's cabbies know the city as well as they should. Pay with small bills and tip at least 15%.

Car hire: All the major international car hire companies operate in New York as well as many of the smaller ones, though car hire in the Big Apple is more expensive than in any other city in the USA. You're better off using public transport because parking is invariably difficult or very expensive.

SIGHTS

Situated at the mouth of the Hudson River in America's north-east, what started at a small Dutch trading post has grown to a bustling metropolis covering some 37 sq. km, accommodating a population of nearly 8 million. New York today is the largest city in America and the third largest in the world. Everything about it is striking. Visually there's nothing but skyscrapers as far as the eye can see; culturally it couldn't be more diverse, with inhabitants from every corner of the globe; and for speed, activity and excitement, there's nowhere comparable. The city never sleeps – wherever you are at whatever time, there's always something to see or do.

The Big Apple, of course, isn't without its dangers. It has a relatively high crime rate and certain parts of the city are virtual no-go areas for New Yorkers and tourists alike. Following general rules of street safety, however – such as planning your route before going anywhere and sticking to the beaten track, not carrying any loose valuables, and not drawing attention to yourself as a visitor – should guarantee safe passage around this truly fascinating city.

New York is made up of five boroughs: Manhattan, Brooklyn, The Bronx, Queens and Staten Island. Though in this section we shall concentrate on Manhattan, nonetheless there is a great deal worth visiting in the other boroughs (See **Excursions**, p.588).

Because of the enormity of New York, it's a good idea to go on one of the many sightseeing tours to get an overview of the city. The Circle Line is a well-known three-hour, 56-kilometre boat tour around Manhattan which takes you past all the different sections

of the city and brings you excellent v
the bustling New York docks.

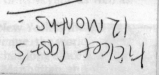

Probably the most famous attractio
STATE BUILDING on 34th Street at Fif
building at the time of its constructio
title but still affords spectacular view
rounds from two observation decks near the top. Open
9.30 a.m.–midnight. It costs $4 to go to the top.

Another good observation point is the WORLD TRADE CENTRE
on Church and Vesey streets, which is made up of twin skyscrapers
– the tallest twin buildings in the world. Observation decks at the
top afford excellent views of both the city and New York Harbour.
The nearby NEW YORK STOCK EXCHANGE has a free Visitors' Gallery overlooking the trading floor, as does the Commodity
Exchange.

A ride on the STATEN ISLAND FERRY gives you magnificent views
of the STATUE OF LIBERTY, the harbour and the city's skyline and
costs only 50 cents for a round trip. You can also take the ferry
boat to LIBERTY ISLAND where you will see the statue close up.
Next-door ELLIS ISLAND used to be New York's immigration centre.
It dealt with 12 million immigrants from 1892–1954 and has since
been turned into a museum recounting the history of immigration
to America.

Neighbourhoods in New York are like mini-states of their own.
CHINATOWN in lower Manhattan, bordered by Baxter, Worth and
Canal Streets and the Bowery, is home to the second largest
Chinese community in the US (San Francisco has the largest) –
watch out for the pagoda-like telephone booths.

GREENWICH VILLAGE stretches from 14th Street to Houston
Street in Lower Manhattan and is the city's haven of counter-
culture students, musicians, struggling artists, and New York's largest gay population. As well as the general atmosphere, usually
enhanced by street performers of one kind or another, there are
also a number of specific points of interest, such as the LIBERAL
CLUB at No 137 MacDougal Street where leftists like Emma Gold-
man and Upton Sinclair used to meet years ago. LITTLE ITALY and
SOHO (south of Houston Street) are similar in atmosphere to the
Village. SoHo is the current haunt of many city artists and there
are lofts and galleries to browse through, as well as quaint cafés,
boutiques, restaurants and off-Broadway theatres.

HARLEM is an area often avoided by visitors – once New York's
most fashionable neighbourhood, it now has a reputation for being
the slum part of town. Ghettos there certainly are and parts of
Harlem are unsafe for visitors, but it isn't without its beautiful

mansions and townhouses, as well other more specific points of interest – for example, the MALCOLM SHABAZZ MASJID MOSQUE, where black leader Malcolm X was once minister.

CENTRAL PARK has also earned its reputation. Bordered by 5th Avenue, Central Park West, 59th and 110th Streets, it's a vast 840-acre parkland which offers visitors a winter ice-skating rink, outdoor restaurants and a zoo. On the West Side opposite 72nd Street is STRAWBERRY FIELDS, a garden memorial to John Lennon. The best way to appreciate the park, however, is to spend a Saturday or Sunday there watching Americans enjoying their leisure time. In summer there are free entertainment and regular free concerts. You can also rent bicycles to tour the park. A word of warning – the park is very dangerous after dark and even for New Yorkers it's a virtual no-go area.

Surrounding the park are many of New York's finest museums, including the METROPOLITAN MUSEUM OF ART on Fifth Avenue at 82nd Street, the largest art museum in the Western hemisphere, housing a suitably grand collection of exhibits; the GUGGENHEIM MUSEUM and the MUSEUM OF MODERN ART. Another museum worth visiting is the MUSEUM OF THE AMERICAN INDIAN on Broadway at 155th Street, which contains the world's largest collection of items relating to Indian culture.

For more lively entertainment, the undisputed centre in New York is TIMES SQUARE and BROADWAY. Broadway, New York's theatreland, runs into Times Square, which is a mass of neon lights, cinemas and other forms of entertainment with a variable sleaze factor. It's another area where it's advisable not to be walking around after the streets have emptied.

As a shopper's paradise, New York is hard to beat. You can buy anything you like here, so long as you have the dollars or the plastic. FIFTH AVENUE and MADISON AVENUE are two of the best-known shopping streets with two of the top stores, Saks and Macys. SoHo and Greenwich Village are good for antique shops and boutiques. Bargain shoppers should treat themselves to a day in ORCHARD STREET on the Lower East Side, especially on Sundays when the streets are closed to traffic and goods are spread out on the pavements. Pick up a free copy of the pocket-sized *Visitors' Guide to Shopping and Services in New York City* from the New York Convention and Visitors' Bureau (see **Useful Addresses**, p.582).

ACCOMMODATION

New York City has a vast range of accommodation, but most of it is expensive and the cheaper places are often located in the sleaziest parts of town. To maximize your chances of getting a reasonably cheap, safe bed, book as far ahead as you can, regardless of the type of accommodation you're going for.

Hostels:

International Youth Hostel, 891 Amsterdam Avenue, 103rd Street (tel. 932 2300). This is a long way from the centre. Huge place but book ahead. $23 for a dorm bed.

Sugar Hill International House, 722 St Nicholas Avenue (tel. 926 7030). Cheap hostel in Harlem with dorm beds for $12 a night.

YMCA Vanderbilt, 224 East 47th Street (tel. 756 9600). A clean and very comfortable hostel in a safe neighbourhood in midtown Manhattan, with facilities including a gym and a pool. Open to men and women. Singles $46; doubles $57.

YMCA West Side, 5 West 63rd Street (tel. 787 4400). Next to Lincoln Centre, the rooms here are comfortable and well looked after. Facilities include an indoor track, 2 pools, racquet courts and a gym. Singles $42; doubles $52.

Hotels:

Carlton Arms Hotel, 160 East 25th Street (tel. 679 0680). Cheap arty hotel from around $50.

Hotel Grand Union, 34 East 32nd Street (tel. 683 5890). From $68.

Hotel Carter, 42nd Street. Massive hotel opposite Port Authority bus terminal. $60 per room. Cram as many people in as possible, but don't tell the management.

Hotel Seventeen, 225 East 17th Street (tel. 275 2845). This is a great NY scene – anything goes. Rooms start at $65 ($90 with private bath).

B&B: Bed and breakfasts in New York City are not quite the cosy B&Bs you might expect in quieter cities or more rural areas. However they give you an insight into the lives of your average New Yorker and remain a fairly cheap option. Most B&B accommodation is now arranged through agencies. If you want to book it from the UK, try Colby International at 139 Round Hey, Liverpool L28 (tel. 051 220 5848). In New York itself a good agency is The Bed and Breakfast Network of New York, 134 West 32nd Street, Suite 602, New York, NY 10001 (tel. 212 645 8134). Expect to pay $60–80 for a double.

FOOD

New York is the dining capital of the United States with over 10,000 restaurants of all kinds offering a wide range of cuisines: you name it and it will be somewhere in the city.

Like most major cities, various areas are noted for specific types of food. Little Italy, for example, is home to the city's best Italian places, while Chinatown has restaurants accounting for every part of the orient. On the Upper West Side of Manhattan along a stretch of Broadway is a selection of establishments that serve eats as varied as French, Spanish, Indian, Turkish, Thai, Jewish and Cuban. Amsterdam Avenue in the West 80s is particularly good for student restaurants and bars. Yorkville around East 86th Street between Third and Second Avenues features numerous Czech, Hungarian and German places. Greenwich Village is good for Mexican food, as well as Spanish and Italian.

Restaurants in Brooklyn and Queens are probably less flashy but even more 'the real thing' than their Manhattan counterparts, as the neighbourhoods cater for their own, be it Jewish, Italian or Greek. Of course you will never be far from a fast-food joint or a pizza place in New York, and the city has taken street food to a new level.

Carmine's, Broadway and 91st Street Family-style Italian place where you can sample a bit of everything.

Cowgirl Hall of Fame, 519 Hudson Street, Greenwich Village. Authentic Southern and Tex-Mex dishes for around $15.

El Pollo, 1746 First Avenue, between 90th and 91st. Great chicken.

Genoa, 271 Amsterdam Avenue. Cheap and usually very busy genuine Italian restaurant.

John's Pizzeria, 278 Bleecker Street. Excellent pizzeria in the Village.

Peking Duck House, 22 Mott Street. Excellent.

McDonalds, 160 Broadway. Big Macs with a touch of class. Seeing is believing.

Zabar's Deli, Broadway and 80th Street. Famous New York deli.

Fashion Café, 51 Rockefeller Plaza at 51st Street. Owned by Naomi, Claudia and Elle. Open 11 a.m.–2 p.m. Lunch for around $20.

ENTERTAINMENT

The 'city that never sleeps' has everything you could ever want – nightclubs, discos, bars, comedy clubs, singles bars – the list is endless. Cover prices can be high though ($10–15 on average) and drinks extortionate, so try and check out prices beforehand. Don't forget to take some form of ID to prove your age. For up-to-the-minute details of what's going on around the city, check with the *New Yorker*, the *Village Voice*, or the local press. Friday and Sunday editions of the *New York Times* also have good information. Alternatively, call the entertainment hotline on 360 3456.

New York has dozens of clubs. Among the current 'in' ones are Roxy, 515 West 18th Street at 10th Avenue, and Tunnel at 222 12th Avenue at 27th Street, and Webster Hall on East 11th Street. Jazz clubs are everywhere, particularly in the Village. The Blue Note at 131 West 3rd Street is a great live jazz club playing both modern and traditional.

Of an evening there are an enormous range of shows and cabaret acts performing around the city, on Broadway as well as off. Broadway shows are expensive: $45 and upwards. However, you can buy same-day half-price tickets for both Broadway and off-Broadway shows at the TKTS booths – these are located on Broadway at 47th Street, at Two World Trade Center, and in Brooklyn at the half-price ticket booth at Court and Montague Streets. The NYC Visitors' Information Center offers 'twofers' – discount theatre coupons and tickets to special exhibits which you can purchase in advance.

The Lincoln Center is the main forum for cultural events and plays host to some of the greatest names in opera, music, dance and theatre, as well as being the regular home to New York's major companies including the Metropolitan Opera, New York City Ballet and the New York Philharmonic. If their prices are out of your range, you can still enjoy a series of free performances in Lincoln Center's parks and plazas. The Music and Dance Booth in Bryant Park at 42nd Street east of Avenue of Americas also offers half-price same-day tickets for many music and dance events.

There is a huge amount of free entertainment around the city. South Street Seaport offers free summer concerts on the pier and a jazz festival in winter, as well as daily street entertainment. In summer there are free entertainment and a number of concerts in Central Park. Big names like the New York Philharmonic, the Shakespeare Festival and the Metropolitan Opera put on free performances in the parks of all five New York boroughs.

EXCURSIONS

Just getting to BROOKLYN HEIGHTS can be a pleasure in itself as you cross the famous BROOKLYN BRIDGE. Brooklyn Heights itself is full of old-world charm and calmer than the more frenetic Manhattan. Its brownstone rowhouses have changed little since its emergence in the 18th century.

A trip to CONEY ISLAND, separated from the rest of Brooklyn by a creek, offers a strange day out in a place which, at the turn of the century, attracted millions of New Yorkers with some of the period's most thrilling rides and amusement arcades, but it is now run down and neglected. To get there takes just the price of the subway. Today Coney Island comprises a beach, a boardwalk dotted with hot-dog and clam bars and miles of near-derelict amusement parks, including three big dippers.

LONG ISLAND, on the other hand, is a thriving island with areas of great scenic beauty and many fine beaches where New Yorkers still like to take their holidays. The western end is the suburban area of Queens and Brooklyn, while the beaches are at the eastern end. FIRE ISLAND, a 65-kilometre strip of sand dunes and barrier beach, can be reached by road, rail or ferry. The island has no roads so the local population get around on foot or by bike. There are superb facilities for hiking, cycling and swimming. Some 48 km from New York on Long Island is JONES BEACH, the most popular beach with New Yorkers. Officially Jones Beach State Park, it covers some 2,500 acres worth of woods and beach area. There's room for over 100,000 swimmers, either in the ocean or in salt-water pools, as well as a three-kilometre boardwalk, good fishing and restaurants. If you want to get off the beach for a while, near Oyster Bay is SAGAMORE HILL, the home of President Theodore Roosevelt, while the Museums at Stony Brook include displays of history, art and science as well as a Fine Arts Centre.

The HUDSON VALLEY was settles by early colonialists on their way to the heart of North America and most of thge valley's attractions are within 1–3 hours of Manhattan. The best way to see the sights is by boat – catch one of the many pleasure craft and ferries that ply up and down the Hudson. Among the sights are the opulent Vanderbilt mansion at Staatsburg; the arts and entertainment complexes around Catskill; and the military academy at West Point. George Washington's HQ during the war of Independence can be visited in Northburgh, as can the home of Franklin D. Roosevelt at Hyde Park, which contains a library and museum dedicated to FDR. The home itself is just as it was at the time of his death in 1945.

San Francisco

AIRPORT FACILITIES

San Francisco International Airport is 26 km from the city's downtown area. The airport is made up of three buildings: the North (N), South (S) and International (INT) Terminals, each interconnected by convenient passageways as well as a complimentary shuttle bus service. All terminals have post boxes and stamp machines, information desks, currency exchange and eating facilities. Duty-free is available in the International Terminal. For further information, ring 761 0800.

CITY LINKS
Bus: There are two main bus services operating from the airport to downtown San Francisco. For a $7 fare, the SFO Airporter runs every 20 minutes to various downtown points. The San Trans bus service also operates between the airport and downtown. The 7B and 7F lines go to the city and buses run every 30 minutes. Fares go up to $1.25 depending on the distance travelled, and exact change is required.
Taxi: Taxis to San Francisco cost around $30. Find them at cab stands (identified by a yellow-striped pillar) on the centre island of the lower level roadway in front of all terminals. Only use taxis which display the gold San Francisco International Airport medallion.

USEFUL ADDRESSES
Tourist office: San Francisco Visitor Information Center, Lower Level Hallidie Plaza, Market and Powell Streets (tel. 391 2000). Open Mon.–Fri. 9 a.m.–5.30 p.m.; Sat. 9 a.m.–3 p.m.; Sun. 10 a.m.–2 p.m.
Post office: 7th and Mission Streets.
British Consulate: 1 Sansome Street (tel. 981 3030).
Emergency services: Dial 911 for police, fire or ambulance.

GETTING ABOUT
The cheapest method of getting around the city is on foot – the centre is compact enough to walk to most places. If the hills are too much for you, take a bus, cable car or tram (street car); all operate a fairly extensive network. Have the exact change ready. Taxis must be booked by phone. All the major national car rental firms operate in the city and rental desks can often be found at major hotels.

For trips further afield, the Bay Area Rapid Transit underground and overground rail system links the city with surrounding communities.

SIGHTS
As the city whose Golden Gate has been the gateway to America for travellers since the early 19th century, San Francisco today is home to a population taken from almost every corner of the earth, and consequently it boasts a rich and diverse culture. Whether you're walking through Chinatown or Little Italy, San Francisco's cosmopolitan atmosphere is evident. Its reputation as the gay capital of the world adds yet another dimension to the city's character. After the great earthquake of 1906 which left half the city razed

to the ground, San Francisco was rebuilt around its remains. As a result, the steep hills on which the city is built today show an attractive blend of old and new, from the famous cable cars and Victorian-style 19th-century residences to the fashionable Japan Center and celebrated Golden Gate Bridge.

San Francisco enjoys cool summers and warm winters. Sightseeing can be a full-time occupation for two or three days. Riding the famous cable cars is not only a convenient way of touring the downtown sights, but can also be an exhilarating way of getting around, particularly if you stand on the rear platforms. The CABLE CAR BARN MUSEUM, at the corner of Mason and Washington Streets, contains the huge steel cables and machinery that power the cable cars.

Another museum which houses treasures from old 'Frisco is the SAN FRANCISCO MARITIME MUSEUM. The main building is in Aquatic Park at the foot of Polk Street, but the exhibits stretch to Pier 43, where the *Balclutha* – one of the great sailing ships and the last survivor of the Cape Horn fleet – is docked. Also of nautical interest is the HYDE STREET PIER, where four restored ships from America's seafaring past are docked: a wooden steamer, a side-wheel ferry boat, a work scow and a three-masted schooner.

FISHERMAN'S WHARF at the foot of Taylor Street is another Bay-side attraction. As the docking area for local fishing boats, it has a wealth of restaurants, fish markets and pavement stalls selling assorted seafood. Nearby is the CANNERY, which gets its name from its former role as a fruit cannery. Now converted into a complex of art galleries, speciality shops and restaurants, it's also a popular area with street musicians and performers. PIER 39 is another major shopping and restaurant complex, whose design reflects the San Francisco of the last century and offers excellent views of the city and its surrounds. You can also enjoy views over the Bay and city from GHIRARDELLI SQUARE, a former chocolate factory which has been converted to a Victorian-style deluxe shopping and restaurant centre. Ghiradelli's Ice Cream Parlor sells legendary ice-cream sundaes.

To sample the cultural as well as the cosmopolitan aspects of San Franciscan life, wander through the city's Chinatown, Little Italy and Japantown. CHINATOWN houses the largest Chinese community outside Asia and its sights and people endow it with a truly authentic atmosphere. As well as the Buddhist temples and endless selection of fine Chinese restaurants, points of interest include the CHINATOWN WAX MUSEUM, the CHINESE CULTURE CENTER and the CHINESE HISTORICAL SOCIETY OF AMERICA. The focal point of JAPANTOWN is the JAPAN CENTER – three-square blocks in size, it houses a complex of shops, coffee houses, a Japanese steam bath, tempura bars and Oriental gardens. Also found here is the PEACE PLAZA, home to colourful festivals such as the spring Cherry Blossom Festival and the Aki Matsuri Festival in the autumn. LITTLE ITALY is located at North Beach and is worth a visit, if not for its pavement cafés and restaurants, then for its off-Broadway theatres, its nightclubs and numerous other forms of entertainment.

Frisco is also home to one of America's finest city parks – the GOLDEN GATE PARK. Besides its beautiful lakes, the exquisite Japanese Tea Garden, botanical gardens and paddock fields with herds of buffalo, the park also contains some fine museums, including the MORRISON PLANETARIUM, the ASIAN ART MUSEUM and the CALIFORNIA ACADEMY OF SCIENCES. Other museums around the city include the SAN FRANCISCO MUSEUM OF MODERN ART in the Civic Center at Van Ness Avenue, the OLD MINT, displaying coins and other related exhibits, and the California Palace of the LEGION OF HONOR at Lincoln Park, which houses various forms of French art.

ACCOMMODATION
Hostels:
San Francisco International Hostel (IYHF), Building 240, Fort Mason (tel. 771 7277). $15.

The International Network Globe Hostel, 10 Hallam Place (tel. 431 0540). $17.

Youth Hostel Central, 116 Turk Street (tel. 346 7835). $10 for dorm beds.

European Guest House, 763 Minna Street (tel. 861 6634). $12.

San Francisco International Student Center, 1188 Folsom Street (tel. 641 1411). From $15.

Grand Central, corner of 10th and Market Streets. From $12.

YMCA, 220 Golden Gate Avenue (tel. 885 0460). Singles from $26; doubles from $38.

YMCA Chinatown, 855 Sacramento Street (tel. 982 4412). Men over 18 only. From $26.50.

Hotels/motels:
Pensione International, 875 Post Street (tel. 775 3344). Clean central guest house with complimentary breakfast.

Pension San Francisco, 1668 Market Street (tel. 964 1271). Central location with morning coffee included.

The Ansonia Hotel, 711 Post Street (tel. 673 2670). B&B with singles from $35; doubles from $45.

Temple Hotel, 469 Pine Street (tel. 781 2565). From $30.
B&B: To arrange accommodation from the UK, try Colby International at 139 Round Hey, Liverpool L28 (tel. 051 220 5848).

FOOD

On the food front, it is hard to find a national cuisine not represented in San Francisco. Chinatown is obviously the place to go for Chinese food; North Beach is home to innumerable Italian restaurants; and for seafood it's best to head for Fisherman's Wharf. French and Japanese cuisine are also well represented – Japantown is the centre for the latter. There are numerous restaurants which feature local specialities – these include Crab Louis, abalone steak, crusty sourdough bread, Bay shrimp and artichoke dishes. Celebrated Californian wines are also a feature of San Franciscan restaurants.

Yamoto, 717 California Street (tel. 397 3456). Good Japanese restaurant with friendly service.

Scoma's, Pier 47 (foot of Jones Street) (tel. 771 4383). Fine seafood.

Gaylord, Ghiradelli Square (tel. 771 882). Indian cuisine with good views of the Bay.

The Hunan, 924 Sansome Street. Great Chinese food.

Trader Vic's, 20 Cosmo Place (tel. 776 2232). Renowned for superb Polynesian dishes.

Tommaso's, 1042 Kearny Street (tel. 398 9696). Pizzas worth waiting for.

Brandy Ho's, 217 Columbus Avenue (tel. 788 7527). Excellent Hunan food.

ENTERTAINMENT

San Francisco has a very lively after-dark entertainment scene – from bars to nightclubs hosting everything from fruit machines to big-name live entertainment. The Firehouse at 3160 16th Street is one of the city's most popular clubs, while the I-Beam at 1748 Haight Street is a well-known live music venue. There's also a fine theatre and concert scene. The Louise M. Davies Symphony Hall at 201 Van Ness Avenue (tel. 431 5400) is home to the San Francisco Symphony; the War Memorial Opera House on the same street (tel. 864 3330) plays host to both the San Francisco Opera Association and the San Francisco Ballet.

For listings pick up the free weekly *Bay Guardian*. The entertainment sections of the dailies also offer details of events.

EXCURSIONS

ALCATRAZ ISLAND is located in San Francisco Bay off the Fisherman's Wharf area. The island's prison is one of the country's leading tourist attractions. Once home to notorious criminals such as Al Capone and 'Machine Gun' Kelly, the penitentiary was closed down in 1963 but today its forbidding corridors and eerie cells are open to the public. To get to the 'Rock', take the round-trip ferry service which departs from Pier 41.

SAUSALITO is a small town 16 km north of San Francisco. From its bygone days as a fishing village, it has become home to a diverse range of fine restaurants, antique shops and art galleries. The local population consists mainly of artists, sculptors and writers, most of whom gather in the No Name Bar. The town has a quaint feel and relaxing atmosphere, as well as a spectacular view of the San Francisco skyline.

About 24 km north-west of the city, the MUIR WOODS are a magnificent collection of towering redwood trees which are centuries old. Walking trails are marked out to take you through some spectacular natural sights.

San Francisco is also in close proximity to some of America's greatest tourist attractions and most popular National Parks. Within striking distance of the city by car are the YOSEMITE and LASSEN VOLCANIC NATIONAL PARKS, and LAKE TAHOE, all showing California at its most beautiful. Yosemite is home to deep valleys, mountain streams, trees, waterfalls and mountain peaks; Lassen Volcanic National Park has hot springs and cold lakes stocked with German brown trout; and Lake Tahoe with its fine beaches and excellent countryside is one of the USA's most celebrated spectacles. All these attractions offer extensive camping facilities to visitors. Book ahead in July/August for the most popular campsites, especially those in Yosemite.

Hawaii

VITAL STATISTICS

Hawaii has a population of around a million and its capital is Honolulu. Having become America's 50th state in 1959, it is now well and truly integrated into the United States and most of its vital statistics are the same. Even though Hawaii is made up of several strong ethnic groups — Japanese, Chinese and Filipinos as well as native Hawaiians — English (or Pidgin) is the local language.

In terms of climate, the lack of seasonal variation makes Hawaii's climate close to perfect. The warmest months of August and September have an average temperature of 27°C while the 'coldest' month of February averages 22°C. Rainfall at the coast is about 51 centimetres annually, but the mountains receive up to 470 centimetres. Waialeale, the highest mountain on the island of Kauai, can be the wettest place on earth with a rainfall of 1.143 metres a year. The islands are consistently bathed with gentle trade-wind breezes which bring a refreshing cool to the heat of the day.

INTERNAL TRAVEL
Air: Aeroplane is the best means of hopping between the islands in terms of speed and convenience. Flights are reasonably cheap. Contact Hawaiian Airlines on 537 5100. Some travel agencies sell inter-island coupon books which work out less expensive than single flights purchased individually.
Local transport: There is a good bus service on Oahu and a skeleton service on Hawaii (Big Island) but public transport is virtually non-existent on other islands. Bicycles, cars and mopeds are widely available for rent.

ACCOMMODATION
Hawaii is notorious for its high-priced accommodation, though out of peak season (mid-December to the end of April) you are likely to find that prices fall. The cheapest accommodation is provided by hostels and YMCAs, though B&Bs are now a growing concern. Camping in state parks is popular and strictly controlled. You can also stay in cabins in the parks if you reserve in advance.

FOOD
The blend of cultures that now make up Hawaii State mean that you can enjoy a fine mixture of Japanese, Filipino, Chinese and more, together with the usual fast-food options. Look out for dishes featuring freshly caught fish and delicious fruits such as guava. On Hawaii (Big Island) macadamia nuts and Kona coffee are particular specialities. Traditional Hawaiian luaus may not be quite the feasts they once were but are still worth a visit. The commercial ones tend to be stingier and less authentic than the charitable or church luaus. If you are visiting one of the islands other than Honolulu, the luaus will be better value there.

WHERE TO GO FOR WHAT
Hawaii State is made up of a group of islands – some are well-developed and populated; others are remote. The best-known island is OAHU, which, with Hawaii's capital city of HONOLULU, is the state's communications, transport and tourist centre. Although

it is believed that Oahu was populated in AD 1000 by Polynesians from Tahiti, or even before that by the Marquesas Islanders, Captain James Cook first sighted Oahu in 1778 and introduced the islands to the Western world. He actually landed on Kauai, north-west of Oahu, and named the archipelago the Sandwich Islands. It was on the island of Hawaii (Big Island), the largest and furthest south of the string, that Cook was slain in a fight with the Hawaiians in 1779. King Kamehameha I, from the island of Hawaii, established the kingdom by conquering the other islands one by one, except Kauai which was peacefully ceded later. The Kingdom of Hawaii survived until 1893 when a bloodless revolution led to the formation of a provisional government and, in 1898, annexation by the USA.

KAUAI, the 'Garden Island', offers magnificent scenery and lush vegetation, waterfalls, canyons and valleys. Notable spots include the Waimea Canyon, the 'hidden' valley of Kalalau, Hanalei Bay, Wailua River, Nawiliwili Bay and Poipu Beach. Colourful tropical plants and flowers make this island quite spectacular. Helicopter excursions are available to show you some of the more inaccessible spots.

MOLOKAI, the 'Friendly Isle', is only just waking up to tourism. Consequently the 6,500 inhabitants are still extremely friendly towards visitors and it's a lovely place for a day-trip. Pineapple plantations, ranching and a surprising African Game Reserve take up most of the island. Try the delicious Molokai bread while you are there.

LANAI, once the centre of pineapple growing, is also relatively undeveloped and offers relaxing opportunities for hiking, deep-sea fishing and relaxation. MAUI, the 'Valley Isle', boasts the largest dormant volcano crater in the world – HALEAKALA – a spectacular sight. Lahaina, an old whaling town, was Hawaii's capital before 1845. The Kaanapali resort area, Hana village and the Iao Valley in the west Maki Mountains are also spots worth visiting.

HAWAII is the 'Big Island', a place of many contrasts, from snow-clad MAUNA KEA (4,139 metres) to the KA'U DESERT. Tropical forests and splendid waterfalls are just some of the natural phenomena to be seen. Sugar, coffee, cattle and macadamia nuts are grown on the island. Good places to visit are the Hawaii Volcanoes National Park, Kealakekua Bay, Kailua-Kona, Kawaihae, Parker Ranch and Waipo Valley, once the home of the Hawaiian kings with a long black volcanic beach.

KAHOOLAWE ISLAND is a low barren uninhabited place. NIHAU ISLAND has a privately owned ranch. Inhabitants there speak Hawaiian and preserve many of the cultural traditions of Hawaii.

To stay on any of the other islands for more than a day you should book accommodation in advance.

FURTHER INFORMATION

Hawaii Visitors' Bureau, Waikiki Business Plaza, 2270 Kalakaua Avenue, 8th Floor, Suite 800, Honolulu HI 96815 (tel. 808 923 1811).

The United States Travel and Tourism Administration, PO Box 1EN, London W1A 1EN.

Background reading: *Let's Go: California and Hawaii* (Pan Books).

Honolulu

AIRPORT FACILITIES
Honolulu International Airport, just 10 km from Honolulu City, caters for Hawaii State's foreign and domestic overseas flights plus inter-island travel. It has one international terminal divided into Arrivals (ground level) and Departures (second level) with the Inter-Island Terminals on either side. Both Arrivals and Departures have information desks and currency exchange, together with food outlets. The Departures level also has shops and duty-free facilities.

CITY LINKS
Airport buses are available to the city and are preferable to the rather expensive taxicabs. Privately operated motorcoach transportation goes from the airport to Waikiki with stops at the major hotels. Car rental companies based at the airport provide a transport alternative.

USEFUL ADDRESSES
Tourist offices: Hawaii Visitors' Bureau, Waikiki Business Plaza, 8th Floor, 2270 Kalakaua Avenue, Suite 800 (tel. 923 1811). The State Visitor Information Service has booths at the major Hawaiian airports.
Main post office: 3600 Aolele Street, Honolulu (tel. 423 3990).
Emergency services: Dial 911 for police, fire or ambulance.

GETTING ABOUT
As tourism is the big money-maker in Honolulu, transport is laid on to every conceivable corner.
Bus: Mass Transit Lines buses (tel. 848 5555) run an extensive network of routes across the city. They all show route numbers

and destinations, and the driver will give you a free transfer ticket for another route should you wish to change buses. 'The Bus', as these bright yellow vehicles are known, will not accommodate luggage.

Taxi: These are plentiful but quite expensive. Random cruising is not allowed in Honolulu so you must phone for a taxi instead of being able to hail one in the street. Recommended companies are Charley's Taxi (tel. 622 4177) and Sida (tel. 836 0011).

Car hire: Available from the airport or numerous places on Kalakaua Avenue, the main street in Waikiki.

SIGHTS

Capital of the Hawaiian Islands since King Kamehameha III made it his residence in 1845, Honolulu is a thriving modern metropolis and one of the United States' most popular holiday resorts. It is a harbour city situated on the south-east coast of Oahu, one of the eight main islands which make up Hawaii State. Downtown Honolulu, with its multi-storey office and apartment blocks, is Hawaii's financial centre where nearly every Hawaiian corporation has an office.

A mere 5 km down the coast is WAIKIKI, one of the world's most famous beach resorts, lined with high-rise hotels where tourists come to see and be seen. Near Waikiki, DIAMOND HEAD is an extinct volcanic crater which forms an outstanding coastal landmark and has a lighthouse at the foot of its 230-metre peak. It is also a great spot for viewing the spectacular windsurfing and wave riding. For more leisurely pursuits, nearby KAPIOLANI PARK has tennis courts, softball diamonds, jogging parks and areas for bowling, football, rugby and polo all set amongst lawns and shade trees. Free Sunday afternoon concerts are given at an outdoor bandstand, while the Waikiki Shell, an outdoor amphitheatre, hosts the Kodak Hula Show.

The NATIONAL CEMETERY OF THE PACIFIC is at Puowaina Drive (via Pali Highway turnoff). Also known as 'Punchbowl', this volcanic crater has become a memorial for US war casualties. Look for the World War II and Korean battle-map murals, the grave of Ernie Pyles (a famous war correspondent) and a terraced shrine for the 'Courts of the Missing'. A viewpoint looks out over the city and the shoreline of Honolulu.

IOLANI PALACE, on the corner of King and Richards Streets, near downtown Honolulu Civic Center, is an Italian Renaissance-style royal palace (the USA's only one) completed in 1882 for King Kalakaua. It was used by Hawaii's government until 1969 and has since been restored to its 1880 style. Iolani Barracks was the former home of the Royal Household Guards and Royal Hawaiian Band concerts are now performed here each Friday noon.

EMMA'S SUMMER PALACE at 2913 Pali Highway was the home of King Kamehameha IV's widow and is fully furnished with displays of her treasures. The KAWAIAHAO CHURCH, 957 Punchbowl Street (near the Civic Center) is built of coral and steeped in Hawaiian regal splendour and history. Sunday morning services are followed by conducted tours.

On Pier 9 in downtown Honolulu, the ALOHA TOWER, a harbourside landmark built in 1926, is now dwarfed by skyscrapers but used to be the tallest building in Honolulu. An observation balcony is open to the public daily. On Pier 5 near Aloha Tower, *Falls of Clyde* is a four-masted, square-rigged ship. Built in Scotland in 1878, it sailed the Hawaiian waters and is now used as a maritime museum.

The FOSTER BOTANIC GARDENS at 180 North Vineyard Boulevard are open daily for picnicking or wandering. On view is a collection of rare plants native to the tropics including a wide variety of palm trees and a wild orchid garden. Free tours are offered. The HONOLULU ZOO is at 151 Kapahulu Avenue in Kapiolani Park, Waikiki.

In the Manoa Valley stands the UNIVERSITY OF HAWAII campus with several distinctive buildings including an Oriental teahouse and garden. Tours of the East-West Center are given free during the week, starting from Jefferson Hall.

Hawaii is rich in museums and art galleries. ALICE COOKE SPALD-ING HOUSE at 2411 Makiki Heights Drive, is full of Asian decorative arts, notably the Michener collection of ancient Japanese woodblock prints. BISHOP MUSEUM at 1355 Kalihi Street has Pacific arts and crafts, Hawaiian royal artefacts and natural history, arts and science displays. The HONOLULU ACADEMY OF ARTS at 900 South Beretania Street exhibits Asian, European, American and Pacific art. The TENNANT ART FOUNDATION GALLERY at 203 Prospect Street shows the works of one of Hawaii's most respected artists, Madge Tennant.

ACCOMMODATION
As one would expect of a vast holiday destination, there is a great diversity of accommodation in Honolulu, though real budget accommodation is relatively scarce and you should book as far ahead as possible.

Hale Aloha (IYHF), 2417 Prince Edward Street (tel. 926 8313). 3-night stay only. From $15. Close to the beach.

Honolulu International Hostel (IYHF), 2323A Seaview Avenue (tel. 946 0591). From $12.

Outrigger East, 150 Kaiulani Avenue, Waikiki (tel. 922 5353). Good accommodation in a handy spot, on the market-place one street away from the beach.

Interclub Waikiki, 2413 Kuhio Avenue (tel. 924 2636). From $15.

Arnott's Lodge and Hiking Adventures Hostel, 98 Apapane Road (tel. 969 7097). Dorms start at $15. Singles/doubles: $26/$36.

FOOD
Hawaiian restaurants serving the local cuisine are actually in the minority in Honolulu – there are so many other nationalities to vie with. Korean, Filipino, German, French, Thai, Mexican, Greek, Indian and Japanese restaurants abound and it's quite common to find yourself eating a cosmopolitan array of dishes within one meal. For cheap eats head for the International Food Court in Waikiki's International Market Place or the Food Market in the Ala Moana Center.

Ono Hawaiian Foods, 726 Kapahulu Avenue. Usually crowded out by locals.

Kanraku Tea House, 750 Kohou Street in Kalihi. Japanese in style and atmosphere – eat sitting cross-legged on the floor.

Perry's Smorgy, 2830 Kuhio Avenue (tel. 926 0184). Full meals from $5.

ENTERTAINMENT
The entertainment capital of the Pacific must surely be the Waikiki with the usual clubs and discos. The Wave at 1877 Kakakaua Avenue (tel. 941 0242) puts on regular live music. The Rose and Crown in King's Village (tel. 923 5833) has a good 'pub' atmosphere. Tourist-oriented typical Polynesian shows are slick and flashy productions with the verve and fire of Tonga, Fiji or Tahiti. The Tahiti Polynesian Revue in Moana's Banyan Court has plenty of grass skirts and war chants. Hawaiian music and dancing is softer, more gentle and melodious. For listings read the *Waikiki Beach Press*, *Hawaii Tourist News*, *Snooper*, *Where* or *This Week*. The daily newspapers will also have entertainment pages.

EXCURSIONS
Getting away from the bustle of city and beach is very quick and easy here. Rural areas and remote beaches on Oahu are only a short drive away. In fact, a circuit tour of the whole island can be

accomplished in one day. One of Hawaii's most famous spots is PEARL HARBOR, whose 1941 bombing by the Japanese finally brought the US into World War II. The USS ARIZONA MEMORIAL is built over the sunken battleship *Arizona* in which more than 1,000 US servicemen died during the attack. Other major sights include BYODO-IN TEMPLE in the Valley of the Temples on Kahekili Highway and the SEA LIFE PARK (Makapuu Point). The magnificent HANAUMA BAY was formed when one of the walls of Koko Head Crater was swept away by the sea and is a beautiful spot for snorkelling. The POLYNESIAN CULTURAL CENTER in Laie is a recreated village representing the indigenous cultures of the peoples of the Pacific, including those of Samoa, Hawaii, Fiji, Tonga and Tahiti, and incorporating live displays.

ANTIGUA AND BARBUDA

VITAL STATISTICS
Red tape: All visitors to Antigua and Barbuda must have a return or onward air ticket. Travellers from the EC, America and Canada, whose stay will not exceed six months, can enter using any of the following forms of identification: a valid passport, British Visitors Passport, birth certificate, voter's registration card, Citizenship Card or Nationalization Certificate. All other nationalities should check their individual passport/visa requirements.
Customs: Arriving passengers are allowed 200 cigarettes or 50 cigars or 250 g tobacco, 1 l alcohol and a small quantity of perfume for personal use.
Health: No mandatory vaccinations. Health insurance is recommended.
Language: English is the official language.
Population: 75,000; the majority are of African descent, the rest being a mix of British, Lebanese, Syrian and Portuguese.
Capital: St John's, population 66,000.
Political system: Independent democracy. The system of government is modelled on the British parliamentary system. Elections are held every five years.
Religion: A wide variety of Christian denominations: Methodist, Moravian, Anglican, Roman Catholic. Plus a scattering of Rastafarian.
Time: Four hours behind GMT in winter, five hours behind in summer.
Money: The currency is the Eastern Caribbean dollar (EC$),

divided into 100 cents. Coins: 1, 2, 5, 10, 25 and 50 cents, EC$1. Notes: EC$1, EC$5, EC$10, EC$20 and EC$100. The exchange rate is tied to the US dollar; rates fluctuate, but as a rule £1 = EC$3.91.

US dollar traveller's cheques are widely accepted; sterling and US dollars can be changed at banks in St John's, in hotels and larger shops. Most credit cards are accepted.

Tax: There's a US$12/EC$30 Departure Tax; a 7% Government Tax on hotel accommodation, and hotels add a 10% tax in lieu of tipping.

Communication: A full national and international direct dialling service is in operation. Public phones are easily found in built-up areas, as are international fax/telex services. A full postal service is in operation.

Electricity: 220/110v AC/60Hz. American-style plugs.

Business hours: BANKS: Mon.–Thurs. 8 a.m.–12 p.m.; Fri. 8 a.m.–1 p.m. and 3–5 p.m.

POST OFFICES: Mon.–Fri. 8 a.m.–12 p.m. and 1 p.m.–4 p.m.

SHOPS: Mon.–Fri. 8.30 a.m.–12 p.m. and 1p.m.–4 p.m. Early closing for shops is mainly on Thursday – some shut on Saturday.

OFFICES: Mon.–Fri. 8 a.m.–12 p.m. and 1p.m.–4 p.m.

Holidays: 1 January; March/April (Good Friday and Easter Monday); first Monday in May (Labour Day); first Monday in June (Whit Monday); 16 June (Queen's Birthday); August (Carnival – dates vary); 1 November (Independence Day); 25 and 26 December.

Climate: Antigua's climate is a very pleasant tropical one, and stays warm and relatively dry year round. Temperatures range from between an average of 24°C in January/February to 28°C degrees in August/September. There is a relatively low humidity; average annual rainfall is 114 cm, with November having the most rainy days.

DO'S AND DON'TS

Few locals seem to resent the explosion of tourism in their fragile homelands, and they are especially accommodating if visitors make an effort to integrate. Remember, no matter how sexy the calypso lyrics or how provocative the dancing, there's also a prim side to this free and easy world. Skimpy clothing away from the beach is not appreciated, and in the evening a shirt and trousers or a blouse and skirt is the standard garb.

There are hustlers and peddlers – selling anything from trashy trinkets to ganja – but the most persistent stick to Jamaica, where crime is at its worst.

WHERE TO GO FOR WHAT

Antigua was discovered in 1493 by Columbus. Although he didn't land, he did find time to name the island – after Santa Maria la Antigua of Seville. It wasn't for another 130 years, however – when a group of Englishmen sailed from the Caribbean island of ST KITTS – that Antigua was claimed for Great Britain, under whose control it has remained to the present day (bar 1966, when it came under French command).

Today, Antigua still has much to offer the visitor, not least a beauty and charm shared by the Antiguans themselves. The largest of the Caribbean's Leeward islands, it's a little over 160 sq. km and sits due north of Guadelupe – south and east of its smaller neighbours Barbuda and Redonda. Known as the 'island with a beach for every day of the year' – a phrase you will become all too familiar with – Antigua does indeed have a myriad of secluded bays and hidden inlets to explore. Although the culture of the island, like that of many others in the Caribbean, is tinged with more than a hint of Britishness, there's little of the stress and rush of modern Western living. It's an infectious atmosphere that sways with the rhythm of calypso and limbo, so who cares if dinner is a little long in arriving? The countryside mixes open grazing land with sugar cane and pineapple fields, and tropical rain forest.

Running along the south-west coast, and finishing inland near the centre of the island, close to the Village of Sweets, runs the famous FIG TREE DRIVE. This picturesque routeway is overgrown with lush vegetation such as wild mango and banana trees. On the east side of Antigua, near the road for Half Moon Bay, sits POT WORKS DAM, a huge tranquil lake set in exquisite surroundings. Near the villages of PARES and PARHAM are the ruins of the first major sugar plantation (dated 1674) and Parham Church which, though partially destroyed by the 1843 earthquake, is still regarded as the finest church in the West Indies.

NELSON'S DOCKYARD, named after the admiral himself – he once served here – contains Admiral House, a nautical museum, and the restored officers' quarters. Clarence House, a splendid Georgian-style royal residence (Antiguan home of Prince William Henry later King William IV), is built half-way up the hill towards SHIRLEY HEIGHTS, which afford spectacular views over Nelson's Dockyard and English and Falmouth Harbours.

Antigua has a distant Indian heritage and, at INDIAN TOWN, a national park in the north-east, can be seen the DEVIL'S BRIDGE.

This natural arch has been carved out over the centuries by crashing Atlantic breakers, and nearby blowholes spout surf and froth high into the air. South of St John's are the MEGALITHS of Green Castle Hill. Their origin is disputed: modern interpretations regard them as nothing more magical than distinctive geological formations, but legend has it that these were built by the Indians in honour of the Gods of the Sun and Moon. BETTY'S HOPE ESTATE – a pioneer sugar plantation currently under restoration – is a throwback to the colonial days and sits amid the splendour of the island's interior.

BARBUDA – about 44 km north-east of Antigua – is renowned for its pink sand beaches, many of which are deserted because the bulk of the 1,200 inhabitants live in the small capital, CODRINGTON.

INTERNAL TRAVEL
Bus: There's no set schedule; in fact the whole service is very casual – not to say patchy. Give it a go though, it's the best way to meet Antigua face to face. There is also a network of minibuses which operate around St Johns.

Taxi: A far more reliable option. Rates are fixed, there are no metered journeys. Taxis are plentiful and they're always available at the airport, the deepwater harbour, St John's, and at most hotels. A new policy means that all taxi drivers are well versed in local knowledge and can act as guides.

Car hire: One of the best methods of getting round the island. There are several local and international hire companies in operation across the island, including the airport. Ask the Tourist Office if you need additional advice. Expect to pay upwards of US$50 a day. For a EC$50, a temporary local driver's permit will be issued on presentation of your own licence. Driving is on the left.

Bicycles: these can generally be hired from hotels.

ACCOMMODATION
There are more than forty hotels on Antigua and Barbuda – from the basic-but-friendly to the extravagantly luxurious. The winter season – December to April – is substantially more expensive. The price escalation varies with different hotels, but expect to pay between 30–65% more. Cheap accommodation can be found in budget hotels, guest houses and beach apartments.

FOOD
Keep an eye out for the unusual, and give it a try: Salt fish, lobster and red snapper, suckling pigs, fresh chicken and anything cooked over a charcoal grill will be delicious. Curries are another popular island option. International menus from places as distant and

diverse as France, Italy and China are also available. Locally made American-style ice cream should round off any meal perfectly. Quench your thirst with a chilled fruit juice, or sip coconut milk straight from the husk. For something stronger, try Antiguan red and white rums – or mix them with juice and spices for a rum punch.

BUDGETING
It's worth knowing that local and imported rum are sold at the same price. Expect a small round of drinks to set you back £5–6. Restaurants serving local Antiguan food are the cheapest, where a meal will cost upwards of £7. At fast-food joints – Kentucky Fried Chicken and the like – expect to pay £3–4. Dining out in hotels is more expensive.

FURTHER INFORMATION

Antigua and Barbuda Tourist Office, 15 Thayer Street, London W1M 5LD (Tel. 0171 486 7073).
Background reading: *The Caribbean*, by James Henderson (Cadogan Guides), *Caribbean Islands Handbook*, ed. Ben Box and Sarah Cameron (Trade and Travel Publications), *A Little Bit of Paradise* (Hansib Publishing Ltd, Hertfordshire, UK), and *Antigua and Barbuda – Heart of Caribbean* (Macmillan Publishers, Basingstoke, UK).

St John's

AIRPORT FACILITIES
V. C. Bird International Airport is about 7 km from Antigua's capital, St John's, and handles direct flights to and from several major international airports worldwide. There is one terminal. Standard facilities are available, including an information desk, bank and foreign exchange services, a hotel reservations counter, restaurant and bars, a post office, left-luggage and lost-property counters, duty-free shops (though stock is limited), a meeting point, and a car rental desk.

Airport Information: check-in times are 120 minutes before international flights, 60 minutes prior to domestic/regional flights. A departure tax of US$10/EC$26 is levied on adults staying longer than 24 hours.

CITY LINKS
Taxis are the easiest and most reliable form of transport from the airport to anywhere on the island. Journeys aren't metered, the

rates are fixed. Average airport fares, include US$10 to St John's US$10; US$20 to Nelson's Dockyard.

USEFUL ADDRESSES
Tourist office: Antigua-Barbuda Department of Tourism, corner of Long and Thames Streets, St John's, Antigua (tel. 462 0480).
Main post office: corner of High and Long Streets, St John's.
British High Commission: Price Waterhouse Building, Factory Road (tel. 462 0008).

SIGHTS
ST JOHN'S, Antigua's capital, is situated in the north-west of the island. The city's museum, itself a historic building, houses a fascinating and varied collection of exhibits including Arawak Indian artefacts, relics of plantation slavery, early primitive tools and even working steam engines. ST JOHN'S CATHEDRAL is a famous tourist landmark not only for its unusual architecture but also on account of its chequered history. The building's interior is encased in pitch pine, intended to secure it against hurricanes and earthquakes, and the figures of St John the Baptist and St John the Divine are said to have been plundered from one of Napoleon's ships. Free admission.

The bustling open-air public market is also worth a visit for its colour and vast array of foods. Further exotic appeal, albeit on a fairly small scale, is created by the Botanical Gardens. FORT JAMES, at the entrance of St John's Harbour, is of historic interest as are many of the island's other fortifications; notably FORT GEORGE, now a picturesque set of ruins and, earliest of them all, FORT BARRINGTON, which is situated on Goat Hill guarding the mouth of DEEP BAY.

Back in the town centre, potter around St John's local handicraft centre, and the Industrial School for the Blind, which produces delicate straw work. Other crafts well worth viewing and buying are on display at Harmony Hall in Brown's Bay Mill, where local Antiguan art is exhibited.

ACCOMMODATION
The following is a sample from across the island. Prices shown are winter/summer rates:

Admiral's Inn, English Harbour, Antigua (tel. 460 1027). Situated in the heart of the island's charter yacht centre, 23 km from the airport, 19 km from St John's. Straightforward accommodation in convivial atmosphere, thirteen rooms. Prices start at approx. US$76 for a single in summer or US$104 in winter.

Falmouth Harbour Beach Apartments, Falmouth Harbour, Antigua (tel. 463 1027). 28 self-catering beachside cottages in English Harbour. Singles: US$90—96 in summer, US$118 in winter.

Antigua Sugar Mill, 10 km from St John's (tel. 462 0857) Twenty two with mod-cons clustered around pool. Sugar mill observation tower nearby, overlooks sea, though not close to beach. Singles US$60 in summer, US$80 in winter.

TimeAway Apartments, 3 km from St John's, seven from airport (tel. 1212 0775). Self-catering. About 200 m from beach, nightlife nearby. Singles: US$50—70 in summer, US$85—95 in winter.

Pigottsville Hotel, Clare Hall, St John's, Antigua (tel. 462 0592). Twenty rooms, close to town centre. Rooms start at US$30—40.

Runaway Beach Club (tel. 462 1318). About 3 km from St Johns. One- and two-bedroom villas with kitchenettes and a pool. US$60 summer, US$80 winter.

For more budget accommodation information options in St John's, call the Antigua and Barbuda Tourist Board in London (details p. 575), and ask for a copy of *Budget Hotels and Guest Houses, St John's and Codrington*.

FOOD

Antigua's broad-based cuisine is matched by the variety of places that serve it. From beachside salad bars and local rice'n'peas vendors through to the large hotels serving top-notch international cuisine there really is something for everyone. What's more the friendly atmosphere encourages culinary exploration, and few local dishes are a disappointment. Distinctive Antiguan flavours combine spices and delicate sauces. Among the places that come highly recommended is:

Shirley Heights Lookout, Shirley Heights, Antigua (tel. 463 1765). Excellent views as well as food. Look out over Nelson's Dockyard and English Harbour, and enjoy specialities such as seafood and grilled steaks. Meals from US$20. Their popular Sunday barbeques continue way into the evening.

ENTERTAINMENT

When it comes to enjoying yourself, rest assured that the full Caribbean repertoire — steel bands, limbo dancing, fire eating, calypso — is not only on tap, it's overflowing. There's also plenty of reggae and jazz. The bulk of the organized nightlife centres on the hotels, though there are plenty of bars and a string of nightclubs in the tourist areas. For a quiet night, pick an intimate bar; there are plenty in the main tourist centres.

Royal Antiguan Casino, Ramada Renaissance Royal Antiguan, Antigua (tel. 462 3733). One of five casinos on the island; it features roulette, blackjack, craps, and one-armed bandits.

Halcyon Cove, Dickinson Bay, Antigua (tel. 462 0256). Expensive, but offers traditional entertainments nightly. Lively atmosphere.

For specific information on what's going on during your stay, pick up a copy of *It's Happening, You're Welcome*.

FESTIVALS AND EVENTS
Sporting events include the international tennis tournament featuring professional and amateur, competitive and friendly matches (men's tournament early January, women's early April); International Sailing Week, an annual regatta which lures Caribbean and international yachtsmen, and provides plenty for land lovers to do too (end April or early May). In May, the island hosts the Culinary Exposition, with tasty treats at their best.

The mid-summer Carnival (late July/early August) is a ten-day cultural festival in the widest sense of the word – a good natured celebration of all that is Antiguan.

EXCURSIONS
Sea excursions are one of the best ways to explore the coastline and wealth of marine life. Snorkel on the edge of the reef, or sail in a glass-bottomed boat trip over the deeper coral gorges. Scuba diving is easily arranged, as are courses for beginners.

BARBUDA offers many secluded delights, from the wooded interior and the tranquil beaches – some of which stretch literally for miles – to coral reefs and sunken wrecks. Not that you'll ever be totally alone, the wildlife is profligate both on land and under the sea. On the island's north-western edge, there's a bird sanctuary. Across the island, on its south-western reaches, sits the MARTELLO TOWER, one of hundreds of seaward look-out points on islands across the Caribbean.

REDONDA is a place for isolation after the partying; an uninhabited craggy islet, it's a favourite spot for bird watchers.

BARBADOS

VITAL STATISTICS
Red tape: Valid passports are required, but for most foreign nationals visas aren't necessary. You may be asked to produce an onward ticket.

Customs: 1 l spirits, 200 cigarettes or 500 g tobacco.

Health: A yellow fever certificate is required for visitors coming from an infected zone. Other vaccinations are not officially required, but inoculation against typhoid and polio is recommended. There are good hospital facilities on the island, including a casualty ward. Health insurance is advisable.

Language: English is widely spoken.

Population: Around 258,000

Capital: Bridgetown, population approx. 10,000

Political system: Independent democracy.

Religion: Christian: Anglican (70%), Methodist, Moravian, Roman Catholic. Also historical Jewish connections.

Time: Five hours behind GMT.

Money: The currency is the Barbados dollar (B$), divided into 100 cents. Coins: 1c, 5c, 10c, 25c, and B$1. Notes: B$2, B$5, B$10, B$20, B$50 and B$100. The currency is tied to the US dollar, but sterling can be changed easily in banks and hotels. £1 = approx. B$2.90. All major credit cards welcome.

Tax: Departure Tax of B$25, except for those on the island for less than twenty four hours. Government Tax on accommodation 5%; hotel service charge 10%.

Communications: International direct dialling facilities are available, and there's a full postal service.

Media: There are two local daily newspapers, *The Advocate* and *The Nation*. British, American and other foreign newspapers are also available. *The Visitor* is a free what's on listings magazine.

Electricity: 110v/50Hz.

Business hours: BANKS: Mon.–Thurs. 8 a.m.–3 p.m.; Fri. 9 a.m.–5 p.m.

POST OFFICES: Mon. 7.30 a.m.–12 p.m. and 1 p.m.–3 p.m., Tue.–Fri. 8 a.m.–12 p.m. and 1 p.m.–3.15 p.m.

SHOPS: Mon.–Fri. 8 a.m.–4 p.m.; Sat. 8 a.m.–12 p.m.

OFFICES: Mon.–Fri. 8 a.m.–4 p.m.

Holidays: 1 January; February (Holetown Festival); Easter, plus Oistins Fish Festival; Whit Monday; first Monday in June (Queen's

Birthday); July (Caricon Day); Crop Over Festival; October (United Nations Day); late November (National Independence Festival of Creative Arts); 25 and 26 December.
Climate: In Barbados, temperatures range from 24–30°C. The heaviest rainfalls occur between August and November.

DO'S AND DON'TS
As on other Caribbean islands, the main 'don't' is the wearing of skimpy clothing away from the beach and poolside. Women shouldn't go topless no matter where they are. Running kit for jogging in the streets is acceptable – it's a popular island pastime – but don't walk into town in beachwear and/or bare feet. Public displays of affection between couples should be kept to tourist areas. Finally, don't take photographs without asking permission.

WHERE TO GO FOR WHAT
Barbados takes its name from the Portuguese 'los barbados' ('the bearded ones'). It was given by the Portuguese explorer Pedro da Campa who, on discovering the island in 1536, was struck by the shaggy, exposed roots of the banyan trees he sighted on the shore. Campa didn't claim Barbados for Portugal, and so it was the British who became the first settlers, in 1627. They ruled for the next 350 years, Barbados only gaining full independence in 1966. The island is 23 km wide and 34 km long and lies 160 km due east of the other Lesser Antilles Islands. It has retained the natural beauty which attracted the first settlers, and is one of the best known islands in the East Caribbean region. Its appeal is indeed wide ranging; from the exotic terrain drenched in year-round sunshine, to the culture and atmosphere that manages to juggle modern-day living with that of 18th century England.

HARRISON'S CAVE at St Thomas is a series of underground caverns with stalagmites, stalactites (make a pact with yourself to remember which is which this time), underground streams and waterfalls. There's an electric tram to take you through. HOLETOWN in St James is where the island's original settlers first landed in 1627. That settlement is commemorated by the Holetown Monument, one of many historical signposts that point to the colonial heritage of the entire Caribbean region. A good time to visit is mid-February, when the Holetown Festival celebrates that first landing.

OUGHTERSON NATIONAL WILDLIFE PARK in St Philip is thick with flora and fauna, including monkeys, alligators, snakes and turtles. There's also a nature trail through a large orchard, and tours of OUGHERTON HOUSE, a classic example of a plantation Great House – a history lesson in itself. SOUTH POINT LIGHTHOUSE in

Christchurch was actually built in Britain. Constructed from iron it was dismantled and shipped across the Atlantic and then reassembled in Barbados.

TURNER'S HALL WOODS in St Andrew is a trip back in time to the Barbados witnessed by the early settlers; the remnant of a much larger tropical forest that covered the island in the early part of the 17th century, it still nurtures such indigenous species as the trumpet tree and the macaw palm.

The COTTON TOWER in St Joseph is one of several old island forts and military signal towers; this precursor to modern communications is now open to the public. At sunset, for a particularly impressive view of the southern half of the island, head for another old watch tower, the GUN HILL SIGNAL STATION at St George's. For a view of the rest of Barbados, climb the narrow road from the village of Hillaby to the summit of the island's highest peak, MOUNT HILLABY (335 m) in St Andrew.

An insight into the grandiose style of living enjoyed by Barbadian landowners in the 17th and 18th centuries is offered by a tour of VILLA NOVA in St John. A well-preserved mansion, once home to a 19-century sugar baron by the name of Edmund Haynes, its adjacent tropical gardens are well worth exploring, too.

For more exotic plant life, head to the ANDROMEDA GARDENS on the east coast. A match for its tropical delights is the stream that winds through the garden, connecting the pools and waterfalls. And if you're still craving natural beauty, make WELCHMAN HALL GULLY in St Thomas your next stop. This natural ravine, 1.25 km long, offers abundant wildlife and excellent views of northern Barbados, especially at dawn and dusk. Keep an eye out for the monkeys while you're there.

Finally, take a trip to St Andrew and the MORGAN LEWIS MILL. Built by Dutch-Jewish settlers to traditional designs, the origins of this restored mill are unmistakable.

INTERNAL TRAVEL
Bus: Barbados' buses are comfortable, reliable and cover all places of interest on the island. There are two types, public buses (blue with a yellow stripe) and privately run mini-buses (yellow with a blue stripe). The fare for any destination is B$1.50.

Taxi: Easily found at the airport, the deepwater harbour and outside hotels, taxis are not metered, so always agree on a price before starting.

Car and bike hire: There are a number of local car hire firms. Prices range from B$80–135 per day to B$400–520 per week. Bicycles are also for rent. Prices start at B$17 per day.

ACCOMMODATION

Prices vary with the seasons: winter (mid-Dec.–mid-Apr.) is high season, while summer (mid-Apr.–mid-Dec.) is low season. There are over a hundred hotels on the island: the budget options are cheap hotels and cottages-cum-apartments. (The Barbados Tourism Authority produces a very useful leaflet detailing cheap hotels called 'Apartment and Cottage Rates'.)

FOOD

Not surprisingly, seafood is a speciality on Barbados. Flying fish, the national mascot, is a particular favourite. Local Bajan cuisine is meaty: look out for pork, chicken and black pudding. Try *cou-cou*, a cornmeal okra dish, or *jug-jug*, a mix of Guinea corn and peas. The usual international dishes can be found, and there's no shortage of fast-food outlets. Tropical fruits and fruit juices are wonderfully refreshing and there are plenty to try. Beer and the famous Barbados rum flow freely just about everywhere.

BUDGETING

A few beers and a couple of local rums will cost about B$10. Local rum will set you back a mere B$0.50. Fast-food prices per person range from B$5 to B$7.50. Bus fares are a flat B$1.50 wherever you go. It's worth hiring a moped or push bike; the island is fairly flat, so cycling is okay. Scooters can be hired for B$32/61 a day, B$155/298 a week for single/double seaters. Beware of taxi drivers: some have vivid imaginations when it comes to charging, so always fix a price first. There aren't any campsites or hostels on the island, see below for details of cheap hotels.

Legal employment opportunities are virtually non-existent. There's very little work available of any kind, but think twice before risking it. In the words of one tourist official: 'if you're reported – you'll get deported.'

FURTHER INFORMATION

Barbados Tourism Authority, 263 Tottenham Court Road, London W1P 9AA (tel. 0171 636 9448).

Background reading: Two excellent guidebooks are *The Caribbean*, James Henderson (Cadogan Guides), and *Caribbean Islands Handbook*, ed. Ben Box and Sarah Cameron (Travel and Trade Publications).

Bridgetown

AIRPORT FACILITIES
Grantley Adams International Airport (tel. 428 7101) is located 10 km east of Bridgetown. There is one terminal handling all flights in and out of Barbados. Facilities include: tourist information desk, bank and foreign exchange services, hotel reservation counter, bars and a restaurant, a post office, shops and duty-free shopping, car-rental desks.

Check-in time prior to international flights is 120 minutes. An airport tax of B$25 is levied on visitors remaining on the island for longer than 24 hours.

CITY LINKS
A well organized taxi service operates between the airport and the rest of the island, and taxis are available round the clock. The average Bridgetown fare is B$30.

USEFUL ADDRESSES
Tourist office: Barbados Tourism Authority, PO Box 242, Harbour Road, Bridgetown, Barbados (tel. 427 2623/4).
Main post office: General Post Office, Cheapside, Bridgetown, Barbados.
British Embassy: Lower Collymore Rock, PO Box 676, Bridgetown, Barbados (tel. 436 6694).
US Embassy: PO Box 302, Bridgetown (tel. 436 4950).

SIGHTS
Admiral Nelson visited Barbados six months before his death, and TRAFALGAR SQUARE in the capital was named in his honour (the statue here was actually erected 36 years before the one in London). Another building with considerable historical significance is the OLD SYNAGOGUE AND CEMETERY, for it was Dutch-Jewish traders from Brazil who in the early 1620s introduced sugar cane to the island. The synagogue was built in the mid-17th century and is the oldest in the western hemisphere; the tombstones in the adjoining cemetery date back as far as 1630. Continuing on a religious footing, take a look at ST PATRICK'S CATHEDRAL: the original building was constructed in the 1840s, but was subsequently burnt down. The one on view today was built in 1899 and has interesting architecture. Still very much in use, it is the hub of Roman Catholicism in modern Barbados.

PELICAN VILLAGE, an arts and crafts centre located near the deep-water harbour in an attractively landscaped setting, has plenty of things worth buying. QUEEN'S PARK is the former residence of the general in charge of the British troops in the West Indies. On the withdrawal of the British regiment, it was turned into grassland. Look out for the 1,000-year-old baobab tree; at 2 metres in circumference, it's one of the largest trees in Barbados. THE FOUNTAIN GARDENS in Bridgetown are a man-made attraction, constructed after piped water was introduced to the island in the late 19th century.

ACCOMMODATION
Budget options fall into two categories: cheap hotels and cottages-cum-apartments.

Maresol, St Lawrence Gap, Christchurch, Barbados (tel. 428 9300). Friendly, clean one/two bedroom apartments close to sea. Prices from US$60.

Travellers Palm, Sunset Crest, St James, Barbados (tel. 432 7722). Pleasant single-room apartments with the beach close by. US$35.

Fred La Rose Bonanza, Dover (tel. 428 9097). Twenty bedrooms with singles from B$25 summer, B$30 winter.

Pegwell Inn, Welches (tel. 428 6150). Singles from B$11 summer, B$13 winter.

Broome's Vacation Home, Pine Gardens (tel. 426 4955). Singles, winter and summer, from B$21.

See the Barbados Tourism Authority leaflet *Apartment and Cottage Rates* for further information.

FOOD
Island cuisine covers the usual international options and local Bajan delicacies.

Flying fish is a speciality and is cooked in a number of ways. Whether it's deep-fried, baked, broiled, stuffed or stewed, flying fish is served in all restaurants, from the sleek to the seedy. Other popular dishes are the sea egg (the roe of a sea urchin), dolphin (the pelagic fish variety, not the one you save by buying the right tinned tuna), red snapper and fresh lobster.

Bajan cuisine offers such delights as tasty black pudding and souse, or suckling pig. There's also a wide variety of tropical fruits available in Bajan restaurants, look out for Barbados cherries and mangoes. For budget meals, stick to Bajan establishments, and local Chefettes for affordable fast food. After dinner, Barbados rum is highly rated the world over, and it's certainly one of the smoothest and richest.

The following selection serve dinner at a cost of B$25–55 per person:

Atlantis Hotel, St Joseph, Barbados (tel. 433 9445). Delicious Bajan cuisine served overlooking Tent Bay (and the view is magnificent). House specialities include turtle steak, flying fish, and spinach cakes.

Fisherman's Wharf, Bridgetown (tel. 436 7778). Tables overlook the careenage.

Witch Doctor, St Lawrence Gap, Christchurch (tel. 435 6581). Caribbean meals in jungle atmosphere.

ENTERTAINMENT
The nightlife is lively, whether its a local rum-hole full of swilling locals, or a more Western-style bar. There are also plenty of clubs and discos. Baxter's Road (on the road north out of Barbados), is a lively place to hang out. Lined with bars and street vendors cooking up food, it's cheap and open almost until dawn. Fisherman's Wharf is another fun place. Harbour Lights nightclub (Bay Street, St Michael), is ten minutes out of town. It's not cheap to get into, but like many hotels and bars on the island it has a happy hour as regular as clockwork. If the drinks aren't reduced in price, you'll have your third one on the house.

The Warehouse (Bridge House, Bridgetown) is a popular place with locals and visitors alike. The live entertainment is good; the air-conditioned dance floor an added bonus.

Cultural evenings are to be had at 1627 and All That (Barbados Museum), which offers open-air dinner and theatre evenings on Thursdays and Sundays. Tuck into a Bajan buffet while you enjoy Afro-Barbadian music and various dance shows covering 400 years of island history. Tickets cost from US$25.

EXCURSIONS
Given the island's small size, many excursions are included in the Sights section, p. 583. There are however, plenty of day trips worth going on if you head out to sea – sailing, swimming or diving. And at least one full day's sunbathing is essential. Popular beaches north of Bridgetown include PARADISE BEACH and PAYNE'S BAY. For a final quick blast of sun before your flight onward or homeward, try SILVER SANDS close to the airport.

BERMUDA

VITAL STATISTICS

Red tape: A valid passport (including British Visitor's Passport) is the preferred form of identification, and is mandatory for all visitors except those from the United States and Canada, who can use a variety of other official documents. Only a handful of nationalities require a visa; visitors from Western Europe, Australasia and North America do not need one.

A return or onward air ticket (or certificate detailing alternative future transportation) must be presented by all visitors, unless prior permission has been obtained from the Bermuda immigration authorities. There are strict controls on people entering the country to seek residence and/or employment. Travellers arriving with open-ended tickets will have their term of stay on the island fixed upon arrival.

Visitors travelling on to the United States must obtain their American visas before arriving in Bermuda.

Customs: Visitors can take in 200 cigarettes and 50 cigars and 450 g tobacco; along with 1 l spirits and 1 l wine.

Duty-free goods are not available at the airport, but may be purchased within 24 hours of departure from shops elsewhere on the island. Goods are delivered to the airport for collection before boarding the plane.

Health: Vaccinations are not required. Health insurance is recommended.

Language: English is the mother tongue.

Population: Around 70,000.

Capital: Hamilton, population 2,000.

Political system: Self-governing British dependent territory.

Religion: Anglican, Methodist, Roman Catholic.

Time: Four hours behind GMT.

Money: The currency is the Bermuda Dollar (BD$), divided into 100 cents. Coins: 1, 5, 10 and 25 cents, BD$1. Notes: BD$1, BD$2, BD$5, BD$10, BD$50 and BD$100. It's pegged to the US dollar, which is widely accepted and of equal value. US dollar traveller's cheques can be used for cash payments. Sterling (in any form) is seldom welcome, but banks will change it. Major credit cards can be used in most places, and the thirteen Bank of Bermuda cash machines accept VISA/Plus cards. £1 = about BD$1.59.

Tax: There is a $15 Airport Departure Tax, and $60 Port Tax (cruise ship passengers will pay this in advance to the shipping company). A 6% Government Room Occupancy Tax is levied on room rates.

Communications: Bermuda has a full, direct-dial domestic and international phone service. Public telephone kiosks can be found all over the island. There are also worldwide telegram and telex links. Postal services are efficient and reliable. Look out for the red post boxes.

Electricity: 110v AC/60 Hz. American plug.

Business hours: BANKS: Mon.–Fri. 9.30 a.m.–3 p.m.

POST OFFICES: Mon.–Fri. 8 a.m.–5 p.m.; Sat. 9 a.m.–12 p.m.

SHOPS: Mon.–Sat. 9 a.m.–5 p.m.

OFFICES: Mon.–Fri. 9 a.m.–5 p.m.

Holidays: 1 January; Good Friday; 24 May (Bermuda Day); first Monday in June (Queen's Birthday); late July (Cup Match and Somers Day); 25 and 26 December.

Climate: Bermuda's climate is sub-tropical, with an average temperature of around 21°C. Summer runs from May to mid-November, with peak temperatures in July and August reaching roughly 30°C; winter and spring temperatures rarely fall below 10°C. The island is saved from frost by the Gulf Stream, and extremes of heat are tempered by sea breezes. There is no rainy season as such.

DO'S AND DON'TS

As they freely admit, Bermudians have clung to one aspect of their British colonial legacy: the English reserve. Although this doesn't make it an unfriendly place, Bermuda is dignified and informal in equal measure. Feel free to sport the brightest pair of Bermuda shorts you can get your hands on, but in other respects behave in a manner befitting the island's pristine avenues and gardens. Away from the beach, it's an offence to appear in public without a shirt or in a bikini top. Although joggers may wear running garb, bare feet and hair-curlers(!) are definitely unacceptable. In hotels, restrict skimpy clothing to the poolside area. Casual gear (smart, in backpacker speak) is okay for restaurant lunches, but stricter dress codes are imposed after dusk.

Before painting the town red, check that your 'overalls' are smart enough. At night, many restaurants and nightclubs expect men to wear a jacket and tie; women should put on something 'elegant and dressy' – so if you didn't pack Dad's blazer, or one of Mum's Laura Ashley numbers, stay away from the smart set.

WHERE TO GO FOR WHAT

Bermuda is not in the Bahamas, nor is it part of the Caribbean. Named after Juan de Bermudez, the Spanish explorer who passed the islands on his way south to the Caribbean in 1503, this isolated outcrop of 150 islands lies 966 km east from Cape Hatteras in North Carolina, the nearest piece of mainland. It's also the northernmost land-mass with coral deposits in the world.

Bermuda's next visitor didn't stay either: he simply carved the initials T. F. and the date 1543 on rock in what is now the Spittal Pond Nature Reserve. Another 66 years were to pass before existence of the islands became known to the British, courtesy of Sir George Somers, who was shipwrecked on Bermuda in 1609. The first Englishman to settle in Bermuda arrived in 1612 and, in 1684 it became a British colony, which it has remained ever since. The islands cover an area of 34 sq. km, and the local population of some 60,000 inhabit a beautiful country full of green hills, pastel houses, rainbow-coloured flowers and fine beaches.

The town of ST GEORGE, in the north-east, is a popular urban attraction. The first capital of Bermuda, founded in 1612, it still displays much of its past. Among its attractions is FORT ST CATHERINE, which contains various exhibitions including historical dioramas, plus replicas of the Crown Jewels; the STATE HOUSE, built in 1620, is one of the island's most significant historical relics; ST PETER'S CHURCH is the oldest Anglican place of worship in the western hemisphere. With your mind still firmly fixed on the past, stroll around KING'S SQUARE; its pillories and antique ship replicas do much to recreate the atmosphere of old Bermuda. VERDMONT, on Collectors Hill Road, is fine example of an 18th-century Bermudan home. Having viewed the antiques, take a breath of fresh air in the beautiful gardens overlooking the sea.

Dipping into the past one more time, head out to IRELAND ISLAND on the western tip of Bermuda's flotilla of land masses. Among the exhibits in the MARITIME MUSEUM are the celebrated Teddy Tucker treasures.

Bermuda has the highest concentration of limestone caves in the world. Both the CRYSTAL CAVES and LEAMINGTON'S AMBER CAVES are situated along the Harrington Sound Road. For a peek at life underwater, the aquarium in tiny FLATTS VILLAGE has a wide range of marine life on show and in performance; there's also a zoo and a fine collection of birds. For more wildlife take a trip out to SPITTAL POND, Bermuda's largest nature reserve. Keen bird-watchers should visit between November and March.

Beach bumming is an essential part of any island holiday. The list of enticingly exotic beaches includes: Stonehole, Warwick, Long, Chaplain and Horseshoe Bay.

INTERNAL TRAVEL

Bus: A regular service operates throughout the island, linking all points of interest. Bermuda is divided into fourteen zones, any trip of three zones or more costs $5. With tokens bought in advance, a three-zone journey costs $2. All buses leave from the Central Terminal on Washington Street in Hamilton City. This efficient service makes island travel remarkably painless, but you must have the correct fare.

Boat: Ferry sailings run between Hamilton and various island ports, average fares $2.50. Mopeds/bicycles are charged at the foot-passenger rate.

Taxi: Carrying a maximum of six people, taxis can be hired by the hour or the day, or metered for specific journeys. There is a 25% surcharge for trips between midnight and 6 a.m.; luggage carried in the boot is charged at $0.25 per item (to a maximum of $2 per trip). Rates are the same all over the island: $4 for the first mile, $1.40 each additional mile.

Horse-drawn carriages: Minimum hire is half an hour. Fares start at $20.

Moped hire: Widely available and popular, no licence is required. Speed limit is 20 mph. Most hotels hire them out. Charges start at $15 for four hours.

Bicycle hire: Slightly cheaper to rent than mopeds. Shout out how much you've saved as you overtake the scooter riders.

Car hire: Self-drive cars cannot be hired on Bermuda. This is to minimize congestion.

ACCOMMODATION

Budget accommodation in Bermuda is a relative term, but cheap places are available and standards are high. Among the economy options are small housekeeping cottages (holiday apartments) available from $50 per night, and small guest houses. Many cheap places have set year-round prices, and good deals can be had by groups of three or more. Many of the hotels, especially the smaller ones, encourage half-board accommodation (bed, breakfast and dinner).

FOOD

Bermuda plays host to cuisine from around the world – Indian curries to Tuscan pasta – but no prizes for guessing that seafood is a speciality. Apart from lobster dishes (actually crayfish) very little is unique to the island, but do give Bermudian cooking a try. Among the local fare that comes highly recommended are large tiger shrimp, tangy mussel pie, and the traditional 'Hop'n'John' which mixes rice and black-eyed peas. Bermuda fish chowder, done with sherry peppers and black rum, and any fresh fish pan-fried or broiled is delicious. In keeping with the nation's heritage, roast beef and Yorkshire pudding are not uncommon options. For dessert, bring yourself back to the reality of your surroundings with bananas baked in rum, or a slice of loquat plum pie.

BUDGETING
You won't have much change from $40–$60 per person for a double room in a B&B Guest House at peak season. Metered taxi fares start at $4 for the first mile, dropping to $1.50 for subsequent miles. Bus fares are $3 for all zones, but you can buy a book of fifteen 14-zone tickets for $18. Ferry fares start from $2.50. To hire a scooter costs $20 for one day and $65 for five days; a litre of scooter petrol will set you back $1.25. On average, a budget meal for two will cost $25–$40. Basic bar drinks cost $3–6. Takeaway alcohol works out at about $8 for a six-pack of beer, $15–$22 for a bottle of spirits. Out on the town expect to pay $6 to see a film, $20–25 to go to the theatre.

Employment opportunities for non-nationals are very limited. Not surprisingly, given Bermuda's size, the government positively discriminates in favour of Bermudians. A work permit must be applied for – and granted – before arriving on the island. If you're feeling persistent, contact the Chief Immigration Officer, Department of Immigration, Government Administration Building, 30 Parliament Street, Hamilton HM 12. Or: PO Box HM 1364, Hamilton HM FX.

FURTHER INFORMATION

Bermuda Tourism (European Representative), BCB Ltd, 1 Battersea Church Road, London SW11 3LY (tel. 0171 734 8813).
Background reading: *Caribbean Islands Handbook*, ed. Ben Box and Sarah Cameron (Trade & Travel publications); *Insight Guides: Bermuda* (APA Publications); and *What's Cooking in Bermuda*, by Betsy Ross.

Hamilton

AIRPORT FACILITIES
Bermuda Kindley Field Air Terminal is located on the eastern fringe of the island, 20 km from the city of Hamilton. With the completion of a new Departures building, there are now two airport terminals.

Available facilities include an information desk (usually open 11 a.m.–6 p.m., depending on flight schedules), an accommodation counter, bars and a restaurant, shops (hours vary with flight schedules, but generally 9 a.m.–6 p.m.), a meeting point, and travel agent counters. Car rental facilities are not available because car hire is not allowed on the island. There isn't an on-site duty-free, either.

An airport departure tax of $15 is levied on adults.

CITY LINKS
Taxis are approximately $25, public buses $3.50 per person.

USEFUL ADDRESSES
Tourist office: Bermuda Department of Tourism, Global House, 43 Church Street, Hamilton HM 12, Bermuda
Bermuda Hotel Association: Camel Buildings, Corner of King and Reid Streets, Hamilton 5–23.
Amex: L.P. Gutteridge Ltd, Harold Hayes Frith Building, PO Box 1024 (tel. 295 4545).
Main post office: 56 Church Street, Hamilton, Bermuda.
British Deputy Governor's Office: Government House, Hamilton (tel. 23600).
US Consulate: 'Crown Hill', 16 Middle Road, Devonshire DV 03, Bermuda (tel. 295 1342).

SIGHTS
Set in PEMBROKE PARISH, on the inner shore of the island's fishhook, Bermuda's capital has plenty of shops, pubs and engaging residential areas. But the sights to track down first are the numerous historical attractions. The CENOTAPH, between Parliament and Court Streets, was built in honour of Bermudians who died during World Wars I and II. In the park behind lies the CABINET BUILDING. Here Bermuda's Legislative Council sits, and close by are several government offices. In the middle of the park, to the right of Reid Street, stands the imposing building of SESSIONS HOUSE in which sits the House of Assembly. The clock tower, on the south-west corner of the building, was built to commemorate Queen Victoria's Jubilees in 1887 and 1897. The Supreme Court is housed here also; keep an eye out for court officials in traditional 'Rumpole' garb.

An intriguing latter-day spot to explore is the CITY HALL of Hamilton. Built in 1960, it has a modern-wind clock tower, while inside is found a small theatre, the MAYOR'S PARLOUR, and various offices of the Corporation of Hamilton; upstairs is the home of the Bermuda Society of Arts, and an exhibition of works by international as well as local artists and sculptures.

The BERMUDA HISTORICAL SOCIETY is located in the Par-La-Ville gardens, and is well worth visiting for its enormous range of exhibits of Bermudiana. Nestling in the gardens is the PUBLIC LIBRARY, which boasts a collection of island newspapers dating back to 1787. Before setting your sights further afield, make time for HAMILTON FORT; this restored Victorian building is as captivating for its history as for the views it affords of the city and harbour.

ACCOMMODATION
Prices shown below are per person for rooms, and per apartment for group bookings. As with all expenditure on the island, US and Bermudan dollars are interchangeable. Expect a service charge of between 5–10%.

Small housekeeping cottages:

Marula Apartments, Pembrook Parish (tel. 292 3985). Fan-cooled rooms set in spacious grounds at water's edge; a five minute ride from Hamilton. Singles $70–100, doubles $40–45. Cottage for four: $150.

Burch's Guest Apartments, Smith's Parish (tel. 292 5746). Informal place with views of north shore; close to amenities, cycles and the like for hire. Singles $55. Doubles $37.50. Three-person apartments: $90.

Blue Horizons, Devonshire Parish. Singles $55, doubles $37.50. Apartment for three: $90.

Pillar-Ville Guest House, Southampton Parish. Singles $45–50, doubles $37.50–42.50. Cottage for four to five sharing: $130–185.

Small guest houses:

Hillcrest Guest House, St George's Parish (tel. 292 1630). Air-conditioned rooms set in gardens; close to beach, shops, bus route. Singles $45. Doubles $32.50 per person.

Que Sera Guest House, Paget Parish (tel. 236 1998). Air-conditioned rooms with pool and patio; set in quiet residential area near Botanical Gardens. Single $45/50. Four-person unit $140.

FOOD
There are more than a hundred restaurants, cafés and bars – including numerous British-style pubs – on Bermuda. Shades of fish and chips on the Costa Del Sol? Not at all; but drinking holes do have suitably stocked bars, and an informal atmosphere. At any of Ber-

muda's cafés, pizza and salad is a reasonably priced lunchtime option. Economical eats at ($25–40 for two):

Hog Penny Pub, Burnaby Street, City of Hamilton, Pembroke Parish (tel. 22534). A tasty, if basic, menu is offered – bangers and mash being one of the chef's specialities.

Rum Runners, Front Street, City of Hamilton, Pembroke Parish (tel. 24737). Head to the pub area for cheap food. There's a good view of the harbour from the balcony. Piano entertainment is laid on after dark.

The Fisherman's Warf, Somers Wharf, St George's Parish (tel. 71730). Romantic candle-lit tables – offer your partner undying devotion over shrimps, beef and exotic salad. Quite pricey.

ENTERTAINMENT

After-dinner shows are laid on by most of the larger hotels, and the island has plenty of nightclubs. However, you're probably better off tracking down one of the smaller local places; ask the staff in your hotel, or any of the cab drivers for suggestions. They may suggest darts and a sing-song in a pub, or some jazz, reggae or a steel band. Karaoke has invaded Bermuda, but for participation-pastimes of a more traditional – if equally public – nature, have a go at limbo-dancing. One of the liveliest shows on the island is found at the Clay House Inn (North Shore Road, Devonshire), with no holds barred whether it's dancing or music. Alternatively, opt for the intimacy of a peaceful calypso evening. Before heading home, finish the night off with a stroll along the beach; there aren't any malarial mozzies here.

Cultural events are hosted regularly, including: classical music, drama, ballet, folk music, and (in keeping with the island's Britishness) Gilbert and Sullivan operettas. The fortnightly *Preview of Bermuda Today* is a what's on listings magazine that will keep you in touch with all the entertainment options.

FESTIVALS AND EVENTS

The Bermuda Festival, a six-week international arts festival, featuring local and international artists specializing in classical music, dance, jazz, drama and popular entertainment, is held each year in January/February.

In March, Front Street, Hamilton, comes alive to the Annual Street Festival, with local music, crafts and fashions on show.

In April and May, Bermudians open their homes and gardens every Wednesday afternoon. Also in May is the Bermuda Heritage Week: actually a month-long sporting and cultural event, ending on Bermuda Day (24 May). Look out for cycling, running, dinghy racing and the Bermuda Day Parade.

EXCURSIONS

Sea excursions go in several directions from Hamilton Harbour, in craft ranging from yachts to catamarans to glass-bottomed boats. Cruise times last for anything between two hours and a full day. Lunch, free bar and some calypso and limbo dancing will sustain your enthusiasm for the marine life and coral reefs. Ask around for available trips, or contact two of the main companies: Williams Marine (tel. 53727), and Kitson & Company (tel. 54506).

Ferry excursions are operated by the Bermudian government. They travel across the Great Sound between Paget, Warwick, Hamilton and Somerset, and are an ideal opportunity to tour the coastline waters of Bermuda for just a few dollars. For further information phone 54506. Taxi tours are a stress-free way to get to know mainland Bermuda. Plan your own route, tell the driver where you want to go, and leave the rest to him – including the running commentary. Drivers will also help plan your route. Qualified guides are distinguishable by the small blue flags on their taxis. One company that offers good set tours is Penboss Taxi tours (tel. 53927) their itinerary takes in Harrington Sound, Somerset and St George's Island. Expect to pay upwards of $75 per day for the car.

You can charter a sailing yacht, complete with skipper, though the rates are expensive. Longtail Cruises (tel. 236 448), Perrah Yacht Charters (tel. 295 0060) and Starlight Sailing Cruises (tel. 292 1834) offer some of the lower rates. The cheapest you'll find will be about $175 for three hours.

Bus, moped, or bike is another tour-the-sights option. You won't have the attentive assistance of a personal guide, but there'll be plenty of people willing to help, and offer their own interpretation of Bermudan history. The best way to see Bermuda's many free attractions – its parks, gardens, bridges, nature reserves, deserted railway line – is on foot. Ask at the Hamilton tourist office for details.

SECTION THREE
ROUND THE WORLD AT A GLANCE

Round the World Temperature Guide °F/°C

	Jan	Feb	Mar	Apr	May	June
Amsterdam	40/4	41/5	47/8	52/11	61/16	65/18
Antigua	84/29	84/29	84/29	84/29	84/29	84/29
Auckland	73/23	73/23	71/21	67/19	62/17	58/14
Bahamas	77/25	77/25	79/26	81/27	84/29	87/30
Bahrain	68/20	70/21	75/24	84/29	92/33	97/36
Bangkok	89/32	91/32	93/34	95/35	93/34	91/33
Barbados	83/28	83/28	85/29	86/30	87/30	87/30
Bermuda	68/20	68/20	68/20	71/22	76/24	81/28
Delhi	70/21	75/24	87/30	97/36	105/41	102/39
Frankfurt	37/3	43/6	48/9	58/14	66/19	72/22
Hong Kong	64/18	63/17	67/19	75/24	82/28	85/29
Kuala Lumpur	90/32	91/33	91/33	91/33	91/33	91/33
Lima	82/28	83/28	83/28	88/31	74/23	68/20
London	43/6	44/7	50/10	55/13	62/17	68/20
Melbourne	79/26	79/26	75/24	72/20	62/17	57/14
Mexico City	70/21	74/23	78/26	80/27	79/27	77/25
Miami	74/23	76/24	79/26	81/27	84/29	86/30
Mombasa	87/30	77/30	90/32	89/32	85/29	83/28
Moscow	15/−9	17/−8	25/−4	45/7	57/14	65/18
New York	37/3	38/3	45/7	57/14	68/20	77/25
Penang	90/32	91/33	92/34	91/33	90/32	90/32
Rio de Janeiro	84/29	85/29	83/28	80/27	77/25	76/24
San Francisco	55/13	59/15	61/16	63/17	63/17	66/19
Singapore	86/30	88/31	88/31	88/31	89/32	88/31
Sydney	78/26	78/26	76/24	71/22	66/19	61/16
Tokyo	47/8	48/9	54/12	63/17	71/22	76/24
Vancouver	41/5	45/7	50/10	57/14	65/18	70/21

These temperatures (in °F and °C) represent the average daily maximum (in the shade) for most of the major destinations covered by this guide. Maximum temperatures normally occur from early to mid-afternoon.

Round the World Temperature Guide °F/°C

	Jul	Aug	Sep	Oct	Nov	Dec
Amsterdam	70/21	68/20	65/18	55/13	41/5	41/5
Antigua	84/29	84/29	84/29	84/29	84/29	84/29
Auckland	56/13	59/14	60/16	63/17	66/18	70/21
Bahamas	88/31	89/32	88/31	85/29	81/27	79/25
Bahrain	99/37	100/38	92/33	90/32	82/28	66/19
Bangkok	90/32	90/32	89/32	88/31	87/30	87/30
Barbados	86/30	87/30	87/30	86/30	85/29	83/28
Bermuda	85/29	86/30	84/29	79/26	74/23	70/21
Delhi	96/35	93/34	93/34	93/34	84/29	73/23
Frankfurt	75/24	73/23	66/19	55/13	45/7	39/4
Hong Kong	87/30	87/30	85/29	81/27	74/23	68/20
Kuala Lumpur	90/32	90/32	90/32	90/32	90/32	90/32
Lima	67/19	66/19	68/20	71/22	74/23	78/26
London	71/22	70/21	65/18	57/14	50/10	45/7
Melbourne	55/13	59/15	63/17	66/19	68/22	75/24
Mexico City	74/23	74/23	72/22	72/22	70/21	70/21
Miami	88/31	88/31	88/31	83/28	79/26	76/24
Mombasa	82/28	83/28	84/29	86/30	88/31	84/29
Moscow	70/21	67/20	57/14	43/6	28/−3	20/−5
New York	82/28	80/27	79/26	69/21	51/11	41/5
Penang	90/32	89/32	88/31	89/32	88/31	88/31
Rio de Janeiro	75/24	76/24	75/24	77/25	79/26	82/28
San Francisco	65/18	65/18	70/21	68/20	63/17	57/14
Singapore	88/31	87/30	87/30	87/30	87/30	87/30
Sydney	60/16	63/17	67/19	71/22	74/23	77/25
Tokyo	83/28	86/30	79/26	69/21	60/16	52/11
Vancouver	74/23	74/23	65/18	27/14	48/9	43/6

These temperatures (in °F and °C) represent the average daily maximum (in the shade) for most of the major destinations covered by this guide. Maximum temperatures normally occur from early to mid-afternoon.

Round the World Air Guide

AIR FARE SEASONS

1 Europe/Mid East/Africa

a. Russia–
Moscow

low	Jan–Jun	Oct–Nov	
high	Jul–Aug	Sept–Xmas period	

b. Bahrain

low	10 Oct–14 Dec	6 Jan–30 Apr
high	15 Dec–5 Jan	1 May–30 Sept

c. Nairobi

low	1 Apr–31 May				
shoulder	Feb	March	June	Oct	Nov
high	1 Jul–30 Sept	1 Dec–31 Jan			

d. Cairo

low	1 Oct–14 Dec	6 Jan–30 Apr
high	15 Dec–5 Jan	1 May–30 Sept

2 Asia

a. Bangkok as
general guide

low	1 Feb–15 June	1 Oct–30 Nov
high	16 Jun–30 Sept	1 Dec–31 Jan

3 Australasia

a. Oz/NZ/
Fiji

basic	1 Apr–30 Jun	
off peak	1 Feb–31 Mar	Jul
shoulder	Jan	1 Aug–9 Dec
	24 Dec–31 Dec	
high	10 Dec–23 Dec	

4 South America

a. Brazil

low	1 Apr–14 Jun	1 Oct–9 Dec
high	15 Jun–30 Sept	10 Dec–31 Mar

b. Mexico

low	1 May–30 Jun	1 Oct–14 Dec
	11 Jan–31 Mar	
high	1 Jul–30 Sept	10 Dec–10 Jan

c. Peru

low	1 May–30 Jun	10 Oct–14 Dec
	16 Jan–31 Mar	
high	1 Jun–30 Sept	15 Dec–15 Jan

5 North America

a. Canada

low	Feb	1 Apr–13 May	
shoulder	Mar	14 May–30 Jun	Oct
high	1 Jul–30 Sept		

b. Caribbean	low	1 Oct–5 Dec	25 Dec–30 Jun
	high	1 Jul–30 Sept	6 Dec–24 Dec
c. Hawaii	low	7 Jan–19 Feb	16 Mar–17 Apr
		8 Sept–3 Nov	
	shoulder	20 Feb–15 Mar	11 May–19 Jun
		4 Nov–19 Dec	
	high	18 Apr–10 May	20 Jun–7 Sept
		20 Dec–6 Jan	
d. USA	low	1 Nov–10 Dec	25 Dec–31 Mar
	shoulder	Oct Apr May	
	high	1 Jun–30 Sept	11 Dec–24 Dec

Your Country-by-Country Checklist

This alphabetical list shows for each country:

r =   Vaccinations or tablets recommended for protection against disease, but note
      that for yellow fever pregnant women and infants under nine months
      should not normally be vaccinated and therefore should avoid exposed to
      infection.

E =   Vaccination is an essential requirement for entry to the country concerned
      and you will require a certificate.

E1 = Vaccination is essential except for infants under one year (but note the
      advice above).

E2 = Vaccination essential (except for infants under one year) unless arriving
      from non-infected areas and staying for less than two weeks. The UK is a
      non-infected area, but if travelling via equatorial Africa or South America,
      seek medical advice.

* =   Vaccination is essential if the traveller arrives from an infected country – i.e.
      where yellow fever is present. This will not apply if your journey is direct
      from the UK.

M =   Meningitis, depending on area visited and time of year.

a) = Depends on area visited.

b) = Limited risk in São Tiâgo Island.

c) = Recommended for all travellers going to the province of Darién.

d) = Certificate only required if leaving Paraguay to go to endemic areas.

Country	Hep. A Polio Typhoid	Malaria	Yellow Fever	Other
Afghanistan	r	r	*	
Albania			*	
Algeria	r	r	*	
Angola	r	r	*	
Anguilla				
Antigua/Barbuda			*	
Argentina	r	r		
Armenia				
Australia			*	
Austria				
Azerbaijan				
Bahamas	r		*	
Bahrain	r		*	
Bali	r	r	*	
Bangladesh	r	r	*	
Barbados	r		*	
Belarus				
Belize	r	r	*	
Benin	r	r	E1	M
Bermuda				
Bhutan	r	r	*	
Bolivia	r	r	* r	
Botswana	r	r		

Country	Hep. A Polio Typhoid	Malaria	Yellow Fever	Other
Brazil	r	r	* r	
Brunei	r		*	
Bulgaria				
Burkina Faso	r	r	El	
Burma see Myanmar				
Burundi	r	r	* r	
Cambodia	r	r	*	
Cameroon	r	r	El	M
Canada				
Cape Verde	r	r b)	*	
Cayman Islands	r			
Central African Republic	r	r	El	M
Chad	r	r	El	M
Chile	r			
China	r	r a)	*	
Colombia	r	r	r	
Comoroe	r	r		
Congo	r	r	El	
Cook Islands	r			
Costa Rica	r	r		
Croatia				
Cuba	r			
Cyprus				
Czechoslovakia				
Djibouti	r	r	*	
Dominica	r		*	
Dominican Republic	r	r		
Ecuador	r	r	* r	
Egypt	r	r a)	*	
El Salvador	r	r	*	
Equatorial Guinea	r	r	* r	
Estonia				
Ethiopia	r	r	* r	M
Falkland Islands				
Fiji	r		*	
Finland				
Gabon	r	r	El	
The Gambia	r	r	*	M
Georgia				
Ghana	r	r	El	
Greenland				
Grenada	r		*	
Guam	r			
Guatemala	r	r	*	
Guiana, French	r	r	El	
Guinea	r	r	* r	
Guinea-Bissau	r	r	* r	
Guyana	r	r	* r	
Haiti	r	r	*	

Country	Hep. A Polio Typhoid	Malaria	Yellow Fever	Other
Honduras	r	r	*	
Hong Kong	r			
Hungary				
Iceland				
India	r	r	*	M
Indonesia	r	r	*	
Iran	r	r	*	
Iraq	r	r	*	
Israel	r			
Ivory Coast	r	r	E1	M
Jamaica	r		*	
Japan	r			
Jordan	r		*	
Kampuchea	r	r	*	
Kazakhstan				
Kenya	r	r	*	M
Kirgizstan				
Kiribati	r		*	
Korea (North and South)	r			
Kuwait	r			
Laos	r	r	*	
Latvia				
Lebanon	r		*	
Lesotho	r		*	
Liberia	r	r	E1	M
Libya	r	r	*	
Lithuania				
Madagascar	r	r	*	
Madeira			*	
Malawi	r	r	*	
Malaysia	r	r	*	
Maldives	r		*	
Mali	r	r	E1	M
Malta			*	
Mauritania	r	r	E2	
Mauritius	r	r	*	
Mexico	r	r	*	
Moldova				
Monaco				
Mongolia	r			
Montserrat	r		*	
Morocco	r	r		
Mozambique	r	r	*	
Myanmar (Burma)	r	r	*	
Namibia	r	r	* r	
Nauru	r		*	
Nepal	r	r	*	M
Netherlands, Antilles	r		*	
New Caledonia	r		*	

Country	Hep. A Polio Typhoid	Malaria	Yellow Fever	Other
New Zealand				
Nicaragua	r	r	*	
Niger	r	r	E1	M
Nigeria	r	r	* r	M
Nille	r		*	
Norway				
Oman	r	r	*	
Pakistan	r	r	*	M
Panama	r	r	E1 c)	
Papua New Guinea	r	r	*	
Paraguay	r	r	d)	
Peru	r	r	* r	
Philippines	r	r	*	
Pitcairn Island	r		*	
Poland				
Polynesia, French (Tahiti)	r		*	
Puerto Rico	r			
Qatar	r		*	
Réunion	r		*	
Romania	r			
Russia				
Rwanda	r	r	E1	
St Helena	r			
St Kitts and Nevis	r		*	
St Lucia	r		*	
St Vincent and Grenadines	r		*	
Samoa	r		*	
São Tomé and Principe	r	r	E2	
Saudi Arabia	r	r	*	M
Senegal	r	r	E1	M
Seychelles	r			
Sierra Leone	r	r	* r	M
Singapore	r		*	
Slovenia				
Solomon Islands	r	r	*	
Somalia	r	r	* r	
South Africa	r	r	*	
Sri Lanka	r	r	*	
Sudan	r	r	* r	M
Surinam	r	r	*	
Swaziland	r	r	*	
Swoden				
Switzerland				
Syria	r	r	*	
Tahiti	r		*	
Taiwan	r		*	
Tajikistan				
Tanzania	r	r	*	
Thailand	r	r	*	

Country	Hep. A Polio Typhoid	Malaria	Yellow Fever	Other
Togo	r	r	E1	M
Tonga	r		*	
Trinidad and Tobago	r		*	
Tunisia	r		*	
Turkey	r	r a)		
Turkmenistan				
Turks and Caicos Islands				
Tuvalu	r		*	
Uganda	r	r	* r	M
United Arab Emirates	r	r		
Ukraine				
Uruguay	r			
USA				
Uzbekistan				
Vanuatu	r	r		
Venezuala	r	r	r	
Vietnam	r	r	*	
Virgin Islands	r			
West Indies	r		*	
French West Indies	r		*	
Yemen Arab Rep. (North)	r	r	*	
Yemen Dem. Rep. (South)	r	r	*	
Yugoslavia				
Zaire	r	r	E1	
Zambia	r	r	* r	
Zimbabwe	r	r	*	

News in English

Keeping in touch with the world news is always advisable for long-haul travellers. The BBC World Service provides the most comprehensive English language service and the following waveband chart will let you know where to find it wherever you are.

Africa
Central and West

kHz	6005	7105	7185	7320	9410	9580	11720	15070	15105	21470	21660	21710	25650
m	49	41			31		25	19		13			11

East

kHz	1413	6005	7185	7320	9410	9580	11750	11860	15070	15420	17885	21470	25650
m	212	49	42		31		25		19		16	13	11

North and North-west

kHz	5975	7185	7320	9410	9580	11750	12095	15070	17705	21710	25650
m	49	41		31		25		19	16	13	11

Southern

kHz	6005	7185	7320	9410	11750	11820	15070	15400	17885	21660	25650
m	49	41		31	25		19		16	13	11

America
Central and Caribbean

kHz	5975	6175	6195	7325	9510	11750	11775	15070	15260	17830
m	49			40	31	25		19		16

North

kHz	5975	6120	6175	9510	9590	7325	11750	11775	15070	15260	17830	21710
m	49			31		40	25		19		16	13

South

kHz	6005	9575	9915	11750	15260
m	49	31		25	19

Asia
Indian sub-continent

kHz	1413	6195	7135	9410	9740	11750	11955	15070	15310	17770	17790	21550	25650
m	212	49	41	31		25		19		16		13	11

South-east and East

kHz	3915	6195	9570	9740	11750	11955	15280	15435	17770	17880	21550	25650
m	75	49	31		25		19		16		13	11

Europe
Central

kHz	1296	3955	6050	6195	9410	9750	12095	15070	17790	21550	21710
m	231	75	49		31		25	19	16	13	

Northern

kHz	648	1296	5975	6050	6180	7120	9410	15070	15420	17695	17790	21550	25650
m	463	231	49			41	31	19		16		13	11

South-east

kHz	3955	5975	6050	6180	7185	7320	9410	12095	15070	17790	21470	21710
m	75	49			41		31	25	19	16	13	

South-west

kHz	3970	5975	7185	7320	7320	9410	9580	9760	9915	12095	15070	17705	21710
m	75	49	41			31				25	19	16	13

Western

kHz	648	5975	6050	7120	7185	7320	9410	9750	12095	15070
m	463	49		41			31		25	19

Middle East

kHz	1323	693	6050	7140	9410	11760	12095	15070	15310	17770	17790	21710	25650
m	212	469	49	41	31	25		19		16		13	11

As a general rule, the lower frequencies usually give better results early in the morning and late in the evening. Likewise better results for higher frequency in the middle of the day.

Airline Two-Letter Codes

It is useful to know these two-letter codes as they are used extensively in timetables, brochures and tickets to identify airlines. The list below is not complete but covers the main ones you are likely to encounter on an around the world journey.

Code	Airline
AA	American Airlines
AC	Air Canada
AF	Air France
AH	Air Algerie
AI	Air India
AM	Aermexico
AN	Ansett Airlines of Australia
AQ	Aloha Airlines
AR	Aerolineas Argentinas
AS	Alaska Airlines
AY	Finnair
AZ	Alitalia
BA	British Airways
BD	British Midland Airways
BI	Royal Brunei Airlines
BU	Braathens SAFE
BW	BWIA International Trinidad and Tobago Airways
CF	Faucett
CI	China Airlines
CO	Continental Airlines, Inc.
CP	Canadian Airlines
CX	Cathay Pacific Airways
CY	Cyprus Airways
DL	Delta Air Lines
EI	Aer Lingus (Irish)
EK	Emirates
FI	Flugfelag-Icelandair
FJ	Air Pacific
GA	Garuda Indonesian Airways
GF	Gulf Air
GH	Ghana Airways
GJ	Equatorial International Airlines of São Tomé
GR	Aurigny Air Services (Channel Islands)
HA	Hawaiian Airlines
HM	Air Seychelles
HN	NLM – Dutch Airlines
IA	Iraqi Airways
IB	Iberia
IC	Indian Airways
IS	Eagle Air
IT	Air Inter
JL	Japan Air Lines
JM	Air Jamaica
JU	JAT (Jugoslovenski Aerotransport)
KE	Korean Airlines
KL	KLM – Royal Dutch Airlines
KM	Air Malta
KQ	Kenya Airways
KU	Kuwait Airways
LB	Lloyd Aero Boliviano
LG	Luxair – Luxembourg Airlines
LH	Lufthansa German Airlines
LO	LOT (Polish Airlines)

LV	LAV – Linea Aeropostal Venezolana	RG	Varig, SA
		RJ	ALIA – Royal Jordanian Airlines
LY	El Al Israel Airlines	RK	Air Afrique
LZ	Balkan (Bulgarian Airlines)	RO	Tarom-Romanian Airlines
MA	Malev (Hungarian Airlines)	SA	South African Airways
MB	Western Airlines	SD	Sudan Airways
ME	Middle East Airlines	SK	SAS – Scandinavian Airlines System
MH	Malaysian Airline System	SN	Sabena – Belgian World Airlines
MK	Air Mauritius		
ML	Midwest Airlines	SQ	Singapore Airlines
MS	Egyptair	SR	Swissair
MX	Mexicana de Aviacion	SU	Aeroflot Soviet Airlines
NG	Lauda Air	SV	Saudi Arabian Airline
NH	All Nippon Airways	TC	Air Tanzania
NM	Mount Cook Airlines	TG	Thai International
NU	Southwest Airlines (Japan)	TK	THY – Turkish Airlines
NW	Northwest Airlines	TN	Australian Airlines
NZ	Air New Zealand	TP	TAP Air Portugal
OA	Olympic Airways	TU	Tunis Air
OK	CSA (Ceskoslovenske Airolinie)	TW	TWA – Trans World Airlines, Inc.
OS	Austrian Airlines	UA	United Airlines
PA	Pan American World Airways	UE	Air LA
		UK	Air UK
PC	FijiAir	UL	Air Lanka
PH	Polynesian Airlines	UM	Air Zimbabwe
PK	Pakistan International Airlines	UN	Eastern Australia Airlines
PL	Aeroperu	UP	Bahamasair
PR	Philippine Airlines	US	US Air
PV	Panorama Air	VA	Viasa
PZ	LAP – Lineas Aereas Paraguayas	VB	Birmingham European Airways
QF	Qantas Airways	VP	Vasp
QM	Air Malawi	VS	Virgin Atlantic Airways
QZ	Zambia Airways		
RA	Royal Nepal Airlines	ZV	Air Midwest
RB	Syrian Arab Airlines	ZP	Virgin Air

Principal Airports Around the World

City Name	3 Letter Code	Name of Airport/s	Distance from City Centre Miles	Km
AFRICA				
Algiers	ALG	Houari Boumediene	12	20
Cape Town	CPT	D. F. Malan	14	22
Casablanca	CAS	Mohamed V	19	30
Dar-es-Salaam	DAR	International	9	15
Djibouti	JIB	Ambouli	3	5
Durban	DUR	Louis Botha	10	16
Freetown	FNA	Lungi Intl.	18	29
		Hastings	15	24
Harare	HRE	Harare	7	12
Johannesburg	JNB	Jan Smuts	15	24
Nairobi	NBO	Jomo Kenyatta	8	13
		Wilson	2	3.2
Tangier	TNG	Boukhalef Souahel	9	15
AMERICAN CONTINENT				
Atlanta	ATL	Hartsfield Atlanta Intl.	9	14
Barbados	BGI	Grantley Adams	6.8	11
Bermuda	BDA	Kindley Field	12	19
Boston	BOS	Logan Intl.	4	6
Buenos Aires	BUE	Ministro Pistarini	32	51
		Aeroparque Jorge Newbery	5	8
Chicago	CHI	O'Hare Intl.	21	35
		Midway	10	16
		Meigs Field	1	1.6
Cleveland	CLE	Cleveland Hopkins	12	19
Dallas/Fort Worth	DFW	DFW International	15	24
		Love Field	4	7
Denver	DEN	Stapleton Intl.	6	10
Detroit	DTT	Metropolitan	20	32
		City Airport	5	9
Edmonton	YEG	International	21	34
		Municipal Airport	3	5
Halifax	YHZ	International	23	37
Houston	HOU	Intercontinental	20	32
		Hobby Airport	10	16
Kansas City	MKC	International	18	29
Las Vegas	LAS	McCarran Intl.	6	10

City Name	3 Letter Code	Name of Airport/s	Distance from City Centre	
Los Angeles	LAX	International	15	24
		Burbank	21	34
		van Nuys	8	13
Memphis	MEM	International	10	16
Mexico City	MEX	Benito Juarez Intl.	8	13
Miami	MIA	International	7	11
Minneapolis/St Paul	MSP	Minneapolis-St Paul Intl.	10	16
Montréal	YUL	Dorval	15	25
		Mirabel	33	53
Nassau	NAS	International	10	16
New Orleans	MSY	International	13	21
New York	NYC	J. F. Kennedy Intl.	14	22
		La Guardia	8	13
		Newark	16	26
Ottawa	YOW	Uplands Intl.	11	17.5
Panama City	PTY	Tocumen International	17	27
Philadelphia	PHL	International	8	13
		North Philadelphia	12	19
Pittsburgh	PIT	Greater Pittsburgh	16	26
Québec	YQB	Québec	9	14.5
Rio de Janeiro	RIO	International	13	21
		Santos Dumont	1	1.6
St Louis	STL	Lambert Intl.	13	21
Salt Lake City	SLC	International	5	8
San Diego	SAN	Lindbergh Intl.	2	3
San Francisco	SFO	International	15	25
Seattle	SEA	Settle/Tacoma Intl.	14	22
Toronto	YYZ	Lester B. Pearson Intl.	17	27
Vancouver	YVR	International	9	15
Washington DC	DC	Dulles Intl.	26	43
		National	4	7
Winnipeg	YWG	International	4	6

ASIA

City Name	3 Letter Code	Name of Airport/s	Distance from City Centre	
Bangkok	BKK	International	19	30
Beijing	PEK	Capital	16	26
Bombay	BOM	Bombay	18	29
Calcutta	CCU	Calcutta	8	13
Colombo	CMB	Katunayake	20	32
Delhi	DEL	Indira Gandhi International	14	20

City Name	3 Letter Code	Name of Airport/s	Distance from City Centre	
Hong Kong	HKG	International	3	5
Karachi	KHI	Karachi	8	12
Kuala Lumpur	KUL	Subang Intl.	14	22.5
Osaka	OSA	International	10	16
Singapore	SIN	Changi	12.4	20
		Seletar	12	19
Tokyo	TYO	Haneda	12	19
		Narita	40	65

AUSTRALASIA

City Name	3 Letter Code	Name of Airport/s	Distance from City Centre	
Adelaide	ADL	Adelaide	5	8
Auckland	AKL	International (Mangere)	14	22
Brisbane	BNE	Brisbane Intl.	7	11
Canberra	CBR	Canberra	4	6
Honolulu	HNL	International	6	10
Melbourne	MEL	Tullamarine	13	21
		Essendon	7	11
Perth	PER	Perth	6	10
Sydney	SYD	Kingsford Smith (Mascot)	5	8
Wellington	WLG	International	5	8

EUROPE

City Name	3 Letter Code	Name of Airport/s	Distance from City Centre	
Amsterdam	AMS	Amsterdam-Schiphol Intl.	9	14
Athens	ATH	Hellinikon	6	10
Belgrade	BEG	Belgrade	12	19
Berlin	BER	Tegel	5	8
Brussels	BRU	National	8	13
Copenhagen	CPH	Copenhagen	6	10
Dusseldorf	DUS	Dusseldorf	5	8
Frankfurt	FRA	Frankfurt Intl.	6	10
Geneva	GVA	Geneva	3	5
Hamburg	HAM	Fuhlsbuttel	8	13
Helsinki	HEL	Helsinki-Vantas	12	19
Istanbul	IST	Ataturk	15	24
Lisbon	LIS	Lisbon	4.5	7
London	LON	Heathrow	15	24
		Gatwick	28	46
		Stansted	34	55
Madrid	MAD	Barajas (Mad.)	10	16
Malta (Valletta)	MLA	Luqa	3	5

City Name	3 Letter Code	Name of Airport/s	Distance from City Centre	
Marseille	MRS	Marseille–Provence	15	24
Milan	MIL	Linate	6	10
		Malpensa	29	46
Moscow	MOW	Sheremetyevo	18	29
Nice	NCE	Cote d'Azur	4	6
Oslo	OSL	Gardermoen	32	51
		Fornebu	5	8
Paris	PAR	Orly	9	14
		Charles de Gaulle	14.5	23
Prague	PRG	Ruzyne	11	18
Rome	ROM	Leonardo da Vinci (Fiumicino)	22	35
Stockholm	STO	Arlanda	25	40
Vienna	VIE	Schwechat	11	18
Zurich	ZRH	Zurich	8	13

MIDDLE EAST

City Name	3 Letter Code	Name of Airport/s	Distance from City Centre	
Abu Dhabi	AUH	Abu Dhabi Intl.	21.7	35
Bahrain	BAH	Muharraq International	4	6.5
Beirut	BEY	International	10	16
Cairo	CAI	International	14	22
Dubai	DXB	Dubai	3	5
Jeddah	JED	King Abdulaziz Intl.	11	18
Jerusalem	JRS	Atarot	6	10
Kuwait	KWI	International	10	16
Riyadh	RUH	King Khaled Intl.	22	35
Tel Aviv	TLV	Ben Gurion Intl.	9	14

Foreign Tourist Offices in the United Kingdom

Where there is no tourist office given, try the relevant Embassy or Consulate.

Algeria	6 Hyde Park Gate, London SW7	0171 221 7800
Andorra	63 Westover Rd, London SW18 2RF	0181 874 4806
Antigua	Antigua House, 15 Thayer St, London W1M 5LD	0171 486 7073
Australia	10-18 Putney Hill, London SW15 6AA	0181 780 2227
Austria	30 St George St, London W1R 0AL	0171 629 0461
Bahamas	10 Chesterfield St, London W1X 8AH	0171 629 5238
Barbados	263 Tottenham Court Rd, London W1P 9AA	0171 636 9448/9
Belgium	Premier House, 2 Gayton Rd, Harrow, Middx HA1 2XU	0181 861 3300
Bermuda	BCB Ltd, 1 Battersea Church Rd, London SW11 3LY	0171 734 8813/4
British Virgin Islands	Suite 388, Great Eastern Hotel, Liverpool St, London EC2M 7QN	0171 283 4130
Canada	62–5, Trafalgar Sq, London WC2N 5DY	0171 930 8540
Cayman Islands	100 Brompton Rd, London SW3 1EX	0171 581 9960
China	4 Glenworth St, London NW1 5PG	0171 935 9427
Denmark	Sceptre House, 169/173 Regent St, London W1R 8PY	0171 734 2637
Eastern Caribbean	10 Kensington Court, London W8 5DL	0171 937 6570
Egypt	168 Piccadilly, London W1V 9DE	0171 493 5282/3
Finland	66 Haymarket, London SW1Y 4RF	0171 839 4048
France	178 Piccadilly, London W1V 0AL	0171 499 6911
Germany	65 Curzon St, London W1Y 7PE	0171 495 3990
Gibraltar	Arundel Great Court, 179 The Strand, London WC2R 1EH	0171 836 0777/8
Greece	4 Conduit St, London W1R 0DJ	0171 734 5997
Hong Kong	125 Pall Mall, London SW1Y 5EA	0171 930 4775
Iceland	172 Tottenham Court Rd, London W1P 9LG	0171 388 5346
India	7 Cork St, London W1X 2AB	0171 437 3677/8
Indonesia	70-71 New Bond St, London W1Y 9DE	0171 491 4469
Israel	18 Great Marlborough St, London W1V 1AF	0171 434 3651
Italy	1 Princes St, London W1R 8AY	0171 408 1254
Jamaica	111 Gloucester Place, London W1H 3PH	0171 224 0505

Japan	Heathcoat House, 20 Saville Row, London W1X 1AE	0171 734 9638
Jordan	211 Regent St, London W1R 7DD	0171 437 9465
Kenya	25 Brook Mews, London W1Y 1LG	0171 355 3144
Korea	Vogue House, 1 Hanover Square, London W1R 9RD	0171 408 1591
Luxembourg	36/37 Piccadilly, London W1V 9PA	0171 434 2800
Macau	First Floor, 6 Sherlock Mews, off Paddington St, London W1M 3RH	0171 224 3390
Malawi	33 Grosvenor St, London W1X 0DE	0171 491 4172
Malaysia	57 Trafalgar Sq, London WC2N 5DU	0171 930 7932
Malta	Mappin House, Suite 300, Winsley St, London W1N 7AR	0171 323 0506
Mauritius	49 Conduit St, London W1R 9FB	0171 437 7508
Mexico	60-61 Trafalgar Sq, London WC2 5DS	0171 734 1058
Morocco	205 Regent St, London W1R 7DE	0171 437 0073
Netherlands	25 Buckingham Gate, London SW1E 6LD	0171 630 0451
New Zealand	New Zealand House, 17th Floor, Haymarket, London SW1Y 4TQ	0171 930 0363
Norway	Charles House, 5/11 Lower Regent St, London SW1Y 4LR	0171 839 6255
Philippines	17 Albemarle St, London W1X 4LX	0171 499 5443
Portugal	New Bond Street House, 1/5 New Bond St, London W1Y 0NP	0171 493 3873
Seychelles	Eros House, 111 Baker St, London W1M 1FE	0171 224 1660
Singapore	Carrington House, 126-130 Regent St, London W1R 5FE	0171 437 0033
South Africa	5/6 Alt Grove, Wimbledon, London SW19 4DZ	0181 944 6646
Soviet Union	Intourist House, 219 Marsh Wall, London E14 9FJ	0171 538 8600
Spain	57/58 St James's St, London SW1A 1LD	0171 499 0901
Sri Lanka	13 Hyde Park Gardens, London W2 2LU	0171 262 5009/ 1841
Sweden	29/31 Oxford St, London W1R 1RE	0171 437 5816
Switzerland	Swiss Centre, 1 New Coventry St, London W1V 8EE	0171 734 1921
Taiwan	Free Chinese Centre, 4th floor, Dorland House, 14/16 Regent St, London SW1Y 4PH	0171 930 9553/4
Tanzania	78-80 Borough High St, London SE1 1LL	0171 407 0566

Thailand	49 Albemarle St, London W1X 3FE	0171 499 7679
Trinidad & Tobago	7th Floor, 113 Upper Richmond Rd, London SW15 2TL	0171 780 0318
Tunisia	77a Wigmore St, London W1N 9LJ	0171 224 5598
Turkey	1st Floor, 170/173 Piccadilly, London W1V 9DD	0171 734 8681
Turks & Caicos Islands	3 Epirus Mansions, Epirus Rd, London SW6 7UJ	0171 376 2981
USA	22 Sackville St, London W1X 2EA	0171 439 7433
US Virgin Islands	2 Cinnamon Row, London SW11 3TW	0171 978 5262
Zambia	2 Palace Gate, London W8 5NG	0171 589 6343/4
Zimbabwe	428 Strand, London WC2R 0SA	0171 836 7755

Also, the British Tourist Authority is based at Thames Tower, Black's Road, Hammersmith, London W6 9EL (tel. 0181 846 9000).

Foreign Tourist Offices in the United States

Australia	1270 Ave of the Americas, New York, NY 10020	489 7550
Austria	545 5th Ave, New York, NY 10017	697 1651
Bermuda	Rockefeller Center, 630 5th Ave, New York, NY 10111	397 7700
Brazil	551 5th Ave, New York, NY 10017	682 1055
British Virgin Islands	370 Lexington Ave, New York, NY 10017	696 0400
Caribbean	20 E 46th St, New York, NY 10017	682 0435
Chile	1 World Trade Center, Suite 5121, New York, NY 10048	
China	159 Lexington Ave, New York	725 4950
Colombia	140 E 57th St, New York, NY 10022	688 0151
Eastern Caribbean	220 E 42nd St, New York, NY 10017	986 9370
Ecuador	167 W 72nd St, New York, NY 10023	873 0600
Egypt	630 5th Ave, New York, NY 10111	246 6960
French Polynesia	200 E 42nd St, New York, NY 10017	757 1125
France	610 5th Ave, New York, NY 10020 *Also covers the French West Indies.*	757 1125
Gambia	19 E 47th St, New York, NY 10003	759 2323
Germany	747 3rd Ave, New York, NY 10017	308 3300
Haiti	1270 Avenue of the Americas, New York, NY 10020	757 3517

Hong Kong	548 5th Ave, New York, NY 10036	947 5008
Iceland	75 Rockefeller Plaza, New York, NY 10019	582 2802
India	30 Rockefeller Plaza, New York, NY 10020	586 4901
Indonesia	5 E 68th St, New York, NY 10021	564 1939
Israel	350 5th Ave, New York, NY 10118	560 0650
Ivory Coast	c/o Air Afrique, 1350 Ave of the Americas, New York, NY 10019	
Jamaica	2 Dag Hammarskjöld Plaza, New York	688 7650
Japan	45 Rockefeller Plaza, New York, NY 10020	757 5640
Kenya	15 E 21st St, New York, NY 10022	486 1300
Korea	460 Park Ave, New York, NY 10016	688 7543
Mexico	630 5th Ave, New York, NY 10020	265 4696
Morocco	521 5th Ave, New York, NY 10175	557 2520
New Zealand	630 5th Ave, New York, NY 10020	586 0060
Panama	630 5th Ave, New York, NY 10020	246 5841
Philippines	556 5th Ave, New York, NY 10036	575 7915
St Lucia	41 E 42nd St, New York, NY 10017	867 2950
St Vincent & the Grenadines	220 E 40th St, New York	986 9370
Senegal	200 Park Ave, New York, NY 10003	682 4695
South Africa	610 5th Ave, New York, NY 10020	245 3720
Spain	665 5th Ave, New York, NY 10022	759 8822
Sri Lanka	609 5th Ave, New York	935 0369
Switzerland	608 5th Ave, New York, NY 10020	757 5944
Taiwan	801 Second Ave, New York, NY 10048	432 0433
Tanzania	201 E 42nd St, New York, NY 10017	986 7124
Thailand	5 World Trade Center, New York, NY 10048	432 0433
Tunisia	630 5th Ave, Suite 863, New York, NY 10020	582 3670
Turkey	821 United Nations Plaza, New York, NY 10017	687 2194
Uganda	801 2nd Ave, New York	
United Kingdom	680 5th Ave, New York, NY 10019	581 4700
USSR	45 E 49th St, New York, NY 10017	371 6953
Venezuela	450 Park Ave, New York, NY 11011	355 1101
Zambia	150 E 58th St, New York, NY 10022	758 9450
Zimbabwe	535 5th Ave, New York, NY 10017	307 6565

Foreign Tourist Offices in Australia

America Samoa	327 Pacific Highway, North Sydney NSW 2060
Austria	19th Floor, 1 York St, Sydney NSW 2000
Canada	8th Floor, AMP Centre, 50 Bridge St, Sydney NSW 2000

Denmark	60 Market St, PO Box 4531, Melbourne, Victoria 3001
Germany	c/o Lufthansa German Airlines, Lufthansa House, 12th Floor, 143 Macquarie St, Sydney NSW 2000
Greece	51-57 Pitt St, Sydney NSW 2000
Hong Kong	Bligh House, 4-6 Bligh St, Sydney NSW 2000
India	Carlton Centre, Elizabeth St, Sydney NSW 2000
Macao	Suite 604, 135 Macquarie St, Sydney NSW 2000 or GPO Box M973, Perth, Western Australia 6001
Malaysia	12th Floor, R & W House, 92 Pitt St, Sydney NSW 2000
Mexico	24 Burton St, Darlington, Sydney NSW 2000
South Africa	AMEV-UDA House, 115 Pitt St, Sydney NSW 2001
Singapore	8th Floor, Gold Fields House, 1 Alfred St, Sydney Cove NSW 2000
Sri Lanka	FP Leonard Advertising Pty Ltd, 1st Floor, 100 Bathurst St, Sydney 2000
Switzerland	203-233 New South Head Rd, PO Box 82, Edgecliff, Sydney NSW 2027
Thailand	12th Floor, Royal Exchange Building, Corner Bridge and Pitt Streets, Sydney NSW 2000

Foreign Tourist Offices in Canada

Antigua	Suite 205, 60 St Clair Ave East, Toronto, Ontario M4T 1L9
Australia	120 Eglington Ave East, Suite 220, Toronto, Ontario M4P 1E2
Austria	2 Bloor St East, Suite 3330, Toronto, Ontario M4W 1A8 or Suite 1220-1223, 736 Granville St, Vancouver, BC or 1010 Ouest Rue Sherbrooke, Montréal, Québec
Barbados	615 Dorchester Blvd West, Suite 960, Montréal, Quebec H3B 1P5 or Suite 1508, Box 11, 20 Queen St West, Toronto, Ontario M5H 3R3
Bermuda	Suite 510, 1075 Bay St, Toronto, Ontario M58 2B1

British Virgin Islands	Mr W. Draper, 801 York Mills Road, Suite 201, Don Mills, Ontario M3B 1X7
Cayman Islands	234 Eglington Ave East, Suite 600, Toronto, Ontario
Denmark	PO Box 115, Station 'N', Toronto, Ontario M8V 3S4
Eastern Caribbean	Suite 205, 60 St Clair Ave East, Toronto, Ontario M4T 1L9
France	1 Dandas St West, Suite 2405, Box 8, Toronto, Ontario M5G 1S3
Germany	2 Fundy, PO Box 417, Place Bonaventure, Montréal PQ, H5A 1B8
Greece	1233 Rue de la Montagne, Montréal QC, H3G 1Z2
Israel	102 Bloor St West, Toronto, Ontario M5S 1M8
Jamaica	2221 Yonge St, Suite 507, Toronto, Ontario M4S 2B4
Jordan	181 University Ave, Suite 1716, Box 28, Toronto, Ontario M5H 3M7 *or* 1801 McGill College Ave, Suite 1160, Montréal, Québec H3A 2N4
Kenya	Gillin Building 600, 141 Laurier Ave West, Ottawa, Ontario
Macao	Suite 601, 700 Bay St, Toronto, Ontario M5G 1Z6 *or* 475 Main St, Vancouver, British Columbia V6A 2T7
Mexico	1 Place Ville Marie, Suite 2409, Montréal 113, Québec *or* 1008 Pacific Centre, Toronto Dominion Bank Tower, Vancouver 1, British Columbia
Morocco	2 Carlton St, Suite 1803, Toronto, Ontario M5B 1K2
Peru	Mr Raziel Zisman, 344 Bloor St West, Suite 303, Toronto, Ontario
Portugal	Suite 1150, 1801 McGill College Ave, Montréal, Québec H3A 2N4
South Africa	Suite 1001, 20 Eglington Ave West, Toronto, Ontario M4R 1K8
Spain	60 Bloor St West, Suite 201, Toronto, Ontario M4W 3B8
Switzerland	PO Box 215, Commerce Court, Toronto, Ontario M5L 1E8
Trinidad & Tobago	York Centre, 145 King St West and University Ave, Toronto, Ontario M5H 1J8
USSR	2020 University St, Suite 434, Montréal, Québec H3A 2A5

650

| US Virgin Islands | 11 Adelaide St West, Suite 406, Toronto, Ontario M5H 1L9 |

Foreign Tourist Offices in New Zealand

Australia	15th Floor, Quay Tower, 29 Customs St, Auckland 1 (PO Box 1646, Auckland)
Great Britain	PO Box 3655, Wellington
Fiji	47 High St, Auckland
Hong Kong	General Buildings, G/F Corner Shortland St and O'Connell St, Auckland (PO Box 1313, Auckland)
Malaysia	Malaysian Airline System, Suite 8, 5th Floor, Air New Zealand House, 1 Queen St, Auckland
Singapore	c/o Rodney Walsh Ltd, 87 Queen St, Auckland

Embassies, High Commissions and Consulates in the United Kingdom

Algeria	54 Holland Park, London W11 3RS	0171 221 7800
Antigua	Antigua House, 15 Thayer St, London W1M 5LD	0171 486 7073/5
Argentina	53 Hans Pl, London SW1X 0LA	0171 589 3104
Australia	Australia House, Strand, London WC2B 4LA	0171 379 4334
Austria	18 Belgrave Mews West, London SW1X 8HU	0171 235 3731
Bahamas	10 Chesterfield St, London W1X 8AH	0171 408 4488
Bahrain	98 Gloucester Rd, London SW7 4AU	0171 370 5132/3
Bangladesh	28 Queen's Gate, London SW7 5JA	0171 584 0081/4 589 4842
Barbados	263 Tottenham Court Rd, London W1P 9AA	0171 636 9448
Belgium	103 Eaton Square, London SW1W 9AB	0171 235 5422
Bolivia	106 Eaton Square, London SW1W 9AD	0171 235 4255
Brazil	6 St Alban's St, London SW1Y 4SG	0171 930 9055
Burma	19a Charles St, Berkeley Square, London W1X 8ER	0171 499 8841
Canada	38 Grosvenor Street, London W1X 0AA	0171 409 2071
Chile	12 Devonshire St, London W1N 2DS	0171 580 6392/4
China	31 Portland Pl, London W1N 3AG	0171 636 1835
Denmark	55 Sloane St, London SW1X 9SR	0171 235 1255
Ecuador	3 Hans Crescent, Knightsbridge, London SW1X 0LS	0171 584 2648
Egypt	19 Kensington Palace Gdns, London W8 4QL	0171 229 8818
Fiji	34 Hyde Park Gate, London SW7 5BN	0171 584 3661/2
Finland	32 Grosvenor Gardens, London SW1W 0BP	0171 235 9531
France	6a Cromwell Place, London SW7 2EW	0171 823 9555
Germany	23 Belgrave Square, London SW1X 8PZ	0171 235 5033
Greece	1a Holland Park, London W11 3TP	0171 727 8040
Hong Kong	6 Grafton St, London W1X 3LB	0171 499 9821
Iceland	1 Eaton Terrace, London SW1W 8EY	0171 730 5131/2
India	India House, Aldwych, London WC2B 4NA	0171 836 8484
Indonesia	38 Grosvenor Sq, London W1X 9AD	0171 499 7661
Rep. Ireland	17 Grosvenor Place, London SW1X 7HR	0171 235 2171

Israel	15 Old Court Place, Kensington, London W8 4QB	0171 937 8050
Italy	38 Eaton Place, London SW1X 8AN	0171 235 9371
Jamaica	1-2 Prince Consort Rd, London SW72BQ	0171 823 9911
Japan	101-4 Piccadilly, London W1V 5FN	0171 465 6500
Jordan	6 Upper Phillimore Gdns, London W8 7HB	0171 937 3685/7
Kenya	Kenya House, 45 Portland Place, London W1N 4AS	0171 636 2371/5
Korea Rep.	4 Palace Gate, London W8 5NF	0171 581 3330
Kuwait	40 Devonshire St, London W1N 2AX	0171 589 4533
Luxembourg	27 Wilton Cres, London SW1X 8SD	0171 235 6961
Malawi	33 Grosvenor St, London W1X 0DE	0171 491 4172/7
Malaysia	45 Belgrave Square, London SW1X 8QT	0171 235 8033
Malta	16 Kensington Square, London W8 5HH	0171 938 1712
Mauritius	32/33 Elvaston Place, Gloucester Rd, London SW7 5NW	0171 581 0294
Mexico	8 Halkin St, London SW1X 7DW	0171 235 6393
Morocco	49 Queen's Gate Gdns, London SW7 5NE	0171 581 5001
Nepal	12a Kensington Palace Gdns, London W8 4QU	0171 229 1954/ 6231
Netherlands	38 Hyde Park Gate, London SW7 5DP	0171 584 5040
New Zealand	New Zealand House, Haymarket, London SW1Y 4TE	0171 973 0368/9
Norway	25 Belgrave Square, London SW1X 8QD	0171 235 7151
Oman	44a/b Montpelier Square, London SW7 1JJ	0171 584 6782
Pakistan	35 Lowndes Square, London SW1X 9JN	0171 235 2044
Papua New Guinea	14 Waterloo Place, London SW1Y 4AR	0171 930 9922/6
Paraguay	Braemar Lodge, Cornwall Gdns, London SW7 4AQ	0171 937 6629
Peru	52 Sloane St, London SW1X 9SP	0171 235 6867
Philippines	9a Palace Green, London W8 4QE	0171 937 3646
Portugal	62 Brompton Rd, London SW3 1BJ	0171 581 8722/4
Qatar	115 Queen's Gate, London SW7 5LP	0171 581 8611
Saudi Arabia	30 Belgrave Square, London SW1X 8QB	0171 235 0831/ 0303
Senegal	11 Phillimore Gdns, London W8 7QG	0171 937 0925/6
Seychelles	111 Baker St, 2nd Floor, Eros House, London W1M 1FE	0171 224 1660
Sierra Leone	33 Portland Place, London W1N 3AG	0171 636 6483
Singapore	9 Wilton Cres, London SW1X 8SA	0171 235 5441

South Africa	South Africa Hse, Trafalgar Sq, London WC2N 5DP	0171 839 2211
Soviet Union	5 Kensington Palace Gdns, London W8 4QS	0171 229 3515/6
Spain	20 Draycott Place, London SW3 2RZ	0171 581 5921
Sri Lanka	13 Hyde Park Gdns, London W2 2LU	0171 262 1841
Sweden	11 Montagu Place, London W1H 2AL	0171 724 2101
Switzerland	16/18 Montagu Place, London W1H 2BQ	0171 723 0701
Syria	20 Rue Vaneau, 75007 Paris (represented by Lebanese Embassy in London)	
Tanzania	43 Hertford St, London W1Y 7TF	0171 499 8951
Thailand	30 Queen's Gate, London SW7 5JB	0171 589 0173
Tonga	New Zealand House, 12th Floor, Haymarket, London SW1Y 4TE	0171 839 3287
Trinidad & Tobago	42 Belgrave Square, London SW1X 8NT	0171 245 9351
Tunisia	29 Prince's Gate, London SW7 1QG	0171 584 8117
Turkey	Rutland Lodge, Rutland Gdns, London SW7 1BW	0171 589 0360
United Arab Emirates	48 Prince's Gate, London SW7 2QA	0171 589 3434
United States	5 Upper Grosvenor Street, London W1A 2JB	0171 499 3443
Uruguay	48 Lennox Gdns, London SW1X 0DL	0171 589 8835
Venezuela	56 Grafton Way, London W1P 5LB	0171 387 6727
Zambia	2 Palace Gate, London W8 5NG	0171 589 6343/4
Zimbabwe	Zimbabwe House, 429 Strand, London WC2R 0SA	0171 836 7755

Embassies, High Commissions and Consulates in the United States

Algeria	2118 Kalomama Rd, NW, Washington DC 20008	328 5300
Argentina	1600 New Hampshire Ave, NW, Washington DC 20009	387 0705
Australia	1601 Massachusetts Ave, NW, Washington DC 20036	797 3000
Austria	2343 Massachusetts Ave, NW, Washington DC 2008	483 4474
Bahamas	600 New Hampshire Ave, NW, Washington DC 20037	338 3940

Bahrain	2600 Virginia Ave, NW, Washington DC 20037	324 0741
Bangladesh	3421 Massachusetts Ave, NW, Washington DC 20007	327 6644
Barbados	2144 Wyoming Ave, NW, Washington DC 20008	387 7373
Belgium	3330 Garfield St, NW, Washington DC 20008	333 6900
Bolivia	3012 Massachusetts Ave, NW, Washington DC 20008	483 4410
Brazil	3006 Massachusetts Ave, NW, Washington DC 20008	797 0100
Burma	2300 S St, NW, Washington DC 20008	332 9044
Canada	1746 Massachusetts Ave, NW, Washington DC 20036	785 1400
Chile	1732 Massachusetts Ave, NW, Washington DC 20036	785 1746
China	2300 Connecticut Ave, NW, Washington DC 20008	328 2500
Colombia	2118 Leroy Place, NW, Washington DC 20008	387 5828
Costa Rica	2112 S St, NW, Washington DC 20008	234 2945
Denmark	3200 Whitehaven St, NW, Washington DC 20008	234 4300
Dominican Rep.	1715 22nd St, NW, Washington DC 20008	332 6280
Ecuador	2535 15th St, NW, Washington DC 20009	234 7200
Egypt	2310 Decatur Place, NW, Washington DC 20008	232 5400
Fiji	1629 K St, NW, Washington DC 20006	296 3928
Finland	3216 3216 New Mexico Ave, NW, Washington DC 20016	363 2430
France	2535 Belmont Rd, NW, Washington DC 20008	328 2600
Germany	4645 Reservoir Rd, NW, Washington DC 20007	298 4000
Great Britain	3100 Massachusetts Ave, NW, Washington DC 20008	462 1340
Greece	2221 Massachusetts Ave, NW, Washington DC 20008	667 3168
Haiti	2311 Massachusetts Ave, NW, Washington DC 20008	332 4090
Honduras	4301 Connecticut Ave, NW, Washington DC 20008	966 7700
Iceland	2022 Connecticut Ave, NW, Washington DC 20008	265 6653
India	2107 Massachusetts Ave, NW, Washington DC 20008	265 5050
Indonesia	2020 Massachusetts Ave, NW, Washington DC 20036	293 1745
Ireland	2234 Massachusetts Ave, NW, Washington DC 20008	462 3939

Israel	3514 International Drive, NW, Washington DC 20008	364 5500
Italy	1601 Fuller St, NW, Washington DC 20009	328 5500
Jamaica	1850 K St, NW, Washington DC 20009	452 0660
Japan	2520 Massachusetts Ave, NW, Washington DC 20008	234 2266
Jordan	2319 Wyoming Ave, NW, Washington DC 20008	265 1606
Kenya	2249 R St, NW, Washington DC 20008	387 6101
Korea	2370 Massachusetts Ave, NW, Washington DC 20008	483 7383
Kuwait	2940 Tilden St, NW, Washington DC 20008	966 0702
Luxembourg	2200 Massachusetts Ave, NW, Washington DC 20008	265 4171
Malawi	1400 20th St, NW, Washington DC 20036	296 5530
Malaysia	2401 Massachusetts Ave, NW, Washington DC 20008	328 2700
Malta	2017 Connecticut Ave, NW, Washington DC 20008	462 3611
Mauritius	4310 Connecticut Ave, NW, Washington DC 20008	244 1491
Mexico	2829 16th St, NW, Washington DC 20009	234 6000
Morocco	1601 21st St, NW, Washington DC 20009	462 7979
Nepal	2131 Leroy Place, NW, Washington DC 20008	667 4550
Netherlands	4200 Linnean Ave, NW, Washington DC 20008	244 5300
New Zealand	37 Observatory Circle, Washington DC 20008	328 4800
Nigeria	2201 M St, NW, Washington DC 20037	223 9300
Norway	2720 34th St, NW, Washington DC 20008	333 6000
Oman	2342 Massachusetts Ave, NW, Washington DC 20008	387 1980
Pakistan	2315 Massachusetts Ave, NW, Washington DC 20008	332 8330
Panama	2862 McGill Terrace, NW, Washington DC 20008	483 1407
Papua New Guinea	1140 19th St, NW, Washington DC 20036	659 0856
Paraguay	2400 Massachusetts Ave, NW, Washington DC 20008	483 6960
Peru	1700 Massachusetts Ave, NW, Washington DC 20036	833 9860
Philippines	1617 Massachusetts Ave, NW, Washington DC 20036	483 1414
Portugal	2125 Kalorama Rd, NW, Washington DC 20008	265 1643
Qatar	600 New Hampshire Ave, NW, Washington DC 20037	338 0111

Saudi Arabia	1520 18th St, NW, Washington DC 20036	483 2100
Senegal	2112 Wyoming Ave, NW, Washington DC 20008	234 0540
Seychelles	820 Second Ave, New York, NY 10017	687 9766
Singapore	1824 R St, NW, Washington DC 20009	667 7555
South Africa	3051 Massachusetts Ave, NW, Washington DC 20008	232 4400
Spain	2700 15th St, NW, Washington DC 20009	265 0190
Sri Lanka	2148 Wyoming Ave, NW, Washington DC 20008	483 4025
Sweden	600 New Hampshire Ave, Washington DC 20037	298 3500
Switzerland	2900 Cathedral Ave, NW, Washington DC 20008	462 1811
Syria	2215 Wyoming Ave, NW, Washington DC 20008	232 6313
Tanzania	2139 R St, NW, Washington DC 20008	232 0501
Thailand	2300 Kalorama Rd, NW, Washington DC 20008	667 1446
Trinidad & Tobago	1708 Massachusetts Ave, NW, Washington DC 20036	467 6490
Tunisia	2408 Massachusetts Ave, NW, Washington DC 20008	234 6644
Turkey	1606 23rd St, NW, Washington DC 20008	667 6400
USSR	1125 16th St, NW, Washington DC 20036	628 7551
United Arab Emirates	600 New Hampshire Ave, NW, Washington DC 20037	338 6500
Uruguay	1918 F St, NW, Washington DC 20006	331 1313
Venezuela	2445 Massachusetts Ave, NW, Washington DC 20008	797 3800
Western Samoa	211 E 43rd St, New York NY 10017	682 1482
Yemen Arab Rep.	600 New Hampshire Ave, NW, Washington DC 20037	965 4760
Zaire	1800 New Hampshire Ave, NW, Washington DC 20009	234 7690
Zambia	2419 Massachusetts Ave, NW, Washington DC 20008	265 9717

Embassies, High Commissions and Consulates in Australia

| Argentina | 1st Floor, Suite 102, MLC Tower, Woden, ACT 2606 |
| Austria | 107 Endeavour St, Red Hill, Canberra |

Bangladesh	43 Hampton Circuit, Yarralumla, Canberra, ACT 2600
Belgium	19 Arkana St, Yarralumla, Canberra, ACT 2600
Brazil	11th Floor, 'Canberra House', 40 Marcus Clarke St, Canberra, ACT 2601
Burma	85 Mugga Way, Red Hill, Canberra, ACT 2603
Canada	Commonwealth Ave, Canberra, ACT 2600
Chile	93 Endeavour St, Red Hill, Canberra, ACT 2603
China	14 Federal Highway, Watson, Canberra, ACT 2602
Colombia	PO Box 391, Double Bay (NSW), Sydney 2028
Cyprus	37 Endeavour St, Red Hill, Canberra, ACT 2603
Denmark	24 Beagle St, Red Hill, Canberra, ACT 2603
Egypt	125 Monaro Crescent, Red Hill, Canberra, ACT 2603
Fiji	9 Beagle St, Red Hill, PO Box E159, Canberra, ACT 2600
Finland	10 Darwin Ave, Yarralumla, Canberra, ACT 2600
France	6 Darwin Ave, Yarralumla, Canberra, ACT 2600
Germany	119 Empire Circuit, Yarralumla, Canberra, ACT 2600
Greece	1 Stonehaven Crescent, Red Hill, Canberra, ACT 2603
Iceland	2 Montalto Ave, Toorak 3142
India	3-5 Moonah Place, Yarralumla, Canberra, ACT 2600
Indonesia	Piccadilly Court, 3rd Floor, 222 TITT, PO Box 6, Sydney
Rep. Ireland	200 Arkana St, Yarralumla, Canberra, ACT 2600
Israel	6 Turrana St, Yarralumla, Canberra, ACT 2600
Italy	12 Grey St, Deaking, ACT 2600
Japan	112 Empire Circuit, Yarralumla, Canberra, ACT 2000
Jordan	20 Roabuck St, Red Hill, Canberra, ACT 2603
Korea	113 Empire Circuit, Yarralumla, Canberra, ACT 2600
Malaysia	71 State Circle, Yarralumla, Canberra, ACT 2600
Malta	261 La Perouse St, Red Hill, Canberra, ACT 2603
Mauritius	16 National Circuit, Suite 6, Barton, Canberra, ACT 2600
Mexico	14 Perth Ave, Yarralumla, Canberra, ACT 2600

Netherlands	120 Empire Circuit, Yarralumla, Canberra, ACT 2600
New Zealand	Commonwealth Ave, Canberra, ACT 2600
Norway	3 Zeehan St, Red Hill, Canberra, ACT 2603
Pakistan	59 Franklin St, Forrest, PO Box 198, Manuka, Canberra, ACT 2603
Papua New Guinea	Forster Crescent, Yarralumla, Canberra, ACT 2600
Peru	94 Captain Cook, Canberra, ACT 2603
Philippines	1 Moonah Place, Yarralumla, Canberra
Portugal	8 Astrolabe St, Red Hill, Canberra, ACT 2603
Seychelles	127 Commercial Rd, South Yarra, Victoria 3141
Singapore	81 Mugga Way, Red Hill, Canberra, ACT 2603
South Africa	Rhodes Place, Yarralumla, Canberra, ACT 2600
Soviet Union	78 Canberra Ave, Griffith, ACT 2603
Spain	15 Arkana St, Yarralumla, ACT, PO Box 256, Woden, Canberra
Sri Lanka	35 Empire Circuit, Forrest, Canberra, ACT 2603
Sweden	9 Turrana St, Yarralumla, Canberra, ACT 2600
Switzerland	7 Melbourne Ave, Forrest, ACT 2603
Thailand	111 Empire Circuit, Yarralumla, Canberra, ACT 2600
Turkey	60 Mugga Way, Red Hill, Canberra, ACT 2603
United States	Yarralumla, Canberra, ACT 2600
Venezuela	Suite 106 MLC Tower, Woden, Canberra, ACT

Embassies, High Commissions and Consulates and Canada

Antigua	Suite 205, 60 St Clair Ave East, Toronto, Ontario M4T 1L9
Argentina	130 Slater St, 6th Floor, Ottawa
Australia	The National Building, 13th Floor, 130 Slater St, Ottawa K1P 5H6
Austria	445 Wilbrod St, Ottawa, Ontario K1N 6M7
Bangladesh	85 Range Rd, Suite No 1007, Sandringham Apartments, Ottawa
Barbados	Suite 700, 151 Slater St, Ottawa, Ontario K1P 5HE
Belgium	The Sandringham, 6th Floor, 85 Range Rd, Ottawa
Brazil	255 Albert St, Suite 900, Ottawa K1P 6A9
China	415 St Andrews, Ottawa

Costa Rica	No 2902, 1155 Dorchester Blvd West, Montréal
Denmark	85 Range Rd, Apt 702, Ottawa K1N 8J6
Eastern Caribbean	112 Kent St, Suite 1701, Ottawa, Ontario K1P 5P2
Egypt	454 Laurier Ave, East Ottawa, Ontario
Finland	222 Somerset St West, Suite 401, Ottawa, Ontario K2P 2G3
France	1 Dundas St West, Suite 2405, Box 8, Toronto 0NT MSG 123
Germany	1 Waverley St, Ottawa, Ontario K1N 8VA
Greece	80 Maclaren Ave, Ottawa, Ontario K2P 0KG
Iceland	5005 Jan Talon St West, 3rd Floor, Montréal, Québec H4P 1W7
India	325 Howe St, 1st Floor, Vancouver, BC
Indonesia	225 Albert St, Suite 101, Kent Sq Building CPO, Box 430, Terminal A, Ottawa, Ontario
Rep. Ireland	170 Metcalfe St, Ottawa, Ontario K2P 1P3
Israel	Laurier Ave West, Ottawa K1R 7T3
Italy	275 Slater St, 11th Floor, Ottawa K1P 5H9
Jamaica	Sandringham Apt, Suite 202-204, 85 Range Rd, Ottawa, Ontario
Japan	255 Sussex Drive, Ottawa, Ontario K1N 9E6
Kenya	Gillin Building Suite 600, 141 Laurier Ave, West Ottawa, Ontario K1P 5J3
Korea	151 Slater St, Suite 608, Ottawa, Ontario K1P 5H3
Malawi	112 Kent St, Suite 905, Ottawa, Ontario K1P 5P2
Malaysia	60 Boteler St, Ottawa, Ontario K1N 8Y7
Mexico	130 Albert St, Suite 206, Ottawa, Ontario K1P 5G4
Morocco	38 Range Rd, Ottawa
Netherlands	3rd Floor, 275 Slater St, Ottawa K1P 5H9
New Zealand	Metropolitan House, Suite 801, 99 Bank St, Ottawa K1P 6G3
Norway	Suite 932, Royal Bank Centre, 90 Sparks St, Ottawa K1P 5B4
Pakistan	2100 Drumond St, Apt 505, Montréal H3G 1X1
Peru	170 Laurier Ave West, Suite 1007, Ottawa K1P 5V5
Philippines	130 Albert St, 606-607 Ottawa, Ontario
Portugal	645 Island Park Drive, Ottawa K1Y 0B8
Saudi Arabia	Suite 901, 99 Bank St, Ottawa K1P 5P9
South Africa	15 Sussex Drive, Ottawa K1M 1M8
Soviet Union	285 Charlotte St, Ottawa K1N 845

Spain	350 Spark St, SUIR802, Ottawa, Ontario K1R 758
Sri Lanka	85 Range Rd, 'The Sandringham', Suites 102-104, Ottawa, Ontario K1N 8J6
Sweden	441 Maclaren St, Ottawa, Ontario K2P 2H3
Switzerland	5 Malborough Ave, Ottawa, Ontario K1N 8E6
Tanzania	50 Range Rd, Ottawa, Canada K1N 84
Thailand	85 Range Rd, Suite 704, Ottawa, Ontario K1N 8J6
Trinidad & Tobago	73 Albert St, Room 508, Ottawa, Ontario K1P 5R5
Tunisia	115 O'Conner St, Ottawa
Turkey	197 Wurtenburg St, Ottawa, Ontario K1N 8L9
United States	100 Wellington St, Ottawa K1P 5T1
Venezuela	Suite 2000, 320 Queen St, Ottawa K1R 5A3
Zambia	130 Albert St, Suite 1610, Ottawa, Ontario
Zimbabwe	112 Kent St, Suite 915 Place de Ville, Tower B, Ottawa, Ontario K1P 5P2

Embassies, High Commissions and Consulates in New Zealand

Argentina	IBM Center, 151-165 The Terrace, 5th Floor, PO Box 1033, Wellington
Australia	72-78 Hobson St, Thorndon, Wellington
Belgium	Williston St 1, PO Box 3841, Wellington
Canada	PO Box 12-049 Wellington B, ICI Building, 3rd Floor, Molesworth St, Wellington
Chile	Robert Jones House, 12th Floor, Jervois Quay, Wellington
China	226 Glenmore St, Wellington
Denmark	18th Floor, Challenge House, 105-109 The Terrace, PO Box 10035, Wellington 1
Fiji	Robert Jones House, Jervois Quay, Wellington
France	1 Williston St, DBP 1695, Wellington
Germany	90-92 Hobson St, Wellington
Hong Kong	General Building, G/F Corner Shortland St & O'Connell St, Auckland
India	Princes Towers, 10th Floor, 180 Molesworth St, Wellington
Israel	13th Level, Williams City Centre, Plymmet Steps, PO Box 2171, Wellington
Italy	38 Grant Rd, PO Box 463, Wellington

Japan	7th Floor, Norwich Insurance House, 3-11 Hunter St, Wellington 1
Korea	12th Floor, Williams Parking Centre Building, Corner of Boulcoutt St & Gilmer Terrace, Wellington N2
Malaysia	163 The Terrace, PO Box 9422, Wellington
Netherlands	Investment House, 10th Floor, Ballance and Featherstone St, Wellington
Norway	38-42 Waring Taylor St, PO Box 1392, Wellington
Papua New Guinea	Princes Towers, 11th Floor, 180 Molesworth St, Thorndon, Wellington
Peru	3rd Floor, 36/37 Victoria St, Wellington
Philippines	Level 30, Williams City Centre, Boulcott St, Gillmer Terrace, Wellington
Portugal	47-49 Fort St, Auckland
Singapore	17 Kabul St, Khandallah, Wellington
South Africa	Molesworth House, 101-103 Molesworth St, Wellington, PO Box 12045
Soviet Union	57 Messines Rd, Karori, Wellington
Sweden	PO Box 1800, Wellington 1
Switzerland	22-24 Panama St, 7th Floor, Wellington 1
Thailand	2 Burnel Ave, PO Box 2530, Wellington 1
United States	29 Fitzherbert Terrace, Wellington

London Area Airline Offices of Major Airlines

Airline	Address	Fares	Telephone numbers	
			Reservations	Admin. & Enqs.
Aer Lingus	223 Regent Street, London W1R 7DB		0181 569 5555	
Aeroflot Soviet Airlines	70 Piccadilly, London W1V 9HH		0171 355 2233	0171 491 1584
Aerolineas Argentinas	Chesham House, 150 Regent Street, London W1R 5FA		0171 439 6288	
Air Afrique	177 Piccadilly, London W1V 0LX	0171 493 4881	0171 629 6114	0171 493 4881
Air Canada	7/8 Conduit Street, London W1R 9TG	0181 759 2636	0181 759 2636	0181 759 2636
Air France	158 New Bond Street, London W1Y 0AY	0171 499 9511	0171 499 9511	0171 491 9511
Air India	17 New Bond Street, London W1Y 0BD		0171 491 7979	0171 493 4050
Air Jamaica	5th Floor, Sabena House, London W1V 0JA		0171 734 1782	0171 437 8732
Air New Zealand	Ground Floor, New Zealand House, Haymarket, London SW1 4TE	0181 741 2299	0181 741 2299	0181 741 2299
Alitalia	205 Holland Park Ave, London W11 4XB	0171 602 7111	0171 602 7111	0181 745 8200
American Airlines	15 Berkeley Street, London W1		0181 572 5555	
Austrian Airlines	50 Conduit Street, London W1R 0NP		0171 439 0741	0171 491 1851
Avianca	Linen Hall, 162-168 Regent Street, London W1R 5TA	0171 408 1889	0171 437 3664	0171 408 1889

Airline	Address	Fares	Telephone numbers	
			Reservations	Admin. & Enqs.
British Airways	PO Box 10, Heathrow Airport, Hounslow, Middlesex TW6 2JA			0181 897 4000
British Midland	2/5 Warwick Court, London WC1R 5DJ		0171 430 2496 /7	
Canadian Airlines	Rothschild House, Whitgift Centre, Croydon CR9 3HN		0345 616767	
Cathay Pacific Airways	7 Apple Tree Yard, Duke of York Street, London SW1Y 6LD	0171 930 4444	0171 930 7878	0171 930 7878
China Airlines	5th Floor, Nuffield House, 41/46 Piccadilly, London W1V 9AJ		0171 494 1261	0171 494 1261
Continental Airlines	Beulah Court, Albert Road, Horley RH6 7HZ		0293 776464	0293 771681
Delta Airlines	Victoria Place, Buckingham Palace Road, London SW1W 9SJ		0800 414767	0293 826100
Egypt Air	296 Regent Street, London W1R 6PH	0171 437 0812	0171 437 6426	
El Al	185 Regent Street, London W1R 8EU		0171 437 9255	0171 439 2564
Emirates	125 Pall Mall, London SW1Y 5EA		0171 930 3711	0171 930 5356
Finnair	14 Clifford Street, London W1X 1RD	0171 629 8039	0171 408 1222	0171 629 4349
Garuda Indonesia	35 Duke Street, London W1M 5DF		0171 486 3011	0171 935 7055
Gulf Air	10 Albemarle Street, London W1X 3HE	0171 409 1091	0171 408 1717	0171 409 0191
Iberia	29 Glasshouse Street, London W1R 5RG		0171 437 5622	0171 437 9822
Icelandair	172 Tottenham Court Road, London W1P 9LG		0345 581111	0181 745 7051

Airline	Address	Fares	Telephone numbers	
			Reservations	Admin. & Enqs.
Japan Airlines	Hanover Court, 5 Hanover Square, London W1R 0DR		0171 408 1000	0171 629 9244
KLM	8 Hanover Street, London W1R 9HF		0181 750 9000	0181 750 9200
Kenya Airways	16 Conduit Street, London W1R 9TD	0171 409 3121	0171 409 0277	0171 409 3121
Korean Airlines	66 Haymarket, London SW1Y 4RF	0171 389 2522	0171 930 6513	0171 930 1957
Kuwait Airways	16-20 Baker Street, London W1M 2AD		0171 412 0007	0171 412 0006
Lufthansa	Lufthansa House, 10 Old Bond Street, London W1X 4EN	0171 408 0322	0171 408 0442	0171 408 0322
Malaysian Airline System	91a Askew Road, London W12 9AX	0181 862 0770	0181 862 0800	0181 862 0770
Middle East Airlines	48 Park Street, London W1Y 3PD	0171 493 6321	0171 493 5681	0171 493 6321
Northwest	49 Albemarle Street, London W1		0345 747800	
Olympic Airways	164-5 Piccadilly, London W1V 9DE		0181 846 9080	0181 846 9966
Pakistan International	45 Piccadilly, London W1	0181 741 8066	0171 734 5544	
Pan Am	120 Cheapside, London EC2	0181 759 1262	0181 759 8000	0181 750 9331
Philippine Airlines	Centrepoint, 103 New Oxford Street, London WC1A 1QD	0171 379 6855	0171 836 5508	0171 836 0828
Qantas	91 Regent Street, London W1		0800 747767	0181 846 0466
Royal Jordanian Airlines	177 Regent Street, London W1R 7FB		0171 734 2557	0171 437 9465
Sabena	Gemini House, West Block, 10-18 Putney Hill, London SW15 6AA	0171 437 6960	0181 780 1444	0181 780 1444

Airline	Address	Fares	Telephone numbers Reservations	Admin. & Enqs.
Saudia/Saudi Arabian	508-10 Chiswick High Road, London W4 5SQ	0181 995 7755	0181 995 7777	0181 995 7755
SAS	52 Conduit Street, London W1R 0AY	0171 437 7086	0171 734 4040	0171 734 6777
Singapore Airlines	143-147 Regent Street, London W1R 7LB	0181 747 1777	0181 747 0007	0181 995 4901
South African Airways	251-259 Regent Street, London W1R 7AD	0171 437 0932	0171 734 9841	0171 437 9621
Swiss Air	3 New Coventry Street, London W1V 4BJ	0171 734 6737	0171 439 4144	0171 439 4144
Tap Air Portugal	38 Gillingham Street, London SW1V 1JW		0171 828 0262	
Thai International	41 Albemarle Street, London W1X 3FE	0171 499 9113	0171 499 9113	0171 499 7953
TWA	200 Piccadilly, London W1V 0DH	0171 439 0707	0800 222222	
United Airlines	58 St James Street, London SW1A 1LD		0800 898017	0800 898017
US Air	Piccadilly House, 33/37 Regent Street, London SW1Y 4NB		0171 734 3001	
UTA	177 Piccadilly, London W1V 0LX	0171 493 4881	0171 629 6114	0171 493 4881
Varig	16/17 Hanover Street, London W1R 0HG		0171 629 5824	
Viasa	19/20 Grosvenor Street, London W1X 9FD		0171 493 3630	
Virgin Atlantic	Ashdown House, High Street, Crawley RH10 1D9		0293 38222	0293 562345
Zambia Airways	163 Piccadilly, London W1V 9DE		0171 491 0650	

Visa Requirements

Country Travelling to:	VISA REQUIREMENTS					Restrictions and Requirements
	Australia	Canada	New Zealand	UK	USA	
Algeria	Yes	Yes	Yes	Yes	Yes	If wish to stay more than 3mths need a permit de séjour obtainable from nearest 'Wilaya'.
American Samoa	No	No	No	No	No	Need visa if over 30 days.
Andorra	No	No	No	No	No	
Antigua	No*	No*	No*	No*	No*	* Must have return ticket.
Argentina	Yes	Yes*	Yes	Yes	Yes	* Tourists don't require visas, others do.
Australia	—	Yes	No	Yes	Yes	
Austria	No*	No*	No*	No	No*	* Up to 3mths; UK up to 6mths.
Bahamas	No	No	No	No	No	
Bahrain	Yes	Yes	Yes	No	Yes	
Bangladesh	Yes/No*	Yes	Yes	Yes	Yes	* Yes, if stay exceeds 3 months. No if stay less than 15 days.
Barbados	No	No	No	No	No	
Belgium	No	No	No	No	No	
Bermuda	Yes*	No*	Yes*	No*	No*	* Must have a return ticket.
Bolivia	Yes	Yes	No	No*	No*	* Tourists don't/Others do

Country Travelling to:	VISA REQUIREMENTS					Restrictions and Requirements
	Australia	Canada	New Zealand	UK	USA	
Botswana	No	No	No	No	No	
Brazil	Yes	Yes*	Yes	No*	Yes	* Need passport endorsed for Brazil (must not expire within 6mths from date of arrival in Brazil), a roundtrip ticket and funds to meet expenses.
British Virgin Is.	No	No	No	No	No	
Burma	Yes*	Yes*	Yes*	Yes*	Yes*	* Valid for 14 days only.
Canada	No	—	No	No	No	
Cayman Is.	No	No	No	No	No	
Chile	No	No	No	No	No	
China	Yes	Yes	Yes	Yes	Yes	
Colombia	Yes	Yes	Yes	No*	Yes	* Must have a valid passport and a return or continuation ticket.
Cook Islands	No*	No*	No*	No*	No*	* Must have valid passport and a return ticket. Need visa after 31 days.
Costa Rica	Yes*	Yes*	Yes*	No	No	* Need visa after 30 days.
Denmark	No*	No*	No*	No*	No*	* Need visa if stay over 3mths.
Eastern Caribbean	No	No	No	No	No	
Ecuador	No*	No*	No*	No*	No*	* Need visa if staying over 3mths.
Egypt	Yes*	Yes*	Yes*	Yes*	Yes*	* Visitors must register with the Ministry of the Interior at al-Mugama within 7 days of arrival in Egypt.

VISA REQUIREMENTS

Country Travelling to:	Australia	Canada	New Zealand	UK	USA	Restrictions and Requirements
Fiji	No	No	No	No	No	
Finland	No	No	No	No	No	
France	Yes*	No*	Yes*	No*	No*	* Up to 3mths.
Gambia	No*	No*	No*	No*	Yes*	* Up to 3mths.
Germany	No*	No*	No*	No*	No*	* Up to 3 mths.
Gibraltar	No	No	No	No	No	
Greece	No	No	No	No	No	
Grenada	No*	No	No*	No*	No*	* Up to 3mths.
Guayana	Yes	Yes	Yes	Yes	Yes	
Haiti	Yes	No	Yes	No	No	
Hawaii	Yes	No	Yes	No	No	
Hong Kong	No[a]	No[a]	No[a]	No[b]	No[c]	[a] Up to 3mths. [b] Up to 6mths. [c] Up to 1mth.
Iceland	No*	No*	No*	No*	No*	* Need return ticket.
India	Yes	Yes	Yes	Yes	Yes	
Indonesia	*	*	*	*	*	* Depends on the reason for visiting. Each individual must find out if a visa is necessary for their particular trip.
Ireland (Rep.)	No	No	No	No	No	
Israel	No*	No*	No*	No*	No	* Free visa on arrival.

VISA REQUIREMENTS

Country Travelling to:	Australia	Canada	New Zealand	UK	USA	Restrictions and Requirements
Italy	No	No	No	No	No	
Ivory Coast	Yes*	Yes*	Yes*	No*	Yes*	* Valid for 3mths.
Jamaica	No†	No*	No†	No†	No*	† Up to 3mths. * Need proof of citizenship and return ticket for visit not exceeding 6mths.
Japan	Yes	Yes^a	No^b	No^c	No	a Up to 90 days. b Up to 3mths. c Up to 6mths.
Jordan	Yes	Yes	Yes	Yes	Yes	
Kenya	Yes	No	No	No	Yes	
Korea (Republic)	No*	No*	No*	No†	No*	* Up to 15 days. † Up to 60 days.
Kuwait	Yes	Yes	Yes	Yes	Yes	
Lesotho	No*	No*	No*	No*	No*	* Not required for stop up to 30 days – tourism.
Luxembourg	No*	No*	No*	No*	No*	* Up to 3mths.
Macao	No	No	No	No	No	
Malawi	No	No	No	No	No	
Malaysia	No	No	No	No	No*	* Up to 3mths.
Mali	Yes	Yes	Yes	Yes	Yes	
Malta	No	No	No	No	No	
Mauritius	No	No	No	No	No	
Mexico	Yes*	No*	Yes*	No*	No*	* Need to get tourist card, which is free of charge.

VISA REQUIREMENTS

Country Travelling to:	Australia	Canada	New Zealand	UK	USA	Restrictions and Requirements
Morocco	No	No	No	No	No	
Nepal	Yes*	Yes*	Yes*	Yes*	Yes*	* Valid for 3mths.
Netherlands	No*	No*	No*	No*	No*	* Up to 3mths.
New Zealand	No	No†	—	No†	No*	† Up to 6mths. * Up to 3mths. All visitors need an onward ticket and sufficient funds.
Nigeria	Yes*	Yes*	Yes*	Yes*	Yes	* Need entry permit.
Norway	No	No	No	No	No	
Oman	*	*	*	*	*	* Not issuing visas at present. To go to Oman you need a sponsor in Oman to apply for a 'No objection Certificate' for you (allows you to travel for 3mths)
Pakistan	Yes*	Yes*	Yes*	Yes*	Yes†	* Up to 3mths. † Up to 1mth.
Panama	Yes	Yes	Yes	No	Yes	
Papua New Guinea	Yes*	Yes*	Yes*	Yes*	Yes*	* Up to 30 days but need a return ticket.
Paraguay	Yes*	No*	Yes*	No	No	* Stay not exceeding 90 days.
Peru	Yes	No	Yes	No	No	
Philippines	No*	No*	No*	No*	No*	* For 21 days as long as have ticket of onward travel.
Portugal	No^a	No^b	No^a	No^b	No^b	^{a} Up to 3mths. ^{b} Up to 2mths.

Country Travelling to:	VISA REQUIREMENTS					Restrictions and Requirements
	Australia	Canada	New Zealand	UK	USA	
Qatar	Yes	Yes	Yes	No	Yes	
Saudi Arabia	Yes	Yes	Yes	Yes	Yes	
Senegal	Yes*	Yes*	Yes*	Yes*	Yes*.	* Plus return ticket.
Sierra Leone	Yes	Yes	Yes	Yes	Yes	
Seychelles	No	No	No	No	No	
Singapore	No	No	No	No	No	
Solomon Is.	No	No	No	No	No	
South Africa	No	No	No	No	No	
Soviet Union	Yes	Yes	Yes	Yes	Yes	
Spain	Yes	No	Yes	No*	No	* Up to 90 days.
Sri Lanka	No*	No*	No*	No*	No*	* Up to 30 days.
Swaziland	No	No	No	No	No	
Sweden	No	No	No	No	No	
Switzerland	No	No	No	No	No	
Syria	Yes	Yes	Yes	Yes	Yes	
Tahiti	No†	No*	No†	No†	No*	† Up to 3mths. * Up to 1mth.
Thailand	No*.	No*	No*	No*	No*	* Up to 15 days. If leave by rail need visa.
Togo	Yes	Yes	Yes	No	No	
Tonga	No	No.	No	No	No	

VISA REQUIREMENTS

Country Travelling to:	Australia	Canada	New Zealand	UK	USA	Restrictions and Requirements
Trinidad & Tobago	Yes	No	No	No	No	
Tunisia	Yes	No	Yes	No	No	Delivered on arrival.
Turkey	No	No	No	Yes	No	Issued on arrival.
Turks & Caicos Is.	No	No	No	No	No	
Uganda	Yes	Yes	Yes	No	Yes	
United Arab Emirates	Yes	Yes	Yes	No*	Yes	* Stay not exceeding 30 days.
United Kingdom	No	No	No	—	No	
US Virgin Is.	Yes*	No	Yes*	No	No	* Also evidence to prove you will be leaving the country.
United States	Yes*	No	Yes*	No	—	* Also evidence to prove you will be leaving the country.
Venezuela	Yes	Yes	Yes	Yes	Yes	Tourist visa.
Yemen Arab Rep.	Yes	Yes	Yes	Yes	Yes	
Zambia	No	No	No	No	Yes	
Zimbabwe	No	No	No	No	No	

Be a Good Tourist

Tourism is the world's largest industry and while most of us think of travel as a good thing because it gives people enjoyment, encourages understanding between races and brings in needed foreign exchange, inevitably it has its negative side too – if uncontrolled it can change the face of the natural environment and break down traditional ways of life.

Many of the problems created by tourism have resulted from the desire to benefit from economies of scale: quite simply, we are now paying the environmental price of holidays that were sold too cheaply to too many people. Now tourists are recognizing the damage done by this industry and, as the Costas lose their appeal, a new breed of 'traveller' is emerging – one who does not leave his conscience at home but who travels with an enlightened approach and an open mind.

So how can you be a 'good tourist'? This brief checklist should provide a few pointers:

- With congestion such a major problem, consider travelling out of season. Even if you have to plan around school holidays, it is possible to travel in the Easter or autumn breaks.

- If you are travelling to a less-developed country, consider the leakage of foreign exchange from the economy. If you take a package in which the airline and hotel are foreign owned, only 22–5% of the brochure price will stay in that country. If you then consume Western goods which are imported you further reduce the profits that country might make from tourism. If you can, stay with locals, and try to consume only local goods.

- Take nothing in your case that you don't strictly need. In countries where waste disposal is poor, don't add to the problem. Remove toiletries, shirts and photographic goods from wrappings before you leave and take shampoos and sunscreens made from natural substances so that, if they get into the water, they won't destroy marine life.

- When arranging transport, look at what the locals do. To soak up the atmosphere without polluting it, use buses, bikes and your feet!

- If you're buying souvenirs, support the local arts and crafts market. But be careful not to buy goods made from endangered species.

- Be sensitive with your camera. Always ask someone before you take their picture, and don't click away in places of worship. Use your camera constructively – to photograph rather than pick wild flowers, for instance.

Being a good tourist is all about leaving as little negative impact as possible and, where you can, making a positive contribution to the environment and people of the place you're visiting. If you would like more information, look at my book, *The Good Tourist*.

I Need *Your* Help

In a book covering as much as this one, inevitably there might be a few things that change between it being handed in to the publisher and it appearing on the shelves. If you find any inaccuracy, please do write and let me know.

Or if you stumble across a great find, drop me a line and we'll add it into next year's edition. And credit you.

Also, if you've done a lot of travelling and have a pair of decidedly itchy feet, and can write and research like a dream (preferably with a proven journalistic background, or a degree in English at least), why not become one of my updating researchers?

Write to me at the address below, with a full CV/letter telling me the interesting and relevant bits about you (which CVs rarely do!) and enclose a photo, and we'll take it from there.

Better still, if you happen to fit all the above criteria but are also a whizz in the kitchen and a source of inspiration, discipline and would be fun for two lively wee schoolboys, consider becoming my live-in P.A./nanny/housekeeper (male or female, we don't mind!) Each year I take on someone who wants to break into the competitive world of travel writing as an assistant. This is a combined role with being our Girl/Boy Friday who also helps in the house, drives kids to school, cooks, etc., etc. If you've experience in that field and can prove to me you're hard-working, great with kids and keen on travel, send on details now.

Write to Katie Wood c/o HarperCollins Publishers, 77-85 Fulham Palace Road, Hammersmith, London W6 8JB.

Looking forward to hearing from you!

INDEX

Landscapes and Memories

An Intermittent Autobiography

John Prebble

'John Prebble's unselfish, compassionate outlook honours the *necessity* of history in all our lives.' James Malpas, *Observer*

No living writer is more responsible for shaping our picture of Scotland and its past that John Prebble. With his great trilogy, *The Highland Clearances*, *Glencoe* and *Culloden*, he has brought alive some of the central, tragic episodes in Scottish history with an immediacy that their readers will never forget. *Landscapes and Memories* is as close as Prebble will come to writing an autobiography. Like memory itself, it moves backwards and forwards between the distant and the recent past, between Prebble's recollections of his own life and of the lives and history he has written about.

'Some of the writing is as unforgettable as Dr Zhivago's journey across Siberia. His own story is as moving as any of those sagas of Scottish rural and military life on which he has so solidly built his reputation. All who read or write about Scottish history stand permanently indebted to Prebble.'

John Ure, *Times Literary Supplement*

'Along with Christopher Hill and E. P. Thompson, he deserves his place in that great generation of romantic English Marxists of the 1930s who have devoted their lives to celebrating the losing sides of British history.' Niall Ferguson, *Daily Mail*

'John Prebble . . . has brought Scottish history to a mass audience in his distinguished books . . . the fit between imagination and reality is perfect.' Frank McLynn, *Independent*

ISBN 0 00 637460 3

Anthony Storr

Music and the Mind

'Anyone who feels like reflecting about the origins, the impact and the significance of music will find Dr Storr's book helpful and stimulating.'   Alfred Brendel

In this challenging book, Anthony Storr, one of Britain's leading psychiatrists, explores why music, the most mysterious and intangible of all forms of art, has such a powerful effect on our minds and bodies. He believes that music today is a deeply significant experience for a greater number of people than ever before, and argues that the patterns of music give structure and coherence to our feelings and emotions. It is because music possesses this capacity to restore our sense of personal wholeness – in a culture which requires us to separate rational thought from feelings – that many people find it so life-enhancing that it justifies existence.

'This beautifully written book, humane, intelligent and thoughtful, is a significant contribution to our understanding of those mysterious movements of the mind.' Adam Lively, *Times Educational Supplement*

'It is a stimulating inquiry aimed at discovering what it is about music that so profoundly moves so many people, in the course of which he describes the physical effects of mescaline, considers the relation of bird-song, the burbling of babies and the language of literature to music, and touches on many other fascinating topics, concluding that its most significant aspect for us is its power to create order out of chaos.'   Frances Partridge, *Spectator*

'Reading Storr's work is always like being taken on a journey through a foreign country by a great enthusiast. It doesn't matter if you don't know the language because he teaches you what you need to know along the way. His knowledge is vast and his enthusiasm infectious . . . Storr is an extraordinarily gifted communicator.'
Mary Loudon, *New Statesman & Society*

ISBN 0 00 686186 5

The Ark's Anniversary

Gerald Durrell

When Gerald Durrell was six he told his mother that he intended to have his own zoo. This is the story of how he achieved his ambition — and how his dream grew into the Jersey Wildlife Preservation Trust, to become a major world force in wildlife conservation.

Whether on the trail of a bank manager or a pigmy hog, whether courting patrons or tracking a Gunther's gecko, Gerald Durrell's enthusiasm remains undiminished as, Noah-like, he gathers in his wonderful collection of rare and exotic animals to save them from extinction.

ISBN: 0 00 637537 5

Douglas Botting

Gavin Maxwell

A Life

The bestselling author of *Ring of Bright Water* (over 2 million copies sold worldwide) was, in the words of *The Times*, 'a man of action who writes like a poet'. Aristocrat, social renegade, wartime secret agent, shark-hunter, adventurer, racing driver, traveller, naturalist, poet and painter, Gavin Maxwell was also one of the most popular authors of wildlife books in the 20th century.

'Here is a life woven from the stuff of high romance, a tragic and fascinating quest.'   ELSPETH BARKER, *Independent on Sunday*
Books of the Year

'Could hardly be bettered . . . Botting's great achievement is to have looked at his friend square in the face, portraying his frailties while remaining loyal to his gifts.'
FRASER HARRISON, *New Statesman*

'Wonderfully written and very penetrating and understanding. What an extraordinary story!'   DAVID ATTENBOROUGH

'Excellent and thorough . . . a gripping story, told here by someone who knew him well, yet can stand back far enough to see this extraordinary character as a whole.'
DUFF HART-DAVIS, *Mail on Sunday*

' . . . Botting has unravelled then rewoven the extraordinary tapestry of Maxwell's life into a fond, frank and endlessly absorbing and moving book.'
JIM CRUMLEY, *Scotland on Sunday*

'Compelling . . . a ripping yarn about a mercurial man told with the verve and romanticism it deserves.'
JOHN MCEWEN, *Sunday Telegraph*

0 586 07109 1